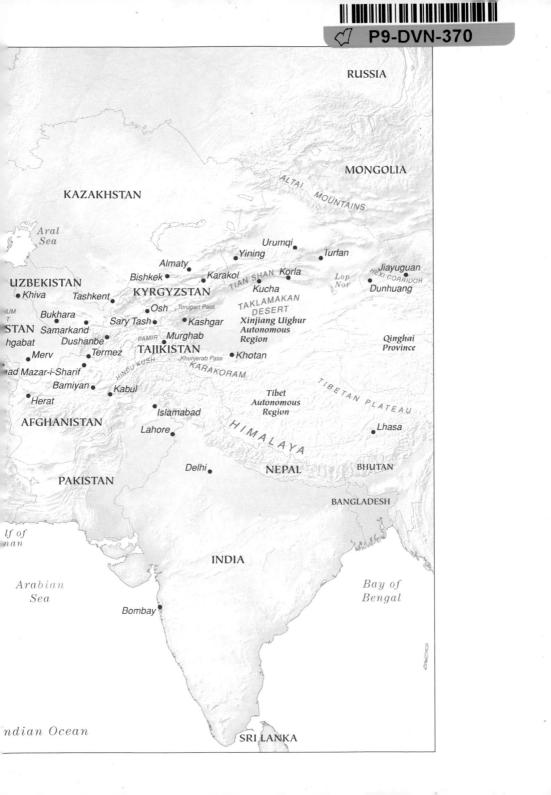

RUSSIA

MONGOLIA

ALTAI MOUNTAINS

KAZAKHSTAN

Aral Sea

Urumqi
Yining
Turfan

Almaty
Bishkek
Karakol
Korla
Jiayuguan
HEXI CORRIDOR

UZBEKISTAN
Khiva
Tashkent
KYRGYZSTAN
TIAN SHAN
Kucha
Lop Nor
Dunhuang

UM T
Bukhara
Osh
Torugart Pass
TAKLAMAKAN DESERT

STAN
Samarkand
Sary Tash
Kashgar
Xinjiang Uighur Autonomous Region

hgabat
Dushanbe
PAMIR
Murghab
Qinghai Province

Merv
Termez
TAJIKISTAN
Khunjerab Pass
Khotan

ad Mazar-i-Sharif
HINDU KUSH
KARAKORAM
TIBETAN PLATEAU

Bamiyan
Kabul

Herat
Tibet Autonomous Region
Lhasa

AFGHANISTAN
Islamabad

Lahore
HIMALAYA

Delhi
NEPAL
BHUTAN

PAKISTAN
BANGLADESH

lf of nan

INDIA

Arabian Sea
Bay of Bengal

Bombay

ndian Ocean
SRI LANKA

LUCE BOULNOIS

Luce Boulnois was born in France in 1931. She studied Chinese and Russian in Paris at the National Institute of Oriental Languages and Civilisations (INALCO) and at University. After graduation, she spent seven years as a translator. It was during this period that her interest in the history of interrelations and material and cultural exchanges between East and West started. Firstly, from the discovery through readings of Soviet and Chinese Central Asia, then, in Cold War time, through professional roles when the region was completely closed off from the outside world and inaccessible to non-Communist Europeans. The result of this work was her first book on the Silk Road published in 1963. It has been re-edited since and translated into nine languages, including Chinese and Japanese. As a scientific worker for almost thirty years in the National Centre of Scientific Research (CNRS), in a research team in the field of Nepalese and Himalayan studies, Luce Boulnois continued to study the history of trade relations and cultural exchanges, with a thesis and various publications on trans-Himalayan trade, Sino-Nepalese relations and Silk Road matters. Retired since 1992, she wrote a new book on the Silk Road, published in 2001 by Olizane, Geneva, and is continuing her historical research on Central Asia and Tibet.

HELEN LOVEDAY

Translator Helen Loveday read Chinese and later obtained a PhD in Chinese art at Oxford University. She has travelled extensively in China and Central Asia, where she became intrigued particularly by the interactions between the Persian and Chinese worlds. She worked as an independent researcher in Far Eastern art for many years and currently teaches Chinese and Japanese art at Geneva University. She is also the assistant curator of the Baur Collections at the Museum of Far Eastern Art in Geneva. She has translated a number of works, including the Odyssey guide to *Mongolia*, and is author of the Odyssey guide to *Iran*.

JUDY BONAVIA-BOILLAT

Consultant editor Judy Bonavia-Boillat, an Australian citizen currently resident in France, lived in Asia for thirty years, including eight years living and travelling in China. She has long been fascinated with the Silk Road, researching its history and culture, much of it from original Chinese sources, and travelling part of it while she lived in China. She has also explored the Pakistan Karakoram Highway into the Hunza Valley. She is author of the Odyssey guides to the *Yangzi River* and the *Silk Road*.

PUBLISHER'S NOTE

In keeping with a recent trend toward 'neutral' language, some contributors to this work (see Silk Road Treasures Nearer to Home and Silk Road Timeline) have opted to use BCE (Before the Common, or Christian, Era) and CE (Common, or Christian, Era), instead of the conventional BC and AD.

Preceding page: Big Goose Pagoda, Xi'an, China (Wong)

Following pages: The Great Colonnade, Palmyra, Syria. A 17th-century Arabic castle, Qala'at Ibn Maan, sits astride a hilltop in the distance. (Grover)

Page 6: Kalyan Minaret and Mosque, Bukhara, Uzbekistan (Grover)

Silk Road

Monks, Warriors & Merchants on the Silk Road

Bodhisattva painting on silk, Khocho, 9th to 10th century AD

Silk Road

Monks, Warriors & Merchants
on the Silk Road

Luce Boulnois

Translated by Helen Loveday
with additional material by
Bradley Mayhew and Angela Sheng

Principal photographers: Wong How Man,
Amar Grover and Adam Woolfitt

Copyright (English Edition) © 2004 Airphoto International Ltd.
Maps Copyright (English Edition) © 2004 Editions Olizane, Geneva
Translated from the French Edition originally published in 2001 by Editions Olizane.
11, rue des Vieux-Grenadiers, CH-1205 Geneva, Switzerland

Translated from the French *La Route de la Soie—Dieux, Guerriers et Marchands* by Luce Boulnois
ISBN: 2-88086-249-3 Copyright © 2001, 2003
by Editions Olizane, 11 rue des Vieux-Grenadiers, CH-1205 Geneva, Switzerland
Web: www.olizane.ch

This English edition published by Odyssey Books & Guides, an imprint of
Airphoto International Ltd, 1401 Ching Ying Building
20–20A Connaught Road West, Sheung Wan, Hong Kong
Tel: (852) 2856-3896; Fax: (852) 2565-8004; E-mail: odysseyb@netvigator.com

Distribution in the United States of America by
W.W. Norton & Company, Inc., 500 Fifth Avenue, New York, NY 10110, USA
Tel: 800-233-4830; Fax: 800-458-6515
Web: www.wwnorton.com

Distribution in the United Kingdom and Europe by
Cordee Books and Maps, 3a De Montfort Street, Leicester LE1 7HD, UK
Tel: 0116-254-3579; Fax: 0116-247-1176
Web: www.cordee.co.uk

Library of Congress Catalogue Card Number: 97-66479
ISBN: 962-217-720-4 (Hardback); ISBN: 962-217-721-2 (Paperback)

Managing Editor: Helen Northey
Consultant Editor: Judy Bonavia-Boillat
Editor: Carey Vail
Design: Au Yeung Chui Kwai
Map Design: Editions Olizane
Translator: Helen Loveday
Index: Luce Boulnois and Editions Olizane/Airphoto International Ltd.

Front cover: Detail, *Majnun Approaches the Camp of Layli's Caravan*, from a manuscript of the *Haft Awrang* of Jami, Iran, 1556–65. Courtesy of the Freer Gallery of Art, Smithsonian Institution, Washington D.C. (repeated on 485); Back cover photo: Wong How Man

Photography by Wong How Man, Amar Grover and Adam Woolfitt

Additional photography and illustrations courtesy of: Museum für Indische Kunst, Berlin 3 (repeated on 488); Royal Geographical Society 8–9 (Ian MacWilliam), 25, 465 and 508 (Sassoon); Peter Fredenburg 12–13; William Lindesay 434, 447, 493, 520–21, 529, 533, 536; Jeffrey Jay Fox 466; Victoria and Albert Museum, Courtesy of the Trustees of the V&A 486, 494 (Daniel McGrath), 496; Shaanxi History Museum 487, 502, 503, 504–5, 506; Patricia Lanza 499; Xia Ju-xian 511.

Production by Twin Age Limited, Hong Kong
Manufactured in Hong Kong

Preceding pages: Crossing the Anjuman River, Badakhshan, Afghanistan
Following pages: On the Karakoram Highway, Xinjiang, China
Right: Thousand Buddha Cave, Shuilian Dong, near Wushan, Gansu province, China (Grover)

To my grand-daughter Gwenola Guyot

Preface

*W*hat do we mean today when we speak of the "Silk Road"? What images are conjured up by these two words, so laden with complex connotations and echoes? Do they correspond to a specific reality?

For some, the Silk Road is a distant travel destination, a place for historical tourism. It refers to China and to Central Asia, which is even more mysterious to us than China because our history and geography books have largely ignored it; its long history attracts us but is confined in our minds to a few key names such as Alexander the Great, Genghis Khan, Marco Polo, Prester John, the *Thousand and One Nights* and Tamerlane, yet we know there are more worlds to discover there.

For others, the Silk Road is Buddhism and its artistic remains, now familiar to us through superbly illustrated books, through films and television documentaries, and through conferences. Since the emigration of hundreds of thousands of Tibetans after 1959, Buddhism has become more widely known in the West, where it arouses both interest and sympathy.

For those interested in the history of civilizations and more particularly in the relations and exchanges between them—which is the subject of the present book— the Silk Road is not a single road but a network of routes, over both land and sea, which, starting from around the time of Roman expansion towards the Middle East in the 1st century BC, linked the Mediterranean world with China, as well as all the countries located between these two farthest points of the Eurasian continent. These were trade connections that operated not directly between these two extremities, but rather between partners at close hand: by land across the entire continent; and by sea through the ports of the Red Sea, the Persian Gulf, India, South-East Asia and China.

For those who love adventure, travel writings of the Silk Road gleam with words like caravan, horseman, nomad, yurt, desert, silence and immensity. These regions, closed to foreigners for so long, now offer up the beauty of their landscape to travel writers, to ascetics, to sportsmen and to romantics from the Mediterranean to the Great Wall.

Right: Kargi Bay, near Cnidos on the southern coast of Turkey. Seen through the columns of a ruined priory, a Turkish cruising ship for holidaymakers lies at anchor. (Woolfitt)

Modern Chinese historians begin their history of the Silk Road with what was for them the "opening to the West": an opening carried out by a diplomatic mission sent in the 2nd century BC by a Chinese emperor to a very distant land probably located in the north of present-day Afghanistan. What occurred thereafter is the story of the Chinese colonial empire, conquering, being conquered and reconquering again and again.

The land routes, which predominated for a long time, were complemented or replaced, at various periods and in various places, by maritime routes which finally became the more important, at least until the advent of the railway through the heart of Asia. These lines of communication have conveyed material and cultural exchange between the great civilizations that developed in this area over the past twenty-two centuries. We, in the East and the West, are the heirs to this exchange.

This trade and transfer of material goods and technical knowledge occurred sometimes peacefully; amicably between neighbours, through diplomatic relations, through gifts between sovereigns, through marriage alliances between royal families or through commercial trade. At other times it occurred through war and conquest, plunder, enforced tribute, capture, slavery, the forcible transfer of specialists and technicians, artists or scholars; or even secretly, through trickery, as in the case of silkworm eggs and sericulture, because silk was for a long time one of the main products traded, hence the term which we are attempting to define here.

And then there is the mixing of peoples when cities were taken and the womenfolk captured, sold in the slave markets, scattered among the victors and buyers, bearing children of mixed blood; when entire communities were forced to move from one land to another, and resettled, mixing with the locals.

And so too have religious beliefs migrated and spread across the Asian continent—Buddhism, Manichaeism, Eastern Syrian Christianity (or Nestorianism), Islam, Roman Christianity—either through the vocation of missionaries, or because of persecution which compelled emigration, via merchant colonies settled abroad, taking with them their own religion, or through forced conversions.

All of that was in the old days, one might say, but can we really be sure that we are not once again in a period of population displacements through economic, ethnic or ideological conflict?

The history of Inner Asia, from the Chinese pole to the Iranian pole, is one of a cyclical unification and disintegration of great empires. Among these, the Chinese Empire, at times concentrated around its historical capitals and its Han provinces, at other times, in a phase of conquest, pushing out towards the Himalaya and the Pamir; sometimes diminished, conquered and subjugated by a foreign dynasty which it inevitably assimilated; at other times divided into several feudal kingdoms, but always born again and growing in power and strength.

The Iranian pole, equally indestructible, has played a political and cultural role in the western half of Inner Asia, as much during the pre-Islamic period as during that of the caliphate.

Between these two poles, empires lasting two or three centuries have appeared and disappeared: the Kushan Empire, the confederations of Huns and Turks, the Tibetan, Mongol, and Russian empires (the latter even approaching the limits of the British Empire), and then the Soviet Empire. The British Empire left Asia only in 1947; the Soviet one crumbled before our eyes in 1991. Is it the weakening of central power that leads to the dissidence of the outermost regions? Or is it the rejection of an authority loathed by a population that feels nothing in common with it? An old adage says that the security of the Chinese capital is at play on its furthest frontiers.

When dynasties decline, empires shrink or lose their outlying regions, their marches and the support of their satellites, the furthest reaches soon break up into a multitude of small kingdoms (sometimes several dozen of them), which then set up changeable alliances and destroy each other in feudal wars. They end up being consumed by a conqueror, who, having devoured all his neighbours, forms once more a great empire under his domination, and the cycle starts over again. Genghis Khan and Tamerlane started their careers on a very narrow base—and the rest is history. These coagulations and dissolutions of empires occur amidst great violence and sometimes true genocides.

In line with earlier tsarist policies towards Central Asia, the USSR believed it could at last turn Afghanistan into a complaisant satellite state, thereby ensuring a firm stand against its rival powers in Asia. However, the Soviet troops who entered Afghanistan in 1979 were forced to pull out without glory or profit ten years later, leaving behind a ruined and divided country, which had been for the Soviet power not a source of victorious success at all, but rather a time bomb.

Following pages: A Tajik wedding procession in the Pamir heads to the bride's home. The groom wears a red and white headscarf. (Wong)

Meanwhile, in 1991 when the USSR collapsed, the general situation in Central Asia seemed from afar to be relatively reassuring. One hoped that this time the drawing of a new political map and the creation of new independent states would be achieved without massacres, open warfare and destruction. In the West, since the fall of the Berlin Wall and the Soviet threat, one believed in a new era free from the Cold War and its nuclear risk looming over a world cut in half. China itself transformed its economic policy and developed commercial relations in all directions, including across the border with the former Soviet states. It attracted foreign investors and partners and relaxed its religious policies. Many of our fears disappeared. Were we now in a world free of Marxist dogma and "two block" policy, moving towards an era of peace, religious tolerance and prosperity?

Some even dreamed of a new caliphate, a renaissance of humanist Islam where arts, sciences and letters would bloom again from Turkey to Xinjiang—as in the splendorous time of Samarkand. However this dream was short-lived.

The twin themes of nationalism and religious fundamentalism were already stirring unrest and were a threat to the political stability and peace of the region. Western and Asian powers became increasingly preoccupied by the spread of Islamic fundamentalism—with the backing of certain powers, either openly or clandestinely, in a dynamic of conflict and terrorism, it introduced itself slowly into the four old Soviet Muslim republics of Central Asia (Uzbekistan, Turkmenistan, Kyrgyzstan and Tajikistan). Meanwhile in Xinjiang the Chinese government was working to neutralize aspirations of independence that combined anti-Chinese feelings and religious attachment to Islam. Observers had already drawn public attention to the economic and strategic importance of the oil and natural gas reserves present in enormous sites in the Caspian Sea, in Kazakhstan and in Xinjiang, as well as other parts of Central Asia, and to the power that would be linked with their possession. Already Russia, China and three, then four, of the newly independent republics (Kazakhstan, Kyrgyzstan and Tajikistan, and then Uzbekistan who joined in 2001) were striving to coordinate efforts to prevent the cultivation and traffic of opium, the enormous profits of which are used by various movements for the purchase of weapons. But nobody could then have imagined what happened on the other side of the world on 11 September 2001.

Right: On the Road, Xinjiang, China (Wong)
Following pages: Bezeklik Thousand Buddha Caves, near Turfan, Xinjiang, China (Wong)

The American reaction to this event was war—a new war—in Afghanistan, with its manifold effects on neighbouring countries. Then another war in Iraq, again led principally by the USA. America has seen its power increase enormously in the last decade. As the foremost military and economic world power it intervenes where it deems fit. So too do terrorists. For this reason the great new fear is not so much the use of nuclear weapons but the threat of chemical and biological warfare.

Today we talk of the Islamic threat, of the risks linked with American imperialism, of incompatible civilizations, of forces of good and evil. How is it possible for nations and provinces with a predominantly Muslim population situated along the Silk Road not to be deeply concerned?

In just a few trimesters we have unwillingly turned a page and chapter in the book of history. But it is still the same history and it is still the same book—with pages we love to reread and pages we would like to forget—but this is impossible, for they are both part and parcel of our very being.

L.B.
Meudon, December 14, 2003

Author's Note

For the transcription of Chinese words, the official pinyin system used in the People's Republic of China has been adopted throughout. The reader should bear in mind that words which appear as homophones in transcription would be easily differentiated from one another in Chinese by their tones and the characters used to write them; the customary habit of distinguishing the two neighbouring provinces of Shanxi and Shaanxi by their spelling has been followed.

Many cities and geographical features have had several different names over the centuries. These are, in most cases, cross-referenced in the index. (See also the chapter on Comparative Place Names, page 507.)

Modern maps in many countries often use very different spellings for the same locality, and the post-colonial period in Asia has led to a great number of changes in place names. Maps are therefore often out of date. Those in the present book tend to provide the name most frequently used in the West at the moment (such as Kashgar, Khotan), even when this is not the current official name in the state to which these cities now belong, and even when they have had other names in the past. To help the reader locate a city, many of the maps show the present provincial borders or international frontiers as faint dotted lines.

The borders of the states and empires shown on the maps in this book (the Kushan, Parthian, Sassanian empires and the Turkish kingdoms, for example) are very approximate: either because they cannot be defined with any precision today, or because they changed frequently. A map which covers a long period of time is by its very nature incorrect for several reasons: in the case of Central Asia, in a few centuries, there were at times thirty-six, then fifty, and occasionally even seventy kingdoms on the same expanse of territory, some of whose names are unknown. Furthermore, our notion of a frontier and of sovereignty does not correspond to a situation which included suzerain, vassal or tributary kingdoms, protectorates and zones of influence, all of which represent degrees between the extremes of full independence and complete annexation.

As for the trade routes, the references to them in ancient texts are generally very succinct. These routes have been established as accurately as can be using various criteria such as texts and observations on the ground. Certain reliable elements, such as known cities, markets and ports, remains of caravanserais and warehouses, can also be depended on. Nevertheless, the placing on a map of these routes which are reconstructed from a combination of data varying from established facts to uneasy hypotheses is an enterprise which is necessarily unsatisfactory.

Right: Masud Minaret, Ghazni, Afghanistan

Contents

The Silk Road Today

Maps

Right: Detail from the dome of the 17th-century Masjed-e Emam, one of Iran's most celebrated mosques, Isfahan, Iran. (Grover)

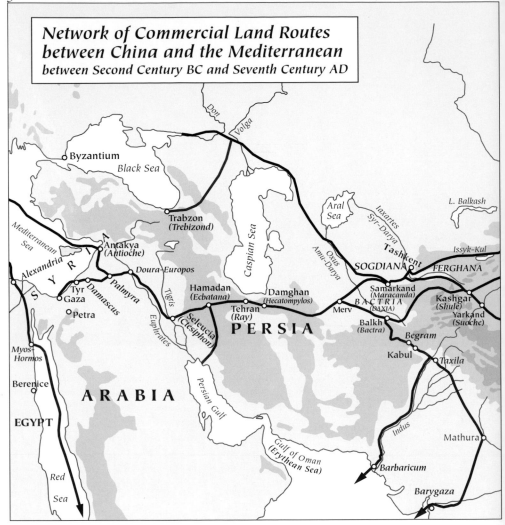

Network of Commercial Land Routes between China and the Mediterranean
between Second Century BC and Seventh Century AD

Network of Commercial Land Routes

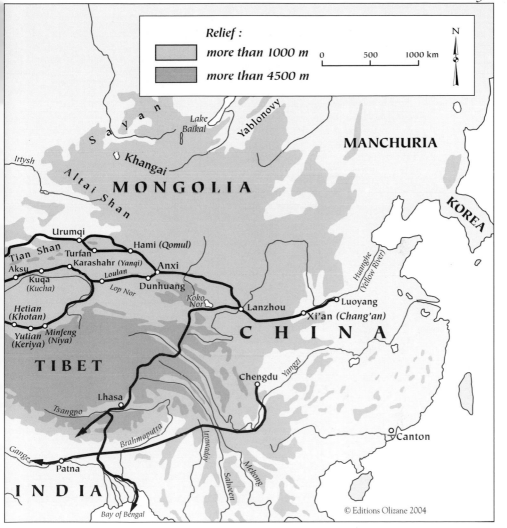

A Uighur woman reels raw silk onto a hand-cranked wooden wheel, Khotan, Xinjiang, China. (Wong)

Chapter One

Serica

*I*n the early summer of 54 or 53 BC—some 700 years after the foundation of Rome—Marcus Licinius Crassus, consul-triumvirate of Rome and governor of Syria, rashly led his seven legions eastwards, beyond the Euphrates, in search of an elusive enemy.[1] But endless days of uncertainty, awaiting a battle that never came, weakened the army's resolve. Since their departure from Syria, a disturbing series of inauspicious omens had been observed: Crassus and his son had stumbled and fallen when leaving the temple in Hierapolis, while Crassus' horse had bolted and drowned in the Euphrates. In this doubtful and anguished mood, the superstitious soldiers, so far from home, could not fail but recall the old curses muttered in the streets of Rome against Crassus. For were they not well aware of the power of maledictions?

Crassus' army officers too fully realized the madness of this war and its unpopularity in Rome. It was even in breach of a friendly accord existing between Rome and the country they were invading. They sensed that its sole objective was the enhancement of Crassus' personal glory, motivated by his jealousy of the other triumvirs, Caesar and Pompey.

Suddenly they were under attack. With an inhuman din, amidst the deafening roar of large leather drums covered in bells, the long-haired Parthian warriors hurled themselves at the Roman legions, showering them with arrows and surrounding them. The Romans, their hands nailed to their shields by the arrows, bewildered and overwhelmed, nonetheless attempted again and again to engage in hand-to-hand combat. But the Parthians remained strategically close enough to shoot, yet far enough away to avoid the melée.

In their rearguard, the Parthians had camels laden with arrows and were amply supplied with other ammunition. Their long spears tore through hard shields and soft padding alike, piercing two men at a time. Their archers succeeded in breaking the Roman tortoise formation, slashing like scythes at the soldiers' and horses' legs, and penetrating beyond the wall of shields.

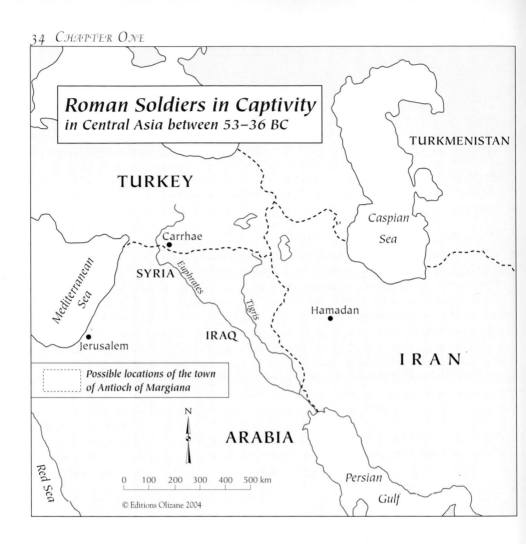

Roman Soldiers in Captivity
in Central Asia between 53–36 BC

TURKMENISTAN

TURKEY

Caspian
Sea

Carrhae

Mediterranean
Sea

SYRIA

Euphrates

Tigris

Hamadan

Jerusalem

IRAQ

IRAN

Possible locations of the town
of Antioch of Margiana

N

ARABIA

0   100   200   300   400   500 km

Red Sea

Persian
Gulf

© Editions Olizane 2004

According to the accounts of Florus and Plutarch,[2] written much later, the Romans at first believed that they were up against a small number of enemy soldiers, for the Parthian general had concealed his main force behind his advance guard. Their armour and helmets, their weapons and standards had been covered with robes and furs to prevent them from gleaming.

But in the bright sunlight, the Parthians had suddenly torn away the covers, revealing their helmets and weapons made from "Margianian iron glittering clean and bright", their horses clad in plates of copper and iron, and their "standards shining with gold and silk". The Romans saw that a vast army

confronted them. Stunned, blinded and deafened by the war cries and the drums of this enemy, outnumbered and weakened by thirst in the June desert heat, the legions fled.

Within a few hours the battle was over and the defeat complete. Crassus had been killed, along with his son, who had served under Caesar in Gaul and been sent by him to fight in Syria beside his father with his Gaul mercenaries. Twenty thousand Roman soldiers perished and ten thousand were taken captive. Thus did the Battle of Carrhae end. The site is today located in Turkish territory, near the Syrian frontier, not far from the Turkish town of Harran, between

Urfa, the Edessus of old, and the Syrio-Turkish frontier. The Roman eagles, far from entering the Parthian kingdom of the Arsacids victorious, entered as prisoners. They were to remain there for thirty-three years until a new political climate saw a few of them handed back to the Romans in 29 BC.

The Roman prisoners, among them foreign mercenaries, were deported to Antioch of Margiana, at the opposite end of the Persian Empire. A few were sent home with the Roman standards; most would never return. Their traces would, however, be picked up in the Orient; after all, ten thousand men do not disappear like a puff of smoke. The survivors of the Battle of Carrhae are but one example among many in Eurasian history of the movement of populations, both civilian and military, which were so often the result of wars in antiquity. It was these movements which contributed to the spread of ideas and of knowledge, to the intermixing of races, and perhaps to the collective memory of peoples.

> *It is very likely that the word* ser *came from the Chinese word for silk, pronounced* si *in Beijing dialect, and was probably the origin of the word "silk".*

What were these Parthian "standards of gold and silk", which so stunned the Roman soldiers? Florus is explicit: *auro sericeisque vexillis*, and *sericeus* means "of silk". Both the term and the object itself were widespread in Florus' time. *Sericum*, "silk"; *serica*, cloth or clothes made of silk. There is no ambiguity over the meaning of the words here: they refer to an expensive cloth of high quality, made on the eastern fringes of the world by a people known as the Seres (*ser*, *seris*, nominative plural *seres*). This referred to Chinese silk and to the people who made it. It is very likely that the word *ser* came from the Chinese word for silk, pronounced *si* in Beijing dialect, and was probably the origin of the word "silk".

But in 53 BC, the word *ser* and its derivatives had not yet entered the Latin vocabulary, and the cloth itself was almost unknown in Rome. Perhaps it had reached Greece as the word *ser* appears in Greek texts slightly earlier than it does in Latin ones. It was used to refer to a distant Oriental people, without any reference to textiles. One Greek author, Apollodorus of Artemita (died 87 BC)

—Artemita was a city in Assyria—used the word in this way. According to him, the conquests of Euthydemos, king of Bactria, had reached the land of the Seres in 220 BC.

Bactria, once a Persian satrapy conquered by Alexander the Great, occupied a region roughly to the south and south-west of the Amu-Darya River, part of present-day Afghanistan and Turkmenistan. After Alexander's death, the Persian Seleucid dynasty divided up the eastern part of his empire. In 255 BC, a satrap from Bactria proclaimed himself independent of the Seleucids, and succeeded in maintaining his independence for over forty years: it was during this period that King Euthydemos conquered his territories to the east, becoming a direct neighbour of the Seres.

However, between 212 and 205 BC, he was forced to accept the suzerainty of the Seleucid king, Antiochus III the Great (223–187 BC), who re-established Seleucid control from Syria to the Amu-Darya, becoming the new master of Bactria. According to Florus, Antiochus III also launched an expedition to Greece where he was defeated by the Romans, in 191 or 190 BC. During this attempted conquest, he camped in Euboea, on the shores of the Euripes, *positis aureis sericisque tentoriis*, "having set up tents of gold and silk". The island of Euboea is a large Greek island in the Aegean Sea, separated from peninsular Greece by the Straights of Euripes. Assuming that Florus is using the term *sericus* in reference to cloth from Seres, this would indicate a very early appearance of Chinese silk on the shores of the Mediterranean.

According to geologists, the southern part of the island of Euboea subsided, leaving only a few islets emerging from the water, including Kea, Pliny's Ceos which we shall be mentioning soon, and which was also associated with a textile closely related to Seric cloth.

The Romans probably took the term *ser* from the Greeks once the long-term presence of Roman soldiers began in Greece, although through what intermediaries the word had appeared earlier in the Greek vocabulary is not known.

The eastward spread of Roman power had begun in 220 BC in Illyria, on the eastern edge of the Adriatic Sea, and was followed by the conquest of the powerful kingdom of Macedonia, temporarily beaten in 197 BC. Roman troops were active in Greece (though possibly not on many of the islands) for decades before they succeeded in transforming all the Greek kingdoms into tributaries or Roman provinces. This was finally achieved in 146 BC. The incursion of Antiochus III into Euboea and peninsular Greece was brief, and he was driven back into Asia. He may have brought with him to Euboea silks and other products from the Far East, but this would only have been an isolated occurrence.

Roman expansion continued towards the East, in Asia Minor: Galatia, Bithynia, Cappadocia and Pergamon were all absorbed into the Roman province of Asia founded in 129 BC. Mithridates, king of Pontus (a kingdom on the Black Sea, to the north of present-day Asian Turkey), fought the Romans for twenty years before his final defeat in 63 BC when Pontus was annexed to the province of Asia. Syria and Phoenicia in turn became Roman provinces in 62 BC, and Palestine became a tributary.

In the meantime, Pompey (consul-triumvir with Crassus and Julius Caesar), had succeeded in freeing the eastern Mediterranean of the troublesome pirates who had effectively controlled it, forming a veritable seafaring power from their bases in Cilicia, on the south coast of Asia Minor. The sea was now open to Roman ships and to those of her allies and tributaries, for the movement of troops and weapons, war booty and slaves, and to trade of all kinds. Soon to be called an empire, Roman power extended as far west as parts of Spain and Gaul, in the east to Asia Minor and Syria, and in Africa to Carthage (which had been destroyed). But Rome was to face a new enemy: Iran had passed, province by province, from the hands of the Hellenized Seleucid dynasty into those of the Parthian Arsacids. It was these Parthians who threatened the Oriental Roman protectorates and provinces when Marcus Licinius Crassus was made governor of Syria, in 56 BC.

In all probability, these *serica*—these precious gold-embroidered silks from the land of the Seres—were first seen by Roman soldiers stationed at their easternmost outposts, either through the intermediary of the Seleucid army (which had contact as much with Greece as it did with Central Asia, and perhaps even the Far East), or of the Parthian army (which was in contact with Bactria in the east and Syria in the west). But one might well ask, why not earlier?

There is nothing to prove that Chinese silks had not appeared at some earlier point here and there around the Mediterranean or the Black Sea. Perhaps as royal gifts, acquired from nomadic "barbarians" from Asia—tribes shunted ever westwards by war until they reached the northern shores of the Black Sea—who had had much earlier contacts with the Greeks. There is nothing to prove to the contrary. It is quite possible that silks were a rare luxury, reserved for the nobility and were handed down, sold or plundered and transported as booty, ending up in a merchant's warehouse, before being purchased by a rich buyer. This is certainly suggested by the remains found in royal and noble tombs. According to reports published in 1993, silk strands, of probable Chinese origin, were found intertwined in the hair of an Egyptian mummy dated circa 1000 BC.[3] The mummy was that of a 30- to 50-year-old woman; she lay in Thebes in a cemetery for king's labourers. The discovery indirectly resulted from UNESCO's

> *The silk strands were very probably of Chinese origin. Their diagnosis was based on the absence of sericin, a gummy protein which is wrapped around the silk fibres of the cocoon; its absence indicates that the thread was treated according to Chinese techniques.*

efforts to save cultural remains from the destruction wrought by the construction of the Aswan Dam. Archaeologists from the Soviet Union and Eastern Europe carried out the excavation work; researchers from Vienna examined the mummy and concluded that the silk strands were very probably of Chinese origin. Their diagnosis was based on the absence of sericin, a gummy protein which is wrapped around the silk fibres of the cocoon; its absence indicates that the thread was treated according to Chinese techniques. This is thought to be one way of distinguishing Chinese silk from the various raw silks which exist or existed in certain Mediterranean countries.

Apart from this discovery, other evidence suggests that silk was quite widespread in Egypt at around the same time it was in Rome, when commercial links with eastern Asia had become more frequent and more important.

Other, slightly less recent archaeological finds have revealed the existence of silks (whether of Chinese origin is not clear) in tombs dating from the 7th century BC in Germany, in the state of Bade-Wurtemberg, and from the 5th century BC in Greece.[4] Their presence, like that of Chinese silk in Egypt several centuries earlier, does not in itself prove that there was steady commercial contact with the silk-producing land on the other side of the continent, but neither does it prove the opposite. In truth, the history of the transmission of products and techniques should be looked at from the opposite perspective than is usually adopted: we should be asking not when, why or how a product, a cultural feature, or a genetic stock (plant, human or animal) passed from one point of the globe to another, but rather how and why it did not occur earlier.

We should begin from the assumption that it should, quite naturally, have spread, and then examine the sequence of obstacles—the withholding of information, commercial and strategic secrets, monopolies, imperialism and fears—all of which played a part. No sooner do we come across the first appearance of silk in the West than we must ask ourselves: why so late? Were the Chinese not already producing gorgeous silks at the time of the Trojan wars, in the time of Moses and even earlier? Even if trade routes or important trade flows did not yet exist, exchange on a lesser, more individual scale could equally well have brought these products to other peoples on the Eurasian continent. Gifts of precious silks between kings were an age-old practice which the Chinese emperors made into a characteristic feature of their policy towards their nomadic neighbours. The plundering which occurred after the capture of towns or palaces was another process through which this exchange could have occurred.

> *Gifts of precious silks between kings were an age-old practice which the Chinese emperors made into a characteristic feature of their policy towards their nomadic neighbours.*

The progress made in archaeological laboratory techniques now allows us to analyse in more detail, and with more certainty, the remains discovered both previously or more recently (and their number grows daily); new hypotheses can be put forward. From one decade to the next, the trade network of antiquity is revealed as being far richer and older than we had previously thought.

There is one more detail from Plutarch's account (written a hundred and fifty years after the Battle of Carrhae), which echoes, as it were, the silk standards of the Parthians. It is his mention of the helmets and weapons "made of Margianian iron glittering clean and bright" which contributed to blinding the Roman soldiers on that fateful day. This iron of Margiana was very probably Chinese iron which, at this period, was highly reputed in Central Asia and Persia, being of much superior quality, owing to the high level of Chinese technology. This, at least, is what the ancient Chinese historians tell us; it is also the opinion of the Latin writer Pliny the Elder (died 79 AD), who wrote in his *Natural History* (Book 34, chapter 41): "But of all the varieties of iron, the palm goes to the Seric, sent us by the Seres with their fabrics and skins. The second prize goes to Parthian iron." Both Plutarch and Pliny were writing at a time when people had become familiar with products from India and from lands beyond.

But where was Margiana? What the Greeks called Margyanê, and the Romans Margiana, extended to the south-east of the southern shores of the Caspian Sea, just south-west of Bactria, within the borders of the present-day Republic of Turkmenistan. It was a prosperous oasis on the lower course of the Murgab River, a dependency of the Parthian government. Pliny, in Book 6, describes it as a sunny land, where vines were grown, surrounded by a beautiful ring of mountains, but difficult to reach on account of the great sandy deserts which separated it from Parthia. This was, therefore, an ideal location to send captive soldiers, and it was there that the Parthian king deported the prisoners from the Battle of Carrhae: Romans, Gauls, as well as mercenaries from other lands, were forced to settle down in Antioch of Margiana to guard the eastern frontiers of the Parthian Empire against the nomads. Antioch of Margiana was the other name of Alexandria-Margiana, one of many eponymous cities founded by

Alexander the Great. Destroyed by the nomads, it had been rebuilt by the Syrian king Antiochus I Soter, son of Seleucus, in the first half of the 3rd century BC, and was renamed after that ruler. That city too disappeared. Some researchers locate it on the site of the later town of Merv, an important cultural and commercial centre in the Middle Ages, during the Muslim period.

Merv was also in turn destroyed, this time by the Mongols, in 1221. The ruins of ancient Merv are still visible, in the Republic of Turkmenistan, just to the north of Bairam-Ali, in the delta of the Murgab River, 20 kilometres south of the modern Karakum canal. Merv is located just north of the canal. Thirty kilometres west of these ruins is the main town of the district of Mary, a town founded in the 19th century on the site of an ancient fortress; it was known as New Merv before being re-baptized Mary in 1937. It is in this area that archaeologists have long searched for Antioch of Margiana and possible locations for its site include present-day Giaur-Kala, east of the ruins of Merv, an area further south, in the valley of the Tedjen River, or somewhere along the upper reaches of the Murgab River.[5]

This same fate befell numerous other cities of Central Asia, destroyed by conquerors from both East and West, razed and then rebuilt on the same site or nearby. Oasis-towns were brought to their knees by the destruction of their irrigation canals. Independent city-states had their populations partly exterminated, while the survivors were enslaved and moved to other regions, few ever managing to escape to freedom. When a city was founded or re-founded, it would sometimes be populated with inhabitants from some other vanquished town, also plundered and destroyed.

Eighteen years after the Battle of Carrhae, in 36 BC, a Chinese army corps fought against foreign troops when it besieged the fortified town of Zhezhe in Central Asia. This town, which was occupied by a Xiongnu chief (after whom the city was named), lay some 700 or 800 kilometres north-east of Margiana, in the north of the Republic of Kyrgyzstan, probably in the valley of the Talas River. Were these Roman prisoners who had escaped from Margiana? Had they been sold or been presented as gifts to friendly princes? Or had they become mercenaries to some nomad chieftain? These foreign soldiers used the famous

Roman tortoise battle formation, a technique in which their large, rectangular shields were raised above their heads, resembling fish scales, forming an impenetrable wall on all sides against arrows and spears. The ramparts of the town were protected by a double row of stakes—another Roman practice. An account of this battle appears in a Chinese dynastic history, the *Hou Han shu*, or *History of the Later Han*, written at the end of the 1st century AD, a text to which we shall refer frequently. The details of these military techniques were considered striking enough to be worthy of mention in this text, although the Chinese author had no notion that soldiers who had originally come from the Far West had ever been present in the fortress. Zhezhe was overrun by a Chinese expeditionary force, which had been sent on a reprisal mission. Part of the population was exterminated, and the remainder captured and enslaved, including 145 soldiers who, for some reason, were not put to death.

Nothing more is heard of these men, but forty years on, in 5 AD, local Chinese chronicles mention a town called Lijian, in Gansu province, just south of Yongchang. The area had long before been conquered by the Chinese who had populated the towns and villages with convicts and displaced persons. Lijian is the name Chinese texts of the time gave to Rome, either broadly to encompass regions of Roman culture and allegiance, or to the western part of what was to be called the Roman Empire. The place name Lijian remained in the local registers until the 5th century.

It was the British Sinologist, Homer H. Dubs, translator, among other works, of the Chinese historical chronicles of the Former Han dynasty, who first brought this episode of history to the attention of Western readers. In a study called *A Roman City in Ancient China*, published in 1957, he examines the possible Roman origin of the soldiers who defended the town of Zhezhe against the Chinese, offering very plausible comments and arguments. The only other possible explanation might be that these military techniques (especially the tortoise formation, which required thorough training) had been learnt by ex-prisoners of the Romans—Parthians, for instance—who had either escaped or been freed, or by others who had had dealings with the Romans, and who, through the vagaries of war, had taught their military know-how to others.

Following the tracks of these reluctant travellers, we are led through time to the early years of the Christian era, for it is then that the word *Seres* appears for the first time in a Latin text—in a much quoted verse from the *Georgics* of Virgil (died 9 AD). After a passage mentioning the forest products of India, Ethiopia and Arabia, Virgil writes (Book 2, verse 121): "*Velleraque ut foliis depectant tenuia Seres?*" (from the immediately preceding text, one must supply two words, and read it as "*Velleraque quid referam ut foliis depectant tenuia Seres*"), translated as: "And why should I tell you how the Seres comb off [card, separate with a comb] the fine down of the leaves?"

> *The theory about the vegetable nature of Seric cloth was to survive for a long while among Latin writers.*

It would seem that for Virgil, the cloth of the Seres was made by combing some sort of substance off the leaves of trees. Is this a form of cotton? Are we meant to think of the raw cocoons, lightly stuck by their gum to the leaves of certain trees, which the Romans had heard of? But this verse is to be found in a chapter on plant products, and the theory about the vegetable nature of Seric cloth was to survive for a long while among Latin writers.

Seric cloth had become widely used in just a few years, at the time of Caesar, Crassus and Pompey. It was still employed mainly for military honours, and contributed in Rome to the splendour of the triumph of Julius Caesar, in 46 BC, when the victorious general astounded the crowds by having silk banners unfurled over the heads of the spectators.

Sixty years on, silk had become common in Roman civilian society. It had become such a fad among wealthy families that, in 14 AD, a few months before the death of Emperor Augustus, an edict from the Senate forbade men from wearing silk, "which dishonours them", and limited its use to women. Later, in other countries, similar sumptuary laws would attempt to offset the excessive spending of a particular social class on luxury goods and the excessive amounts of money leaving the country. These laws had both a moral and an economic goal: to avoid ostentation and a lowering of moral standards, to preserve the old virtues of simplicity, and to prevent waste and commercial imbalance caused by the import of luxury goods. Beautiful, shimmering silk, sometimes associated with gold ("cloths of gold and silk" was an expression which appears time and again in Florus as well as Marco Polo), was all the more prized because it was imported from distant lands, and was a symbol of luxury, along with gems, ivory and rare perfumes. It scandalized the moralists and worried the economists. Latin writers from the 1st century AD on would often express similar sentiments.

New words were soon added to the old *sericum, serica, sericeus,* and *Seres* of Latin vocabulary: words such as *sericatus,* "clothed in silk", and later *sericarius,* "silk merchant", *sericoblatta,* "clothes of silk dyed purple". But what exactly was this Seric cloth, *sericum*? Where did it come from, and by what route did it arrive in the Parthian kingdom, and onwards to Greece, Egypt and Rome?

Chapter Two
The Land of Silk

That which is properly known as silk is the unbroken thread unwound from the cocoon of the silkworm, *Bombyx mori*, which feeds mainly on the leaves of the white mulberry tree (*Morus alba*). This caterpillar turns into a chrysalis, but is not permitted to transform itself into a moth, so that the cocoon is not perforated. Thus a continuous unwound thread is what distinguishes cultivated silk from the various forms of wild silk, made from the cocoons of other caterpillars, in which the moth leaves the cocoon by piercing a hole through it, thus breaking the thread which the caterpillar has wound around itself. In this instance, the silky substance has to be woven just as one would cotton, and the thread obtained is less fine and inferior in quality than thread from an intact cocoon. Wild silks, produced by various insects, exist in many parts of the world from Assam to Madagascar; the Mediterranean countries also produced their share of them, around the same time that Seric cloth appeared there. This has led to a certain confusion in the use of the various terms for these fabrics, as we shall see.

A continuous unwound thread is what distinguishes cultivated silk from the various forms of wild silk.

Let us summarize the life cycle of the silkworm, at least in so far as it is known in our temperate climes and with the present-day species of caterpillar. The fertilized egg turns from yellow to grey in the first two days after it is laid. This egg, the size of a pin head, goes through a period of rest (diapause) which lasts ten months, the first five months of which are spent in a warm environment, between 22° and 24° C, followed by five months in the cold, but above freezing, at 5° C. At the end of these ten months, the egg is ready to hatch. It is encouraged to hatch by progressively increasing the temperature to 24° C in a humid atmosphere, nowadays carried out in an incubator. In earlier times, this reheating, which lasted twelve days, was done in various ways. The peasant women of 19th-century France are said to have kept the eggs next to their skin under their bodices. In China, at the beginning of the 20th century, they were placed under the bed quilt. In the 6th century, according to one Byzantine author writing three centuries later, the Central Asian technique was to cover them with fresh manure.

> *The caterpillar weaves its cocoon with its "saliva", using a thread secreted by its silk-producing glands, winding it round itself in a figure-of-eight pattern.*

At last the egg hatches: out comes a minuscule larva, weighing half a milligram, which will soon increase its weight 10,000 times, feeding on an exclusive diet of mulberry leaves. After about five weeks, during which it sheds its skin four times, the caterpillar weaves its cocoon with its "saliva", using a thread secreted by its silk-producing glands, winding it round itself in a figure-of-eight pattern over a period of about four days. The substance which it secretes is composed mainly of fibroin wrapped in sericin, which will become the silk thread.

Once its cocoon is completed, the caterpillar turns into a chrysalis and over a period of 10 to 12 days transforms itself into a moth. The moth then secretes a liquid called coconase, which softens the thread and allows it to leave the cocoon by parting the threads. Almost as soon as the moths have left their cocoons, they mate, and egg laying begins one day later. But this natural cycle occurs only in the case of cocoons, set aside for reproduction; the rest are scalded or suffocated before the chrysalis can turn into a moth and make its exit hole. The process known as reeling (unwinding the thread from the cocoon) can now begin. With those cocoons reserved for reproduction, about two months elapse before the hatching of a new generation of eggs.

For a very long time, the cocoons were scalded, a process which both kills the chrysalis and softens the gum in which the cocoon is wrapped, essential for the unwinding of the silk thread. Today, the chrysalis is suffocated by exposing the cocoon to hot air, in an oven; after this, cocoons can be left for several months before reeling.

The ten-month incubation period of the eggs is an important element when considering the history of the spread of sericulture. It was this delay, with its succession of hot and cold periods, which allowed the transport of the eggs without killing them and preventing them from hatching before they could be properly fed. These were

> *The ten-month incubation period of the eggs is an important element when considering the history of the spread of sericulture.*

times when journeys took months, sometimes years, and when the goods transported were subject to very variable and sometimes extreme temperatures. Historical or semi-historical accounts which mention the export of silkworm eggs over very long distances across Central Asia, in the 5th, 6th and 7th centuries AD, do not explain what measures were taken to prevent the eggs from hatching too early. The problem simply does not appear to have arisen. And yet this detail, which is no longer important to modern sericulture, is tremendously significant when we consult these texts. How much credibility can we give these texts if it turned out that it was impossible to transport silkworm eggs for three or six months, or even longer, without them hatching, despite extremes in temperature? If it was indeed possible to do so (and assuming the Chinese and Central Asian silkworms prior to the 8th century shared the same traits as modern ones), it was nonetheless no easy task.

Once the chrysalis has been suffocated, the cocoon can be unwound intact, with its continuous thread measuring between 600 and 2,000 metres in length. Having softened the sericin around the cocoon by boiling it in water, the end of the thread can be teased free. The threads from several cocoons are twisted together so as to form a single thread of raw silk, which is coiled into skeins; this process is known as throwing. The silk is now ready to be dyed and woven.

In China, the origin of the invention of the reeling process has its own myth. Both historical records and archaeological finds confirm the great antiquity of silkworm breeding and reeling (although the language of these ancient texts does not allow one to determine precisely at what period the cocoons were first scalded before the appearance of the moths in order to obtain a continuous thread). As silkworms for wild silk and mulberry trees were

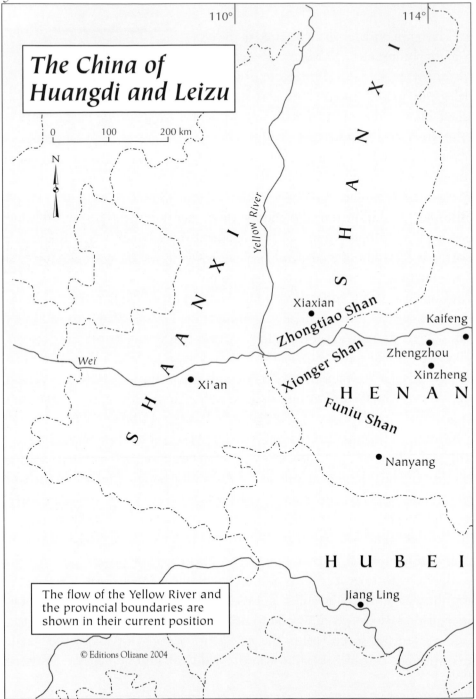

The China of Huangdi and Leizu

0   100   200 km

N

110°

114°

S H A A N X I

S H A A N X I

Yellow River

Xiaxian

Zhongtiao Shan

Kaifeng

Xionger Shan

Zhengzhou

Xinzheng

Weï

Xi'an

H E N A N

Funiu Shan

Nanyang

H U B E I

Jiang Ling

The flow of the Yellow River and the provincial boundaries are shown in their current position

© Editions Olizane 2004

118°

122°

38°

HEBEI

Gulf of
Bo Hai

34°

SHANDONG

Yellow River

Shou Qiu

Qu Fu

Yellow Sea

JIANGSU

Nanjing

Shanghai

Suzhou

Tai
Hu

Changjiang
(Yangzi)

Huzhou-
Wu
Xing Xian

ZHEJIANG

indigenous to the region, and the climate was favourable, it is not surprising that there developed a textile industry exceptional both for the quality and the quantity of its production.

Chinese tradition attributes the invention of most arts and crafts to Emperor Huangdi, the Yellow Emperor, also known as the Great Inventor, the third of the legendary wise emperors, whose reign is traditionally dated at between 2674 and 2575 BC.[6] His predecessors, Fu Xi and Shennong, who reigned successively between 2852 and 2674 BC, are said to have invented agriculture, husbandry, fishing, medicinal herbs and trade, to mention but a few. Huangdi is credited with the invention of feeding techniques, the use of hemp instead of animal furs for clothes, the construction of huts to replace caves, boats and animal-drawn carts as a means of transport, weapons, pottery, copper containers, music and the calendar. His wife Leizu is said to have invented silkworm breeding, the reeling of cocoons and the making of silk clothing.

Leizu, whose name is composed of the character *lei*, comprising the elements for "woman", "field" and "silk thread", and the character *zu*, meaning "ancestor", came from the Xiling clan. According to the *Shiji*, a historical text written by the Grand Historian Sima Qian (died 86 AD), "Huangdi took as his first wife a daughter of the Xiling clan, called Leizu." She was the first to teach her people to breed silkworms, to unwind the cocoons and to make clothes with the thread. Later, she was considered the goddess of the silkworm and as the second most important woman in the history of China, the first being Nüwa, wife of the legendary Emperor Fu Xi. According to tradition, the Son of Heaven himself ploughs the land and the empress herself tends the silkworms, symbolizing together the two pillars of the Chinese economy in ancient times. And indeed for centuries, until the last Chinese dynasty, the sovereign would symbolically carry out the rite of ploughing the first furrow of the year in person.

Where was the kingdom of Huangdi located and where did the mulberry trees grow which fed Leizu's silkworms?

LOCATION OF SERICULTURE IN CHINA

Traditionally, Huangdi is said to have been born at Shouqiu, in the province of Shandong, about three kilometres north-east of the city of Qufu, where the second legendary Emperor Shennong had set up his capital. This region was part of the kingdom of Lu, future birthplace of Confucius (6th century BC). It was here that the famous "thousand mulberry trees of Qi and Lu" grew, and the *Shijing*, or *Book of Odes*, a compilation of some 300 ancient poems attributed to Confucius and one of the great classics of Confucianism, calls this area the "land of mulberry trees". The province of Shandong has long been known as a silk-producing region, both of wild and cultivated silk. However, one modern historian, Zhang Qiyun, suggests that the homeland of Huangdi's clan, the Bear Clan, was not located in Shandong but in Henan province, at Xinzheng, in the district of Kaifeng, just south of Zhengzhou. He posits that the name, "Yellow Emperor", would have derived from the name given to this region, known in Chinese as "Yellow Earth" because of the colour of its fertile loess soil. Basing his theory on similarities between place names and clan names, Zhang Qiyun considers that the clans of Huangdi and Xiling originated from the area around the Funiu mountains, in the west of Henan province, a region where the silkworm is indigenous and which still produces wild silks today. This would therefore make Henan the oldest, or at least one of the oldest, areas in which sericulture was practised. In 1926, Chinese archaeologists unearthed a cocoon in a Neolithic tomb in the far south-west of Shanxi province, near the village of Xiyin, in the district of Xiaxian, at the foot of the Zhongtiao mountains. This region of Shanxi is not far from the supposed homeland of the third legendary emperor and his wife in Henan. In 1958, some silk felt, a silk belt and fragments of raw silk were discovered in a Neolithic site in the province of Zhejiang, carbon 14 dated as 4,750 years old. This site is a village to the west of Wuxing Xian (now Huzhou), in the north of the province, near the southern shore of Lake Taihu, south-west of Shanghai. This cocoon and these pieces of silk are the oldest archaeological traces of the silk industry, not only in China, but in the entire world.

While the Chinese Empire was gradually taking shape, extending west and south from the middle course of the Yellow River, silkworm breeding and the art of weaving were developing, spreading and being perfected. Both reached a technical level and a quality which were unequalled elsewhere in the world, and silk was to become a mass-product of such high quality that for more than a thousand years it would be the main export of China, and one which remains important today.

> *It is women who are credited with the skill and know-how associated with the manufacture of cloth, mainly silk and hemp.*

As far back as one can go in the ancient texts, it is women who are credited with the skill and know-how associated with the manufacture of cloth, mainly silk and hemp. Once silkworms began to be bred and kept inside the house (around 1000 BC?), this activity can be considered as having become part of the daily life of three-quarters of Chinese villages. Women and girls spent a large part of their time nurturing the silkworms (the Chinese term for "breeding" animals also means "to nourish" or "bring up"). Fresh mulberry leaves had to be cut several times a day to feed the ravenous caterpillars. Mulberry trees were planted everywhere. Properly fed, maintained at a constant and warm temperature in a clean space, and placed at the right moment on racks, the silkworms would happily weave their cocoons. As soon as this was finished, they were scalded, and the reeling and throwing processes would begin, twisting together the fibres from several cocoons into a single thread. It was all a question of patience, care, skill and time. Weaving, dyeing and embroidery were other arts in which the Chinese excelled, and still excel.

The reign of the great Emperor Yu, legendary founder of the Xia dynasty, is traditionally dated from 2205 to 2197 BC, and was marked by a period of cataclysmic flooding. The kingdom was divided into nine fiscal regions, six of which were silk-producing: these were the regions (*zhou*) of Yu, Qing, Yan, Xu, Jing and Yang. The remaining three, Ji, Liang and Yong (two of which were the westernmost regions of China at that time) manufactured no silk. Information on the economic geography of this period is to be found in a text known as the *Tribute of Yu*, which lists the local products each region was to send as tax to

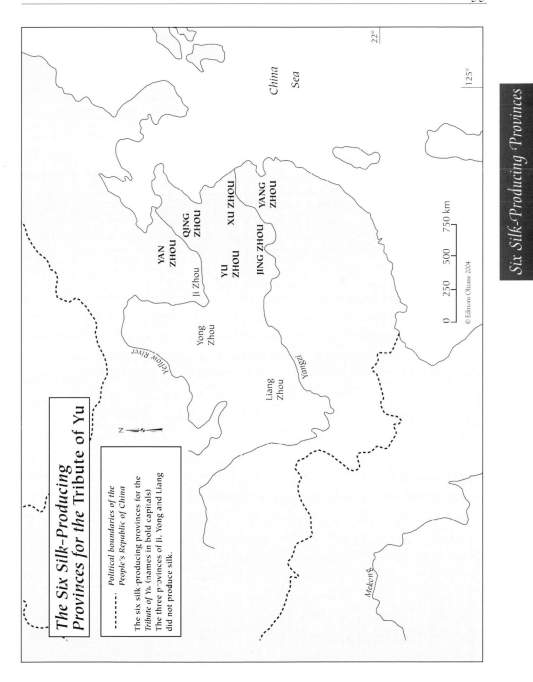

The Six Silk-Producing Provinces for the Tribute of Yu

- - - - - - - *Political boundaries of the*
People's Republic of China

The six silk-producing provinces for the
Tribute of Yu (names in bold capitals)
The three provinces of Ji, Yong and Liang
did not produce silk.

N

YAN
ZHOU

QING
ZHOU

XU ZHOU

YANG
ZHOU

Ji Zhou

YU
ZHOU

JING ZHOU

Yong
Zhou

Liang
Zhou

Yellow River

Yangzi

Mekong

China
Sea

22°

125°

0   250   500   750 km

© Editions Olizane 2004

Six Silk-Producing Provinces

the emperor. This tax was paid in kind: cereals, metal, silk, leather, bamboo and tortoiseshell. The *Tribute of Yu* has come down to us through the centuries as a section of one of the Chinese classics said to have been compiled and rewritten by Confucius, the *Shujing* or *Book of Annals*.

Mulberry trees and silk are very much present in the classical Confucian texts, reflecting both their antiquity and their importance in Chinese life. To the Western eye, the silkworm may not be particularly attractive, and yet, according to the *Shijing*, or *Book of Odes*,[7] it is said of a beautiful girl that "Her hands are like soft young shoots, her skin is like lard; her neck is like the tree-grub, her teeth are like melon seeds, her head is cicada-like, her eyebrows are silkworm-like." Another ode compares the mulberry tree which, so luxuriant when it is young, little by little becomes debilitated, exhausted by the continuous lifelong plucking of its leaves, to the debilitated and exhausted population, weakened by misery (the comparison may even suggest that that which weakens some may fatten others...).

> *To the Western eye, the silkworm may not be particularly attractive, and yet, according to the Shijing, or Book of Odes, it is said of a beautiful girl that "Her hands are like soft young shoots, her skin is like lard; her neck is like the tree-grub, her teeth are like melon seeds, her head is cicada-like, her eyebrows are silkworm-like."*

Even the ideograms of the Chinese written language confirm the ancientness of these practices: among the inscriptions on bone or tortoiseshell dating back to the Shang dynasty (second millennium BC), one comes across the characters *can* (silkworm), *sang* (mulberry tree) and *si* (silk).

During the so-called Warring States period (403–221 BC), the silk industry had already reached its peak. No other archaeological excavations in the world have brought to light such beautiful cloth from such an ancient period. By this time, brocades as well as light fabrics such as gauzes and crêpes had been invented in China; there were felts, taffetas and even serged armour. The richness of the textile vocabulary then is highly significant. Dyeing and embroidery had also reached a very high technical and artistic level. In a tomb dated approximately 300 BC, in Hubei province, just west of Jiangling (on the north bank of the Yangzi River), the body of a man was unearthed, dressed in over ten types of silk, with six padded silk counterpanes and embroidered silk covers. One set of clothes, made of silk gauze, is embroidered with dozens of tigers chasing their quarry across a decor of mountains and fantastic rocks. The embroidery, in relief on the front side of the cloth, is almost invisible on the back, a technique similar to the double-faced embroidery of Suzhou, in Jiangsu province (just west of Shanghai), that is still famous today.

Three hundred years before the Christian era, Alexander's empire had been divided up after his death and the Asiatic part of it had passed into the hands of the Seleucid kings. The early Chinese kingdoms were separated from the Seleucid Empire by nomad clans and tribes, as well as by immense and often barren open spaces. Greek texts of the time of Alexander knew nothing of China or of silk, and the contemporary Chinese texts made no mention of Western countries. The West was for the Chinese a mythical land where the kings and queens of old legends lived, such as Xiwangmu, the Queen Mother of the West, riding her phoenix-drawn chariot. It was inhabited by fabulous hybrid men and animals, which haunted the Kunlun mountains, a chain still known by that name in modern geography. But closer still, to the west and north, in their immediate vicinity, lived the enemy: the Xiongnu and the Mongol horsemen, nomads and barbarians.

It was to guard against these nomads, who harried the population living on the frontiers, that the Chinese emperor, Qin Shihuangdi (died 210 BC) built the Great Wall. Having conquered and drawn together under his supreme authority the neighbouring feudal states, he took, in 221 BC, the title of First August Emperor, *Shihuangdi*, *huang* being the equivalent of the Roman *Augustus* (no link with Huangdi, the Yellow Emperor). He devoted himself to unifying, consolidating, defending and governing the Chinese Empire, a ruler feared as much by his subjects as by his enemies. Apart from the construction of the Great Wall, a gigantic undertaking which led to the sacrifice of vast numbers of men, he is credited with the unification of writing, of units of measure, of laws and with the construction of roads. He is also responsible for the burning of the books of the Confucian school. Today, one visits not his mausoleum—the tumulus has been identified at Lintong, near the city of Xi'an, and has yet to be opened—but the astonishing terracotta army which was buried nearby. This is one of the most visited sites in China, and was discovered entirely by chance in 1974. Over six thousand clay statues have been unearthed, statues of warriors and horses, wearing helmets and armour, slightly larger than life-size, all different, sculpted in clay and buried near the imperial mausoleum which they have guarded in silence for twenty-two centuries.

The Great Wall (the Wall of Ten Thousand Li), sections of which still stand, served to protect the Chinese Empire against its nomadic enemies for many centuries, with the help of two other tools: cavalry and diplomacy.

As we have seen previously, according to the text of the Greek Apollodorus, Euthydemos, the king of independent Bactria, had extended his conquests eastwards, until he found himself near the land of the Seres in 220 BC. In all likelihood, this proximity led to hostilities, and any exchanges between them took the form of raids, plundering or extorted tribute. Indeed, booty was but one of the ways in which precious goods travelled. A notorious example of this, in more recent times, can be seen in the peregrinations of the Trojan treasure across Germany and Russia. Silk was a precious commodity, and it is perhaps as such that war chiefs and foreign courts first saw it. If, instead of being beaten at the Battle of Carrhae, the Romans had been victorious, they would have captured the Parthian standards and might have decorated their own temples, palaces and triumphant chariots with silk, and would have become familiar sooner with this new and superb exotic fabric.

Chapter Three

Adventures of a Diplomat-Explorer: The Opening of the Road to the West

C hinese historians date the first diplomatic and economic relations between China and the West to the 2nd century BC. This was when the "Western Territories" (Xiyu) were "opened up", to use the Chinese expression, by the famous westbound mission of Zhang Qian, in the Han dynasty, "in the third year of the Qianyuan era of the reign of Emperor Wudi", 138 BC. The aim of the mission was a strategic one, to establish military alliances with the heads of those tribes who were enemies of the Xiongnu, in order to take the latter from the rear.

The Xiongnu (long considered the ancestors of the Huns, a theory now contested) had become particularly powerful and aggressive in the period which followed the reign of Qin Shihuangdi, First August Emperor. At the beginning of the Han dynasty, founded in 206 BC, a confederation of Xiongnu tribes continually threatened China's security to the north and north-west, despite the Great Wall, carrying out raids, plundering the wealth of the sedentary agriculturists and artisans, following a pattern which was to last until modern days. Across the vast expanse of steppe and semi-desert which stretches from the Caspian Sea to Peking (Beijing), the nomads' main economic resources were the products of the breeding and hunting of animals. They were neighbours to prosperous kingdoms—large realms or small oasis-states—where agriculturists, artisans and merchants had developed a way of life which was culturally and artistically more sophisticated, as well as materially and technically more advanced than theirs. China, Iran, Russia and the fertile irrigated oases of Central Asia produced what these nomad people could not: cereals, textiles, goods made according to the latest technical advances of the period and, later on, tea and weapons.

The nomads were horsemen as well as archers; they carried out raids, fleeing after their attack, and were almost impossible to catch. For a sedentary nation, the best defence against these attacks was to build defences: the Great Wall of the First Emperor, fortified towns which could survive long sieges behind their towers and ramparts, numerous small forts guarding passes, routes, gorges, and customs posts. A string of fortifications stretched right across Central Asia, like a dotted line across a map, and the exchange of goods and ideas was concentrated at these points, either in the form of trade or diplomatic presents, or of attacks and plunder. Some of these fortifications are still standing while others are now in ruins. The Chinese Empire, the Iranian or Hellenized kingdoms of Central Asia, the Persian Empire, and later the Russian Empire have all been affected by the presence on their doorstep of these nomadic peoples.

The Chinese regarded the nomadic Turks and Mongols, with whom they had to deal throughout their history (even being conquered by them in the 13th century), in the same way that the Europeans would later see the Huns, and then the conquering Mongols of Genghis Khan: as uncultured and bloodthirsty barbarians, closer to wild beasts than to men. The fear that these nomads instilled still remains in people's imagination both in the East and the West. Chinese sculptures from the Han period show them with brutish faces, while the Christian maps of the Middle Ages placed the Mongols at the very extremity of Asia and identified them with the Gog and Magog of the Bible.

Our main sources today on the history of the reign of Han Wudi, his expeditions westwards, the expansion of Chinese influence into Central Asia, and the opening of China to the West are the *Qian Han shu*, or *History of the Former Han* (a text which covers the first half of the Han dynasty, from 206 BC to 9 AD, written at the end of the 1st century AD) by Ban Gu, and the *Shiji*, the *Record of the Historian*, written by Sima Qian, who died in 86 BC.[8] According to these, the Xiongnu had succeeded, around 140 BC, in forming a powerful kingdom, threatening all its neighbours. The wars against them had cost the Chinese so much money, so many horses and soldiers, either killed or taken captive, that Emperor Wudi of the Han tried a diplomatic approach: he sent an envoy to the Yuezhi, another nomadic people who had earlier been defeated by the Xiongnu, to obtain a military alliance with them. The chief of the Xiongnu had killed the king of the Yuezhi, and made a drinking cup from his skull, as was the custom of his people. He had driven the Yuezhi out, forcing them to emigrate thousands of kilometres further west, as far as the banks of the Amu-Darya, in the land of Daxia, the old Bactria of the Hellenized Persian Empire.

At the same time, the envoy was to gather any information he could on the countries he passed through or near, to establish contacts with them and set up alliances. It was a mission of diplomacy, strategy and intelligence.

> *To lead this expedition to the west, the Chinese emperor chose an officer from the palace guard named Zhang Qian, a native of Chenggu district, in south-west Shaanxi.*

But how was he to reach the Yuezhi? Not only was the route unknown, but he would have to pass through the territory of the Xiongnu, who blocked the way. For a long time, the Xiongnu had controlled the roads, maintaining a state of insecurity and preventing communication between the numerous small kingdoms that made up Central Asia. They would brutally attack travellers and merchants they came across, killing them and plundering the caravans.

EXPEDITIONS WESTWARD

To lead this expedition to the west, the Chinese emperor chose an officer from the palace guard named Zhang Qian, a native of Chenggu district, in south-west Shaanxi, just east of Hanzhong. He was at least thirty years old, courageous, extremely strong, very resolute and tenacious, capable of winning men over and was well acquainted with the Xiongnu, as well as with the situation in the Western Territories. He was joined by ninety-nine men, most of them junior officers or simple soldiers, as well as a few paupers. Among them was a certain Ganfu, a skilled archer, a Xiongnu who had been captured during the war against the Chinese. At first, he had been made a servant working for an aristocratic family in Shandong. But he felt very bitter towards the Xiongnu, having been mistreated in his own country and having suffered a great deal, and so he was freed and enrolled into the Chinese army. He proved a sure and very effective assistant for Zhang Qian.

They left in 138 AD from the capital Chang'an, the present-day city of Xi'an. Several centuries later, this famous expedition was illustrated among the frescoes of the cave-temples of Mogao at Dunhuang, in Gansu. Cave 123 shows Zhang Qian taking leave of the emperor just before his departure.

What followed then was a scarcely believable adventure. But of the hundred men who set out from China, only two were to return.

Zhang Qian led on his horse, carrying the insignia of his imperial mission: a bamboo pole over two metres long, with three tufts of yak-tail hair attached to it. This yak hair can reach two metres in length, and has always been an emblem of power across a large part of continental Asia.

They headed north-west, through southern Gansu province, crossing the Yellow River and entering what is known as the Hexi Corridor ("west of the river"), a territory which extends over hundreds of kilometres along the foot of the Qilian mountains and which is part of present-day Gansu. But they were to find that this area was occupied by the Xiongnu.

Shortly after leaving the Great Wall behind them, they took a wrong turn and came unexpectedly upon a strong detachment of Xiongnu horsemen. Unsurprisingly, the skirmish ended with the capture of the Chinese who were led to the king's residence. "The land of the Yuezhi is to the north of my territory", argued the king. "What right does the House of Han have in sending an ambassador there? If I wanted to send an ambassador to a country located south of China, would the House of Han allow me to do so?" Zhang Qian was roughly treated and then enslaved to an aristocratic Xiongnu family where he remained for eleven years, pasturing sheep and cows. During this time he married a Xiongnu slave and had one son.

One day, an opportunity of escaping presented itself. An unknown number of Chinese prisoners fled, taking with them dried food and water, and travelling westwards on foot as fast as they could. They "ate out in the wind and slept in the dew", according to the Chinese expression, and suffered from both hunger and thirst, from which several of them died. Fortunately, Ganfu and several

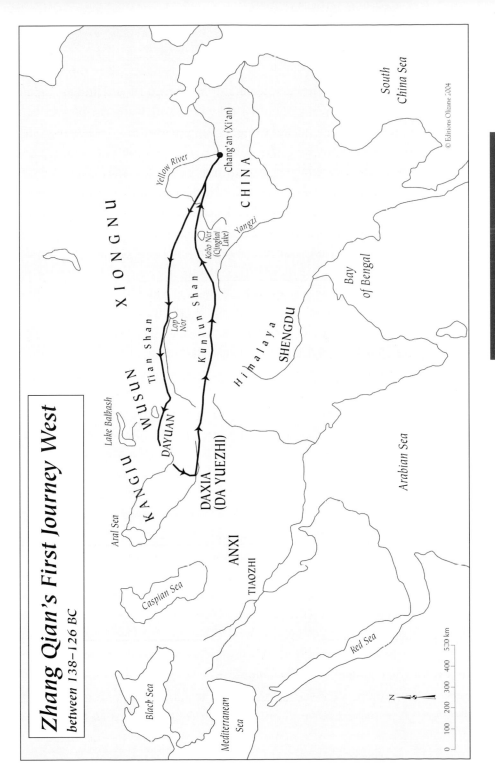

Zhang Qian's First Journey West
between 138–126 BC

South
China Sea

© Editions Olizane 2004

XIONGNU

Yellow River

Chang'an (Xi'an)

CHINA

Yangzi

Koko Nor
(Qinghai Lake)

Lop
Nor

Tian Shan

WUSUN

Kunlun Shan

SHENGDU

Himalaya

Bay
of Bengal

Lake Balkhash

KANGJU

DAYUAN

DAXIA
(DA YUEZHI)

Aral Sea

ANXI

TIAOZHI

Arabian Sea

Caspian Sea

Black Sea

Red Sea

Mediterranean
Sea

Z

0   100   200   300   400   530 km

others, who were skilled archers, were able to hunt for food, and managed to sustain the small troop. Crossing hills and valleys, orienting themselves by the position of the sun, the moon and the stars, they arrived after a difficult journey on the shores of a vast salt lake, the Lop Nor. This was the ancient kingdom of Loulan, unfortunately occupied by Xiongnu soldiers. Near the lake, they hunted and made provisions of food to continue their journey. They enquired about a route which would lead them to the Yuezhi, and followed the Tarim Basin along its northern edge.

What is now the Chinese province of Xinjiang was, at that time, divided into a multitude of small principalities, some of which were no more than fortified towns in the middle of an oasis. Zhang Qian and his companions passed through the kingdoms of Weili (present-day Weili Xian, just south of Korla, in central Xinjiang), Qiuci (near Kucha, or Kuqa, slightly further west), Shule (near Kashgar), and several others, eight in all. Finally, having skirted round a chain of mountains, they arrived in the kingdom of Dayuan, a peaceful and prosperous country of approximately 300,000 inhabitants, where they were warmly welcomed. This land was none other than the valley, or rather the depression, of Ferghana, encircled by high mountains, and located on the upper course of the Syr-Darya River (Naryn and Kara-Darya), in the far south-east of Uzbekistan, next to Kyrgyzstan. During the Muslim period, it was known as the kingdom of Kokand. The Chinese mission had arrived, by chance, in this blessed valley, the "pearl of Central Asia". It was, however, to play an unexpected role in Chinese foreign policy.

China was not entirely unknown to the king of Dayuan who had heard of it as a powerful and wealthy country. Zhang Qian remained in Dayuan for a time, discovering foods strange to the Chinese: grapes, carrots (which the Chinese called "*hu* turnip", *hu* being the term used to refer to anything which came from Central Asia), as well as garlic and sesame. Above all, he discovered that Dayuan produced wonderful horses, and that it grew a grass that was the best possible forage for these animals, alfalfa or *musu*.

The king of Dayuan was obliging enough to have the Chinese mission accompanied as far as Kangju (in the ancient region of Sogdiana, between the Amu-Darya and Syr-Darya rivers). Zhang Qian had now arrived where the empire of Alexander had ended. The king of Kangju in turn guided the Chinese travellers as far as the land of the Yuezhi. They had at last reached their destination.

The Yuezhi, or Da Yuezhi ("Great Yuezhi"), at that time occupied the territory of ancient Daxia, Bactria. Under pressure from the Xiongnu and finally driven out by them, they had settled in this fertile land where they enjoyed a prosperous and peaceful life. They were certainly sympathetic towards the aims of the Chinese government, and missed their old lands, but China was too distant, and a combined pincer movement almost impossible to carry out, as the Xiongnu were too powerful and too close at hand. The king could not make up his mind. Zhang Qian waited for a year and then, not having obtained the alliance which had been the goal of his mission, he decided to return home.

In order to reach China, he changed itinerary: by taking the south road around the Tarim Basin, he travelled south of the Kunlun mountains and crossed the modern province of Qinghai. But the Xiongnu were everywhere, and once again the travellers were captured, clapped in irons, and put to hard labour. This time Zhang Qian thought he would never survive. But the old Xiongnu king died of illness in 126 BC, and taking advantage of the internal power struggle which followed his death, the survivors of the Chinese mission succeeded in escaping once again, this time fleeing eastwards. Their bad luck seemed to have left them at last. They reached the Chinese capital, but only three of them remained: Zhang Qian, his Xiongnu wife and his faithful Ganfu —one Chinese and two Xiongnu. Of Zhang Qian's son, no mention is made, nor of any of his other companions. Difficult as it may be to believe, during these 13 years of hazardous travel, Zhang Qian had managed to hang on to his ambassador's insignia, the pole of yak-tail hair.

The adventures and dangers which the Chinese envoy had endured deeply moved the capital. When Zhang Qian presented to the emperor, with two hands, his ambassador's pole in the Imperial Palace, Emperor Wudi, filled with emotion, granted him the rank of a high dignitary, and recompensed Ganfu with an honorific title.

In his report, Zhang Qian detailed all that he had seen and learnt about the Western Territories, which greatly interested the emperor, who questioned him over and over about it. Although the alliances made were indeed uncertain, Zhang Qian's mission had, nevertheless, achieved much more than it had set out to do: it had unlocked to China an entirely new part of the world, with its many kingdoms and their products, so useful and so curious. Reality would one day far exceed the dreams of Emperor Wudi, who had never imagined that the Chinese Empire might reach the Pamir and Karakoram mountains, still unknown to him.

> *It is hardly surprising that today Zhang Qian is one of the best known of China's national heroes. His name is also associated with what we now call the Silk Road: what was to emerge as a result of his mission was a major flow of transcontinental trade in which silk would, for a long time, play a key role.*

It is hardly surprising that today Zhang Qian is one of the best known of China's national heroes. His name is also associated with what we now call the Silk Road: what was to emerge as a result of his mission was a major flow of transcontinental trade in which silk would, for a long time, play a key role.

EXPEDITIONS SOUTHWARD

Let us return to the year 126 BC. In order to reach these far-off lands and to establish commercial relations and alliances with them, it was necessary, first of all, to find a route which was not obstructed by the Xiongnu. When in Daxia, Zhang Qian had noticed in the marketplace, "fabrics from Shu and bamboos from Qiong", two typical products of Sichuan, which were instantly recognizable to a Chinese. The kingdom of Shu covered the central and south-western parts of the present-day province of Sichuan. Qiong is still the name given to the mountain massif west and south-west of Chengdu, the capital of Sichuan, in the very heart of the province. How did these two Chinese products come to be sold so far from their place of origin?

In answer to this question, the inhabitants of Bactria told Zhang Qian that their merchants travelled to Shengdu to buy them, Shengdu being the Chinese name for northern India, a land located several thousand *li*** to the south-east of Daxia. There, the land was low-lying, hot and humid, and teeming with herds of elephants. But Daxia was 12,000 *li* from the Chinese capital, Chang'an, and if one were to follow the road Zhang Qian had taken, one would encounter the Xiongnu. If one chose to travel further south, one would have to cross the land of other hostile peoples, the Qiang, who lived in present-day Qinghai, to reach the Chinese capital. And then there were the deserts. And yet, they assured Zhang Qian, the road from Daxia to Sichuan was free of Xiongnu, free of bandits and accessible.

Accessible? From Bactria to India, yes; so says chapter 123 of the *Shiji*. But what about from China to India, via Sichuan? An attempt was made and an expedition set out under the leadership of Zhang Qian. The Chinese reached Yibin, in the south-central area of Sichuan, quite easily, but just south, in the region between Yibin and Kunming, in Yunnan, they could not find a way through. Spending over a year here, they made more than ten attempts, all in vain. Finally, as other difficulties arose, they gave up and returned to the Chinese capital. However, though communication turned out to be impossible or too risky between the north and Sichuan, there had been long-standing and very active contacts between Sichuan, Yunnan, Burma, Assam and India. India also had relations with many countries of Central Asia and the West. We shall return again later to the "fabrics from Shu and bamboos from Qiong".

In 115 AD, Emperor Wudi sent Zhang Qian on a third mission, with 300 men. This time, he followed a route which passed north of the Tianshan mountains, and headed for the Wusun, a people living to the south and east of Lake Balkash, in the Ili region. This was once again a strategic operation, to persuade the Wusun, who had also in the past been driven out by the Xiongnu, to return to their ancient territories, in order to "cut off the right arm" of the Xiongnu. But once again, the Chinese alliance did not seem to offer sufficient security to the Wusun, and once again China was considered too distant, and the Xiongnu too close.

---

* *Nowadays, the li is equal to about 576 metres; in ancient times, it may have been slightly different.*

Zhang Qian then divided his company up, sending envoys to the other kingdoms he had visited before, Dayuan, Kangju, Yuezhi and Daxia. Just over a year later, all these states sent ambassadors to the Han court, and from that time on official missions regularly travelled back and forth. Zhang Qian himself returned to Chang'an, bringing with him, with the help of Wusun guides, a small embassy from the Wusun ruler, accompanied by several dozen beautiful horses as a gift to the Chinese emperor. Zhang Qian and his various envoys returned with new products and surprising information from these far-flung, unknown lands. Zhang Qian died in 104 or 103 BC, at the age of about sixty, having spent a good thirty years of his life on perilous and difficult journeys, having endured too the ingratitude of princes—he was in disgrace for a certain time, around 123 BC, for having been defeated by the Xiongnu. But in the end, the emperor once again bestowed honours upon him, and posterity remembers as a model this warrior-diplomat-explorer who "opened" the road to the west.

Missions to the west had revealed to the Chinese the existence of several large kingdoms such as Anxi (Persia; Anxi may refer to the Parthian dynasty of the Arsacids), the closest country to Daxia where Zhang Qian had himself lived; Shengdu (India), Tiaozhi (a land in the Middle East which we shall identify later on), Yancai (identified with the Allan people, who are described in other texts as living north of the Caucasus), and finally, the furthest one, Lijian. The kingdom of Lijian designated either the whole or the easternmost part of Roman territory. This was the first time that the Roman world appeared in Chinese written history.

While Zhang Qian had been living in Daxia, during his first mission, the king of Anxi had invited him to visit his kingdom. It was some time later, however, between 115 and 105 BC, that a Chinese delegation led by one of Zhang Qian's envoys from the land of the Wusun, was able to take up this invitation. The Parthian king, whether through excessive honour or great prudence, sent a general with 20,000 soldiers to the frontier to greet him. The meeting was very positive, and was followed by mutual exchanges of ambassadors and gifts. As they did with other kingdoms of Central Asia, the Chinese envoys "carried with them credentials and gifts of silks".

It is in this way that Chinese silks began to arrive in Western countries—no longer as an exceptional occurrence—in ever greater quantities, and with variable frequency. There must have been delays along the way: according to contemporary witnesses, a return journey between China and the Western Territories took between three and eight years.

GIFTS AND TRADE

The giving of presents implies gifts in return; this is what we mean by "exchange", but not yet trade in the sense we usually give the word today. At what moment did these "presents" between kings turn into economic trade between nations? Was it when the value of the gifts from both parties were equivalent in value? When does one pass from the stage of barter in kind to that of trade proper? Is it once the value in an exchange of goods is calculated in terms of a currency,

Many kingdoms would acknowledge their status as vassals or protectorates of China, and the goods they sent would be called "tribute". Thus a "tribute system" developed, a Chinese concept according to which the emperor, the centre of the world and a cosmic axis, the father of his subjects and of his vassals through the Mandate of Heaven, received tribute from them as an expression of this relationship.

and any difference in value between the exports of the two parties is paid in cash, first as metal coinage, and then as symbols where the face value is guaranteed by the nation minting it?

In Zhang Qian's time, this flow of goods which was beginning to circulate in both directions between China and Persia, sustaining several other kingdoms on the way, is referred to by Chinese historians as "gifts" between rulers. Several decades later, when China's conquest of Central Asia began in earnest, many kingdoms would acknowledge their status as vassals or protectorates of China, and the goods they sent would be called "tribute". Thus a "tribute system" developed, a Chinese concept according to which the emperor, the centre of the world and a cosmic axis, the father of his subjects and of his vassals through the Mandate of Heaven, received tribute from them as an expression of this relationship. The Chinese character *gong* was used for both the taxes paid to the emperor by the Chinese provinces, in the ancient days of the *Tribute of Yu* (*Yu gong*), and for what we specifically call tribute, a payment made by a foreign sovereign. The term *gong* would for a long time designate both these, until national taxes and payments from abroad were finally differentiated in the Chinese vocabulary.

It should, however, be noted that during the twenty centuries or so that this tribute system theoretically lasted, tribute was not a unilateral payment, unlike, for example, the tribute paid to Rome by vanquished lands. The Chinese emperor offered "presents" in return to the ambassadors of tributary nations, to be given to their own sovereign, of a value at least equal to that of the tribute received. These exchanges were gradually codified, as much in their contents as in the ceremonies which accompanied all official acts regarding an embassy. The tribute was, officially, essentially a political symbol. In practice, it occasionally happened that the suzerain-vassal relationship was pure fiction, and that the exchange of tribute-gifts concealed an undeniable commercial reality. The following scenario applies for slightly more recent periods but may well have been applicable earlier as well: the goods which arrived in Chang'an entered the imperial treasury, where part was put aside for the emperor and the court, and the remainder was sold to merchants who redistributed it among their customers in China. What the Chinese court sent, could, in the case of silk, for example, come directly from the taxes paid in kind by the subjects of the Chinese government, or could be bought by the treasury as a "gift" to the foreign king. In other words, this was in effect large-scale trade tightly controlled by the Chinese state. Since historical texts lay more emphasis on political and military events or the activities of the court, rather than on commerce, which was considered a humble activity, these texts do not tell us very much about the manner in which the exported or imported products circulated down to the level of the individual consumer. Later, particularly under the Tang dynasty, texts would openly mention the merchant corps, but there is no doubt that external commerce had always been, and continued to be, highly regulated and controlled by the imperial government.

It is also possible that merchants joined official caravans from one or another kingdom in order to enjoy armed protection, and were authorized to carry out trade of certain goods as long as this did not hinder the interests of the governments concerned. This has always been the case in analogous geographic environments and particularly throughout Central Asia.

At the time of Emperor Wudi, China could not pride itself on having vassals among the kingdoms of the Western Territories. However, there is one clear trend: according to the annals, the rulers of the small kingdoms which Zhang Qian and his envoys passed through sent their sons to the imperial court. It would therefore seem that this practice, aimed at sealing relations with foreign kingdoms, was already well developed: by attracting the son, or one of the sons of a ruler to the Chinese court, not only would he become steeped in Chinese culture, but he was a guarantee of his father's friendship, as he was in a sense a hostage. Was it entirely voluntarily that these kings sent their sons, for years, into the hands of such a powerful ruler? Chinese princesses were sometimes asked in marriage by "barbarian" kings, and this might be agreed to; again, this was meant to seal the friendship between two nations, and these girls too were, in a sense, hostages, although perhaps in a less dangerous way. Some of them played a particularly important role in the diffusion of techniques and religious beliefs, as we shall see soon.

Thus Chinese presence was affirming itself in the Western Territories, and this led the government to set up fortified posts to keep the road open, founding the prefectures of Jiuquan and Wuwei, in 121 BC, and Zhangye and Dunhuang, in 111 BC. Finally, in 59 BC, the Western Territories commandery or protectorate was created, headed by a sort of governor-general, named "Protector-General" (*Duhu*), assisted by two military commanders.

LIJIAN

Further west, the most important and the most powerful kingdom appeared to be that of Anxi (Persia). It was for this reason that a Chinese envoy had been sent to establish contacts with its ruler, as we have seen above. In return, a Parthian embassy reached the palace of Wudi between 110 and 100 BC;

according to Sima Qian, it brought gifts to the emperor, including five skilled conjurers (jugglers, perhaps?) from Lijian.

What exactly Lijian corresponded to is difficult to establish, as it is described in such a vague manner in the texts of the period. Some have suggested Petra (under its alternative name, Rekem), Syria or the Eastern Roman Empire, as well as Hyrcania or Alexandria in Central Asia. Paul Pelliot and Homer Dubs, as well as others after them, opted for Alexandria in Egypt. Later, Lijian was retrospectively considered by Chinese historians as having designated the Roman world, or perhaps only its eastern section. Other terms were also to be used in Chinese for the Roman Empire.

What else did the Parthian envoy bring with him? Probably a type of mandolin with an almost spherical box; its name was transcribed in Chinese as *pipa*. Presumably, musicians also accompanied the instrument, which was adopted in China, and later in Japan as well.

This exchange of embassies between China and the Parthian kingdom of the Arsacids occurred during the reign of the Parthian king, Mithridates II (124–91 BC). The Parthians, whose origins may be traced back to the same type of westward migration that we have met in the case of the Yuezhi and Wusun, had brought together under their dominion the pieces of the dislocated Seleucid Empire. The reign of Mithridates II seems to have been marked by defensive clashes, in the east, against nomads. This agrees with Chinese records that tell us of the aggressive omnipresence of the Xiongnu and the establishment of the Yuezhi in ancient Bactria. An alliance with the Chinese Empire could prove useful in neutralizing a common enemy, which was precisely the aim of Chinese diplomacy.

By the end of his reign, Mithridates II had extended his control in the West as far as the Euphrates and Armenia. He had now come up against the power of Rome, which controlled all of Greece and almost all of Asia Minor, dominated the seas in the eastern Mediterranean, and was to establish itself in Syria, soon to become a Roman province. There was to be a succession of wars and temporary treaties between Parthia and Rome.

When the Battle of Carrhae occurred, Persia and China had been in regular contact for fifty or sixty years, which meant that silks and other Chinese products had had plenty of time to penetrate the material culture of Iran.

Sima Qian provides us with a succinct description of the kingdom of Anxi, located several thousand *li* to the west of the Greater Yuezhi, a land of sedentary agriculturalists who cultivated rice, wheat and vines, and made wine with the grapes. It was a very large state, which extended over several thousand *li* and included several hundred towns, both large and small. It was also a land of merchants who, over land or water, dispatched their goods among neighbouring nations, even at a distance of several thousand *li*. Silver coins bearing the face of the ruler were used; when one king died, the coins were recast with the face of his successor. Their language was written on parchment in horizontal rows.

Tiaozhi

Several thousand *li* west of Anxi, according to information brought back by Chinese missions, was the land of Tiaozhi: "It overlooks the Western Sea. It is hot and damp, and the people cultivate the fields and grow rice. There are large birds [ostriches] with eggs as large as pots. The population is very large." This brief description of a land which appears to have been important must not be neglected, and ends with these curious comments: "It has skilful conjurors. And further the elders of Anxi say that they have heard that in Tiaozhi are to be found the Ruoshui and Xiwangmu, though they have never seen either of them."[9]

Had the elders of Anxi heard of the mythological story of Xiwangmu, the Queen Mother of the West? And where, in the 2nd century BC, was Tiaozhi? Later it would be located in Mesopotamia, Mecena, roughly that part of present-day Iraq which gives on to the Persian Gulf and includes the lower reaches of the Tigris and Euphrates rivers. The French Sinologist Edouard Chavannes suggested Characenia, that is Susiana, in Persia, just east of the Tigris. Like the names of several other states, the same term was re-used over several centuries, and did not always designate exactly the same geographic territory, as the political frontiers of states were constantly shifting.

As for Ruoshui, the second character *shui* means "water", and is often specifically used for rivers. The first word means either "weak" or "dead". Father Hyacinthe Bitchurin, in the 19th century, translated the expression as "dead waters". Chavannes, in the early 20th century, translated it as "weak river".

The reports of the Chinese envoys describe several other countries, and in certain cases these are the only precise and dated documents which we possess on them, even if they are very brief.

From the very beginning there is one very obvious leitmotiv in this history, and that is war. Wudi's mission to the West to establish military alliances led in its wake to horses being used to fight the wars, silk being exchanged for horses and soldiers being sent to obtain them by force.

Other exchanges also occurred as a collateral result, through the compassion of the gods or, who knows, through the intelligence of man, from this rather dark primary cause, war. But have we not always known, since Homer, that the gods can play a double game?

Chapter Four
The Power of a Kingdom Rests with its Horses

*W*hen Zhang Qian returned from his third mission, around 105 BC, he brought back horses from the land of the Wusun. Either he himself or his envoys had also brought back from the Ferghana Valley alfalfa seeds and vine "seeds" (probably grapes or grape pips, for how could the actual plants have survived such a journey?), as well as many other products. The most important of these were the alfalfa, the horses and the news, which he had already relayed on his return from his first mission, that there existed in Ferghana a race of exceptional horses which could be used to improve the Chinese cavalry and would be of vital help in controlling the Xiongnu and all nomad enemies who threatened China and prevented it from communicating with the West.

In classical historical sources, such as the *History of the Former Han* and the *Shiji*,[10] a significant amount of space is devoted to the efforts of the Chinese government to acquire horses. This was to remain a constant feature throughout China's pre-modern history, as the empire was continually threatened by aggressors whose strength lay in their cavalry; aggressors who were themselves horse breeders and therefore held a great advantage over the Chinese.

In the ancient world, from China to Greece and Mongolia to Persia, the horse was indeed the source not only of power, but of the very survival of the state. Man had succeeded in taming, controlling and making the horse do his bidding, and once he could use the strength and speed of the horse, was able to master both time and distance, first of all with horse-drawn chariots (attested to in ancient China as well as in ancient Greece) and then universally with cavalry. Man and his horse had been transformed into a mobile war machine, ultra-fast, capable of carrying several weapons, armour and provisions for days. Those who owned the most resistant horses (resistant to fatigue, and different types of terrain and climate), as well as the fastest, would have a strong advantage in any conflict.

Consequently, the nation which bred and possessed these horses, which owned stallions and mares of the best stock, which had the best pasture land, the best climate, and understood the art of breeding, held a considerable asset in its favour. Inversely, a large state which wanted to be powerful, or simply hoped to avoid being conquered by another, but did not possess this advantage, had to find ways of obtaining this essential element of warfare, through exchange, trade, shady dealings or agreements between rulers, by guile or by force.

China is a land of agriculturalists, turning its soil into fields for the cultivation of cereals. It is poor in pasture land, and could never become a great horse breeder. It would therefore always have to import them.

HORSES FROM DAYUAN

Before the expeditions westwards, China had to rely mainly on a large-headed pony which grew long hair in winter, and whose hooves wore down fast, so that it was unfit for use in mountainous areas and on long journeys. The problem of hooves, for nations which apparently did not shoe their horses, seems to have played a determining role in the story of the horses from Dayuan. These horses had very hard hooves which wore down very slowly, whereas during Chinese military operations it was necessary to allow the animals long periods of rest so that their feet could recover from the wear and tear and the horn could mend. The Chinese therefore required much larger contingents of horses and the cost of war consequently increased. Between the years 121 and 118 BC, after the campaigns against the Xiongnu which had led to the loss of more than 100,000 Chinese horses, the situation was indeed a perilous one. Three problems had to be resolved: acquiring rapidly a species of horse better adapted to war against nomads; importing stallions and mares and arranging a breeding program in the imperial stables; and developing the cultivation of alfalfa as fodder. The latter was by far the easiest, and the new fodder was easily obtained. The best which was said to exist was called *musu* in Chinese, a word probably derived from the language spoken in Dayuan, a Turkish, Mongol or Iranian term, or which may even have come from the place of origin of the plant, probably Media, a region of Persia just south of the Caspian Sea, in the north-western part of modern Iran.

The Greeks, who knew of alfalfa very early on, called it *medike poia*, the Median grass, from the 5th century BC on, and this name has remained in modern Italian as *erba medica* and in the scientific name *Medicago sativa*. This providential plant passed from one country to another, under various names which mark the military or non-military treks of cavalry, just as a series of visas on a passport reveal the itinerary and stopovers of the modern traveller, and arrived in the eastern Mediterranean, from where the Arab cavalry exported it to Spain, and the Spanish conquistadors to America. In China, it was introduced, acclimatized and cultivated thanks to Emperor Wudi who was given alfalfa seeds by Zhang Qian.[11]

Obtaining horses was a completely different matter.

Emperor Wudi, the historians repeatedly tell us, was a passionate lover of fine steeds. One day, as he was divining with the help of ancient texts, the trigrams revealed to him the arrival of divine horses from the north-west (divine in the sense of supernatural). He therefore sent an embassy to the king of the Wusun, who did indeed reside in the north-west, south of Lake Balkash, to request horses from him. The king twice sent him a thousand horses. The emperor tried several of them in person and was impressed by their abilities: they could climb mountains, jump over ravines and gallop as if they flew. They were called heavenly horses, *tianma*. One of the deliveries of a thousand horses sent to Emperor Wudi in 109 BC (a gift apparently related to Zhang Qian's stay with the king of the Wusun), arrived with a request for a matrimonial alliance: the king asked for the hand of a princess of the imperial Han family. He was indeed to obtain it, as we shall see later.

The horses of Wusun were undeniably marvels, but even more marvellous were the horses from Dayuan which Zhang Qian had discovered further west. Not only did their hooves wear down only slightly, but they were larger and more resistant than the usual horses of the Chinese army: they could carry heavily armed men, could cover "a thousand *li* a day", and they had "a double spinal column", that is, they had two rows of muscles either side of the spine, which was said to be more comfortable for the rider. They also had one strange peculiarity: they sometimes secreted a reddish sweat, which was why they were also called "blood-sweating horses".[12]

Countless poems have been composed in China about these horses, both real and imaginary, and the greatest painters have immortalized them. And, more than anywhere else, horse legends abound in Central Asia. Natural and supernatural stories have come down the centuries, embellished as they did so, and modified with new elements. Stories of marvellous, celestial, supernatural horses, or simply horses with exceptional qualities, already appeared in the historical texts of the Han period on Gansu and the Western Territories. A thousand years later, these stories reappeared in a new form, such as in the Tibetan epic of Gesar and his horse Kyang, with its reddish-brown coat, its black mane and its white nose, a heavenly horse in the real sense of the word since it could fly through the air and carry its master in an instant across half of Tibet. Its father was the White Horse of the Sky, its mother the Blue Mare of the Spirits of the Lake.[13]

One such Central Asian legend explains how to obtain a heavenly horse: in the high mountains, wild horses cannot be captured, so one must set piebald mares loose at the foot of these mountains. The mares will mate with the wild horses, and the foals which are born will have "sweat of blood". These foals were therefore hybrids of wild horses and domesticated mares.

According to a different legend, brought back in the 7th century AD by a Chinese pilgrim, they were the result of crossbreeding between domestic mares and lake dragons, which, in order to mate, would emerge from the water in the shape of a horse. This produced a race of dragon-horses which were very difficult to tame, very fierce, but which gradually became docile and made the region famous for the quality of its horses.[14]

This story of dragons is perhaps related to a trick played during the reign of Emperor Wudi. It happened in 113 BC (or in 120 BC according to different sources), near Dunhuang, by a large marshy pond called Wuwa, surrounded by vast prairies. A Chinese government official named Bao Lizhang had been sent there as punishment for a crime he had committed, to farm land allocated to the military colony and to look after a herd of horses. The wild horses would often come to drink at the marsh. Among those who returned most frequently, Bao noticed one exceptional animal, a horse of strange beauty, of a beauty that was a wonder to behold.[15]

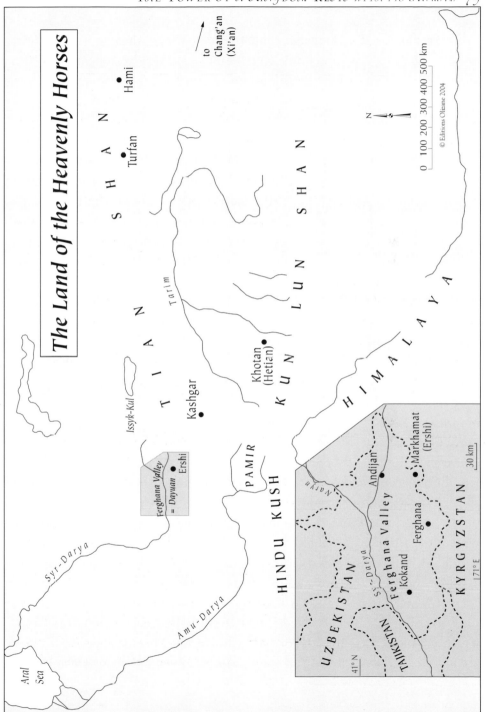

The Land of the Heavenly Horses

to Chang'an (Xi'an)

Hami

Turfan

T I A N   S H A N

Issyk-Kul

Kashgar

Tarim

Khotan (Hetian)

K U N   L U N   S H A N

PAMIR

Ferghana Valley = Dayuan • Ershi

HINDU KUSH

H I M A L A Y A

Syr-Darya

Amu-Darya

Aral Sea

0 100 200 300 400 500 km

N

© Editions Olizane 2004

UZBEKISTAN

TAJIKISTAN

KYRGYZSTAN

Andijan

Markhamat (Ershi)

Ferghana Valley

Ferghana

Kokand

Naryn

Syr-Darya

30 km

41° N

171° E

What did Bao do? He made a clay figure of a man, dressed it in his own clothes, placed a lasso and bridle in its hands, and set the puppet up on the water's edge. The beautiful horse was at first surprised, but then grew used to the figure, and continued coming to drink every day. When he was well accustomed to it, Bao one day stood in the place of the clay mannequin, wearing its clothes and holding in his own hands the lasso and bridle. Once the horse began to drink, he threw the lasso and bridle over its head and tamed him. Then he offered the horse to the emperor, known for his passion for fine horses. Bao hoped by this exploit to obtain a pardon, and be allowed to return to his homeland in Henan and to his family. But so that the horse should be associated with some miraculous event, he invented an extravagant story, telling how the animal had come forth from the waters of the pond, and had leaped out in a single bound. The emperor was very pleased with this, not only because the horse was superb, but also because this supernatural incident came on top of another auspicious sign, the discovery near the Hall of Imperial Sacrifices, of a precious three-legged cauldron. The appearance of sacrificial vessels from antiquity was always considered a good omen. The emperor thereupon composed two odes, the "Song of the Heavenly Horse" and the "Song of the Precious *Ding* [Cauldron]". He had a weakness for ritual obligations and any manifestations of the supernatural, and he had showered with honours and presents a magician who had done nothing but deceive him. In his mind, the horse was a gift, a personal favour from a divinity whom he particularly venerated. He sang in his ode of this god-given horse which, as it galloped, oozed red foam and sweat, and which could run over 10,000 *li*: only a divine horse such as this could be a worthy companion to the "dragon which crosses the sky, slicing through the clouds and mist".[16]

Only a divine horse such as this could be a worthy companion to the "dragon which crosses the sky, slicing through the clouds and mist".

Where was this pond, this lake, this marsh bordered by rich pasture land, which produced these horses? For ages, scholars have been competing in their attempts to identify it, although its general location, somewhere near Dunhuang, has been known for some time. There are two possible sites, both of which have their supporters (this is not an insignificant debate, because both Chinese and foreign tourists are fascinated by the story). Some hold the location to be the artificial lake or reservoir of Huangshuiba, four kilometres from Nanhuxiang (the "borough of the southern lake"), itself located south-west of Dunhuang, on the banks of the Dang River. The waters from several sources collect in this reservoir, forming an oasis of greenery and prairie land in the middle of the desert. The other possible location is the pond of Wuwa, south-east of Dunhuang, on the banks of the same river, a highly picturesque place known from other legends, a small crescent-shaped lake called "the Spring of the Crescent Moon".

There is a second story told in the *History of the Former Han* of a horse rising from this pond, this time set in 95 BC, a story even more imbued by the climate of omens and the supernatural which so prevailed in the reign of Wudi: the emperor, having captured a white unicorn (perhaps during a hunt) on Mount Longshou in the east of Gansu, offered it in sacrifice to his ancestors in the Imperial Temple.[17] In the same year, a heavenly horse rose from the waters of Wuwa, and gold was found on Mount Taishan, a sacred mountain in Shandong. The emperor deduced from this extraordinary combination of events that "it was necessary to modify certain things to be in harmony with these auspicious omens", and decreed that from then on, gold ingots would be cast in the form of unicorn's and horse's hooves (according to commentators, the unicorn is said to have identical hooves to those of horses). This was, of course, carried out. The vassal rulers were given these gold ingots called *madijin*, "gold horse hooves". Many centuries later, they have occasionally been found in the ground, and turn out to be elegant in shape and made of fine gold. There are probably a few more examples to be found in the collections of numismatists.

Are these stories a memory of the famous heavenly horses? The Madisi, the "horse-hoof temple", located about 50 kilometres due south of Zhangye, in Gansu, near the border with Qinghai, is said to have been built on the site of one of the old staging posts built along the route which these horses followed from the kingdoms of Central Asia to the Han court. One Chinese author links this with the horses of Wudi. And one account tells how travellers are shown the print of the hoof of Gesar's horse on the wall of a cave in the monastery.[18]

However fine the horses of Wusun were, however divine those which rose from the pond of Wuwa, the war was pressing and the horses from Dayuan were even better. They were obtained in exchange for silks, much appreciated everywhere, stimulating a regular flow between China and Persia. But one day the king of Dayuan changed policy, and refused to part with his horses.

Around 107 or 106 BC, a Chinese envoy came to offer him large quantities of gold in exchange for horses. The king refused to hand them over, and hid them. The Chinese envoy, who had only a few hundred men with him, was offended, behaved in a discourteous way, was expelled and finally killed. The emperor decided on reprisals and in 104 BC assembled an army (its ranks filled as usual with criminals and outcasts), which left for the capital of Dayuan, the fortified town of Ershi (Eulshe), to bring its ruler to reason, avenge the insults and seize the much-coveted horses.[19]

The city of Ershi has now disappeared. Its ruins can be seen in the modern Republic of Uzbekistan, near the village of Markhamat, in the *oblast* of Andijan, north-east of the city of Ferghana. This was a blessed land, with abundant fruit, horses, vines and alfalfa. The king had little to fear from the Chinese. How could a large army travel so far from its bases and feed itself, when it could not find provisions along a road which crossed hostile regions and deserts? Not much risk of that, was there? And anyway, nothing had ever happened in the past.

New generations of horses were thus assured (later, Dayuan was to send a couple of fine horses regularly every year), and the Chinese cavalry would from then on be as powerful and efficient as that of the Xiongnu and other mounted archers.

And indeed, the first Chinese expedition ended in catastrophe. A second campaign was then organized, and an expeditionary corps of 60,000 soldiers (all the riff-raff had been gathered together), with 100,000 oxen, 30,000 horses, 10,000 donkeys, mules and camels, a stock of pre-cooked and dried rice, and a large quantity of weapons, set out under the command of General Li Guangli, in 103 BC. As well as officers, there were engineers whose task was to divert the waters of the river which fed the town of Ershi.

By the time the army arrived before the walls of the city, the number of soldiers had diminished by half. The siege itself lasted for forty days. The town elders reckoned that the enemy only wanted the horses, and much pain and hardship could be avoided if a certain number of these horses were handed over to the Chinese. But the king was obstinate in his refusal to give in. The elders killed him and sent an envoy to General Li Guangli, carrying the king's head, and made the following proposition: the Chinese would choose and take with them a certain number of horses and mares, and would then withdraw, without entering the city. They would be given food. If this proposition was not accepted, all the horses of Ershi would be slaughtered.

The Chinese had also suffered from the siege. They could not prolong it indefinitely with the provisions they had. The besieged, on the other hand, seemed not to be running out of food. As for water, the Chinese had indeed diverted the course of the river to cut the town's supply, but foreign engineers had arrived—or were about to arrive—from the land of Qin, who knew how to dig wells and ensure the arrival of water in the city. Finally, reinforcements were said to be on their way from a neighbouring country. The Chinese general decided to accept the propositions which were presented to him. The expeditionary corps, or what remained of it, left, taking with it several dozen horses of very good quality, and 3,000 mares and stallions of second and third choice. Only a thousand were to survive, arriving in 101 BC in the Chinese capital, where they were placed in the imperial stables. New generations of horses were thus assured (later, Dayuan was to send a couple of fine horses regularly every year), and the Chinese cavalry would from then on be as powerful and efficient as that of the Xiongnu and other mounted archers. Representations of horses in Chinese sculpture reflect the change in species that occurred at this period. Heavenly horses, literally flying through the air, without wings, appear in Chinese iconography. At Leidai, near Wuwei in Gansu province, the tomb of a general of the Later Han dynasty (25–221 AD) has been unearthed which contained ritual figurines, including chariots and 39 bronze horses. One of these horses appears to be galloping through the air: three of its feet do not touch the ground and the fourth rests on a flying bird, perhaps a falcon judging by its eye. This flying horse has been shown throughout the world, and can be seen today on the cover of art books and tourist pamphlets, even as a miniature sculpture, on the office tables of Chinese tourist agencies.

During the Han, Tang (618–906) and following dynasties, until the 18th century, the need to acquire horses was an important factor in Chinese policy towards the nomads. The horse was always used as an article of exchange and a means of applying pressure between the two parties, depending on their respective power. The Wusun had made use of the horse early on to press their request for a Chinese princess for their king, which they obtained. But the Chinese too invested vast numbers of men and amounts of money to force Dayuan to provide its horses when the simple offer of gold was insufficient. Even if China did not always have supremacy, it did at least have its own ways of bringing pressure to bear, first of all through silk, which was in great demand everywhere and of which China was for a long time the only producer. Later, towards the 10th and 11th centuries, silk was replaced by tea which was now drunk throughout Asia, and China would remain the sole producer of tea until the middle of the 19th century. Silk for horses, or tea for horses; it was only when the Chinese Empire dominated its nomad neighbours militarily, or had annexed their territories, that it was able to obtain horses as tribute or as tax. These were paid with money, or in kind, or partly in both, as the fiscal system became coin-based. Finally, horses would be bought through usual trade procedures.

Among the events of the campaign of 104–101 BC, one feature of particular interest is the intervention of the engineers from Qin, experts at digging wells. The same character *qin* refers either to China (Da Qin, Great Qin), or to the territories of Lijian under Roman domination, or perhaps just those of the eastern Mediterranean, which several centuries later would also be called Folin. Most modern commentators of the *Shiji* and the *History of the Former Han*, though not all, identify these engineers from Qin as ordinary people from the Mediterranean world, and why not? A few prisoners of war, transferred, or bought, or renegades who had been saved by their technical knowledge? Or voluntary émigrés hiring themselves out? Qin is a vague term; does it refer to Romans, Syrians, Egyptians from Alexandria, Greeks, Jews? Others, such as Chen Liang writing in 1983, consider that Qin is China, and believe that the Chinese taught the people of Dayuan to dig their wells, just as they taught them to cast iron. There must certainly have been Chinese deserters here and there, or soldiers, prisoners of the Xiongnu. There may also have been captives who were then sold to other masters. This was just one aspect of the mixing of nations and the transmission of techniques across the Eurasian continent. There is a curious example of this in the case of a Swede in the 18th century, Jean Renate, captured by the Russians at the Battle of Poltava in 1709, sent in semi-liberty to Siberia, then integrated into a Russian colony which later led a military operation against the Dzungars. The Russian column was attacked and captured, and the Swedish engineer found himself a prisoner of the Dzungars. He taught them to cast canons. But, he was no traitor: the Dzungars were the enemies of his enemies. After 24 years in captivity, Jean Renate finally returned to his native country. Such stories are numerous in Central Asia, constantly swept by the winds of war.

From the reign of Han Wudi on, the history of Central Asia is dominated by the colonial dynamism of China, which became an empire, extending north, west and south in almost the same fashion, the same rhythm, and at the same time as the Roman Empire, on the other side of the Eurasian continent. Today, the Roman Empire has disappeared politically, whereas after two thousand years of alternating phases of expansion and contraction, and of recapturing, losing once again and reconquering its foreign marches and dominions, present-day China, the People's Republic of China, includes, and even extends beyond, the territories which the Han dynasty once dominated or influenced, reaching as far as the foot of the Pamir mountains.

Chapter Five
Armies and Caravans into the Unknown

*T*he ancient historical annals devote much more space to military events than to economic data; the most neglected aspect is generally trade. We know more about battles, heroic deeds and acts of treason than we do about what was sold in the marketplace and details of imports and exports. All attention is focused on the fame and glory of the sovereigns, not on the material life of the people. And when there is a mention of the latter, commerce comes last; indeed, in several of the great civilizations, trade and merchants were treated with contempt. Texts from the Han period, for example, mention "gifts" and "tribute", as well as the rare and curious objects presented by foreign rulers, but do not really inform us about commerce, except in connection with silk and horses. Yet the Chinese rulers went to such enormous expense

> *The Chinese rulers went to such enormous expense to open up, maintain and extend ever further the road westwards, to establish and maintain relations with countries located six months or a year away.*

to open up, maintain and extend ever further the road westwards, to establish and maintain relations with countries located six months or a year away (and which were not always suppliers of horses). Was all this solely in order to secure alliances against the Xiongnu, their descendants or their nomadic cousins, and to protect Chinese territory? Surely not. In any case, once they became the masters of the road westwards, and felt less threatened by their weakened neighbours, the Chinese government strove not only to maintain relations with the kingdoms of Central Asia, but also to reach the countries furthest to the west, even as far as the land "where the sun sets".

> *Even the proudest of states must recognize that economic exchange is a necessity for all people. It was not just through pride of conquest that so many Chinese soldiers in the Han and Tang periods perished in the mountains and deserts of Central Asia, but also to maintain the flow of men and goods.*

Was this done out of geographical curiosity, combined with hopes of commercial links, the desire for useful products, such as metals and medicines, as well as technical knowledge? Probably a mix of all these. Even the proudest of states must recognize that economic exchange is a necessity for all people. It was not just through pride of conquest that so many Chinese soldiers in the Han and Tang periods perished in the mountains and deserts of Central Asia, but also to maintain the flow of men and goods.

This led to the creation of bridgeheads, of fortified bases and garrisons. As Chinese domination progressed westwards, it took different forms: direct administrative colonies, protectorates, various degrees of suzerainty, semi-independence, forced friendship, armed persuasion and arbitrary alliances when interests were found in common. Chinese presence was established first in Gansu, the western "horn" of China, a prolongation towards the north-west of the Hexi Corridor, extending into the heart of the desert, and then into all the oasis-kingdoms which had been set up along the double road leading north and south across the Tarim Basin.

Emperor Wudi's interest in exchanges with a country as distant as Bactria is clearly revealed by the fact that, as soon as he learnt that Zhang Qian had seen products there which had arrived from Sichuan, via India, he sent him off to locate that trade route. As we have already mentioned, his mission failed. When the Chinese government conquered the region of Canton (Guangzhou), around 111 BC, the inhabitants of neighbouring Sichuan grew afraid and sent tribute to the Chinese court. It was thought that they would no longer dare oppose the passage of Chinese missions. But this was not to be. Once again, missions were attacked and plundered, and the project of reaching the Western Territories through Sichuan was once again abandoned. The region on the borders of

Sichuan, Yunnan and Tibet, inhabited by various hostile groups, who were invincible in the mountainous terrain, has always prevented the passage of foreigners. In the 18th and 19th centuries, the British in India repeatedly tried to reach China by a land route through north-east India, Assam, Bhutan, Tibet or Nepal, but always had to abandon the idea.

However, preventing foreigners from passing did not prevent goods from circulating. It was simply a matter of the difference in profit which successive merchants could make, and of the price which was paid, at the end of the journey, by the buyer. The Chinese government concentrated all its energy on the routes crossing the Western Territories: colonial armies, expeditionary corps, punitive expeditions. The term "pacification" is used in Chinese with the same military connotations as in English. The fact of the matter was that it was necessary to re-conquer and re-pacify the region continually.

Having created, as we saw above, between 121 and 111 BC, the prefectures of Jiuquan, Wuwei, Zhangye and Dunhuang, fortified posts were built at the Yumenguan and Yangguan passes. Progressing westwards, military posts were set up, and state commissioners named who were responsible for the security of the military colonies and for providing fresh supplies to the officials sent to foreign countries. In order to increase the population of these new towns and settlements, large numbers of convicts were deported to them. After the creation in 59 BC of the protectorate of Xiyu, the Protector-General, the equivalent of a modern colonial High Commissioner or Governor-General, became the key to the entire colonial and military adventure in the West.

The problem of providing supplies was a crucial one as the land could not feed the extra population. It was solved through the establishment of agricultural garrison-farms on requisitioned land on which convicts were put to work (one example of this is the case mentioned earlier of Bao Lizhang, condemned to work as a peasant, and who succeeded in escaping from this fate by capturing a superb wild stallion and making the emperor believe in its supernatural origin). Who were these Chinese convicts? Indeed, they were not only criminals but also included, among others, low-ranking officials who had committed minor crimes, fugitives, resident merchants (in other words, non-itinerant merchants) who had been entered on the market register, former resident merchants, as well as the children and grandchildren of those who had been entered on the market register.[20] We know that merchants did not enjoy a high social status in ancient China, and that certain schools of thought despised commerce, but it is difficult to understand this legislation which pursued merchants down to the third generation.

The road westwards, as it is briefly described in the *History of the Former Han*, began at the passes of Yumenguan and Yangguan, before splitting into two branches. The southern fork crossed the kingdom of Shanshan (long vanished but which is often mentioned in the Han period, and was perhaps located west and south-west of Lake Lop Nor), followed round the northern slopes of the Nanshan (Southern) mountains, and then continued westwards "in the direction of the flow of the river" as far as present-day Yarkand. It crossed the Onion mountains (the Pamir), and led to the Great Yuezhi and Anxi. The river mentioned is probably the Tarim or one of its tributaries.

The other road, known as the Northern Road, stretched from the kingdom of Western Qushi (which included Turfan), near the Northern mountains (the old name for the Tianshan), and continued downriver as far as present-day Kashgar. Crossing the Pamir massif westwards, the road then led north to the kingdoms of Dayuan, Kangju and Yancai.

The Protector-General, who lived in the very heart of the Western Territories, some 1,500 kilometres from the Chinese frontier, had supreme control over all the garrison commanders, and closely watched the neighbouring kingdoms of Wusun, Kangju and the other western states, keeping the emperor informed. His mission, according to the historian Ban Gu, was to "reassure those who were peaceful, and to put down through force those who were not".

The first phase of contact between China, Persia and the kingdoms located in between lasted about 240 years. Then the Han dynasty lost control of these regions, from 9 to 73 AD, because of troubles within and enemies without. Finally, during the Later Han dynasty, the Chinese general Ban Chao managed to re-establish Chinese dominion over the Western Territories, at least for a few decades.

The introduction into China of so many previously unheard of Western products is generally attributed to the reign of Han Wudi, although this, according to historians, is partly legend. We know that this ruler, who was infatuated with power, authoritarian, sometimes cruelly harsh, and who had a passion for horses, was prone to believe in the supernatural when it came to the imperial cult towards heavenly beings. He was so fond of war that it ruined the country. But he was very interested in everything which arrived from foreign lands. In his park, perhaps better termed a reserve, he erected a building reserved for storing those curios sent as gifts and tribute by foreign rulers, or which Zhang Qian and other envoys had brought back with them: ostrich eggs from Persia, dishes made of rock crystal, small tables inlaid with jade from Khotan, pearls, precious stones, and objects of tortoiseshell, rhinoceros horn, or made from the feathers of rare birds. In the park lived a Persian lion, peacocks, one or two elephants, camels, blood-sweating horses and other exotic animals. Vines and alfalfa had entered China, as well as other new plants, such as sesame, linen (or "*hu* hemp", that is hemp from Central Asia), carrots, garlic, types of coriander, onions, cucumbers, beans, a "red flower" which was perhaps carthamus or saffron, as well as other plants and trees such as the walnut and the pomegranate. In addition, there were also medicinal substances, musical instruments from Iran and conjurors or acrobats from Lijian.

More caution is needed when reading the story of an ambassador from the West who is said to have brought to the emperor in 90 BC a glue so powerful that it could stick back the broken ends of a bow string, as well as clothing made from the fur of the *jiguang*. Both of these warrant comment.

This story is related in a work attributed to Dongfang Shuo, who is said to have been in the good graces of Emperor Wudi and seems to have held a post in the imperial reserve. His book, entitled *Hainei shizhou ji* (*Tales of the Ten Isles in the Sea*), describes foreign lands as perceived by the Chinese at the time, and mentions the relations which the emperor had with them. The embassy that brought them "glue and *jiguang*" is recounted in two chapters devoted to the "Western Sea"; their country is the Island of Phoenixes and Unicorns (*feng lin zhou*), located in the middle of the Western Sea, measuring 1,500 *li*, and surrounded on all four sides by the Ruoshui, the "weak river" or "dead waters" that we have already met above in the stories of the "elders of the kingdom of Anxi". So we are faced with three enigmas: the superglue, an animal known as *jiguang*, and the land of phoenixes and unicorns surrounded on all sides by a river of a very strange nature.

It should be borne in mind that the *Hainei shizhou ji* is generally considered a web of fantasy, full of supernatural elements, and that its author was a humorist who "excelled at making jokes" (according to one very serious dictionary). But even jokes, dreams and poetic imagination may be significant.

According to this tale, an envoy from a western kingdom brought as tribute to the emperor four ounces of an extra-strong glue, green in colour, known as "glue for mending bow-string", or "mud (paste) for mending metal". In addition, he also brought clothing made of *jiguang* fur. The emperor, who did not realize how useful these two items were, did not make much of them. He felt that this western country, though it had sent tribute from so far away, had nothing much to offer. The tribute was stored away in the treasury depot for foreign products, and the emperor was in no hurry to send the ambassador back with gifts worthy of the tribute received.

Some time later, while the emperor was out on a tiger hunt in his reserve, the string of his bow snapped. Immediately, the envoy from the western country, getting down from his horse, came over with a hundredth of an ounce of the glue. He wetted the bow-string with saliva and stuck the two ends together again. The emperor was astonished. He ordered several strong men to pull the string, but they could not manage to break it. Not only did this glue indeed stick the string back together again, but it could be used to repair metal objects. The emperor verified this as well, and began to realize that he had seriously underestimated the value of the tribute he had received.

This glue, explains the author of the tale, is made in the following way: in the country located in the middle of the Western Sea, live flocks of phoenixes and herds of unicorns. There are mountains, rivers, lakes, marshes, as well as a hundred types of wonderful medicinal plants and many immortals (the author uses the term in the Daoist sense). The phoenix beaks and unicorn horns are boiled and then left to steep together, after which an ointment is made from them: this is the glue for mending bow-strings and metal objects.

As for the clothing made of *jiguang* fur or skin, it is said to be yellow in colour, and if soaked for several days in water, does not run. If it is thrust into fire, it does not burn. It is made, says the author, from an animal of the same type as divine horses (*shenma*). Several dictionaries confirm that it is a horse's skin, saying that the *jiguang* has a white coat, red mane and eyes the colour of gold. In ancient times, it seems that these clothes were worn in certain ceremonial circumstances at court.

When the ambassador returned home, Emperor Wudi, in order to make up for his mistake, expressed his profound thanks, and presented him with gifts of cinnamon of the highest quality and dried ginger, both of which were precious medicinal products unknown in his native land.

The story does not say from which western land the man had come, nor from where the *jiguang* hide originated. But the glue, as we know, was produced in the land of "phoenixes and unicorns". And we have seen that this land was surrounded on all sides by the Ruoshui river. Are we to consider this river, as one dictionary states, as "a fluid half-way between air and water, from the land of immortals"? According to the *Hainei shizhou ji*, "the down of wild swans will not float on it, and one cannot cross it", while another text explains that "this water will not support swan down". Does this mean that it is so light that a swan's feather will sink into it? One author states that these waters cannot be crossed by boat, but yet another, more recent, says that one can sail on it in boats made of pieces of leather sewn together. But where is it? The two characters for Ruoshui nowadays refer to the Zhangye River in Gansu. But in ancient texts, the whereabouts of this river varied, though it was always said to be beyond the western passes of China. For some, it ran along the foot of the Kunlun mountains or some other unidentified mountains; for others, its source was to be found in the north, in the "Kingdom of Women", which it skirted round to the east, before turning southwards to the sea. This subtle and mysterious river therefore seems to have zigzagged across an imaginary West, winding around the lands of the women and the phoenixes and unicorns, sweeping into its over-light waters a mixture of reality and legend. We may one day unravel its mystery, but so far no one has ever managed to do so.

JIBIN

We return to the real world with the relations which Han Wudi inaugurated with one of the greatest Western countries beyond Parthian Persia: Jibin, located some 7,000 kilometres from the Chinese capital, and thought to be either present-day Kashmir or the region of Kabul.[21] Embassies were exchanged. But during the 1st century BC, these relations were often interrupted, and Chinese missions were frequently roughly treated. The kings of Jibin did not fear China, which was too distant. The kingdom was formidably defended by its natural barriers: "hanging roads", a terrifying route through gigantic mountains, with a path less than two feet wide, over ravines of incalculable depth (the description brings to mind the Karakoram Pass). Those who fell were smashed to pieces before they had even hurtled down half the slope; there was no choice but to walk along in single file, roped together. The travellers suffered from severe headaches, and from the fierce sun beating down on the naked rocks. And then they had to cross several independent states where they endured all sorts of rebuffs; all requests for food and help were denied. How many caravans, men and beasts were abandoned, lost in the desert, never to return! Why bother to maintain relations with a country that does not fear one, which does not behave properly and which is of no use to one? Particularly when it is clear that it is not for diplomatic reasons that it keeps up relations with China, but solely for reasons of commerce. For instead of sending important people or members of the royal family as ambassadors, they sent only vile merchants, who, in the guise of bringing gifts, only wanted to do business!

Jibin had seemed to be an interesting partner. According to the History of the Former Han, it was a large country, wealthy thanks to its agriculture (cereals, alfalfa, vines, fruit trees), and its artisans who could weave wool, embroider with silk, sculpt and make objects in gold, silver, copper and tin.

Thus pleaded, around 30 BC, a Chinese official to the emperor, taking pity on those who had been sent on these fearful journeys to accompany, as etiquette demanded, important ambassadors home. Why, he insisted, risk the lives of useful people for useless ones? And yet, Jibin had seemed to be an interesting partner. According to the *History of the Former Han*, it was a large country, wealthy thanks to its agriculture (cereals, alfalfa, vines, fruit trees), and its artisans who could weave wool, embroider with silk, sculpt and make objects in gold, silver, copper and tin. Trade was controlled by laws, and the author describes gold and silver coins with the image of a rider on horseback on the obverse and a human face on the reverse. Four valuable products are mentioned: pearls, coral, yellow amber and *liuli*. These were imported into Jibin: the country was not located near the sea, and therefore did not produce any coral or pearls. Neither did it produce yellow amber. As for the term *liuli*, it is thought to have come from the Sanskrit *vaidurya* which, at the time of the Former Han dynasty, perhaps still designated lapis lazuli, mined in Badakhshan. This is one of the "Seven Treasures" of Buddhism; later, or perhaps already at this period, it designated coloured glass, a speciality for which Syria and Egypt were famous. At the beginning of the Christian era, India was also a producer of it (China knew how to make glass at the time, but this Western glass was highly reputed). Whatever its provenance, this *liuli* was therefore an imported product in Jibin (in the 5th century, foreigners from the land of the Yuezhi were to travel to the Chinese capital and teach there the art of coloured glass-making).

North-west of Jibin was the land of the Greater Yuezhi (the same territory as Bactria), and to the south-west it bordered on the eastern frontier of the land known then as Wuyishanli, itself a neighbour of Tiaozhi and Lijian to the west. The landlocked kingdom of Jibin, therefore, received goods from coastal regions (pearls from the Persian Gulf or Ceylon, and coral from the Mediterranean, and possibly from the Red Sea or the Persian Gulf), lands which also produced *liuli*; it also received yellow amber from somewhere. Several amber-producing regions were known in antiquity; one of these was on the shores of the Baltic Sea, in eastern Prussia, where this fossil resin was extracted by a Germanic tribe. It was already known to the Greeks in the time of Homer, and today is still the most famous amber-producing region. Amber was also collected along the south-eastern coast of England and along the coasts of Denmark, as well as in the Electrid Islands (*electrum* is one of the ancient names for amber), in the Adriatic Sea. But it could also have come from India or Upper Burma, assuming that the sites which are known there today were already quarried at that period. Although Chinese officials, both civil and military, pretended to look down upon trade, it is clear that other nations did not harbour the same prejudice.

What did China send back to the many rulers of kingdoms both large and small (sometimes with a population of only 1,800 or 1,000 inhabitants) from which it received gifts and tribute? Essentially, silk and high quality iron, the same iron used by the Parthian soldiers when fighting the Romans (the texts mention "weapons" but do not clearly state whether iron in pigs was also exported). Lacquer and bamboo objects, bronze mirrors, plants such as ginger, cinnamon and rhubarb also spread westwards. The creation of military agricultural colonies, and the attention which the emperor gave to the development of agriculture in these settlements, may have led to the diffusion of Chinese cultivation and irrigation techniques, unless on the contrary, the Chinese borrowed some of these from the farmers living in the oases. Chinese know-how in manufacturing iron and iron weaponry was passed on to certain kingdoms of the West by Chinese specialists. In this respect, one particularly interesting passage from Sima Qian has been commented on by Joseph Needham in his *Science and Civilisation in China*.[22] Talking about the countries which extended from Dayuan to Anxi, that is from Ferghana to Persian Parthia passing through Sogdiana, Bactria and Margiana, Sima Qian writes "they produced neither silk nor lacquer, did not know how to cast iron in order to make pots, pans and other objects, until deserters who had fled from a Chinese embassy settled in the region, and taught them to cast iron to make weapons and other useful objects. And when the people from these lands obtained from the Han yellow and white metal, they used it not only to cast coins, but to cast utensils." Joseph Needham then comments on the expressions "yellow metal"

> *Communications were interrupted with the Western Territories during seven or eight decades of the first century of the Christian era.*

and "white metal" which, rather than referring to gold and silver as is usually the case, may instead indicate alloys of copper and tin, copper and nickel, silver and tin, or other alloys used by the Chinese for their own coinage. According to Chinese historians, communications were interrupted with the Western Territories during seven or eight decades of the first century of the Christian era.

During this period, commerce by sea routes between the Mediterranean and India developed considerably, as well as through the Red Sea and the Persian Gulf, an itinerary which was completed

During this period, commerce by sea routes between the Mediterranean and India developed considerably, as well as through the Red Sea and the Persian Gulf, an itinerary which was completed by a land route which took the goods from northern India through Kashmir to the western borders of Iran, joining Central Asia.

by a land route which took the goods from northern India through Kashmir to the western borders of Iran, joining Central Asia. In addition to this, caravan routes linked Afghanistan, Iran, Iraq and the eastern Mediterranean. This period, which was one of great political and economic development of the Roman Empire (the reign of Augustus, the First Emperor, ended in 14 AD), also saw the development in the Roman Empire of active trade, both by land and by sea, with the countries bordering the Mediterranean, the Black Sea and the Red Sea, as well as with the kingdoms of Arabia and the Caucasus, with Persia, India and even Ceylon. The dynamism of the Mediterranean, combined with Roman military power, had also, though slightly later than had occurred in China, opened a way to those distant, unknown lands, to India, Taprobane, Serica and Scythia. The Westerners too had their tales of the "Ten Islands in the Sea".

Chapter Six

The Geographer in Antiquity and Women's Extravagance

To the Chinese of the 1st century AD, Lijian and Tiaozhi were the westernmost nations of the world, since beyond them was the place where the sun set. In Pliny the Elder's *Natural History*, we read that opposite Mount Atlas, thought to have been located on the Mauritanian coast, lay the island of Atlantis. From there, one could sail on to the Gorgades Islands, once the abode of the three Gorgons. And beyond that, there were, it was said, the two Hesperides Isles. "Some people think that further on are the Fortunate Islands," wrote Pliny the Elder, and beyond that the sun set.

The geographical knowledge of the Romans concerning Europe, northern Africa, the kingdoms bordering the Red Sea, the Middle East, Asia Minor, the shores of the Black Sea, the Caucasus, Persia and India had grown considerably after the reign of Augustus. In the case of the Orient, they were able to add to the information which the Greeks had given them, data culled from direct reports and first-hand accounts about new nations. Book 6 of the *Natural History* is devoted to Asia, and clearly demonstrates that the Romans knew of the existence of several nomadic people to the north of the Black Sea and the Caucasus, as far as the Ural mountains, as well as of the Scythians, a universal term for the nomads who lived further east. They knew of the Caspian Sea, which they believed to be a gulf of the Scythic Ocean (the Arctic Ocean), and of the Oxus and Syr-Darya rivers. They knew that Bactria and Sogdiana were situated on the the eastern edge of the Parthian kingdom, and that in Sogdiana stood the town of Alexandria, founded by Alexander the Great, "where altars have been built to Hercules, Bacchus, Cyrus, Semiramis and Alexander [...]

there is the limit reached by all the conquerors", wrote Pliny. And that is where the geographical knowledge of the Romans had ended for a long time. But now, they could extend it slightly further, although their description of Eastern Asia was still very uncertain. Pliny believed that by following the eastern coast of the Caspian Sea and then that of the Scythic Ocean, one could skirt eastwards round the continent and arrive in the Orient. He described thus what we would call Siberia, Mongolia and Central Asia:

"The first part of the coast after the Scythian promontory is uninhabitable on account of snow, and the neighbouring region is uncultivated because of the savagery of the tribes that inhabit it. This is the country of the cannibal Scythians who eat human bodies; consequently the adjacent districts are waste deserts thronging with wild beasts lying in wait for human beings as savage as themselves. Then we come to more Scythians and to more deserts inhabited by wild beasts, until we reach a mountain range called Tabis which forms a cliff over the sea; and not until we have covered nearly half of the length of the coast that faces north-east is that region inhabited. The first human occupants are the people called the Seres, who are famous for their woollen substance obtained from their forests (*primi hunt hominum qui vocantur Seres, lanicio silvarum canitiem*); after a soaking in water they comb off the white down of the leaves (*perfusam aqua depectentes frondium canitiem*), and so supply our women with the double task of unravelling the threads and weaving them together again (*unde geminus feminis nostris labos redordiendi fila rursusque texendi*). So manifold is the labour employed, and so distant is the region of the globe drawn upon, to enable the Roman matron to flaunt transparent raiment in public (*tam multiplici opere, tam longinquo orbe petitur ut in publico matrona traluceat*). The Seres, though mild in character, yet resemble wild animals, in that they also shun the company of the remainder of mankind, and wait for trade to come to them."

The Land of the Seres

After this, in chapter 20 of Book 6, are the names of three rivers which Pliny places in the land of the Seres, followed by a series of names of rivers or people which no longer seem to be linked to the description of the Seres.

Who really were the Seres? One hesitates between the Chinese, that is to say the Han, or some nation from Central Asia. Or could the term have referred to the whole of China and its protectorates? Pliny died in 79 AD; at this period, as far as we know, sericulture had not yet crossed the western frontiers of the Chinese Empire, and it was forbidden to export either silkworm eggs or mulberry seeds. The manufacture of silk thread was a tightly guarded secret and was to leak out only some time later. If the Seres were the people who made *sericum*, and if the main definition of the latter is to be a product of the Seres, we end up with a circular argument which is of no particular help to the geographer. Pliny's text places the Seres, in other words, somewhere far to the east of the Caspian Sea, between the Scythians and the Oriental Sea, and the mention of this sea would seem to indicate that he probably included the actual coast of China in this kingdom. If one consults later texts mentioning the Seres or Serica, they almost always appear to be indeed referring to China, although at other times, a kingdom of Central Asia seems more likely.

The passage about silk, this down or wool obtained from the forests, shows that nothing at all was known at that time about sericulture, or even about its animal origin. Had Virgil not classified it in his chapter on tree products? Pliny did likewise. He does not call this cloth *bombycina*, as he does for all caterpillars' threads from Cos and Assyria, forms of wild silk which have nowadays disappeared but which seemed to have been familiar to Pliny, who gives us a detailed description of them, although how accurate he was we do not know. But let us return to the few terms concerning what Roman women did with this product which had travelled so far, and the manner in which they wore it: *redordior* is almost always translated as "unravelling". Its first sense is "to undo that which is woven" (*ordior*: to make a weft, as a spider spins its web). This is confirmed by the words that follow, *rursus texere*, "to weave a second time". But what exactly is this referring to? If it is the action of unravelling that which is woven, then the raw material which our Roman woman must have used was not a thread, but cloth. Some authors have even suggested that the threads of this (Seric) cloth were pulled, to be then rewoven differently, to make a looser, lighter, transparent cloth. Or, they may have used threads of some precious material woven in with the textile fibres. But this remains only a hypothesis. Furthermore, one should bear in mind that the cocoon is itself a woven object, and that consequently the word *redordior* might mean "to unwind a cocoon", that is carding and spinning it, or unwinding it (the reeling process). This would in turn imply that the Romans received not just silks from the Seres, but cocoons. However, we know that China did not export these.

WOMEN OF SERICULTURE

Pliny uses same words, *redordiri* and *rursus texere*, for another kind of cloth, the *bombycina*, produced from a caterpillar from Assyria, which he describes in chapter 26 of Book 11, mainly devoted to insects. These are large larvae, with two horn-like projections, which become caterpillars, and then chrysalises, ie *bombyx*. These insects, writes Pliny, produce webs like spiders from which the luxurious *bombycina* cloth is made for women's dresses. "The process of unravelling these [silk threads] and weaving them again (*redordiri rursusque texere*) was first invented in Ceos by a woman named Pamphile, daughter of Plateas, who has the undeniable distinction of having devised a plan to reduce women's clothing to nakedness."

The Chinese princess Leizu had invented silk manufacture, and the Chinese people consider her a benefactress. The daughter of Apollo perfected, in a Greek island, a cloth of the similar type, but no one is grateful to her. The island of Ceos, once the Hydrussa of the Greeks, is the island presently known as Kea, located slightly south of the island of Euboea, in the Aegean Sea.

The transparency of the cloths, as well as their extreme lightness, did not upset only Pliny: Seneca too deplored the fashion for these cloths "which aid neither the body nor modesty".

Pliny mentions these over-light fabrics and the decadence of morals a third time, in chapter 27 of Book 11. "Silk-moths", he writes, "are also reported to be born in the island of Cos" (here he is referring to the island of Kos, far to the south-east of the Kea mentioned above, near modern Bodrum on the Turkish coast). His description, which he admits comes from rumours, is difficult to interpret, as it does not necessarily refer to a caterpillar–cocoon–chrysalis process, but does end up with the formation of a light feathery matter around the animal, which has to be "softened with moisture, and then thinned out into thread with a rush spindle [*in fila tenuari*, spun, and not unravelled and rewoven]. Nor have even men been ashamed to make use of these dresses, because of their lightness in summer; so far have our habits departed from wearing a light cuirass that even a robe is considered a burden! All the same we so far leave the Assyrian silk-moth to women."

WOOD OF THE FOREST

Concerning these ancient and vanished textiles, as well as the first Latin descriptions of the Seric cloth—the "fine fleece of the leaves" of the forests of the Seres, according to Virgil; the "wool of their forests", and the "white down of the leaves" which can be detached after "a soaking in water", according to Pliny—one cannot help making a parallel, perhaps a less bold one than it first appears, with other textiles from ancient periods produced in Sichuan, Yunnan and Burma and which may, from the Han dynasty on, have reached Bactria and Persia along the trade routes, and from there the Mediterranean world. If the fabrics themselves did not make the journey, at the very least the descriptions of their manufacturing process may have. Ancient Chinese sources and dictionaries mention a cloth made from a white down which forms on the leaves of certain trees and which is thoroughly soaked. This tree is the white *tong* tree, a variety of *wutong*, and almost the Chinese national tree. The white *tong* tree grows abundantly in Upper Burma and Yunnan, and the manufacture of this cloth was a speciality of the ancient Burmese kingdom of Piao, on the border with Yunnan. "The leaves of this tree carry a white down; this down is collected, washed, twisted [that is to say it is spun by twisting], and woven to make clothes."[23] There can be no possible confusion here with cotton, which is always referred to by other terms and is clearly differentiated from all other textile materials in these sources.

The similarities between these descriptions are disconcerting. But equally remarkable is the variety, the abundance of textile production throughout the world, the ingenuity, the aesthetic imagination and the technical virtuosity of man. Has the textile industry not always, in almost every economic history, and particularly that of China, been of prime importance? As evidence of this one can cite the incredible richness of the vocabulary in this domain, both in Chinese and in other languages. There exists a seemingly unending list of words whose dictionary meanings are not understood precisely, or which have shifted somewhat through the centuries. Many are foreign words borrowed phonetically, which have been transformed as they pass from one language to the another, and words which reflect ethnic mixings: the textile industry covers the whole breadth of life in society, from the elementary need for protection from cold to the most irrational luxury.

Whether through sheer coincidence or some other reason, when one mentions the cloth of the white *tong* tree it is difficult not to think of the forests of the Seres, of Zhang Qian's "cloth from Shu and bamboos from Qiong", four characters from the *Shiji (Shu hu Qiong zhu)* which are worth their weight in studies and commentaries. Everyone agrees on the bamboos from Qiong, though one may wonder why such voluminous and heavy goods were sent to the banks of the Amu-Daria River. Opinions differ, however, as to the nature of the cloth from Shu, and articles devoted to this problem bring to light an astonishing world of unknown fabrics in our own region.

The Kingdom of Shu

Shu, a kingdom in Sichuan, passed under Chinese control very early on (whereas Chinese might was to come up against stronger resistance from the inhabitants of Yunnan for a long time). It has always been a land of skilful weavers, either of hemp or of various types of ramie (*Boehmeria nivea*), or, from the Han period on and conceivably even earlier, of silk. They are perhaps the only people to have perfected, at the time of the *Tribute of Yu*, more than 3,000 years ago, a method of weaving wild animal fur, such as bear or fox fur, into a rather rough cloth which was sent as tax to the Chinese emperor. Sichuanese hemp was renowned for its high quality. The merchants of Shu, according to texts, exported their hemp cloth all over. The fabric which Zhang Qian saw was certainly, according to Sang Xiuyun, linen or a cloth made from ramie or nettles.[24] One

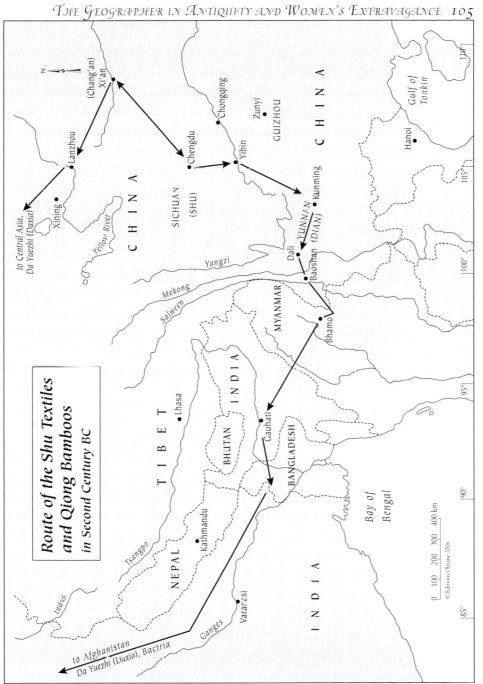

Route of the Shu Textiles
and Qiong Bamboos
in Second Century BC

Route of the Shu Textiles and Qiong Bamboos

© Éditions Olizane 2004

type of very fine hemp cloth, with a very tight weave and a slightly shiny yellow appearance, was famous from the second millennium BC on and was stored in large bamboo segments, known as "Qiang bamboo", after the name of the proto-Tibetan people who manufactured it. This is one reason why some authors believe that the fabric which Zhang Qian found so striking in Daxia was a hemp cloth; another reason is that silks from Sichuan were not yet as famous at this period (around 128 BC). They were, however, soon to become so, and even to supersede the manufacture of hemp in the region.

From the beginning of the Christian era at least, Sichuan and Yunnan were renowned for their "fine cloths" of silk. These provinces have always been made up of a mosaic of ethnic groups (some of the 56 ethnic minorities of the present-day Chinese People's Republic), each with its own language, customs and decorative art. The Di, a group from the kingdom of Shu who lived to the north of Chengdu, made and exported a silk cloth in which the silk thread was made up of strands of different colours twisted together and then woven, producing very attractive coloured effects.

A couple of dozen names of fabrics are known for the specific silks of the prefectures and kingdoms of Sichuan and Yunnan. All of these may have reached India, Afghanistan and Central Asia via various trade routes. Indeed the merchants of Shu first passed through Yunnan, where they bought goods that interested them, before continuing further on, through Upper Burma, towards Assam and Bengal. It was apparently somewhere in northern India, or directly from merchants of Daxia, that the Indian traders came to stock up on supplies.

The fact that the merchants of Shu were compelled to cross Yunnan has led to the suggestion that the name "cloth from Shu" may also refer to fabrics bought along the way, and therefore to the attractive cloths of Yunnan. This would not be the first time that an item is given a mistaken name of origin, which is an indication not of its producer but of the route it has followed. Another example of this is turquoise, which arrived from Persia via Turkey.

Did these merchants therefore buy and take back to Bactria, under the name of "cloth from Shu", a Yunnanese fabric, of a unique kind, made not from leaves, twigs or bark, but from the flowers of a tree? This is a speciality of the Ai Lao, who lived in the Yongchang region, probably present-day Baoshan, in western Yunnan, between the Mekong and Salween rivers, not far from the Burmese border. Once again, the cloth comes from the *wutong* tree, which produces tender, supple and shimmering white flowers, which shine like silk, and can be threaded and woven into wide strips, before being washed or soaked. The cloth is then pure white and cannot be stained.

What has become of these marvels? Dictionaries confirm the authenticity of their existence. Perhaps they could still be made today, in this period when we invent in our laboratories all sorts of composite and synthetic fabrics, with their own descriptive vocabulary which will amuse and intrigue our descendants.

THE MEDITERRANEAN WORLD

The world of textiles in Greco-Latin antiquity was less elaborate. The main textiles of the Mediterranean world were wool and linen. In the time of Pliny, cotton muslin from India and Seric silk were already known, but the latter, being much sought after, still arrived in small quantities and was very expensive. This was a luxury product for the wealthy classes. But in an empire which was reaching its peak, the landed aristocracy, colonial governors and victorious generals possessed enormous fortunes. These fortunes, we know, were less the result of Roman industry than of profits made from war and the economic exploitation of conquered lands. The agricultural workforce was in part supplied by defeated, enslaved populations.

Among those who had direct contact with Rome was a class of merchants, Syrians, Greeks and Jews, who crossed the Red Sea or followed the caravan routes across the Middle East, towards the ports of India and Central Asia. These merchants endeavoured to keep up with the demand for luxury products that this wealthy society generated, a society which was often idle and proud, criticized for its debauchery and for abandoning the fundamental virtues which had made the greatness of Rome. Was it wise or proper to eat foie gras, cock crest stews, snails fattened on cooked wine and oysters brought from Lucrin Lake, 200 kilometres from Rome? To spend one's days in the baths and one's nights drinking and throwing precious stones at the feet of famous courtesans?

Having wild beasts brought from Egypt for the Games or burning a fortune's worth of perfume and rare herbs at home? And what a scandal that banquet had been at which Lollia Paulina, Caligula's wife, appeared ornately dressed, literally covered in emeralds and pearls, particularly knowing that everybody knew that they came from the treasure of her grandfather, Lollius, and represented the spoils brought back from the provinces! Lollius, who had extorted gifts from all the kings of the Orient and been dishonoured by embezzlement. So disgraced was he that he was made to take poison "so that his granddaughter could show herself, in the candlelight, covered in 40 million sesterces" worth of jewels.

Silk was not yet, however, present except in very small quantities, and was not commonly used for tunics, veils or togas. At first, it was used in small pieces, as ornaments dyed purple, embroidered and inlaid on tunics or togas of white wool and soft cottons, or of byssus from Palestine, a linen or cotton cloth. It was made into bands, borders, squares and badges. Perhaps the available pieces of silk were woven by mixing threads of silk with threads from other textiles, or rewoven into a looser cloth, as we have seen above.

The first Roman to be dressed entirely in pure silk was apparently Emperor Heliogabalus (218–222), the "mad Caesar", a Syrian and a sun-priest in the Syrian religion; the least Roman of all Roman emperors, and renowned for his extravagance. However, Pliny's criticisms do demonstrate that in his time women were already wearing entire pieces of clothing made of silk.

Perhaps silk was also already being used in some parts of the empire to wrap the embalmed bodies of eminent people. This practice, which was current in China, would later be adopted in Christianity for the bodies of saints and their relics.

For what reason was one prepared, in the Roman world just as in Asia as far west as China, to pay fabulous prices for a fabric which, until then, one had lived perfectly well without and which one could have continued ignoring without changing the smooth running of the world, without preventing humans from falling into the traps laid by the gods, or without stopping that little rascal Eros from shooting his arrows left and right? For no other reason than that luxury is luxury and that fashion is fashion.

THE COLOUR OF SILK

Everyone knows the virtues of silk, its beauty, its luxurious and shiny appearance, its suppleness, softness and comfort. Warm in winter, cool in summer and light to wear. A fabric which hardly creases, is relatively resistant and unaffected by rot; it can be made into ethereal veils and sumptuous brocades; it can be embroidered with threads of gold or silver, or even painted. And finally, Chinese silk, which is naturally white or very pale cream in colour, can be dyed very easily, particularly in purple. It is in all ways superior to other light Mediterranean cloths, to the wild silks mentioned earlier. These, incidentally, seem to have disappeared from the market shortly after this period, despite having sufficient importance in the eastern Mediterranean to have found an unexpected echo in a Chinese historical text, the *History of the Later Han (Hou Han shu)*, which deals with events between 25 and 221 AD. In the chapter describing Da Qin, the Lijian of old, we are told that in Da Qin there were wild silkworms.

In Rome, the issue of dyeing had taken on an ever-increasing importance in the cloth industry. The traditional white of ancient clothes was still popular, but it had become the custom to place coloured ornaments on a white background. The most sought-after colour was purple; this colour had in fact become standard wear in certain circumstances linked to religion or power. In chapter 60 of Book 9 of his *Natural History*, Pliny writes: "The rods and axes of Rome clear a path to the colour purple; it marks the honourable status of boyhood; it distinguishes the senator from the knight; it is called in to secure

"The rods and axes of Rome clear a path to the colour purple; it marks the honourable status of boyhood; it distinguishes the senator from the knight; it is called in to secure the favour of the gods; and it adds radiance to every garment, while in a triumphal robe it is blended with gold." ...
Generals and emperors wore as military dress a cloak dyed entirely purple.
But women were forbidden to wear the colour—except princesses.

the favour of the gods; and it adds radiance to every garment, while in a triumphal robe it is blended with gold." The togas of the augurs and the magistrates were decorated with bands of purple; triumphal togas, which were granted to certain high dignitaries, were decorated with bands of purple and gold embroidery. Generals and emperors wore as military dress a cloak dyed entirely purple. But women were forbidden to wear the colour—except princesses.

After the fall of Troy, when Aeneas stood before Laurentum on the coast of the Tyrrhenian Sea, with those of his chosen companions who remained, in that memorable story of immigration which Virgil embroidered into the *Aeneid*, he sent to King Latinus an embassy of supplicants, bearing gifts of a gold libation cup from his father Anchises, a sceptre and a tiara from Priam, and cloths made by Trojan women, "purple vests were weav'd by Dardan dames" (verse 248 of Book 7). In response, Latinus offered Aeneas and each member of the Trojan embassy his finest steeds, "each with a saddle-cloth of embroidered purple" (verse 277).

Although this prestigious dye seems to have been reserved for a minority, it had gained some economic importance through its trade and the price it fetched. The production of this dye is one of the oldest industries of the Mediterranean, going back to Phoenician times. One legend tells how the Phoenician god Melkerth was out walking one day with his dog on the beach; the dog bit into a shell and his mouth was stained red. The god used the liquid from the shell to dye a tunic which he then offered to his beloved. The most beautiful purple is that from Tyre and Sidon. In Pliny's time, it was even, he says, all that remained of the glory of Tyre. Shells producing purple were also fished off the coast of Africa, more precisely in the "Purple Isles", which may well be the Canaries, as well as in Greece, on the coasts of Laconia, south of the Peloponnese. An industry of purple dyeing also existed at Basra, on the Persian Gulf. Pliny does not refer to the purple from Spain, which is mentioned in the *Aeneid* in verse 581 of Book 9, as the "red dye from Spain", used to stain the "mantle with pictured scenes in needlework" of one of the warriors who fought alongside Aeneas in the battles which arose as a result of his marriage.

Purple was first used to dye wool and linen; it is mentioned time and again in the oldest texts of the Bible: in *Exodus* 26, Yahwe commands Moses to make, for the Ark of the Covenant, a "tabernacle with ten curtains of finely woven linen, and violet, purple and scarlet yarn". Similarly, the veil of the Holy of Holies, the entrance curtain to the tent, and the sacerdotal clothes of Aaron and his priests were to be made in the same way.

The term "purple" in fact covers a wide range of hues from bluish-purple, dark red and violet to scarlet, according to the shell used and its place of origin. The most sought-after was always a reddish-purple colour, the colour of blood. For a long time, this was reserved for sacerdotal and royal purposes. Darius, king of the Persians, and Alexander the Great of Macedonia, wore clothes of purple. Similarly, in Rome, it was first of all reserved for the kings, and then, as the age of the kings passed, it was used by the highest-ranking magistrates. It gradually became simply an external sign of the patriciate and of wealth, with the exception of certain types of purple of superior quality which the emperors always kept for themselves. Nero even decreed the death penalty for anyone who wore imperial purple, and later, under the Byzantine emperors, such edicts would be periodically renewed.

The liquid which provides this superb though costly dye is contained in a sort of "vein" of the shell, which ejects it as it dies. Pliny devotes several chapters to its production (Book 9), distinguishing between various types of purple-producing mollusc (*buccinum, purpura, murex*), which are further characterized by "the ground they live on" (mud, seaweed, reefs or pebbles). He explains its manufacture thus: the molluscs had to be gathered alive, and then crushed (with or without their shells according to their size), before being left to steep in salt for three days. The liquid produced was then reduced over a low fire, in a leaden pot, for ten or so days, so that the contents of a hundred amphora (equivalent to 1,944 litres) was reduced to 500 pounds in weight. Then the cloth was simply soaked in the dye. The long process, from the initial fishing through to the final stage of its production, plus the constant high demand for the dye, explains the high price it commanded. And what of Tyrian purple, which is dyed twice in the juices of two different shells, producing a bright red with a shimmering appearance? What of silk dyed with purple? Pliny finishes his five chapters devoted to purple by mentioning the adulterations and changes it underwent, a subject he brings up in connection with most other costly dyes, medicinal products and perfumes that he describes in his work, counterfeit products which plagued trade just as banditry followed caravans.

In the 3rd century, under Alexander Severus, the manufacture of purple became a state monopoly. Reprimanded by the Church, the use of purple nevertheless penetrated the Christian world, around the 5th century, under the respectable form of parchment dyed with purple, on which the text of the Bible was written, sometimes in gold letters. The purple industry, ruined by the collapse of the Eastern Roman Empire at the end of the 5th century, sprung up again under the Byzantine Empire, and was revived in the western Mediterranean by King Roger of Sicily, before finally disappearing at the end of the 13th century.

The dye itself seems to have been exported, around the 1st century AD, via the Persian Gulf to the Indian port of Barygaza (see the following chapter). However, despite the fame of purple-dyed cloth in the Western world, no mention of it is to be found—at least so far—in literary sources from the Far East, even from India, either as an import from the West or as one of its particularly beautiful products.

Yet commercial relations between the Roman world and foreign countries, and particularly with Eastern states, were becoming increasingly important; though many of the older austere Romans regretted this, it was much to the liking of the merchants, navigators, sailors and producers of export goods throughout the Roman world, as well as in Arabia, Parthia, India and beyond. As is well known, trade benefits the middlemen more than the producers themselves. What upset Pliny, Seneca and others like them was that the purchase of luxury goods—and the majority of products from these very distant lands were luxury goods—was not balanced on the Roman side by equivalent exports, and therefore produced a considerable trade deficit. "In no year," writes Pliny in chapter 26 of Book 6, "does India absorb less than fifty million sesterces of our empire's wealth, sending back merchandise to be sold with us at a hundred times its prime cost." The cost of luxury is mentioned again in chapter 41 of

Book 12: "And by the lowest reckoning India, China and the Arabian peninsula take from our empire 100 million sesterces every year—that is the sum which our luxuries and our women cost us." Pliny incriminates India mainly because of its pearls, Serica because of silk, and Arabia because of perfumes and above all incense. The loss would therefore be of some 50 million sesterces in the case of Serica and Arabia combined. Half a century earlier, Tiberius had already deplored the import of "these articles which serve female vanity, jewellery and small luxury objects which drain all the wealth out of the empire and, in exchange of trinkets, send the empire's silver to these foreign nations, when it is not to the enemies of Rome". As for the Roman trade deficit, historians are not all in agreement on that point.

THE WEST WIND TO INDIA

Sea trade between the western coast of India and the states bordering the Persian Gulf had existed for centuries, and Indian merchants had not waited for the reign of Augustus to sail to the Red Sea. But it does not appear to have been until the beginning of the Roman Empire that sailors and merchants from the Mediterranean—Syrians, Greeks and Egyptians—ventured into the Red Sea and visited the coasts of India. By then, Pompey had rid the eastern Mediterranean of the pirates who had prevented its navigation. The Romans, with their powerful naval and military might, now controlled these waters. A second event of importance was (according to Pliny, who relates this episode in chapter 26 of Book 6), the discovery, by a Greek mariner named Hippalus, around 100 BC, of how to make use of the *favonius* wind, the west wind, in other words the monsoon winds, to travel much faster from Cape Syagros in Arabia—a cape identified by some authors as the Cape of Ras Fartak, some 800 kilometres east of Aden, on the southern coast of Arabia—to the Indus delta. The distance between this cape and the Indian port on the mouth of the Indus is some 1,850 kilometres in a straight line, a distance which Pliny gives accurately to within six per cent. In the first centuries of the Christian era, this west wind would be called *hippalus*, after the name of its "discoverer".

Arab and Persian sailors had certainly understood the movements of the monsoon for some time. This "discovery" is therefore more the adoption, by Greek and Syrian sailors, and more generally by sailors from the Mediterranean under Roman protection, of a navigational practice which they had not known about previously, and which the Arab and Persian sailors had perhaps not wanted others to hear of. The dangers of sailing between the Red Sea, the Persian Gulf and the Indian coast, for those who did not understand the monsoon regime, had prevented maritime expeditions there for a long time. One can make a link between Hippalus' find and an event related in almost the same year, in chapter 118 of the *History of the Later Han*. The author of this text, Fan Ye (died 445), largely based his account of the Western countries on a report presented to the emperor around 125 AD by Ban Yong, son of general Ban Chao who re-conquered Central Asia, and nephew of Ban Gu, the historian of the Former Han period.[25] The chapter on Anxi, the Parthian kingdom, states that in 97 AD the Protector-General Ban Chao sent Gan Ying on a mission to Da Qin (a term which had superseded Lijian to refer during the Later Han to the Roman Empire). "When he arrived in Tiaozhi, he found himself on the coast of the great sea. He wished to cross it, but the sailors of the western frontier of Anxi told him: 'The sea is vast and great; with favourable winds it is possible to cross within three months, but if you meet slow winds, it may take you two years. It is for this reason that those who go to sea take on board a supply of three years' provisions. There is something in the sea which is apt to make a man homesick, and several have thus lost their lives.' When Gan Ying heard this, he gave up on his project."

Da Qin

The state of Tiaozhi mentioned in this account is located to the south-west of Anxi, its capital, some 60 days' ride from the Anxi frontier. It therefore seems that the word refers to a region including the lower reaches of the Tigris and Euphrates rivers, as far as the sea coast, since the capital is described as surrounded by sea on three sides. The state of Tiaozhi, says the *History of the Later Han*, was later conquered by Anxi.

In another paragraph, devoted to Da Qin, which we shall return to, the historian writes that Da Qin received ambassadors from neighbouring countries, letting them make use of the staging posts along the road from the frontier to the royal capital where, upon arrival, they were presented with gifts of gold pieces. "The king of this country", one reads further on, "constantly desired to have diplomatic relations with the Han. But Anxi, wanting to be the [only] trader of Chinese silks, opposed this plan and set up obstacles so that there could be no personal communication with China." The Parthian kingdom, as we have seen, enjoyed good relations with China, bought large quantities of silk from it, and sent much appreciated gifts via its ambassadors (even sending in 87 AD a live lion and an animal known as *fuba*, said to resemble a unicorn; in 101 AD, it sent another live lion and giant birds from Tiaozhi, birds which laid eggs as large as jars, and which were probably ostriches, from then on known in China as "birds of Anxi"). But did all these gifts represent an adequate counterbalance to the influx of silk? We do not know full details of what Anxi sent in return, as the Chinese chronicles mention mainly curios and rarities. The few acrobats, musicians, lions and ostriches could not have been a fair equivalent economically, and silver or gold coinage does not seem to have made up the difference. Other products must have been involved, originating either from Anxi itself, or in large part from the eastern Mediterranean or even further west, from countries for whom Persia was playing the role of middleman, a role which it would strive to retain for centuries.

Tiaozhi may have followed the same policy for maritime routes, that is to discourage the Chinese, using the pretext of dangers at sea, from getting a foothold in Da Qin. The *History of the Later Han* tells us that Gan Ying "reached Tiaozhi and crossed Anxi. He went as far as the edge of the Western Sea and saw Da Qin. Beyond the passes at Yumen and Yang [the limits of China], for more than 40,000 *li*, there is no country which he did not visit thoroughly."

It was only 60 years later, as far as we know, in 166 AD, that the first Roman ambassador reached the Chinese court, by sea, via Jenan (Vietnam). According to the French Sinologist Edouard Chavannes, musicians and jugglers from Da Qin had already reached Burma in 120 AD, but never an embassy. Furthermore,

> *The state of Da Qin was wealthy, well organized and well administered. Its justice, its system of elected monarchy by which the king was deposed if calamities occurred during his reign, the opulence of the sovereign's five palaces, with their pillars of rock crystal, built in the capital which was over 100 li in circumference, all of these were greatly admired.*

was this a genuine embassy, sent, as it claimed, by Andun (Marcus Aurelius Antoninus)? This seems doubtful in view of the miserly gifts which it took with it: elephant ivory, rhinoceros horns and tortoiseshell, which were not rarities in China, though this may not have been realized in the West where these objects were indeed valuable. Emperor Huandi certainly did not query the official character of the embassy, but he did have reservations over the veracity of the reports which he had received concerning Da Qin: they must be exaggerated as this state did not send rare or precious products, and could not therefore be the powerful and wealthy country he had been led to believe.

What did the *History of the Later Han* have to say about Da Qin? Whether it was correct or not, its description was certainly more detailed than the information available at the time in Rome about the Seres, Serica and silk. The state of Da Qin, the author starts off, is also called Lijian. As it is located west of the sea, it is known too as the Kingdom to the West of the Sea (*Haixi guo*). It is a vast kingdom, with more than 400 cities and several tens of smaller kingdoms are subject to it. The inhabitants devote themselves to agriculture and grow a large number of silkworm mulberry trees. Chavannes understands this sentence as "they plant great quantities of the mulberry tree of the silkworm", in other words, according to him, the people of Da Qin plant a type of mulberry tree which can be used to feed silkworms, without specifically stating that silk worms are raised there. Grammatically, the Chinese could be understood to say that they both raise silkworms and plant mulberry trees, as later texts claim. Chavannes chose the interpretation which corresponded to the current opinion at the time, that sericulture was not known in the West at this period. Given that, one may wonder why, of all the known varieties of tree, such quantities of that particular type of mulberry were planted?

The state of Da Qin was wealthy, well organized and well administered. Its justice, its system of elected monarchy by which the king was deposed if calamities occurred during his reign, the opulence of the sovereign's five palaces, with their pillars of rock crystal, built in the capital which was over 100 *li* in circumference, all of these were greatly admired. Mention is made of the honesty of its merchants, its good quality silver and gold coinage (we even know the relative value of gold and silver, 10 to 1, as was the case for a long time in China). The merchants traded along maritime routes with the kingdom of Parthia and with India, and this commerce brought them profits of 1,000 per cent (compare this to Pliny's recriminations). We have an idea of the physique of the inhabitants, tall people, who resembled the Chinese, one reason why the state was called Da Qin (Qin is the same character as the one used in ancient texts to designate China). This is slightly puzzling, but what interested the author of the *History of the Later Han* most were the products of Da Qin, which were indeed remarkable: "It is from this country", he writes, "that all the various and rare objects from foreign states come." From this we can deduce that although the inhabitants of Da Qin did not travel to China, their merchandise certainly reached there, via merchants from other countries, particularly from India and Persia.

Of these products, some are easy to identify, and others present certain problems of interpretation. It is clear that the land of Da Qin held much gold, silver and other valuable substances, that the state produced coral, amber, red cinnabar, a type of green jasper and light fabrics of various colours, as well as cloth embroidered with gold. It seems likely that *liuli*, which has been identified as the Sanskrit *vaidurya*, and which originally designated lapis lazuli, here refers to coloured glass, an ancient product which was familiar to the states of the eastern Mediterranean. The term "fire-washed cloth" is usually interpreted as an asbestos cloth. The "delicate cloth which some say is the wool of sea sheep, but which is really made from cocoons of wild silkworms" may refer to the filaments which cover certain Mediterranean mussels, mentioned in other texts and which form a sort of "marine silk". The Arab author, Al-Muqaddasi, writing at the end of the 10th century, describes a mussel which was gathered in the Mediterranean and which he calls *abû qalamûn*: "a creature which scratches itself on the rocks on the seashore. It leaves some of its fur there, which has the softness of silk and the colour of gold. The people do not leave a thread of it behind, because it is very rare. It is gathered, and cloths woven from it; and in the course of a day it assumes various colours. The ruler has forbidden the export of it, though, of course, some is exported secretly. One garment made of it may fetch ten thousand *dînârs*."[26]

Other expressions from the *History of the Later Han* are enigmatic, such as the ring which shines at night ("ring" seems to indicate here a flat disc pierced with a round hole in the centre, rather than a finger ring). This brings to mind various gems which shine at night and which are met in a number of traditions from the *Romance of Alexander* to the *Thousand and One Nights*. *Langgan* is a term which crops up in the oldest Chinese texts such as the *Tribute of Yu*, but has never been identified. It may at times have referred to a type of coral, but in this text coral is mentioned by its more usual name, *shanhu*. And what exactly are the "moon-bright pearls", the "rhinoceros which frightens chickens", and the "ointment which makes gold"? On the other hand, one product known here as *suhe*, was to have a long career in the history of commerce: this was a compound scent made from the juices of various perfumes heated together. The term *suhe* was to refer to several different substances at different periods.

The *History of the Later Han* attributed this product to Da Qin, and not to Persia or to its south-western neighbour, while Pliny believed that the ruinous perfumes which the Romans used to excess originated in Arabia.

Information of a different type was also provided about Da Qin: when following the land route across the state, it was not brigands which had to be feared but wild animals, tigers and lions, and it was recommended to travel in caravans of at least one hundred armed men. Was this once more a ploy on the merchants' part to discourage the over-inquisitive or potential informers? Perhaps not, because mentions of dangerous wild animals appear elsewhere too, both in connection with Da Qin, in Chinese texts, and with the states neighbouring the Seres in Latin and Greek texts of the same period, genuinely giving the impression that the countryside, not to mention the forests and deserts, were infested with these beasts. The Chinese author of the *History of the Later Han* does not mention snakes although they seem to have been very common at the period. It is no coincidence that the pharmacopoeia of the Greek and Roman world in the first centuries of the Christian era was renowned for a compound called theriac, which could heal animal bites, hence its name, derived from the Greek *ther*, or wild beast.

One should not expect merchants to have made geographic knowledge public, whether they actually held it or not. They had their own reasons for not doing so. The author of the *Natural History* deplores, when talking about sailors, that "the great crowd which sails does so only through love of profit and not for science, without thinking, in its blindness and its avidity, that navigation itself becomes much safer through science." No doubt he was right. But of all those who left, either overland or by sea, how many ever returned? One in two? One in three? One in ten? At sea, it was the merchants and sailors who were at risk, not the sedentary Roman citizens. Why then, having faced all these dangers, should they reveal to the public and to potential rivals, perhaps even to their enemies, the knowledge which had been acquired at such a price, and which represented part of a merchant's capital? There is no doubt that this knowledge was passed down from father to son, from brother to brother, within each family or community, as were many other professional secrets.

Pliny is wrong when he criticizes the merchant class. For one thing, it is thanks to them that we have guides and manuals of geography and trade, a few of which have reached us, books which circulated and contained if not secrets of the trade, at least basic knowledge about the routes, safety measures, commercial partners and goods to be traded. Furthermore, whether indeed "driven by love of profit" or by other motives, these merchants—through their travels and contacts, the objects, knowledge and traditions they carried with them in both directions, the foreign languages they learned or at least grasped notionally—played the role of middlemen and messengers, between different peoples in the same way that translators did (many of whom probably came from merchant families).

The sea route was certainly, at this time, far more dangerous than the land one when travelling from the shores of the Mediterranean to the Indian coast. Nevertheless, owing to obstacles produced probably more through human and political causes than through natural ones, trade at this period turned to these maritime routes and developed vigorously along them; and they in turn were made slightly less fearsome thanks to an understanding of the monsoon winds.

Chapter Seven

Dangers in the Erythraean Sea

Those who go down to the sea in ships,
Who do business in great waters;
These see Yahweh's works,
And His wonders in the deep.
For He commands, and raises the stormy wind,
Which lifts up its waves.
They mount up to the sky; they go down again to the depths.
Their soul melts away because of trouble.
They reel back and forth, and stagger like a drunken man,
And are at their wits' end.
Then they cry to Yahweh in their trouble,
And He brings them out of their distress.
He makes the storm a calm,
So that its waves are still.
Then they are glad because it is calm,
So He brings them to their desired haven. (Psalm 107)

Early Jewish and Christian sailors would sing this psalm from the Bible, praying to God to save them from danger, and it was still sung some eighteen or twenty centuries later, by British sailors of the Royal Navy. The sailors armed themselves against pirates, but against the fury of the sea, they needed divine help. In the 13th century, Al-Shadili, one of the great Muslim mystics, who crossed the Red Sea regularly to go to Mecca, composed a "Litany of the Sea", *Hizb al-bahr*, which he recited every day while on board ship. Since then, Muslim travellers have recited it whenever they face danger at sea. Ibn Battûta, himself a great traveller at the beginning of the 14th century, has left us the words of this prayer, through which he implored for divine mercy:[27] "O God, O Mighty, O Forbearing, O All-knowing, Thou art my Lord [...] Thou aidest whom Thou wilt, for Thou art the Powerful, the Compassionate. [...] do Thou establish us and succour us, and subject to us this sea as Thou didst subject the sea unto Moses, and as Thou didst subject the fire to Abraham, and as Thou didst subject the mountains and the iron to David, and as Thou didst subject the wind and the demons and the jinn to Solomon. Subject to us every sea that is Thine on earth and in heaven, in the world of sense and in the invisible world, the sea of this life and the sea of the life to come. [...] Grant us a fair wind according to Thy knowledge; waft it upon us from the treasures of Thy Mercy, and carry us thereon with conveyance of Thy favour, [granting us] therewith preservation from sin and wellbeing in our spiritual and our material life and in the life to come; verily Thou art disposer of all things."

Buddhist sailors and caravaneers, meanwhile, on the routes of Central Asia or in the Indian Ocean, appealed to Avalokitesvara, the bodhisattva of travellers, to protect them from drowning, bandits and pirates.

The Red Sea, Erythraean Sea, Gulf of Arabia, Indian Sea, all these names were used in the first centuries of the Christian era to designate the Red Sea and that part of the Indian Ocean from Cape Guardafui to the western coast of India—the sea which conveyed all the marvellous products of Arabia, Africa, India and beyond. This was the sea which brought frankincense and myrrh, ivory, rhinoceros horn and tortoiseshell, spices and pepper, cotton and silk muslins, in other words everything which, according to the moralists, was later to cause the fall of the Roman Empire. These moralists would forget that the Erythraean Sea also brought iron from India and Serica, which was used for weapons and armour, as well as numerous medicinal substances.

Detailed descriptions of the trade with the countries around the Red Sea and with India are given in Pliny's Book 6, and more particularly in the *Periplus of the Eyrthraean Sea*, a manual intended for sailors and merchants, written in Greek by an unknown author (a Syrian or perhaps an Alexandrian?), sometime between the first half of the 1st century and the beginning of the 3rd century AD. In this text, the range of geographical information about the known world is extended much further, to India and even into the Far East.[28]

The journey appears always to have begun at Alexandria, with a first stop at Juliopolis, three kilometres away. From there, one travelled up the Nile for twelve days with the "etesian winds" as far as Coptos (Kuft, Koft or Qift on modern maps). The distance from Juliopolis to Coptos was 309 Roman miles (457 kilometres, one Roman mile being 1,479 metres), according to Pliny. Pliny reckoned the distance from Coptos, where one left the river to travel by caravan overland, to the port of Berenicê on the Red Sea, to be 257 Roman miles, a distance which was covered in twelve days, with nine staging posts along the way. Berenicê, or Bender-el-Kebir on some maps, is now once again referred to as Berenicê (for example, on the National Geographic Society map of the Middle East, 1991, scale 1:5,877,000). Another apparently important port was Myos Hormos, located near Coptos, much further north than Berenicê, which also served Coptos and Alexandria.

On the opposite coast, on the eastern shore of the Red Sea, was the port of Leukê Cômê, linked by caravan to Petra and from there to the Mediterranean port of Gaza. This was an important commercial port for Arab ships until Petra's position diminished and was finally superseded by Palmyra, following the Roman Emperor Trajan's (98–117 AD) conquest. (It is said that the unbaptized Trajan was one of the only two pagans ever to have been admitted to Heaven, having been delivered from Hell by the prayers of St Gregory.)

TRADE WITH INDIA

Berenicê and Myos Hormos were the ports of departure for India, from where one could make use of the *hippalus* winds. Pliny describes the journey from Berenicê in mid-summer. The first commercial port of call, after thirty days of travel, was Ocelis (Okêlis, Ocilia), in Arabia, thought to be located either at Seh Sa'id, on the Straights of Bab-el-Mandeb, near the island of Perim, or at Kanê (Qana), at Hisn el-Ghurab, slightly further east along the Arabian coast. But according to Pliny, it was best to leave Ocelis and sail directly to the Indian port of Muziris, which could be reached in forty days with the *hippalus* winds. Muziris has been identified by some scholars as Kodungalur, known as Cranganore on the older British maps, on the south-western coast of India, just north of

Cochin. However, Pliny counsels against using this port because it was frequented by pirates, and recommends instead that of Bakarê, slightly further south.

When all went well both on land and at sea, the journey from Alexandria to the first Indian port would therefore last 94 days, without counting stopovers and waiting periods at each change of transport.

From the southern coast of Arabia one could also follow another route, different from the one Pliny indicates, which reached India slightly further north, at a port in the Indus delta, Barbaricum (Barbaricon), just south of modern Karachi. One could also travel to Barygaza, which corresponds to the present-day Broach, just north of the port of Surat, which had trade links with the Persian Gulf. Barbaricum and Barygaza both served hinterlands that produced the goods the foreign sailors were seeking. It also connected the maritime trade with that of "Scythia", that is to say Central Asia, using routes which crossed northern India, the Himalayan region, Kashmir and Afghanistan.

Before turning to India, let us look more closely at the ports of the Red Sea. Apart from those which we have just mentioned and which were particularly concerned with trade with India, several other ports sold products from Africa or Arabia, some of which were also exported to Western Asia. On the African side, besides Berenicê, the ports of Adulis, Massillon and Opônê also exported goods produced in their hinterlands. Adulis (near present-day Massawa, or Mits'iwa), the port of Abyssinia and Sudan, served Axum, the capital of the Abyssinian kingdom, in modern Ethiopia. It was the largest ivory market of the Red Sea, near large elephant and rhinoceros hunting grounds, rhinoceros horn being in great demand. This coast also supplied tortoiseshell. Ivory, rhinoceros horn and tortoiseshell were exported not only to the Roman world and the countries of the Mediterranean, but also to India and beyond. (We have mentioned the mistake made by the merchants of Da Qin in the middle of the 2nd century, thinking that they were taking the Chinese ruler a fine present.) Another port, Ptolemais, located slightly further north on the African coast according to the *Periplus*, specialized in the export of live elephants.

The region of Cape Guardafui, also known as the Promontory of Spices, was a great producer of several varieties of *cinnamomum* (cinnamon), as well as an excellent form of incense. The quantities of exported cinnamon were such that

specially large boats were used, which left from the port of Mosyllon, probably
Ras Hantara, on the north coast of the Horn of Africa, near the tip of Cape
Guardafui. Opônê, slightly further along the south coast of the Cape, also
exported cinnamon, incense and tortoiseshell.

CINNAMON

Cinnamomum is usually translated as cinnamon, although the term also
designates cassia (*Cinnamomum cassia*). The two are not quite synonymous;
cinnamon being the dried inner bark of the branches of the cinnamon tree (C.
verum), rolled into little cylinders, or "quills", the form in which it is still sold
in shops today (hence its name, said to be derived from the Hebrew for "tube").
The cinnamon tree is a member of the laurel family, and is closely related to
the cassia tree.* It is possible that cinnamon and cassia were names given to
different parts of the same tree, as there is some confusion, through the centuries,
over the use of these terms (as there is for many other commercial plant
products). In any event, cinnamon was much more highly prized than cassia,
and even more so than *malabathrum*, a term which seems to have designated
the leaf of the cinnamon tree, imported from India. Cinnamon and cassia were
not the exclusive products of the Horn of Africa (where they are no longer to
be found today): cinnamon trees grew abundantly in China as well as in South-
East Asia.

Europe would later import large quantities of cinnamon from the Far East.
In the first centuries of the Christian era, cinnamon and cassia, as well as a
number of other aromatic plants, had both religious and medicinal uses.
Cinnamon had long been a component of anointing oils used by the Hebrew
people, and in the perfumes of the king of the Parthians. It is still a subject of
discussion whether Solomon's *Song of Songs* is a love poem or a mystic ode, for
in it his beloved is compared to "an orchard of pomegranates, an orchard full of
rare fruits; spikenard and saffron, sweet cane and cinnamon with every incense-
bearing tree, myrrh and aloes with all the choicest spices." Cinnamon also
appears in the pharmacopoeia of the Greco-Roman world, and is mentioned by

* In the USA, the term cinnamon can legally be applied to C. cassia, whereas the British pharmacopoeia
requires cinnamon to be the product of C. verum.

the Greek physician Dioscorides in the 1st century AD, who ascribes multiple therapeutic virtues to it, as well as by another famous Greek physician, Paul of Aegina, in the 7th century.[29]

The aloes from the island of Socotra, much used in medicines and in funerary rites, was also exported to the Mediterranean. This island is located about 250 kilometres north-east of Cape Guardafui. The Red Sea also produced a shell, which when crushed gave out a fragrant substance, *onycha*, used in various compound perfumes.

FRANKINCENSE

On the opposite shore of the Red Sea was Hadramaut, on the southern tip of the Arabian Peninsula—the land of myrrh and most of all of frankincense. At the time of Pliny it was the kingdom of the Sabaeans, the wealthiest of the Arab tribes thanks to the forests of aromatic trees which grew on the western mountain slopes and along a coastal strip where there was sufficient rainfall. It was known as Arabia Felix, or the Arabia of Aromats. At that time it was above all the land of the frankincense tree, *thus* in Latin, belonging to the *Boswellia* genus. These jealously guarded forests for centuries ensured the fortunes of their owners, and were the object of an important trade with the countries of the eastern Mediterranean and Persia. Frankincense itself is an oleoresin, a gum resin which drips from incisions made in the bark of the tree. It is dried in the air then shipped and sold in small pieces and grains, which can still be seen in many Christian countries, although its use in Roman Catholicism has diminished significantly.

Frankincense is used either alone or as a compound, essentially as a perfume burnt during religious ceremonies, a custom which Christianity adopted from earlier religious practices. The necessity of obtaining incense for the great religions of antiquity, such as Judaism and the Greek and Roman religions, explains its particular importance in commercial trade. Later, it was used in more profane fields and in medicine.

Its use for religious purposes probably goes back as far as the beginning of religious belief, because of the pleasant fragrance it gave out when burnt. In Yahweh's prescriptions to Moses concerning the building of the sanctuary and the cult to be practised there (the sacerdotal code), some thirty or more centuries ago (the text in *Exodus* which mentions this event was written five or six centuries later), it is said that the grand priest shall burn each day, on an altar of acacia wood covered in pure gold, the "sweet incense". In addition, a scent for burning was to be made for the exclusive worship of Yahweh. This sacred perfume contained resin, a "sweet-smelling unguent" (*onycha*), galbanum and "sweet spices and pure frankincense". This "oil of holy ointment, an ointment compound after the art of the apothecary" should not be prepared for any other use than for "meeting Yahweh": "Whosoever shall make like unto that, to smell thereto, shall even be cut off from his people."

The religious use of incense was also widespread throughout the Greek world: Pliny tells us how, in the 4th century BC, the young Alexander, in his father's palace in Macedonia, was reprimanded by his teacher Leonidas for having placed too much incense on the altars. "Wait to do that," said Leonidas, "until you have conquered the countries which produce it." Alexander would later conquer Arabia, and as a belated answer to his teacher, sent him an entire ship full of incense! Admittedly, the ship, which he had plundered along with its contents, did not cost him much, and it is always worth having the gods on one's side, whether one be the son of Amon or an incarnation of Dionysus.

The Bible does not tell what quantities of gold, myrrh and frankincense the three Eastern magis brought to Bethlehem, guided by their star. Christian iconography, which has represented this scene thousands of times, only shows very small pots. But there may have been a caravan following them, filled with gifts worthy of the King of Israel. Thirty-three years later, one Friday evening, Joseph of Arimathea and Nicodemus, brought "a mixture of myrrh and aloes, about a hundred pounds. Then they took the body of Jesus, and bound it in strips of linen with the spices, as the custom of the Jews is to bury," and placed Christ in the tomb, according to the Gospel of John.

During Rome's period of greatest prosperity and wealth, under the empire, the demand for frankincense, as for all perfumes and costly substances, increased tremendously. Prices rose, and production could hardly satisfy the demand. A very significant text by Pliny, in chapter 41 of Book 12, tells us about its use, which later became abuse, in Roman funerals: "Arabia, which is styled 'Happy',

[…] puts her happiness to the credit of the powers above, although she owes it more to the power below. Her good fortune has been caused by the luxury of mankind even in the hour of death, when they burn over the departed the products which they had originally understood to have been created for the gods. Good authorities declare that Arabia does not produce so large a quantity of perfume in a year's output as was burned by the Emperor Nero in a day at the obsequies of his consort Poppaea. Then reckon up the vast number of funerals celebrated yearly throughout the entire world, and the perfumes such as are given to the gods a grain at a time, that are piled up in heaps to the honour of dead bodies!"

MIDDLEMEN

Some merchants from Alexandria tampered with their goods. But the control over the harvest, which was subject to various prohibitions and religious obligations, as well as the rules over its transportation, made for the trade of a very pure product, which could be bought in Petra or Gaza, where it arrived by caravan. This is the itinerary which Pliny describes in chapter 30 of Book 12, a compulsory one from which it was forbidden to leave on pain of death. It was probably the main route before the development of maritime transport. Numerous taxes were levied on the merchandise along this route, first of all the tithe in honour of the god of the Sabaeans, Sabis, which covered the caravan's travel costs for several days. Then there were the dues to the king of the Gebanites, another mandatory transit point; after that, the sixty-five staging posts before reaching the port of Gaza on the Mediterranean. In addition to this were the sums of money to be given to priests, king's secretaries, guards, soldiers, gate-keepers, "all along the route they keep on paying, at one place for water, at another for fodder, or the charges for lodging at the halts, and at the various tolls-gates; so that expenses mount up to 688 *denarii* per camel before the Mediterranean coast is reached; and then again payment is made to the customs officers of our empire. Consequently, the price of the best frankincense is 6, of the second best 5, and the third best 3 *denarii* a pound." The same litany of complaints, or over state or private racketeering reappears in many merchants' accounts from all over the world and at all periods, telling of the parasites who lived off the movement of trade. A good many of these staging posts could probably be avoided once Roman maritime power had succeeded in gaining relative control of the Red Sea, and the sailors who benefited from this could load in one port, and navigate directly to another one, thus reducing the number of over-greedy middlemen.

The two principal ports where incense was loaded were on the Arabian coast; the first of these, Muza, near Moka or perhaps even Moka itself, slightly north of Ocelis, could, as we have seen, be reached in thirty days' sailing from Berenicê, and was the main point of departure for India. Muza was not a staging post on the way to India, but was the great port for the export of frankincense and myrrh until the Middle Ages. The second port was Kanê, also mentioned above, the incense port both for the countries of the Mediterranean and the ports of the Persian Gulf, as well as for Barbaricum and Barygaza on the western coast of India.

Before the *Periplus*, and before direct travel between Egypt and India, there had existed another port, Eudaemion, on the Arabian coast, at the entrance to the Red Sea. Indian sailors travelled as far as that port, where goods and ships from India and Egypt congregated, but did not have the right to go beyond it. Whichever direction one came from, one could go no further. But the town was destroyed during a war and was never rebuilt.

MYRRH

In addition to frankincense, we have also mentioned myrrh. This was another particular product of the region, much in demand for perfume and medicine, and used for centuries by Egyptian embalmers. The botanical name of the bush is *Commiphora abyssinica* or *Balsamodendron myrrha*, and it belongs, like frankincense, to the Burseraceous family of trees and shrubs. It is also an oleoresin, used since ancient times as a compound in perfumes to be burned, in all scented oils, an anointing oil reserved for the high priests and in worship carried out according to the Jewish sacerdotal code of prescriptions (like frankincense), as well as a royal unguent reserved for the Parthian kings. It was also a component of perfumes used for secular purposes, in the Egyptian and Greco-Roman pharmacopoeia, and in Paul of Aegina's list of pharmaceuticals.

OTHER AROMATICS

Bdellium, which belongs to the same family as myrrh and was used in much the same way, was also in great demand. This grew not only in Arabia and East Africa, but also in India and in Bactria, and bdellium from the latter was even more sought-after than that of Arabia. Its botanical names are *Balsamodendron mukul* or *Balsamodendron roxburghii*. Apart from frankincense, myrrh, cinnamon, aloes and bdellium, the countries giving onto the Red Sea also produced *costus* (*Saussurea radix, Saussurea lappa*), the roots of which were used in perfume and medicine. It also grew in Syria, as well as in the Himalaya and Tibet, but that of Arabia was considered the finest. Finally, two other aromatics were cardamom, the seeds of a plant of the ginger family which thrived in Arabia, India, Armenia and on the shores of the Bosphorus, and agalloch, an aromatic wood.

Were some of these medicinal substances, spices and perfumes exported to India? Storax and incense were exported to Barbaricum. It is highly likely that certain products left there in the form of compound perfumes and medicine. If Arabia was the mother of aromatic substances, Persia was renowned for its compound perfumes (scents which were used as much to hide odours and for health reasons), and Greece for its highly reputed medicine. Fragrant substances imported from India would also enter into these compounds, which could contain hundreds of different elements.

As we have seen above, the Chinese described *suhe*, mentioned in the *History of the Later Han*, as a product of Da Qin, made from the juices of several plants boiled together. This contradicts the view of some authors who believe that, in the first centuries of the Christian era, the term *suhe* must refer to storax, the gum resin of *Styrax officinalis*, from the Styracaeae family, which is obtained, like frankincense, from incisions made in the tree trunk. Several centuries later, *suhe* was thought to designate *Liquidambar orientalis*, liquidambar or liquid storax, an amber-coloured resinous sap (hence its name), which comes from a bush of the Hamamelidaceae family. This latter *suhe* was imported by the Chinese from South-East Asia. In addition, one 13th century Chinese author, Zhao Rugua, writes that the "fragrant *suhe* oil" came from Dashi, which at that time generally designated several of the Arabian kingdoms. The same author mentions a perfume from Persia, *anxi xiang*, yet again using the term Anxi, which originally referred to the Persia of the Arsacids, the Parthians. But for him, this product was imported into China from Sumatra, although this does not prevent it from having come from even further afield. The kingdom of Anxi is said to have sent some as "tribute" to the Chinese emperor between 566 and 572, and again between 605 and 617. According to Joseph Needham's research, the words *anxi xiang* may have first designated bdellium, and then later Sumatran benzoin.[30]

THERIAC

Did the reputation of Greek medicine, so highly considered in the Western world, ever cross the eastern seas and reach the land of the Seres? Direct contacts were rare. We know of the Roman embassy (if it really was one) in the year 166 which arrived at the Chinese court, by sea, and which brought with it gifts which had obviously been acquired at one of the ports of call, perhaps in the Red Sea. Among the few official embassies of the Roman Empire to reach China, a particularly interesting one arrived in 667, sent by the Byzantine Empire, which presented Emperor Gaozong with theriac. Theriac had been famous for seventeen or eighteen centuries in the West. It was a medicine made up of several hundred different substances, the product of Greek medical science, and had first been made on a large scale in the time of Dioscorides and Galen, in the 1st and 2nd centuries AD. Used specifically against bites and stings of poisonous animals—dogs, snakes, scorpions and sea animals—it was also used to treat a wide range of other ailments. Kept secret and monopolized by some, rediscovered and improved upon by others, the formula of this theriac was used in Europe until the 18th century. The famous French apothecary, Moyse Charas, who lived during the reign of Louis XIV, hoped to break the monopoly which Venice held at the time on the manufacture of this medication, and produced in Paris the "great theriac of Andromace". He published the formula in his *Traité de la thériaque*, first printed in 1668. Moyse Charas was an important figure in the history of the transfer of medical knowledge. His best-known work, a *Royal Galenic and Chemical Pharmacopoeia*, published for the first time in 1676, was a huge success, and was certainly the first European medical work to be translated into Chinese.[31]

Let us turn back to the first centuries of the Christian era, when trade with India through the Red Sea was growing. What did the Greek, Syrian and Arab sailors buy and sell in those Indian ports?

If we were to follow the main ports of call mentioned in the *Periplus*, and to choose the direct route from Cape Guardafui or from Kanê, one would land at Muziris, Bakarê or Nelcynda (Neakyndon, Melkyda or Nincildea in other sources). The latter is a port less than a hundred kilometres south of Muziris, not directly on the coast but on the estuary, perhaps some 10 kilometres east of Kottayam. These were the three main points for the export of pepper and *malabathrum*, the leaf of the Indian cinnamon tree. Enormous quantities of these two products were shipped from there, along with pearls, diamonds, sapphires, various other gems, silks, *spica nardi* and tortoiseshell from "Chrysê" (perhaps the Malacca peninsula or Sumatra?).

Spica nardi, or spikenard, comes from the Greek *nardostakhys* (used, among others, by Paul of Aegina), from which is derived its modern botanical name, *Nardostachys jatamansi*. This is a vivacious spice of the Valerian order which grows abundantly throughout the Himalaya; its leaves and roots were—and are still—used for perfumes and medicine. Nard (*nardus*, *nardum* or *nardos* in Greek and Latin texts), a term frequently met with in the Middle Ages, is thought by some to be a Gramineae (*Cymbopogon schoenanthus?*); its roots produce an essential oil used in perfume, medicine and cosmetics. This plant is abundant in the Punjab, Baluchistan and Iran. Other scholars, perhaps confusing it with *Nardostachys*, believe it refers to *Valeriana spica*. Pliny writes, in chapter 26 of Book 12, that nard is a shrub the leaf of which "holds a foremost place" in perfumes. The word nard has obviously designated different plants according to different writers at different times. The identification of these plants is often very difficult; not only do their trade terms not necessarily follow their scientific appellations, but most of these medicinal plants were transported in a dried form, in pieces or even powdered, sometimes packed into cakes, at other times adulterated, or used in compounds which were often trade secrets.

Instead of sailing towards Muziris, it was possible to leave Egypt in July and sail directly to Barygaza, the export port of *spica nardi*, *costus*, bdellium and *lycium,* all of which had been brought from countries much further north, from Kashmir and other Himalayan regions. *Lycium* is a bush used in medicine, cosmetics and dyeing. Ivory, agate, carnelian, pepper, cotton cloth and cotton thread, silks and probably silk in skeins could also be bought there. The silks in all likelihood came from China. Cotton and cotton cloth were to India what silk was to China, its main industrial product and its most important export.

Barygaza was a service port for the trade route across northern India and Kashmir, and led to Central Asia. This land route completed the maritime route by connecting the Red Sea to Central Asia without passing through Persia, thus allowing trade in Indian products on the way. It represented the most important branch of the transcontinental Silk Road. It opened up the kingdoms of Inner Asia to the outside world, and played an even more important role when, in times of war and political troubles, China lost control of the Western Territories and the eastern half of the Silk Road was closed as a result. The port of Barbaricum held a similar position, in the delta of the Indus River, as a point for loading and unloading goods which were traded in the town of Minnagara, "a city of Scythia subject to the Parthian princes", located further inland, where remains of buildings dating back to Alexander could still be seen at the time.* *Costus, lycium,* nard, turquoise, lapis lazuli, cotton, indigo, silk in skeins, "Seric fur" could all be bought there, products of India, of the Himalaya, of Badakhshan and of China.

Indigo, a blue dye produced by the leaves of a plant of the *Indigofera* which grows abundantly in India, was, during the 16th to 18th centuries, one of the main Indian exports to Europe. It is probably this dye which is called *indikon* in the *Periplus, indicum* in Latin, which simply means "Indian", but which is actually used to designate several different substances at different times: not only the vegetable dye, but also a mineral, in which case the word is an abbreviation for "Indian stone", mentioned in the pharmacopoeia of the physician Dioscorides.

---

* *Ruins of fortresses attributed to Alexander are to be found as far as the present-day region of Sindh in Pakistan, just north-east of the Indus delta. "Scythia" should therefore be taken not as referring to a particular kingdom, but more widely as a region apparently subject, at the time, to the Parthians. Perhaps Minnagara was a large commercial emporium, a frontier town and customs post, bordering on the Kushan kingdom?*

In the plural form, as *indica folia*, it is an expression which refers not to indigo but to a different "Indian leaf", *malabathrum*, the leaf of the cinnamon tree, another important export. The multiplicity of these "Indian" objects in the vocabulary reflects the importance of commercial trade with India.

PEARLS

Pearls were one of the most sought-after products in Rome, as well as throughout Asia. Pliny the naturalist and moralist devoted more pages to them than to any other product, seven chapters in Book 9, including one or two pages deploring the use of them. "Moral corruption and luxury spring from no other source in greater abundance than from the genus shell-fish. [...] It had been insufficient, forsooth, for the seas to be stowed in our gullets, were they not carried on the hands and in the ears and on the head and all over the body of women and men alike. What connection is there between the sea and our clothing, between the waves and waters and woollen fabric? We only enter that element in a proper manner when we are naked! Granted there is a close alliance between it and our stomachs, but what has it to do with our backs? Are we not content to feed on dangers without also being clothed with them?" And he adds further on: "Women glory in hanging [pearls] on their fingers and using two or three for a single earring; [...] nowadays, even the poor people covet them—it is a common saying that a pearl is as good as a lackey for a lady when she walks abroad! And they even use them on their feet, and fix them not only to the laces of their sandals but all over their slippers. In fact, by this time, they are not content with wearing pearls unless they tread on them, and actually walk on the unique gems!"

These passages reflect the importance of the relatively recent demand for pearls and consequently of their import, all of which is confirmed by the *Periplus*. They came from the Indian Ocean, and were bought in various ports, Muziris, Bakarê, Nelcynda, but according to the *Periplus*, the largest pearl market was Argaris, on the eastern coast of India, near the southern point of the Indian peninsula. It was nearby, at Kolchoi, that the most productive pearl fisheries were found. Opposite it, the island of Palaesimundu, also known as Taprobane, in other words Ceylon, now Sri Lanka, also produced and exported pearls. For Pliny, the three most important pearl-producing areas of India were Taprobane, Stoidis, an island in the Indian Ocean some 50,000 feet (about 74 kilometres) from the Iranian coast of the Persian Gulf, near the Straits of Hormuz, and Perimula, a promontory on the south-eastern coast of India. The author of the *Natural History* seems singularly interested in these trinkets which he so criticized the Romans for using, and describes their qualities according to their provenance. According to him, the most highly valued ones came from the coast of Arabia on the Persian Gulf.

The *Periplus* mentions pearl oyster fishing up the coast of the Persian Gulf, naming two ports at the end of the Gulf, Apologus and Ommana, not far from Spasinou Charax, near the mouth of the Euphrates. These ports traded with Barygaza, from which they bought copper, sandalwood, ebony and teak, and themselves exported pearls, purple dyes, wine, dates, clothes, gold and slaves to Arabia and India. This implies that the pearls that could be bought at Barygaza probably came from the Persian Gulf.

Taprobane had been known to the Romans for a long time, but it was only during the principate of Claudius (41–54 AD) that a freed slave in the service of Annius Plocamus, who was in charge of tax collection in the Red Sea on behalf of the Imperial Treasury, was "blown along by the north winds" as he was sailing round Arabia to the Straits of Hormuz. These winds brought him within fifteen days to the port of Hippuros in Taprobane, a journey of some 900 marine miles (about 1,667 km). "He was entertained with kindly hospitality by the king, and in a period of six months acquired a thorough knowledge of the language; and afterwards in reply to the king's enquiries he gave him an account of the Romans and their emperor. The king among all that he heard was remarkably struck with admiration for Roman honesty, on the grounds that amongst the money confiscated the *denarii* were all equal in weight, although the various figures on them showed that they had been coined by several emperors. This strongly attracted his friendship, and he sent four envoys, the chief of whom was Rachias," writes Pliny in Book 6. Pliny devotes eight chapters (84 to 91) to Taprobane, to its geography, natural resources, agriculture, fishing ("mainly of turtles"), and to the longevity of its inhabitants. His description includes one rather strange passage: Rachias stated that the island of Ceylon lay opposite the south-eastern coast of India, extending for over 10,000 stadia or 1,850 km (1,250 miles) in length, that is to say more than four times its real size. He also says that the island faced the land of the Seres, beyond the Hemodi mountains (a term generally used for part of the Himalaya).

The Seres he describes are indeed strange, being of "more than normal height, and have red hair and blue eyes, and they speak in harsh tones and use no language in dealing with travellers." In order to trade with them—and Rachias' father had done this—it was necessary to use a system of silent barter, on opposite banks of a river. This was carried out in the following way: the merchandise proposed by A was deposited on one side of the river. The merchants of B would cross over, and place their goods beside the first, according to what they proposed in exchange. They would then return to the other bank. The merchants of A would come back and, if the exchange satisfied them, would take away B's goods and leave theirs on the ground, which B could then pick up. If A was not satisfied, they would turn away, leaving everything on the ground! B would cross back and add to their own pile of merchandise, and so on until the supplement corresponded to the other party's expectations, and each side went away with its acquisitions. This manner of trading with the Seres is also described by Pomponius Mela in the 1st century AD, by Solinus in the middle of the 3rd century and by Ammianus Marcellinus in the 4th century.[32] It would seem that this practice was not confined solely to Seres. Several examples of this type of trading are known in historical accounts from various countries, which may have arisen either through lack of translators, or from a refusal to have direct contacts with foreigners. In many cases, it occured, as here, between two nations living on either side of a frontier river.

Much has been written about this passage of Pliny's, as about other aspects of Rachias' information, about these Seres who presumably were not actually Seres, and could not in any case have been located so close to Ceylon. The French scholar Jean Filliozat has clearly shown that the authors of antiquity confused two separate people with the same name, or with names which were phonetically similar: one from Kerala, near Ceylon, and the other an Indo-

European people from Central Asia who were quite unrelated to the former.[33] On the question of the silent barter among the inhabitants of Ceylon, there exists a 5th-century Chinese account which echoes these controversial Latin texts. The Chinese Buddhist monk Faxian, who lived for two years in Ceylon around 409–411 AD, writes in chapter 38 of his travels: "The country originally had no human inhabitants, but was occupied only by spirits and dragons [the Chinese translation of the Indian *nâgas*]." According to Hindu myths and legends, the island was indeed inhabited by demons known as *rakshasa*. But these demons and dragons had an almost human behaviour: they engaged in trade. "Merchants of various countries carried on a trade [with them]. When the trafficking was taking place, the spirits did not show themselves. They simply set forth their precious commodities, with labels of the price attached; while the merchants made their purchases according to the price; and took the things away. Through the coming and going of the merchants, when they went away, the people of their various countries heard how pleasant the land was, and flocked to it in numbers till it became a great nation." In chapter 37, the Chinese traveller mentions a hundred small islands all around Ceylon (Shizi), which almost all produced beautiful gems and pearls. Some of them, and one minute one in particular, produced the *mani* pearl, a very bright and very pure pearl used to make the most precious Buddhist prayer beads. This pearl symbolized the Buddha, and the king was entitled to three of every ten pearls found.

Taprobane, the fair land, frequently appears in the history of travel and of trade, in Hindu mythology and in Buddhism. Ceylon was converted to Buddhism in the 3rd century BC, and according to one legend, the Buddha Sakyamuni is said to have lived there, leaving his footprints in the ground. One of the Buddha's teeth is still revered there as a sacred relic.

COINS

In the first centuries of the Christian era, Ceylon seems to have been a sort of huge cash-register, a treasury of coinage and money from various countries which indicates the multiplicity and importance of its trade. Tens of thousands of coins—Indian, Roman, Kushan, Sassanian Persian and Chinese—have been unearthed there. In the first three centuries AD, the island had active commercial relations with northern India and with Western states, either directly or through the intermediary of Indian sailors. Silver *denarii* of nine Roman emperors have been found, as well as a few copper coins from Alexandria, and silver coins from northern India and from the Kushan Empire. From the 4th century on, with growing economic crises in the Roman Empire and in Egyptian commerce, Sri Lanka became the largest maritime trade centre of the Indian Ocean. Tens of thousands of bronze and copper Roman coins (no longer silver ones) have been discovered there dating to the 4th and 5th centuries, issued in the mints of Rome, Alexandria, Carthage, Antioch, Constantinople and other Mediterranean cities. The numerous Sassanian and Byzantine coins date from the 6th and 7th centuries,[34] while Arab coinage marks the period when sailors from the caliphates visited Serendib, as Ceylon was also known.

Roman coins have also been found in many places in India, several hundred scattered pieces in all. There is further evidence to confirm the existence of relations between Rome and India, hinted at in written sources, mentions of Roman embassies to India or Indian embassies to Rome in the 1st century BC. Among other things are the ruins found near Podukê, not far from Pondicherry, on the Coromandel Coast. The *Periplus* mentions the existence of three ports close to one another in the south of the Indian peninsula: Kamara, Sopatma and Podukê. In this area, slightly south of Pondicherry, the village of Virampatnam (Arikamedu), has been known since the 18th century for its ancient brick and earth ruins and its old wells, the remains perhaps of a vast warehouse. Just before the Second World War, several interesting finds were made at the site: necklace-beads of glass, carnelian, agate, jasper, garnets and coloured quartz, a carved carnelian ring perhaps representing Augustus but definitely of Roman manufacture, and fragments of pottery typical of the famous Italian manufacturing centre of Arezzo (Arretium) in Tuscany, all dating to the 1st century AD.[35] The same site also yielded stone tools, mill stones, polishing or grinding stones, semi-precious stones either in the process of being cut or still uncut, suggesting that there must have been a sizable stone workshop there. Was this a trading post, a branch of some Roman enterprise or a genuine colony?

Were these local artisans making Roman-style objects for export? Whatever the answer, Roman products arrived on the Coromandel Coast from the first half of the 1st century AD onwards, and this site remained active for several centuries more.

Further along the eastern coast of the Indian peninsula, Western navigators knew of the existence of the Ganges delta, through which *malabathrum* and "Gangetic nard" transited, as did two types of cloth, *pinikon*, and the "excellent *sindones* which are called Gangetic". According to Greek dictionaries, *pinikon* is a marine linen, a fibre collected from a seashell, a product we have already met in the Mediterranean. As for *sindon*, it may refer to either a fine cotton or linen cloth, a light tunic, a veil or a shroud. Of course, it is very tempting to equate these with the light cotton muslins that have always made the reputation of the Indian textile industry.

The region was said to possess gold mines, and gold coinage was certainly in use there. Gold was also a characteristic product of an island near the Ganges delta, known as the "furthest extremity towards the east of the inhabited world", Chrysê, from the Greek for "gold", often identified as the Malacca peninsula, or perhaps the island of Sumatra. According to the *Periplus*, this is where the best tortoiseshell was to be found.

And what did lie further east? Nothing, nothing but ocean, for the *Periplus*, for Pliny, for the geographers of the 1st century such as Pomponius Mela and Strabo: this was the edge of the inhabited world. The coast, according to them, did continue, however, but turned northwards, following what we call Indochina and China in a long straight line. Later, in the 2nd century, Ptolemy would extend the known world slightly further east, imagining a vast gulf to the north of which he placed Seres. As we have seen earlier, a few rare citizens or subjects of the Roman Empire had landed in these regions, probably in Burma or Vietnam, and from there had reached the Chinese capital. Were they so few? In Vietnam too, there is evidence of relations with the Roman world, if not of actual Roman presence. In 1944, in the province of Oc-Eo, about 20 kilometres from the Gulf of Thailand, a French scientific team led by Louis Malleret discovered an archaeological site which yielded Chinese and Indian objects, as well as a certain amount of gold and silver jewellery, with carvings of Roman origin or of Roman inspiration, most of them in carnelian, as well as medals from the period of the Antonines (2nd century AD), and a few other objects.[36]

These objects, writes Malleret, "provide the proof that during the 2nd and 3rd centuries of the Christian era, the site of Oc-Eo produced artists who carved intaglios in the purest Roman style and were capable of reproducing its skilled techniques. This is not flotsam which has been swept by some distant current from the Western world and shored up here, lost on the extreme edges of a peninsula in the Asiatic world. These are the creations of an art incorporated into the domestic and social lives of the inhabitants of this land."

One cannot help linking these ruins with those of Arikamedu in India, and with the traces of Roman techniques, military this time, left in Central Asia after the Battle of Carrhae; all of these appear to be scattered witnesses of something, but of what exactly? Of trade, of a few deserters, of prisoners of war who escaped or were sold, of shipwrecked sailors making a new life for themselves, of small groups of Greeks, Jews or Syrians settling down, with their trade and their gods, in some welcoming land? We are all free to imagine these odysseys, whose only remains are a few antique objects in a museum, measured, examined, sorted, analysed by all sorts of machines, dated, catalogued, labelled and mute behind their safety glass.

Travelling up the coast from south to north from Chrysê, the *Periplus* mentions "a very great inland city called Thinaï", located in what we would now call China, from where cotton (*erion*: cotton or wool, but most likely referring here to the former), *nema* (thread) and *serikon* (silk) were taken by foot across Bactria as far as Barygaza, and along the Ganges to a region called Mimyrikê, Damirica or Limuria.

With Ptolemy,[37] the Far East becomes slightly more detailed and closer to reality: Chrysê has now become a peninsula, and the coast, from there on, curves inwards into a wide gulf, the Great Gulf, on the shores of which lies Kattigara, the port of the Sinae. The capital is Sinae, or Thinaï, north of Kattigara. These were the two main towns of this land. The meridian where the capital was located marked the easternmost edge of the known inhabited world. Nevertheless,

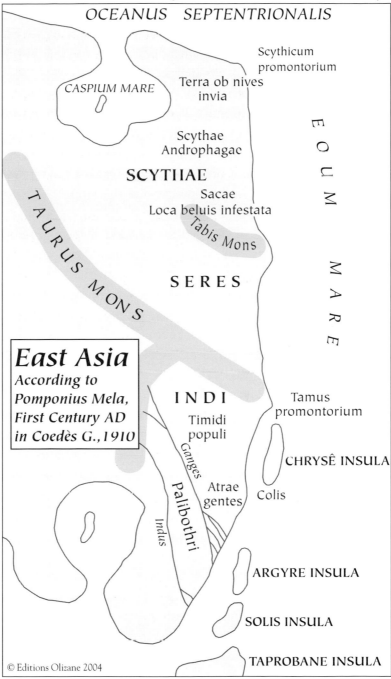

OCEANUS SEPTENTRIONALIS

Scythicum promontorium

CASPIUM MARE

Terra ob nives invia

EOUM MARE

Scythae Androphagae

SCYTHAE

Sacae
Loca beluis infestata

Tabis Mons

TAURUS MONS

SERES

East Asia
According to Pomponius Mela, First Century AD in Coedès G., 1910

INDI

Timidi populi

Tamus promontorium

Ganges

Atrae gentes

Colis

CHRYSÊ INSULA

Palibothri

Indus

ARGYRE INSULA

SOLIS INSULA

TAPROBANE INSULA

East Asia According to Pomponius Mela

for Ptolemy, the Sinae people were not the Seres; the latter were located further north, and it seems that one travelled there not by sea, but preferably overland, following routes which will we shall see further on.

Sailing from the "Gangetic Gulf", the Gulf of Bengal, to the port of Kattigara led one past a number of unusual islands, some of them interesting, others disturbing. Some were sources of gold or silver, several were inhabited by cannibals, others by monkey-tailed satyrs. The so-called "stone of Heracles", on the ten grouped islands of Maniolae, was said to immobilize and restrain ships built with iron nails; the reputation of this stone was to continue in the West throughout the Middle Ages.

Although geographical knowledge was gradually being extended eastwards, it nevertheless appears that most trade between the Roman Empire and the suppliers of Indian products, as well as of iron and silk from the Seres, was concentrated on the one hand along the caravan routes which led to the eastern Mediterranean—routes which sometimes passed through Persia (first Parthian and then Sassanian)—and on the other hand to Barbaricum and Barygaza, the destinations of the routes from the Himalayan regions and the kingdoms of Central Asia, along which Chinese products were carried. As for Chinese merchants themselves, no text, no source, no country mentions their presence, or that of their agents, for the first centuries of the Christian era in the Mediterranean world, in the Red Sea or in the Indian Ocean. On land, they are also absent from caravans west of the Pamir mountains.

Reading these well-known Greek and Latin texts, it is interesting to note that there is more information on what was to be bought in the East and much less on what the Roman Empire sold there. The various fears and criticisms over trade deficits have already been mentioned. The presence of Roman money—of gold and silver coinage—almost everywhere could be interpreted as evidence of insufficient export of goods. One looks in vain, in the case of departures to the Far East, for mentions of trade in cereals, wine and oil, as was known across the Mediterranean, with millions of amphorae left either on the sea floor or in the ports. Nevertheless, Greek, Italian and Syrian wines were appreciated and exported throughout the Red Sea region, as well as to India, particularly to Barygaza. From the Roman world also came wine, perfumes (such as *suhe*), copper and tin, probably linen, and two much sought-after products which fetched a very high price in Asia: coral from the Mediterranean, and coloured glass, a speciality of Syria, Alexandria and Italy, before becoming one of the Rhine region.

THE KINGDOM OF THE KUSHAN

The Persian Gulf was never a Roman protectorate. It was the province of the Arabs and the Parthians, then of the Sassanids, and like the Red Sea, was crossed by trade ships, which maintained an active trade with India. The Parthians, however, could not prevent the world's sailors from sailing the Red Sea and crossing the Indian Ocean to trade in the ports of India, Indonesia and Indochina. But they could and did control the main caravan route from Central Asia, attempting to block Roman expansion into the eastern Mediterranean and monopolizing for themselves the sale of eastern products, mainly that of silk. During the first centuries of the Christian era, they always maintained good diplomatic and commercial relations with China but were, for the most part at war with the Romans, or at the very least, were great rivals. This rivalry between Persia and its largest western neighbour, the struggle for control over the outlets of the great trade routes to the Mediterranean, was to continue into the next centuries, during the Sassanid dynasty and the Byzantine Empire. Later still, the caliphs and then the sultans of Constantinople would attempt to keep the Christians away from the shores of the Mediterranean, preventing them in the Middle Ages from "sailing even a plank on the sea". The European powers did not succeed in ending this blockade which affected products from the Far East until sufficient progress had been made in navigation and weapons technology, until Africa could be circumnavigated with ships with sufficient dissuasive fire-power; this was achieved in 1497 by the Portuguese.

During the first three centuries of the Christian era, the catalyst which provided much of the energy and vitality along the inland trade routes between Asia and Central Asia, the latter itself a crossroads between China and Persia, was not so much the development of trade with the Roman Empire, but the formation of a new political power. This new entity set itself up between India, the Parthian kingdom and Central Asia, occupying the land from Bactria to the mouth of the Indus River, corresponding to the caravan routes and their outlet to the sea. This new power—which encouraged trade, was tolerant of religions and was itself a hybrid of multiple influences—was the kingdom of the Kushan.

Chapter Eight
The Seven Treasures

*W*e have mentioned Kushan coinage and the trade between Barygaza and Barbaricum, and Inner Asia. Greek and Latin texts of the period apparently do not explicitly mention the kingdom or the empire of the Kushan, although the Chinese continued for several centuries to call it Da Yuezhi. As Zhang Qian's mission had revealed, this kingdom was descended from one of the five Yuezhi tribes driven out by the Xiongnu which had settled in Bactria. The Chinese gave different names to each of the five tribes; one of these, the Guishuang, was the one which we know as the Kushan. But although aware of this origin, certain texts such as the *History of the Later Han*, and again the *Bei shi*, the *History of the Northern Dynasties*, written during the Tang dynasty, nevertheless retained the term Da Yuezhi. This tribe subdued the other four and then proceeded to absorb its neighbours, finally forming an empire, in the age-old cyclical process peculiar to Inner Asia (the Xiongnu, the Turks in the 5th and 6th centuries and the Mongols under Genghis Khan in the 13th century all followed the same pattern).

The chronology of Kushan history has been much debated. Their first king, Kudjula Kadphises, probably reigned from 30 to 78 AD. The most famous ruler, Kanishka I, is sometimes said to have begun his reign in 78, while others place it later, between 100 and 126 at the earliest, or between 120 and 146 at the latest.[38] The Kushan kings fought their nomadic neighbours, the Chinese, and Anxi, Parthian Persia. According to the Chinese annals, they captured Kabul, Kashmir and then India (this must refer to only one or a few of the kingdoms of northern India), where they killed the king and replaced him with one of their generals. It is possible that by conquering these Indian kingdoms and turning them into protectorates, they were able to control the ports of the north-west, among others Barbaricum. The Kushan dynasty prospered for about three centuries, from the end of the 1st to the end of the 4th century, which coincided with the peak of the Parthian Arsacid dynasty of Persia and the beginning of the Sassanid dynasty (226–651) which succeeded it. It was also contemporaneous with the Chinese Later Han (25–220), Wei (220–264), Jin (265–317) and Northern Wei (386–535) dynasties, as well as the smaller dynasties existing during this period of division of the Chinese Empire. Finally, it was also contemporary with the Roman Empire, which split into two in 330 with the transfer of the capital to Constantinople, the "second Rome".

The centuries of Kushan rule, a "very powerful house" according to Chinese historians (and indeed the Chinese generals who fought it in Central Asia did not always emerge victorious), were characterized by favourable policies towards trade and cultural exchange, and encouragement in religious, artistic and technical fields. This empire was itself the result of the merging of various Iranian and Greek influences: it had first incorporated one Persian satrapy, and then became part of Alexander's empire before belonging to the Seleucid kings. Other influences arrived from the steppe culture from which the Yuezhi originated, as well as later from Indian culture, once Indian territories were annexed. These four civilizations, Iranian, Greek, "Scythian" and Indian were perhaps a temporary blend from the political point of view, but one which has left us lasting vestiges. From Indian civilization came a powerful religious movement, Buddhism, which reached Central Asia and China at the time of the Kushans. Its spread, encouraged by the Kushan rulers, was inexorably tied in with the dynamism of trade. Commerce and Buddhism were to go hand in hand, each benefiting the other, wealth providing material support for the religion through donations, and the donor receiving spiritual assistance in return for his gifts. More prosaically, the trade routes and the armed caravans allowed missionaries to travel in relative safety.

In China, there had been 65 years of interruption in relations with the West. During this time, according to the historical annals, the Western Territories had dissolved into dozens of small kingdoms, more or less independent from the Xiongnu. Then, the Later Han had succeeded in re-establishing Chinese control, setting up once again military outposts and a Protector-General; not, however, without numerous rebellions and incidents. In 91 AD, the Chinese general Ban Chao, who had conquered all of the Western Territories, was named Protector-General, residing in Kucha, while Turfan became the military headquarters. This was a period of great imperialism for China, which established its dominion over more than fifty kingdoms (varying in size from 350 to 32,000 families), all of which "submitted themselves and sent hostages". A complete colonial administration was once again organized, and historians have described at length the economic and military development of these Western Territories. This was the basis of Chinese claims to these territories, for eighteen or nineteen centuries thereafter, with varying degrees of success.

Inevitably, war with the nomads flared up once more, and from 105 to 107 AD, the Western Territories rebelled and China's control ebbed and waned. In order to have a few years of relative security for traders to carry out their business, Ban Yong, son of Ban Chao, the founder of this colonial empire, was named military commander in 123. He had been brought up and trained in Central Asia, and succeeded in re-conquering seventeen kingdoms. The reports that Ban Yong filed were to provide the basic information on Central Asia at this period contained in the *History of the Later Han*. But decline and chaos were once again on the horizon, and it was during one of these periods of *pax sinica*, in the last decade of the 1st century AD at the latest, or just before the time when communications were cut off, that a mission, whether official or private is not clear, set out by land. For once, we know of its existence not through Chinese annals (which make no mention at all of it), but through Ptolemy, who came across it through an account, now lost, by the Roman geographer Marinus the Tyrian, writing at the end of the 1st century, of a trip made to Serica by the Greek Maës Titianos.

Merchants tell many tall tales, but who else could one believe, since apart from a few prisoners who had been freed or had escaped and miraculously returned home, only they had seen these far-off lands with their own eyes and returned to tell the tale. It was obviously in their interests to keep all possible competition away, to discourage others in advance. It was for this reason that tempests, snowfalls, mountains and precipices, wild beasts, bandits, pirates, hostage takers, demons, sirens and divine powers were all embellished and exaggerated. And indeed, apart from the supernatural elements, much of it was often true.

Furthermore, it was clear that the Persian government had a policy of preventing Chinese silk from reaching Western countries by any other means than through Persia itself. This left only one solution: to establish direct contacts oneself, following the safest route.

Between Da Qin and China, two routes, or rather two half roads, are known to us from different sources. The first is described in the *History of the Later Han*, while the second is the route followed by Maës Titianos, and written up by Marinus the Tyrian.

According to the *History of the Later Han*, when travelling east to west from Dunhuang, one reaches the passes of Yumenguan ("Jade Gate") and Yangguan ("Sun Gate" or the "Gate on the Sunny Side of the Mountain"). Yumenguan is located about 68 kilometres north-west of Dunhuang—a town renowned for its cave murals—and Yangguan about 50 kilometres south-west of it.* These two famous passes, where customs and police controls were carried out, were the real gateways to China although located in the middle of the desert. Yangguan can only be identified today by the ruins of a watchtower which date to the Han dynasty. The route mentioned in the *History of the Later Han* crosses the kingdom of Shanshan, south of Lake Lop Nor, and leads to the Onion mountains (the Pamir), which give onto the Western states via two routes, the southern and the northern branches. The southern road follows the northern side of the Qilian, Altyn and Kunlun mountains, as far as Suoche, or Shache, present-day Yarkand, crossing the kingdoms of Jumo, Jingjue and Jumi. After leaving the Pamir this route terminated in the kingdoms of Da Yuezhi and Anxi.

The northern route leads first from Shanshan to Yiwu (Hami) and Gaochang (near Turfan), the land of the Former Qushi. It then skirts the Northern mountains and follows the course of a river, arriving finally at Shule (near Kashgar). Further west, the northern route crosses the Pamir and arrives in the valley of Ferghana, Kangju (Sogdiana) and the land of the Yancai. The *History of the Later Han* also mentions a route which led north from Gaochang/Turfan

---

* Care must be taken not to confuse Yumenguan, a frontier post in antiquity to the north-west of Dunhuang, with the town of Yumenshi, a stop on a branch of the main Lanzhou–Urumqi railway line, about 245 km east-south-east of Dunhuang, or with Yumenzhen, on the Lanzhou–Urumqi line, about 198 km east of Dunhuang. Dunhuang itself is not directly on the railway.

to Jinmancheng, which has been identified as Dsimsa (Jimsar on modern western maps, or Jimusaer on recent Chinese maps), east of Urumqi, and north of Turfan on the railway line. This was the territory of the Later Qushi. In other words, this was more or less the same route that was mentioned in the *History of the Former Han*. With the exception of the names of the kingdoms and the people living there, these two routes were to change very little in the following centuries. The reason for this is simple. The path of trade routes was dictated by the geographical features; by the need to skirt around mountain chains or cross them by the only practical passes; by using the few existing watering places and pastures for the animals; by including oasis settlements where food and water could be bought and goods traded, and avoiding the deserts as much as possible. The mountain chains to the north and south all touch the Pamir. It is likely that Chinese presence in this area never amounted to much more than a few embassies or military detachments because beyond this point the old Chinese texts become less and less detailed. The main partners of the Chinese were the Yuezhi (followed by the Kushan) and the Parthians, but the Chinese had little direct contact with the countries beyond.

> *The path of trade routes was dictated by the geographical features; by the need to skirt around mountain chains or cross them by the only practical passes; by using the few existing watering places and pastures for the animals; by including oasis settlements where food and water could be bought and goods traded, and avoiding the deserts as much as possible.*

THE STONE TOWER

Coming from the other direction, as a Greco-Roman merchant or geographer, the route to far-off Asia also ended in the same region, being described in great detail from the Mediterranean as far as the Stone Tower, and then becoming vague. Let us look at the route followed, according to Ptolemy, by Maës Titianos and his travelling companions. The first surprise is that according to Marinus

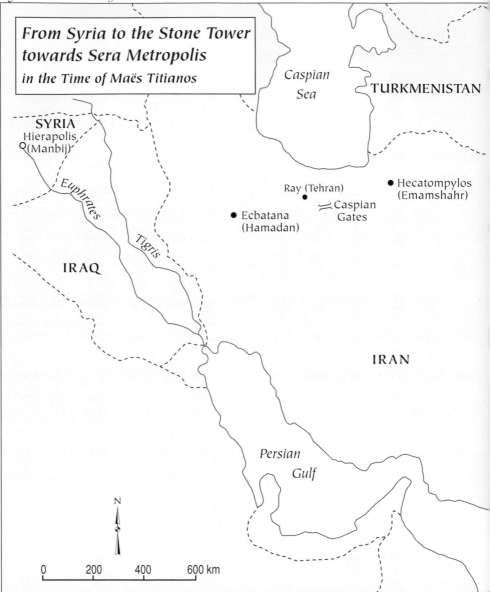

From Syria to the Stone Tower towards Sera Metropolis
in the Time of Maës Titianos

Caspian
Sea

TURKMENISTAN

SYRIA
Hierapolis
(Manbij)

Euphrates

Tigris

IRAQ

Ray (Tehran)
Caspian
Gates

Ecbatana
(Hamadan)

Hecatompylos
(Emamshahr)

IRAN

Persian
Gulf

N

0   200   400   600 km

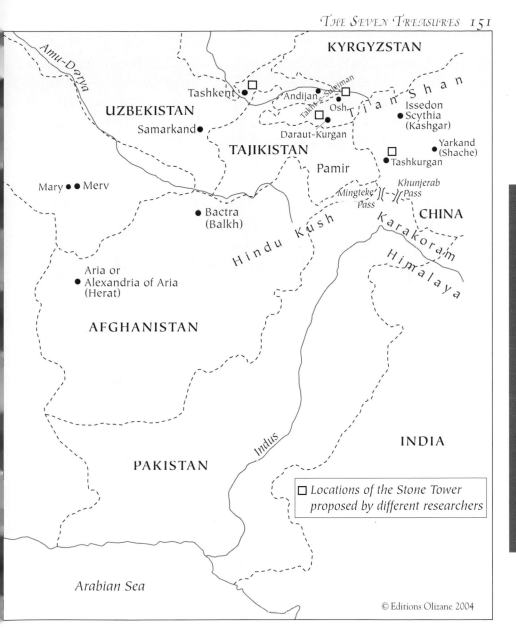

KYRGYZSTAN

Amu-Darya

Tashkent

UZBEKISTAN

Andijan

Takht-e-Suleiman

Osh

Issedon
Scythia
(Kashgar)

Samarkand

Daraut-Kurgan

TAJIKISTAN

Yarkand
(Shache)

Pamir

Tashkurgan

Mary ● ● Merv

Khunjerab
Pass

Mingteke
Pass

CHINA

Bactra
(Balkh)

Hindu Kush

Karakoram

Himalaya

Aria or
● Alexandria of Aria
(Herat)

AFGHANISTAN

Indus

INDIA

PAKISTAN

☐ Locations of the Stone Tower
proposed by different researchers

Arabian Sea

© Editions Olizane 2004

From Syria to the Stone Tower towards Sera Metropolis

the Tyrian, Maës, "a certain Macedonian, who was also called Titian, son of a merchant father, and a merchant himself",[39] passed through the Parthian kingdom. He crossed the Euphrates at Hierapolis (near Manbij, just north-east of Aleppo in Syria), followed part of the Tigris valley downstream, and reached Ecbatana (Hamadan in Iran), passing through the Caspian Gates. These are the *Portae Caspiae* of Pliny (Book 6, chapters 15 and 17), which separated Media and Parthia: here, an interminable narrow gorge cuts through the mountains which run along the southern coast of the Caspian Sea. Carts could only advance in single file between the vertical cliff faces, their progress rendered even more difficult and dangerous by the waters which ran down the rocks and flowed at their feet, and the swarms of snakes which haunted the area. Some writers have identified this defile as that of Sirdara, 60 kilometres south-east of Tehran.[40]

Once the Caspian Gates had been crossed, Maës headed towards the Parthian Hecatompylos, present-day Emamshahr (or Shahrud, in Iran), slightly further to the north-east, and then towards Antioch of Margiana, Aria (Alexandria of Aria, now Herat, in Afghanistan), Bactra (Balkh), the Comedarum mountains (in the Hindu Kush, the Pamir, or the Hissar?), and from there finally reached the Stone Tower, "where the mountains which join the Imaus begin", in other words the Himalaya. At this point, the caravans would regroup, rest and restock supplies to face the seven-month journey to Sera, or Sera Metropolis, the capital of the Seres. Marinus the Tyrian estimated the distance at 36,200 stadia (reckoning 26,280 from Hierapolis to the Stone Tower; which would place Hierapolis some 62,480 stadia from Sera, assuming the stadium used by Ptolemy was indeed the Roman one, equivalent to a total distance of 11,551 kilometres). This is unlikely to be the distance as the crow flies, but rather the distance covered on the ground. Ptolemy gives shorter distances, noting that Marinus the Tyrian himself accuses Maës and his companions of having exaggerated them, as merchants often did.

But where is the Stone Tower which Ptolemy and Marinus the Tyrian mention? Several locations have been proposed. Tashkurgan, in Xinjiang, on the Kashgar–Islamabad road which enters Pakistan after crossing the Karakoram. Or Tashkent, in Uzbekistan, or Daraut-Kurgan in south-western Kyrgyzstan.

One author suggests Takht-e-Suleiman, the mountain which dominates the town of Osh in Kyrgyzstan.[41] Tashkurgan, Daraut-Kurgan and Takht-e-Suleiman are all on routes which cross high mountain chains and lead to Kashgar, from where the north and south branches of the road to China diverge. The ancient tales describe only very briefly the countryside and the obstacles encountered on the way. Modern travellers, however, have given us descriptions of the formidable obstacles and the seemingly insurmountable dangers encountered en route—mountains up to 8,000 metres in height and passes often between 4,500 and 5,500 metres.

After the mountains came the desert, and with it the searing heat, the winds and the demons skilled at luring travellers out of their way, separating them from their caravans, and letting them die of thirst and hunger. One such legend, retold down the centuries by caravaneers, soldiers and oasis dwellers, was repeated by a Chinese Buddhist monk in the 4th century, and another Chinese monk in the 7th century, by Marco Polo in the 13th century and by the Jesuits in the 17th century.[42] Bandits also roamed there, but there did exist pleasant oases too, prosperous kingdoms, and further, much further on, at the end of the road, the land of silk, Sera Metropolis.

In the Asia perceived by Pliny and his contemporaries, one could theoretically have reached Serica from the Caspian Sea by following the coast eastwards, and then overland from north to south. But the Scythian man-eating wild animals, ice, snow storms, or "the contrary will of some divine power", barred access to it from this side. In the south, Serica gave on to the Sinae, and here we come back to the description of the Great Gulf and the Far Eastern coastline given by Ptolemy himself.

It is difficult to determine who the Sinae were in relation to the Seres. Ptolemy does not seem to think that the two nations had any contact. "The navigators say," he writes, "that above Sinae is the region of the Seres and their capital Sera. To the east lies an unknown region which has stagnant marshes in which grow reeds so thick and large, that catching hold of them, and upborne by them, men can walk across them. [They say further] that not only is there a way from there to Bactria through the Stone Tower, but also a way to India through Palimbothra. The journey from the capital of the Sinae to the port of Kattigara runs to the south-west."[43] Palimbothra, also known as Palibothra or Pataliputra, now the modern Indian town of Patna, was at the time "a very large and very rich city, capital of a great kingdom on the banks of the Ganges, the Prasi, the most powerful and the most famous people of northern India", according to Pliny.

The Sinae and the Seres were considered the easternmost people of the inhabited world, and the capital of the Seres, Sera Metropolis in Latin, and that of the Sinae—Sinae, Thinaï or Thinae—were, with the port of Kattigara, the furthest cities in the east. To the east and south of the Sinae were "unknown lands"; to the west, was "India beyond the Ganges". But who were the Sinae? A Burmese kingdom? Was it south-west China, that is to say Sichuan and Yunnan, part of which were Chinese prefectures and the rest semi-independent or independent principalities? In the first centuries of the Christian era, Chengdu, the capital of Shu, in Sichuan, was a city as large as China's imperial capital, Chang'an, and the merchants of Shu, as we have seen, travelled as far as India with their goods.

Clearly, Ptolemy's text is similar to the Chinese historical sources, the earliest of which is chapter 123 of Sima Qian's *Shiji*, so many times referred to by historians.[44]

SICHUAN TO ASSAM

The road which left Chengdu first went south (the route through Tibet seems not to have been used, according to certain historians, until the 7th century, under the Tang dynasty) to Yibin and on to modern Kunming, in Yunnan (then the state of Dian), before continuing westwards to Dali. From there onwards, the land was nothing but gigantic upthrusts running from north to south, interminable chains of mountains between which the Mekong, Salween and other great rivers had carved out gorges and ravines, unnavigable in these regions. Tracks a few feet wide, hugging the cliff face, which were familiar to the local "barbarian" tribes, the Yi, Man and Ai Lao, were common hazards for the "merchants from the land of Shu". South-west of Dali one passed through the prefecture of Yongchang, near the modern town of Baoshan. Then, after crossing more rivers and mountains, one entered Upper Burma along several different routes, arriving at Kamarupa, present-day Gauhati, in Assam, and finally reaching Bengal, the end of the long trek for the Sichuanese merchants. Here, the goods were passed over to Indian merchants. The Ganges and the Northern Indian Plain were not difficult to cross, and that is probably why the merchants of Daxia had declared to Zhang Qian that there was an easy and practicable route between their land and the land of Shu! Nevertheless, travelling from the Indian Plain to the north of Afghanistan, whichever route followed (and there are no details in the texts about these), was not without its eventful moments, as they led their caravans from staging post to staging post.

SERICA

Where should one try to place Serica on a modern map? To the west of it is Scythia, where Ptolemy lists several peoples and towns, among them an "Issedon Scythia", which might, according to some, be Kashgar, the "Scythia beyond the Imaus mountains" referring to the whole of Chinese Turkestan, that is Xinjiang and part of modern Gansu. To the north and east were unknown lands. To the south, were the Sinae and their port, and "India beyond the Ganges". But if Issedon Serica is indeed, as the drawing in G. Coedès' book, based on Ptolemy, suggests, the capital of the kingdom of Khotan, that would imply that the notion of "Serica" stretched further west than China itself, as Khotan at this period was frequently an independent kingdom. And it is not clear at all where to locate the capital of the Seres, Sera Metropolis, which may not be Chang'an. Furthermore, Ptolemy lists the names of fifteen towns in Serica, including Issedon Serica, almost none of which can be identified by modern historians. How many of the dozens and dozens of names of towns and peoples of Central Asia which filled the texts of Greek and Roman, Chinese and Arabic geographers, have been identified? These references are the only remaining trace.

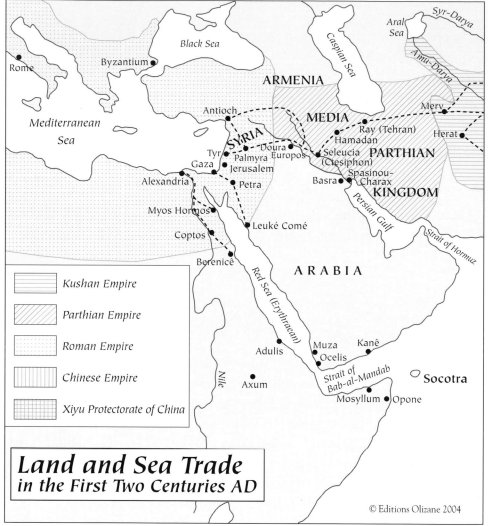

Land and Sea Trade
in the First Two Centuries AD

© Editions Olizane 2004

Chinese sources give only vague indications of routes to the west, and Western sources are equally vague about those to the east. Although Ptolemy provides a more detailed commercial network than was known earlier, with more ramifications, it is still difficult to draw a map from it; in any event, it would be a map which might have been valid at one given moment, but would soon be out of date, and at best one can only gain a few indications.

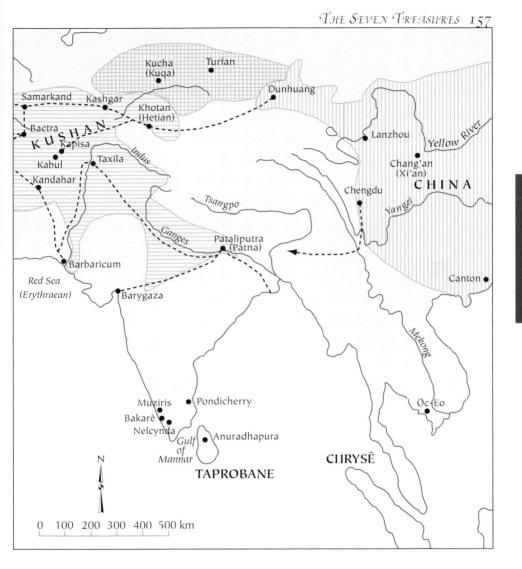

But all these roads led to silk: demand for it never diminished and its source seemed inexhaustible (there may even have been, at certain times, an over-production of it in China). It was not only silk which was in demand, but silk thread for weaving. Evidence of this comes from the demand for silk weavers. The texts rarely state clearly whether a customer was buying silk in skeins, but there would have been no need to attract or kidnap so many silk weavers if silk thread had been unobtainable. Apparently, China exported silk thread in large quantities.

The Chinese deserters who taught several kingdoms in the Western Territories how to make iron or steel according to Chinese techniques—techniques which then passed to the Parthians—also taught the art of weaving silk in the same regions. This does not imply that there had been no earlier knowledge of weaving in these countries, but silk weaving was a special skill. The next stage would be to discover the secret of sericulture, still unknown in a large part of Eurasia, and to obtain silkworms. Persia was possibly one of the first commercial partners of China to succeed in doing so.

According to Aly Mazaheri,[45] the breeding of silkworms in Iran goes back to the reign of the Kushan king, Kanishka. Having beaten the Chinese in 114–116 AD (according to the chronology followed by the author), somewhere in Central Asia, Kanishka is said to have taken a number of Chinese workmen (or workmen from a Chinese protectorate or an ally of China) back with him to northern India. They were made to settle in the Punjab, then under Kushan domination, where they founded a new town, Cînapati.* The first part of the name, "Cîna", may well indicate, as is often the case, a link with China. These expatriates, who were very numerous, are said to have introduced the art of breeding silkworms. Where the worms or the eggs came from, this semi-legendary tale does not say.

CîNAPATI

The name Cînapati, transcribed into pinyin as Zhinapudi, reappears several centuries later, in the account of the Chinese pilgrim Xuanzang who crossed the region in the middle of the 7th century.[46] In this case, it designates both a kingdom and its homonymous capital. Reading Xuanzang's description, we come to understand who these expatriates might have been: hostages, a common method of guaranteeing an alliance or allegiance. Xuanzang indeed explains that King Kanishka had become very powerful, and that the "Fan to the west of

---

* *The Sanskrit letter correctly transcribed as "c" is pronounced as the English "ch". This has sometimes been written "ch" or "tch", particularly in older translations. To avoid confusion, the preferred transcription "c" is used throughout in this work.*

the river", frightened, had sent him hostages, whom he treated well. He provided them with separate winter and summer residences—their winter residence was Cînapati. Some writers place this kingdom between the Sutlej and Ravi rivers, tributaries of the Indus, and the capital slightly further north, or perhaps further south at Amritsar, in the Punjab. It may be located

> *It is this cîna which calls China to mind, and indeed, in a certain number of Sanskrit words, cin or tsin means "Chinese" or "of Chinese origin".*

somewhere near the present-day town of Patti, between Amritsar and Kasur, just west of the Biyas.

These hostages introduced peaches and pears into the Punjab, two fruits hitherto unknown in India. They were named *cînani* and *cînarajaputra* (while the Indians called the peach a fruit from China, the Greeks and Romans called it a Persian fruit, *persica mela, persicum*). It is this *cîna* which calls China to mind, and indeed, in a certain number of Sanskrit words, *cin* or *tsin* means "Chinese" or "of Chinese origin".

Despite giving us all these details, Xuanzang does not tell us anything about the introduction of the silkworm into the region, although he was the first to mention the story of the clandestine transfer to Khotan of silkworm eggs by a Chinese princess in 400 AD. In his description of the countries he crossed, some sixty or so kingdoms and principalities in all, Khotan is the only case in which he mentions the breeding of silkworms.

Samuel Beal, in his annotated translation of the text, acknowledges the difficulty of translating the somewhat obscure term "Fan to the west of the river", which another Sinologist has translated as "tributary princes west of the Yellow River", but could be rendered as "united tribes of the Fan people", the Fan being, at that period, the Tibetans. So were these hostages Chinese or not? Beal quotes a biography of Xuanzang which states that the hostages sent to Kanishka included the son of the Chinese emperor. We have seen that it was the custom between kingdoms to send hostages who were closely related to the ruling sovereign. The consideration with which these people were treated is an indication of their high status. If the weavers and silkworm breeders mentioned by Mazaheri were Chinese, they must have been part of the retinue accompanying these political hostages. Whatever the case, they were people from the north-west of China or from neighbouring territories.

In Xuanzang's account, the only passage which explicitly mentions Indian textiles lists several types:[47] *jiaoshiye*, from the Sanskrit *kauseya*, which he calls "the product of the wild silkworm"; a cloth known as *die*, which generally refers to cotton (and this is the most likely explanation here), but which dictionaries also define as a "cloth of fine wool" in ancient times; *como (kshauma)*, a sort of hemp; *jianbolo (kambala)*, which has been translated either as "fine sheep wool" or "fine goat hair" (which brings to mind cashmere, or *pashm*, which is the under fleece of goats from the high Tibetan plateau); and *helali (karala)*, "made from the fine hair of a wild animal", which was highly prized. The latter evokes the famed *tuz*, a sort of wild *pashm*, which comes from wild antelopes from the Western Tibetan plateau, now almost extinct, a textile that, like *pashm*, is one of the specialities of Kashmir, which Xuanzang visited.

KEDJARAN

According to Mazaheri,[48] the Sassans, an Indo-Iranian family, emigrated or expatriated from India, took large quantities of raw silk from Cînapati to Kedjaran, a town on the Iranian coast of the Persian Gulf, and introduced the breeding of silkworms to the south of Fars province. This family, which grew wealthy, established marital alliances with the Persian aristocracy; one of its members, Ardeshir I, became the founder of the great Sassanid dynasty. When Ardeshir became king, the city of Kedjaran, or Kedjaweran, was already a wealthy merchant town thanks to the local breeding of silkworms. Around the year 1000 AD, the Persian poet Ferdusi was to write a famous epic, the *Shahnâme*, which centred on Ardeshir, Kedjaran, a silkworm which had turned into a dragon and young girls who bred silkworms. Sericulture and the silk industry took off in Persia, according to Mazaheri, at the end of the 3rd century, and from then on became an important branch of the country's economy.

Logically, at the time of King Kanishka, silkworm breeding could have spread right across India. In actual fact, we do not know for sure at what period India became a great producer of fine silks. For one, the country was already reputed for its textiles, particularly its cotton muslin, and had large numbers of skilled weavers. Secondly, silks made from the thread of wild cocoons which was carded, spun and woven had always existed in India, among other places in Assam. No precise legend has formed around a particular event telling of the introduction of Chinese silkworms into India, but these do exist in other countries, and we know for example that in the 2nd century AD, silkworm eggs reached the ruler of Japan (where wild cocoons of a particular species were already known). Korea is said to have bred cocoons several centuries before the Christian era. We also know that sericulture was introduced into Central Asia around the 5th century, and to Byzantium in the 6th century, as we shall see later. But no equivalent historico-legendary event for India exists in the texts; silk weaving is mentioned there, in some ways, as an obvious fact which knew no beginning. A foreign provenance for silk thread is not mentioned anywhere. Nevertheless, there does exist an indigenous word (*kauseyam*, *kauseya*) which is applied to wild silks, as well as to all natural silks.

A classical Indian political treatise, the *Arthashastra*, attributed to Kautilya, a minister of King Candragupta (died 289 BC), and written either in the 4th century BC or just after, does provide some information on the textile industry in northern India at the time of the Maurya dynasty.[49] Materials that were spun (work carried out by women) were the following: wool, bark, cotton, cheesecloth, hemp and linen. No mention is made of silk. On the other hand, woven fabrics (work carried out by men) are listed as rough linen, fine linen, silk, antelope hair and cotton. In addition, in the chapters on agriculture, the breeding of silkworms is not referred to, and neither is the cultivation of cotton plants. Should one conclude from this that for many centuries Indian weavers used silk thread from wild cocoons bred locally? And when did this change? Xuanzang's text does not bring up the question of silkworm breeding either, and yet generally speaking, these two subjects—the growing of cereals and the presence or absence of silkworm breeding—are rarely left out from Chinese travel accounts, or from the texts of geographers and historians.

On the other hand, the term Cînapati, designating either a town or a state in the Punjab, also appears in the time of Kautilya in the *Arthashastra*, with a different meaning which was to become common: here it refers to a fine cloth, and more specifically a silk cloth produced in the land of Cîna, or China. At least, this is the way that it has generally been understood.

The word "Cîna" is the transcription of the Chinese name for the Qin dynasty (221–207 BC) which preceded the Han. This term still designates China today, and is often used as a generic term. The term *patti*, *pati* or *patta* generally designates a fine cloth, or a silk cloth, and compound words derived from this include terms for silk weaver, silk thread, etc. It is often synonymous with *kauseya*, silk. Thus the city of Cînapati may well be linked to the arrival in the Punjab either of Chinese silks or of weavers, and perhaps even of Chinese techniques of sericulture, or of silkworm eggs themselves. And yet, according to Xuanzang, this name designated an entire kingdom, although no such kingdom is listed among the great silk-producing or silk-weaving centres.

The Chinese character Qin (following the modern pinyin transcription) used for the dynasty of that name has had other meanings too. In the first centuries of the Christian era, it replaced "Lijian" in Chinese texts to refer to the Roman Empire, the Da Qin, or "Great Qin". The same term can sometimes be applied, according to some writers, to a much more limited region and to a population living in north-eastern India: in the eastern Himalaya, Assam, Upper Burma, and the frontier regions of Tibet and Yunnan. In a study devoted to the Cînapati of the *Arthashastra*, Rao Zongyi, taking into account ancient Indian sources such as the *Laws of Manu*, a text which goes back to the beginning of the Christian era, and the *Mahabharata*, written between the 4th century BC and the 4th century AD, insists on the fact that "what is known as Cîna in the Hindu epics is the region located in the eastern part of India, on the edge of Tibet and Burma".[50] The native people of Assam would have belonged to it. Should one then make a connection here with the Sinae, the Thinaï of Ptolemy, located south of Serica and linked by a trade route to India and Bactria, as we have seen previously?

But here we are far from the court in Chang'an and from imperial power, and there is no link either with the Roman Empire. Later, from the Tang period on, Cîna, for the Indians, and Sin or Mahasin (Great Sin) for the Arabs, would refer to China, and the Greek monk-traveller Cosmas Indicopleustes, in the 6th century, would call China "Tsin".

But goods circulated, regardless of politics or tolls and taxes levied. In the first centuries of the Christian era, several precious products feature in historical texts among the goods which reached China via the Central Asian kingdom of Kushan. The texts at this period, as in all other periods, mention precious substances—gems, gold, silver, perfume, rare medicines, and valuable fabrics— much more frequently than they do everyday goods, even though the latter may have been the object of a much larger volume of trade, and were more essential to the life and power of the state. But highly valuable, yet at the same time small and lightweight goods, could be transported over vast distances for a relatively high profit. This is why the texts tell of sumptuous silks, but very little of wool; they talk about musk, but little about cereals; more about peacocks, parrots and hunting falcons than about donkeys or sheep. The very important trade of vital products, which is carried out over short rather than long distances, is hardly ever mentioned in these texts. In comparison with very valuable items, they are treated by ancient historians with the same disregard with which a victorious general treats the common soldiers after a brilliant military campaign. And yet, one wonders whether the gems and pearls weighed as heavily in the global volume of imports and exports as these rapt narrators would have us believe.

Coral, a Buddhist Treasure

We have seen the importance which Pliny gave to the purchase of pearls in the Roman world. They were exported in great quantities to Central Asia and China, and of course to the whole of India. Another precious material that was to circulate very widely for a long period of time was coral. At that time, and for a long while afterwards, the Mediterranean was one of the world's largest suppliers of coral. This marine product is in fact a primitive animal, but until the 18th century it was generally thought to be a vegetable and even earlier a mineral. It was classified in the West only as a semi-precious material, but seems to have been considered more valuable elsewhere. Coral has been found on the Eurasian continent in Celtic and Scythian tombs long predating the Christian era, and from the beginning of that era appeared throughout Asia, in Persia, India, the Himalaya, Central Asia, China, and later in Tibet and Mongolia. Demand for it increased as Buddhism spread from Central Asia to China: coral and pearls feature among the so-called Seven Treasures of Buddhism, and so became some of the most sought-after objects in countries where Buddhist religious centres, monasteries, temples, stupas and rulers appeared. Thus archaeological finds of coral are also, in a way, indicators to the spread of Buddhism.

The first centuries of the Christian era, particularly after the reign of Kanishka, were a decisive period in the history of this religion. In a climate of religious tolerance, supported by the generosity of merchant donors and even the king himself, Buddhism spread freely across the entire Kushan Empire, which was crisscrossed by the great commercial trade routes. An empire which eventually extended from Bactria to the shores of the Caspian Sea, to the Tarim Basin, the Himalaya, Kashmir, and the middle reaches of the Indus and Ganges river valleys. At exactly the same period when Christianity was spreading in the West, beyond the Persian frontiers, Buddhism expanded eastwards, with its missionary monks, its many monastic and theological centres, its innumerable stupas and statues, and translations of the Buddhist canon. More and more lay groups embraced the new faith. Among these were merchants who settled in small merchant colonies which developed in the great trade centres in north-western China, as far as Chang'an and Luoyang.

It was from Central Asia that Buddhism entered China, apparently as a result of the legendary dream of Emperor Mingdi (reigned 58–76 AD) of the Han dynasty, first told in the *History of the Later Han*. The arrival of the new faith in China centred on royalty, as with many other innovations. In his dream, the emperor saw a tall man, all in gold. From the top of his head shone a bright light. The emperor gathered his ministers round and asked them to interpret his dream. They told him that: "In the West is a divinity known as Fo, his height is of sixteen feet and he is the colour of gold." The emperor yearned to find out about the doctrine of this Fo (the Chinese name for the Buddha). He sent a mission to India and present-day Afghanistan; there, the envoys came across texts and statues, which they brought home from the land of the Kushan, along with the two first translators of Sanskrit Buddhist canonical texts into Chinese. These two Indian religious men, She Moteng (Kasyapa Matanga) and Zhu Falan (Dharmaratna), settled in the then Chinese capital Luoyang, where they began the translation of several Buddhist sutras. The emperor had a monastery built for them, outside the town, called the Temple of the White Horse (Baimasi), in commemoration of their arrival, mounted on a white horse, carrying their precious sutras. This is said to be the first Buddhist temple ever built in China and is still visited as such today, although the original buildings have long since disappeared.

This first temple and these earliest translations into Chinese mark the beginning of an ongoing religious saga, that is the arrival in China of a foreign religion. Buddhism developed deep and lasting roots in China, and found itself a place as one of the three main philosophical and religious currents there, alongside Daoism and Confucianism. Other foreign religions were to arrive over the centuries: Nestorian Christianity, Manichaeism, Islam, Judaism and Western Christianity, some of which have disappeared from China, while others survive only as minority religions, the most influential being Islam, particularly in Xinjiang. The brief forty-year long Marxist interlude attempted unsuccessfully to suppress them all, native as well as foreign religions.

Buddhism, first introduced into Tibet in the 7th century, was then driven out and later reintroduced. It passed from there to Mongolia in the 16th century, despite having been eradicated from continental India. Today, it has disappeared from most of Central Asia, leaving behind its treasures in sand-covered cities, mural paintings hidden in the depths of hundreds of caves, innumerable manuscripts, treasures which have slept for ages in the deserts and mountains, only to be awoken in the 20th century by archaeologists.

Various religions have crossed the Asian continent like waves flowing from west to east; the opposite direction, curiously, from the great military and economic migrations.

Sapta Ratna

How did a religion of detachment, of renunciation, of indifference to the world in which we live, which advocated the life of the errant mendicant monk or a monastic life of the most frugal simplicity, end up accumulating precious materials such as gold and gems? How did the great landed monasteries acquire their wealth, and the Potala and Tashilumpo in Tibet their fabulous treasures? How did the patchwork monk's robe and his simple begging bowl lead to tombs weighing several tons of gold each, housing the embalmed corpses of the great reincarnated Lamas? The same questions could certainly be asked of other religions which look down upon worldly goods. In the Buddhism of the Kushan period the role of the lay donor had already developed as a form of devotion: wealthy donors acquired merit, and saved time, as it were, in the chain of future reincarnations towards the final goal, entry into Nirvana, by subsidizing financially the monastic community, the building of stupas, or the decoration of religious buildings. These donors were often rich merchants, who were particularly encouraged in this. Their gifts came in the form of precious metal, or gems, as well as fine silks, used for banners, hangings or clothing for the statues decorating the temples. These precious materials were the *Sapta Ratna*, the Seven Treasures of Buddhism. The links between Buddhism, its monasteries and its religious community, the acquisition of merit and hope for future reincarnations, on the one hand, and trade and the wealth of the Seven Treasures on the other, have been wonderfully explained by Liu Xinru in a work about trade and religious exchanges between China and India during the first six centuries of the Christian era.[51]

What are the *Sapta Ratna*? In the traditional Buddhist concept, they were originally what constituted sovereignty: the wheel, symbol of the Law; an elephant and a horse, symbols of royalty; a precious stone; a Queen; a minister; and the head of a lay family, who gathers the riches for the king.[52] Then, the concept of the Seven Treasures began to encompass materials more closely associated with jewellery and metalworking. This is reminiscent of the *Nava Ratna*, the nine precious materials of Hindu symbolism, one of which is coral, and which are associated with the planets. By the Kushan period, the list was much the same as today, namely gold, silver, pearls, lapis lazuli, rock crystal, followed by several terms whose meaning has been much discussed. These are "red pearls" (which may have been small beads of coral or carnelian or some other red stone), or some unidentified substances (commentators hesitate between coral, amber and diamond for one of them and between coral, agate, and ammonite for the other). But when one crosschecks the texts in which they occur, it appears that all these terms may be considered with some certainty to designate coral. Coral is present in the archaeological records of the period, and is to be found throughout the Buddhist world, where it is still very much in demand.

Luckily for archaeologists (or for tomb robbers!), the decoration of stupas and temples, as well as statues sometimes covered in gold, coral and turquoise, led to concentrations of these valuable materials in, on, and under religious buildings. The custom had developed very early on for donors to provide for the future upkeep of a temple or a stupa by burying gold and jewels in its foundations or near the foot of the building. At the same time, this was a rite of propitiation in the Buddhist world. Robbers and conquerors quickly developed the reflex of checking what could be found there. Archaeologists, in a rather different frame of mind and with more precautions, have done likewise, and found there the answers to many of their questions.

These precious materials had often come from very distant lands. The pearls and coral came from coastal regions—the Indian Ocean, the Persian Gulf, the Red Sea, the Mediterranean. Lapis lazuli came from Badakhshan. Gems, gold and silver came from all over. Silk came from China. All of this arrived along trade routes, thanks to the merchants. In this commercial network with both economic and religious facets, the merchant occupied high moral ground. Unlike the view held in the Roman and Christian worlds, and in the Hindu civilization, the merchant, seen as virtuous and honest, was not at all looked down upon in countries where Buddhism predominated. Merchants are not shown in a good light in the Gospels, whereas in the *jatakas*, the moral tales describing the previous lives of the Buddha, the Buddha himself was several times incarnated as a merchant or a caravaneer. In Islam, the Prophet Mohammed was born into a family of merchants, and for several centuries the Muslim world was the leader in trade. "I was a merchant among merchants", we read in the first lines of the very first tale of the *Thousand and One Nights*, whose stories abound with merchants.

Coral had already reached China before the Kushan period, and Buddhism probably only increased the demand for it. The term which indisputably refers to it in Chinese, *shanhu*, is a word which has never had any other meaning, and appears for the first time in the *History of the Former Han*, written in the 1st century AD, referring to valuable objects which could be seen in the court of the Former Han emperors.[53] It appears too in the description of Western countries, in chapter 96 of the same *History*, as a product from Jibin. The earliest occurrence of the term is, according to one Chinese dictionary, in the *Shiji*.[54] In the first case mentioned above, *shanhu* refers to a coral branch. This was a form of gift or tribute presented to sovereigns or to eminent men, frequently referred to in both Western and Eastern history until the 18th century. It was indeed a rarity, and if polished coral in the form of small beads of varying size already had much value, a fine branch of intact coral, with a good depth of colour, could fetch extravagant prices, and was a present worthy of a king. In principle, the coral fisheries reserved the finest branches for the local sovereign who would offer them to his peers. In the Mediterranean, given the fishing techniques used, it was difficult to gather coral branches without breaking them; then they had to be transported intact to the other end of the world. Coral was mainly exported in the form of beads, or small cylinders, which could be left intact or pierced and threaded, or as small fragments which could be individually hand crafted as desired.

The Chinese appear at first to have known nothing about its nature or of its marine origin since it is said to be the product of a country without any access to the sea, a country to which the *History of the Former Han* also attributes the production of pearls. It is then mentioned, in chapter 118 of the *History of the Later Han*, as a product of Da Qin, the Roman Empire. In the *Bei shi*, or *History of the Northern Dynasties*, which roughly covers the 5th and 6th centuries but was written at the earliest in the 7th century, coral is mentioned in chapter 97 as a product of the kingdom of Bosi, that is Persia, as well as of Fuluni, "north of Bosi". The latter state is difficult to locate, and is characterized only by the presence of a river to the east of the capital which flowed from north to south, in which strange birds dwelt, some of them resembling humans, others a camel or a horse, and which could only live in water. Apart from coral, this country also supplied amber, and lions lived there in large numbers.

The *Sui shu*, the *History of the Sui Dynasty*, which covers the end of the 6th and the beginning of the 7th century, also attributes coral to Persia. It is in the *Tang shu*, the *History of the Tang Dynasty*, a text written as always during the following dynasty, in this case the Song, probably in the 11th century, that we find precise details about the aspect of coral in situ and ways of fishing it. In chapter 221 of the *Xin Tang shu* section, we read that coral grows in Folin, the "Da Qin of old, some 40,000 *li* from the Chinese capital", as well as in Bosi. Surprisingly, the text describes the fishing techniques used in Folin, in the "Western Sea", that is the Mediterranean: "In this sea, is an island of coral. Using large vessels, the inhabitants of this sea send large iron nets down to the sea floor. The coral grows there on large rocks. At first, it is as white as a mushroom; after one year, it becomes yellow; after three years, it is red. Its branches are entangled, reaching three or four feet in length, and get snared in the iron net which uproots it. The people on board ship pull the nets out of the water. If one does not fish at the right season, nothing is obtained and the coral rots."

This method of gathering coral by raking the seafloor corresponds perfectly to the Italian technique known as the "cross of St Andrew". The idea was to gather the coral by haulage; a large cross of wood or iron, weighted in the centre with lead, to which pieces of fishing nets or unbraided rope were fixed, was let down to the sea floor and dragged along by the boat so as to rake the coral bed. The branches of coral were snared in the net, and the traction ripped them off and dragged along anything else caught by it. This technique caused great damage, breaking many of the branches, hence the rarity of fine, large, intact branches. This method was probably used early on in addition to simple diving, once the coral beds which were near the surface of the water had been exhausted (coral fishing for beads for necklaces goes back to pre-historic times). The Musée de la Vieille Charité in Marseilles houses the central part of one of these Roman crosses of St Andrew, dating to a couple of centuries before the Christian era. Pliny also describes a similar process.

How did a Chinese historian, living at the other end of the world, hear about coral fishing techniques in the Mediterranean? Probably from Muslim merchants who, in the Tang period, visited the ports of southern China, and would have been familiar with the Mediterranean world. It must have been a similar traveller who brought to the attention of the author of chapter 221 of the *Tang shu* the existence in Folin of "a cloth made from the hair of a water-sheep" known as "cloth of the Western Sea", a description reminiscent of Pliny's "silk of marine mussels" and other names given to this long-vanished cloth.

According to the *Tang shu*, coral three feet in height was to be found in Persia. It must have been centuries since coral of such dimensions had been seen, at least in the Mediterranean.

In 1991, the Oceanographic Museum of the Principality of Monaco exhibited a large red coral fragment, with five or six branches, approximately 80 centimetres in height. It came from Japan, an important coral producer in modern times, but which has not been exploiting its coral beds for the past 2,000 or 3,000 years as the countries of the Mediterranean have done.

The term "coral", as used in this book and indeed in the sources mentioned, refers to *corallium rubrum*, "jewellers' coral", or "red coral of the Mediterranean" (although it does not come exclusively from that sea, neither is it always and only red in colour). There are pink, white and black corals as well, though it is undeniably the red which has been most in demand throughout the world. Until the 19th century, the Mediterranean was the main supplier.

Red coral played a role in Greek mythology, where it was considered to be the blood of Medusa, one of the Gorgon sisters, who could turn to stone those whom she looked upon. Medusa was decapitated by Persius and her blood ran into the sea where it solidified. It is hardly surprising that this marine product was attributed some extraordinary origin, and it has certainly been credited with various supernatural powers and properties throughout the Old World, as have certain other gems.

In chapter 11 of Book 32 of his *Natural History*, Pliny writes that "As much as Indian pearls are highly prized in our countries, so the Indians attach high value to coral." It is indeed an established fact, he notes slightly sceptically, that people have this conviction. He lists the fishing sites: the best coral, the most highly valued, is that of the "Gaul Gulf", the Gulf of Lions in France. Then come the Stoechade Islands near Marseilles; the Aeolian Islands (the Lipari Islands north of Sicily); Cape Drepanum (Trapani, on the west

Coral is more than a decorative object. It can keep misfortune at bay, protect against the evil eye, harmful spirits and tempests. When worn on the body, it is a protection, a talisman. This belief has persisted until this very day in the Mediterranean, and Corsican babies are still presented with a tiny hand made of coral, in the shape of a closed fist with the thumb sticking out.

coast of Sicily); Graviscae, in Etruria, on the western coast of Italy; and finally coral fished in the Bay of Naples. He also mentions Erythris, probably Erythris of Ionia, but says that the coral is too brittle, despite being red, and is therefore less appreciated. Beyond the Mediterranean, Pliny is more vague: there is some to be found in the Red Sea, but it is blacker (black coral from the Red Sea is referred to in the accounts of Commander Jacques Cousteau, the famous French oceanographer of the mid-20th century).

Pliny believed that the "berries", which are soft and white under water, harden and become red in colour upon contact with air. The most highly prized coral is that which is the reddest, has the most branches, and is neither stony nor hollow. The finest is "as highly prized by men in India as the largest pearls (*uniones*, "the unique ones") are by the women in our land", he repeats once more as if fascinated. And why are the Indians so enamoured of it? "Their soothsayers and diviners think that it is an excellent amulet to ward off danger; in this way, coral is for them an object of ornament and of religion." But this is not only an Indian belief; in the West too, and particularly in Italy, coral is more than a decorative object. It can keep misfortune at bay, protect against the evil eye, harmful spirits and tempests. When worn on the body, it is a protection, a talisman. This belief has persisted until this very day in the Mediterranean, and Corsican babies are still presented with a tiny hand made of coral, in the shape of a closed fist with the thumb sticking out. According to Pliny, a branch of coral hung around the neck of a child is said to keep him safe. In the Christian world, from the 15th century on, a number of Italian paintings of the Virgin holding the infant Jesus show the baby wearing a necklace of coral beads, or a coral pendant; in others, the Virgin holds a coral branch in her hand. This symbolism is difficult to justify from a purely Christian point of view. Coral is therefore a product which carries with it a certain innate power, and which as such, has crossed frontiers reaching India and then the Buddhist world in general. In Nepal, in Newari society, it is still the custom to place a piece of coral in the mouth of a deceased person.[55] One could go on giving more examples of its dual role, as much protective as decorative. It is also known as an antidote and a medicine, and is present in all ancient and modern pharmacopoeias, both Western and Eastern. All these reasons help explain its widespread distribution through trade, and why its production could never satisfy demand. Coral grows only 5 millimetres a year, and much patience is therefore required before a site is replenished.

At the time of the *Periplus of the Erythraean Sea*, the great port for the export of coral to Africa and the East was Alexandria. From there, the coral was then shipped to Kanê, the incense port, and to the Indian ports of Muziris, Barbaricum, Barygaza and Bakarê. It was probably from the Indian ports that it was distributed not only to India but also to Kashmir, Afghanistan, Central Asia and China. But even before this, coral had been exported to Western Europe, where it has been found in archaeological excavations. From there, we can follow its traces further east across the Asian continent, in the ancient tombs of tribal chiefs and other warriors.

As Pliny tells us in a few words in Book 32, even before these exports to India, the Gauls had decorated their swords, helmets and shields with coral. The demand for its export was such in Pliny's time that hardly any was to be had in the regions where it was produced. Archaeology confirms what the ancient texts tell us: from the time of the foundation of the port of Marseilles by the Phoceans in 600 BC, a trade route was set up between Marseilles and the north-east of France, up the Rhone Valley, bringing the products of the Mediterranean to the Celtic tribes which, at that time, were wealthy and prosperous. In several sites scattered across the Champagne region, tombs thought to date between 500 and 300 BC have revealed numerous objects decorated with coral which illustrate the use of this precious material in Celtic decoration.[56] Beads in the shape of pearls, olives and fine strips, small branches hung as pendants, and above all cabochons and stoppers of coral, set into bronze or iron, decorate helmets, scabbards, sword handles, harness fittings, fibulae, torques and bracelets. But several researchers have noticed the disappearance of coral from the countries inhabited by the Celts from the end of the 4th century BC. This disappearance may be due either to the weakening and decline of Celtic groups, or to the scarcity of coral induced by considerable exports to the East.

Among the Celtic Gauls, coral was replaced first by a blood-red enamel, said to be a Celtic invention,[57] or by coloured glass. Later, towards the end of the 3rd century AD, garnets appeared, inlaid into cloisonné—a cheaper replacement for enamel; garnets continued to be prominent in the metalwork of the high Middle Ages. The red coloured garnet was obviously cheaper to import as a coral substitute. In Asia, coral was often replaced by other red materials, such as carnelian.

Coral beads and inlaid cabochons, similar to those found in the Champagne region, have also been found in England and Germany, Hungary, as well as in the Scythian burial sites north of the Black Sea, on the lower reaches of the Syr-Daria, near the frontier of Kazakhstan and Uzbekistan, and as far east as Siberia. In the 18th century, the Russian governor of Siberia sent a number of gold belt plaques inlaid with coral to the Kunstkamera Treasure of Peter the Great; unfortunately, they cannot be dated with certainty but probably belong to the 5th, 4th or 3rd centuries BC.[58]

Glass-Making

During the Han and Kushan periods, another Western product very popular in Asia was glass, and particularly coloured glass. Western countries did not have a monopoly on glass-making. But the quality and sheer beauty of their glasswork, the fruit of long experience going back to the 7th century BC, explains the enthusiasm which it generated and the large volume of glass exports to the East and elsewhere from the beginning of the Christian era.

According to Pliny, who devotes two chapters to glass in Book 37 of his *Natural History*, it was invented in Phoenicia, in present-day Syria, in the marshy region of Cendebia, next to Judea, at the foot of Mount Carmel. The sands there were particularly suited to glass-making. The Phoenicians transmitted their knowledge to the Carthaginians, and from there the technique spread to Alexandria. At the beginning of the Christian era, Italy began to compete with the Egyptian and Syrian glass-makers with its workshops on the Adriatic coast, at Aquilea and Arretium (Arezzo). The latter was already known for its pottery, remains of which have been found as far away as India. Glass-making techniques then reached Lyons, before spreading even further north with the founding of the Rhine glass industry, which was to flourish in the 3rd century.

This glassware came in various forms. Beads of coloured glass paste for necklaces have been found along all the trade routes from England to the Far East, and from the Ukraine to Central Asia: round, oval, pear or cylinder-shaped, disc or even amphora-shaped, opaque or translucent glass, in shades of blue and green, or multi-coloured. These were probably not objects of great value. In a completely different category were blown or moulded objects of opaque or translucent glass: vases, cups, flasks, phials. Coloured glass techniques were highly developed, to the point where good imitations of gems could be made, which led to a trade in fake stones, sometimes passed off as genuine. The Cabinet des Médailles of the National Library in Paris houses several examples of Mediterranean glass from the beginning of the Christian era or just before, from places such as Alexandria, Greece, Rhodes, Cyprus and Italy. These include a head of Medusa made of light green, opaque glass paste; minuscule amphorae decorated with yellow stripes on a blue ground; blue glass paste from Alexandria;

several glass containers in translucent blue or green, and a few genuine wonders, including gold-based glasses from the 3rd or 4th century AD, and an Alexandrian glass cup known as "millefiori", almost translucent, in blended hues of turquoise and purple.

Although Pliny states that Indian glass was of a quality unequalled elsewhere because it contained crushed rock crystal, cadmium, nitre and ophirium, it was nevertheless Mediterranean glass which gave rise to a long distance export trade, as confirmed in both Western and Eastern texts.

Glass export to India is mentioned in the *Periplus*. Axum and Barygaza imported lead glass, Muziris, Nelcynda and Bakarê imported untreated glass, and Barbaricum glass dishes. From the Indian ports, these objects reached the Kushan kingdom and China along the land route.

China also made glass well before the Christian era, as borne out by finds from Chinese tombs from the 5th century BC. It may also have imported Indian glass. But during the first centuries of the Christian era, it was Western glass that took precedence.

The first Chinese terms designating glass seem to have come from Sanskrit or Pali words for precious stones. *Liuli*, the earliest term for coloured glass, is said to come from the Sanskrit *vaidurya* or the Pali *veluriya*, which referred to lapis lazuli, or any other blue or green stone. It was also one of the Seven Treasures of Buddhism. It is probably in this sense that it is mentioned in chapter 96 of the *History of the Former Han* where it is listed among other products from Jibin, alongside coral, yellow amber and pearls. Later, it would be used to designate coloured glass, and particularly the foreign coloured glass which so attracted Chinese buyers.

In the *History of the Later Han* (chapter 118), the production of *liuli* is attributed to Da Qin, and is listed in the same order as in the *History of the Former Han*: coral, amber, *liuli*. There is no doubt here that it refers to coloured glass. The same text also contains the earliest mention of the "gem which shines in the night". Joseph Needham has suggested that this refers to a false stone, made artificially phosphorescent, part of a prosperous branch of the glasswork industry which produced fakes, according to some authors.[59]

Later still, a new word, *boli*, appears in Chinese as the common term for glass in general, although originally it may have referred more specifically to transparent, uncoloured glass. It probably came from the Sanskrit *sphatika* or the Pali *phalika*, designating rock crystal, also one of the Seven Treasures of Buddhism.[60]

The *History of the Northern Dynasties*, the *Bei shi*, mentions in chapter 97 that Persia, or part of Persia, produced coloured glass. Other kingdoms mentioned include the Da Yuezhi, none other than the Kushan Empire, which the Chinese writers continued to call by the name of its original tribe. Li Yanzhou, the author of the *Bei shi*, does not say that coloured glass was made there, but he does mention an important fact concerning the role its inhabitants played in the spread of this technique. In 424, during the reign of Tai Wudi (424–452) of the Northern Wei dynasty, which followed the Han, "the inhabitants of the Yuezhi kingdom traded in the capital [the capital of the Wei was Datong, in northern Shanxi province], declaring that they knew how to make glass of different colours from stone. They therefore mined minerals in the mountains and experimented with melting [glass] in the capital; the attempt was successful, and their glass even exceeded in brightness and radiance the glass imported from Western countries. For this reason, the sovereign ordered this glass to be brought to the palace. The melting of glass was taught to one hundred or so people. The glass made was transparent and of bright colour. All those who saw it were astonished, as if it had been made by the gods. Since then, the price of coloured glass has decreased throughout the empire and is no longer considered an object of great value."

Who were these glass-makers who arrived from the Kushan kingdom? And from what area of this multi-ethnic empire did they come? Were they locals or émigrés from some other region? We know nothing about them. Indeed, what was even left of the Kushan Empire at the beginning of the 5th century? Encroached upon from all sides, it had already lost many of its provinces to the Gupta dynasty which, in the meantime, had formed a large Indian kingdom, and to the Sassanid dynasty which had replaced in 227 the Parthian Arsacid dynasty and turned Persia into one of the great world powers. According to some chronologies, the Kushan Empire no longer even existed. The entire political map of the continent had collapsed after the 3rd century. In 221, the Han dynasty had fallen apart, destroyed by internal troubles and external invasions by nomadic groups. In its place, several kingdoms had emerged, and the Turco-Mongol invasions had devastated, burnt and depopulated northern China. Wolves and tigers roamed around the ancient capital of the Han, and emperors were taken prisoner and turned into slaves. Finally, a nomad chief from the Turkish Toba group was proclaimed emperor of China, founding the Wei dynasty which ruled over northern China from 386 to 535. It was Tai Wudi, a Sinicized Toba, who once again began building relations with some of the dozens of small principalities in Central Asia, which had been fighting among themselves continually since the end of the Han. Once again diplomatic missions set off for China.

The Roman Empire had begun a process of decline which paralleled that of the Chinese Empire. For Rome, the 3rd century was one of internal troubles, of economic ruin, monetary collapse and misfortunes, all aggravated at the end of the century by the invasion of the Goths. Relations between the Roman world and India slowed down, Roman gold and silver coinage stopped circulating along the trade routes. But it too was to regain power.

It was to this new reality that glass-makers from the Yuezhi kingdom arrived at the Wei court. This was the beginning of a new period of openness which was to last several decades. The art of glassware had now been acquired by the Chinese, apparently freely and peacefully. The costly purchasing of luxury goods abroad was now over! And indeed, given the circumstances, they were perhaps no longer arriving in China in any case. In a similar move, in order to free himself from ruinous imports of Chinese silk, one Central Asian king succeeded in obtaining the one treasure which was even more valuable than the Seven Treasures of Buddhism: silkworm eggs, and the knowledge needed to breed them and to make silk. "Little treasures" was the affectionate nickname which the Chinese breeders gave to the worms, the source of their material well-being, though it is difficult to come across anything as ugly and smelly. But beauty can come forth from ugliness as the lotus flower rises from the muddy bed of a pond. The eggs of these "little treasures" made their journey to the West thanks to the marital alliance of a prince.

Chapter Nine
Silk Princesses

*T*he account of the silkworm's journey is first told to us by the Chinese Buddhist monk Xuanzang, who, on his return from India between 640 and 645, crossed Central Asia by the southern route, passing through the independent kingdoms of Kashgar and Khotan (or Yutian in Chinese). The events he speaks of occurred some two centuries before his time, in the first quarter of the 5th century, when relations between the Chinese government and the Western Territories were once again being established.

According to Xuanzang, the king of Yutian wanted to obtain silkworm eggs and mulberry seeds. But the Chinese court refused to supply any; determined as they were to maintain their monopoly on the manufacture of silk, the export of both the eggs and the seeds from China was strictly prohibited. The king of Yutian then solicited the hand of a Chinese princess in marriage, as a token of his allegiance to the Chinese emperor. This request fitted in well with the emperor's policy towards the Central Asian kingdoms, and so was granted. An ambassador was sent to the Chinese court to fetch and escort the royal fiancée to her husband. But the ambassador also had another mission, to tell the young lady that "our country has neither silk or silken stuffs. You had better bring with you some mulberry seeds and silkworms, then you can make robes for yourself."[61] The Princess concealed the two items in her headdress and managed to smuggle them through the Chinese frontier.

This is the first part of the monk's version, told towards the end of the account of his travels, the *Da Tang xiyu ji*. There exists an oral tradition which gives a different version of the story, more sympathetic towards the Chinese princess because it appeals to her goodwill. It has also been embellished somewhat, although it has not been confirmed by historians. This is the version as it is found in a compilation of tales from Dunhuang, published in Shanghai in 1986:[62]

"In times gone by, when the finest Chinese silks reached the kingdoms of the Western Territories through the passes of Yumenguan and Yangguan, because the journey was very long and transport difficult, when they arrived, they were worth their weight in gold. But this was of little consequence to the princes and nobles, particularly in the kingdom of Yutian. The wealth of that kingdom came from its jade production, and it was with jade that they paid for the silk, but they bought so much silk that there was less and less jade in the kingdom. Wracked by worry over this, the king of Yutian lost both his appetite and his sleep.

There was in the kingdom a devoted and wise minister, Yuchimu, who understood why he was declining. He explained to the king that he had learned, by enquiring among the merchants, how silk could be manufactured in the kingdom: all that was needed was to get hold of mulberry seeds and silkworm eggs, as well as the necessary specialists. But the king answered that he already knew this, that he had previously sent merchants, in secret, to buy seeds and eggs, but that it was absolutely impossible to do so because of the strict Chinese prohibition and the tight control they imposed; there was no possibility of crossing the frontier posts at Yangguan and Yumenguan with these forbidden objects in one's possession, as the inspections and searches were very thorough. And the risk was very great.

But there was a way, said the minister. In the old days, the king of the Wusun had obtained a Chinese princess as wife, and she had brought with her silkworm eggs and mulberry seeds. You are a great king, why should you not ask for the hand of a princess, and arrange things so that she brings with her these two items, as well as technicians?

And so Yuchimu was sent off to the court [unfortunately neither of the two versions of this story provides the name of the Chinese emperor, which would have allowed the event to be dated, but the princess was said to be called Lushi]. The request was granted, an auspicious date for the departure was fixed, the innumerable cases, presents, dowry and personal affairs of the princess were prepared, the list of servants who would dwell with her in far-off Yutian was drawn up, and an escort was arranged.

Meanwhile, Yuchimu managed to have a secret meeting with the young girl: he explained to her that the kingdom of Yutian produced jade, but no silk. Now that she was leaving for Yutian to be queen and mother of the kingdom, it would be of great benefit if she were to bring wealth to her new people. 'If you brought to Yutian silkworm eggs and mulberry seeds, the whole nation would feel infinitely grateful to you.'

The princess hesitated. It was certainly desirable to bring prosperity to the people, but how was she to disobey orders, how could she get the objects through customs?

The minister implored her on bended knees. The king of Yutian had repeated over and again that he was not asking the princess to bring with her [as part of her dowry] gold, silver, gems or pearls, but only this: silkworm eggs and mulberry seeds. The princess would think up a plan, the princess surely would not want to break the heart of the king, her husband, and this old minister…

The princess thought about it for half a day, and finally said: all right, but not a word to a soul, this business must not reach anyone's ears, let me think it over, I shall arrange something, so it will be done.

A few days later, the lengthy princely cortege, powerfully protected, set off on the road west, with the chiming of thousands of camel bells, escorted as it left by members of the imperial family. As so many others had done, this young girl of imperial blood was leaving for ever her parents, her country, her friends, her civilization, to serve as the seal for an alliance with a supposedly 'barbarian' sovereign living months away from her native city.

Having arrived in Dunhuang, the caravan stopped for two weeks to make the necessary preparations before crossing the great desert, and then set off for the Yumen Pass. There, the officer guarding the pass examined all the travellers and their luggage very carefully: the guards who accompanied the princess, her servants, even the headdress of minister Yuchimu which was checked inside and out. At last, they were allowed to cross the pass.

Once out of the pass, the minister respectfully asked the princess whether the silkworm eggs were there, whether she had them on her. She smiled and said:

'Yes, I have them on me.'

'Indeed?'

The princess took off her headdress of cinnamon leaves and took out of her chignon of crow-black hair the silkworm eggs:

'See, Minister, you can set your mind at rest! According to the rules set by my sovereign, it is not permitted to touch the head of a person of a princely or noble rank.'

Here at least was one of the three objects! The minister then respectfully asked: and the mulberry seeds…

The princess asked one of her servants to come forward and open her medicine chest: all sorts of herbs and plants were stored in it, and there, among the various seeds used in medicine, were the mulberry seeds, which are a genuine part of the pharmacopoeia. They had escaped the attention of the police officer as he inspected the coffer.

That accounted for two of them! But there was still something missing: had the princess not brought with her a male servant, a specialist in the art of silk making?

'Minister, do not worry, the specialist is one of my servants.'

Yuchimu was astounded: a woman? Women capable of breeding and raising silkworms, of planting mulberry trees and of weaving? What a strange question! Girls in China, he was told, all learn to plant mulberry trees, to care for silkworms, to treat the cocoons; to weave; this is all women's work. Three skilled specialists had been chosen before the princess' departure and brought along as servants. They all laughed over this, the minister bowed to the princess, and quickly sent off to his sovereign in Yutian a fast courier on horseback to tell him of the joyful event and to prepare a grandiose welcome reception for the princess."

Since then, according to this text, silkworm eggs, mulberry trees and weaving techniques passed to Yutian, then to India, and from there eventually reached Europe.

The rest of the story can be read in the brief text of Xuanzang. When she arrived in the kingdom of Yutian, the princess stopped first of all at a site about three kilometres south-east of the capital, where the monastery of Lushi would later be built, named after her and which Xuanzang would visit. From there, the princess was conducted in great pomp to the royal palace, where she deposited the eggs and seeds.

"In the spring-time, they set the seeds, and when the time for the silkworms had come they gathered leaves for their food; but from their first arrival it was necessary to feed them on different kinds of leaves, but afterwards the mulberry trees began to flourish. Then the queen wrote on a stone the following decree, 'It is not permitted to kill the silkworm! After the butterfly has gone, then the silk may be twined off [the cocoon]. Whoever offends against this rule may be deprived of divine protection.' Then she founded this *sanghârâma* [monastery] on the spot where the first silkworms were bred; and there are about here many old mulberry tree trunks which they say are the remains of the old trees first planted. Since then this kingdom has possessed silkworms, which nobody is allowed to kill, with a view to take away the silk stealthily. Those who do so are not allowed to rear the worms for a succession of years."

This passage certainly contains surprising information. For what reason was it forbidden to kill the cocoons and the butterflies allowed to escape, thereby ruling out the possibility of obtaining a continuous thread, and in effect treating the cocoon as raw silk? Was it for technical reasons or because of the Buddhist principle of not killing living beings? Or did this prohibition apply only to the main breeding site, which would need to produce eggs to keep the species going in the kingdom? Whatever the reason, Khotan has long been a producer of cocoons and silks. But let us look at a few other princely marriages linked to the spread of sericulture.

There is, first of all, the story of the Chinese princess who married a king of Wusun. There may in fact have been several of them, and the particular event we are referring to cannot be dated precisely. Neither can we be sure of the level of development of sericulture in ancient times in the land of Wusun. Furthermore, there is some debate over the marriage of the king of Yutian which some commentators have placed at a much earlier period, at least a century before the generally accepted date of the beginning of the 5th century. In any event, the Chinese monk Faxian, who passed through Khotan around 400 AD, describes the Buddhist monasteries there, as does Xuanzang, but does not mention any which might correspond to the Lushi temple or might have been built by the Chinese wife of the king of Yutian, nor does he make any reference to a story about silkworms. But being a religious man above all else, perhaps he was not interested in this episode in the history of textiles, although he would certainly have visited such a monastery during his three-month stay and mentioned it had it existed.

In 635, during the Tang dynasty, another Chinese princess is known to have taken silkworm eggs to Tibet, carrying them in her wedding basket, with, among many other things, a statue of the Buddha. This was Princess Wencheng, who was married to the king of Tibet, Song-tsen Gampo, and who encouraged both Buddhism and silkworm breeding in her adoptive country. But at that period, the secret of the manufacture of silk had already reached the Middle East and the Byzantine world, and China no longer held the monopoly over its production.

Are we really to believe that the three pillars of silk production, eggs, the mulberry tree and Chinese know-how, had never filtered west of the Great Wall before the 5th century AD? That this was genuinely the best-kept secret, the best-protected monopoly, in the history of techniques? Or is it not rather, as is so often the case, that the introduction of a beneficial industry to a kingdom centres around the king and around one particular event, thus fixing it in historical memory, just as one attributes to mythical sovereigns or their wives, or even to a benevolent divinity, the inventions of mankind? How many untold attempts at smuggling cocoons had preceded the princely marriage described in the revered texts? If one considers the economic importance of silk, a merchandise which was virtually a currency and which could be exchanged and sold everywhere, and the enormous expense which the purchase of silk represented to all non-producing countries, it is difficult to believe that there have been so few successful attempts over so many centuries.

As minister Yuchimu had promised, the "silk princess" was considered a national benefactress in Khotan. A wooden panel discovered in the early 20th century by the British archaeologist Marc Aurel Stein in a small ruined sanctuary at Dandan-Uilik, near the oasis of Domoko, just east of present-day Khotan on the southern branch of the Silk Road, is thought to have been her portrait. (Yotkan, a few kilometres from Khotan, is said to be the site of the ancient capital of the king of Yutian, visited by the Chinese monks whose tales have reached us.) This somewhat damaged wooden panel, one of several, was placed upright against the base of a statue. It dates either from the 6th or the 7th century.[63] Stein identified the panel as illustrating the introduction of sericulture to Khotan: the Chinese princess herself is shown with a round, full face, long black hair, a large headdress and a basket full of cocoons beside her. Standing to one side is a feminine figure, with a different headdress pointing with her outstretched arm to the top of the princess' head. Another female figure, with her hair dressed like the previous one, is surrounded by objects which could serve to weave or spin (a loom, a reel for thread and a spinning wheel?).

THE GOD OF SILK

A fourth figure, a male, is more difficult to interpret. He has sometimes been called the God of Silk. Roderick Whitfield in *Caves of the Thousand Buddhas* sees in him "a four-armed deity who may be the patron of weaving associated with the silk legend". This figure, sitting cross-legged in Iranian fashion on a cushion, is wearing long boots; in his four hands he holds various unidentified attributes, one of which—a sort of knife with a triangular blade—may have been used to cut threads. Like the other three figures on the panel, he is surrounded by a nimbus. The same figure can be seen on another panel from the same site, again painted in an Iranian style (probably of Sogdian influence), and has been baptised the "Iranian bodhisattva": like the previous one, he is seated cross-legged, wears long black boots and a closely fitting Iranian costume in shades of green, has black hair, a thick black beard and moustache, and a nimbus; his four hands are holding attributes similar to those of the princess panel.

The name which the Khotanese gave to this male figure is not known. He holds the tools of a workman, wears the costume and headdress of a prince or a knight, has the four arms of a divinity, but not necessarily a Buddhist one (on the other side of the same wooden panel is a painting of the Hindu god Shiva). All of this confirms, if need be, the importance of sericulture and of textiles in this kingdom. Did Khotan in turn try to preserve jealously for itself, as long as possible, this veritable living goldmine that was the silkworm?

One hundred and twenty or thirty years later, this source of wealth was once again seized somewhere in Central Asia, perhaps in Khotan, and presented to the sovereign of Da Qin (Folin), Emperor Justinian, who reigned over Byzantium from 527 to 565. In the meantime, sericulture had probably reached northern Iran, where the provinces located south of the Caspian Sea produced their own cocoons very early on. In present-day Uzbekistan, in the heart of the Ferghana Valley, it is said to have appeared in the 4th century AD, that is before it was even known in Khotan. The city of Marghilan (Marghinan) in Ferghana, which has existed since the 2nd century BC at least, was known from the high Middle Ages on for its silk made from local cocoons; much later, it became almost the silk capital of the USSR.[64] Uzbekistan and Kyrgyzstan have been cocoon producers for so long that history has no trace of the beginnings of sericulture there.

> *People in Central Asia preferred to be paid in silks rather than in Chinese copper coins.*

One may wonder what so many kingdoms did with so much silk? This was not a strategic product, it was not indispensable to life, nor to the defence of the nation, it was not a weapon or a medicine, so where did this widespread passion come from? Apart from its qualities as a textile and the beauty of the cloth, or perhaps because of these, silk came to have great financial value, and could be likened to a currency. It had the properties of a currency: being divisible up to a certain point, easy to preserve and to transport, accepted and exchanged everywhere, and finally, having a relatively stable value. In other words, silk was similar to a precious metal. Thus it was bought not only to be used as a textile, but to be sold against other products or stocked and kept as a safe investment, as one would with coins. It was sold and sold again from merchant to merchant, it was used to pay dowries, debts, the work of an artist or a scholar. It was the gift par excellence. It was used as an offering in Buddhist temples, or as a gift from a king as reward for a service. In the 4th, 5th and 6th centuries, writes Liu Xinru, people in Central Asia preferred to be paid in silks rather than in Chinese copper coins.

Originally, silk was a tax, going back to the time of the *Tribute of Yu*, when the stores of the state treasury were filled with silk sent as a payment in kind by the people. Its production and circulation reached, at the beginning of the 4th century, prodigious quantities. Figures dating from this period bear this out: the supply of silk kept in the capital, Luoyang, is said then to have amounted to some 4 million bolts.[65] In the following century, the quantity of silk supplied through tax was more than could possibly be stocked, and so was distributed as salary to all civil servants.

Silk was widely used in Buddhism for banners, generally painted, embroidered or woven with religious motifs, which decorated temples and stupas. These can still be seen in certain Buddhist countries in the form of very long, wide bands of silk that are hung from the ceiling. There are also immense draperies that, at the great feasts, were unfolded over huge spans of monastery walls, as tall as a three-storey building.* There are said to have been thousands of Buddhist buildings decorated in this manner in Central Asia from Kashmir to Gansu in the first centuries of the Christian era. Furthermore, it was also the practice to pay in bolts of silk the monks who recited on request texts or prayers at religious services, carried out the liturgy, or translated sacred texts. They themselves could use silk to pay fines they might incur for faults they had committed in monastic life. One Buddhist sovereign of a northern Chinese dynasty of nomadic origin, at the beginning of the 5th century, wanted to pay a Kashmiri monk, Fotuo Yeshe, 10,000 bolts of silk for his translation work of Buddhist texts into Chinese. The monk refused, but the five hundred Chinese and foreign monks who worked with him on his translations were paid with the bolts.

> *The Christian vision of the world had little in common with luxury, abundance and pleasure, and so silk was once more disapproved of.*

In the West, beyond Persia, in the declining Roman Empire, which had split up and then coalesced again in its eastern half, Christianity was spreading. The persecutions had ended, and Emperor Constantine I, who reigned from 306 to 337, established freedom of

---

* This custom still exists: in August 1999, the world's largest embroidered Buddha was shown in Dalian, in the province of Liaoning in north-east China, at the Tibetan Popular Art Festival. This satin curtain measured 45 m by 35 m, and weighed 3.5 tons. It has also been shown in other Chinese cities (information from the Xinhua News Agency).

religion, thus protecting the Christians. He himself edged more and more towards the Christian faith, finally being baptized just before he died. He transferred the capital to ancient Byzantium, founding the city which bears his name, Constantinople, and reunified the divided empire. Christianity spread through all levels of the population and reached Western Europe. The Christian vision of the world had little in common with luxury, abundance and pleasure, and so silk was once more disapproved of.

Saint Jerome (died 420), in a letter entitled *To Laeta, on the education of girls*, recommends that a young girl "look down upon cloths made from silkworms, the fleece of the Seres and gold thread". He also spoke out against the use of perfume. Once again, this familiar moral attitude towards silk reappears, shared by other religions which extol poverty and renunciation. However, as in Buddhism, the beautiful and the valuable became integrated into religious practice over time, as a sign of veneration. While Christians wore austere clothes, while liturgical cloths and vestments were imperatively made of linen, as Pope Sylvester (died 335) firmly reminded (it was only some centuries later that silk would be prescribed for certain liturgical cloths), the most sumptuous of silks entered the Church first to wrap the relics of saints,

> *The fact that sericulture had been introduced to Iran in the 3rd century or even earlier, and that Sassanid Persia kept a firm monopoly over any silk cloth and thread transiting from China to the Mediterranean countries, had turned the silk industry into one of the pillars of the Persian economy.*

and then as wall hangings or banners. The two oldest pieces of silk in France served as shrouds enveloping the bodies of saints: the cope of St Mexme, at Chinon, thought to date to the 4th century;[66] and the shroud or tunic of St Germain, who was bishop of Auxerre in the 5th century.

Before the middle of the 6th century, part of the silk cloth and all the silk thread skeins came from Persia or, via Persia, from China. The fact that sericulture had been introduced to Iran in the 3rd century or even earlier, and that Sassanid Persia kept a firm monopoly over any silk cloth and thread transiting from China to the Mediterranean countries, had turned the silk industry into one of the pillars of the Persian economy. It became one of the causes for the wars which were waged for several centuries between Persia and Byzantium.

Had the Europeans made any progress in their knowledge of silkworms? The texts which we have contain some surprises. We have seen how Virgil, and after him Pliny, writing in the 1st century AD, referred to down from the leaves of a tree, which was soaked and carded. The Greek geographer Strabo, who died around 21 AD, mentioned that the Seres often made a cloth from "certain barks of shelled byssus", but in the 2nd century, the Greek geographer and historian Pausanias counters Strabo's theory and reveals the animal origin of Seric cloth: "The threads of which the Seres make their garments are produced, not from a bark, but in the following manner. In the country of the Seres, there is an insect which the Greeks call a *ser*, but to which the Seres themselves probably give a different name. In size, it is twice as big as the biggest beetle; but in all other respects it resembles the spiders that spin under the trees, and in particular it has, like the spider, eight legs. The Seres rear these creatures, and build houses for them adapted both for winter and summer. The product of these insects is found in the threads which they wind about their feet. The people keep these insects four years, feeding them on millet; but in the fifth year, knowing they will not live longer, they give them a green reed to eat. This is the food that the insect likes best of all, and it crams itself with it till it bursts with repletion; and when it is dead they find the bulk of the thread inside."[67]

In the middle of the 3rd century, Solinus, a Latin writer, takes up the descriptions of Virgil, Strabo and Pliny, and comes back to the plant origin of silk: "The Seres, by sprinkling the leaves of the trees, detach the flakes with the water; they use this tender and fine down by treating it with water. This is what is called *sericum*, admitted to our shame into our customs; it is the passion of luxury which has brought women first, and now even men to use these cloths which serve more to show the body than to hide it."[68]

In the second half of the 4th century, the Latin historian of Greek origin, Ammianus Marcellinus (who lived in Antioch and fought in the wars in the East), reproduces yet again the same description of the Seres: "The land is wooded, but without thick forests. On these trees a form of down of great softness and fineness is collected by moistening the leaves several times. This is then spun and it becomes silk, that cloth once reserved for the noble classes and which everyone wears today."[69] Other writers, such as Claudius at the end of the 4th century, and Ausonius, in the beginning of the 5th century, also mention these forest fleeces. Apart from Pausanias, all of them, for five centuries, endlessly retransmit the story of the tree down soaked in water. And yet in the descriptions of bred cocoons, the only encounter with liquid is during the scalding of the finished cocoon. This may then be a badly interpreted echo of this operation, but one cannot help thinking also of the "tree down" mentioned in chapter 6: an ancient product of Yunnan and Upper Burma, which comes from the leaves of a variety of *wutong* tree, in the form of a white down which is abundantly washed, then woven to make cloth. One can imagine how the manufacture of this cloth may have been misconstrued into a story passed on by a traveller. We have seen that clothes from the same regions did reach Bactria in the 2nd century BC—and perhaps mingled there with other stories of textile techniques, to become mistakenly understood as the manufacture of silk. The question remains open but this is a possible explanation.

Chapter Ten

Transfers

*I*n other fields too, we find somewhat surprising information in the few documents which have come down to us about the way in which people living at opposite ends of the world pictured each other. Let us consider some Latin and Greek texts on the Seres, and a few Chinese texts on the inhabitants of Da Qin, or Folin. One cannot help wondering where they found their information, beginning, for instance, with the physical appearance of these distant foreigners. Ovid, who died in 18 AD, gives the Seres a swarthy complexion (*colorati*). Pausanias, in the 2nd century, writes that according to some, the Seres are of Ethiopian race; according to others, they are Scythians crossbred with Indians. We have already seen how the Seres were described by the ambassador of Ceylon in Rome as blue-eyed, red-haired, of above average height, with a harsh voice and unwilling to speak to foreigners. Obviously, a rather vague notion of who the Seres were had hovered over the immense and still imprecisely understood territory of Asia before it came to designate the Chinese themselves. For some reason, from the 1st century AD, the Seres had a reputation for extraordinary longevity: for Strabo, they could live more than 200 years; for Lucan, in the 2nd century, they lived over 300 years.[70] Pliny is more modest, allowing them a lifetime of only 140 years. Was this some echo of the Chinese Daoists?

Pliny's description of their strange manner of carrying out trade, by silent barter, has already been quoted. Several later writers were to take up this rather original trait, but until the end of the 2nd century texts on the Seres are rather brief: Pomponius Mela limits himself to a few words about them, remarking that the Seres are a nation fond of justice. Pliny writes that they are civilized, mild in character (*mites*), but shun the company of others. From the end of the 2nd century, the descriptions become fuller, and Bardesanes, a philosopher, scholar and poet from Edessus, who converted to Christianity around 222 AD, presents the Seres as models of virtue, impervious to the harmful influence of the stars:[71]

"Among the Seres, the law forbids murder, prostitution, theft, the adoration of statues. In this vast land, one sees neither temple, nor prostitute, nor adulterous wife, nor thief dragged before justice, nor murderer, nor victim of a murder. For neither the star of the shining Ares passing across the Meridian can compel any spirit to kill a man with iron; nor Cypris in conjunction with Ares induce any of them to have dealings with the wife of another, although in their land Ares holds the centre of the sky throughout the day, and though the Seres are born every day and at any hour." Similar texts can be found in the works of two other writers of the same generation.

> *"To the east, and beyond the two Scythias," writes Marcellinus, "the summits of lofty walls form a circle and enclose Serica, an immense land of commendable fertility, which touches on Scythia in the west, and on frozen wastes in the east and north, and stretches in the south as far as India and the Ganges".*

Finally, in the 4th century, a long passage from Ammianus Marcellinus[72] presents a Serica which covers not only China but all of Central Asia, inhabited by "diverse peoples", such that one wonders what the ancient authors meant by Seres, a notion sometimes as vague as that of Da Qin to the Chinese. We seem to be closer here to the Serindia of the 6th century than to present-day China within the Great Wall. And yet the Great Wall is mentioned by Marcellinus, certainly for the first time in Greco-Latin literature, albeit with a rather fanciful course. "To the east, and beyond the two Scythias," writes Marcellinus, "the summits of lofty walls form a circle and enclose Serica, an immense land of commendable fertility, which touches on Scythia in the west, and on frozen wastes in the east and north [this excludes the coast of China], and stretches in the south as far as India and the Ganges [thus including Qinghai and Tibet]."

"The names of these mountains are Anniba, Auzacium, Asmira, Emodon and Opurocarra. Two rivers, the Oechardes and the Baltis, flow down the fast slopes of these plateaux and then, having slowed, cross a vast stretch of land.

The appearance of the soil is very varied; here it is flat, and there, a gentle depression and cereals, fruit, cattle, are all abundant. Diverse people live in this fertile land. The Anthropophagae, the Annibae, the Sizygae and the Chardae face the north wind and winter. The Rabannae, the Asmirae and the Essedones, the most illustrious among these peoples, watch the rising sun. In the west are the Athagorae and the Aspacarae, and towards the south the Baetae who live in the high mountains. Towns are few in number but large, wealthy and populated. The most famous and the most splendid are

"The Seres, of all the races of man the most peaceful, are unfamiliar with war and the use of weapons... They seek after a life as free as possible from all disquiet... when strangers cross the river into their country to buy silks or other commodities, they exchange no words with them, but merely intimate by their looks the value of the goods offered for sale..."

Asmira, Essedon, Aspacara and Sera. The Seres, of all the races of man the most peaceful, are unfamiliar with war and the use of weapons. Rest they like above all else and so they are very easy-going neighbours. In their land the climate is soft and healthy, the breath of the winds always temperate. The land is wooded, but without thick forests… They seek after a life as free as possible from all disquiet, and shun intercourse with the rest of mankind. So when strangers cross the river into their country to buy silks or other commodities, they exchange no words with them, but merely intimate by their looks the value of the goods offered for sale; and so abstemious are they that they buy not any foreign products."

Who could Ammianus Marcellinus' informants have been? We have mentioned the Roman embassies sent to the Far East in 120 and 166, but it was mainly the sailors and merchants who brought back all sorts of first-hand accounts mixed with hearsay. Some of these tales, like many legends, would pass on from author to compiler from generation to generation, and consequently become distorted. Despite the unique value of the Chinese dynastic histories, which date almost every event very precisely, they are nevertheless characterized by two distinctive traits. These texts circulated after the end of the dynasty they described, sometimes two centuries later. The events recorded (embassies, wars, treaties, etc), may be reliable because they are based essentially on archives and authentic contemporary reports dating from the period described. But when it comes to the description of a country, the compiler may be influenced by the situation in that country at the time of writing, which may have changed considerably since the period he is supposed to describe, hence the vagueness of the frontiers of such far-off regions as the Roman Empire. Furthermore, certain identical passages reappear from one dynastic history to the next, as if they had been transposed through the centuries, carrying with them out-of-date information.

We have mentioned in chapter 6 the passages in the *History of the Later Han* concerning foreign relations in Da Qin, its trade with India and Persia, its unsuccessful attempts to have direct commercial relations with China, and its manner of receiving ambassadors. We have listed its wonderful products, in their Chinese interpretation: the precious metals, coral, amber, glassware, perfumes, asbestos, the moon-bright pearl, the night-shining gem, the rhinoceros which frightens chickens, unknown fabrics such as the water-sheep cloth and the coating, or ointmemt, which can make gold. The *History of the Later Han* also provides a remarkable variety of small details about government and daily life: the king's black carriage, surmounted by a white canopy; the description of the man who follows the carriage, holding a bag in which the king's subjects may place petitions; his five palaces with columns of rock crystal, which the king would visit alternately one day in five to deal with business of state; the administration run by thirty-six department heads; the existence of an elected monarchy rather than a hereditary one.

If we turn from the *History of the Later Han*, written in the 5th century, to the *Bei shi*, the *History of the Northern Dynasties*, written no earlier than the 7th century, and then to the *Tang shu*, the *History of the Tang*, which was not set down until the 11th century, we find elements concerning "Da Qin, the old Lijian", and then "Folin, the Da Qin of old", which reappear from one text to the next but which may in reality have ceased to exist, as well as mysterious products which do not become any more comprehensible with time.

We may wonder why that empire was given one of the names for China: in the *History of the Later Han*, "the inhabitants are tall and have regular features, they resemble the inhabitants of the Central Kingdom, which is why this country is called Da Qin". In the *Bei shi*, "the inhabitants are tall and well-built; their clothes, their carriages, their flags, all resemble those of the Central Kingdom, which is why in foreign countries they are called Da Qin."

This was clearly an empire of considerable importance. According to the *History of the Later Han*, Da Qin extends for several thousand *li* and includes almost 400 cities. Several dozen small principalities came under its authority. In the *Bei shi*, Da Qin stretches over 6,000 *li* and has a very large population. In the *History of the Tang*, Folin extends for 10,000 *li*, has around 400 cities, with several dozen small principalities under its domination, and maintains a standing army of over a million soldiers.

However, the names of the capitals and main cities vary between the three texts, and are almost always so corrupted as to be unidentifiable. On the other hand, practical details about its administration do appear: the story of the civil servant following the king's carriage with a bag in which to hold petitions and complaints appears in all three texts. So too does the system of government based on a division of the kingdom into sectors, and the system of postal relays. Among its products, the mysterious night-shining gems and the moon-bright pearls continue throughout. The amber and coral from the *History of the Later Han* reappear in the *History of the Tang*, as does the fabric made from aquatic sheep-down. And in the *History of the Tang*, the inhabitants of Folin still shave their heads, the king's palace is in full glory, with its coloured glass, its rock crystal, its gold and its gems on the walls.

But the chapters of the Chinese dynastic histories devoted to Western states are not interested only in Da Qin. The *Bei shi* describes, in the 5th and 6th centuries, some seventy-five kingdoms to the west of Dunhuang. Among the most important ones—important either for the size of their population or the number of words devoted to them—are Bosi, or Persia (most probably a region covering present-day Iraq and a large part of Iran),* then Khotan, Turfan, Karashahr, Kucha and Sogdiana. Most of the seventy-five kingdoms are given only a few dozen words each.

The list of products from Persia from this period is the longest in this chapter on the Western countries. This suggests that China must have had many direct relations with this country, which it never attempted to conquer, against which it never waged war, and which was probably a good commercial partner, as well as the state of transit for the silk sold in the Mediterranean countries. In the *Bei shi*, Persia is credited with the production of coral, amber, the *suhe* perfume, red cinnabar and rock crystal, which had all previously been listed under Da Qin. Persia also produced gold, a very pure copper, mercury, tin, various good quality stones (probably including turquoise), diamonds, large fine pearls and *liuli* glassware. In addition, different types of woollen cloth, which are given a variety of names, red-coloured deer leather, silks, different plants used for perfumes, black pepper, and "thousand-year-old" dates candied in honey. Also mentioned are fine horses, large donkeys, camels that could travel 700 *li* a day, lions, white elephants and the eggs of a giant bird, probably the ostrich. The government system, irrigation, weapons, clothing, as well as customs ("they place their dead in the mountains") are all described. Exchanges of embassies with northern China in 518–519 and 554–556 are also mentioned.

The Chinese monk Faxian had passed through the kingdom of Khotan around 399–400. Faxian observed his surroundings through the eyes of a Buddhist, and marvelled at the king's piety, the tens of thousands of monks and nuns living in the many monasteries, and the thousands of stupas dotted around. He saw dazzling Buddhist ceremonies with processions of carriages, statues covered in flowers, silk banners and, everywhere, the Seven Treasures. He does not describe the royal palace but the new royal monastery, covered in sculptures, gold leaf and solid silver. This monastery, he writes, received the precious items in donations from the six kingdoms to the east of the Pamir. The inhabitants had

---

* The text says that "Bosi is the Tiaozhi of old", which must have included at least the lower reaches of the Tigris and Euphrates. However, in the Bei shi, the kingdom of Anxi, which we have considered as representing Iran, has now shrunk considerably and is described in only a few words, while the new state, Bosi, has one of the longest paragraphs in the book.

a passion for religious music, which was most beautiful. In contrast, the author of the *Bei shi* is less enthusiastic: yes the country was entirely Buddhist, and the king very devout. And yet it was a state without decency or justice, where there was nothing but theft and debauchery. It was a relatively large kingdom, 1,000 *li* in length and as much in breadth, with five large cities and several dozen smaller towns. Thirty *li* to the east of the capital was a river which produced large quantities of jade, which was the country's main source of wealth. The soil was very suitable for growing wheat, hemp and mulberry trees (as mentioned earlier, this does not refer to sericulture as such), and fine horses and fast mules were also bred there. The country's customs and justice are again mentioned, and we have an indication on the ethnic type of the population in the 6th century: west of Turfan, it is the only population to resemble the Chinese physically, all the other groups having sunken eyes and a large nose. Unfortunately we have no description of the Chinese and of China from a Khotanese text.

> *Khotan had... sufficiently close ties with China to have contracted a matrimonial alliance with it. It was not a great military power... and therefore needed China's support against the continual incursion of nomads. Located on a branch of the Silk Road, it was a necessary commercial staging post, and the largest producer of jade in the whole of Asia.*

Khotan had, as we have seen, sufficiently close ties with China to have contracted a matrimonial alliance with it. It was not a great military power, perhaps because of the importance of Buddhism, and therefore needed China's support against the continual incursion of nomads. Located on a branch of the Silk Road, it was a necessary commercial staging post, and the largest producer of jade in the whole of Asia.

About 3,000 *li* south of the capital of Khotan, south of the Pamir, was a strange kingdom, governed by women, where men devoted themselves purely to military affairs. It was called the Kingdom of Women (Nüguo), and had been run in this way for generations. This was a kingdom of middling size on a

Central Asian scale, with a population of 10,000 families (some principalities had only 300). What do we know of it? It had a palace, one principal and one surrogate queen. We are given some indications about religious practices (including human sacrifice every year to a divinity of the forests), funerary customs, a method of divination by reading the entrails of a bird, clothing (long hair and leather shoes), a liking for hunting and no regular taxation. But what distinquished it from other kingdoms were its products: local copper, cinnabar, musk, black oxen (the usual description for a yak), very fine horses and exceptional quantities of salt, which was exported to India in large amounts and for great profit. The musk, yaks and salt all undeniably indicate Qinghai and Tibet. The first relations between the Kingdom of Women and China occurred in 586, during the Sui dynasty, when the kingdom is said to have "sent tribute". According to the *Bei shi*, nothing more came of this. Interestingly, the government of the People's Republic of China, which has searched through historical sources to find anything which would legitimize the inclusion in ancient times of Tibet into Chinese Empire, has never made use of that particular "tribute".

The theme of a kingdom run by women appears in several travelogues from various periods. One of these kingdoms, in Tibet, quite distinct from the Amazons of our Greek writers, is still the subject of scientific papers; another, located probably in the Indonesian islands, reappears in the 16th century, after having been mentioned in the *Thousand and One Nights*.

The Ancient Jigsaw

Many of these kingdoms and peoples are no more than names. What useless curiosity urges us to want to bring them to light? We open up tombs—those which have not yet been plundered—and we dig up cities buried in the sands. We unearth with great care pottery, weapons, jewellery, coins, silks, mummies and skeletons in the tombs of kings and nobles (the cemeteries of the poor yield little, and their bodies are but compost for future fields). Sometimes, rubbish tips of broken objects, lying at the foot of city walls, reveal something of the lives of the common people. The six thousand or so clay soldiers of the army of the First Emperor, buried near Xi'an, tell us about the weapons, the clothing, the physical features of the soldiers. But it needed the conceit of an emperor for them to be created. Of the real soldiers, those who died twenty-three centuries ago fighting the Xiongnu, and of so many others, nothing remains, other than perhaps a local legend about wailing ghosts, or of places which people are afraid to cross at night.

Central Asia is still a treasure trove of archaeological discoveries, despite all that has disappeared. Hundreds of square kilometres of frescoes at Dunhuang, monasteries in Xinjiang, fortified castles and towns in Khorezm, tombs filled with objects in solid gold, hoards of gold, silver or bronze coins, statues, and caches of manuscripts in known or unknown languages. Ten or twenty centuries later, we study these remains analysing them in laboratories and using computers. We try to put together the pieces of the puzzle, comparing them with each other, we decipher alphabets and texts, we compare them to the old historical sources we have known for ages. Sometimes, we question one section of our knowledge, and start again with a new hypothesis, never being satisfied—so tenacious is the need to understand. Periodically, a new scientific technique helps us move towards a conviction. All these analyses allow us to date an object, to determine its physical or chemical structure, to suggest its origin. Does not the word "vestige" come from the Latin *vestigium*, meaning first of all, "sole of the foot", and then "footprint"? But these traces have much more to tell us if we know how to decipher them: they tell us of armies, merchants, slaves, monks, artists, scholars, artisans, rampart and canal builders, kings and queens. And all of them had their gods, their angels, their demons, their prophets.

Goods could move without men leaving their own country, by passing from hand to hand, from person to person, through exchange at the frontier. It was general practice for professional transporters to convey the merchandise through their own country as far as the frontier, where they exchanged it or sold it to merchants from a neighbouring country, sometimes paying customs duties. The necessity of using several interpreters is often mentioned.

TRADE CENTRES AND TRANSIT CENTRES

Another stage occured when caravaneers were authorized, thanks to inter-state arrangements, to cross the frontier with the goods which the merchants had handed to them, and to travel as far as a certain caravanserai, market or bazaar, where these goods were sold to other merchants, or stocked in warehouses. At large commercial crossroads such as Kashgar, Yarkand, Kabul, Lanzhou and Samarkand trade centres were organized with a system of state control, customs and government services, large warehouses and hostelries. There were representatives there from the large trading houses, as well as people selling or renting camels, horses, and mules, suppliers of food, forage, and water. Of course, the great capitals such as Chang'an and Luoyang provided similar services on an even grander scale, including permanent merchant colonies.

> *Other desert oasis settlements along the Silk Road, whose hinterland produced very little and had a limited buying power, were mainly places of transit. They provided somewhere for both man and beast to rest and recuperate between two difficult stages of the journey.*

Other desert oasis settlements along the Silk Road, whose hinterland produced very little and had a limited buying power, were mainly places of transit. They provided somewhere for both man and beast to rest and recuperate between two difficult stages of the journey. They also offered a form of safety. Here, one could change caravaneers and pack animals as many of the latter died along the way. The caravans were assigned to a certain circuit, on one side of a particular frontier in accordance with tribal or political arrangements. One of these staging posts was the Stone Tower. It is not described as a large trade centre, but only as a place to gather one's strength and reorganize before facing the great desert to the east. Coming from the other direction, from China itself, it was at Dunhuang that one stopped for one or two weeks to prepare the men, animals and merchandise, while stocking up on food, forage and water before crossing the great desert to the west.

Great caravans would be joined, for security reasons, by various private individuals, small merchants, monks and artists, who, for some personal motive undertook these long and always hazardous journeys.

These caravans included hundreds, sometimes even thousands of animals, with a solid armed escort, and were accompanied by servants, aides, camel drivers, and by the owner's (or owners') agents, or a member of his family, a son or nephew learning the trade, or even the owner himself. It is not clear exactly how far each particular group journeyed during the first centuries of the Christian era: the merchants of Shu travelled from south-west China to India, where Indian merchants took these goods as far as Bactria. Persian merchants went as far as China, Sogdian ones to China, India and sometimes as far as Vietnam. As an exception to this, the Greek Maës Titianos travelled from the eastern Mediterranean to somewhere in Central Asia, and one of his companions went as far as the land of the Seres. But the Persians' goal of preventing the Romans from having direct relations with the Chinese was certainly the reason why this trade was carried out mainly by sea at the time.

As for official caravans, those that carried ambassadors, "gifts" and "tribute", these would be accompanied by officials, soldiers and servants who would travel the entire distance and back.

These great caravans would be joined, for security reasons, by various private individuals, small merchants, monks and artists, who, for some personal motive undertook these long and always hazardous journeys.

These voyages could last from several months to several years —travel accounts generally indicate an average progress of 25 to 30 kilometres a day for a merchant caravan.

These voyages could last from several months to several years—travel accounts generally indicate an average progress of 25 to 30 kilometres a day for a merchant caravan. Travellers would have observed the changing landscapes, inhabitants and products, but only a tiny part of all of this has been written down.

Ambassadors, on the other hand, wrote reports upon their return. The Chinese ambassadors' accounts were used as the basis for the chapters on the Western states in the dynastic histories and other official sources. Merchants' accounts included their own observations as well as the tales and stories, the hearsay and the legends, which the men must have told each other in the evenings around a meal, during a halt, or while travelling at night, when it was too hot to walk by day. Conversations must have been held in two or three languages. But as each individual travelled only a segment of the transcontinental road, the tales and information changed hands as they moved along.

CUPIDITY AND FOREIGN SLAVES

There was more continuity along the sea route, and the sailors from Alexandria or Syria, as well as those from Arabia travelled directly to India and Sri Lanka. The Indians visited all of India and Indonesia, and went by land to Burma, Afghanistan and Central Asia. India and Ceylon and the Roman Empire maintained relations until the decline of the 3rd century. But if two or three Roman embassies did reach the coast of China, we do not know of any in the other direction: no Chinese embassy is mentioned in Rome or Constantinople.

The merchants, ambassadors and religious missionaries travelled of their own free will. The conquering generals too. But, as is revealed in historical texts, more people travelled against their will, and it is they who have contributed immensely to the transfer of technical knowledge and religious beliefs, as well as to the mixing of peoples.

The hoards of people temporarily or definitively displaced far from their homelands are an expression of the brutal reality of the history of the Old World. Through war, the population of entire cities, and sometimes of entire regions, was exterminated, sold into slavery or deported. Over and again, the chronicles state in just a few words: "He seized the town, it was plundered and burned, and all its inhabitants killed or taken into slavery." Capturing a town was first of all a punishment for not having surrendered immediately. Even if it did surrender, it could still be plundered, on the slightest pretext, as occurred in Rome at the time of the Celtic invasions. This was a way of demonstrating one's strength, of setting an example, in order to terrify the adversary. It was above all a way of seizing his wealth: royal treasures, the treasures of churches and monasteries, and the private riches of the inhabitants. Cupidity was often the main motive behind the attack of a city. But the greatest wealth which one could seize was undeniably a human being for this commodity could be used, sold or discarded.

During antiquity, man was the principle method of production. His physical strength was the main source of energy; his intelligence, his technical training and his skills made him ever valuable. Women, when young, were valued for their beauty. Skilful workers, musicians and dancers could be certain of staying alive. A woman could always be sold again to work in the home, to spin and embroider, as a servant and of course in bed. Children could be trained for all tasks according to their capabilities, both in town and in the countryside. Thus, once part of the fighting force had been eliminated, and then the old, the sick, the handicapped, and if necessary the babies, the victors would divide among themselves the women, the children old enough to work and the remaining able-bodied men. The sharing was done according to hierarchy, as was the rest of the booty. Great battles also made thousands of prisoners available, all young and fit for work.

War was therefore the main source of slaves, maintaining for centuries a constant supply of workers. Wars have even sometimes been fought for no other reason than to acquire a greater workforce. When wars began to decrease, other ways were found of obtaining slaves: through punishment, or buying them in the marketplaces. In most cases, the slaves were foreigners. A frequently encountered figure in Chinese and Latin texts of the first centuries of the Christian era is the foreign slave. Furthermore, several countries prohibited by law the buying or selling of their own citizens, and only hardened criminals could be sentenced to become slaves in their own land.

The number of available slaves maintained itself more or less automatically in part through children born to parents who were either both slaves or whose mothers were slaves and whose fathers were their first master or owner; this naturally gave rise to considerable mixing of the population. A large military defeat was equivalent in many ways to an immigration, and then to descendants of mixed blood, the posthumous revenge of the vanquished.

Alexander the Great, who destroyed as many cities as he created, fortified in 328 BC a town on the Oxus, called Alexandria Oxiania, which was settled with the inhabitants of the indigenous settlement it replaced. Among other settlements founded in Bactria was Ai Khanum, located in the extreme north of Afghanistan, near the Tadjik border, on the left bank of the Pyanj, at the point where that river and the Koktcha meet, just north of Kunduz. In 1977–78, the central treasury building was excavated, revealing a treasure thought to date sometime before 145 BC, and to be that of King Eucratides, the last Greek king of Bactria, accumulated not through trade, but through the looting of India. Many valuable Indian objects were found, including rock crystal and agate inlay which may have decorated a throne, a disc inlaid with shells and glass paste (perhaps the back of a mirror?), agate, carnelian, as well as lapis lazuli and coral beads worked in India.[73] After its discovery, it was first thought that the site of this settlement must be that of Alexandria Oxiania. Recently however, new elements have led historians to revise this theory and to suggest instead Termez, on the right bank of the Amu-Darya, as the possible site of that city, while Ai Khanum could be identified as Ptolemy's Eucratidia.[74]

In this way, wealth circulated, little by little, ship by ship, from camel to camel, slowly accumulating into a substantial volume of trade, and on which people along the trade routes made a living; or it could be suddenly plundered by a conqueror, amidst war cries and murder; split up and sold, only to form a new hoard for another sovereign or war chief. And so it would start all over again. These violent upheavals greatly facilitated the movement of capital, precious materials, stocks of silver coins, and particularly gold around the world. Where did the gold which Alexander plundered in Bactria in 327 come from? Was it, as Herodotus claims, the gold which the Arimaspes took from the griffins, somewhere in the Urals? Was it gold from the Altai, or from Zeravshan in Uzbekistan?

The Macedonians and the Greeks plundered so much, say the historians, that Alexander had his soldiers' breastplates lined with gold, weighing them down and inconveniencing them when they fought. Furthermore, overloaded with booty and fearing they would lose it all, they forced Alexander to put an end to his conquest of the world, and demanded to return home. Many Macedonian soldiers did return safely, probably still clutching their gold. How many times since then was it melted down and cast again in some other form? Did some of it end up in a treasure pillaged by the Goths, the Vikings or the crusaders when they took Constantinople? Cast as Roman *aurei*, did it return to its country of origin to pay for iron or silk? Did it lie at the bottom of the Erythraean Sea, or the Mediterranean, in the coffers of a shipwrecked boat? Did it shine on the cupolas of a Muscovite church or the dome of the Invalides in Paris? Was it used to write golden letters in a Bible or a Koran? Was it, on the other hand, safe in the treasure of the Templars, or of the Third Reich, the reserve of a state bank, in some numismatic collection, or did it modestly shine on the wedding ring of a Christian peasant? The same could be said of silver, continually molten into ingots, coins, jewellery, liturgical or profane art objects.

In the year 260 of the Christian era, the Sassanian Persians, having defeated the Romans even more thoroughly than at Carrhae, captured Emperor Valerian, and after taking Antioch, deported the city's entire population to Persia. Bishop Demetrius, taking all the Christians with him, volunteered to follow the convoy of prisoners to preach Christianity in this foreign land. In 360, after another victory against the eternal enemy, the king of Persia, Shapur II, captured the silk workers of Roman Syria and moved them near Susa, in Persia. In 645, during the Tang dynasty, when a Manchu city in the present-day province of Liaoning refused to surrender to the Chinese, 14,000 of its inhabitants were made slaves and many of them transferred to the Chinese capital.

During the conquest of Central Asia by the Arabs, Bukhara was destroyed in 709, and half the population deported. In 711–712 Samarkand was taken, and its temples and statues destroyed. During the conquest of Khorezm, in 712, Kuteiba drove out the Jewish physicians, who fled to Khazaria, burnt the books and imposed on the Sogdians an annual tax in silk and slaves. In 713, he took and burnt Tashkent. In 750, a Chinese general of Korean birth, Gao Xianzhi, also captured Tashkent—which in the meantime had been rebuilt—seized a large quantity of lapis lazuli, gold, camels and horses, massacred the old and weak, enslaved the young, and took the king prisoner. The following year, this same Chinese army, still under the command of Gao Xianzhi, was defeated at the Battle of Talas, in the region of present-day Djambul in Kazakhstan, by the troops of the Arab general Ziyad ibn-Salih al-Khuza'i. He took a large number of prisoners, among them silk weavers and paper makers, an event which had considerable consequences for both Muslim and Christian civilizations.

Captive soldiers could be sent to guard fortified posts on the furthest frontiers, a common custom in both Persia and China, or form a particular guard in the palace. Since a large proportion of the world's soldiers were mercenaries they might be content with such a fate. This practice reappears in the 18th century in Central Asia under the emirs, who would offer Russian soldiers captured during raids on the Russian frontiers the chance to serve in their own army, promising them a fine career if they converted to Islam.

The Trade of Knowledge

Prisoners sometimes succeeded in escaping and soldiers sometimes deserted. There were defectors among the servants of a diplomatic mission, for example, or unwilling colonialists, or simply individuals who could make a better living from their talents in a neighbouring country, or those fleeing justice. These people may have been the moving force behind more transmission of techniques and know-how than has ever been granted in the histories, since Sima Qian's mention of Chinese refugees teaching Central Asians and Parthians the Chinese techniques of steel making.

Among these involuntary expatriates, one must not forget the hostages, usually close relatives of a ruler, as well as their retinues which were expected to expatriate themselves with them. We have mentioned the hostages of the Kushan king; other cases are even more famous, such as that of the Parthian hostage An Shigao, a member of the Arsacid lineage, who lived in the 2nd century in the Han capital, translating numerous texts from the Buddhist canon into Chinese. These young princes also contributed to the exchange of knowledge between civilizations, living long years in foreign courts where they would meet scholars and artists.

Apart from merchants, prisoners of war, hostages and various displaced people, another agent of interrelationship was that of princely marriages as we have seen. The Chinese dynastic histories always present the Chinese princesses as having been "granted" by the emperor to a foreign sovereign whom he deigns to honour. If the opposite occurred, the annals make no mention of it. Sometimes, however, these marital alliances were obtained by force, for example by the Tibetans in the 7th century. On another occasion, a refusal on the part of the Chinese court to a request from a Kushan king led to war. The system of princely marriages cementing an alliance was, of course, practised between all kingdoms, just as it was between the monarchies of Europe. Every sovereign married either himself or his daughters into the neighbouring ruling families. Although these princesses, in the period we are considering, were often Buddhist and contributed to spreading or consolidating Buddhism in that part of the world, it does not appear, unfortunately, that the system prevented war, any more than it did in Europe. It did, however, contribute to the meeting of civilizations through the intermediary of these representatives from the highest levels.

In what category should one class musicians, as voluntary or involuntary travellers? Were they independent, or paid by a patron, or simply slaves? One reads of kings sending as a gift to his peers a troupe of musicians and dancers of both sexes, just as one reads of acrobats, jugglers and magicians sent as tribute. The texts often mention female slaves who had received a good musical education. Of all the ancient arts, there is one that escapes us: we have examples of architecture, sculpture, painting, metal working, but we have lost the music, just as we have lost the perfumes. And yet music occupied a large place in the lives of the wealthy classes, and musicians and dancers from Iran, Khotan, Kucha and Sogdiana were famous in China and throughout Central Asia. They have been painted on the cave walls of Dunhuang, of Penjikent in Sogdiana (with a harpist in shades of pale green), at Khotan and elsewhere. *Pipa* players, flutists and dancers have become familiar figures, frequently reproduced. Sometimes we have the texts of the words they sung, but we have lost the melodies, the timbres and the manner of singing.

These different doctrines were not often in conflict: religious tolerance seems to have reigned for a long time in most of the kingdoms of Central Asia, where foreign religions, either triumphant or in flight from persecution, were made welcome.

Occasionally, sovereigns also invited, on the basis of their reputation, eminent foreign personalities in the fields of architecture, astronomy, medicine, and particularly scholars and astrologists who knew or pretended to know methods of making drugs of immortality and other secret recipes.

There also existed another category of traveller, those who set off without weapons and riches, journeying in small groups, following the same routes as the armies and caravans, facing the same difficulties and dangers, but with a completely different goal. These men had nothing to sell, they took with them only books, doctrines, beliefs, another method of reaching salvation. These were the Buddhist, Nestorian, Manichaean monks, missionaries and pilgrims, who, well before the arrival of Islam, spread and firmly established these three religions from Persia to China. The caravanserais of the merchants were also those of the gods. These different doctrines were not often in conflict: religious tolerance seems to have reigned for a long time in most of the kingdoms of Central Asia, where foreign religions, either triumphant or in flight from persecution, were made welcome. Buddhism was present for sufficiently long to have left there some of the most beautiful works in the world heritage of art.

Chapter Eleven
Transmitters of Faith

*W*e mentioned earlier the dream of Emperor Wudi of the Han and the arrival at the Chinese court of the first representatives of the new doctrine from the West, Buddhism. This doctrine spread through China, first slowly and in a limited way, and then, from the second half of the 2nd century AD onwards, much more widely. It could not have failed to reach China through its western dominions, as it had already spread across Central Asia, particularly during the tolerant rule of the Kushan kings. When the Chinese monk Faxian crossed the continent along the southern branch of the Silk Road in 399–400, during the Eastern Qin dynasty, he travelled from Buddhist kingdom to Buddhist kingdom, from monastery to monastery, and tells us of the many wonders which he saw.

This great traveller, known under his religious name of Faxian, was born in Shanxi into the Gong family, and was placed in a monastery as a child. He became a monk when he was twenty, and five years later, left Chang'an for India, with a few other monks, in search of complete and authentic texts from the Buddhist canon. At the time, there was a shortage of these texts in China, despite the efforts of translators. The copies of the sutras they were using were not reliable, and in many cases sections of the text were simply missing. The monks who undertook this long journey were motivated by a strong desire to find original and complete texts, particularly of the *Vinayapitaka* on monastic discipline. They wanted to learn Sanskrit and study the texts with Indian masters in the best monasteries, in order to translate them themselves into Chinese upon their return. They also desired to go on pilgrimage to the places where the Buddha was born, where he had lived and where he had preached. Faxian was one of the first to fulfil all of these goals.

In Chinese Buddhism, more than in any other religion, the translators have been remembered and honoured. There were an enormous number of religious texts to be translated into Chinese from Pali and Sanskrit, with the immense difficulties which this entailed in attempting to render religious and philosophical notions which had no equivalent in Chinese concepts.

Buddhism, like Christianity, was a religion of missionaries, a universal religion of salvation. It is a religion of the book, although founded, like Christianity, on the acts and words of one who wrote nothing. Its propagation, and therefore the salvation of others, rests not only on the faith and devoutness of the missionaries, but first on the knowledge and the conscientious work of the translators. As an indirect consequence of this, salvation also rests on techniques of textual reproduction, that is on the book in the physical sense of the word— on writing, copyists, woodblock printing, parchment, bark, papyrus, paper.

The Role of Translators

The first translators known to us were two Indian monks who arrived in Luoyang "with their sutras carried on a white horse", during the reign of Han Mingdi: She Moteng, whose Indian name was Kasyapa Matanga, and Zhu Falan, or Dharmaratna.[75] But it was mainly in the middle of the 2nd century that the new religion began to make rapid inroads in China, thanks to the work of the translators and to imperial protection (though the emperors were not necessarily Buddhist themselves, they encouraged this doctrine). It also had a particular appeal to various levels of the population, so much so that in 300 AD there were said to have been over 180 religious establishments in Luoyang and Chang'an, the two capitals, and a total of 3,700 monks.

The origin and biographies of the various translators are noteworthy, and once again reflect the types of transmission that we have seen earlier. Among the most famous translators was An Shigao, a Parthian prince who was probably a hostage at the Chinese court, where he arrived around 148. He is said to have renounced his right to the throne, and to have translated 35 texts. An Xuan, an Iranian merchant, arrived in Luoyang around 181, where he began translating and teaching. Lokakshema, or Zhiloujiachen in Chinese, a Yuezhi, translated an enormous number of Mahayana texts in the second half of the 2nd century.

The 3rd century was a period of great monastic development in China when much translation was undertaken. Famous translators such as Zhi Qian and Kang Senghui worked in the kingdom of Wu, one of the "Three Kingdoms" into which China was then divided and which covered the south of the country.

Zhi Qian came from a Yuezhi family which had settled in Luoyang at the end of the 2nd century, and spoke several Central Asian languages. Kang Senghui's ancestors were Sogdians who had lived in India for several generations before settling as merchants in what is now Hanoi. Born in Hanoi, Kang Senghui was an orphan and became a monk at the age at ten; he studied Chinese when he arrived in China at a very young age.[76] The most famous translator of the 3rd century, however, was Dharmaraksha, Zhu Fahu in Chinese, descended from a Yuezhi family that had lived in the Dunhuang military post for several generations. It was there that Dharmaraksha was born and became a monk at the age of eight. By then, the lack of texts was already keenly felt by Chinese Buddhists, but many were available in the Western Territories. Dharmaraksha was to travel with his religious master to several kingdoms, encountering thirty-six different languages, written in a variety of scripts. He studied several of these and acquired a number of books, before returning to China and devoting the rest of his life to the translation of 149 texts. He died around the year 300 at an advanced age.

These famous translators did not work alone, they were assisted by entire teams, which included a number of foreigners. Dharmaraksha, for example, worked with Parthians, Sogdians, Khotanese, Kashmiris, Indians and Yuezhi.

FAXIAN

A century later, however, there was still a shortage of canonical texts in China and, despite the large number of Buddhist monasteries present throughout the Western Territories, it was deemed necessary to travel to India itself to find the authentic word of the Law. This is how, in 399, Faxian, then 25 years old, set out on a mission which was to last fourteen years. We have the details of this journey from his personal account.[77]

Faxian crossed the sandy desert and visited thirty kingdoms, passing through Zhangye, Dunhuang, Shanshan, Karashahr, Khotan, crossing the Onion mountains (Pamir), venerating a tooth of the Buddha at Jiecha (perhaps Skardu, in Baltistan, in modern Pakistan-administered Kashmir). It was a cold and harsh land where one crossed high mountains covered in snow all year round, haunted by "venomous dragons which spit forth poisonous winds, and cause showers of snow, and storms of sand and gravel. Not one in ten thousand of those who encounter these dangers escapes with his life." These were the "Snow Mountains", the Karakoram or the Himalaya, which Faxian crossed.

Finally he arrived in northern India, in the small kingdom of Toli (difficult to identify), where a number of monks of the Hinayana school lived. There was in this kingdom an extraordinary statue of a strange origin. Once upon a time, an arhat (a disciple of the Buddha who has arrived at a state of perfection, and attained Nirvana), using the supernatural powers he had acquired, sent a skilled craftsman to the Tushita heaven. He was to contemplate and memorize the physical appearance of the bodhisattva Maitreya, the Buddha of the Future, in order to make a wooden statue of him. This occurred, Faxian was told, 300 years after the Buddha's entry into Nirvana, that is to say around the year 180 BC. Faxian saw the statue in the year 400 AD: it was "eighty cubits in height, and eight cubits at the base from knee to knee of the crossed legs". On certain days it would give out a light. Was this a vision of the statue which was supposed to have manifested itself in a dream to Emperor Mingdi? Kings' dreams were often interpreted as premonitions of major historical events; not only in China but also in Greece, in the Bible and among the first Christian emperors. Miraculous statues that move of their own volition, or refuse to be moved by men, or which are created in some supernatural fashion, are frequent in religious legends.

Further on, the travellers had to face fifteen days of perilous travel along high mountain slopes, along the precipitous banks of the Indus River, treading the vertiginous pathways chiselled into the rock face, climbing some seven hundred ladders, which ended with a suspended rope bridge across a river, over 80 feet wide. Over the next sixteen centuries, terrifying experiences of this kind have been regularly described by travellers who have had to cross the Hindu Kush or the Himalaya. But this was the only route for pilgrims and missionaries, and "no place is impenetrable to one who is motivated by sincere faith". Faxian was told that it was after the erection of the statue of the bodhisattva Maitreya that monks arrived from India carrying the books with them. From then on the doctrine began to spread further east.

Faxian and his companions, either together or separately, crossed Afghanistan and Pakistan before travelling down the Ganges valley. They stopped for the usual summer retreat, and it was perhaps then that they met, in a monastery in Jibin, a famous monk, Buddhabadra (Fotuobatuoluo in Chinese), known for his great knowledge and holiness, who was travelling from monastery to holy site. They beseeched him to go to China as a teacher and religious master. Thus it was that just before the return of Faxian himself, Buddhabadra, accompanying one of the other Chinese monks who was returning home, arrived in China and began the translation work that he was to carry out in collaboration with Faxian. This eminent master, who had also entered a monastery as a child, is generally believed to have been Indian. His birthplace was probably Kapilavastu, the capital of the kingdom of which the Buddha's father was once king, and which is located in modern Nepal, near the Indian frontier. Sometimes he is considered a Nepalese, although this region was not actually a part of the kingdom of Nepal at that period. In the present-day context of good Sino-Nepalese relations, he is often presented as the first Nepalese to have visited China.[78]

Faxian passed through Taxila, then through Purushapur (Peshawar), always on the lookout for texts, but never failing to venerate relics and souvenirs of the Buddha, be it a tooth, an alms bowl, bones from his skull, his mendicant's stick, his monk's robe, or even his golden-coloured shadow on a cave wall. But Faxian had not yet succeeded in acquiring a copy of the *Vinayapitaka*. Everywhere the Indian monks were astonished at seeing a pilgrim who had come from so far. At Kapilavastu, he was filled with sadness, for there had once been a city there, a palace, a king, and now there was nothing but emptiness and desolation. The entire population of what had once been a kingdom memorable among all now amounted to a few monks and 20 or 40 families of common people. The gardens of Lumbini, dear to the heart of every Buddhist, had reverted to jungle. Faxian continued his travels to all the memorable sites commemorating various phases of the life of the Buddha: his enlightenment, his preaching and his death. Finally, he descended into the heat of the Ganges Plain where he visited all the holy sites.

At Pataliputra (Patna), capital of the kingdom of Magadha, he was at last able to obtain a copy of the *Vinayapitaka*. In the years since he had left on his pilgrimage, he had found masters able to transmit the text orally, but not the text itself. Pataliputra had been the capital of Ashoka, and its innumerable stupas and sculpted pillars expressed the religious fervour and political power of that kingdom. Two great monasteries, one of the Hinayana and the other of the Mahayana school, still attracted large numbers of monks and students. Faxian remained at Patna for three years, during which he copied the most complete version of the *Vinayapitaka*, one which included the largest number of annotations. He also found other texts that were missing in China which he studied with his knowledge of Sanskrit.

Travelling down the Ganges, Faxian boarded a large merchant ship in a port at the mouth of the Hoogli River. It was the beginning of winter and the favourable winds took them to the island of Ceylon in fourteen days. Faxian called it Shizi, a translation of its Indian name, Singhala, or "land of the lion". This was an ancient name said to have been derived from that of the kingdom's founder, an Indian merchant and sailor named Singh, "lion". It seems to be a recurring aspect of this island to have many names and for navigators to come upon it by chance. We have already mentioned the Roman sailors who lost their way in the Erythraean Sea, swept off course by the winds, and came upon Taprobane by chance. Another similar story is told in the *Thousand and One Nights*: in an attempt to reach some Indian or Indonesian port, a ship's captain fell upon this unknown island, an enchanting island, welcoming, full of riches, which he called Serendib. Although he did not find what he was looking for, in his search, he found something ten times better. The English language has kept an echo of this tale in the word "serendipity", the faculty of making happy and unexpected discoveries by chance, and the expression "Serendipity effect" used in scientific publications, be it in chemistry or physics, for a providential secondary effect.

Like Magadha, Ceylon was, at the beginning of the 5th century, a great centre of Buddhism. The Buddha was said to have gone there to convert demons and dragons. Faxian describes all the splendours of this triumphant religion there, stupas and temples adorned with the seven precious substances, as if the island itself were made of gems and pearls. There were precious relics too, a tooth of the Buddha and his footprints. Devoutness and religious studies flourished. It was also a land of trade, receiving all sorts of foreign merchants and goods, from India, Arabia, and, no doubt, perhaps also China. One day, Faxian was admiring an enormous green jade image of the Buddha holding a priceless pearl in his right hand.[79] He had been travelling for several years already and his eyes had beheld nothing but unfamiliar lands and people. His Chinese companions were no longer with him, and "a constant sadness was in his heart". Suddenly, as he was standing before this jade statue, "he saw a merchant presenting as his offering a fan of white silk", as was the custom in China, and Faxian broke down in tears.

Faxian spent two years in Ceylon, then boarded a large ship, carrying more than 200 passengers bound for China, taking with him Sanskrit texts unknown in his homeland. The ship was assailed by storms and the Buddhist monk prayed to Guanyin, the Chinese form of the bodhisattva Avalokitesvara, to protect the travellers. The ship survived, and three months after leaving Ceylon, they reached Java. Here they remained for five months, probably simply to repair the boat, "for this was a land where Brahmanism flourishes, and all sorts of errors concerning Buddhism that it is not worth mentioning". After boarding the ship once more, another tempest hit them a month later. Once again they escaped, but the Hindu merchants on board, believing that it was the monk who was the cause of their misfortune, wanted to leave him behind on the nearest island. Were the Chinese Buddhists to lose the fruit of these thirteen years of research? Faxian had already struggled hard to save his precious documents, when the merchants had thrown their own goods overboard in order to aid the ship's progress. Thanks to the intervention of several other travellers, it was decided he should keep them. Seventy days after leaving Java, their provisions and water were exhausted, and the sailors had lost their way. They should have arrived in Canton long ago. The captain changed direction, and fortuitously, twelve days later they sighted land, and the Chinese passengers recognized the vegetation of China. They had in fact reached the southern coast of the Shandong peninsula.[80] The crossing had lasted more than five months, and the year was now 413. But Faxian's mission was accomplished: fourteen years after departing, he returned with his invaluable collection of texts. He settled in Nanking where he met again with Buddhabadra, and with him devoted the rest of his life to translation. He also wrote an account of his travels, some 14,000 to 15,000 words long, while his translations totalled "more than 100 times 10,000 words".

KUMARAJIVA (LUOSHI)

While Faxian was travelling abroad, another great translator had come to China. He arrived in 401, two years after Faxian had left, and was to die in Chang'an in 409, a few years before he returned. He too accomplished an extraordinary feat of translation of Buddhist texts. The Chinese called him Luoshi, but he is generally known by his original name, Kumarajiva. He is considered by the Chinese to be one of the four greatest translators ever. His biography is indeed out of the ordinary. His father came from an Indian kingdom. Renouncing an official post which had been offered he left, travelling eastwards across the mountains. Hearing of his reputation for knowledge and wisdom, the king of Qiuci (Kucha), a small but flourishing kingdom, invited him to stay as spiritual counsellor, and soon gave him his younger sister in marriage. She bore him a son, Kumarajiva, who became a monk at the age of seven. He became renowned for his understanding of the sacred texts, having been taught by the greatest masters of Jibin. All the Buddhist kings wanted to invite him to their court but he chose to return to Kucha.

His reputation reached King Fujian, of the Later Qin dynasty (384–417), one of the Buddhist kingdoms in northern China of Hun origin. Fujian, hoping to be the sole beneficiary of the wise man's advice, decided to have him kidnapped. Taking advantage of the fact that a war had broken out in the Western Territories, he ordered his best general, Lüguang, to leave for Kucha with 70,000 soldiers. At their farewell dinner he explained to the officers that his desire to defeat Kucha was not that he wanted its territory, but because he wanted Kumarajiva, for "men of great wisdom are a nation's supreme treasure".

The order was therefore given to capture him and bring him back as soon as possible. Thus in 383, Lüguang destroyed Kucha, annexed it and defeated another thirty kingdoms on the way. He captured Kumarajiva, without neglecting to plunder the wealth of the Western Territories and return with it, packed on the backs of 20,000 camels.

Having arrived at Liangzhou, modern Wuwei in Gansu, the victorious general learnt that his ruler had just been killed by an army chief, Yaonong, who had taken control. Without proceeding any further, he settled down in Liangzhou, first as governor then, later, proclaiming himself the founder of a new dynasty, the Later Liang (386–403). The story of this ephemeral kingdom is one of drunkenness and debauchery; Lüguang soon died, and one of his two sons killed the other. During this time, Kumarajiva, powerless to do anything, and a foreigner in a court which had no interest in religious questions, spent his time deepening his knowledge of Buddhist texts and his study of Sanskrit, learning Chinese and familiarizing himself with Chinese literature. He remained in Gansu fifteen or sixteen years.

But the assassin and successor of King Fujian, Yaonong, planned to retrieve Kumarajiva. The new king of Liang refused to let him leave. When Yaonong died his son, in turn, carried on with his father's plan, and for the second time a war was waged to kidnap the holy man. In 401, the king of Liang, heavily defeated, was compelled to hand Kumarajiva over to the victor. Allowed to settle in complete freedom in a pavilion in the middle of a park, a few *li* south-west of Chang'an, the survivor of all these enforced travels devoted the rest of his life to translating Buddhist scriptures into Chinese. He died in 409. Today, in the district of Luxiang, near Xi'an, the temple where he worked and where his ashes have been kept may still be visited.[81]

Kumarajiva was a man of enormous erudition. He had many Chinese disciples as well as students, among them eminent religious men. His deep understanding of the Sanskrit texts, the elegance of his style, the sum of his work (he translated seventy-four texts), have assured him a place among the greatest. He was a contemporary of St Jerome, translator of so many Christian texts from Greek to Latin, who spent fifteen years on the edition of the Bible later known as the *Vulgate*.

It has often been remarked that the 5th century before the Christian era witnessed the simultaneous appearance of the great milestones in human thought: Plato, Socrates, Confucius, Laozi, and Sakyamuni, the historical Buddha. The period from the 2nd to the 5th century after the birth of Christ also witnessed the simultaneous expansion of Buddhism in Central Asia and China, and of Christianity throughout the Roman Empire, then in Persia, and then even further east.

> *The period from the 2nd to the 5th century after the birth of Christ... witnessed the simultaneous expansion of Buddhism in Central Asia and China, and of Christianity throughout the Roman Empire, then in Persia... These two religions... obviously did not bring together in a single generation nations which until then had been deprived of any belief. On the contrary, both of them sprang from another, earlier, great religion.*

These two religions, which today represent over a third of the world's population (2.28 of the 6 billion inhabitants of the earth), obviously did not bring together in a single generation nations which until then had been deprived of any belief. On the contrary, both of them sprang from another, earlier, great religion. Both faced difficult obstacles, and from time to time benefited from political support.

CROSS-FERTILIZATION

What indigenous Central Asian beliefs did Buddhism supplant before reaching China? Bactria and Sogdiana had been deeply imbued with Iranian and Hellenized Persian culture. Zoroastrianism, or Mazdaism, has left many archaeological and literary traces there. Hinduism had also reached those living nearest India. But there were also the beliefs and cults of the people from the steppes, and those of the Tibetan population before the introduction of Buddhism. These have all been classified as shamanism, through lack of a better term, and all are poorly understood because these civilizations left no written texts. Many of these cults have become obsolete, though not entirely forgotten, for they have left some traces in the symbolism and the superstitions of the descendants of those who were once faithful to them.

In China, Buddhism penetrated discreetly into a powerful, centralized state, deeply rooted in its two fundamental doctrines, Confucianism and Daoism, which had sprung from the very origins of Chinese civilization. These have had little impact west of China, but they did influence the Korean, Japanese and Vietnamese civilizations further east. Confucianism was difficult to export, being based on the belief that the emperor of China was the pivot of the world, and owed his rule to the Mandate of Heaven. As Son of Heaven, and father of the people, he perpetuated the cult of the ancestors. Daoism did not spread much beyond China before being indirectly introduced into Japan in the 7th or 8th century AD. In its land of origin, it has lived on until the present day with its dual character: on the one hand, encompassing wisdom, philosophy and techniques of psychic and physical phenomena, but abandoning, in modern times,

> *Buddhism in China was, at times, protected by some emperors, to counterbalance the over-powerful influence of the Confucian literati, but was not an imposed state religion. It was the Northern dynasties, of Hun origin... who were the most active in encouraging its establishment. This is an oft repeated paradox, ... that the most warlike people, those with the most brutal morality, adopt a religion which professes compassion and peace.*

research into alchemy and a potion for immortality; on the other hand, and its most popular aspect, is the interpretation of supernatural powers by priests and soothsayers. These two doctrines, which go back to the very dawn of Chinese history, remained dormant during the decades of Western modernization and Marxist communism, hardly scratched by the Cultural Revolution. Visibly or invisibly, they are part of the Chinese mental heritage, just as Greek philosophy and art, the Christian monarchic system and cathedrals are part of the mental heritage of the Western world.

Buddhism in China was, at times, protected by some emperors, to counterbalance the over-powerful influence of the Confucian literati, but was not an imposed state religion. It was the Northern dynasties, of Hun origin, who had set themselves upon the Chinese throne, who were the most active in encouraging its establishment. This is an oft repeated paradox, comparable in Christianity also, that the most warlike people, those with the most brutal morality, adopt a religion which professes compassion and peace. Nevertheless in China, Buddhism was never dominant and it was persecuted several times. In 845, under the Tang dynasty, when all foreign religions were forbidden, the monks were scattered and Chinese subjects forced to renounce their Buddhist, Manichaean or Christian practices. The enemies of Buddhism criticized its monasticism for its rejection of two fundamental social duties, working and having children. Likewise, after the introduction of Buddhism into Tibet in the middle of the 7th century AD, it was driven out in the mid 9th century by the local Bön clergy. Reintroduced in the 11th century, Buddhism was once again heavily oppressed in the 20th. Buddhism's elimination from India was finally achieved by the Muslim conquest, and it sought refuge in Nepal and Tibet. It was after the Muslim conquest, and the adoption of Islam by the Turks, that Buddhism was also gradually driven out of Central Asia, from the 8th century on.

According to the accounts of various observers and to archaeological discoveries, Central Asia had been mainly Buddhist even before Faxian picked up his pilgrim's staff and set off in search of the Law. We have seen that it was Indians, Parthians and Central Asians who translated the Indian texts for the Chinese. Can one translate religious texts if one is not oneself a follower of that faith? Had these Parthians also become Buddhist in Central Asia, or had they been Buddhist before they arrived there, in other words were there Buddhists in Persia, and how far west had Buddhism spread? Had it reached Arabia or Europe?

The expansion of Buddhism is apparent as far west as Margiana, where the ruins of Giaur-Kala, the Merv of antiquity, reveal the presence of a monastery with stupas which probably contained relics. Between the 3rd and 5th centuries

AD, Merv was an important trade centre, much visited by Indian merchants who had crossed Bactria. It may be that some of these merchants were Buddhists who established a colony at Merv and built monastic complexes and stupas in an Indian style.[82] In the ruins of Giaur-Kala, Chinese cinnabar, shells from the Indian Ocean, semi-precious stones, and inscriptions in Brahmi and Kharoshti have been found. This community too must have suffered during the phases of religious persecution by the Sassanian kings from the reign of Shapur I (241–272) on. Shapur, who conquered Margiana and annexed it to Persia, destroyed the Buddhist sanctuaries during his campaign in the Kushan state, while the Zoroastrians persecuted all other religions. During the reign of his successors, between 273 and 283, a powerful Zoroastrian movement succeeded in obtaining the condemnation of Mani and of the Manichaeans in Iran. They either destroyed or converted for their own cult all the religious buildings in Merv belonging to the Jews, Buddhists, Brahmins, "Nazaraeans" (Christians) and "Zandiq" (Manichaeans). The Persian conquest of Kushan territory ended under Shapur II (309–379); the Buddhist buildings of Termez (in modern Uzbekistan, on the Amu-Darya, on the Afghan frontier) were destroyed and the Christians in Iran were persecuted. These anti-religious persecutions ceased at the end of the 4th century. In Merv there followed a massive influx of Buddhist monks from India, while a new convent of Christian hermits was built to the north of the Buddhist structures. These two foreign religions were once again driven out and their buildings destroyed, in the 6th century, this time definitively.

DUNHUANG

In contrast, Buddhism flourished right across the region under Chinese influence. At the time when the protection of the defeated Kushan kings was vanishing from their old territories now annexed by Zoroastrian Persia, one of the most extraordinary corpora of Buddhist art—a high point in the heritage of humanity—was being created in the rock caves of Dunhuang. Today a small sub-prefecture in Gansu of no economic or strategic importance, Dunhuang became a Chinese prefecture at the very beginning of the Han dynasty influence in Central Asia. In the 4th century, it was an important administrative and commercial centre on the Silk Road, and a large Buddhist centre. Twenty-five kilometres south of the town, hundreds of caves were dug into the huge cliff-face on the edge of the desert; 496 of these caves are in a good state of preservation, housing more than 45,000 square metres of murals and 2,415 statues, the majority of which are Buddhist. The first painted caves date from the end of the 4th century, and the last ones from the 13th century, with a peak during the Tang, from the 7th to the 10th centuries. A thousand years of painting, preserved thanks to the extreme aridity of the environment, show the various artistic influences, Greco-Buddhist, Chinese and Mongol Lamaist, which gradually blended into one another. In the half-light, the visitor can still glimpse scenes of life on the border, of kings and donors, of ethnic groups from all the Central Asian countries, itinerant merchants, pilgrims, bandits, caravans and *feitian* or *apsaras*, divine beings flying across the Buddhist sky. There are untold numbers of paradises, but also a few figures from classical Chinese mythology, such as the Queen Mother of the West. Good fortune and the caution of those who concealed this miraculous site over time prevented its destruction, even during Dunhuang's most troubled periods.

Gansu, Xinjiang and part of Afghanistan are littered with the remains of the triumphant omnipresence of Buddhism during at least eight centuries. Many vestiges have also been found in Uzbekistan and Turkmenistan. But what is left of the beliefs prior to the great Buddhist period, apart from the foreign Hellenic influence? Many gods have perished there, but how did they perish?

And how did the cults of Mithra, of Baal and Astarte, of the Syrian Sun god, of the Egyptian Isis, of Apollo, of Aesculapius, disappear from Mediterranean Europe? The Roman Empire, supranational and cosmopolitan, mixed people and ideas. It was all very well making the cult of the emperor mandatory, but we know from Latin writers that the gods and the virtues of antique Rome were no longer truly venerated. The religions of the Greco-Roman world lost all vitality as the empire disintegrated politically and economically. They did not come back to life with the growth of the Byzantine Empire, but they did show remarkable artistic longevity, in sculpture, painting and architecture, imbuing Western European civilization with their Classical style right up into the 19th century.

Of the different Oriental religions which gained ground around the Mediterranean, Christianity came out in the lead. Having been persecuted for a long time, it was to become the dominant religion, and in turn exclude all others.

CONSTANTINE

At the end of the 3rd century, Asia Minor and Egypt had been mostly Christianized, the West much less so. The expansion of the new religion began accelerating after 311, when an Edict of Toleration of all religions was proclaimed by Emperor Galerius, followed in 313 by an edict from Constantine I, authorizing Christianity as well as all other religions throughout the empire. It is believed that Constantine himself was converted to Christianity and baptized just before his death in 337.

Except during the brief reign of Julian the Apostate between 361 and 363, Christianity, strongly supported by the highest authorities, continued to grow, particularly once it was imposed by the successors of Constantine. In 391, pagan cults were banned and the pagan temples in Roman Egypt were closed; the following year, the same prohibitions were extended to the whole of the empire. From 408 on, pagans were progressively excluded from official functions, from the army, the administration and from the right to be judicial witnesses. Finally, in 529, under the Byzantine Emperor Justinian, only Christians were allowed to live in the empire, with pagans facing banishment and the confiscation of their goods. Only Judaism was authorized, under supervision. At the end of the 6th century, the vast majority of the population of the old Western Roman provinces had also been baptized. But some pagan survivals would persist for a long time.

Concurrently, within Christianity itself, various movements were excluding each other, while the councils attempted to organize a unity in Christian dogma. The political authorities imposed not only Christianity, but a single and unique form of Christianity, which was more and more closely associated with their aims.

While an evangelical missionary movement of some intensity was developing in all directions, a struggle against heresies began after the First Council, the Council of Nicea, in 325: Arianism, Manichaeism, Montanism, all became subject to repression and expulsion. After the Council of Ephesus in 431, it was Nestorianism; after the Council of Chalcedony in 451, it was Monophysitism. Repressions and expulsions resulted in the immigration and the dissemination in other countries of those who remained faithful to the condemned doctrines, and would not repudiate their beliefs. Thus certain heretics found refuge in Persia, only to be driven out later by yet further religious persecution. They moved to Central Asia, and in some cases even to China.

The main reason behind the great schism in the 5th century, which split the Christians into two large entities which were mutually exclusive, was a difference in the conception of the nature of Christ—divine and human. This changed nothing of the message, but this theological point appeared to be so essential that the disagreement around it led to condemnations, expulsions, brutality and emigration. It is true that power struggles between the great theological centres of Alexandria and Constantinople on the one hand, and Antioch and Edessus on the other, also played a part in this.

At the time of the Council of Ephesus which declared Dyophysitism (more commonly known as Nestorianism after the Bishop of Constantinople, Nestorius) a heresy, a number of Christian communities were already established in Persia. They had originally settled there after a mass deportation following King Shapur I's victorious campaign against the Eastern Roman territories in 260. He sent into the heart of Persia hundreds of thousands of prisoners captured in Cilicia, Cappadocia, and particularly in Syria, thus effectively implanting Christianity deep into his own empire.[83] The population of Syria had been in large part Christian, some of whom were descended from Christianized Jews who had been compelled to flee Jerusalem. In addition, Christianity had also been preached in Persia by missionaries, and had even reached the upper echelons of society, whose sons were sent to study at Edessus. The new religion was developing dynamically in Persia, albeit with periods of persecution, depending on the convictions of the king and the power of the Mazdaian clergy.

It was the descendants of these Persian Christians who were later to travel east, either through missionary zeal or a need to flee.

The term "Syrian" was not the ethnic designation of a people, but referred simply to an inhabitant of Syria, that is to say a Jew, a Greek, a Palmyrenian, a Roman, or a person from another neighbouring state who had settled in Syria. We have met the Syrians as merchants on the trade routes, a polyglot nation which travelled widely, many of whom where translators, and who made substantial contributions to the translation of the Bible. If Greek was the language of the Church for a large proportion of Christians, and the most prestigious language of culture, Latin was gradually gaining on Greek in the western part of the Roman Empire, and had supplanted it in liturgy. At the end of the 4th century, St Jerome's *Vulgate*, translated into Latin from the Hebrew and Greek, rivalled an earlier Latin Bible, also translated from the Greek, written in Carthage more than a century before. The Bible, or at least the New Testament, had been translated or was being translated into various languages; Coptic, Ethiopian, Georgian, Armenian, Gothic. The Syrians spoke a branch of Aramaic, often called Syriac, in which they wrote their sacred texts; Aramaic was to become the vehicle which spread the Christian doctrine further east. Being bilingual or trilingual, the Syrians also translated books written in Greek or Syriac into Pahlavi, or Middle Persian, the language used in Persia at the time.

In both Christianity and Buddhism, each of which covered a very wide multi-ethnic area, translation was considered a pious work, and many monks devoted ten or twenty years of their life, sometimes even more, to spreading the sacred texts. Despite St Luke's account in the *Acts of the Apostles*, the Holy Spirit did not really release the translators from their task of spreading the Word of Christ. The apostles were not able to hand down the gift which came to them from Heaven, in the form of a tongue of fire, on that day of Pentecost—the gift of preaching in all languages: "And they were all filled with the Holy Ghost, and began to speak with other tongues, as the Spirit gave them utterance." And people from all nations who were in Jerusalem "heard them speak in his own language". This miraculous gift, which would have invalidated the curse of the Tower of Babel, was soon lost, if we are to believe the long and still ongoing story of translators. How many bloody controversies and misunderstandings could probably have been avoided if this gift had been part of the Apostolic accomplishment! But perhaps the text of the apostle Luke has been misunderstood, or badly translated? No similar miracle of the gift of languages exists in the Buddhist tradition.

The Christian communities of Persia depended first and foremost on the patriarch of Antioch. In 424, the Mesopotamian Church, as it was sometimes known, declared itself independent and set up its own patriarchate at Ctesiphon. For political as much as for religious reasons, a quarrel then arose concerning the dual nature of Christ, and the Nestorians were compelled to leave the territory of the Byzantine Empire. The Persian Church chose to rally to the side of the Dyophysitists and broke off completely with Byzantium. Persia became a bastion of Nestorianism and welcomed many monks driven out of Byzantium. When in 489, the Byzantine emperor Zeno closed the school at Edessus, expelling the students and teachers, many of whom were Persians, and burning its library, the Persians reopened the school at Nisibis, on the frontier between Byzantium and Persia. So long as they clearly divorced themselves from Byzantium, Persian Christians were not harassed by the government. Indeed this was not the time for the latter to be making enemies at home for Persia was caught in a vice between its old enemy, Byzantium, and a new enemy, the Hephtalite Huns who were racing across Central Asia. They had taken Merv and Herat in 484, killed King Firuz, captured his son, and imposed peace on the Sassanian kingdom, forcing them to pay tribute.

THE HUNS

The 5th century was marked by a new wave of invasions of nomadic peoples, moving from east to west as periodically occurred across Eurasia. The White Huns, or Hephtalites, who are generally grouped as Turks or Turko-Mongols, had occupied Sogdiana since 430, and harassed the Persian frontier. Other Huns, led by Attila, had ravaged Europe, destroyed and depopulated seventy cities, and compelled the Byzantine Empire to pay it tribute. This was the century of the rise to power of the Turks who would become the most formidable partners of Tang China after having reigned several times over the northern part of the Chinese Empire. Having driven out the Kushan, the Huns occupied Khorezm, all of Sogdiana, Tokharestan and Bactria, plundering and ruining the sedentary kingdoms. Their capital, perhaps first of all located in Badakhshan, was then transferred in the 6th century to Paikend, near Bukhara. In the east, they also conquered the region of Kashgar, and in the west Wakhan and Kashmir.

The Persian Christians, even those of high birth, found themselves in a difficult situation. On the one hand, Byzantium and Sassanian Persia were hereditary enemies, and frequently openly at war, and the Christians risked being considered as an inside enemy, friends of Byzantium. But it was difficult for them to seek Byzantium's help as a protector of Christianity, having themselves been declared heretics by Byzantium; to do so, they would have to renounce their beliefs concerning the nature of Christ, and declare Mary the "Mother of God". Nevertheless, attempts at reconciliation were made. Finally, the Christians also found themselves up against the militant hostility of the very powerful Mazdaian clergy. Their story in Iran has been one of ongoing alternation between tolerance and persecution on the part of the authorities.

The Huns were to play an unexpected role in the spread of Christianity. They were nomadic people, whose neighbours were sedentary with more complex religions, whom they conquered piece by piece, and whose religions they frequently adopted. The Huns and several Turkish nations such as the Uighur had become Buddhists, Christians or Manichaeans. At the time when the heir to the Sassanian throne, Kavadh (Qobad), was a hostage living with the Huns near Merv, there were already Christians established in Merv and Sogdiana. Earlier, action taken by the Mazdaians had scattered the foreign religious communities there, but they had later been re-established. Under the Hunnish government, Christianity was so well received that a strong proselytizing movement developed there, encouraged by the Persian Nestorian Catholicos, in 498.

The Huns had placed the young Qobad on the Persian throne, and their khan had married a Sassanian princess, sister of Firuz. But Qobad, having backed a social policy which did not favour the aristocracy and the Mazdaian clergy, was deposed and imprisoned by his own nobility. He succeeded in escaping, seeking refuge with the Hun khan, whose wife was his aunt, where he was made welcome. In 498, the Catholicos Babai sent a missionary, Bishop Paul, to convert the Hephtalites.[84] It so happened that the khan's sister fell ill; the Nestorian Bishop successfully cured her, and then baptized her. From then on, conversions became more and more numerous and Dyophysitist Christianity prospered among the Hun community (the Visigoths and the Vandals, who arrived from the West, also converted to Christianity, but to Arianism).

There were many ... occasions when a script was invented to spread a religion. The Tibetan alphabet was created from Sanskrit, in the 8th century, by a Buddhist monk who used it to propagate Buddhism in Tibet. The Slavonic alphabet, the father of Cyrillic, was created in the 9th century by two Byzantine monks from the Greek alphabet and used to evangelize Russia.

But the Word had to be spread, and therefore translators were needed. Bishop Paul formed a team to translate the Bible into the language of the Huns, and painters of illuminated manuscripts to make the text more accessible. He had to create an alphabet for this language which still had no script, and invented one using elements from the Pahlavi and Sogdian alphabets, both derived from Aramaic. This hybrid of Aramaic letters would later be used to write the Turkish languages, particularly Uighur, and Mongol.

There were many such occasions when a script was invented to spread a religion. The Tibetan alphabet was created from Sanskrit, in the 8th century, by a Buddhist monk who used it to propagate Buddhism in Tibet. The Slavonic alphabet, the father of Cyrillic, was created in the 9th century by two Byzantine monks from the Greek alphabet and used to evangelize Russia.

Relations between the Hephtalite khan and Persia were further consolidated by the marriage of Qobad to his niece, daughter of the khan, thus enabling him to return to the Sassanian throne. But what happened to the Nestorians in Sogdiana? Despite hard times (the destruction of the Hun kingdom by new

Turkish conquerors in the middle of the 6th century), they were still present, at least in the middle of the 7th century. In this context of tension between Persia and Byzantium, of hostility from the Mazdaian magi and of Turkish politics, let us first look at the particular role played by two monks, whose motivations this time had nothing to do with the nature of Christ.

EMPEROR JUSTINIAN

Emperor Justinian had been ruling Byzantium since 527. One of the economic problems faced by the Byzantine Empire was that its trade with eastern Asia had to contend continually with a blockade set up by the Persian governments. The latter prevented in every possible way the transport of goods between the East and Byzantium and its allies, other than that through their own territory. They fixed their own prices and chose their own customers. This concerned above all Chinese silk, either raw, in thread form or woven cloth. The Persians had their own silk industry, and were already breeding silkworms, while the Byzantines had silk workshops, organized as a state industry, but were compelled to buy the raw material abroad. Unfortunately, the only supplier available to them was Persia whose prices were exorbitant. The Byzantine taxation system was more suited to stifling the industry than allowing it to prosper, as its rules and regulations were paralysing, and the losses in foreign trade exasperating. Emperor Justinian I tried in vain to find a way round the Persian obstacle and to establish relations, if not with the producers of silk, at least with a cheaper middleman. And after all, it was not necessary to enrich one's own enemy. A solution would be to produce raw silk themselves, but how were they to do this?

The vagaries of politics brought him strange visitors, "monks from India", according to Procopius of Cesarea (died 562), in his *War of the Goths*, (Book 4 chapter 17), or a "Persian", according to Theophanus of Byzantium, who died in 817.[85] Later writers believe that they were more likely to have been two Persian Nestorian monks. According to Procopius, these monks were received by Emperor Justinian in Byzantium in 550 or 551, and announced that they came from India and that they had lived for a long time in Serindia, where sericulture was practised. They knew how silk was made. They explained that

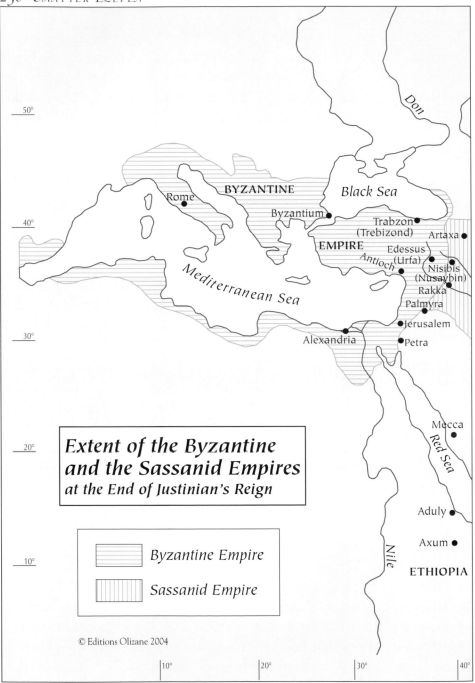

Extent of the Byzantine
and the Sassanid Empires
at the End of Justinian's Reign

Byzantine Empire

Sassanid Empire

© Editions Olizane 2004

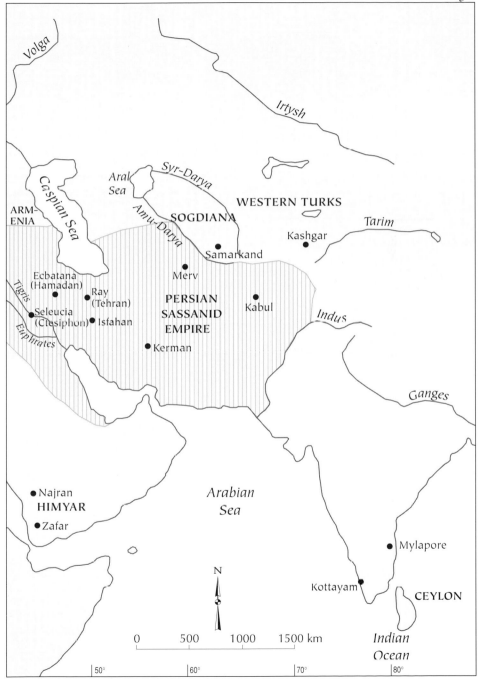

Volga

Irtysh

Aral
Sea

Syr-Darya

WESTERN TURKS

Caspian Sea

Amu-Darya

SOGDIANA

Tarim

ARM-
ENIA

Kashgar

Samarkand

Ecbatana
(Hamadan)

Merv

Ray
(Tehran)

PERSIAN
SASSANID
EMPIRE

Kabul

Indus

Tigris

Seleucia
(Ctesiphon)

Isfahan

Euphrates

Kerman

Ganges

Najran

HIMYAR

Arabian
Sea

Zafar

Mylapore

N

Kottayam

CEYLON

0   500   1000   1500 km

Indian
Ocean

50°   60°   70°   80°

Extent of the Byzantine and the Sassanid Empires

it came from certain caterpillars but that these were impossible to obtain alive. However it was easy to produce them for the "grains" or eggs of these worms were produced in large numbers. Long after they were laid it was possible to cover the eggs with dung, and after being heated for a sufficient amount of time the worms would hatch. They were prepared to bring Justinian the eggs that would produce these caterpillars. The idea was, obviously, to export them secretly from Serindia. Having questioned the two men for a long time, the Byzantine emperor entrusted them with this mission, promising them great rewards, and the two travellers left. They returned in 553 or 554, carrying, as they had pledged, silkworm eggs, which they had managed to keep in good condition through the method described above. Then they bred the caterpillars, feeding them on mulberry leaves, and the silkworms went through their normal cycle. Thus, according to Procopius, did sericulture begin in Byzantium.

> *The introduction of the silkworm into the Byzantine Empire did not lead to an immediate revolution in trade. Justinian's policy of economic interventionism was just one of the main causes of this stagnation: he turned the production of cocoons into an imperial monopoly, confined to his personal workshops, and thus stifled the Byzantine silk industry, still obliged to look to foreign imports of raw material.*

In Theophanus' version, it was a Persian who returned from the Seres, successfully concealing the silkworm eggs in a hollow staff, according to some, or in a coffer, according to others. In either case, they were hidden and ready to hatch.

How the monks were rewarded, if indeed they were monks, is not told. If they were Nestorians, why would they have favoured thus an empire which did not recognize Nestorianism? Were they on a political mission from an enemy of the Persians?*[86] Or were they working on their own?

The introduction of the silkworm into the Byzantine Empire did not lead to an immediate revolution in trade. Justinian's policy of economic interventionism was just one of the main causes of this stagnation: he turned the production of cocoons into an imperial monopoly, confined to his personal workshops, and thus stifled the Byzantine silk industry, still obliged to look to foreign imports of raw material.

MOHAMMED

The Byzantine weavers were always to depend on imported silk thread, which did not prevent them from producing superb silks during the entire Middle Ages. But sericulture proper, the cultivation of the mulberry tree and the breeding of silkworms, was developed only later by the Muslim rulers and spread throughout their territories. In 571, according to one tradition, and before 579 according to others, Mohammed, founder of a new monotheistic religion, was born in Arabia, in a tribe which specialized in international trade. This religion was soon to win over not only many souls, but a large number of thrones. In 651, the Sassanian dynasty was overthrown by the Arab Muslim conqueror, and Persia was now a caliphate. Sericulture was developed south of the Caspian, in Azerbaijan and in Armenia, and then, as the Muslim conquests spread, in Syria. In 741, the Syrian troops of the Emir of Barbary, which had arrived in Spain from Africa to crush a rebellion against Arab dominion there, introduced sericulture and silk weaving to Almeria. In the 9th century, the Arabs set themselves up in Sicily and introduced sericulture in Palermo. In the 11th century, Sicily once again passed into Christian hands via the Norman conquests, and under King Roger of Sicily sericulture and silk techniques were

* According to N. Tajadod, the two monks came from Ceylon, lived in China, and presented themselves to the Nestorian Catholicos in Persia, who at the time had been exiled in the mountains of Azerbaijan by the Persian government, during a phase of Christian persecution. The monks produced a small coffer full of wriggling silkworms, and explained that they had with them a chest-full of silkworm eggs which they had managed to export clandestinely from China, and which they were prepared to sell to the highest bidder, such as the Sassanian sovereign. The Catholicos, as revenge against the king of Persia for persecuting Christians, advised them instead to go and propose their goods to the court in Constantinople. Unfortunately, N. Tajadod, in this chapter as in the rest of his book, does not give any reference or indication of his sources.

transmitted to Venice. From Italy, in the 14th century, the popes introduced the mulberry tree and silk weaving to the Avignon region, in the south of France. Silkworms were then bred at different periods in various areas of France. Louis XI and Henry IV showed some interest in sericulture, but it was François I who brought in Italian specialists, and in 1545 founded the Fabrique de Lyon around which the production of cocoons developed. The breeding of the silkworm, which had spread either through coercion, trickery or by peaceful means, took some thousand years to reach France after having crossed the western frontier of China.

Chapter Twelve

Byzantium, Persia, the Turks and the Sogdians

From the beginning of his reign, Emperor Justinian had been seeking to circumvent the obstacles created by Persian control not only of the land route towards Central Asia, but also of certain ports on the sea routes to the Far East. The Byzantines were hoping not so much to buy silk directly from the Seres as to find cheaper and less hostile suppliers than the Persians.

In order to loosen this Persian net, the Byzantine government decided upon a diplomatic approach with the Christian kingdoms to the north of the Persians and on the Red Sea.

The Kingdom of Ethiopia, on the African coast of the Red Sea, which had been Christian since the 4th century, had, in 523, a king strongly dedicated to the defence of his fellow Christians. Previously, Ethiopia had imposed a Christian king of its own choice on the kingdom of Himyar, located opposite it, on the Arabic coast of the Red Sea, a kingdom which included Yemen and beyond. However, King Yusuf, or Joseph, the son and successor of that Christian king, had begun persecuting Christians in his kingdom.

Yemen was not an entirely Christian kingdom, but did have a large Christian community. Evangelization had begun there in 340, when an envoy of the Roman Empire, Theophilos the Indian, had arrived, with a gift of two hundred Cappadocian horses, requesting the king of Himyar's permission to build churches in his kingdom, for the Christians who lived there. The aim was at the same time to extend Roman influence in southern Arabia, to counter that of Shapur II in Mesopotamia and the Persian Gulf.[87] But the conversion of the Himyarites to Christianity had to contend with a very influential and proselytizing Judaism, as well as indigenous beliefs. Although Christianity had begun to spread in the kingdom in the 4th century or at the beginning of the 5th, it seems that Yemen turned massively to Judaism after the conversion of one of its kings, at the end of the 4th century. Some of its subsequent kings were Christians, but most of them were Jewish, although they never imposed a state religion.

King Joseph, who reigned from 522, broke with this policy, and opted solely for Judaism; he began persecuting Christians, as much through religious conviction as in the hope of loosening the Ethiopian hold over the country and avoiding pressure from Byzantium. In 523, he attacked and captured the town of Najrân, the stronghold of the Himyarite Christians and a crossroads on the caravan routes, burnt the church and massacred the nobles, clergy and nuns who refused to convert to Judaism. Previously, he had massacred the Ethiopians living in the Himyarite capital, Zafar, and turned the Christian church into a synagogue. These events naturally figure in Christian martyrology.

In 524, Kaleb, the king of Ethiopia, landed with his troops in southern Arabia, took Zafar, defeated the Himyarites, rebuilt the churches, and set a Christian king upon the throne. The hold of Ethiopia over Himyar was to last about forty years.

Ethiopia and Yemen controlled all comings and goings of ships in the Red Sea from the east; the only other route was through the Persian Gulf, controlled by Persia. With Christian kingdoms in Ethiopia and Yemen (Himyar), the Christian Byzantine Empire could hope to set up political and commercial alliances to divert to the Red Sea and the Byzantine ports part of the trade flow monopolized by the Persians. The Ethiopians would profit from the silk bought directly from the Indians, as would Byzantium, by paying a lower price for it than from the Persians, and, according to Roman historian, Procopius, being no longer compelled to pay in metal coins.

Emperor Justinian sent his ambassador Julianus to Ethiopia and Himyar, requesting, in the name of their common religion, that the two sovereigns join him against the Persians. The embassy failed, as the king of Himyar did not feel strong enough to confront Persia. The Ethiopians could not buy silk directly from the Indians, as the Persian merchants not only effectively controlled the ports where the Indian ships made their first stopover, but were also in the habit of buying by the shipload. In those circumstances, there was little choice but to continue buying silk from Persian merchants, mainly in the customs port of Nisibis (Nisibin, present-day Nusaybin, on the Khabur River, a tributary on the left bank of the Euphrates, on the frontier between modern Turkey and Syria), which for a long time was the sole supply point. Later, trade was also possible at Callinica (possibly Rakka, or Ar Raqqah, located in present-day Syria, on the left bank of the Euphrates), and at Artaxa (Artachat, on the left bank of the Araxes, in modern Armenia, just south of Erevan).

It was in these towns that goods from Central Asia and beyond arrived after crossing Persia by land; Indian products or goods arriving in the ports of the north-western coast of India were transported by land as far as Afghanistan from where they reached Central Asia and Persia. Similarly, goods arriving by boat from India via the Persian Gulf, or which were produced in the countries on the Persian Gulf, arrived via Persia in these same customs towns. Persia, which was in a phase of great military and economic power, therefore monopolized a good proportion of the land and sea transport. Its merchants and ships travelled everywhere, controlling certain ports in India and even in Ceylon, as well as those in the Persian Gulf. As we have seen, Persia was sufficiently feared by the kingdoms around the Red Sea to have eliminated all competition for goods coming from India. Thus, their western neighbours had no choice but to turn to the Persian middlemen to buy their silks and silk thread, cotton muslins, pepper, spices, aromatic plants and perfume.

Persia, which was in a phase of great military and economic power, ... monopolized a good proportion of the land and sea transport. Its merchants and ships travelled everywhere, controlling certain ports in India and even in Ceylon, as well as those in the Persian Gulf.

Persian industry itself produced many beautiful silks, glassware, ceramics and other fine goods, but the silk monopoly was by far the most important. Just as in the Byzantine Empire, this trade was tightly controlled and regulated by the state, which profited greatly from the imposition of heavy and multiple taxes on it. The trade of raw silk was a state monopoly. The Persian silk industry was also a major buyer of silk thread which was woven into very fine cloth, with easily recognizable motifs and styles; from fragments found in archaeological sites in many Western countries as well as in Central Asia, one can trace the spread of the textile.

Much more is known about the art of Persian silk weaving in the middle of the 6th century than about the production of cocoons. We know that the king of Persia had kidnapped a number of weavers in Syria and sent them to Iran. But authors disagree about the breeding of silkworms. If this already existed in some areas, the production was probably nothing like sufficient for the needs of Persian weavers. They must have relied heavily on silk from China and from Central Asia, since sericulture had been known and introduced into Khotan about a century and a half earlier, and from there must have spread to Serindia, from where the Nestorian monks apparently brought back silkworm eggs.

In 562, after decades of war, the sovereigns of the two great empires, Justinian and Khosroes, signed a treaty of "perpetual peace" (which did not last very long), in which clauses on trade occupied a prominent place. Nisibis and another customs town were opened to the Byzantines, and the trade of raw silk was permitted. There appeared to be no avoiding Persia.

THE TURKS

Despite Christian missionary work carried out with Byzantine support beyond the Caucasus among the Huns, the baptism of a Hunnish prince, and good relations with the Hephtalite Huns, the Byzantine government had been unable until then to make good use of a religious community to conclude material alliances with these people. Yet, this was a promising northern route to bypass the Persian monopoly. One occasion did present itself after a change in the political and ethnic map of Asia, with the arrival of a new wave of conquerors, the Turks. Descendants of populations which had settled much earlier in the Altai, the Türküt, or Tujue to the Chinese, whom we call Turks, swept across Asia from east to west. In 552, they split into Western and Eastern Turks, the former occupying Turkestan. Istemi, or Dizabul, the head of the Western Turks, first of all allied himself with the armies of the Persian King Khosroes, and defeated the Hephtalites in 565. The Hephtalite kingdom disappeared. The Sogdians, vassals of the Hephtalites for a hundred years, passed under the domination of Dizabul. Under one master and then another, these Sogdians had continued to develop their civilization, and to carry out their commercial activities. It was through the silk trade that they became known to the Byzantines. Their story is told us by a 6th century writer, Menander Protector.[88]

The Sogdians were merchants and caravaneers who traded in all the oases along the Silk Road, and even set up branches in China. They would have liked permission to do so in Persian territory too, and to sell there the silks they had bought elsewhere; they appear even to have sought, if the text has been correctly interpreted, to be allowed to cross Persia to reach Byzantium. They asked their new masters, the Turks, allies of the Persians (an alliance sealed by the marriage of Dizabul to the daughter of Khosroes), for permission to approach the Persian sovereign.

The Persians did not want to welcome foreign merchants in their land, and even less to allow the Turks or their allies to infiltrate their territory, and to spy on the country. This was an unwavering feature of their policy. When the embassy from Sogdiana, led by a high official called Maniah, arrived with a certain quantity of silk, requesting access to and passage through Persia, King Khosroes delayed giving his answer. Then, on the advice of his counsellors, he bought all the silk from the Sogdians, and burnt it before them to show that what they had brought was of no interest to Persia.

THE SOGDIANS

The Sogdians returned home and reported these events to Dizabul. The latter, who very much wanted to set up an agreement with Khosroes, sent another embassy. This time, the king poisoned several of its members, letting it be known that they had been victims of an epidemic, frequent in Iran. But Dizabul was not taken in, and was understandably filled with hatred.

Maniah suggested to the Turkish khan to seek out the friendship of Byzantium, by sending an embassy which he was prepared to lead. It was, of course, necessary to take the route through the Caucasus, passing north of the

Caspian Sea, to avoid Persia. The Turkish embassy reached Byzantium in 568–569, bearing credentials and an important gift of silk for Emperor Justinian II. The emperor welcomed them very graciously, and enquired about the Turkish kingdom (he seemed not to have heard of the disappearance of the Hephtalite kingdom). The Turkish ruler proposed an alliance treaty and promised, for his part, to attack the Persians: it was in their common interest to resist Persian power and its monopoly on the silk trade. Justinian sent a return embassy to accompany the Turkish mission home.* It was led by Zemarchus, prefect of the Oriental cities, and was greeted in magnificent fashion by Dizabul. Silk tents were set up, with an abundance of gold and silver, and all this somewhere in the Altai, which greatly astonished the Byzantine envoys who did not expect to see such luxury among the "barbarians". Feasts and celebrations followed, with reciprocal presentations of gifts, and, in short, a treaty of alliance and trade was agreed upon: the Byzantines would buy silk directly from the Turks or from their vassals, the Sogdians. Zemarchus and his embassy were in turn escorted back to Byzantium by another Turkish delegation. They returned, as far as we can make out from the text, along the shores of the Aral Sea, then passed to the north of the Caspian, crossing the Emba, Ural and Volga rivers, and through the land of the Volga Bulgars. Zemarchus then learned that 20,000 Persians were waiting to ambush them in the woods along the Kuban River, north of the Caucasus. He tricked the Persians by sending them off on a false trail, thus avoiding the trap, and the travellers carried on to Trabzon, and from there finally reached Byzantium.

The alliance lasted ten years, until the death of Khan Dizabul. Several exchanges of embassies occurred during this period, between 569 and 576, always following the route north of the Caucasus, a route which had always existed but which was difficult and perilous because of the physical obstacles along it:

* If one looks at the much later account by Theophanus of Byzantium, one reads, rather surprisingly, just after the story of the arrival at the Byzantine court of the monks carrying silkworm seeds, that "later, Emperor Justinian taught the Turks how [these worms] were born and worked; they were very surprised, as the Turks then occupied the markets and ports of the Seres which previously had belonged to the Persians." This episode could not have taken place before the stay of the Turkish embassy in Constantinople. It is not possible that at this point the Sogdians did not know of sericulture! But in that case, which Turks and which Seres is Theophanus writing about?

high mountains, deserts, wide rivers and the climate. Despite this, it was to remain much used during the following centuries.

The 6th century is said to be the peak of the Sogdian civilization. In their own native territory, between the Amu-Darya and Syr-Darya rivers, as well as slightly further west according to the period, they developed a culture known to us through its superb artistic remains. More than any other, this trading and travelling people played the role of middleman in the transfer of goods, techniques and religious beliefs across continental Asia. They maintained this role, even when they were no longer independent, and while dominated by the Hephtalites or the Turks. Some of them remained in their land of origin, others emigrated and formed colonies in the oases of Central Asia, as far as China. When we talk of the Sogdians, we are referring either to the Sogdians in Sogdiana itself, or to their diaspora, regardless of the reasons which led to their emigration.

They appear at the forefront of the silk trade with their western neighbours, Persia and Byzantium, striving to improve business and opening up markets. The name of the envoy who guided the embassies to these two countries, Maniah, has led some to conclude that he was Manichaean, and others that he was a Buddhist.[89] Sogdiana was indeed a multi-religious state. Fundamentally, it was Mazdaian (Zoroastrian), like Persia of which it had been a satrapy for a long time, but it also included a large number of Buddhists, Nestorian Christians and Manichaeans. Several new religions, particularly the great monotheistic ones,

> *Sogdiana was indeed a multi-religious state. Fundamentally, it was Mazdaian (Zoroastrian), like Persia of which it had been a satrapy for a long time, but it also included a large number of Buddhists, Nestorian Christians and Manichaeans. Several new religions, particularly the great monotheistic ones, were founded at this period, and were spreading right across Asia and Europe, as far as the northern and eastern coasts of Africa.*

were founded at this period, and were spreading right across Asia and Europe, as far as the northern and eastern coasts of Africa. At the same time, another phenomenon occurs, that of successive waves of conquering migrations, of Turkish or Mongol peoples jostling one another out of the inexhaustible reservoir of Eastern Asia. These conquerors, mainly nomadic people with a simple material culture, would give up their own religions in large numbers to adopt those of the conquered nation, whereas the opposite occurred during the Muslim conquest. In the first centuries of the Christian era, the Huns, the Goths and the Turks became Buddhists, Nestorian or Aryan Christians and Manichaeans. In the 9th century, the Turkish kingdom of the Uighurs became the only kingdom of which Manichaeism was ever the official religion. Later, the Turkish kingdoms would turn to Islam. Genghis Khan and his descendants would become Buddhists, Muslims and Nestorians. As for the original religions of the Turkish Mongol people, religions which we sometimes call shamanistic out of convenience, very little is known about them as they have left no written texts. They were supplanted or diluted by the new religions, and little by little lost their priests and their faithful. Today only oral traditions remain, in an impoverished popular form, a few material remains such as tombs or engraved stones, and a few residual customs. But these are not enough to tell us about the form they took when the cavalry of Attila the Hun stood before Paris, or when the Toba Turks plundered the Chinese capital, letting their horses out to pasture in the imperial gardens, before founding the Wei dynasty, and adopting Buddhism.

Before the Muslim conquest which eliminated Buddhism and Manichaeism from all the states of Central Asia, this region had been a crossroads where these religions lived freely side by side.

The Sogdians are said to have contributed much to the eastward spread of Manichaeism. The founder of this religion, Mani, a Persian born in Babylonia in 216, preached, from 240 on, a new doctrine of salvation in which the dualistic concepts of Mazdaism mingled with the Jewish and Christian beliefs which had been those of a religious community to which Mani had belonged, 20 years earlier, in Persia itself. It was known as the Church of Light, the doctrine of the Two Principles, and its followers considered Mani the last heavenly messenger, the final successor to Zoroaster, Buddha and Jesus, the seal of the prophets.

This was a universal religion, a religion of the book, the only one of the revealed faiths of which the founder himself wrote down the revelations and its doctrine. It was also a religion of missions and proselytism. Its doctrine was intransigent, pessimistic, austere, one in which the dualism between matter and spirit led to disregard for the former, to the point of refusing to have children, of treating an illness, or advocating suicide by inanition; this at least is the dark picture drawn by Christian authors, who opposed it for centuries. As surprising as it may seem, this doctrine spread very rapidly both east and west, during Mani's lifetime and after his death (pressurized by the Mazdaian clergy, the king of Persia, Bahram I, had him executed in 274 or 277).

In a burst of missionary zeal Manichaeism reached Egypt in the 3rd century and Roman North Africa at the end of the 4th century (we know that St Augustine, Bishop of Hippone, in modern Algeria, had embraced this doctrine in his youth before fighting it vigorously). It then spread across half of Europe, where it was regularly outlawed and persecuted as a heresy, but reappeared periodically in such movements as that of the Bogomils and the Cathars. The latter became the targets of the Albigensian crusades of the 13th century, during the reign of the French king Louis VIII. In the East, Mani had preached as far as the frontiers of India. In the Persian Empire itself, Manichaeism survived, with phases of persecution, under the Sassanids and then the caliphs, until the end of the 10th century. It was driven out of the Byzantine Empire in the 7th century. But Manichaeism also had a missionary dynamism which was independent of its ordeals; during one of these zealous periods, it reached Sogdiana, China and then the Uighur kingdom, to be driven out once again in the middle of the 9th century. Small groups were able to survive, more or less clandestinely, throughout Central Asia and in China, for several centuries more.

The Sogdians spoke an East-Iranian language, and wrote using the Aramaic script. Sogdian became the international language of Central Asia, thus reinforcing the role of the Sogdians as spreaders of culture. This role became even more important during the Tang dynasty. The sites of Qotcho, near Turfan, and Dunhuang have revealed a large number of manuscripts written in Sogdian, and the Aramaic script was to serve as the basis for the creation of new alphabets for writing Uighur and Mongol.

Sogdiana, the ancient Kangju of the Chinese, the land of canals, with its capital at Samarkand (Marakanda, Afrasiab), passed in the 6th century under the domination of a Turkish khan. The Turks essentially levied taxes, but they also encouraged commercial activities among their vassals, contributing to the safety of travellers. Thus, the peripatetic Sogdians were described by foreign historians as a nation of merchants, not warriors. According to religious texts found at Dunhuang, they would appear to be above all Buddhists, Manichaeans or Nestorians. But the remains in Sogdiana itself—murals, stone or wood sculpture, funerary caskets—suggest a society of horsemen and a people living according to the religious practices of Zoroastrianism. The murals of the Palace at Penjikent, near Samarkand, show scenes of feasts and tournaments, of iron-clad horsemen and archers. They have narrow faces, long fine noses, black moustaches with, occasionally, black beards and black, almond-shaped eyes. Other frescoes show us a local divinity, that of the Amu-Darya, Anahita, the goddess of water and fertility, holding a pomegranate in her hand; or a young dead prince, solemnly mourned in a palace, a practice reminiscent of the Zoroastrian cult celebrated in an annual rite of a ceaselessly dying and reborn divinity. It is again Zoroastrianism which is denoted by the large ossuaries filled with rectangular, ceramic or sometimes alabaster, four-footed funerary urns, in which the bones of the dead were placed once all the flesh had been picked off by animals and birds of prey. These urns have been found in their hundreds in the ruins of Sogdiana. Penjikent, Varahch near Bukhara, Maymurg, Balalyk-Tepe in the Surkhan-Darya Valley, Afrasiab, Tali-Barzu, Kafyr-Kala and Ak-Tepe have all left traces of this civilization.

Western sources ignore the Sogdians completely, while the Chinese dynastic histories continue to describe the land of Kang: the *Sui shu*, or *History of the Sui Dynasty* (589–620), written during the following dynasty, describes, in chapter 83, a powerful state, which had annexed seven or eight of its neighbours, with a code of law and marriage and funerary customs similar to those of the Turks, and where sacrifices were offered to the ancestors. And yet the chronicler states that they were Buddhist. They were skilled merchants, and many foreigners travelled to their land to trade; their ruler even sought to attract them. They used the same writing system as the Turks. Their eyes were sunken, they had large noses and wore thick beards. They played different sorts of drums, lutes, five-stringed guitars and flutes. The climate in their country was warm, largely suitable for the cultivation of cereals; they enjoyed horticulture, grew fruit trees and vines—making a wine which aged well—and bred horses, camels and donkeys. They produced gold, sal ammoniac, various incenses, white pearls, deer hide and musk, silks and cloth. During the Daye reign period of the Sui dynasty (605–617) they sent a mission for the first time to the Chinese court bringing local products as tribute.

Archaeological remains have revealed the spread of Sogdian artefacts throughout Central Asia, including carved wood decorated with vine leaves and bunches of grapes, precious gold and silver tableware, wool carpets and armour of chain mail (soldiers wearing this armour are represented on many Central Asian and Iranian paintings). Whether they had learnt this technique from the Chinese, the Persians or the Tibetans, or whether they had invented it themselves is unclear, but this Sogdian chain mail remained much sought-after for several centuries. The Sogdians had known for a long time how to make glass, and are said to have transmitted to the Chinese the techniques of wine-making.

COSMAS THE MONK

One noteworthy product of the land of Kang mentioned in the *History of the Sui* is musk-deer hide. Musk was not a novelty to the Chinese, who had known of it for a long time, but it was not until the 6th century, probably, that musk appeared in Europe. One may wonder why of all the fragrant and medicinal substances which were exported from Western or Middle Eastern countries to Asia and vice versa, musk was known so late in the West. Perhaps there has been some misunderstanding related to the vocabulary used for it.

The first firm mention of musk in a Western source appears to be in the *Christian Topography* of Cosmas the Monk, or Cosmas Indicopleustes, that is "one who has travelled in India", a Greek merchant from Alexandria who followed the maritime route in the 6th century, visited India in person, and brought back much detailed information about Ceylon, China and Ethiopia.

On his return to Europe, he became a monk in the Sinai and wrote, around 545, under Justinian, an account of his travels. Both Greek and Latin versions of it exist. This account was much read in Europe and later in Russia (where some very beautiful manuscripts of it exist, translated into Old Slavonic from the Greek).[90] In the chapter on India and Ceylon, he describes, surprisingly, the musk deer, calling it by its Indian name: "The musk is a small animal, and in that country they call it 'kastury'. They hunt it, killing it with arrows, and take from it a mass of blood which it has near the navel, after having tied it. It is this part of the animal which smells nice, and this blood is what we call musk; the rest of the body is discarded as useless." In the Greek text, the word for "musk" is *moschos*.

The Sanskrit name for musk, and the modern Nepalese word is *kasturi*; in Nepalese, a related word, *kasturo*, designates the musk deer. Nepal, until 1973 (when the musk deer was declared a protected species and hunting was prohibited in many countries), was a large exporter of musk, mainly to Japan, the biggest customer in modern times. In the wooded regions of the Himalaya and of Tibet, the population of musk deer was very large until the 17th century, and it is surprising that musk had not reached the ports trading with the West before the 6th century. Nevertheless, for climatic reasons—this product spoils easily during a long sea trip—musk from Tibet, the Kingdom of Women, and Sogdiana, mentioned in the old Chinese texts, could have reached at a much earlier date the countries which would later become big buyers of it along the land route.

Musk cannot be identified among the aromatic or medicinal substances mentioned by the Greek and Latin classical authors: neither Pliny, nor the *Periplus*, nor the Greek physician Dioscorides in the 1st century of the Christian era, describe anything which could be equated with musk. Although the word *muscus* in Latin and *moschos* in Greek appear in these texts, they designate something else (the word existed but was clearly being used for a plant product, a sort of tree lichen as well as for some marine product). It is possible that St Jerome was referring to a musk-bearing animal in the letters in which he criticizes the use of perfume: he writes, in a letter to the virgin Principia, concerning the morals of the pagan widows which Christian widows must not adopt: *"Illae enim solent... fragrare musco mure"*, "they are wont to scent themselves with mouse musk". Furthermore, in a letter to Demetrias, still on the subject of what women should not do, he uses the expression *peregrini muris olentes pelliculas*, the "fragrant skins of the foreign mouse".[91] What exactly is this fragrant mouse whose skins come from abroad? It is tempting, in the absence of such mice in other texts, to think of it as a musk gland, sold in its natural state, still containing the musk: a small purse-like bag covered in hair, giving off a powerful smell, and looking somewhat like a mouse.

Even if musk was not completely unknown as a perfume in the 4th century, it was however not used in the Byzantine world as a medicine (which was its most common use in the East) before Cosmas the Greek.

But what is musk? It is the secretion from a gland of a small male deer, *Moschus moschiferus* (the term *muscus* was replaced at some point by the term *moschus*, linked to the Greek *moschos*, which may be derived from the Persian word for this substance), the size of a young roe deer, which lives in the wooded hills of Eastern Asia: the Himalaya, Tibet, Qinghai, Sichuan, North Vietnam, the Altai, Korea, Manchuria and Siberia. It is a graceful little animal with a brownish, sometimes blackish coat, and with fine legs and muzzle. It has two long white teeth, like small tusks, curving downwards, protruding from the upper jaw. It lives alone or in small groups, up to an altitude of 4,000 metres (12,000 feet), and is quite at home in the steepest areas, fearing neither snow nor the harsh winters. It feeds on grass, leaves from trees and bushes, moss and lichen. Its musk is highly valued depending upon its smell, which varies according to its local diet: the musk from Tibet and North Vietnam is much less esteemed than that from Siberia.

The musk is produced in an excrescence, or sac, located beneath the skin of the abdomen, behind the navel. The sac is about six centimetres long and three centimetres wide, coated with glands which exude a thick and oily substance, with a pungent smell, and of various colours (yellowish, browny-red, or almost black), which is pure musk. This sac, which weighs about thirty grams, is an organ related to sexual activity. The smell is so strong and lasting that only tiny amounts of the product are used at a time. To obtain the sac, the animal is hunted down and killed (legendary tales are told of the musk sac falling to the ground after the male rubs itself against a rock when the sac feels overfull). It has been hunted in all sorts of ways—with bows and arrows, dogs, nets, decoys and snares—even in Buddhist countries. Although today it is an endangered species, it must certainly have been abundant in the past, particularly when the very steep regions which it is so partial to supported only a small human population.

> *Tibetan musk is mentioned among the scents which the blessed will breathe in Heaven, alongside Persian rose, basil from Samarkand, citron from Tapurastan, violets from Isfahan, saffron from Qom, water lilies from Shervan, aloes nadd from India and amber from Sikhr.*

In China itself, musk had been known since ancient times, but probably more as a medicine than for its scent. One of the main characteristics of the musk deer, according to ancient Chinese dictionaries, was its non-fear of snakes. Indeed, as the deer would feed on snakes, the musk was thought to be an antidote to snake venom. In early medicine, both in the West and the East, the omnipresence of snakes led to a large number of medicines listed as antidotes, either to snake venom, or to all animal venoms (the Greek physicians perfected this under the name of theriac). This was the main virtue of the musk deer, *shexiang* in Chinese, or "*she* scent", a character written with the key for "deer" and which exclusively designates the musk deer. The Chinese Treasury received musk as tax or tribute from several provinces and countries: many districts from the provinces of Shaanxi, Shanxi, Gansu, Henan, Hubei and Sichuan supplied it, as did Xinjiang, Tibet, Qinghai, North Vietnam and Mongolia, as well, apparently, as Sogdiana.

Musk must have been known in Persia in the 6th century, during the reign of Khosroes II, at least as a perfume. Aly Mazaheri quotes a Sassanian text from the period, in Pahlavi, in which Tibetan musk is mentioned among the scents which the blessed will breathe in Heaven, alongside Persian rose, basil from Samarkand, citron from Tapurastan, violets from Isfahan, saffron from Qom, water lilies from Shervan, aloes *nadd* from India and amber from Sikhr.[92] It seems also to have had a ritual use, as Zoroastrians rub it into their beards and eyebrows during the celebration of their cult of Ahura Mazda.[93] The Manichaeans used it in a compound perfume for Mani, made from aloes wood, amber, water lilies and Tibetan musk.[94]

As a drug, the properties of musk have been known for a long time and

> *Apart from its reputation against snake venom, musk was used as a stimulant, a cardiac tonic, an antispasmodic, an aphrodisiac and an aid against melancholy. It was said to dissipate harmful influences, spirits and demons, noxious miasmas, to heal wounds and ward off nightmares.*

were used in Chinese medicine, and perhaps just as early on in Indian medicine. Only much later and to a lesser extent did Greek medicine and its European descendants adopt it. Apart from its reputation against snake venom, musk was used as a stimulant, a cardiac tonic, an antispasmodic, an aphrodisiac and an aid against melancholy. It was said to dissipate harmful influences, spirits and demons, noxious miasmas, to heal wounds and ward off nightmares.[95]

The musk deer is not the only curious animal which Cosmas mentions in India. He also talks about the *rinokeros*, which needs no translation, the *taurelafos* or bull-deer, the *kamelopardalis* or giraffe, the *monokeros* or unicorn—which he admits not to have seen himself—a sea calf, the dolphin and the tortoise, the last three of which are well known. He also mentions a new animal, an *agrioboous* or wild bull, which is probably a yak, as the author adds various details (assuming the text we have has not been interpolated subsequently) which are always applied to yaks, such as the use of its tail in India and other places as an emblem of power. As the yak lives at high altitude and in a very particular zone running northwards from the Himalaya, it is likely that Cosmas never actually saw one, but he may have seen its very long, fine tail hair, often shining white, attached to the end of an ornate baton, which was well-known in India. Yak-tail hair has been exported for centuries from the Himalayan countries and Tibet.

The *Christian Topography* also reveals the commercial importance at this period of the island of Ceylon, "which the Indians named Sielediba and the Greeks Taprobane and which was the most fabulous port of the whole of the Indes". This is once again the celebrated island of the Chinese pilgrim Faxian, more than ever a commercial crossroads between both ends of the world, and more than ever the source of the most highly prized stones. Its wealth in rubies and other gems (which we call zircons and aquamarines today) attracted merchants from the world over: ships arrived mainly from India and Ethiopia as well as from China. Faxian, at the beginning of the 5th century, had met Chinese merchants there. In the middle of the 6th century, Chinese boats came regularly and in large numbers to trade in the main port of the island (they seem not to have sailed further west). The islanders, according to Cosmas, traded silks, aloes wood, cloves and clove wood, as well as sandalwood, with the Chinese. They sent their goods as far as Persia, Omiritis, Himyar and Ethiopia (to the port of Aduly). Naturally, they was a very active trade with the large ports of peninsular India: Malê where pepper came from (Cosmas mentions five main pepper ports in India), while Sindu, the "gateway to India", must be located in the Indus estuary. "Calliana has a flourishing trade, as well as Sindu; there one can find musk, *castoreum* and *spica nardi*"; the musk and nard came from the Himalayan region, if not from further afield. From this one can infer that these products must have reached the sea trade network, and there is no reason why they should not have spread to all the places where this network extended.

> *Cosmas mentions a "pagan" temple, "located on a hill where there is a ruby shaped like a pine cone of an incalculable value. When the sun shines on it, it lets off a great fire which dazzles and amazes one."*

Cosmas hardly mentions pearl fishing in Ceylon, which had perhaps become less important by his time. On the other hand, he does mention a "pagan" temple, "located on a hill where there is a ruby shaped like a pine cone of an incalculable value. When the sun shines on it, it lets off a great fire which dazzles and amazes one." This extraordinary ruby will reappear later in the account of Marco Polo's travels.

Cosmas calls China "the land of Chin", at the end of the inhabited world, beyond which there is nothing to the East but sea, where one does not sail. "If one stretched a rope from Chin to Greece, it would pass through the centre of the world." The world vision of this Christian from Alexandria is based largely on Biblical geography, particularly in his reference to the four rivers of Paradise, and the lands of the Red Sea and India. Concretely, Cosmas knew of the existence of the Hephtalite Huns, he provides evaluations of distances, and was convinced that the silk which came from the Far East arrived much faster in Persia along the land caravans routes than by the sea route. This is the reason why, he writes, Persia has such an abundance of silk. There is no doubt that the sea journey was much more dangerous than the land route, given the ships of the period. The various accounts of ancient journeys tell of many more deaths caused by shipwrecks than land disasters.

There is no doubt that the sea journey was much more dangerous than the land route, given the ships of the period. The various accounts of ancient journeys tell of many more deaths caused by shipwrecks than land disasters.

In his discussion of a king of Ceylon, Cosmas mentions what happened to a (Greek?) merchant, Sopater, who had lived about 35 years before the time of writing, which means he must have been alive around 510 AD. He arrived in Ceylon from Aduly, at the same time as an ambassador sent by the Persian ruler; the king greeted them together and questioned each of them about their own land. He wanted to know which of the two was the more powerful. Sopater, who carried Roman gold coins with him, suggested that the king compare the sovereigns' portraits. The gold coins were produced, bearing the image of the prince, of good quality gold and well cast: the merchants, says Cosmas, always choose the best coins to take to foreign lands. The Persian coinage was not of gold but of silver, and was not so well manufactured. The king of Ceylon concluded that the Romans were superior and more powerful and treated Sopater with great honour.

The *Christian Topography* devotes long passages to Ethiopia, with its port of Aduly and its capital, Axum. In its hinterland, near the source of the Nile (where it was thought to be located at the time) gold was mined, which the merchants and agents of the king of Ethiopia came to buy using the system of silent barter which has already been mentioned in other parts of the world. Against this gold they exchanged oxen, iron and salt. Ethiopia, and the kingdom of Himyar opposite it, were both producers of incense. Incense, condemned as an idolatrous custom by the Christian communities in the first centuries, was introduced in the 5th and 6th centuries into liturgical practice, and the need for incense in the West led to a new boom in this trade,[96] which remained prosperous until the first half of the 20th century.

When Faxian was in Ceylon he was interested in Buddhism. Cosmas, on the other hand, was little concerned with this entirely "pagan" population although he does note the existence of a church "for the Persian Christians who frequently visit it. It is served by a priest and a deacon who received the holy orders in Persia. They have the full ecclesiastical liturgy." No doubt these Persian Christians were Nestorians. At the time of Cosmas, the patriarch who consecrated all the bishops of Asia had his see at Ctesiphon, and covered the island of Socotra as well as the bishopric of southern India. Nestorian crosses have been found in Ceylon.[97] Furthermore, Cosmas mentions the presence at Calliana of a bishop ordained in Persia.[98]

JUDAS THOMAS

When did the first Christian communities form in southern India? At present, what we have is a mixture of legendary traditions and material evidence, but this question has recently been revived among historians. At the root of it is the *Acts of Thomas*, an apocryphal text written in Syria in the 3rd century, at Edessus, one of the larger centres from which Christian missionaries went forth. Translated into Greek, then into Latin, this text was very widespread in the 6th century. According to this tradition, after Pentecost the apostles divided among themselves (by drawing lots) the areas where they would go to preach and to which they would devote their lives; India fell to Judas Thomas, also

known as Didymus, the Twin. He did not want to go, but the Lord himself
appeared before him and ordered him to go, making him board ship in the
following manner: a merchant from India, named Abbanes, was at that time in
Jerusalem, where he had been sent by his sovereign, King Gondaphar
(Gondophares, Gundaphorus) on a mission to bring back a good carpenter. As
Thomas was a carpenter, the Lord sold him to the merchant as a slave, signing
a bill of sale with the following text: "I, Jesus, the son of Joseph the carpenter,
acknowledge that I have sold my slave, Judas by name, unto thee Abbanes, a
merchant of Gundaphorus, king of the Indians."[99] According to the legend,
this occurred in the year 50 or 52 AD. Abbanes took Thomas back to northern
India (to Taxila according to one interpretation); Thomas converted the king,
performed miracles, worked as a missionary, founded churches and then,
according to one version, left for southern India, landing at Cranganore,
preaching and converting in Kerala, and finally travelling to another kingdom,
in the region of Madras, where he died as a martyr in the year 72. He was buried
at Mylapore, near Madras. The cathedral Sao Thomé of Madras, built by the
Portuguese in the 16th century, is said to have been raised over his bones.

There are many variants and many marvellous episodes to the legend, still
very much alive, of the Christians of Saint Thomas. And there is also a trace of
it at the other end of the sea, far from Edessus: the ecclesiastical historian Gregory
of Tours, who died in 598, writes that in his time the tomb of Saint Thomas was
venerated somewhere in India. There exists another legend about the founding
of a Christian community by a different Thomas, a merchant this time, Thomas
Kinayi, sent to southern India by the Christian patriarch of Ctesiphon, with a
bishop and Mesopotamian families, in the middle of the 4th century.[100] His
mission was to revive a declining Christian community there.

Of the text of the *Acts of Thomas*, only the name of a King Gondaphar, who
reigned during the years in which the tradition places the mission of the apostle,
is borne out by material evidence: the name appears on coins found in
Afghanistan in the 19th century. But this is a meagre proof for an entire legend.
On the other hand, Nestorian stone crosses, dated to the 6th century, have
been found in two regions of southern India where there exists a very old oral

tradition of Christian origin: two granite crosses, one with an inscription in Pahlavi, were found at Kottayam, a town located near the coast of Malabar, just south of Cochin. These crosses are kept in the Church of Valya Palli. Another cross, also bearing an inscription in Pahlavi, was found by the Portuguese in 1545 near Mylapore, where Saint Thomas was said to have been martyred, and is kept in a chapel built on the site.

Is the presence of Saint Thomas in India to be compared to that of Saint Paul in Corsica? Are religious landmarks attributed to a great saint or a canonized king in the same tradition as the attribution of technical invention to a king or princess? The reality is perhaps that during the winds of persecution aimed at the Nestorians, the Christians, the Jews or the Manichaeans, persecutions which led to emigration, and during the great periods of missionary zeal, many other Thomases, many other Christian or Jewish communities, may have set off to settle in India, without any trace of them remaining today, until a vestige, a sign, a local tradition sets an inquisitive mind on a trail.

Chapter Thirteen
Tang China, Islam, the Turks and Tibet

C hinese history is a sort of cosmic pulsation in which, like a heart beating in systoles and diastoles, the territory of the Chinese Empire dilates and retracts, at times stretching from Manchuria to the Pamir, at others stopping at the Great Wall, sometimes dismembered into several kingdoms, or subdued by a conquering foreign power. Dynastic founders are figures of exception, men of war, reunifiers of the empire, sovereigns with grand designs. Then China grows in strength, pushes back its frontiers, absorbs and Sinicizes its conquerors (Huns, Turks, Mongols, Manchus), neutralizes its enemies, sets up protectorates and buffer states, develops its commercial trade and welcomes foreigners, be they technicians, scientists, artists, or priests of a new religion. This is what happened in the Tang dynasty (626–907). Its founder, Li Shimin, reigned under the name of Taizong from 627 to 650, and incarnated, as Wudi of the Han had before him, a powerful, warlike, dynamic, imperial China, seething with new ideas and contacts. The reign of Xuanzong (713–756), slightly later, is considered the peak of Tang civilization in all fields. At the high point of the dynasty, in 750, China was probably the greatest power in the world.

The 7th century saw the reconquest of Central Asia, and was a thriving period for the Silk Road. At the beginning of the century, the political powers located at either end of the road, Sassanian Persia and China, formed two great poles of development, always on good terms with one another, and sharing a common interest in trade. Between these two poles, were the Turkish confederations, which had been asserting themselves since the middle of the 6th century, turning the many smaller states into vassals or protectorates, harassing the Chinese borders on one side, but kept at bay on the other by the Persian rulers. Profits from trade played a major role in their relations. Further to the west, the Byzantine Empire had not succeeded in breaking through the

Persian barrier, and remained a mere customer of the Persians. For Byzantium, the 7th century was a period of internal troubles and external disasters, and half the territory over which Justinian had ruled was lost. As for Western Europe, it was still suffering from the after-effects of the successive waves of invasions which had devastated it.

Two new powers were in gestation at the time, the Islamic Arabs and the Tibetan kingdom. Islam, a newly revealed religion, was born into a tribe of caravaneers and merchants of large-scale trade. The Arab conquest began just after the death of Mohammed in 632, and in a dozen years placed Mesopotamia, Palestine, Syria and Egypt under its dominion, striving to convert them to Islam. The conquerors crossed the Euphrates in 635, took Ctesiphon in 638, and while they were capturing Damascus, Jerusalem and Alexandria, the Sassanian dynasty came to an end with the death of King Yazdgard III, killed in 635, and the flight of the heir to the throne, Firuz, to China. Under the protection of the Chinese emperor, he was to live for the most part in Central Asia. The Sassanian dynasty disappeared completely in 651, making way for the Umayyad Caliphate. And the thrust eastwards of the new power did not end there: it gradually absorbed half the Turkish or independent kingdoms of Central Asia, and it would finally take the full weight of Tang military power to block its advance. On the economic front, the arrival of a power prepared to encourage trade and stimulate production and industry over such a vast territory, from Central Asia to Morocco, was to turn out to be

> *The creation of an immense Muslim multinational network was to encourage not only the exchange of products, but the circulation of science, techniques, ideas and texts, such as Greek medical and philosophical texts which would be rediscovered in Europe after passing through Arabic translations. Furthermore, the activity of Muslim merchants, both on land and at sea, would greatly contribute to the growing wealth of Chinese trade during the Tang dynasty.*

a powerful engine for economic exchange, once the period of conquest was over. The creation of an immense Muslim multinational network was to encourage not only the exchange of products, but the circulation of science, techniques, ideas and texts, such as Greek medical and philosophical texts which would be rediscovered in Europe after passing through Arabic translations. Furthermore, the activity of Muslim merchants, both on land and at sea, would greatly contribute to the growing wealth of Chinese trade during the Tang dynasty: these merchants arrived in increasing numbers in the great southern Chinese ports. The conquest of Persia by the first caliphs, meanwhile, offered them all the geographic advantages and the commercial channels which had previously enriched Sassanian Persia.

The Chinese state, consolidated under its new dynasty, had stabilized its economy through tax and agrarian reforms, and for a time succeeded in keeping at bay the threat of the Eastern Turks in Mongolia (in particular by taking advantage of the intrigues which divided the clans). It subjugated the kingdoms of Manchuria and Korea, and strove to control its settlements in the various oasis-kingdoms, all the while carrying out its policy of princely marriages. The oases of the Tarim River basin lay across the heart of the great East–West trade routes, and were at the very centre of Buddhist dynamism in Eurasia. But China would nevertheless have to face the Western Turks, the Tibetans and the Arab armies, either in turn or at the same time, if it was to maintain its control and influence.

It was in the middle of the 7th century that political, commercial and cultural relations between China and Tibet were initiated and grew. In 630, the Chinese had, for the time being, subjugated the Western Turks. They began their expansion westwards by recapturing Gaochang (Qotcho in Turkish, near Turfan) in 640 (they were to keep Turfan until it was taken back by the Tibetans in 792). Turfan, Hami (Turkish name: Qomul) and Beiting (Turkish name: Beshbalyk, thought to be near the modern Jimusaer, or Jimsar, in Xinjiang) were made into three Chinese prefectures, under direct administration in both civil and military matters. Beyond Turfan, the Chinese re-established their military presence on the "four fortified sites": Kucha, Khotan, Karashahr and

Kashgar, and set up protectorates in Anxi, the "pacified West",* and Beiting, the "northern court".

Relations with Tibet were ratified in 641 by a marital alliance. More through compulsion than enthusiasm on his part, Emperor Taizong gave Princess Wencheng in marriage to King Song-tsen Gampo, a well-known event that is still illustrated in children's books. Along with the marriage request, the envoy from the Tibetan "barbarians" brought a gift of a large quantity of gold (600 kilos?) in ingots and works of art. This detail, mentioned in the Tang annals, reveals not only the wealth of the Tibetan gold sites (the country's reputation as a producer of gold was to grow in the following centuries), but also the skill and talent of the Tibetan goldsmiths, a nation considered little more than savages. Again in 658, the king of Tibet offered the Chinese emperor an artistic creation described as a city made of gold, with gold horsemen and animals.

Princess Wencheng, a Buddhist, took with her a statue of the Buddha which was later placed in the Jokhang Temple, one of the most highly venerated pilgrim sites in Lhasa. As we have seen, she also took silkworm eggs with her, as well as Buddhist books and Chinese culture. She was a good and wise queen, and from that time on Chinese influence has never ceased in Tibet, whatever the balance of power between the two states (before the Mongol conquests of the 13th century, this was as much in favour of Tibet as of China).

During this period of good relations between China and Tibet, which lasted only a few years, one event occurred which led to a military alliance between the Chinese, the Tibetans and the Nepalese against the king of Magadha, in northern India. Never before had Chinese armies ventured so far. It is very likely that Chinese soldiers were not seen again in the Himalaya until the invasion of Nepal by Emperor Qianlong's army in 1792. This episode demonstrates that movement between India and Tibet, through the Himalayan passes, and between Tibet and China, was far from uncommon after the 7th century. Nepalese history backs this up and tells of the marriage of a Nepalese princess, Bhrikuti, to the same king of Tibet, Song-tsen Gampo, who also had one or more Tibetan wives (although the authenticity of the event has sometimes been questioned by historians, it is at the very least an accepted tradition).

*Not to be confused with Anxi, "Persia".

This princess is said to have introduced Buddhism into Tibet, where the various clans and principalities had until then been followers of the indigenous Bön religion.

This expeditionary corps formed of Chinese, Tibetan and Nepalese soldiers to India was the follow-up on a previous contact: in 643, an embassy from Taizong had been sent to the court of the king of Magadha, Harsha Shiladitya.[101] The embassy crossed Tibet, then the Himalaya through the Kirong Pass into Nepal; after a visit to the king of Nepal, Narendra Deva in the Kathmandu Valley, it reached the Ganges Valley and the kingdom of Magadha. It returned to China with a Brahman, invited by the emperor. Some time later, in 648, a second mission left for India led by Wang Xuance, who had been a member of the first embassy. This time, following a power change in the Indian kingdom, the Chinese embassy was attacked and almost completely massacred; all the gifts it had brought were stolen. Its leader, practically the only person to escape with his life, took refuge on the Tibetan frontier, from where he rallied the kings of Tibet and Nepal to his cause. They sent troops to help him, and he defeated and captured the new ruler of Magadha, taking him as well as his wife and sons back to the Chinese court, along with two thousand Indians and an untold number of cattle. Among the Indian prisoners was a doctor, an expert in longevity drugs, or so he said, whom we shall meet again in the course of the history of the Tang dynasty. Travelling to northern India or Nepal from Tibet apparently became unremarkable from this period on, and several Chinese Buddhist pilgrims were to use this route. Later, there were to be other exchanges between the Chinese and Indians, and in 651, the king of Nepal sent an embassy directly to the court of Taizong. These new relations encouraged the introduction into China of such cultural elements as Indian astronomy, mathematics and medicine, as well as Buddhist philosophical texts.

This military expedition to the kingdom of Magadha was an exceptional event. The Chinese who went to India were principally "eminent religious men in search of the Law", that is to say Buddhist monks who, like Faxian two centuries before (and another Chinese monk, Songyun, at the beginning of the 6th century), travelled to Buddhist monasteries to find canonical texts, to be taught by the great masters, to deepen their knowledge of Sanskrit in the most highly reputed monasteries, to venerate the holy sites such as Kapilavastu and Sarnath, and then to return to China and to devote their lives to the translation and teaching of the sacred texts. The most famous of these pilgrims during the Tang period was Xuanzang (603–664), but there were several others in the 7th and 8th centuries, such as Yijing who set off around 670. Some reached India through Tibet and Nepal. Xuanzang's journey took place during the years between 629 and 644, and he followed the land route across Central Asia. Apart from his enormous work as a translator, he has remained famous for the account of his journey, called *Da Tang xiyu ji*, or *Records of the Western World Compiled during the Great Tang Dynasty*. In this, one finds descriptions of all the countries he crossed, with geographical, political and economic information as well as a history of Buddhism; in all, it is a collection of documentation which has been quoted time and again ever since. His descriptions concern all of Central Asia, Afghanistan and northern India. The adventures he mentions inspired a humorous novel in the 16th century, episodes of which have been enacted on the stage: who in China has not heard of the *Tale of a Journey to the West* by Wu Cheng'en and the exploits of the monkey-pilgrim?

We have mentioned the passage from Xuanzang concerning the introduction of the silkworm into Khotan, one of the kingdoms that he describes in most detail. When he passed through Khotan in 629–630, it was an independent, fervently Buddhist kingdom, a land of temples, monasteries, hermits, statues of the Buddha and pious legends. It was after reading Xuanzang's text in the early years of the 20th century that the archaeologist Marc Aurel Stein, one of the founding fathers of archaeology in the Tarim Basin, resolved to retrace his footsteps and to explore the region which had once been Khotan. Stein's own adventures there and his fascinating published account encouraged others to set off in their turn.

Xuanzang's notes on the products of the countries he crossed are brief but useful. He mentions gold, silver, copper, jade and other minerals, as well as the textile industry, silk, wool, carpets, coins of gold, silver and copper (though he notes that many countries do not use coinage). He makes little mention of trade, although he calls attention to the great gathering of goods and merchants from various foreign countries which converge on Samarkand (which he did not himself visit, and which he does not call Kangju as most Chinese still did at the time).

Two or three years before Xuanzang's first journey to Central Asia, Sogdiana, or Kangju, had, according to chapter 221 of the *History of the Tang*, for the first time (at least the first time during the Tang), sent an embassy with gifts to the Chinese court. The trade routes were once again safe to travel, although Xuanzang still had to deal with robbers during his journey. In 631, the kingdom of Kangju requested the protection of China, but Emperor Taizong hesitated: "How will I send troops 10,000 *li* from here?" Much later, an embassy brought him a live lion as a gift. To thank them for coming so far, the emperor had a poem composed in honour of the envoys. After that, an embassy arrived every year. One of them brought red and white cherry trees, which the emperor had acclimatized in his gardens. Twice during the 7th century, this kingdom, according to the *History of the Tang*, sent "golden peaches" and "silver peaches", the golden peaches were as large as goose eggs, and golden-yellow in colour.[102]

During the same period, in 623, the king of Gaochang (Turfan) sent to the imperial court a small performing dog, six inches tall and a foot long, which could stop a horse and hold a lamp in its mouth (the tale is also told in chapter 221 of the *History of the Tang*). This performing dog came from Folin, the name which had generally taken over from Da Qin to designate, according to the period, either the Roman Empire, including Rome, or the "second Rome", that is the Byzantine Empire, or the eastern part of the latter. In the 7th century, Emperor Justinian's empire had been heavily reduced by the Arab conquest which had deprived it of Armenia, Syria, Palestine and Egypt. The Arabs had occupied part of Cappadocia and devastated the islands of Cyprus, Rhodes, Cos and Crete. In its description of Folin, the *History of the Tang*, written in the 11th century, reproduces word for word the information in the Han annals on Da Qin, such as the pearl bright as the moon shining in the night, the postal relays, the civil servant carrying a bag to hold citizens' complaints, the cloth made from the down of the water-sheep, etc. But it also provides new data, some of which is very surprising, including the description of coral fishing in the Mediterranean, mentioned earlier.

It cannot be claimed that there were steady diplomatic relations between Byzantium and the Chinese court. Nevertheless we know of two embassies in the 7th century, during the reign of Constant II, in 643 and 667. The first brought, from the king of Folin, red glass and an unknown substance, *boduoli*, a name which has not been identified. The second came by sea, and brought a surprising gift, theriac. How are we to interpret this?

> *During the entire Tang period, the Chinese government would continue its search for foreign medicines ... Indeed, the Tang period, up into the middle of the 9th century, was a period of exceptional opening to the world, with an interest first in Turkish fashion (hairstyle and boots), then in Indian culture (astronomy, mathematics, medicine, Buddhist philosophy), and always in musicians and dancers from Central Asia, as well as in all foreign religions.*

Was this a present which was known to be welcome because the court had announced that it was looking for a precious and costly compound medicine such as this (it was said to cure all animal bites, and its composition required as many as 600 different ingredients)? In the West it was highly acclaimed, and was considered a tour de force of the Greek physicians and the old school of Alexandria; had its reputation then reached China? Or was this a commercial enterprise, to create a market in the Far East? The scientific level of Greek medicine is indeed mentioned in the Chinese description of Folin which states that "they have in that country excellent physicians who, by opening the brain and extracting the worms, can cure the darkening of the eye". In addition to these expert surgeons, the Chinese analysts mention several other curiosities from Folin: fire-breathing magicians, as well as a green bird which sits near the sovereign's throne, and warns him by crowing if his food contains poison. It is a country 40,000 *li* away from the Chinese capital, and in the latter such marvels are not seen, there is no such surgery, no warning about poison, and no universal anti-venom. During the entire Tang period, the Chinese government would continue its search for foreign medicines. This is but one aspect of the interest which it and Chinese society showed for everything from abroad. Indeed the Tang period, up into the middle of the 9th century, was a period of exceptional opening to the world, with an interest first in Turkish fashion (hairstyle and boots), then in Indian culture (astronomy, mathematics, medicine, Buddhist philosophy), and always in musicians and dancers from Central Asia, as well as in all foreign religions (these would end with the persecutions of 845). It was a spirit of internationalism and assimilation which affected literature, painting and sculpture.

For China, the first half of the 8th century was a long period of prosperity, security, low prices, active commerce, easy and safe travel, when roads and canals were well maintained. In the wake of this unprecedented prosperity, a monetary system replaced the old barter system, in which textiles were the main form of currency. Taxes and commerce were monetized. Foreign merchants poured into China, forming important colonies in the large cities. The first capital of the Tang, Chang'an, had a population of two million inhabitants, as well as a large district of merchants, the Western Market, where Turkish, Uighur, Tokharian, Sogdian, Arab, Indian and Persian traders gathered, the latter being the most numerous. In all, there were thousands of foreign merchants, all of them tightly controlled and very organized, with head merchants representing their national or ethnic community, according to a system which is commonly seen elsewhere in international trade. The descriptions of trade in China include practices observed

It was at the beginning of the 8th century that tea began to be commonly drunk in China, a custom which then spread among the Uighur.

almost everywhere, such as the obligation to submit goods to control, customs taxes and levies, the right of pre-emption by agents from the court who chose what they wanted to buy before the goods were put on the open market, all sorts of bans on imports and exports (for example, an edict of 714 prohibited the export and sale to foreigners of silk crepe, damasks, gauzes, embroideries, yak tails, iron, gold and pearls).

The Arab merchants, present in large numbers in the port of Khanfu (Canton), paid on arrival an import tax in kind amounting to a third of their cargo. One of the harshest laws was that if a foreign merchant died in China, all his belongings in that land were handed over to the Chinese government, a frequent enough clause in the history of world trade.

Another law prohibited foreigners, some of whom had lived in China for years, from ever leaving the country if they married a Chinese woman, let alone taking their wife and children with them. This clause remained in Chinese law until the end of the 19th century.

Despite all these constraints, the profit to be gained made it all worthwhile, and there was no shortage of volunteers. All the products of the world arrived at the Chinese capital, either by land, or by sea. In the latter case, the goods were unloaded, then shipped north by river or on the Grand Canal. In the Western market of Chang'an, silks, clothes, saddles, meat, medicines and tea were traded. It was at the beginning of the 8th century that tea began to be commonly drunk in China, a custom which then spread among the Uighur.

Luoyang, the second capital of the Tang, was said to have a million inhabitants. Yangzhou, located both on the Yangzi and the Grand Canal, was the centre of the salt monopoly, and an important hub for banking, gold and the tea trade; it too welcomed goods from the world over. Several thousand Persian and Arab merchants did business there. Finally, there was Canton, with about 200,000 inhabitants, well described by Arab travellers, with its enormous port filled with ships from India, Persia and South-East Asia. It was the largest market of aromatic plants and medicines in Asia, where one could also find silks, porcelain—another developing export—and slaves. The town had a large district of foreign residents and a special commissar to deal with the foreign merchants.

Trade was exceptionally prosperous there (and Persian and Arab tales carried its reputation throughout the world) until a series of internal and external disorders ruined it for some time. In Yangzhou, in the 8th century, thousands of Arab and Persian merchants were massacred, as happened too in Canton, in 879, during a social revolt. In Chang'an, in the 9th century, the Uighurs became hated for their insolent behaviour and their practice of dishonest usury, and they and their religion, Manichaeism, were finally banished. In a wave of xenophobia, in 845, all foreign religions, Buddhism, Nestorianism, Manichaeism and Mazdaism, were prohibited, the monks dispersed, the priests driven out, and all their goods confiscated.

The organization of foreign trade under the Tang reflected two different circumstances according to whether this trade was carried out by land, along the Silk Road, or by sea,

> *The organization of foreign trade under the Tang reflected two different circumstances according to whether this trade was carried out by land, along the Silk Road, or by sea, through the large southern ports.*

through the large southern ports. The notion of tribute and gift still persisted in connection with Central Asia, although in practice these were commercial exchanges. Economic and diplomatic relations were marked by the necessity for state security, for the age-old threat from the neighbours to the north and west was still present. There was the constant problem of the supply of horses for the Chinese army. The same difficulties existed in maintaining military control over territories located 3,000, 6,000, or 9,000 *li* from the capital, a control which drained the state finances, was costly in human lives, and necessitated a complex civil and military administration for the transport of food and armaments. In comparison, commerce in the maritime ports was relatively easily controlled and did not entail the same constraints.

UMAYYAD CALIPHATE

After the disappearance of the Sassanian dynasty and the emergence of the Umayyad Caliphate, the Arab forces at first advanced only very slowly eastwards. In the middle of the 7th century, the Arab conquest had not yet reached beyond Merv and Balkh. In the middle of the 8th century, the caliphate conquered Tokharestan (the Bactria of old) with its cities Balkh, Kabul and Badakhshan; a large part of ancient Sogdiana including Samarkand and Bukhara; Khorezm, along the lower reaches of the Amu-Darya, with Khiva and Urgench; Ferghana and the region located north of the Syr-Darya as far as the Chu River. These regions were in fact a swarm of small semi-independent kingdoms—as many as seventy-two—which passed from one leader to another, as well as a few larger kingdoms which maintained their independence for slightly longer. Conquests were temporary, and were often followed by rebellions from the ill-treated or ransomed inhabitants; armies advanced and retreated, cities were lost and recaptured.

Alliances and enmities switched continually between the Western Turks, the Chinese, the Arabs and the Tibetans. Small oppressed kingdoms appealed for help to their neighbours, or to China. Short-lived federations of princes were formed then disappeared. Each of the four great powers which encroached upon one another in Central Asia was also weakened at times by internal unrest, temporarily reducing its potential for strike, with the others attempting to take any advantage. The "four garrisons" of the Chinese Far West, Khotan, Kashgar, Kucha and Karashahr, changed hands several times. The history of the fortresses and cities of Central Asia at the time was nothing but a chaotic succession of cavalcades, sieges and battles. Occasionally, the inhabitants would escape just in time and emigrate, forming foreign colonies in China or elsewhere. Every large-scale military operation involved the displacement of populations as well as of public and private wealth, of treasures from the state or from monasteries, or the contents of commercial warehouses, such as those of Samarkand or Baykend. In the case of large cities, the booty was often fabulous. A new phenomenon can occasionally be noted, the disappearance of books or religious objects which the conqueror could not tolerate. And from 720 on, the caliphs endeavoured to convert the populations of their newly conquered lands to Islam.

Tibet had until then been a relatively minor player in the political game in Asia, but the kingdom which developed in the 7th century in the Yarlung Valley of Central Tibet, including what would later become Lhasa, was in a period of expansion, advancing north-east against the Turks and the Tangut. The king, Song-tsen Gampo, threatened to carry on as far as the Chinese capital if he were not given a princess in marriage, a request he obtained in 641. After a few years of Sino-Tibetan alliance, the Tibetans advanced north-westwards, towards the Karakoram mountains, occupying the Wakhan Corridor (between Afghanistan and Pakistan), and descending towards Kashgar. Allied to the Turks, they briefly captured this city-kingdom from the Chinese. This marked the beginning of a conflict between the Chinese and the Tibetans which was to last until the end of the Tang dynasty, a time which also witnessed the Arab conquest and Turkish resistance, with alternating periods of supremacy of one or the other power.[103] Tibet and China would fight over control of the Pamir, Khotan and Dunhuang which were under the Tibetans for much of the 8th and 9th centuries. Under the Abbasid Caliphate, in the time of Harun al-Rashid (786–809), Tibetan troops backed a rebellion against the caliphate in Samarkand; Harun al-Rashid in person advanced towards his eastern provinces to re-establish authority there, but died on the way. His second successor, his son al-Mamun, established his capital at Merv and declared a holy war in every direction, including towards Tibet. Around 814, the Muslim army defeated the Tibetans in the Karakoram and sent a general and Tibetan officers as prisoners to Baghdad.

Tibet's era as a great power ended in the middle of the 9th century. Internal troubles, rivalry between the great noble families, between Buddhists and followers of the Bön religion, the persecution of Buddhism by King Lang Darma, and the assassination of that king by a Buddhist monk in 842, led to the collapse of Tibetan unity and the loss of all their conquests: Dunhuang, Hami, Khotan, Gaochang (Qotcho), all the towns to the north-west and north-east which had been annexed. By 866, nothing was left of the Tibetan empire and power.

Fighting had already broken out between the caliphs and China in 751, on the banks of the Talas River, almost twenty years after the Arab invasion had been blocked at the other end of the world, at Poitiers in France, by Charles Martel.

The Chinese court and the caliphate had gone through a period of good relations in 741–742. An Arab embassy had been welcomed in Chang'an and had left with a purple robe, a gold belt and an official Chinese title; these were ritual gifts. Then the Umayyad dynasty, facing internal dissension, made its presence less strongly felt in its eastern territories. China was fighting the Tibetans over the Pamir and Wakhan. In 747, a Chinese general of Korean origin, Gao Xianzhi, was named "Assistant Protector-General of the Pacified West", and "General Commissar for the Troops and Horses of the Four Garrisons". Leaving Kucha with 10,000 soldiers, he travelled through Aksu and Kashgar to these high mountainous regions where he inflicted a heavy defeat upon the Tibetan army. He subjugated the kingdom of Bolor, in the Pamir, taking the king and his Tibetan wife back to Chang'an as prisoners. At this time, in 750, the Chinese capital was a crossroads of sovereigns come to pay homage or brought in semi-captivity. The Tang were masters of the Tarim, Dzungaria, the Pamir and Wakhan, and were allies of Ferghana.

Gao Xianzhi, who had "brought the seventy-two kingdoms back to allegiance", was named military governor of the four garrisons. But one year later, he could not prevent China suffering one of the greatest defeats of its entire history, the first and last battle fought between the Chinese army and that of a Muslim empire.

MUSLIM VICTORY

In 750, following an attack and an anti-Chinese move by the king of Tashkent and various Turkish groups, Ferghana appealed to China for help. Gao Xianzhi, whose responsibility this was, besieged and captured Tashkent, defeating his Turkish ally as well. Having plundered the city, killed the old and the weak, and sold the inhabitants into slavery, he had the kings and the Turkish and Tibetan chiefs implicated in the affair taken to Chang'an as prisoners. But the son of the king of Tashkent had succeeded in escaping and fled to Samarkand, governed by Ziyad ibn-Salih al-Khuza'i, the commander for the caliphate. He asked the governor of Khorassan to send reinforcements.

In 751, Gao Xianzhi, warned of the approaching Arab army, advanced westwards with his troops, swollen by Turkish Qarluq and soldiers from Ferghana. The army of Ziyad ibn-Salih included troops from Sogdiana and Khorassan. The two armies fought for five days before the city of Atlakh,[104] near Taraz, present-day Djambul, in Kazakhstan. Betrayed by the Qarluq who went over to the enemy, the Chinese were routed and retreated through a gorge packed with fleeing refugees. Gao Xianzhi managed to escape, but thousands of Chinese soldiers were captured and led on foot to Samarkand.

The Muslim general did not, however, continue his advance further east, and for a long time, Chinese and Arab-Persian Muslim influence would be separated along this line.

Paper Making

Among the thousands of Chinese civil and military prisoners captured by Ziyad ibn-Salih were silk weavers, metalworkers and paper makers. Until then paper seems to have been a Chinese monopoly, at least as a medium for writing, distinct from Egyptian papyrus, tree bark as used in Russia, or the leaves of trees as used in India. The silk weavers were all transferred to Kufa, in modern Iraq, then the capital of the caliphate, where they remained until 762, when they were moved to Baghdad, the new and recently founded capital. One of these involuntary travellers, named Duhuan, was fortunate enough to be able to return to his homeland in 762. The tale of his adventures, of which the original text has been lost, is reproduced in a Chinese encyclopaedia: according to Duhuan, the Chinese artisans and artists taught the Arabs in Kufa how to weave light silk, to work with gold and silver, and the art of painting. He even cites the name and home province of these Chinese masters.

Paper was a more important cultural revolution than the spread of sericulture... Firstly it led to the easy and cheap reproduction of written texts and secondly it led to the birth of printing. Books—holy books of the Buddhist canon, Confucian classics, historical annals, scientific and medical works—containing all human knowledge were produced in large numbers and at relatively affordable prices.

The Chinese paper technicians were transferred to Samarkand, the great centre of book production. There they taught their conquerors the technique of paper making, and so Samarkand became the foremost centre of this industry in the Muslim world and the source of supply for Christian countries.

Paper was a more important cultural revolution than the spread of sericulture had been to the economy. Firstly it led to the easy and cheap reproduction of written texts and secondly it led to the birth of printing. Books—holy books of the Buddhist canon, Confucian classics, historical annals, scientific and medical works—containing all human knowledge were produced in large numbers and at relatively affordable prices. After the Chinese, the other civilizations, Muslim and Christian, were all to benefit from it.

The Chinese had invented paper seven or eight centuries previously, but did not at first use it for writing. During their long history they wrote on bone or tortoiseshell, engraved bronze, carved stone and strips of bamboo, and painted on silk, at the time when other nations were writing on clay tablets, on layers of wax, on papyrus, or on parchment. The use in China of paper as a medium for writing derived from the early invention of a rather crude paper, used for wrapping and made either from waste silk matting, hemp fibres or bamboo. This has been confirmed in archaeological finds from the 1st century BC.[105]

The invention, or rather the perfecting of a paper which could be used for writing, has been attributed to a certain Cailun, born in Sichuan, a eunuch and steward-general in the palace, who is said to have developed it by improving existing concepts (soaking, crumbling, sticking together, spreading and drying). He presented his technique to Emperor Hedi of the Han in 105 AD, as recorded by Fan Ye in the 5th century, in the *History of the Later Han*. The raw materials he used were mulched tree bark (often mulberry) and the lignified substance found under the bark, as well as hemp, old cloth and even old fishing nets, all of which could be found in large quantities and very cheaply. This substance was then stuck together with glue, gypsum, gelatine and starch. The result was a thin, supple sheet on which it was easy to write with brush and ink, a method of writing already used for centuries on silk and bamboo. This invention could not be traced back to the legendary emperors, but at least it could be associated with the imperial palace—for though Cailun is credited with its invention and Emperor Hedi decreed its use, it was no doubt in reality the result of trial and error over generations of artisans. At the time, this product's most valuable property was apparently still not exploited: that of being highly suitable for woodblock printing and xylography, and later typography, what we in our rather narrow circles would call the Gutenberg civilization.

The Chinese techniques of paper making had long since spread to Indochina, Korea, Japan and India, and Chinese paper was not unknown in the Muslim world when the Chinese defeat in Kazakhstan led to the capture of these technicians in 751. When paper appeared in the West, it was not at first considered an acceptable medium for administrative documents; instead, Egyptian papyrus and sheepskin parchments were most commonly used. In Muslim Persia, under the Umayyads, papyrus was the standard medium. The dynasty which replaced them in 750, just before the Battle of Talas, the Abbasid dynasty, first of all opted for parchment; then, at the end of the 8th century, under the Caliph Harun al-Rashid, the vizier Jafar adopted paper in the form made in Samarkand. One of the reasons for this was that when it was scratched or washed it would leave traces, unlike papyrus and parchment, and his choice was therefore dictated above all by the desire to avoid the falsification of documents.[106] In the West, too, it was this very fragility of paper which for a long time meant that it was rejected for official documents. The same vizier Jafar founded, in 794–795, the first paper making factory in Baghdad, probably with the help of technicians from Samarkand, a town of which his brother was then governor. Other production centres were then set up in Syria, Sicily, Andalusia, Morocco and Egypt. Gradually, from the 10th century on, the Christian Western world began to give up using papyrus and bought its paper supplies from these Muslim centres. Damascus was for a long time the main supplier, and paper was often called *charta damascena*, *charta* designating all written documents (on papyrus, parchment or any other medium), and then more particularly paper. Marco Polo would call Kubilai's paper money *monnoye de charte*.

In the 11th century, control of the Mediterranean began to pass from the hands of the Muslims to those of the Christian kingdoms: Roger the Norman reconquered Sicily; Pisa, Genoa and Venice began to dominate the seas, and gained access to Syrian ports where they bought Eastern products. With the Crusades, Venice became the first maritime transporter of the Christian world. It was during the Crusades that the Christian prisoners of the Saracens began to learn about paper making, prepared, according to Maalouf, from wheat straw,[107] although it was mainly hemp that was used in Syria.

Outside Muslim Spain, it was perhaps in France, in the Hérault in 1157, or in Italy, that the first European paper factory appeared: in 1250, the town of Fabriano, near Ancona, was the main supplier in the non-Muslim west.

WOODBLOCK PRINTING

In China, the Confucian texts had been engraved on stone in a "forest of stelae" to insure their longevity; after all, Chinese history had already experienced one great burning of the books under Qin Shihuangdi, the First Emperor. At some undetermined period, logically when paper of sufficient quality became available, texts began to be reproduced by making rubbings of the stone engravings, by applying paper to the stone and stamping it with ink. This was the first step towards printing; it is a simple and quick procedure, which can provide innumerable numbers of copies and which was much used later by archaeologists, before the advent of photography, to take down inscriptions without harming the original. It was but a short step from there to replacing the heavy stone stelae with moveable hardwood boards, which take less time to carve than stone: this was the invention of xylography, or woodblock printing. The texts would be produced page by page, until the board was worn down. The planks were transportable and easy to store, and the raw material relatively abundant.

This is how the first Buddhist texts were printed in China; the oldest printed book is the *Diamond Sutra*, one of the great canonical texts of Buddhism, found at Dunhuang, and dated to 868. The next two oldest books are Chinese calendars dated 877 and 882, also from Dunhuang, discovered among the thousands of manuscripts hidden in caves where they had been placed for safety. These three texts, and many others which were uncovered at the beginning of the 20th century by Western and Japanese archaeologists, were "bought" and taken to England by Marc Aurel Stein; they have since been kept in the British Museum in London. The *Diamond Sutra* is a scroll, one of the old forms of book, composed of sheets of paper stuck end-to-end. It measures 4.65 metres in length and 33 centimetres in width. The quality of the characters and of its engraved illustration reflects the level of technical mastery which the Chinese had reached then, and suggests that this technique had already been in use for perhaps as much as a century.[108] Later, the paper would be folded into an accordion shape, which allowed pagination and made for easier reading. Later still, a bound cover was invented. This woodblock printing, in small separate sheets, continued to be carried out by Tibetan monks after the invention of modern typography, almost until the present day. Monastery libraries contain large numbers of books composed of superimposed leaves held together between two decorated planks of wood, and wrapped in silk, bearing a label with the name of the text to allow one to find it on the shelves. At the end of the 20th century, the monastery of Derge, in a Tibetan district of modern Sichuan province, a monastery that had long been famous as a printing centre of Buddhist texts, still used this xylographic process for its publications.

The extreme aridity of the deserts of Central Asia allowed mummies, textiles and texts on paper to be exceptionally well preserved. For large religious texts, certain Buddhist countries also used paper treated with poison to protect them against insects and rats, although this does not fit well with the prohibition on killing living beings.

TYPOGRAPHY

The next stage of course was printing with moveable characters—characters made of baked clay—which appeared in China much later, in the 11th century. The process was a rather long and complicated one which did not at first challenge xylography. It was not until the 13th century that moveable characters in metal were perfected, and this, along with various other small improvements, allowed the speeding up of composition, which is far more difficult with four or five thousand different characters than with alphabets of twenty-six or thirty letters. The parallel invention of moveable characters by Gutenberg in Germany, around 1450, seems to have been a completely independent creation, although it has sometimes been suggested that the basic idea came from the numerous encounters provided by the Crusades, but no account or detailed evidence bears this out.

The development in the Tang period of paper books, whether manuscript or printed, in China and in Central Asia, is clearly demonstrated by the mass of texts which have been found in archaeological sites such as Dunhuang and Qotcho (Gaochang), as well as by new mentions of a book trade. It would appear that before this, books were not bought and sold; one ordered a copy and paid the copyist. Naturally, a book was a rare and expensive article. Thus once several impressions could be made from the same carved woodblock, the trade in books began.

The Arab conquest had been blocked at Poitiers, in France, in 732, in Kazakhstan in 751 by the victory at Talas, and at about the same time in the Caucasus by a khanate at the height of its power just around 750: the Khazars. They protected Byzantium from the Arabs. Just when, in the East, the great powers facing each other were China, the Islamic caliphate, the Turks and the Tibetans, in the West, it was the caliphate, the Byzantine Christian Empire, and the Kazakh kingdom which confronted one another.

RELIGIOUS CONVERSIONS

The Khazars were originally a Turkish people speaking a Turkish language, who had emigrated in the time of Attila, in the 5th century, making their way northwards to the north of the Caucasus, and settling down in the steppes between the Volga, the Don and the Caucasus. They displaced the Bulgars and other Turkish groups before imposing suzerainty over them, and began encroaching on the Byzantine world by occupying parts of the shores of the Black Sea. From 652 on, they had had on many occasions to fight the Arab conquerors, and to do so made an alliance with Byzantium. A daughter of the Kazakh khan, converted to Christianity and baptized under the name of Theodora, married the heir to the Byzantine throne becoming empress in the middle of the 8th century. The kingdom had several successive capitals, the third and most important of which was Itil, founded in the 8th century on the Volga River. The town was built on a bend of the river, on both banks, with a fortified western section protecting the two palaces, and an eastern section which was essentially reserved for the Muslim population, with numerous mosques, baths and markets. Power was divided between the khan, the religious ruler, who had to be Jewish and descended from a certain line, and the *bek* who exercised temporal power. The population was mixed, with a Jewish aristocracy, Muslims, Christians and a rural mass of followers of the Turkish religion of the steppes. Around 740, the khan of the Khazars had converted to Judaism, and part of his people followed suit. This conversion may seem surprising, but another Turkish group, at the same period, at the other end of Asia, had converted en masse to Manichaeism. Conversions to Judaism were not exceptional, another case in point being the kingdom of Himyar.

In the case of the Khazars, this conversion appears to have had a political motivation: a desire for independence from both Christian Byzantium and the caliphate, two states in which a rise of intolerance was noticeable at the time, and which tended to consider the adoption of a religion as implying the acceptance of the tutelage of the leaders of that religion, be it Byzantium or Baghdad. A large number of Jews fled to the Kazakh kingdom from Byzantium during several periods of persecution in the 6th and 7th centuries, and again under Leon III in the 8th century. Other Jews had left Asia Minor when it was conquered by the Arabs, and large numbers of them were driven out of Khorezm by Kuteiba, the conqueror of Central Asia, after the campaign of 712–714. Among these Jews from Khorezm were a number of scholars and doctors.

This conversion in the 740s corresponded perhaps to a less orthodox form of Khorezmite Judaism, and after 760–770, the need was felt to carry out a great religious reform: scholarly rabbis were invited from Baghdad, and even from the Byzantine Empire.

The key feature of the Khazar kingdom was that it was dedicated to trade. It served as a middleman between the Arab-Persian Muslim world, which now dominated part of Central Asia, the Byzantine world, the Slav tribes to the north and Khorezm, which in the Middle Ages was a flourishing state in the lower valley of the Amu-Darya. A trade route linked Itil to Gurganj, the Urgench of old, a city which had existed since the 1st century AD, near present-day Kunya-Urgench in Turkmenistan, not far from the left bank of the lower reaches of the Amu-Darya.*

* *This should not be confused with the modern city of Urgench, located on the Amu-Darya in Uzbekistan, which was founded in the 17th century by Emir Abdulgazi who transferred there the remaining population of the town of Gurganj, the old Urgench.*

The khanate disappeared at the beginning of the 11th century, not because of the Muslim empire, but because it was defeated by the allied armies of Byzantium and the Varangian prince of the first Russian state, the principality of Kiev.

Another example of the conversion of a Turkish people to a religion and a civilization which were totally foreign to it, was the adoption by the Uighur of Manichaeism as a state religion, resulting in an even more ephemeral result: the Manichaean Uighur kingdom did not last a century. Curiously, the official conversion occurred about twenty years after that of the Khazar khan to Judaism. In 762, in order to put down a serious rebellion which threatened the very existence of his empire—the An Lushan rebellion—the Tang Emperor Suzong appealed to one of his eastern Turkish allies, the khan of the Uighur. During this campaign in China, the khan recaptured for the emperor the capitals Chang'an and Luoyang, where he met a Manichaean priest. Manichaeism was discreetly present in China, with one or two temples in the capital. In a very short period of time, the khan converted to this religion, along with all his subjects. Thus for about eighty years, Manichaeism became an official state religion, a unique historical event. For political reasons, to placate its ally, the Chinese government protected this religion and authorized the construction of numerous temples. However, the Uighur, who formed a large community in Chang'an and elsewhere in China, soon made themselves most unwelcome through their behaviour, particularly their practice of excessive usury in trade and business, becoming such a nuisance that relations with the Chinese deteriorated. The Uighur kingdom was attacked by other Kyrgyz khans, and soon annihilated. In 843, the Chinese government took measures against the Uighur residents in China and banned Manichaeism throughout the empire. This proscription was reinforced in 845 when all foreign religions including Buddhism were forbidden, although the latter had been present in China for 700 years, and would soon flourish again. Many Uighurs emigrated west. There may well have been a few Manichaean faithful scattered in Central Asia, and perhaps in Tibet, from the 9th century on, but none remain today. Chinese Xinjiang, the modern Uighur Autonomous region of Xinjiang, is Muslim or atheist, and Tibet is very largely a Buddhist country with some Bön faithful.

The doctrine of Mani therefore had a relatively official, though brief, presence in China. The old Iranian beliefs, Mazdaism or Zoroastrianism, were very discreet and longer-lasting; the Chinese called them the doctrine of the "God of the Hu Heaven" (of the Western Barbarians), or the "doctrine of fire". In very ancient times, Mazdaism had been implanted in Sogdiana, and must have been brought to China by the Sogdians, from the 4th century AD on, according to Zhang Guangda.[109] He has found in the dynastic annals, as well as in manuscripts from Dunhuang and other archaeological sources, the proof of its presence, particularly in funerary rites which are typical of Zoroastrianism, such as the exposure of corpses to wild animals. Followers of this doctrine are known to have been present at the court of the Northern Wei, and again under the Sui. During the Tang, in 631, a magus, disciple of Zoroaster, appealed to Emperor Taizong and was granted the right to build a temple in the capital. The presence of Iranian doctrines in China is not surprising when one considers the number of Persian merchants who lived in the Chinese capital, and the frequency and regularity of relations between China and Persia in the past.

No traces of Mazdaism have been found in China following the 845 edict prohibiting foreign religions, although this does not mean that it did not continue to survive there very discreetly, as forbidden religions do when their followers are sufficiently few in number not to present a political danger.

Nestorian Christianity had developed and grown many roots in Central Asia and China. Under the first caliphs, the Christians enjoyed some freedom in Iran, and their patriarch, Timothy I (780–823), based at Ctesiphon, had consecrated a bishop for China and created a Tibetan province. A period of active proselytizing began in 635, attested to by a famous stone stele, now kept in a museum in Xi'an. This black stone stele, over two metres tall, is engraved with a long text for the most part in Chinese characters, with a few lines in Syriac. It was erected in 781 near Chang'an, and probably buried by a priest or by Nestorian followers when the 845 edict was proclaimed; it was found by chance in 1623 or 1625 during excavation work. Jesuit missionaries who were living in China at the time became interested in this unique document, which testified to the age-old presence of Christianity in China. The discovery generated a lot of excitement, but it unfortunately became clear that this was not Roman Christianity, but a heretic sect, Chaldaean Christianity, otherwise known as Nestorianism. Nevertheless, the text was studied at length, and is still being studied today. Father Athanase Kircher, a Jesuit, published a Latin translation of it in 1667, with a host of commentaries, in a famous work entitled *China illustrata*, printed in Amsterdam, and soon translated into several Western languages.

This *syro-sinicus* or *sinico-chaldaeus* monument tells of the introduction into China of the "religion of light" by a figure named Aluopen, who had come from Da Qin during the reign of Taizong. He was welcomed by the emperor who had the books he brought with him translated. These he examined, along with the images (paintings or statues?) which went with them, ordering that this doctrine should be preached in the empire, and that a monastery be built for twenty-one men. The text, which relates this event and describes the doctrine, is the work, according to Father Raquin,[110] of a learned Persian monk named Adam, or Jingjing in Chinese; he knew Sanskrit and helped an Indian Buddhist monk to translate Sanskrit Buddhist texts into Chinese. He "was well versed in Buddhism, Daoism and Confucian philosophy". The vocabulary employed and the ideas presented use expressions and notions of Buddhism or Daoism, a common procedure at the time in translation work of this type, which only adds to the great mingling of religious notions in this period of tolerance and openness between 630 and 840. The Nestorians, protected by several Tang emperors, preached and apparently converted many. When the 845 edict drove all foreign religions from China, a certain number of these Christians emigrated to neighbouring countries. In Central Asia, Nestorians were numerous until the end of the Mongol period in the 14th century. Their presence in Tibet has left sufficient traces to have fostered in Europe, in the 17th and 18th centuries, the belief that the country had once been Christian and perhaps still was, and that it would been easy to re-evangelize it.

Chapter Fourteen
The World Marketplace of Sinbad the Sailor

*W*hen it comes to the history of trade, the annals of the Han and Northern dynasties are primarily interested in the rarities and curios which arrived among the "tribute" brought by one or another distant embassy. Was it because of the Chinese scholars' contempt for trade? We have much more information about economy and trade for the Tang period, when additionally, the large number of foreign visitors to China and Central Asia, ranging from the Japanese monk Ennin to the Arab merchant Suleyman, resulted in travel accounts which present an outsider's view of the situation within China.

The Chinese also began to travel further afield then; pilgrims such as Xuanzang and other Chinese monks went to India, and many civil and military officials were sent to the protectorates in Central Asia. A few Chinese merchants appeared in Ceylon. Nevertheless, the Chinese remained land-bound, and there appears to be no Chinese equivalent in the Tang to the Arab accounts of sea journeys such as that of the merchant Suleyman. Arab travellers have described Canton, one of the largest ports in the world at the time, but no Chinese merchant or traveller has described Siraf or Alexandria.

In order to understand the position foreign trade occupied in the Muslim civilization, and the reverberations it set up in the minds of an entire people, one has only to read the *Thousand and One Nights*, which contains a striking number of stories about merchants, doubtlessly gleaned here and there in the caravanserais and ports. These tales are thought to have been first written down in the 10th century, although Harun al-Rashid and his famous vizier Jafar as well as the beautiful Zobeyda, who is often mentioned in the tales of Scheherazade, were contemporaries of Charlemagne(742–814). What we see portrayed in this text is a world of trade in which, for one reason or another, out of fear or grief, the presence of an enemy, or simply the desire to see another land, the hero leaves his hometown, and buys in cash or on credit a shipload of goods to sell, even if he is not originally a merchant. He hires caravaneers, camels, mules, donkeys or horses, then makes arrangements with a ship's captain or a shipping agent, and leaves for two or three years, to Sin al-Sin and Sin-i Kalan and to Khanfu (Canton), picking up on the way legends about the Wak Wak Isles and the Kingdom of Women, the Valley of Diamonds and the Rok bird, but also buying and selling for profit. He returns rich and triumphant, with stories of yields of a thousand per cent, of cheap gold, of robes worthy of a prince, of first quality musk, with a black slave, strong and faithful; or he returns ruined after a shipwreck, from which he only just escaped with his life; or he does not return at all. A mobile society, without watertight castes, in which one has a chance to start over again, thanks to trade.

These stories tell us of bazaars, with their rules and regulations, of troublesome officials, of Persian magicians, devious swindlers, learned and wise sheikhs, impoverished porters. The merchants, princes, viziers, beautiful young women, slaves, genies, locked or not in a bottle, these are the habitual characters of the *Thousand and One Nights*.

The multiple role of the merchant is clearly demonstrated: he is not only a trader but a diplomatic envoy, a messenger, a courier, an informer, a guide. One example among others, a very significant one, is the tale of Aziz, of Prince Diadem and Princess Donia, which is told on the 128th and following nights. Aziz is the son of a great merchant. He has been assigned the task of finding out about a distant princess, Princess Donia, in the Seven Isles of Camphor and Crystal. A caravan is about to leave, so he quickly buys goods of great value and joins it. He intends to return with her within three years. A year later he arrives at the court of King Shahrahmân, father of Princess Donia.

To summarize in a few words, he gathers his information, and returns to give his report. Yes, the princess is indeed very beautiful. The King of Persia, Soleyman-Shah, sends him back from Isfahan to the Camphor Islands with a new mission, to request the young lady's hand in marriage to his son, Prince Diadem. He returns from this second journey with bad news: unfortunately the idea of marriage is abhorrent to the princess and her father will not force her. So Soleyman-Shah decides to conquer the kingdom of this insolent ruler. His advisers succeed in convincing him not to, and Prince Diadem then makes up his mind to go in person to win over the beautiful young lady (although he has never seen her, Aziz' reports can be trusted). All three of them set off, the prince (disguised as a merchant), the vizier and Aziz (on his third journey). He serves as guide and counsellor, all the while carrying out his trade, since they are to pass off as tradesmen, the vizier being the merchant, and the two young men his nephews to whom he is showing the world.

On arriving in the capital of King Shahrahmân, they settle down in the great bazaar, where they rent rooms and warehouse space for they have a large shipload of goods, mainly textiles, and probably many servants. They arrange their bundles in the warehouse and begin by resting for four days. Then they decide to ask for premises in the silk bazaar (Diadem, disguised as a merchant, wears a magnificent robe). The sheikh of the silk bazaar allocates them a shop in the middle of the souk so that they can display their most beautiful fabrics. Our heroes have many adventures, which naturally end well, for Prince Diadem returns home with

> 'There was no better disguise for a vizier and a prince than as merchants, and this was to remain true throughout Asia for a long time. In the West, the favourite guise was that of a monk.

his fiancée. In this story, we have a merchant, himself a merchant's son, entrusted with difficult assignments, negotiating a princely marriage, taking part in a subterfuge, guiding his companions because of his knowledge of these countries and routes, and his experience in travel and trade. There was no better disguise for a vizier and a prince than as merchants, and this was to remain true throughout Asia for a long time. In the West, the favourite guise was that of a monk. Who would suspect three merchants of wanting to marry or kidnap the daughter of a king? Who would doubt the seriousness and good intentions of a silk merchant who displays in the bazaar in the capital, as the prize piece of his collection, a cloth which is described in the "133rd night of the caliph" as: "A cloth which had been set so as to form but one dress for some *huri* or marvellous princess. As for describing it, or enumerating the jewels with which it was enriched or the embroidery under which the weft disappeared, only the poets, inspired by Allah, could so do in rhyming verse. At the very least, it must have been worth, without the covering, 100,000 gold dinar." Indeed, the covering itself was a most extraordinary fabric: it was "fringed with gold tassels, made of a Damascus velvet across which ran, light and coloured, designs of flowers and birds with, in the middle, an inebriated elephant dancing. And from this whole parcel issued forth a perfume which excited the soul."[111]

Even in the stories which are not tales about merchants, it is rare that one does not meet a traveller. The Muslim world of the 9th, 10th and 11th centuries was a civilization of textiles, of trade and travel. These three things were to stimulate indirectly the economic life of its customers and suppliers, not only China in the Tang and early Song dynasties, but also all of Indonesia, India, East Africa, North Africa and Central Asia. It was the Muslim world which would supply Christendom with eastern products, except where they were sworn enemies. Muslim merchants were to be seen in all the ports, bazaars and fairs.

Apart from these tales, we have a much richer mass of documentation in Arabic or in Persian for the Middle Ages than we do for the Christian world at the same time: firm geographical descriptions, either from tales of travelling merchants or other sources, as well as historical, scientific and literary works. Christianity was fenced in, in large part by the Muslim powers which blocked all its exit routes. The Muslim world, on the other hand, was mobile, like a tent which could be easily taken down and transported; it was, in many ways, supranational and multi-ethnic. Its cohesion was achieved through its single religion and a single way of life. Its mobility, and the economic and social importance of its commercial network, made it not only the conveyor of its own cultural and material goods, but also the middleman, the translator, the messenger of products and cultures from different lands in which its countrymen lived for varying periods of time.

The extensive Muslim world of the 8th and 9th centuries—the first two great centuries of Islam—was contemporary with the height of Tang culture, but in the 9th and 10th centuries, it was the empire of the caliphs which became the greatest world power. This empire stretched from Morocco to the Aral Sea and beyond, covering a large part of Africa and Europe, with its centre in Baghdad. Islamization, always encouraged, sometimes enforced, followed the conquest, and occasionally even occurred spontaneously. Many Turkish groups converted to Islam without being compelled to do so, for others had converted to Buddhism or Manichaeism. There were even Chinese Muslims, as in addition to the foreign merchant colonies in the Chinese capital and in Canton, the Muslim religion attracted converts among the local population.

But what was the nature of this immense commercial network which supplied the three continents of the Old World, Europe, Asia and part of Africa?

Let us set aside once and for all the curios and rare goods: the ruby which shines in the night, the moon-bright pearl, the artistic creations in gold and rock crystal, the golden peaches of Samarkand, the acrobats and dwarfs, the jugglers and the performing dogs, even the musicians and dancers. All of this was intended to satisfy the curiosity and splendour of the courts. It was something quite different which made these journeys of two or three years worthwhile for the thousands of expatriate merchants, from Chang'an to Baghdad, from Siraf to Canton, from Samarkand to Ceylon, despite the cost of feeding or replacing thousands of pack animals and horses, of armed escorts against bandits on land and pirates at sea, despite the shipwrecks and the long distances between the trading posts.

In our descriptions of trade in this book, we have naturally left out the voluminous and heavy goods, such as firewood, salt, cereals, animals on the hoof, as well as food products and other consumer goods, which were of little value in comparison to transport costs. These basic survival necessities were in fact traded locally over very short distances, as were raw materials such as

> *Apart from textiles, which were the biggest industry in the world, most trade in terms of value consisted less in precious objects than in basic or indispensable products such as horses, slaves, weapons, metal to be used for coins and other minerals, leather and furs, substances used in metallurgy, for dyeing or in other industries, as well as medicines and aromatic substances.*

minerals or untreated wool. Long-distance trade, on the contrary, tended to favour goods with a high monetary value which were lightweight and took up little space, on the condition that they were not perishable: silks, gems, gold, pearls, good quality weapons, medicine, aromatic substances. Otherwise the transport costs, the running of the commercial network, the losses and the risks would not have been worthwhile. But a few commodities, such as weapons, metals, or some industrial products, were of such necessity that they would be imported even if they were expensive.

It is likely that, apart from textiles, which were the biggest industry in the world, most trade in terms of value (albeit with varying profit margins) consisted less in precious objects than in basic or indispensable products such as horses, slaves, weapons, metal to be used for coins and other minerals, leather and furs, substances used in metallurgy, for dyeing or in other industries, as well as medicines and aromatic substances.

SILK

China still exported silk, both raw and worked, in large quantities—at times the state warehouses held millions of bolts of silk—but Chinese silks were not the only ones being traded. In the Tang period, the Persian output of fine silks grew considerably, being exported both to the East and the West, disseminating Sassanian decorative motifs from Byzantium to Japan. These very specific motifs continued to be reproduced long after Islam tried to prohibit the representation of living creatures. They were taken up and perpetuated in the West by the Byzantine weavers: the Byzantine silk industry, which was as fine as the Persian, thrived during the artistic renaissance which flourished in Byzantium from the end of the 9th century, under the Macedonian dynasty.

Among these easily recognizable motifs are facing figures or animals either side of a central axis, very often a tree or a fire altar. These motifs are often placed in a medallion fringed with a border of pearls or floral designs. The most common key elements are lions, leopards, eagles, griffons, riders and elephants. Despite the prohibitions on depictions of creatures in Islam, these motifs continued for a long time as silk ornaments under the caliphs, among an abundance of birds, flowers and leaves. The Byzantine silk industry adopted many of these animal motifs—animals which were not all known at the time in Europe—and which spread throughout the Christian West. The symbolism in these motifs was apparently of little concern, even when used on the sumptuous silks enveloping the relics of Christian saints. The cloth known as the "cope of Saint Mexme" in France, which dates from the 4th century, was decorated with leopards chained to a Zoroastrian fire altar. In the 8th or 9th century, the shroud of St Austremoine, today in the keeping of the Textile Museum of Lyons, shows a classic Sassanian motif of a royal hunt: medallions enclosing two riders one on either side of a tree, each pursuing a lion with his lance. Another silk in the same museum (though not mentioned as having been used to wrap relics), shows a frieze of a repeated motif of two men on foot, facing either side of an invisible axis, each fighting a lion. The motif of the hunt, and above all of royal hunts, was widespread in the art of many countries, and particularly common in Persian textiles.

In the 8th and 9th centuries, the Prophet's prohibition, at least for men, to wear silk was a thing of the past. "Do not wear clothes of silk and brocade", he had said, "and do not use vases of gold and silver on your table; the infidels have these in this life, we shall have them in the next". To the pure and the just, the Koran promises that "they shall wear green robes of fine silk and thick silk brocade" and that "he who wears silk shall have no part in future life". In principle, men were only allowed to wear a cloth edged with silk two fingers wide or strings of silk. Clothes had to be made of cotton, linen or wool. These restrictions did not apply to women, or to fabrics used as fittings in tents or houses, which were an essential feature of nomadic peoples' furnishings. After the surrender of Jerusalem, where the conquerors plundered large quantities of silk, the first caliph, Caliph Omar, punished those Muslims who had allowed themselves to wear silk. Later, there arose a similar situation to that of the Christian West, with St Jerome's admonitions about cloth and perfume. Even if men abstained from wearing silk, the development which occurred in sericulture and the silk industry within the Muslim world is amply justified by the perfectly legitimate purchasing of women's clothing, carpets, draperies and bed covers, not to mention exports.

If the motifs derived from the Sassanian tradition spread over a very wide area, the same cannot be said of Chinese designs in the West. This might suggest that in the Tang period China exported large amounts of raw silk and very little worked cloth, supplying countries which even though they bred silkworms, never produced sufficient thread to satisfy the demands of their own industry.

Gradually, motifs more in conformity with Islam—geometric designs, interlacing, arabesques, ornamental calligraphy—began to appear on textiles, but the influence of the pre-Islamic Persian tradition was never completely eliminated.

Many of the names of fabrics indicate their place of manufacture, an additional proof of the itinerant nature of textiles. Various sources also mention particularly beautiful cloths, veritable symbols of these deeply monarchic societies with strict hierarchies, fabrics made exclusively for kings.

During the same period, weaving techniques were also spreading from one country to another with displaced workers: brocades, damasks, satins, felts, serges, muslins, gauzes. Terms such as *cendal*, a silk taffeta, samite, a more valuable cloth of serged silk, and *paile*, a rich drapery of golden silk, appear in the medieval vocabulary of the West. There were many others, more or less precisely identified (a French historian, Francisque-Michel, writing in the middle of the 19th century, devoted more than 700 pages to this problem), not to mention the Arabic and Persian vocabulary for types of cloth which have also given rise to solid dictionaries. In general, many of the names of fabrics indicate their place of manufacture, an additional proof of the itinerant nature of textiles. Various sources also mention particularly beautiful cloths, veritable symbols of these deeply monarchic societies with strict hierarchies, fabrics made exclusively for kings, which could not be exported on pain of harsh punishment, such as a caliph's robe woven at Tennis in Syria, certain Byzantine silks reserved for use in the palace and Chinese silks which were not allowed to be sold to merchants. In particular the cloth made of marine silk, from the hair of the *abû qalamûn*, as soft as silk and golden coloured, mentioned by Al-Muqaddasi in the 10th century as a product of North Africa. The sovereign forbade its export, but, says the author, it was exported in secret. Unfortunately this cloth is known to us only through literature, and no museum has been fortunate enough to preserve any. It is not even represented in painting. Like the dragon and the unicorn, we can but dream of it.

COTTON

Among those textiles which were exported in large quantities was cotton. India was in the forefront of this production, as well as Central Asia, where its cultivation had been introduced from India very early on, and where the Chinese encountered it in the Han period. The Chinese seem not to have developed it straight away for they imported cotton from Central Asia and Indo-China in the 3rd century. The cultivation of cotton is thought to have reached Mesopotamia in the 7th century, at the same time that northern Syria became a large producer, while India retained its number one position in the world. In the 8th and 9th centuries, several kingdoms of Central Asia produced fine cotton cloth, and the industry has continued there in modern times: the ex-Soviet republics of Central Asia have been great producers of cotton, thanks to irrigation, as well as growers of mulberry trees for silkworm breeding. In 1965, Uzbekistan was the main Soviet producer of cotton thread, supplying 70 per cent of Soviet production, and second in cotton cloth. In the Tang period, China imported cotton cloth mainly from Kucha and Ceylon.

Iran has had a long tradition of woollen products, particularly carpets. Weaving and carpet making spread to all regions under Iranian influence; the carpets from Iran, Sogdiana (particularly Bukhara), and from several other kingdoms in the Western Territories were famous, and exported to China and elsewhere. These included woven and embroidered carpets. Chinese imports of "dance carpets" from Central Asia are often mentioned. The wool used for these carpets was sheep's wool (silk would also be used later). Woollen cloth featured too among the exports of these sheep-breeding kingdoms, and a fine woollen cloth could be made from camel hair.

Tibet and Mongolia were large producers of sheep's wool (as well as hair and under fleece from yak, goat, camel and wild animals), but at first wool was used for making felt. This textile, relatively primitive and rough, was nevertheless well adapted to the rigorous, cold climate. It was also very practical for making the tents of these nomad breeders. The Tibetans, who were beginning to make a name for themselves from the 7th century on, were thought to dress exclusively in felt and animal skins. The Chinese princess Wencheng succeeded, so the legend goes, in persuading her husband, the king of Tibet, to change this habit and to wear silk undergarments.

Asbestos

Other textiles have been traded in smaller quantities: hemp, ramie and wild silks (which Chang'an did not spurn as tribute) from Assam, Japan and Korea. One more textile, a rare and expensive one, served as a gift between sovereigns, and has been known for centuries: the Chinese called it the "cloth which can be washed in fire", the Greeks *amiantos*, "that which cannot be soiled", we know it as asbestos. This substance can indeed be cleaned by being plunged into fire, from which it emerges as white as snow and unharmed, being fire-resistant. The Chinese believed that it was an animal product, the hair of a white rat, and a similar belief led in Europe to the legend of the salamander (this is a later term of Arabic origin). The Romans knew of this non-combustible cloth and, at the beginning of the Christian era, mined it in Cyprus and India. For the Chinese, it came from countries in the West, and the *History of the*

Later Han mentions it as a product of Da Qin. Several embassies from the Western Territories had, in the 3rd century AD, presented it to the Chinese court. The Persians and the Arabs also knew of asbestos cloth. The mineral itself is found in the form of soft fibres, which can be worked and then woven into a cloth; as such, it was used at the time for the safekeeping of precious objects, or to protect oneself from fire. Later, in the 13th century, there are mentions of Arabic soldiers wearing asbestos clothes when pouring flammable liquids on assailants during the siege of a city. It was Marco Polo who revealed to Western readers the mineral rather than animal nature of this fibre. In his time, it was to be found in Badakhshan and north of Hami, on the northern slopes of the Tianshan mountains.

HUMAN TRADE

But of all goods, the most valuable has always been man himself. Between the 8th and the 11th centuries, just as in preceding centuries, almost every country in the world functioned thanks to a servile work force. This was real slavery—when the slave could be bought, sold or put to death—and not the serf system

Slavery, which has existed ever since there have been wars, was not considered an anomaly, but as part of the natural order of things.

which was established gradually in European societies at the same time, nor the forms which still existed in Russia before 1861 and in Tibet before 1953.

Slavery, which has existed ever since there have been wars, was not considered an anomaly, but as part of the natural order of things. There were, however, significant restrictions on it, in the Muslim as well as the Chinese world, in the Christian as well as the Jewish one. Although any foreign slave could be bought or sold, a member of one's own nation or religious group could not legally be made a slave, except as a state-imposed punishment for some serious crime and in some cases debt. In China, one could not buy a Chinese slave, or in a Christian country a Christian slave, unless it was to enfranchise him. Similar dispositions also existed in certain Muslim countries. Thus on the whole, a slave was usually a foreigner or the descendant of a foreigner.

The main source of slaves was of course war, that great producer of prisoners. The victorious side would employ them for heavy public work—in the mines, building canals, ramparts and fortresses—or would make use of their military competence. This was widely practised in Muslim countries until modern times. The Persians and the Romans had done it before them, and the Chinese, the Turks and the Mongols did likewise. A skilled archer or an expert in fortifications was quickly put to use. Those whom the state did not need were sold to private owners. They carried out the heavy agricultural or construction work, as well as domestic chores. All artisans and technicians were used according to their specialization. Women and young girls were used for domestic work, cleaning, spinning, weaving, sewing, in the kitchen or looking after children. Certain young girls were fortunate enough to be educated as musicians, poets or dancers. There was also a particular category of slave, that of the eunuchs, who were operated on and sold in a few European towns (Cordoba and Verdun), and in Africa, Iran and Khorezm.

While the Christian world held some reservations over slavery, and was one of the first social systems to abandon it, the Muslim world, and to a lesser extent Tang China, were still fundamentally slave societies.

When wars ended in a region, or when the capture of cities no longer provided enough hands for labour, or when the social system no longer produced slaves, other sources had to be found. One then turned to one's weaker neighbours, to the least evolved foreign minorities, or to the large slave markets which were supplied through other wars and raids, or nations compelled to sell their children. The great reservoirs of the slave trade were the Turks, Slavs and East Africans.

Under the Tang, in the 7th century, as China conquered and swept the "barbaric" hordes before its armies, large numbers of prisoners were taken, mainly Turks, captured in their thousands in the Mongol steppes and the deserts of Serindia, as well as Manchus and Koreans. The civil population suffered the same fate. After the punitive expedition of Wang Xuance in 648, two thousand Indians, men and women, were brought back to China, including the king and queen of Magadha.

Mongolian and Central Asian nomads often served as horses' guards, grooms and as riders following in the retinues of nobles. An intelligent and cultured state slave could reach a high position in the palace, or in industry, as a guard, a translator or a trusted confidant. The least enviable fate was being sent to the southern frontiers of the Chinese Empire, the land of fevers, of headhunting aborigines and wild beasts. This was the sad fate, in 851, of many Tibetan and Uighur prisoners. State slaves were often used in the building and upkeep of the Great Wall and other fortifications, or digging canals.

Apart from slaves of military origin, one could buy men, women and children from the slave merchants in Tang China, all of them foreign, never Chinese. These were Persians, captured by pirates and held in slave villages on the island of Hainan, or Turks bought in the market in Bukhara, where they might end up after being kidnapped. Nomadic raids right across the deserts and oases which stretched from the Caspian Sea to Issyk-Kul, now in Turkmenistan, Uzbekistan and part of Kazakhstan, to kidnap men and sell them to the slave markets, were a veritable institution until the middle of the 19th century. The Russians were victims of this in the 18th century. In the Tang period, in the 9th and 10th centuries, other categories of Russians, if that term can already be used then, had ended up in the markets at Bukhara, Samarkand and Urgench: Slav slaves sold by the Khorezmites, who had bought them from Itil in Khazaria. These Slav tribes, who lived in the Russian forests and rivers on the banks of the Don, the Dnieper or Volga rivers, were not members of a powerful nation, and did not have an army strong enough to defend themselves. At first, they were raided and ransomed during incursions by the Varangians or Rus, Vikings who had come down from Scandinavia. After the establishment of the principality of Kiev under the domination of these Rus princes, in the 9th century, they continued to supply, mainly through kidnapping, the slave markets of neighbouring countries: Itil, Armenia, Ray, Baghdad, Urgench, Samarkand and Bukhara, but also Cordoba, Venice and Fustat (Cairo). Some of these men passed through the castration centres; we know that Jewish contractors were involved in such a centre at Verdun, in France, where the Slavs destined for Western Europe arrived. The Slav contribution to the markets was, according to Maurice Lombard,[112] such that their homeland, the forests of Central and

Eastern Europe, was called Bilâd as-Saqâliba, the "land of the slaves". Of the three main slave reservoirs, it was the principal one, the others being the Turks in the steppes of Central Asia, and the Africans from the savannah and the edges of the African bush.

The Turks, the great losers of the Muslim conquest and of the Chinese reconquest of Central Asia, were sold in large numbers on the markets of the Samanid kingdom (including present-day Uzbekistan), as well as on those of Iran and Mesopotamia. The Abbasid Caliphate bought them in huge numbers, and in the Muslim empire they served mainly—tens of thousands of them—in the sovereign's personal guard. These were the mameluks. These princely guards eventually became dangerously powerful in the hands of their freed Turkish officers, and had the power to make and break caliphs.

In China, one could also buy young girls from Korea or Manchuria, slaves from South-East Asia, Cambodia and Malaysia, as well, though illegally, Chinese subjects belonging to the minorities from southern China.

The third of the great slave reservoirs, Africa, does not concern Eastern or Central Asia, although black slaves did appear at the Chinese court of the Tang, as gifts from a sovereign, but they were of major importance to the wealth and power of the Muslim states. Nubians from the Upper Nile, Ethiopians, Somalis, Sudanese from West Africa, and particularly the Zanj, a Bantu people from East Africa, from the island we now call Zanzibar, were all victims of this trade. The Zanj often appear in the *Thousand and One Nights*, and in authentic travel accounts. Captured during raids, or bought very cheaply by local chiefs, they were redistributed in Egypt, Arabia and Mesopotamia. Many of them became eunuchs, and seem, at least in the tales, to have guarded the harems.

Maurice Lombard has emphasized the major importance of slavery for the economy of the Muslim world and the fact that from the 11th century on, when the great conquests were over, the sources of slavery began to run dry. The Slavs were converting to Christianity, and consequently could no longer be sold to the Muslims, according to the principles which were then applied. The Turks had become Muslim, and could no longer be enslaved, which left only the Africans. A crisis in the servile workforce followed.

HORSES

For China, the acquisition of horses was as vital as the slave trade was for the caliphs. The Tang empire, dynamic and martial, had as big a need of them as ever. When Li Shimin founded the dynasty, he had only 5,000 horses, of which 2,000 had been taken from the Turks. A state without horses stumbles and falls, so the emperor began breeding them in the state stud farms and pastures. But this did not satisfy the demand of an empire whose frontiers were extending in every direction, and of the Chinese armies, constantly in the field bivouacking more than 10,000 *li* away from the capital. The acquisition of horses remained a dominant feature of Chinese politics when it came to potential suppliers, all the more so in that the enemies to the north and west, the Turks, the Tibetans and the Arabs, had plentiful supplies of horses, and better breeds.

Horses continued to be traded for silk, and then also for tea, or for the protection of a powerful emperor or for the hand of a Chinese princess; these were old habits. But when the empire seemed in difficulty, they were exchanged for exorbitant sums of money, such as when the Uighur demanded 40 bolts of Chinese silk for every horse at the end of the 8th century. At the beginning of the 9th century, the Chinese government gave them a million bolts of silk taffeta for 100,000 inferior horses.[113]

At what price does one accept sending a daughter from one's lineage to bear children for a barbarian king? In 642, a princess was refused to a Turkish khan who had made an offer of 3,000 horses. The following year, one was granted to another Turkish khan who sent 50,000 horses, along with camels, oxen and goats, accompanied by a royal prince, who was probably a hostage resident in the imperial court. Horses arrived from every direction, the majority, in their thousands, from the north, from the Turks. These were short but very resistant animals, Mongol ponies, the same as were used earlier by the Xiongnu. The Tibetans bred and sold horses of the same type. But when relations began to deteriorate, and the supplier became the enemy, there were no more horses, and even the Tibetans had to kidnap them.

The best horses came from the West: a larger breed, faster and stronger, known since Han times. They came from Ferghana in Uzbekistan and from

Kyrgyzstan, Kucha and Khotan. The very finest became the steeds of princes. Emperor Taizong (626–649) had six favourite ones, whose names have come down to us and who were carved in stone for his tomb in Shaanxi (four of these carvings have been transferred to a museum in Xi'an, and the two remaining ones are in the University of Pennsylvania Museum, in Philadelphia). He also received magnificent Afghan horses from the king of Kapisa, a kingdom to the north of Kabul, at the time when the pilgrim Xuanzang was passing through. All these fine horses were celebrated by poets and painters. It was during the reign of Xuanzong, in the first half of the 8th century, that Han Gan, considered the most famous horse painter in the history of Chinese painting, worked. They are known also from the numerous Tang ceramic statuettes in museums which bring back to life the journey across Central Asia, with its camels, horses, caravan drivers, barbarians and pilgrims. But as realistic as these statues are, the same legendary aura which we noted for the Han still lived on: foals born of wild horses, a dragon-horse which emerges from a lake and heavenly horses. Between campaigns, the Chinese cavalry would play polo, a game which was perhaps of Iranian origin and which was said to have been introduced into China by members of a Tibetan embassy in 709.

The Muslim empire had several large horse-rearing regions under its control, not only in Central Asia, but also in Iran where a big, strong race was bred, capable of carrying warriors protected by heavy armour. Armour was gradually becoming heavier and more sophisticated, finally developing into the cataphractary, the equivalent of our steel-clad knight, like a shrimp in an articulated shell. This horse was bred in large numbers on the edge of the Iranian plateau which gives onto Mesopotamia. For centuries, these horses were exported to India, through the Persian Gulf, by sea, as is mentioned in many travellers' tales. In India, the horses survived with great difficulty, as Marco Polo was to remark, and had to be imported continually.

Apart from these horses of Iranian race, the subjects of the caliph had no trouble obtaining beautiful pure-bred Arab horses and small Barbary horses from North Africa, which carried the Arab conquerors to Africa and Spain. Crosses between these two breeds produced new ones with their own characteristics.

The West was of course also fighting wars with horses. However, it is interesting to note that while the names of the horses of the Chinese Emperor Taizong have been retained, and poems written about them, in the case of Emperor Charlemagne and his barons, of King Arthur or of Attila, it is the name of their swords which has been remembered: Charlemagne's *Joyeuse*, Roland's *Durandal*, Arthur's *Excalibur* (which had magical powers) and Attila's *Astur* (which made the person who held it invincible).

WEAPONRY

The third pillar of war, after men and horses, was weaponry. According to some historians, the Tang dynasty owed their power to the superiority of their weapons. In the history of this part of Asia, the main weapons were the bow and the sword—the lance was secondary.

Without necessarily being a specialist in this field, one can observe, reading the texts, a recurring situation, unchanged since the Han, which would only be modified by the arrival of the cannon which destroyed fortifications. This related to the different approaches taken by sedentary agricultural civilizations, tied to their fields and cities, and nomadic civilizations of animal breeders. The former protected themselves behind ramparts and fortresses, with watchtowers from which they could send fire or smoke signals from one position to the next to raise the alarm, as was done from the Great Wall to Khorezm and from Troy to Carcassonne. In the Han period, the Chinese had even invented the adjustable arrow loop, which allowed one to shoot safely from a wide range of angles. In addition, the Chinese fought as much as possible in close combat, using infantry as much as cavalry, resorting as much to the sword as to the bow or crossbow, and continually perfecting their armour. Their traditional enemies, the nomadic Xiongnu, Mongols and Turks were above all cavalrymen and archers, avoiding pitched battles and hand-to-hand combat, preferring quick raids, constant harassment and kidnapping. They withdrew behind a cloud of arrows rather than drawing their swords; they were elusive, but helpless when facing fortifications. Their strength resided in the speed of their horses and their skill at shooting.

The same distinction holds true in the case of Crassus' legions facing the Parthians, or the 18th-century Russians in Central Asia confronted by their neighbours from the steppes. They advanced along the rivers, building small fortresses as they went, and were constantly harassed and raided on the fringes of their growing empire by the Dzungar, Kazakh or Kyrgyz nomads. More advanced technically, the sedentary people perfected the best weapons, and did their utmost to prevent these weapons from falling into the hands of their enemies. In the 18th century, the Russians, great metalworkers and cannon makers, prohibited (or at least tried to prohibit) the sale of these weapons to the people from the steppes. The Chinese of the Tang period attempted to control the export of their swords and to prevent their Turkish enemy from obtaining them. Generally speaking, the transport and possession of weapons and armour was strictly controlled in China, and any breach of the law could lead to a three-year sentence as a slave. Any individual found with a set of armour and three crossbows in his possession could be banished to the frontiers. The clandestine manufacture of weapons was punished even more severely. Furthermore, any weapon entering China had to be declared, and was placed in the arsenal. Nevertheless, weapons smuggling was a flourishing business.[114]

The Tang sword could be long or short, with a single sharp edge. Was Chinese iron still among the best in the world? Most of these weapons were made in China, but the techniques for making iron, or rather steel, had been transmitted by the Chinese to the Parthians long before, according to Chinese texts. According to other authors, Seric iron may in actual fact have been Indian. It is not surprising that this technique eventually spread to all of China's neighbours, although the tales which mention the capture of weavers rarely refer to the transfer of metalworkers; we have seen only two cases of this: the Chinese deserters who took refuge with neighbours of the Parthians, during the Han, and the gold and silversmiths after the Battle of Talas.

The Turkish nations also had a long tradition of working iron. But the day came when the iron mines inevitably became exhausted, just as the forests next to the mines which provided the charcoal indispensable for ancient metalworking were also used up through over-exploitation. The metalworking industry is by necessity an industry which has to periodically move location. In the Tang period, there appears to have been a shortage of iron ore resources in the Chinese world, despite a ban on its export from China. The Muslim world was poor in iron ore, although there was some to be found in present-day Uzbekistan, in Ferghana and in Upper Zeravshan, and it was plentiful in the region of present-day Ura-Tyube in Tajikistan. The caliphate's main sources of supply were Lebanon, Spain, North Africa and the Caucasus. Indian steel was highly appreciated, and was imported to the large steelworks of Damascus and Toledo where it was fashioned. Swords made of this steel were also bought directly from India, and were reputed for their strength, sharpness and flexibility. Indian steel was made of ore from the land of Zanj, on the eastern coast of Africa, the same region which supplied gold and slaves.[115]

Chinese iron must have retained its reputation since the tale of the 600th of the *Thousand and One Nights* recounts how the hero arrives in a marvellous land, at a tall mountain of blue rock, in which there is a cave shut by a door of Chinese iron.

In the Christian West, rich iron deposits were known in the Alps, and the Tyrol and Styria became renowned centres of weapons manufacture. Other iron-producing regions included the Rhineland, Lorraine and Champagne, as well as the Pyrenees.

The commercial circuit of iron and swords is somewhat surprising; admittedly, these goods were neither fragile nor perishable, but they were heavy, and in addition, the journey was not always legal or risk-free. Pig iron and sometimes even the ore itelf were transported by land or by sea over large distances, which implies that the buyer had great need of them. The swords of the Franks were famous, and Muslim customers bought them either in Andalusia, or through the "land of slaves", the Slavs. They travelled along the Russian rivers and the Caspian Sea, transiting through Khazaria. From there, they could reach Iran, or Khorezm along the north of Caspian, and the great trade centres of Urgench, Bukhara and Samarkand. These Frankish swords may originally have been made from iron ore from the Tyrolean Alps or from Lorraine. In the Mediterranean, the Christian kingdoms in principle abstained from selling swords to Muslim customers, but it is known that the Republic of Venice, the main non-Muslim conveyor, willingly broke these rules when it came to business. The Venetians had no scruples about unloading in the Muslim ports shiploads of swords which had been made in the Christian forges of Lorraine and transported down the Rhone Valley to the ports of Provence.

There was of course another classic way of getting hold of weapons, through war itself. On the battlefield, or off the backs of the vanquished, the victor could collect armour and weapons by the thousands or tens of thousands. This was an important part of booty. In addition, high-ranking officers carried ornate, richly decorated weapons, inlaid with precious materials, sometimes gilded in gold or silver.

Bows and arrows, the only weapon which could strike at a distance (the javelin, much used by the Greeks and Romans, does not seem to have been known in Asia), had been perfected many times. There were bows for foot soldiers and for horsemen, bows made of mulberry wood, nomads' bows reinforced with animal horn and sinews, and crossbows. China bought or made all of these. It also imported special bows, such as the famous great bows of Khorezm which only the strongest men could bend. Chinese arrows, made of bamboo or wood for hunting, or with long steel heads for war, were in no way inferior to those of other nations. Among the specialities from different countries which the Chinese court received as tribute were whistling arrows from the Mongol nomads, poisoned arrows from the kingdom of Nanzhao, in South China, sword blades from Manchuria and armour of various origins.

Han dynasty armour had been made of plates of leather (already at the time of the *Tribute of Yu* vassals sent leather for this purpose, either cow, deer or rhinoceros hide). Under the Tang, these leather scales were reinforced with circlets of metal. At the same time, armour appeared which was made from plates of iron sewn onto a cloth backing, covering each other like the scales of a fish. From the 8th century on, a new type of metal armour spread across Asia and Europe: the coat of mail, or chain mail, which is familiar to us from the European Middle Ages, is also seen in Persian and Arabic paintings and surprisingly, in illustrated manuscripts from Dunhuang. Each element of the chain is riveted to the next, and in China it was known as chain armour. The result is a very supple armour which envelops the body like a cloth, protecting it more fully than the preceding forms. It is also much less cumbersome, less paralyzing than the complete plate-armour worn by knights which can be seen in our museums. This was a major invention but to whom do we owe it? Not to the Chinese, who may have learned of it first from the Tibetans, unless they received a set from Samarkand, at the beginning of the 8th century. It was probably invented by the Iranians. In any event, it spread very fast in every direction.

Because of its texture, chain mail could not be decorated in the luxurious way metallic plates could. It could not be engraved, inlaid or damascened. All this splendour had to be applied to the helmet or the harnessing of the horse. Nevertheless, as supple as it was, chain mail, covering the body from head to toe, leaving only the eyes apparent, weighed heavily on the man and horse that bore it.

Another important element of armaments, leather, was also partly imported into China, and the foreign supplier was once again the nomad breeder. Although less leather was used than previously for armour itself, the demand for different types of leather was still very great as it was used for harnessing, saddles, ropes and ties, bows and arrows, riders' boots, leather sheets in which to wrap objects for transport, water containers and various utensils. All these were made of horse, deer, sheep or ox hide, from both domestic and wild animals. The importance of leather in war is revealed in an amusing way by the following episode about the king of Khotan and the King of the Rats, as recorded by the pilgrim Xuanzang after he had visited this kingdom in 629.

There was in Khotan a particular species of large desert rat, with fur the colour of gold and silver, which had something supernatural about it. At that time, under imminent attack from the Xiongnu, the king of Khotan, only too aware that his army was inferior in numbers, regretted having never made offerings to these creatures. He apparently made up for this and implored their help in this difficult situation. That very night, he saw in a dream a very large rat who told him to attack the Xiongnu the next morning, assuring him that he had nothing to fear. The enemy was already camped outside the capital. Before dawn, the Khotanese army set out, and swept down suddenly upon the Xiongnu. Caught unawares, they ran to their horses and chariots, but to their surprise the leather of their armour, the saddles and harnessing, the strings of their bows, the laces on their clothes, everything which was made of leather had been eaten during the night by the rats. The Khotanese had no difficulty in killing, capturing and breaking up the disorganized, terrified army, which felt that there had indeed been a divine intervention. And this is why, so Xuanzang explains, the desert rat is venerated in the kingdom of Khotan. In gratitude the king had a temple built where sacrifices were made to these rats. Even at the time of Xuanzang's visit, offerings were regularly made. And should offerings fail to be made, some misfortune would certainly befall the kingdom.

DYES AND OTHER VALUABLES

Fortunately, war was not a constant, and the arts and crafts of peacetime also demanded that trade provide a variety of useful products, particularly in the dyeing process of the textile trade. Dyes played an important role in international commerce until the advent of synthetic chemicals in the early modern period. India exported indigo to almost every country; this blue dye was extracted from the leaf and twigs of a bush (*indicum*), known in the West since the beginning of the Christian era and still traded in the 17th and 18th centuries. It was not used only for textiles, but also for cosmetics and in painting. In Persia, it was made into kohl eyeliner, and it was from Persia, or Samarkand, that China received it. A widespread red dye was *sapan*, or brazil-wood, obtained from a tree which grew abundantly in Sumatra and is often mentioned in the Middle Ages. Another red dye, a costly one, used for silk, came from the lacquer insect and was imported into China from Amman and Cambodia. Gamboge, a wood which produced a resin, was used by Far Eastern painters as a yellow pigment; it too was exported from Siam and Cambodia. Other pigments of mineral origin included orpiment or arsenic trisulphide, which gave a very fine yellow, and was exported by Cambodia and the Indochinese state of Champa. It was much sought after by painters, and was used as far afield as Dunhuang in some silk paintings. Blue came from lapis lazuli and green from malachite, both of which were spreading both eastwards and westwards. Litharge, or lead monoxide, used in painting, was exported by Persia. None of these products took up much space, but more voluminous goods, equally essential, filled the long-distance caravans:

alum, indispensable for the leather and paper industries, came from Gansu, Turfan, Byzantium or Persia; sal ammoniac from Kucha and Sogdiana; borax was exported from Tibet; and nitrates came from the salt lakes in Central Asia. From across the seas came Indonesian sulphur, while soda arrived from the South Seas.

Gold and silver was present in many countries. Whether or not used as coinage, they contributed to the balance of trade, that is to pay for purchases when the country buying did not have a volume of goods to export corresponding in value. It is a recurrent theme throughout the history of trade that Western nations had to pay for their Asian imports with massive amounts of coinage and precious metal. Either they did not produce enough goods to equal the value of their imports, or what they produced was not sought-after in Asia. The pre-industrial period is said to have been, according to some theories, a period when production was always inferior to demand, at least on the international market (though on the domestic market the situation must have been different). There was, for example, an over-production of silk in China at certain times. Precious metals and coins compensated for this, preventing the mechanism of trade from coming to a halt. Thus the abundance of these coins in certain distant sites demonstrates the commercial deficit of their country of origin. Certain valuable objects, however, such as works of art or ritual objects, form a case apart as they were not intended to be sold again and circulated in different ways, either as gifts or as plunder.

Gems, fine stones, jade, pearls, ivory, coral and amber travelled with a syncopated rhythm: the very finest pieces were in general reserved by the king. They entered the Treasury, either the king's own or that of the person to whom he presented it as a gift. Those destined to be sold passed through the hands of merchants, and often ended up at the other end of the world. A valuable object would sometimes be bought and sold several times, but the first non-commercial buyer generally had no intention of selling it again. This type of object could stay in a family for generations, or be given to a religious establishment, from where there was a strong chance that it would not travel again for two or three more centuries. Short of war, revolution, theft or fire, it might well remain there for a thousand years.

If, on the contrary, it was stolen or plundered, the object would once again change hands and travel on. Then it was difficult to trace. It might be re-molten, taken apart, modified, it would probably be sold again, which would place it back in the commercial circuit, or it would end up in another palace, in another state treasury or a church, and be once again immobilized for a few centuries.

As trouble loomed on the horizon, the more astute would frequently bury their treasures in a secret location, so well hidden that if its proprietor died, it might be found again only centuries later. This is what archaeologists and historians hope for. The Dunhuang manuscripts and many funerary treasures have reached us in this way. Modern museums may perhaps succeed in preserving them for a time, although bombardments have already reduced to ashes many a treasure which was thought to be safe for eternity. Gold and silver from all over the world, jade from Khotan, lapis lazuli from Badakhshan, Persian turquoise, Baltic amber, diamonds from India, emeralds from Africa, rubies from Ceylon, all of these travelled extensively in all the ways listed above, in these few centuries of active trade and violent exchange, and still continue to do so to some extent. Other more fragile objects, such as coral, pearls and glass, may have disappeared totally, as well as most cloth.

PLANTS

What cannot be resurrected either is the atmosphere of Tang China; the world of scents, associated with bodily health and the divine, two fields which are completely unrelated in our Western conceptions. In the Tang period, the upper classes lived in a cloud of incense and perfume; perfumed bodies, perfumed baths, pouches of scent, temples filled with the smoke of incense. Religious life was permeated with it; Buddhists, Confucians, Daoists and Nestorians continually burnt aromatic substances. Most of these perfumes were meant to be burned, and were made up of various ingredients, many of which were imported. By land, they came from India, Persia and Byzantium. By sea, they came from Arabia, and South-East Asia. Central Asia and Tibet were mainly producers of musk. All-pervading incense was used as much for therapeutic reasons as devotional ones: certain illnesses were thought to be caused by the influence of evil spirits and a fumigation either appeased them or drove them away. Burning incense for the gods encouraged them to behave benevolently and protect one from misfortune; religion and health were connected. Chinese medicine was deeply influenced by Daoist beliefs.[116]

Among the ingredients of these compound incenses for burning were plants native to China, both from the north and south, such as cinnamon, camphor, basil, citronella, nard, *costus*, aniseed, turpentine and gardenia. Other aromatic plants were imported, such as frankincense (*thus*) and myrrh from Arabia, bdellium or "perfume from Anxi" from Persia and other Mediterranean countries, all of which we have met as items of trade in earlier periods; musk came by land from Tibet, Sogdiana and Gansu; *onycha*, the operculum of a seashell, from the Chinese coast or the islands. The import of other aromatic substances from Indonesia and Indochina (Cambodia, Annam, Champa) was also gradually developing: sandalwood, aloes and other fragrant woods, liquid storax, benzoin, cloves and ambergris, known in Chinese as "dragon saliva", which was gathered in the sea at various points in the Indian Ocean. And there were many more substances. Canton, until the end of the 9th century, was the world's greatest bazaar of aromatic substances.

The Arabic and Persian merchants who visited not only Canton, but also the ports of Sumatra, Java, Ceylon and India, stocked up on these precious goods and on spices for their own market, as well as for sale to Christian countries. The Muslim civilization made widespread use of perfumes for personal purposes, especially rose, jasmine and violet essence. The West probably once again developed a taste for this during the Crusades, from the 12th century on.

There exists a concrete description of a journey to Canton and of trade in that port by an Arabic merchant called Suleyman, in the middle of the 9th century, predating the turmoil which ruined trade there. The tale is followed by remarks by another person, who did not make the journey but who adds interesting information written around 916, just after the unrest.[117] The great trade port with eastern Asia, on the Iranian coast of the Persian Gulf, was Siraf, which was visited by sailors from Java, Malaysia, India, China, Arabia, Mesopotamia, Socotra, East Africa, Persia, Syria and Byzantium. The crossing from Siraf to Canton took five months: one month to reach Muscat, another month from there to Kulam of Malaya, a port in southern India, where Chinese ships paid transit rights, and then on to the Langabalus Islands (the Nicobar Islands?), taking care to avoid a few islands inhabited by cannibals. A month after Kulam, one arrived at Kalahbar, in Java, before continuing on to the island of Tiyuma, to Kundrang, Champa (Cochinchina and Annam), and finally Canton. No stopover in Serendib, Ceylon, is mentioned, although Suleyman probably did visit it. He describes the products from there, as well as those from the Indian Ocean off the coast of Zanj, among the 1,900 islands scattered between Muscat and Ceylon: this is where ambergris was collected in the sea. In Ceylon, pearls, rubies, topaz, gold, aloes wood and conchs could be bought. Suleyman uses the Indian word *shank* which refers to conchs used in Buddhist ceremonies. He also mentions that many Jews, Manichaeans and followers of other religions live in Serendib, as this country was tolerant and allowed each person to practise his own faith.

Aloes wood could be bought in several ports of call and sold in Canton. Suleyman visited none of the regions producing musk, but he does provide a fairly long description of the animal, mentioning that it was hunted on the borders of China and Tibet.

Merchants were well advised to take with them, or buy along the way, certain specific products to sell in Canton: ivory, incense, copper, tortoiseshell, rhinoceros horn (belts of rhinoceros horn plates made in India were much in demand in China), fragrant woods and aromatics from South-East Asia, ultra-fine muslin from India and ambergris from the Indian Ocean. These are just a few of the many products exchanged during these commercial ventures.

Two particularly interesting passages in Suleyman's tale read as portents of the even greater role which the Chinese Empire would play in international trade somewhat later: two new products are mentioned, which the Chinese would monopolize for a long time, just as they had silk. Suleyman refers to (although he does not say that he bought any) "a clay of superior quality with which bowls are made which are as thin as glass bottles; the liquid inside them can be seen through them." This is, of course, porcelain.

Further on, he writes of "a sort of dried herb which the Chinese drink in hot water. This herb is sold in all the cities, for a very high price. It is called *sah*. It is slightly more fragrant than clover, but has a bitter taste. Water is boiled and poured onto this herb: this infusion works as an antidote

Silk, tea and porcelain would, in modern times, become the pillars of Chinese external trade.

against all indispositions." This is tea (pronounced *cha* in Mandarin), which was beginning to reach all levels of the Chinese population, before becoming an essential foodstuff among the Tibetans and Mongols. From the 11th century at least, horses would be bought in exchange for tea and no longer in exchange for silk. Later, this fashion would spread among the Russians, but only from the 17th century among the Europeans. As for porcelain, at the end of the Tang, it was beginning to be exported westwards. Silk, tea and porcelain would, in modern times, become the pillars of Chinese external trade.

As well as aromatic substances, there were also spices, which were used both as therapeutic scents and ingredients in cooking: pepper, cinnamon, ginger, cloves and nutmeg have never left our tables since the time of the *Periplus of the Erythraean Sea*. A new category of goods, that of medicines, also reflects the dynamism of trade at this period, although the vocabulary used for these is often difficult to identify positively. Along with the buying and selling of medicine was a parallel trade in medical books, medical knowledge and physicians themselves.

In Chinese medicine, which has a very old and sophisticated tradition, a large number of scientific works, medical encyclopaedias and guides to medicinal plants had already been written. Traditionally, the legendary Emperor Shennong is credited with teaching his people the therapeutic virtues of plants, in the third millennium BC. China was rich in native medicines and apart from those sent by "tributary" states, it also imported some from abroad. It also exported its own drugs. The list of these products is long, and apart from aromatic substances such as musk, it includes rhubarb from the Tibetan border and Gansu; ginseng from Manchuria; zedoary (from the Persian term *jadwâr*), a non-poisonous aconite, a herbaceous plant which grows abundantly in the Himalayan countries, China and Tibet; saffron, or carthamus, which grew among other places in

> *The problem of the preservation of medicinal substances over very long journeys meant that the land route was often preferred to the sea route, for example in the case of rhubarb and musk, as the humidity at sea quickly spoilt this type of product.*

Kashmir; bezoars, concretions found in the stomach of ruminants; bear bile, snake venom, young deer horn, tiger bones, rhinoceros horn and wild products from the forests, as well as various mineral substances. The trade of all these medicines was tightly controlled, at least in China, as both customers and merchants were wary of adulterations. In addition, the problem of the preservation of medicinal substances over very long journeys meant that the land route was often preferred to the sea route, for example in the case of rhubarb and musk, as the humidity at sea quickly spoilt this type of product.

Under the Tang dynasty, the attraction of the first emperors for everything foreign was particularly noticeable in their search for drugs and pharmaceutical products, medical books and experts in this domain. The first Tang emperors were very interested in Indian medicine and science, had Indian medical books translated into Chinese and invited Indian physicians to China. They were not the only ones to do so: the influence of Indian medicine had already been present at the Persian court at the time of Sassanians, and increased under the Muslim caliphate from 750 onwards.

The reputation of Greek medicine has already been noted in Chinese historical annals, as illustrated by the episode of the gift of theriac. Jewish physicians were much sought after everywhere. Arabic medicine was in full development. This "Judeo-Arabic medicine", as it has been termed by M. Lombard,[118] was based on Greek medicine, translated into Syriac, Armenian or Arabic (the translators were often Nestorian Christians), which had passed from Greece to Syria, Baghdad, Cairo and then Cordoba, where the Spanish Jews translated the medical works into Latin, the form in which they reached the centres of the Christian West. This basic Greek knowledge was then developed in the Muslim world, particularly in Iran where scientists added to it the learning from the ancient East, as well as that of ancient Iran and India.[119]

ALCHEMY

Another form of knowledge that had fascinated several Han emperors and stimulated them to turn to Indian science at one time was the manufacture of drugs of immortality. This was one of the fundamental notions of Daoism, the search for longevity, and then for immortality, in a worldly and corporeal sense. Daoism flourished during the Tang, and several emperors, including Taizong, greatly encouraged the search for immortality drugs, or rather for an elixir, which several of their predecessors had already sought. The aim was to make use of botanical, zoological, mineralogical and especially chemical knowledge to prepare an elixir which would prolong human life beyond old age, by rejuvenating the body and its spiritual elements so that the adept could live for several centuries and finally reach the status of eternal life, becoming a real immortal within an ethereal body.[120] A being with a light, purified body, yet still made of matter and of this world; such a being could sometimes be met, wandering through the mountains and forests, or ascending to heaven. So many cases have existed and been recorded that there are even collections of biographies of immortals.

Drinking this elixir was one way of becoming immortal; to prepare it, either plants or inorganic substances were necessary. During the Tang, the search for the formula centred mainly on the latter. In antiquity, several emperors had sent missions across the world to find the plant of immortality; this mythical plant which blossoms in so many tales, in the *Thousand and One Nights*, in our Western fairy-tales, or in the *Ten Isles in the Sea*, already mentioned earlier, was to be picked on an island in the Eastern Ocean. The first Chinese emperor, Qin Shihuangdi, sent a Daoist admiral and five hundred young men and women on a sea journey to find it; none ever returned. In the *Shahnâme*, written by the Persian poet Ferdusi, King Khosroes I, in the 6th century, sent an envoy to fetch this plant from the Himalaya.[121]

Some authors have remarked upon the parallels between the *soma* of Hinduism, the *haoma* of ancient Iran, the peach of immortality of Chinese mythology which grows in the Kunlun mountains (the Far West of Chinese mythology), and with the tree whose fruit confers immortality—the second forbidden tree in the terrestrial paradise—which Adam and Eve did not have time to touch because they had been driven out after having eaten the fruit of the first tree. In other words, somewhere on this earth, there must be a plant or a stone which grants immortality.

Great kings have great means at their disposal: how many chemists, alchemists, scholars and botanists worked for the Chinese emperors! Since this elixir had never been prepared from native resources, it was considered necessary to turn to outside help. Emperor Wudi of the Han had done so, and Taizong also tried. On one particular occasion Taizong enlisted the help of an Indian scholar. After his campaign in northern India, Wang Xuance, who had survived the attack on the Chinese embassy and defeated the Indian king with the help of Tibetan and Nepalese troops, returned to China in 650 with the king and other Indian prisoners. Among these, according to the *History of the Tang*, was a *fangshi*, a term used to designate Daoist alchemists, adept at carrying out chemical experiments. This particular *fangshi*, called Nalomi Sopomei in the Chinese transcription, claimed to be two hundred years old and to be able to live several more centuries. The emperor provided him with lodgings in the palace, and ordered him to prepare the drug of immortality, placing him under military surveillance. The *fangshi* requested incredible plants and special minerals, which had to be sought throughout the empire. Agents were sent to several different Indian kingdoms, in search of a stone from the Banchafo River, since he claimed that a stone idol guarded this river which possessed peculiar properties: sometimes the water would be burning hot, sometimes cold, it could dissolve grass, trees, gold and iron, and if one puts one's hand in it, it would cook it immediately. There were also many other strange things straight out of the visions of an opium addict. But the leaves of one required tree remained inaccessible, as it was defended by a gigantic venomous snake, and the leaves could only be taken by shooting at them with four-headed arrows. In the end, it was decided to send the alchemist home, but unable to make the journey, he finally died in Chang'an. Thus ends the story of the first Indian alchemist at the Tang court.

During the reign of Gaozong (650–741), who also wanted to take the drug of immortality, or at least to prolong his life, an Indian from East India, called Lugaido, arrived at court, offering his services as an alchemist. But nothing came of this either.

Two curious and completely unrelated details that appear in this context of relations with India seem to suggest a definite association with Daoism. The first event occurred while Wang Xuance was in India when, on the point of departure, an Indian king asked him to send him a "portrait of Laozi". The second is that spinach seeds were sent to China by the Nepalese, where they were acclimatized. This would be no more interesting than the import of the turnip, were it not for the fact that this plant is useful for offsetting the side effects of the drug of immortality.

Daoists also worked on mineral substances, either preparing drinkable gold, or perfecting compounds which included highly toxic materials such as mercury, arsenic and lead. These led to heavy losses among alchemists and their customers, and at least two Chinese emperors are thought to have died from them.

Setting aside the charlatans and accidents, it is very likely that in this great mixing of ideas, people, techniques, scientific knowledge and religious beliefs which was occurring then right across the continent, notions of alchemy and chemistry, and knowledge about matter and the human body were passed around between specialists, perhaps away from the courts and from the egocentricity of the rulers, as these were fields in which discretion was a virtue in many countries in these ancient times.

Several historians of ideas and science have raised the question about the relationship between Greek alchemy and Western medieval alchemy on the one hand, and what is known about Daoist practices or ancient Chinese practices in general. In modern times, nobody has discussed this better than Joseph Needham, in a few chapters of his *magnum opus*, *Science and Civilisation in China*, which he said only he and his wife have ever read in its entirety. On the 24th March 1995, the "honorary Daoist", the "Erasmus of our times", departed from this world at the age of 94.

In intellectual and religious fields, within the Daoist, Buddhist, Muslim, Nestorian, Manichaean and Judaic currents which were intermingling in Asia, two new items appeared in commerce: books, which we have already mentioned, and Buddhist relics, in the same way that the trade of relics prospered in the Christian world. "Let the dead bury the dead", and "Do not make relics of my body", they had said. Vain words. The teeth of the Buddha, his alms bowls, the Crown of Thorns, the hands or legs of saints, all of these could be bought, sold, stolen, pawned, and all attracted pilgrims.

At the end of the 9th century, the Tang dynasty was teetering, undermined by internal rebellions. These disorders led to the ruin of the dynasty, and the ruin multiplied the disorders. Trade in Chang'an was reduced to a trickle. Fires broke out in Canton, and the city was plundered and destroyed in 878 by Huang Chao's bandit rebels. Its inhabitants were massacred: without counting the Chinese victims, 120,000 foreigners, Muslims, Jews, Christians and Mazdaians, who lived and traded in Canton, all perished. Huang Chao had the mulberry trees cut down, which put an end to the production of cocoons in the region and to the export of silk to Arab countries from that port. The merchants deserted Canton. Sea communications were interrupted.

In 907, the Tang dynasty collapsed; not only had the central power once again lost control of its native lands and its colonial empire, as well as its influence in Central Asia, but China itself broke up, following the usual cycle of fragmentation and unification. This was the period of the Five Dynasties, which lasted until 960. Then, a sixth dynasty predominated and founded the Song empire, with its capital at Kaifeng. With the re-establishment of a unified imperial central power, it was the port of Quanzhou, which the Arabic merchants named Zaitun, which became the great maritime rendezvous of world trade.

Chapter Fifteen

Oriente Poliano, Cloths of Gold and Silk

*I*n 1954, the Istituto Italiano per il Medio ed Estremo Oriente celebrated the seven hundredth anniversary of the birth of Marco Polo by convening in Italy an international congress attended by many eminent specialists. The acts of this congress were published by the IsMEO in 1957, in Rome, under the title *Oriente Poliano*.

In 1954, Europe was just emerging from the post-war period; the remaining shortages limited travel, but the main obstacles were the Iron and Bamboo curtains which divided the world into the Communist "Eastern bloc" and the capitalist "Western world". This was the period of the Cold War. China was out of bounds, the USSR more tightly closed than ever. East of Iran, the Silk Road was no longer travelled by Europeans or Americans except in their dreams. This phase of closure was to last thirty years.

In order to break down these barriers, at least in the minds of historians, they got together at a congress, which at the time was not as frequent an event as it is nowadays. What better response to give to these policies of closure than to talk of the Venetian hero of communication between Europe and Asia?

MARCO POLO

Oriente Poliano, the Orient of the Polos, was, to be more precise, the Orient of the *Description of the World*, one of the titles given to Marco Polo's account of his journey and all that he saw and heard between 1271 and 1298, during 27 years of travel and living in Asia Minor, Persia, Central Asia, China, Indonesia and India, along the great trade routes of the end of the 13th century. This was a period when the descendants of Genghis Khan reigned over a large part of the world, and Venice and Genoa reigned over European trade with the East.

Is there anyone, today, who does not know something of the adventures of Marco Polo? For centuries books and archives have been examined, and probably everything which can shed some light on his curriculum vitae has been unearthed. And yet, it is still keenly discussed, and proofs and absences of proof are examined with untiring passion to try and answer the question, *Did Marco Polo go to China?*, to quote the title of a book by Frances Wood, published in London in 1995. The author, a Sinologist, is Head of the Chinese Department at the British Library in London. This work has rekindled an old debate which had been dormant over the authenticity of Marco Polo's tale, and, with the help of British television, its reverberations have now reached far beyond the usual circle of specialists. But before coming to that, let us begin with the irrefutable, the precedents to this famous journey to China. The story begins in 1260.

The three Polo brothers, merchants from Venice, had set up a trading post in Constantinople and another in Sudak, in the Crimea, then a tributary of the Golden Horde, the westernmost khanate of the Mongol Empire. Two of the brothers, Mafeo and Nicolo, were in charge of the Crimean post. There they bought furs from northern Russia, wheat from the Ukrainian plains, salted fish from the Sea of Azov, silks and spices from Asia, and slaves taken from the neighbouring Qipchak tribes. For over sixty years, the Venetians had occupied a dominant position, almost a monopoly, in the Mediterranean and the Black Sea over trade with the Muslim world, whether with the Turks or the Islamic Mongols. Their consul in Constantinople was almost the second most important figure in the state; they controlled several large Greek islands, were the foremost naval power in Christendom, the maritime transporters of the Crusades, and money-lenders to barons and kings. If anyone benefited from two centuries of Crusades, it was Venice.

At the time when the Polo family was divided between Venice, Constantinople and Sudak, it had been a hundred and sixty-five years since Pope Urban II had called upon the entire Christian world to take up arms and travel overseas to deliver Jerusalem and Christ's tomb, the most sacred of all pilgrimage sites in Christendom, from the hands of the Muslims. In 1095, these were the Seljuk Turks, one of the greatest Muslim powers of the Middle Ages.

Originally from Central Asia, these Turks had converted to Islam a century before, and emigrated westwards. This was the First Crusade, a period of great spirituality and sacrifice. For several generations, many Christian kingdoms sent their rulers, and sometimes several members of the royal family, as well as their barons, knights and many monks, with all the necessary rank and file, to fight the enemies of Christ, for the love of God and the salvation of their souls. It was also hoped to convert a few Saracens, as the Muslims were called, who, on their part, referred to those from Christian nations as "Franks" (this term, in varying forms, designated Westerners in general throughout Asia until the 17th or 18th century).

Jerusalem, which had belonged to Byzantium since the 4th century, was the subject of dispute between Byzantium and Sassanian Persia during the first half of the 7th century (in 630, the Byzantine emperor Heraclius had brought back to Byzantium the Crown of Thorns, an extremely precious relic to the Christians). But Jerusalem was also claimed as the third holy city of Islam, and conquered in 638 by Caliph Omar. It remained under Muslim domination during the Egyptian Fatimid in the 10th century, then under the Seljuks, whose oppression led to the Pope's First Crusade appeal.

These overseas expeditions had to be financed, troops had to be fed and transported on ships, and weapons and horses bought. Only rich countries could take on these expenses. Nevertheless a moral obligation was felt to participate in the Crusades and the lords, who covered their own expenses and those of their men, and even the kings were forced to borrow money. The Venetians, ship builders and owners, fulfilled the dual role of transporter and moneylender. They lent against security—and what security! In 1237–1238, the merchant bankers of Venice even took the Crown of Thorns itself as a guarantee against the presumably colossal sum which the penniless government of Constantinople borrowed. The Crown of Thorns was almost put up for sale but the Venetians wanted to keep it. The king of France, Louis IX, a pious king who would later be known as Saint Louis, bought it back before the deadline expired, in 1238. The relic was taken to Paris, where it still remains, having by some extraordinary stroke of luck escaped all later conquests and revolutions, all the fanatics, bombardments and fires.

English and French knights left in large numbers; a king of England and a king of France became crusaders; Louis IX took part in two Crusades, being taken prisoner and held for ransom in the first one, in 1250. During the second, in 1270, he died of illness besieging Tunis, without ever having seen Jerusalem. Richard the Lion Heart was also taken prisoner and freed against a large sum of money. King's ransoms were part of a nation's budget.

Jerusalem was taken by the crusaders in 1099. Godfrey of Bouillon founded the Frankish Kingdom of Jerusalem, which covered mainly the coastal area of Syria and Palestine, over which several French knights ruled, and which would last two centuries. The City of Jerusalem itself was taken back by Saladin, the Sultan of Egypt and Syria, in 1187. The Third Crusade ended in 1192 with a treaty between Richard the Lion Heart and Saladin, which allowed the Franks to keep the Palestinian coast from Tyre to Jaffa, without Jerusalem, which remained in Muslim hands. Although the Christians could travel there on pilgrimage, the real centre of Christian Palestine then became Acre. Jerusalem changed hands twice more between Franks and Saracens until the disappearance of the Christian Kingdom of Jerusalem in 1291.

The story has been told elsewhere of how the spiritual drive which lay behind the First Crusade was later perverted and how the defenders of the Holy Sepulchre turned into unscrupulous adventurers, carving out fiefs for themselves in conquered land, ravaging, burning and plundering. The worst case was the capture of Constantinople by the crusaders in 1204, an "act of international brigandage", which set Christians against Christians, Roman Catholics against Orthodox Greeks. The former lacked funds, and Constantinople was bursting with wealth. The crusaders owed money to the Venetians. The Latins and Greeks had hated each other for a long time and had anathematized the other since the split of 1054. The city was completely plundered, and one of the crusader princes, Baldwin of Flanders, was named Emperor of Constantinople, founding the ephemeral Latin Empire which lasted only fifty-seven years.

After 1204, the Venetians, who had helped the crusaders, acquired such power that the Latin Empire was divided between them and the Franks. Venice obtained, in addition to part of the booty, all the privileges mentioned above, including the complete exemption of taxes and customs duties in Constantinople and throughout the empire, a large borough of the capital, rights in the islands, and in practice the control of the straits between the Mediterranean and the Black Sea, as well as the monopoly on the election of the patriarch. Neither of its Italian rivals, Genoa and Pisa, obtained such conditions. It was in these privileged circumstances that Venetian merchants, like the Polo brothers, had prospered. Unfortunately for them, the situation then changed radically.

The Latin Empire of Constantinople had weakened and was about to be reconquered by the Greeks, who had withdrawn for half a century to Nicea, in Anatolia. The Genoese, the rivals of the Venetians in the Mediterranean, made an alliance with the Greeks of Nicea. In mid-July 1261, the allied forces of the Genoese and the Greeks of Emperor Michael VIII took back Constantinople, drove the Latins out, and re-established a Greek dynasty—although illegitimate—that of the Paleologues, which reigned over what remained of the Byzantine Empire until 1453. Rapidly, the Genoese began to take the place of the Venetians with the same commercial and political advantages which Constantinople had granted the latter under the crusaders.

Was it due to this possibly predictable situation that, in 1260, the two Polo brothers, competent and experienced merchants, decided to travel, well provided with jewels, to Khan Berke, the khan of the Golden Horde, a grandson of Genghis Khan, who resided at Sarai on the Volga? Did they want to explore new business markets? Berke had converted to Islam, but this does not seem to have disturbed our Venetians. However, we shall see that they were to play an active role in the service of the Christian religion. Christendom was running out of breath in the East, weakened by its perpetual internal dissensions. But there was no real unity either between the heirs to Genghis Khan's empire, or between the Muslim dynasties themselves.

The empire conquered by Genghis Khan, his sons and his grandsons, from 1206, stretched from their homeland in the heart of the Mongol plateau, across half of China, Central Asia (including Khorezm, Afghanistan, Iran) and the Russian steppes as far as Kiev and the Crimea. The great Russian princes paid tribute to them. The Mongol armies, which seemed invincible, had in 1242

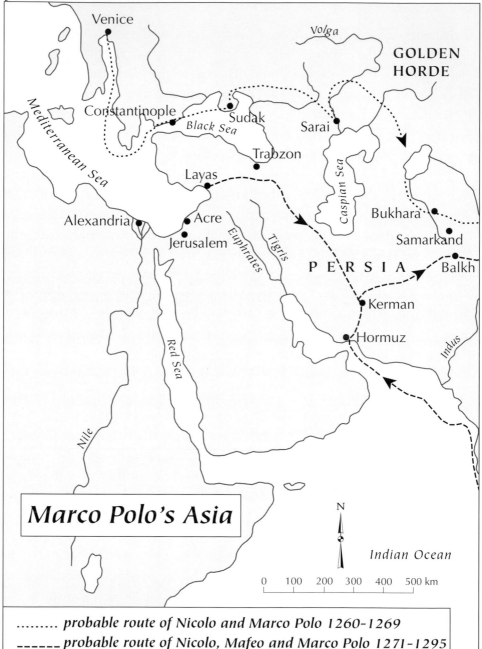

Marco Polo's Asia

.... probable route of Nicolo and Marco Polo 1260-1269
------- probable route of Nicolo, Mafeo and Marco Polo 1271-1295

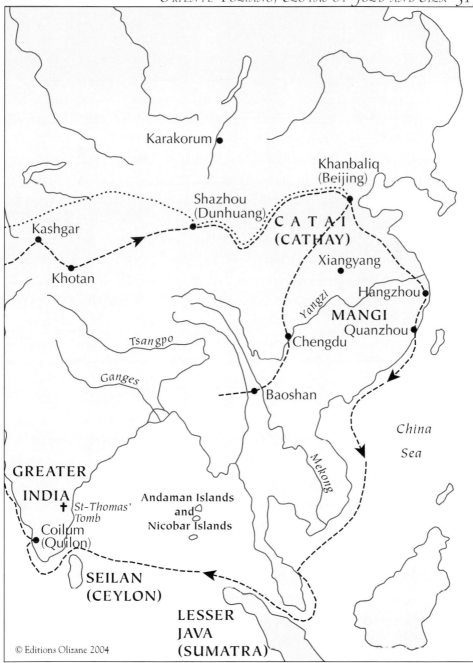

Marco Polo's Asia

camped before the walls of Vienna. The massacres, the devastation which marked their passage had made them appear as a divine punishment in the eyes of the Christians. And yet, tales told by travellers from Syria and Palestine, which had become a genuine crossroads of exchange and contact since the Crusades, had spread the rumour that far to the east, beyond the sultans and the caliphs, there were Christians among these Mongols.

A new wave of Mongol conquerors was approaching: one of the grandsons of Genghis Khan, Hülegü, who had been granted rights over Persia, where the Mongol sovereigns were known as ilkhans, had launched a military campaign. He had just defeated the Ishmaelites, also known as the Assassins, and in 1258, put an end to the caliphate of Baghdad. The last Abbasids took refuge in Egypt. In 1260, the troops of the ilkhan occupied Muslim Syria, including Aleppo and Damascus. The Muslims were threatened on either side, and the Mongols seemed once again about to conquer the rest of the world. The Mameluks of Egypt, sovereigns of Syria and Palestine, challenged them and stopped their advance— definitively this time—at Ain-Djalut in Galilee, taking back Gaza and Damascus.

Can the enemies of one party be the salvation of another? The Christians of Acre, seeing the Mameluks advancing, sent ambassadors to Hülegü, asking for peace and assistance. The ilkhan, tolerant as were all Genghiskhanid sovereigns, and having plans of his own, freed the Christians who had been captured in his territory, promising to leave the Christians in peace and to return to them their Kingdom of Jerusalem.

But let us follow the Polo brothers on their journey to the other Mongol Khan, Berke. They arrived at Sarai, where they were welcomed, and offered their jewels to the khan, who was pleased with them. He gave them jewels worth twice their value in return, according to the account of their trip. After staying a year they wished to return via the Black Sea. This was in 1261–1262. The route home, however, was cut off by a conflict which had broken out between the two cousins, Hülegü and Berke, and it was impossible to travel without being captured. They therefore decided to try a different direction, and arrived at Bukhara, in the territory of the descendants of Djagatai, one of

Genghis Khan's sons. There, they were trapped for three years. Around 1265, an embassy from Hülegü to the Great Khan passed through. The ambassador suggested that they accompany him and be presented to the khan, Kublai, who would certainly welcome them graciously. Their safety was guaranteed, and thus our two Venetians arrived among the retinue of a Mongol diplomatic mission to the Great Khan, five years after their departure from Sudak. Kublai received them in his summer capital, Shangdu, located north of Peking, in the present region of Inner Mongolia.*

Kublai, the Great Khan of all the Mongols since 1260, the emperor of China and the founder of the Yuan dynasty, controlled northern China, and slowly moved into southern China where the legitimate Chinese dynasty of the Song had retreated. When the two Polo brothers were presented to him in Shangdu, he was busy building his new capital, Dadu, which would become Peking, providing him with a power base nearer to the heart of the Chinese civilization which he had in large part adopted. Chinese historians consider him an authentic Chinese emperor, but nevertheless one who, wishing to counteract the influence of Confucian scholars and being distrustful of possible nationalistic feelings towards the foreign conqueror, appealed to non-Chinese specialists as technicians or consultants, military men, physicians and artists. He employed Persians, Indians and Nepalese, Muslims, Buddhists and Christians. In matters of religion, Kublai particularly favoured Buddhism although he welcomed all Chinese and foreign religions, not without some suspicion towards Daoists for their magic and their secret powers. He was sufficiently interested in Christianity to give the Polo brothers to understand that it was not impossible that he would himself convert to that religion.

But which Christianity? This time it was to be that of the Pope and of Rome.

There were already quite a few Christians in Asia: Marco Polo, a few years later, tells us that Nestorian Christians (*nestorins, crestiens nestorins*) could be met everywhere from Persia to China. We know from other travellers that some lived in Mongolia, and that several wives of the Mongol khans were Nestorians, as was Kublai's mother.

---

* *Shangdu, also known as Kaiping, is the modern site of Duolun, in Inner Mongolia, near the border with the province of Hebei.*

There were also Christians of other orders in China. In Peking, Kublai had an Imperial Guard of Orthodox Christians, Allans, a people who came from north of the Caucasus, whom we have already met in antiquity. These Allans were brought to China by the Khan Möngke, brother of Kublai.[122] Did the latter make a distinction, as any Christian would, between the Nestorians and the others?

In any event, he asked the Polo brothers, with whom he discussed religion in the Tartar language, to return to Italy bearing a letter for the Pope in Rome, requesting him to "send as many as one hundred persons of our Christian faith; intelligent men acquainted with the Seven Arts, well qualified to enter into controversy, and able clearly to prove by force of argument to idolaters and other kinds of folk, that the Law of Christ was best, and that all other religions were false and naught; and that if they would prove this, he and all under him would become Christians."[123] He also requested of the Polo brothers that "upon their return they should bring with them, from Jerusalem, some of the holy oil from the lamp which is kept burning over the sepulchre of our Lord Jesus Christ."*

So here is a Mongol khan, an administrator and warrior, who is knowledgeable about Christianity, and with him Italian merchants, skilled at trading furs, gems, cloth and spices, discussing religion, in the Tartar language, as if they were experts. We may wonder which of them—the Great Khan, Marco, the writer or a copyist—inserted the expression the "Seven Arts", a very Western notion from the period. The mention of the seven liberal arts of the university curriculum, that is the *trivium* (grammar, rhetoric and dialectic), and the *quadrivium*, the four mathematical arts (arithmetic, music, geometry and astronomy) would suggest that, if Kublai was indeed aware of the system, he was in need of engineers and scientists, and not just scholars of religion.

Could this have been an early attempt at what was to follow later with the Jesuit astronomers of the 17th and 18th centuries, who brought both the scriptures and science to China? By attempting to convert first the court and the nobles and reckoning that the masses would then follow?

* This is the Church of the Holy Sepulchre in Jerusalem, built over Christ's tomb. In Sir John Mandeville's Travels, written just a century later, one reads in chapter 10: "And there is a lamp that hangeth before the sepulchre, that burneth light; and on the Good Friday it goeth out by himself, [and lighteth again by him self] at that hour that our Lord rose from death to life."

The events in the West made this turn out differently, assuming that Kublai's desire for conversion was indeed sincere, and not simply a pious, semi-fictitious story or one which was adapted to the taste of the period.

The Great Khan gave the Polo brothers a passport and proof of their official mission, a golden tablet engraved with the royal seal and signed according to the custom of his state, in which it was said that the three messengers, the two Italians and an imperial envoy who was to accompany them, were the envoys of the Great Khan. Upon seeing this order of mission, all the local authorities throughout the Mongol Empire were required, at every relay-post, to supply them with lodging, food, horses and ships, and escorts if necessary, as well as anything else which they might need. This was indeed done.

The important Mongol envoy sent by Kublai with the Polo brothers fell ill during the journey and could no longer continue. The two brothers took only three years to reach in 1269 the port of Layas (Lajazzo, or Ayas, today Payas, in modern Turkey, at the north-eastern corner of the Mediterranean, just north of Iskenderun), the end of the land route in Mongol territory, from where they continued on to Acre.

Christianity was then without a Pope. The previous one had died in 1268 and the brothers now had to wait for the election of the new apostle before they could fulfil their mission for the Great Khan. The Polos decided, during this enforced holiday, to see their family.

It was indeed time to do so. When Nicolo had left Venice, his wife was pregnant, and in the meantime she had died, leaving him one son, Marco, now 15 years old. He was to join the next journey, and to become the famous Marco Polo.

The Polos' future no longer lay on the shores of Black Sea, but in Cathay. Since 1261, the circumstances had changed to the disadvantage of the Venetians. It was now the Genoese who dominated Constantinople and the Black Sea. Furthermore, the situation of the Christians in the Levant had worsened to the extent that a new Crusade was called for. The king of France, Louis IX, was about to set sail for the Holy Land with his son Philip, heir to the throne. Louis had become increasingly pious, to the point of jeopardizing his kingdom by refusing to leave his only remaining son behind. For the sacred cause, he had tried several times to establish relations with the Mongol authorities. On the one hand, he hoped for help and an alliance with a new sovereign sympathetic to Christianity, who might even be Christian. If not, there was always the hope of converting him. After all the King of France was one of the most powerful kings of Christendom.

For 25 years, the Pope had sent messengers and embassies to the Mongol sovereigns, making reference to common interests in so far as religion and safety were concerned. For a long time, ever since the legend of Prester John had been circulating, it was thought possible that somewhere at the end of the world was a Christian king (perhaps Prester John himself), and that this king might make himself known through an envoy or a letter. (Prester John was a legendary character widely believed to have been a pious Christian king in the East; firstly his kingdom was thought to be in India, then to the west of Mongolia, where it appears on maps of the 12th century, and even in the late 19th century, as the legend persisted, in Ethiopia.) A great plan was afoot, particularly now that the major danger for Christians was Islam, and that the terror which had accompanied the first Mongol conquests was dying down. In 1245, Pope Innocent IV had sent several missions to the Great Khan composed of men of the frock: three Dominicans, including Andrew of Longjumeau, who left from the Holy Land, and the Franciscan friar John of Plano Carpini (Giovanni de Plano Carpini) and Benedict of Poland, who left from Central Europe.[124] They reached either vassal khans, or the Great Khan himself (Plano Carpini arrived in Karakorum to see the enthronement of the Great Khan Güyük). They all returned with the same answer: "You must come yourself at the head of all your kings and prove to us your fealty and allegiance."

Louis IX, during his first trip abroad, was staying in Cyprus in 1248, waiting to embark for Palestine, when one of these monks returned with this answer. Later that year, still in Cyprus, he received a delegation from the "great king of the Tartars", led by someone named David, perhaps a Nestorian, who announced to him on behalf of the Great Khan that the latter was ready to help conquer the Holy Land and to free Jerusalem from the hands of the Saracens. Louis IX sent back two preachers with magnificent presents including a scarlet tent to be used as a chapel, with images inside "representing the essentials of the

Christian faith". The answer came back in 1251 through the intermediary of Andrew of Longjumeau, at Cesarea where Louis was then residing. Once again, it was an arrogant message to the effect that unless Louis became a vassal and sent a yearly tribute of gold and silver, he and his subjects would be destroyed. In addition, the Great Khan claimed to have defeated Prester John and had him put to death.[125] The chronicler of this legend concluded by saying that Louis regretted ever having sent the preachers. But the envoy named David may have been an impostor. False letters were commonplace between so-called Christian kings, beginning with that of Prester John which had started the whole legend.

In 1253, Louis, who was still in Palestine, at Jaffa, learned that a descendant of Genghis Khan, Khan Sartaq, had converted to Christianity. He sent to Mongolia a Flemish Franciscan, William of Rubruck, who was living at the time in the Holy Land, bearing a letter of congratulations. The monk, hoping to make conversions, or at least to comfort the Christians scattered across Mongolia, set off via Constantinople, the Crimea and Kazakhstan, and arrived almost a year later at Karakorum. This was the residence of the Great Khan Möngke, to whom he had been sent by Sartaq, who it turned out was not in fact a Christian. He stayed there for six months, and then returned home. Upon his arrival in Cyprus, in 1255, he learned that King Louis had returned to France. He wrote an account in Latin of his travels, one of the most important texts of the Middle Ages on the Mongol Empire, and a fascinating read, full of a wide variety of information.[126] Though providing great pleasure to us, the outcome of this journey was a disappointment to the Christian king as the answer of the Great Khan was still the same as before: come as vassals and send tribute.

Slightly later, in 1262 or 1263, as the Polo brothers were themselves travelling towards Mongolia, Louis IX, then in France, received another letter from a Mongol khan, this time from Hülegü, the ilkhan of Persia. The letter had been translated into Latin in April 1262, and was brought by an ambassador from the ilkhan, a Hungarian; it was addressed to "King Louis and to all the princes, dukes, counts, barons, knights and other subjects of the kingdom of France." Hülegü declared himself to be the "destroyer of the perfidious Saracen nations, the benevolent champion of the Christian faith."[127] He affirmed his benevolence towards the Christians of his empire, announcing to King Louis that he had freed all the Christians in his lands who had been imprisoned or enslaved. In Karakorum, he wrote, they had received with great satisfaction the fine tent brought by Andrew of Longjumeau, but had thought that the Supreme Chief was the Pope, and had not realized until much later that the Pope was a spiritual leader only and that the most powerful Christian king was the King of France. Hülegü had the intention, after taking Aleppo and Damascus from the Mameluks, of attacking them in Egypt and destroying them. Unfortunately, he did not have any ships to do so, and was appealing to the King of France to supply him with some and thereby help restore the Kingdom of Jerusalem to the Christians.

This alliance proposal would have been tempting had it not been for all the previous letters and had the sender not styled himself "Great Khan of the entire world". The king took the advice of his counsellors, and with a letter of thanks, sent the embassy to the Pope. No agreement was ever reached.

Since 1245, there had been many letters and declarations of intent. In 1269, Mafeo and Nicolo Polo arrived with another message from the Great Khan, requesting doctors, theologians, scholars and savants. And the messengers seemed to believe that the Great Khan was indeed ready to convert, asking for oil from the lamp of the Holy Sepulchre. It would appear that this khan was not demanding that anyone should become vassal or send tribute. Unfortunately, there is no written trace of these messages, and we have to believe the account left later by Marco Polo.

But this highly attractive request, so appealing to Christianity, coming from one of the most powerful sovereigns of the world, could not be answered: two years went by, and still there was no Pope. Nicolo remarried, and set off once again with his brother to Jerusalem, leaving his new wife behind with child, but this time taking along his son Marco. The year was 1271. They would return to Italy in 1295.

Such were the lives and deaths of the wives of merchants and travellers in general. Ibn Battûta, the famous Maghrebi traveller of the 14th century, tells how he left his pregnant wife in Damascus, in 1326, learning only long after, while he was in India, that she had borne him a son. Returning to Damascus in

1348, after his travels across Asia, he learnt that his son had been dead for 12 years; he says nothing of his wife. During his travels, he married several times, and lists his children born along the way. Several literary traditions contain songs or poems mentioning the absence of merchant husbands, and the melancholy of the solitary wife, perhaps left forever: the *Song of Silu*, a poem from the Kathmandu Valley, on the wife of a Newar merchant absent for years in Tibet; or a Chinese poem from the Tang period, the *Song from South of the River*, on the young wife of Li Yi, a merchant traveller who spent his life far away. In the West, such songs of loneliness referred to the knights of the Crusades. But let us return to the Polo brothers.

In the absence of a Pope, they took their orders from the legate in Acre, and with his authorization, went to Jerusalem and obtained oil from the lamp which burns in front of the tomb of Christ, as Kublai had requested. They returned to Acre, where the legate gave them official letters attesting that the Pope had not yet been elected, and that the two envoys had therefore not been able to fulfil their mission. Our travellers then returned to Layas, only to learn that a new Pope had been elected: he was the very legate from whom they had received their orders, now called Gregory X, who ordered them to return immediately to him at Acre, which they did.

The head of Christianity was indeed hoping to convert the Mongols, but for the time being it was important to obtain military aid from the Persian ilkhan Abagha, a nephew of Kublai, against the Muslim enemy power. But these new projects of military alliance and hopes of conversion were no more successful than earlier ones had been.

Furthermore, Gregory X, although certainly hoping to obtain something from these contacts which Kublai had initiated, and despite sending him valuable presents (including crystal jewels), as well as the precious holy oil, did not bother, or did not manage to send him the hundred scholars of Christian doctrine and of the Seven Arts as had been requested.

On the subject of princely gifts, Marco Polo's account refers to a region located somewhere around Urumqi in Xinjiang, which he calls the province of Ghinghin Talas, and makes mention of asbestos mines, a substance he calls "salamander", as it was still commonly thought this animal lived in fire. He describes asbestos cloth, its resistance to heat, and its ability to be washed and purified by fire, becoming as white as snow. "They preserve at Rome a napkin woven from this material, in which was wrapped the *sudarium* of our Lord, sent as a gift from one of the Tartar princes to the Roman pontiff." This gift was indeed worthy of an effort in return. Unfortunately, the Polos took with them, not one hundred men, but two Dominican friars, "men of letters and of science, as well as profound theologians". The Pope gave them "licence and authority to ordain priests, to consecrate bishops, and to grant absolution as fully as he could do in his own person".

Only two men of letters for such a great country, for such a grand project of ordaining priests and bishops? Optimism was outdoing reality. What was the Pope's genuine intention? In the end, no men of letters arrived before Kublai: no sooner had they left than our travellers encountered the dangers of war in Armenia, and the two missionaries, afraid, sought refuge in Acre. The Polos carried on, taking with them the Holy Oil and the religious mandates which they themselves as lay people could not use, as well as the Pope's gifts. The best gift was in fact young Marco, who was to make the glory, the power and the wisdom of Kublai known throughout the world. He arrived, with his father and his uncle, in the summer capital of the emperor, in 1275, after three and a half years of hardship and continual bad weather since their departure from Layas. Marco was presented by his father to the Great Khan, and fortunately pleased him. The return of these two friends and this young man was feted with "mirth and merry-making" and the Italian guests were "well served and attended to in all their needs".

Marco, polyglot like all merchants, aged just over 20, very rapidly assimilated the language, customs and civilization into which he had been plunged. "He learnt in a short time and adopted the manners of the Tartars, and acquired a proficiency in four different languages, which he became qualified to read and write." The young man became a favourite with the khan, and his career, which was to last for seventeen years, began under the most favourable auspices. Marco was to carry out various missions for the emperor throughout the country, much of which he describes in his account.

Being in favour with an absolute sovereign may bring with it a shower of benefits and honours, but it often has its drawbacks, described time and again in tales and biographies: that is that the sovereign simply will not let him leave. That is was what happened to the Polos. But at long last an opportunity to depart presented itself in 1291. The ilkhan of Persia, Arghun, nephew of Kublai, had lost his wife, and to conform with her wishes, he wanted to marry a girl from the same Mongol tribe. He therefore turned to Kublai, and a young girl was chosen from the appropriate family line. Putting forward their knowledge of lands and seas, the Polos succeeded in being chosen to conduct the bride-to-be as far as Persia, after which they would be allowed to return to their own land.

Having fulfilled their mission and after several other adventures on the way home, the three travellers arrived on the coast of Italy in 1295.

Did they return rich and wealthy? It is believed that they probably did. Of all the events which occurred between 1271 and 1295, the texts which we have tell us only what Marco did, or at least when he went on imperial missions, but make no mention of any commercial activity, of the setting up of any trading post or of clients or contracts. His father and his uncle are almost absent from the tale once they arrive before the emperor on their second journey. They appear only in one military instance, the siege of a town, where in actual fact they could not have been. What did the three of them do for so many years? Did they lead completely separate lives? Yet, the *Description of the World* contains many passages about coinage, bank notes, prices, the values of gold and silver relative to one another; the main commercial products are mentioned in a very general fashion, but one which leaves us with a rapid overview of the economic geography of the regions visited.

Furthermore, there are traces of the Polos in Venetian documents after their return, in commercial or notarial documents, loans, accounts, wills—among others Marco Polo's will dated 9th January 1324—and documents concerning inheritance (he left a wife and three married daughters). There is no doubt the Polos continued to prosper in trade.

But before settling down in Venice again, Marco had one last adventure, to which we probably owe the *Description of the World*: in 1298, or perhaps in 1296, during a naval battle in the Mediterranean between the Venetians and Genoese, Marco was captured by the latter, and imprisoned in Genoa until the end of the conflict. He was finally freed at the end of 1299. In prison, he found himself in the company of another Italian prisoner, a writer, Rustichello of Pisa. Marco used the long months in prison to dictate his memoirs. It was, he himself admits, this stroke of luck which led to the writing of his book. Without this enforced leave, without the hand of a writer, would it ever have seen the light of day? In prison, he had the time to tell his story in detail, to answer the questions of his companion, who wrote it all down and copied it out. Marco the polyglot probably recited it aloud in his Venetian dialect. Rustichello probably took down his notes in Italian, and then wrote a text in what is known as Franco-Italian: that is he wrote in French, the language of prestige and perhaps the language of the public he was aiming at, but a French full of Italian terms and turns of phrase.

The original manuscript is lost but over one hundred and forty manuscript copies are preserved in several large European cities. These are translations, copies of copies, in Franco-Italian, French, Tuscan, Venetian and Latin, which have served as a basis for later printed editions. These copies, sometimes illustrated, were made during the 14th and 15th centuries. Some are complete, others are not, and often seem to be based on the simultaneous use of several versions as they are not identical. The illustrations of these ancient manuscripts have been superbly reproduced in very fine editions. Today we live in a period of annotated editions, with introductions and historical, geographical and linguistic notes. We are also in a period of questioning and critical analysis. But for several centuries, the text was read as it stood, giving rise to amazement and doubt. Were these wild tales, exaggerations based on truth, or an authentic account? Or rather, was it a mixture of all this?

What exactly does he tell us in his book, the *Description of the World*, or the *Book of Marvels*, this traveller and merchant who had seen a thousand wonders, and whose nickname was *Il Milione*? What does he tell us of the greatest trade port in the world, to which ships from all nations sailed, bringing back to the

Mediterranean ports spices and silk? There is much mention of silk. One could even have given Marco Polo another nickname other than *Il Milione*, that of *Cloths of Gold and Silk*, given the number of times which this expression reappears in the text.

Marvels and splendours, screened by memory, amplified with time, and perhaps embellished too by memory or by a trick of the writer? According to Marco Polo the Venetian, from Asia Minor to the coast of China, through Iran and Iraq, but particularly in China, there was nothing but cloths of gold and silk, or silk and gold, or gilt silk.

Marco Polo was probably not originally an expert in textiles, but as a trader, seduced by the surprising beauty of luxury cloth, he appreciated these products which sold so well throughout the world. According to him, Europe got the least beautiful of the beautiful cloth, and at what a price! But he provides very few specific names of cloth, while "cloth

> *Nasich and nach come from the Arabic nasidj, silk brocades, also called baldachins (or baldaquins) of silk, the term baldachin being derived from Baldach.*

of gold and silk" comes back as a leitmotif. He mentions *cendaux* (several times), *nach*, *nasich* (once), *soie gelle* (purple silk, once), *mosolin* (muslin, once) and *quermesis* (once). In the case of China, where more than anywhere the descriptive vocabulary for silk is so rich, there is not a single word designating the textiles produced there. For cloths other than silk, one finds relatively general common names, cotton, linen, *bougran* (cotton cloth), *chenevaz* for hemp cloth, camelot for camel-hair cloth. These are words designating the substance itself, not the manufacturing technique. But his absence of precision may after all come from the ghost-writer, Rustichello.

The words *nach*, *nasich* appear first in his story as products from Baldach (Baghdad). One modern commentator, Stéphane Yerasimos, indicates that *nasich* and *nach* come from the Arabic *nasidj*, silk brocades, also called baldachins (or baldaquins) of silk, the term baldachin being derived from Baldach.[128] It is unsurprising that words of Arabic origin should be used for a product from Baghdad, but the same words will be found in Marco Polo's texts for cloths made at the other end of the world, on the north-western edge of China.

This problem of vocabulary has strengthened the suspicion that Marco Polo's tale may not be a direct account. However, it is also possible that the writer, Rustichello, had asked the narrator to give approximate Italian translations of the expressions from Chinese or from other languages, which were difficult to explain, and would mean nothing to the public. It is equally possible that Marco, now back in Italy, adopted once more his usual vocabulary, that of the merchant world, current in Europe. In all periods, there has been a professional jargon, an international lingo, made up of terms from various languages, understood by all in the trade, and used all along the commercial routes.

The word *cendal* (or sendal in English) appears several times in Western texts, and is frequently used to designate, according to one dictionary, a silk cloth, or half silk, comparable to taffeta. But the term samite which is also common and designates a raw silk cloth, sometimes interwoven with gold and richer than the *cendal*, comes from Syria and Asia Minor, which one would expect to be mentioned. Once again this may simply be the result of the then current terminology.

The silk geography provided in the *Description of the World* takes us in the first part of the text from the Mediterranean to Peking along the land route, which the elder Polo brothers had already travelled. As soon as he set off from Layas, Marco was struck by the beauty and the very low price of silks.[129] In Turkomania (part of present-day Asian Turkey), were large quantities of "silks of crimson and other rich colours"; in Georgia "they have a great abundance of silk, and make cloths of silk and gold, the finest ever seen by man as there is much silk there and many silk workers"; in the kingdom of Mosul, in modern Iraq, are "the finest cloths of silk and gold known as muslins" which were widely exported; in Baldach (Baghdad), a large city, "is a manufacture of silks wrought with gold, and also of damasks, as well as velvets ornamented with the figures of birds and beasts"; in Tauris (Tabriz, in north-western Iran) the inhabitants make "various kinds of silk, some of them interwoven with gold, and of high price"; in Persia, conquered by the Mongols, the city of Yasdi (Yazd in modern Iran) produces "a species of cloth of silk and gold [...] known by the appellation of *yasdi*, and is carried from thence by the merchants to all parts of the world";

another region of Persia, Kierman (Kerman) was renowned for its embroiderers and "work with the needle, in embroideries of silk and gold, in a variety of colours and patterns, representing birds and beasts, with other ornamental devices. These are designed for the curtains, coverlets and cushions of the sleeping places of the rich; and the work is executed with so much taste and skill as to be an object of admiration."

Strangely, to the east of Persia and as far as the frontiers of China, there appears to have been no sericulture or silk industry, neither at Kashgar, where the cultivation and weaving of cotton, linen and hemp are mentioned, nor in Samarkand, nor in Khotan, which is particularly surprising since this town was known for its production of cocoons and silks, nor at Pem (Pera, later called Keriya and now Yutian, in Xinjiang), mentioned as a producer of cotton, nor in the other oases further east in Xinjiang and Gansu.

Finally, the journey takes us to the ancient kingdom of Tangut (which covered part of modern Gansu and Ningxia, in north-western China) and to modern Inner Mongolia, where the narrator discovers camelot, cloth made from camel hair, and some particularly fine ones in white camel hair. In the same province of Tangut, near present-day Xining, he discovers something which was not yet known in Europe, "a very fair white wool, as fine as silk, supplied by oxen and wild cows as large as elephants, very fine to look upon", black and white, with hair three hands in length. He brought some back to Venice, he writes, "as a marvel which has been judged such by all". Marco Polo had quite obviously brought back not yak hair, which is a rough fibre generally made into tents or sacks for transporting goods, but the fine under fleece of this animal, which produces a very fine and silky thread, or the superb yak-tail hair which in Asia is an emblem of authority. If one is to believe Chinese dictionaries, the famous commander Zhang Qian's standard, which this envoy of the Han Emperor Wudi managed to bring back to his ruler after thirty years of adventures, must have been a standard with tufts of yak-tail hair.

As it nears the residence of the Great Khan, the tale takes us to the north-western fringes of China, in a region which is difficult to locate precisely (Ningxia, Gansu, Shaanxi, Inner Mongolia?), where the inhabitants were

Muslim or idolatrous (this term usually designates Buddhists in the text), or else Nestorian Christians. Here once again the silk industry reappears, with vocabulary which we have encountered earlier in Baghdad: "They make cloth of gold and silk which is called *nascici*, and another type of cloth called *nac*, and cloths of silk of different sorts. Just as in our lands we have cloths of wool of diverse nature, so they have all forms of cloths of silk and gold."

From the moment they arrived at Cambaluc, or Khanbaligh in Mongol, the "city of the Khan", modern Beijing, our travellers found themselves plunged into an extraordinary abundance of silk, exported in great quantities: "no fewer than a thousand carriages and pack-horses, loaded with raw silk, make their daily entry; and gold tissues and silks of various kinds are manufactured to an immense extent. And this is no marvel as in all the surrounding regions there is no linen so that all things have to be made of silk. It is true that in some places cotton and hemp may be had, but not sufficient for their needs; but they produce little of this and the great quantity of silk which they obtain at a good price is better than linen or cotton." At the time, Peking was one of the great trade centres of the world, attracting goods from China as well as other Asian countries.

> *The character jin is composed of two elements, the element for "gold" (or originally "metal", but usually taken as meaning gold), and the element for "silk". Each of these two elements can exist independently of the other as a word in itself.*

Silk was produced in Cathay, that is northern China, as well as in Mangi, southern China. In Hebei, at Giogiu (Ginguy), which corresponds to present-day Zhuoxian, "they make cloth of silk and gold and very fine *cendaux*".

Let us examine this expression "cloths of gold and silk": it cannot refer in every case, given the enormous quantities mentioned, to silks weighted down by gold thread, as certain lamés are. Sumptuous cloth such as this had existed and does still exist, for example, for Indian wedding saris, and there are mentions of fabrics almost entirely woven with threads of silver or gold for Western monarchs, but these must have been exceptional products for a royal clientele, and the cloths of gold and silk which appear like a refrain in Marco's text are of a different league. These must be fine brocades in which the quantity of metal used was relatively small, but which showed a very high degree of technical skill and artistry. Perhaps this expression is simply a broad term, the equivalent of a common Chinese word, *jin*, which designates silk in general. The character *jin* is composed of two elements, the element for "gold" (or originally "metal", but usually taken as meaning gold), and the element for "silk". Each of these two elements can exist independently of the other as a word in itself. The term *jin* which we have just mentioned means "silk brocade", and by extension "splendid, brilliant, magnificent". Furthermore, when the two words "gold" and "silk" are used separately, one after the other in the expression "gold and silk", this by extension refers to "wealth", the same connotation as in all languages.

Still in Hebei, at Cacanfu, "they weave gold tissues, as well as every other kind of silken cloth"; at Tundifu (modern Dongping), "silk is produced here in wonderfully large quantities"; this city "has under its jurisdiction eleven cities, that is to say places of great trade, having abundance of silk". An enumeration of all these rather repetitive quotes would be tiresome; suffice it to say that there were mulberry trees, silk, and cloths of silk and gold in three districts in Shaanxi, as well as in the provincial capital, Quengianfu (Xi'an); in Jiangsu, a large producer, at Zhenjiang, Changzhou, Suzhou and other towns; in Zhejiang, where silk was the object of much trade, and was very profitable for the taxes it brought to Kublai's government in the port of Quinsay (Kin-sai), the name Marco Polo gives to modern Hangzhou. "Quinsay is the biggest city that is to be found in the whole world." It was a city of a hundred miles in circumference, with 1,600,000 homes, 12,000 wood or stone bridges, huge markets, twelve guilds of different crafts, each guild owning 12,000 houses with between ten and forty workmen in each. The greater part of the inhabitants of this city, to which Marco Polo devotes more pages than to any other, "are always clothed in silk, in consequence of the vast quantity of that material produced in the territory of Kin-sai, exclusively of what the merchants import from other provinces."

The same abundance is seen in southern China, where silk was produced and woven in several districts of the province of Fujian, which also produced cotton, and in Sichuan, at Cuigiu (perhaps Yibin) and at Sindufu, which is the modern provincial capital, Chengdu.

In the district of Yibin, the account mentions "cloth from tree bark which is very fine and worn in summer, by men as well as by women". South-western China, as we have seen, had, some fourteen centuries previously, been a producer of a particularly fine "wild" cloth from the forests. Whether or not this bark cloth was traded at all in Marco Polo's time, the fact that he mentions it reflects the attention he gives to textiles. He is not as interested in other products, and this mention seems also to prove, in my view, his presence (or that of his father or his uncle) in this area: this type of cloth does not appear to have been part of general world knowledge then, nor to be a strange enough phenomenon to have become one of the legends which followed in the wake of travellers.

Tibet was also under the control of the Great Khan. Marco Polo seems not to have been into the heart of Tibet, but he may have travelled in what are now the westernmost districts of Sichuan and Yunnan which give onto the modern Autonomous Region of Tibet. These districts, which include the Kham region, were of Tibetan culture, and were politically part of Tibet at certain periods. When Marco Polo wrote his account, the Tibet he describes almost certainly included these districts along with Central Tibet, which explains why he presents Tibet as a silk producer, although part of the country had been devastated by the Mongol conquerors, and one could ride for days and days across deserted land haunted by wild animals. "In this province, there is camelot and other cloths of silk, gold and fustian"; but a few lines further on we read that the inhabitants "are dressed very poorly, as their clothes are made of animal skin, of hemp cloth or of rough boquerant". Was sericulture known in Tibet? In its south-eastern part, near Sichuan and Yunnan, and in the districts we have just mentioned, it may well have been: sericulture was supposed to have been introduced into Tibet in the 7th century by the Chinese princess who married King Song-tsen Gampo.

In the last part of his account, which corresponds more or less to his return journey, Marco Polo does not mention sericulture or the silk industry in the countries cited. Reading him one would think that India did not produce any silk, as only cotton is mentioned for a number of Indian kingdoms. No silk either, other than in the holds of ships, in other ports along the sea route before and after India.

This then was the textile geography of Marco Polo, sometimes precise, often a superficial overview, but always influenced by the fascination which these silks exerted on him.

IBN BATTÛTA

The same omnipresence of sumptuous cloth and fabulous court luxury appears in the writings of Ibn Battûta, a Muslim traveller from the Maghreb who journeyed across the world for thirty years between 1325 and 1355. He visited, among other places, the Middle East, Central Asia, India, Ceylon, Indonesia and, briefly, China. Following the usual land and sea routes, he often passed through cities and countries described by Marco Polo forty or fifty years before, providing interesting points of comparison between the two accounts.

Ibn Battûta was a pious scholar, not a merchant, which did not prevent him from offering interesting economic information. He was fascinated, like all the travellers in these monarchic centuries, by the luxury and opulence which surrounded military and political power. Like Marco Polo, he emphasizes the respect with which he was treated by the great of this world, and the favours and good graces he received.

Valuable silks feature prominently amid the visible testimony of wealth and power which rulers deliberately displayed before their people and their guests. Describing the sumptuousness of the court of Mohammed Uzbec Khan, ruler of the Golden Horde, "one of the seven greatest and most powerful kings of the world", Ibn Battûta, who visited this court in 1334, emphasizes the abundance of "cloths of gilt silk". For the khâtûn, the khan's wife, these silks were encrusted with jewels, and her chambermaids wore on their heads "a silk veil embroidered with gold and jewels at the edges". Each of the six slave girls who accompanied her were dressed in robes of silk gilt. "In front of the khâtûn are ten or fifteen eunuchs, Greeks and Indians, who are dressed in robes of silk gilt, encrusted with jewels [...] behind the khâtûn's wagon there are about a hundred wagons, in each of which there are four slave girls, full grown and young, wearing robes of silk..."[130] Further on, the Khâtûn Bayalûn, wife of Sultan Uzbec and "daughter of the king of the Greeks", visits her father "that she might give birth to her child at the latter's residence", in Constantinople the Great. She enters Byzantine territory accompanied by "her mamlûks, her slave girls, pages and attendants, about five hundred, wearing robes of silk embroidered with gold and jewels", herself wearing a "mantle embroidered with jewels, with a crown set with precious stones on her head, and her horse was covered with a saddle-cloth of silk embroidered with jewels".

One quickly tires of these spectacular accumulations, this ostentatious power, luxury and wealth, the hundreds of slaves serving the few eminent figures whose destinies were often flamboyant but ephemeral. Perhaps these glittering scenes, these retinues of hundreds of slaves clothed in silk, these tens of thousands of horseguards, these tons of gold, these basketfuls of gems, are all in part imaginary, amplified by the vividness of the overwhelmed traveller's memory, by spontaneous exaggeration, or by the desire to impress the reader?

Christians or Muslims, merchants or scholars, diplomats or troubadours, all the authors of the period are as if affected in their reasoning and their imagination by what were visible symbols of power. This was the time of absolute monarchs and knights, of slaves and eunuchs, of perpetual war, of conquests and plunder and the amassing of wealth under some religious pretext or without a pretext at all. All this through pure cupidity or swollen pride; pride which the Catholic Church had made into one of the seven cardinal sins.

The significance of silk, in the economy and imagination of a European Christian in the Middle Ages, did not simply include the fact that it was beautiful, and costly (and that luxury was in principle blameful). Apart from its luxury, silk had, as in China, financial value, in the same way that an ingot of gold or gems did; as we have seen previously, it had all the characteristics of a currency. And it was used as currency and as a safe investment. It is through this dual aspect as objects of economic value and of luxury that silks affected the imagination in the same way that gold did. Gold, silver coins, jewels and silks were the first valuables to be taken when a city was pillaged. Part of the silk which arrived from the East was preserved intact, as were ingots of gold or jewels, in coffers, and appear in notaries' inventories, after their owners' death, as a dowry, or as security against a loan, even for ransoms. It was offered to the churches, brought as dowry by nuns upon entering the convent. Travellers who took silk with them were guaranteed sales along the way, and in certain countries, it was even preferable to carry silk rather than cash. The Franciscan William of Rubruck, during his journey to Mongolia in 1253, experienced this in the Crimea, where he suffered from hunger because no one would sell him food, as he could give no silk in exchange. But the regulations of his order forbade him from carrying such a luxury object with him. For the same reason he could not wear the padded silk clothes which a Mongol lady offered him against the cold.

Silk was used to wrap relics or sacred objects, and it also bought treason. In the *Song of Roland*, the text of which was probably fixed by the beginning of the 12th century, we see the ambiguous nature of silk, like that of gold. When, in 778, Charlemagne was fighting the Saracens in Spain, he was tricked by the enemy in Saragossa: the town was inevitably going to fall into Frankish hands, and the Saracens made him believe in their surrender and their conversion to Christianity. Charlemagne quietly left Spain through the Roncevaux Pass, where his rearguard, with Count Roland, was treacherously attacked. This was the doing of the perfidious Ganelon, who, it was said, sought vengeance against Charlemagne and Roland. For his treachery, he received from the enemy great gifts of gold and silver, cloth and clothes of silk, mules and horses, camels and lions. Charlemagne arrived too late to save his rearguard, and Roland, Oliver and Archbishop Turpin died. A few days later, bereaved by the loss of his knights and having buried with great honour the thousands of French dead, Charlemagne could not bring himself to leave behind the bodies of Roland, Oliver and Turpin, and so "He bade their bodies opened be, Took the hearts of the barons three, Swathed them in silken fabric (*E tu les quers en paile recuillir*), Laid them in urns of the marble white."[131] The three bodies were taken back to France on three biers, each covered in a silken sheet from Galaza (*Bien sunt cuverz d'un palie galazin*).

The Christian moralists, beginning with St Jerome, railed against silk in the same way they did against pearls and perfume, but silk found a place for itself in the Church through the intermediary of relics and their wrappings. It entered by the side door into the domain of pious objects, for example as the silk pages inserted in the famous manuscript Bible known as the "Manuscript of Theodolphus", preserved today in the Notre-Dame cathedral of Puy-en-Velay (France), which had been given in 835 by a monk named Theodolphus, Bishop of Orleans. This Latin Bible, written in black, gold and silver letters on white, purple and violet vellum, is unusual in that the vellum pages are separated by inserted leaves, most of which are in silk, with some in cotton, goat hair and mixed cloth, and which have been dated from the 9th to the 16th century.[132] Silk later entered the liturgy itself: originally, when the rites were first set down, only linen was authorized in the celebration of Mass, as a commemoration of the clothes of Christ and of his shroud, and particularly of the tablecloth of the Last Supper. The obligation to use linen exclusively for certain priest's vestments and for altar cloths in Roman Catholicism lasted until the liturgical reform of 1962. But over the centuries, silk was authorized for some of the liturgical cloths, and even became compulsory for certain of the vestments of the celebrating priest, such as the chasuble, stole and maniple, for the veil of the chalice and the pavilion of the ciborium.

Furthermore, silk also entered the ritual of the coronation of the kings of France: these rites stipulated that the new king—whose chest had to be bared to receive unction with the chrism, the holy oil—should wear a purple silk shirt for the ceremony. The forbidden, tolerated, recommended or compulsory use of silk, all was minutely detailed in the ecclesiastical statutes and canons, as was its use in social life, through morals and decrees, in strictly ordered societies in which choice of costume and ornament was not entirely free but reflected social hierarchies.

In the Muslim and Chinese worlds, much less in the Christian world, the gift of a ceremonial robe of precious silk was highly symbolic: this was a gift from a king to a subject, from a prince to another king or another prince, a practice which recurs throughout history.

Another common practice until the beginning of modern times (which began in different centuries in different parts of the world), was the plunder of stocks of silks during the pillaging of a city. The crusaders should have been pious Christians since they risked their lives to free Jerusalem and the tomb of Christ from the hands of the infidels, but they did not scorn these silks which had been so reviled by the early saints. The Fourth Crusade, was, as we know, diverted from its original aim, Palestine, and ended up with the capture of Constantinople by the French and the Venetians. This victory was followed by pillage on a colossal scale. The city was taken in April 1204, on the day following Palm Sunday, writes Geoffrey of Villehardouin who was present at the scene. The next day, the organized pillage of the two palaces and of their immense treasures began: "The booty gained was so great that none could tell you the end of it: gold and silver, and vessels and precious stones, and samite, and cloth of silk, and robes of ermine, and every choicest thing found upon the earth ... Greatly did they rejoice and give thanks because of the victory God had vouchsafed to them, for those who before had been poor were now in wealth and luxury. Thus they celebrated Palm Sunday and the Easter Day following in the joy and honour that God had bestowed upon them." The booty was shared equally between the French and the Venetians, once the former had paid the latter the transport costs owed them: the Venetians were supplying ships and sailors for the Christian pilgrims, and this plunder suited everyone as funds were running low.

Marco Polo, like other travellers, does not leave out the other items which so stimulated people's imagination at the time: gold, gems, pearls and spices, all of which sustained this distant commerce. But he also mentions, more than other authors do, weapons, horses, falcons, furs, leather and, more rarely, medicinal and aromatic substances. The passages concerning these products are sometimes simple enumerations, but at other times, he tells us the legend which goes with them, as in the *Romance of Alexander*, in the *Thousand and One Nights*, or in John Mandeville's *Travels*, or which can be traced back to Pliny or the *Periplus of the Erythraean Sea*. These legends, which merchants, sailors and caravaneers carried with them from one end of the world to the other, were sometimes given new settings, far from their place of origin, as they followed groups of emigrants settling in new homes with their tutelary gods and holy books. And once they entered a book of tales, there was no stopping them.

FUR TRADE

One of these legends which echoes down the ages concerns furs. There was a considerable trade in fur at the time, from Siberia, Russia, and China. Because of the abundance of wild animals there and as houses were barely heated and travellers had to endure interminable months out of doors, furs were in great demand. In two chapters of his account, Marco Polo describes the Land of Darkness, that is to say northern and eastern Siberia, east of the Ural mountains, where, according to the narrator, for a large part of the year "the sun is invisible, and the atmosphere is obscured to the same degree as that in which we find it just about the dawn of day, when we may be said to see and not to see". The inhabitants are of "dull" intellect and barbarians, living like beasts; but they "catch vast multitudes of ermines, martens, arcolini, foxes and other animals of that kind, the furs of which are more delicate, and consequently more valuable, than those found in the districts inhabited by the Tartars, who, on that account, are induced to undertake plundering expeditions". The Tartars were the Mongols, the masters of neighbouring Russia which was also a source of "great abundance [of] furs of ermines, arcolini, sables, martens, foxes and other animals of that tribe". The Tartars succeeded in stealing these furs in the following manner: "They avail themselves of those months in which the darkness prevails, in order that their approach may be unobserved; but, being unable to ascertain the direction in which they should return homeward with their booty, they provide against the chance of going astray by riding mares that have young foals which they leave behind under proper care, at the commencement of the gloomy region. When their works of darkness have been accomplished, and they are desirous of revisiting the region of light, they lay the bridles on the necks of the mares, and suffer them freely to take their own course. Guided by maternal instinct, they make their way directly to the spot where they had quitted their foals; and by these means the riders are enabled to regain in safety the places of their residence."

This story of mares and foals also appears in the *Romance of Alexander*, ascribed to Pseudo-Callisthenes, one of the numerous legendary biographies of Alexander the Great, much read in the West in the Middle Ages.[133] Alexander set out to explore the northern lands where the sun never shone, as far as the Land of the Blessed. He never reached it; having walked for days "seeing daylight but without seeing the sun, the moon, or the stars", warned by birds who told him in Greek that he should not attempt the impossible but return home, he left this Land of Darkness by "following the direction of the Great Bear for twenty-two days, travelling towards the neighing of the foals", because on the advice of a veteran, he had taken care to set out with mares whose foals were left behind. This practice, which hinges on the maternal instinct to find their young, must have been known to all animal breeders and hunters. It appears earlier in a famous passage of another classic, *The Histories*, written by the Greek Herodotus, in the middle of the 5th century BC, a century before Alexander.[134] In this, it was not mares and foals which were used to penetrate an uninhabited region, but female camels and their young because of the speed with which the females ran to join their offspring. The aim of the expedition was to gather particles of gold extracted from the soil by giant "ants". This anecdote has come down the centuries to us, modified along the way, debated, rejected and re-examined in all possible ways. Today, it is thought that the ants were in fact probably marmots and that the location of this original method of mining minerals was Ladakh.[135]

In his *Travels*, John Mandeville, in the 14th century, mixes everything, gold, the ants, the foals and the female camels, and places all of this on the island of Taprobane, Ceylon, where the giant ants become dogs which guard mountains of gold.[136] In his text, one can recognize phrases from Herodotus' passage. According to Mandeville, the ants themselves purify this native gold.

This is just one example of erring themes in literature, which one suddenly encounters in a tale when one least expects it.

One last word about the Land of Darkness: almost a century after Marco Polo, Ibn Battûta describes it as a land which can only be reached by crossing a frozen, uninhabited desert for forty days, "in small wagons drawn by large dogs", which "have claws and so their feet remain firm on the ice". Without these dogs the travellers would be lost. These travellers were in fact rich merchants, well stocked up with provisions; they came to buy furs, but unlike the Tartars in the time of Marco Polo who stole the skins and furs, they no longer actually entered the Land of Darkness: once again, silent barter was carried out on the frontier, and the foreigners left with marten, ermine and squirrel furs, all of very great value in the outside world. Ibn Battûta adds "those who go to those parts do not know who it is who do this trading with them, whether they are of the jinn or of men, for they never see anyone".[137]

GOLD TRADE

Gold was naturally of interest to everyone. On this point, Marco Polo's text appears to be more realistic and concrete than other accounts, and he gives with a merchant's precision the value of gold relative to silver, which until the 19th century was the most common way of evaluating it in commerce. Thus we know from various sources that in the 18th century, the Europeans bought American gold from the Spaniards at 14 or 15 grams of silver for one gram of gold, while they could buy gold in China at a rate of 1 to 10, and for 1 to 9 or even less in Tibet.

For the trader, the most important thing was not whether a particular country had any gold, but at what price it could be bought, assuming that that country did not prevent it leaving its territory. Marco Polo is said to have incited Christopher Columbus to set off on his trip by his description of gold production on the island of Cipangu (Sypangu), Japan. This country was rumoured to have too much gold, and did not know what to do with it all, but it was too distant, ships rarely sailed there, and nobody bought the gold. One of the palaces was plated with fine gold, more than two fingers in thickness, from the roof down to the floor. Marco Polo did not actually see this palace, because he almost certainly never went to Japan. Realistically, however, he gives indications about gold from islands in the China Sea, Tibet and Yunnan where gold could be bought at a rate of 1 to 8 in the region of present-day Kunming, of 1 to 6 slightly further west in Yunnan, and of 1 to 5 even further west, between the Mekong and Salween rivers, which is the lowest rate that can be found in these commercial documents. Merchants therefore came from afar in large numbers loaded with silver to buy gold.

This region, with its centre at present-day Baoshan, was called Sardandan (Zardandan) by Marco Polo, the translation of a local Persian word meaning "gold teeth", as the inhabitants plated their teeth with a sheet of gold. Much more gold was said to come from the land of Caugigu, probably North Vietnam. The precise way in which the author describes southern China and its surroundings, compared with those of Japan, and his silence over other gold-producing areas of the world he should have known is interesting to note.

TRADING IN PEARLS AND GEMS

Pearls too were still much sought after, pearls from the islands in the China Sea, or from Japan, but particularly from the pearl fisheries which supplied the entire world, known since antiquity and still as productive as ever, between the northern coast of Ceylon and the south-eastern coast of the Indian peninsula. In his chapter on Maabar, Marco Polo describes this fishing in detail; it is carried out between the beginning of April and mid-May, in a stretch of shallow sea, just south of Bettala, thought to be modern Puttalam on the north-western coast of the island. The oyster pearls were collected by local divers and paid for by the merchant companies that arrived during the season with the necessary ships and small embarkations. The divers went down to a depth of between four and twelve feet; the oysters were opened and thrown into large buckets of water on board the ship, where they remained until decomposition caused the flesh to rise to the surface, leaving the pearls at the bottom.

These few feet of depth seem rather modest, but there was real danger for the divers: man-eating fish, probably sharks. These could, however, be neutralized by magic; this was the task of certain magicians called Brahmins (*abrivamain* in one manuscript) "who, by means of their diabolical art, have the power of constraining and stupefying these fish, so as to prevent them from doing mischief". They were hired by the merchants for this purpose and were paid a twentieth of the value of the pearls. As pearl fishing is done by day, they interrupted the effect of their magic at night, so that no diver would dare fish fraudulently under the cover of darkness. Apart from the twentieth part paid to the Brahmins, the merchants had to pay a tenth of the pearls' value to the king.

In addition, the latter had the right to reserve for himself the best pearls, and no pearl of a half-saggio or above (a saggio was equal to 4.72 grams) was allowed to leave the kingdom. Furthermore, the king bought them for double the market price. All this, as well as the salary of the divers, still left more than enough for the companies to make a rich profit, as pearls "are in such great quantities that they cannot be counted; and know that the pearls which are found in this sea are distributed through the world, and I tell you that the ruler of this kingdom obtains from this great quantities in duties and treasure".

Marco Polo also mentions pearls from a lake in the province of Gaindu, located in the Xichang region, in the valley of the Yalong River, in the south of modern Sichuan. On the other hand, he does not mention the pearl fisheries of the Persian Gulf. These would be described, several decades afterwards, by Ibn Battûta, who also talks about those off Ceylon. The fisheries of the Gulf were located between Bahrain, on the Arabian side, and Siraf, a port which has now disappeared, near modern Taheri, on the Iranian side. There, the king took one fifth of the fishing as royalties.

"The king is reported to possess the grandest ruby that ever was seen, being a span in length, and the thickness of a man's arm, brilliant beyond description, and without a single flaw. It has the appearance of a glowing fire, and upon the whole is so valuable that no estimation can be made of its worth in money."

Precious gems, which were so abundant in Asia, are much focused upon in our Venetian merchant's text. The island of Ceylon was the source of a great wealth of rubies, sapphires, topazes, amethysts, garnets and other stones. But at the time it was particularly famous for its rubies, finer than in any other part of the world. "The king is reported to possess the grandest ruby that ever was seen, being a span in length, and the thickness of a man's arm, brilliant beyond description, and without a single flaw. It has the appearance of a glowing fire, and upon the whole is so valuable that no estimation can be made of its worth in money." Its reputation crossed the seas, the Great Khan

Kublai heard of it, and sent an embassy to the king to ask him to sell him the ruby, for which he proposed "the value of a city". But the king of Ceylon refused: this gem had belonged to his father and his ancestors, and it was his duty to hand it down to his sons and their descendants. Marco Polo and the embassy returned with the king's answer, but not before Marco saw the ruby with his own eyes: "When the sovereign held it in his closed hand, it stood out from his fist both above and below." Surely, this was the ruby which Cosmas Indicopleustes had already made mention of in the 6th century. Ibn Battûta also mentions the precious stones of Ceylon, particularly the rubies, but also the topazes and sapphires. All the women of the land wore necklaces made of a variety of stones and the king's white elephant was bedecked with very large gems. Beside the king, Ibn Battûta once saw a ruby bowl as large as the palm of a hand, full of aloes oil.

There were also fine rubies in Badakhshan (Badascian) where, in Marco Polo's time, it was believed that the king was directly descended from Alexander the Great and his wife, the daughter of King Darius. These *balasci* rubies were mined exclusively in a mountain located in Afghanistan, on the Upper Amu-Darya, and only on the king's command; he then used them as gifts or tribute, or sold them to merchants, who could export them. The king controlled their mining in order to ensure their scarcity. Badakhshan also produced sapphires, but it was especially famous for being the world's main producer of lapis lazuli (or lazurite), mentioned by every writer over several centuries. According to Marco Polo, this stone was also found in the province of Tenduc, in modern Inner Mongolia, a province which he believed was the ancient kingdom of Prester John, in his time part of Kublai's dominion.

As for diamonds, Marco Polo mentions the most famous producer of them, and according to him the only one, the Hindu kingdom of Mutifili, which has been identified as the kingdom of Telingana, on the Coromandel Coast, between Madras and Machilipatnam. Once again in this context we meet one of those remarkable legendary echoes which accompany the prosaic history of trade: how diamonds are gathered with the unwitting assistance of eagles. According to this legend, there are three ways of collecting the gems. They are found in very high mountains and are swept down by violent rains and torrents into the floors of the gorges, along with everything else in the way. When the waters recede, men pick them up in the sandy deposits. This is tiring work because of the excessive heat, and dangerous because of the large venomous snakes, sometimes man-eating, which seem to live there to protect the diamonds and prevent them being taken (gems guarded by snakes and dragons are another recurrent theme).

The second method is to throw strips of meat dripping with blood down into these very deep and inaccessible ravines, onto their diamond-studded floors. The eagles which live in the vicinity, attracted by the numerous snakes on which they feed, "pursue [the pieces of meat] into the valley and carry off with them to the tops of the rocks. Thither the men immediately ascend, drive the birds away, and recovering the pieces of meat, frequently find diamonds sticking to them."

But the eagles may not always be driven away before they have fed, unavoidably swallowing in the process some of the diamonds stuck in the meat. This is when the third method is used. Fortunately, eagles cannot digest diamonds, so the men "watch the place of their roosting at night, and in the morning find the stones amongst the dung and filth that drops from them". According to one version, if they catch an eagle, they may even kill it and slit open its belly to retrieve the gems.

This story reappears of course in the *Thousand and One Nights*, in the tale of Sinbad the Sailor, without such a precise localization. The same tale is also to be found in the 4th century, in a text by Saint Epiphany, the bishop of Constantia in Cyprus, *De XII Gemmis*, who places it among the Scythians.[138]

According to Marco Polo, diamonds were found only in the kingdom of Mutifili, but "in such great quantity, and so fine and so large, that the whole world is full of them. And do not think that it is the best diamonds which reach our lands of Christians; they are taken to the Great Khan and to the kings and barons of his various regions and kingdoms; for they have the great treasures of the world and buy all the costly jewels. The ones which reach our countries are none else than what is discarded."

Marco Polo also mentions the turquoise of Cherman (Kerman in modern Iran), and what he calls jasper and chalcedony (*jaspre* and *cassidoine*), in the province of Ciarcian (Charchan, or Qiemo in Xinjiang). In this oasis-kingdom, which like many others, had been devastated by the Tartars, "run several large streams, in which also are found chalcedonies and jaspers, which are carried to sale in Cathay, and such is their abundance that they form a considerable article of commerce". One may wonder why Marco Polo makes no mention of jade, either there or in Khotan. But, although jasper (as well as chalcedony which is a variety of the former), is a mineral quite distinct from jade, it is possible that the texts of the Western Middle Ages used the word jasper to designate several stones which were not clearly differentiated in the mind of non-specialists. Furthermore, it was only much later, it would seem, that a specific word for jade appeared in a European language.

Among other precious minerals, Marco Polo mentions a few silver mines, such as those of Badakhshan.

One fact that he reveals to the public is the mineral nature of asbestos, which he calls "salamander" (*salemonde*). It was extracted in the kingdom of Ghinghin Talas, probably located in the region of Urumqi. We referred earlier to the story of the asbestos cloths sent as a gift to the Pope by the Great Khan. It was generally thought in Europe that this substance was the skin of a salamander, an animal believed to be able to live in fire, a belief which goes back to Latin antiquity, and which our traveller refutes. He saw with his own eyes, he says, what it is and how it is extracted and treated in Kublai's kingdom. It is neither a beast nor a snake, but comes from a vein in the mountains. It is a fibrous substance, which "after being exposed to the sun to dry, is pounded in a brass mortar, and is then washed [...] The fibres thus cleaned and detached from each other, they then spin into thread and weave into cloth. In order to render the texture white, they put it into fire, and suffer it to remain there about an hour, when they draw it out uninjured by the flame, and is white as snow." In the same way, when the cloth is stained, it is simply cleaned by passing it through fire again.

Metals

On the subject of metals, our traveller mentions the iron mines in the kingdom of Kerman in Iran, which also produce "steel" and "ondanic". According to S. Yerasimos, this word comes from the Greek *indianikon*, which refers to Indian iron,[139] it also appears in old dictionaries as *andanique, audainne* and *andaine*. As for the "steel" which he says is found in that form in these mines, an impossible occurrence to a modern metallurgist, there must be some sort of misunderstanding over the vocabulary used. Not only does Marco Polo distinguish between iron mines and steel mines, and locates a steel mine in Ghinghin Talas, but steel mines also reappear in a travel account of the 17th century, which was much less affected by fantasy than that of our 13th-century traveller.

Iron and leather were used to make both offensive and defensive weapons. The Chinese as well as the Persians were highly proficient at this; Kerman produced all sorts of weapons, bows, quivers, harnesses, saddles and spurs. In China, Quengianfu, modern Xi'an, in Shaanxi province, "made very fine leather and all the necessary equipment for armies". An important leather industry had developed to supply both men and horses, as was the case in Europe during the same period. Apart from domestic animal skins, hides of deer, rhinoceros and other wild animals were commonly used for armour and leather coverings.

In the military domain, Marco Polo mentions one event which, unfortunately for the author's credibility, is without any doubt incorrect. This is the role which his father, his uncle and he himself are said to have played in the siege of Xiangyang. In 1267, Kublai, already master of northern China, decided to conquer the south, where the legitimate Song dynasty had retreated. The key to this conquest were two fortified towns, Xiangyang and Fancheng, located opposite one another on either side of the Han River (an affluent on the left bank of the Yangzi), in the north of Hubei province. Kublai's troops besieged Xiangyang from 1268 to 1273 without managing to capture it or to starve it, and finally only succeeded in ending the siege with the help of two Muslim engineers, Ismail and Ala al-Din, sent by the Persian ilkhan, Kublai's nephew. At the end of 1272, these two engineers built siege machinery, mangonels and catapults, capable of throwing enormous rocks. They bombarded the fortifications of the two towns, which finally fell. The siege of Xiangyang is so described in the Chinese annals, in the *Yuan shi*, the *History of the Yuan Dynasty*, and by a contemporary foreigner, the Persian Rashid al-Din, vizier of the ilkhan, a doctor, scholar and savant, the author of numerous texts on the history of his times.[140] But Marco Polo, in a long passage, gives a different account. According to him, it was the three Polos, his father, his uncle and himself, who offered their services to the emperor, or rather the services of two men who were with them, a German from Germany and a Nestorian Christian, who knew how to build mangonels or trebuchets capable of throwing projectiles of three hundred pounds. The author insists on the fact that the Mongols knew nothing of this machinery and that it was the first time that any had been constructed in their land. The machines were built and the city, terrified by the devastating bombardment, surrendered. But this intervention by the Polos could not have occurred because as far as we know, in 1272 and 1273, they were not in China.

HORSE TRADING

In both war and peacetime, the world in those days needed horses. China under Mongol domination had no trouble obtaining them, as the Great Khan controlled probably three-quarters of the horses on the Eurasian continent. On the other hand, Marco Polo emphasizes the absence of horses in India, and describes the way in which the Indian kingdoms acquired them, even quoting prices. The best steeds from Persia and Arabia, and the horses from Turkomania left for India mainly from the ports of the Red Sea and the Persian Gulf. The largest place of export of horses to India was, for centuries, Hormuz, Marco Polo's Curmos, a port at the entrance to the Persian Gulf which had first been located on the continent and then, in 1315, was transferred to a nearby island. Indian merchants came there in droves, bringing indigo, spices, rare cloths and ivory to exchange for the horses. These could also be bought at Chisci (Qish) on the same side of the Persian Gulf, at Dufar, in the present Sultanate of Oman, and in the Red Sea, at Scier (Shihr) and Aden. Among the great Indian horse buyers were the kings of Maabar, a kingdom which, as we have seen, had grown rich thanks to its pearl fisheries, and which spent a large part of its revenue on buying horses, as Marco Polo explains at great length. Why buy so many? Because in India, they die. First of all due to the climate, and secondly through incorrect feeding: "For food, they give them flesh dressed with rice, and other prepared meals", and so the horses die. And the merchants selling them, says the narrator, ensure that this situation continues by failing ever to bring grooms with the horses, thus guaranteeing themselves a handsome profit every year.

The export of horses was plagued by acts of piracy. At Tana, near modern Mumbai (Bombay), a Hindu kingdom which exported incense, leather and cotton cloth, groups of corsairs held sway who, with the king's consent, kidnapped many of the horse-bearing ships. They divided the booty with the king, who took all the horses, while they kept the rest, the gold, silver and precious gems; "this is not a kingly deed", writes the narrator.

Other animals also had market value: elephants from Zanzibar, both for the live animal and for its ivory, as well as falcons and other birds of prey from, among other places, Persia and Tibet.

Spices, used both for cooking and as medicine, including pepper, ginger, galangal, cinnamon and cloves, were produced in many regions of India, South-East Asia, South China and Tibet, supplying an immense world trade. European countries could not live without them, and the Muslim world used them abundantly.

India sold various tinctorial plants such as indigo, which grows in many regions, and brazil-wood (*bresilium, brasile*, a red dye whose name, according to the Oxford English Dictionary, may be derived from the French or Spanish word for "glowing embers"), produced in the Nicobar Islands, Ceylon and Quilon, the south-western point of India.

Perfumes and medicine (perfumes for burning were often used for therapeutic reasons), were also much sought after: sandalwood from the Nicobar Islands and the African coast of the Red Sea, incense from Tana, Ethiopia and southern Arabia, ambergris from the whales of the Red Sea and Indian Ocean, as well as the waters off Somalia, Zanzibar and Socotra; finally, musk, which was still very abundant then. Marco Polo describes the latter in some detail, even, unusually, providing one of its local Asiatic names, *gudderi*, the Mongol term (the Greek traveller Cosmas Indicopleustes had already given, several centuries previously, its Indian name, *kasturi*, still unchanged today).

This substance, the animal which secretes it and the method of hunting it, are described twice, once in the section on the Xining region in modern Qinghai, and once again for Tibet. At Silingiu, Xining, then part of the province of Tangut, under the domination of the Great Khan, they produced the best and finest musk in the world. Marco Polo describes the animal, and says he took back with him to Venice the dried head and foot of a musk "gazelle", as well as musk in his pocket, and a pair of small teeth. Musk was also to be found in South China and Tibet, where the animal was hunted with very fast trained dogs. He notes that the odour comes from the "apostume" which contains the musk, located near the animal's navel, which when overfull, sheds its contents, and "such is the quantity [of these animals] that the scent of them is diffused over the whole country".

> *This country was so full of musk fallen from the bodies of these animals that it could be picked up by the handful, and when his horses left Tibet, arriving at the Chinese frontier, the dust carried on their hooves was scented with musk.*

This is reminiscent of a passage from a Persian epic, penned by a contemporary of Marco Polo, the *Sikander Nâme*, written by Nizami around 1200 AD. In this legendary biography of Alexander the Great, the hero, having defeated the king of India, left the country because the health of his horses was deteriorating. To conquer China, he had to cross Tibet. This country was so full of musk fallen from the bodies of these animals that it could be picked up by the handful, and when his horses left Tibet, arriving at the Chinese frontier, the dust carried on their hooves was scented with musk.

Among the medicines (including musk) that Marco Polo mentions are camphor, of which the best in the world was worth its weight in gold and came from the kingdom of Fansur, on the island of Sumatra; snake bile from the borders of Yunnan and Burma; rhubarb from Gansu; *tutie* and *spodium* from the kingdom of Kerman, the former being a zinc oxide drug for the eyes, and the latter, according to the narrator, the residue of the combustion of the former.

The geography of these aromatic, tinctorial and medicinal substances in the *Description of the World* may seem colourful to us but is in fact very succinct and incomplete, if we compare it for example to the compilation by Marco Polo's contemporary Zhao Rugua on Chinese and Arabic trade in the 12th and 13th centuries.[141] It becomes obvious that our Venetian was, in this field as in others, scattering his text with scraps of information, often correct from what we can gather from elsewhere, with a little commentary or an anecdote here and there, but without any desire to be coherent or complete. If we summarize his economic information, we are left with the impression that we have only part of a text, probably that part which was most apt to interest the public. Did Rustichello of Pisa or a copyist, a translator or the narrator himself, either voluntarily or involuntarily, cut from the heterogeneous mass of information that which he judged to be lacking in interest, shocking or untimely? Of course, we have also to bear in mind the discretion of merchants when it comes to business. This text was not, after all, a trade manual. The Polo family surely knew much more than we read in the text which we have at hand. But who is to say that there are not other documents, which have yet to be revealed?

Chapter Sixteen
Tall Tales from Afar?

arco Polo obviously did embellish certain passages of his text, and, whatever he may claim, he did not always clearly distinguish between what he actually saw and what he heard. His account of the siege of Xiangyang is even a case of flagrant deceit. Almost everyone agrees on this, and indeed, from the very moment of the Polos' return to Venice, their tale was not wholly believed. But the elements which are disbelieved differed at various periods; we do not believe in miraculous trees and lamps, in the intervention of evil powers, or monsters, whereas Marco Polo's Western contemporaries did not believe in Kublai's paper money. This subject is dealt with in great detail in one chapter of the account, in which the author tells of the material used (mulberry bark), the location of the Seque (the Venetian word for the Mint), the values of the different coins in terms of Venetian currency (*tornesel* or *tournois*), the minting of them and their circulation. It is even one of the most credible passages and one most easily ascribed to a merchant. Despite the unbelievable marvels in it, the *Description of the World* has remained one of the cornerstones, if not of Western human economic geography in the Middle Ages, at least of Western popular knowledge about the rest of the world. It influenced scholarly knowledge afterwards because although a passage may seem incomprehensible or questionable, it can always be a clue, albeit misconstrued, to some reality. The text has been continually quoted, with reservations, but nevertheless quoted, in academic works, and for a long time influenced European cartography of Asia. Apart from the obvious pleasure which can be had reading it and the charm exerted by its language, it also provides a mass of historical information, either first- or second-hand, on the mentality and vision of the world at the end of the 13th century. Although many men travelled in Asia it so happens that this one set down his memoirs and that they were copied, and then printed, in sufficient numbers for them to have reached us.

But, did Marco Polo go to China! This question, which we raised at the beginning of the preceding chapter, has in the last few years rattled European

Orientalists, medieval historians and a few Chinese historians. Of course, it is not an entirely new mystery; some of the most important Western language writers have debated it, such as L. F. Benedetto, Henri Cordier, Louis Hambis, J. Heers, A. C. Moule, L. Olschki, Paul Pelliot and Henry Yule to mention just a few. Either they considered that, yes Marco Polo had gone to China, or they gave him the benefit of the doubt. In 1966, a specialist in Mongolian studies, Herbert Francke, once again raised the issue, and in 1981 an article in *The Times* of London by Frances Wood brought the problem to the attention of the general public. This was followed by articles by Clive Clunas in the same newspaper, and then by very widespread correspondence, often indignant, which lasted for years. Frances Wood presented her arguments and her point of view in her book *Did Marco Polo go to China?* published in 1995, preceded by an article in early November 1995 in *The Sunday Times*. Conferences and a documentary film produced by British television greatly increased the audience, while the case defending the authenticity of Marco Polo's voyage was pleaded in China by Professor Yang Zhijiu. The book created a storm in Western academic circles, among Sinologists, medievalists and Mongol specialists, but also among a wide public of non-specialists. In France, the *Courrier international* of 12th to 18th September 1996 devoted three pages to the affair, including a résumé of another article which had appeared in the *Far Eastern Economic Review* in Hong Kong, signed by Matt Forney and devoted to the Chinese historian Yang Zhijiu, who since 1991 had been attempting to refute the anti-Polo arguments. All this to say that the debate had now been thrown into the public arena. But what are the arguments put forward denying that Marco Polo ever set foot in China?

In actual fact, the problem is less what he wrote than what he or his ghost-writer did not write. He never mentions the Great Wall, or the custom of binding small Chinese girls' feet to prevent them from growing or the habit of drinking tea. Another negative argument, a more serious one this time, is the fact that the Chinese annals and archives never mention any of the Polos, nor anything which might identify them, while Marco Polo asserts that he was mandated by the Chinese government to carry out certain tasks, which was the case of numerous other foreigners of whom we do indeed have mention. Neither is there any reference to his official presentation to Kublai upon his arrival in China. There is no trace of his role as official escort of the Mongol princess to the ilkhan of Persia, nor of his role as Kublai's ambassador to the king of Ceylon where he was sent to buy the king's famous ruby. Yes, everyone agrees that he exaggerated and "bluffed", but is this sufficient to assert that he never entered China, Cathay or Mangi?

Other arguments have been put forward, including a linguistic argument: for instance, none of the objects from China are given a Chinese name, or one derived from Chinese; on the contrary, the vocabulary used is influenced by Persian. Though doubt exists, the destruction of a myth is not a smooth process. This argument, no longer restricted to the academic world and which somehow affects our entire heritage, came to a head during a UNESCO program called "Silk Roads—Roads of Dialogue" (1990–1997). This program, coinciding with the development of tourism in Chinese Central Asia and in China in general, stimulated the interest of a much wider public for everything associated with the Silk Road.

To a wider cultured public or simply a generally inquisitive public, Marco Polo, as a theme, has played an important role in the development of the travelogue and the history of travel which has characterized publishing in the West over the last thirty years. Beside academic publications and research work, it has given rise to a vast number of popular works from children's books and comics (in the great explorers, adventurers and discoverers category), to scenarios of romantic, beautifully shot films (with the inevitable love story between the young Marco and some princess). A glance at the catalogues of large libraries reveals the rapid growth of publications on this figure who has become a gold mine for certain branches of publishing. In tourist brochures, one can no longer take a step between Venice and Beijing without being "in the tracks of Marco Polo". He has been adopted as a privileged émigré by all Western countries. And there was to be no question of doubting the authenticity of his account, even less that of his sojourn in China.

What was Frances Wood's conclusion in 1995?[142] She states that one part of the text is credible, the details of the prologue, particularly the first journey of Nicolo and Mafeo Polo. "I think it is quite likely that the elder Polos travelled a long way across the deserts of Central Asia, […] perhaps to Karakorum or a Mongol encampment nearby, and returned, protected by the gold safe-conduct tablets of one of the Mongol leaders. Marco's participation and the whole second trip seems unlikely, even allowing for exaggerations." Marco Polo therefore probably did not travel as far as Karakorum, and even less to Peking. Wood is inclined to think that he probably never went further than his family's trading posts on the Black Sea and in Constantinople. And yet, according to the same author, that does not prevent him having had excellent sources, be it in merchant circles or in other written texts, Persian or otherwise. Even if it is only second-hand, the *Description of the World* is a valuable source of information on China and the Middle East in particular. "His usefulness as a recorder of information otherwise lost is similar to the case of Herodotus (*c.*484 BC to *c.*425 BC), who did not travel to all the places he described and who mixed fact with fantasy tales, but whose work is nevertheless not to be discarded lightly." The same could be said of many other historians and travellers. The debate, carried on in articles, books and television programs, is certainly far from over.

Even more recently, a new controversy occurred. In 1997, a large publication appeared on the market, the translation of a manuscript ascribed to a certain Jacob of Ancona, a Jewish merchant who had travelled in China and lived in Zaitun (Quanzhou) as a merchant, just a few years before the Polos. He left Zaitun to return to Italy in 1272, the year in which the three Polos were to travel across Central Asia to the northern Chinese capital, subsequently leaving China in 1291. The story behind this text is even stranger than that of Marco Polo's manuscripts. The work was published as *The City of Light* (*La città lucente* in the Italian original), a name given to Quanzhou because of the countless lights which shone there all through the night. It was presented as the English translation by David Selbourne, a British writer of works on political philosophy, of an Italian manuscript dating from the end of the 13th century and early 14th century, written by Jacob of Ancona. This manuscript is said to have been kept hidden among family archives for 700 years for reasons to do with relations between the Roman Church and the Jews. Its existence was revealed to Selbourne, the latter claims, by a mysterious visitor when he was living in Urbino, in Italy, in 1990. This visitor, the owner of the manuscript, was prompted to show him the text by Selbourne's personality and his interest in the history of Judaism and the Jews, as well as by the fact that Selbourne was a scholar and spoke Italian.[143] It tells of the journey and sojourn in China of a Jewish merchant. It describes the Jewish merchant colonies in Quanzhou and in various Asian ports, the commerce carried on there, the situation in Quanzhou on the eve of its conquest by the Mongols and the base nature of the city, and the author's relations with the Chinese,

> *What is presented here is the world of the Jewish merchant network in the Middle Ages, which is all the more interesting because, in general, Christian or Muslim authors of this period hardly ever mentioned Jewish merchants in their travel accounts.*

be they scholars or merchants, some of whom were advocating resistance to the Mongols, others backing advantageous surrender. There are long chapters on philosophical and political debates in which Jacob, a pious scholar, exposes his Jewish conception of the world, and above all his religious faith, debating with Confucians and Christians on the duties of the state and the citizen, individual freedom and economic liberalism. One chapter also exposes at length the persecutions and injustice which the Jews suffered at the hands of the Roman Church and the Christian kings, and on many occasions the author attacks Christianity itself, which he classifies as idolatry. This is apparently why the manuscript was kept hidden by its owners in Christian countries.

What is presented here is the world of the Jewish merchant network in the Middle Ages, which is all the more interesting because, in general, Christian or Muslim authors of this period hardly ever mentioned Jewish merchants in their travel accounts. This was a closed world, a separate world, nevertheless connected to the Christian one through the necessities of trade, for example, the paradoxical link whereby Christian merchants in the Middle East bought from the Jews the incense necessary for liturgy, and Jewish merchants sold it to them, despite this being an impious act. This at least is what Jacob tells us. For all this to become known to us, it was necessary for *The City of Light* to be published. This was no easy task. It began with a surprising visit, and a proposal to be allowed to read a manuscript, but only at the place where it was kept; this text was never to be reproduced, and the translation would have to be done in that same secret location. The name of the owner, who is not a Jew, and lives "in Italy, in the Marche", was never to be revealed, neither could the whereabouts of the manuscript. No photocopy or photograph or any type of reproduction of a page, or a fragment of the manuscript should ever be made, much less published. The mysterious visitor plays the role of a visiting angel, and then disappears.

A precursory sign occurred in the form of a long article in *The Sunday Telegraph* dated 18th February 1996. The headline read: "Scooping Marco Polo". The article was signed by Matthew d'Ancona, a friend of Selbourne's. He had no family ties with the author of the manuscript, "Giacobbe ben Salomone d'Ancona, grandson of rabbi Israel di Firenze". The names were a simple coincidence. This article announced the future publication of the text, briefly described, and reproduced a few paragraphs from the first chapter, translated into English. "It was in the year 1270, which is to say 5,030 years from the creation of the world, blessed be He, upon the sixteenth day of April and the twenty-third day of Nisan when Giovanni Confalconiere was *podestà* and Matteo Angeli and Gacomo Bladioni were captains of the people, that I, Jacob, son of Salomone of Ancona and grandson of the great Rabbi Israel of Florence, may his memory be recorded, merchant of Ancona, embarked on board ship for my departure to Greater India and the farthest shores of the earth." There followed an article in the *New York Times* on 22nd September 1997[144] announcing the publication of the book shortly in New York, by Little, Brown and Co. After this came a very rapid and lively response on the part of several American and European specialists of Jewish and Chinese history, who strongly suspected a fake, to the extent that the New York publisher decided not to bring out Selbourne's work.

But the British sister company, Little, Brown and Co of London, nevertheless published it, suggesting that the debate should be held once the specialists and experts had read the text and not beforehand. This led to a ferocious battle in the press and on the air waves, with Selbourne being charged with being either the victim of a hoax, an "accomplice" or even the "faker" himself. Refutations and arguments were presented on both sides. It was translated into French in 2000. The original, which none can consult, was, we are told, written in vernacular Italian, and interspersed with terms in Hebrew, Arabic and Latin. It contains many words transcribed phonetically from Chinese, and difficult to identify. Selbourne appended to his translation a number of commentaries both on the language used and the events, as well as an index and a glossary. The original manuscript is said to have been written not in Jacob's own hand, but by a copyist at the beginning of the 14th century, and it ends by giving the name of the copyist, which is that of Jacob's wife's family.

We cannot list all the controversies connected with this editorial adventure, which still remains unconcluded, and which has led many university experts in various fields to take up their pens and write bestsellers on the subject, particularly between 1996 and 1998. The fiercest attack came from two specialists in Hebrew and Middle Eastern history, in an article in *The Times Literary Supplement* of November 1997, which begins "The literary hoax is an ignoble, but ancient, art…" and continues with a very violent attack on all levels. Selbourne answered this in the following issue, with humour and in no uncertain terms, finally stating that his intervention had guaranteed the integrity of the original text, that Jacob's galleon had reached the high seas, and that nothing could now stop it. The book is selling well, which must please Selbourne, as he mentions in the acknowledgments page that the mysterious owner of the document not only gave him authorization to publish a translation, but generously vested the translation rights in him…

Among critics, we find the Sinologists Frances Wood and Jonathan Spence. But once more, Chinese scholars have defended the contested work, perhaps most vociferously amongst maritime and history specialists conversant with Quanzhou's (Zaitun's) contacts with the outside world where most of Jacob's tale occurs. At their head is Wang Lianmao, director of the Quanzhou Maritime Museum, who wrote in 1998 in *The Sunday Times*, "On the basis of historical facts, and in particular of Quanzhou culture, most specialists have come to the conclusion that it is authentic." "This verdict," wrote M. Phillips in *The Sunday Times* on the 11th October 1998, "was dynamite." It marked a turning point in this story—the doubters were now doubted. Other authoritative voices rose in favour of the text, with the support of Chinese researchers, particularly after a conference of Chinese specialists held in Quanzhou in February 1999, according to Selbourne who attended the meeting. Since then, Jacob's galleon has been sailing well; in 1999, the book was translated into Chinese and thirteen other countries had requested translation rights.

> *Whether the ship was a real ship or a ghost ship, whoever its author, translator or ghost-writer may have been, whatever the inspirations may have been, these mermaid songs have not finished sweeping us along with Jacob of Ancona's galleon, to countries from which, thanking God for preserving their lives and fortunes, they brought back in their holds the treasures of China, the Indes, Ceylon, the Persian Gulf and the Red Sea.*

There are more riches in this galleon than one might think, including in the field of ideas. Selbourne says he was inspired by it when he wrote his *The Principle of Duty: An Essay on the Foundations of the Civic Order*. Whether the ship was a real ship or a ghost ship, whoever its author, translator or ghost-writer may have been, whatever the inspirations may have been, these mermaid songs have not finished sweeping us along with Jacob of Ancona's galleon, to countries from which, thanking God for preserving their lives and fortunes, they brought back in their holds the treasures of China, the Indes, Ceylon, the Persian Gulf and the Red Sea. Buying here, selling there, evading dangers, facing tempests and after what was a short return trip for the period—three years and a month—Jacob returned to Ancona, in May 1273.

With him came a wealth of silks, cotton, pepper, ginger, cinnamon, nutmeg, cloves, saffron, rhubarb, myrobalan and all sorts of plants, nard, musk, balm and frankincense, myrrh and storax, indigo, brazil-wood, sandalwood, gems sewn into his clothes, a fine quantity of amber, pearls, coral and much gold. He brought back to his beloved wife, "a necklace of coral and gold most delicately worked" from Ceylon, where he had also bought "a necklace of pearls of great value and a bracelet of amethysts so that I might have them as dowry for my daughters".

It would not have needed more than this to tempt a Genoese named Christopher Columbus to his fate, were it not for the fact that he had already read the account of the famous Venetian with his cloths of gold and silk from Cathay, and his gold from Sypangu; travelling from east to west, he was going in the wrong direction and could not reach Japan, but instead found America, a fine example of the serendipity effect.

Chapter Seventeen

The Emergence of the Great Sea Powers and the Birth of the French Silk Industry

The Song dynasty, which reigned over the whole of China from 960 to 1126, and then over southern China from 1126 to 1278 before being overcome by the Mongol dynasty, was in many fields, particularly philosophy, literature and the arts, a time of crystallization of Chinese thought, to use René Grousset's expression; this was the "delicate Song civilization, the blossoming of Chinese culture".[145]

The term "crystallization" suggests an ultimate stage of evolution of a mineral, beyond which there can be only disintegration or dissolving. But it is also the very essence of this civilization, which sought shelter within itself, excluding all the Turkish and Mongol influences which marked the northern dynasties and the conquerors which came from the north. Furthermore, through force of circumstance, the heart of China proper moved southwards, and the Chinese began to develop their navy. Chinese merchants had for a long time been sailing to Ceylon and the port of Siraf (after 970, this port was destroyed by an earthquake and abandoned for Hormuz), probably on non-Chinese ships in the 10th century. By the 13th century, they travelled on large sea junks built in China, which sailed further and further, both east and west.

According to D. Lelièvre,[146] in the 13th century, China possessed the most powerful navy in the world. The Chinese had been using the compass regularly since the 11th and 12th centuries (it was not really adopted in Europe until the

14th century), and furthermore, at the end of the Song period, they had learned how to use explosives, in the form of grenades and bombards, in naval warfare.

During the Song dynasty, Arabic, Indian, Malay and Persian merchants were frequent visitors to the port of Quanzhou, from where they took home news of southern China, while the Western countries had contacts with northern China, with the government of the Mongol Yuan dynasty, with Kublai and his descendants. The preoccupations of the Christian kingdoms were mainly of a religious or politico-religious nature.

The foreign Yuan dynasty which reigned over China until 1368 was, as we have seen, with its founder Kublai, tolerant towards all religions and trends of thought, and particularly defended Buddhism and Christianity. The politico-religious contacts which were set up between the Yuan emperors and the Tibetan lamas of the Sakya school helped China control the administration of Tibet (the politically correct history of the People's Republic of China traces the integration of Tibet into the Chinese state back to the Yuan dynasty).

Nestorianism went through a prosperous period in Mongol China and the Yuan government too used it to political ends. At this time of relative peace under *pax mongolica*, when land communications, however distant, were safe, the main intermediaries and messengers between the Yuan emperors, the ilkhan of Persia and the Christian kingdoms were monks. The Nestorian patriarchate was still located in Persia, which was governed by a descendant of Genghis Khan. It so happened that among the Catholicos from 1281 to 1317 was a Chinese Nestorian monk, known as Mar Jaballah III, born near Peking. He left China in 1275–1276 to travel to the holy Christian sites in Jerusalem, accompanied by another Nestorian monk known in Europe under the name of Rabban Çauma. The latter came from a Turkish Öngut family which had settled in North China. The two monks were held up in Baghdad, where the former became Patriarch and the latter bishop. In 1287, the ilkhan Arghun sent Rabban Çauma as ambassador to Europe; he travelled through Constantinople, Naples and Rome, where the election of a new Pope was imminent. He went to France, where he met King Philip IV the Fair and King Edward I of England, then returned to Rome, where he was received by the new Pope Nicholas IV. He spent the Easter festivities of 1288 in Rome, receiving communion from the Pope. Then he returned to Persia, and gave his sovereign an account of his mission. That the Nestorian Christians had been considered heretics in the eyes of the Roman Church seems to

> *France was one of the most powerful Christian kingdoms and was the one which had been most eager to set up an alliance with the Mongols against the Muslims.*

have bothered no one, either in Rome or elsewhere.

In 1289, Arghun sent to the Pope and to the kings of England and France a new embassy led this time by a layman, the Genoese Buscarel, who had long been in the service of the ilkhan.[147]

Why France? France was one of the most powerful Christian kingdoms and was the one which had been most eager to set up an alliance with the Mongols against the Muslims, an alliance which the ilkhan Arghun was also hoping for. But the present king was no St Louis. The latter's grandson, Philip the Fair, though profoundly Christian, and though mindful of the duty of Christians to become crusaders, did not himself journey to the Holy Land, nor contribute to a new crusade. He had received Arghun's envoy, Rabban Çauma, with full honours in 1287, permitting him to visit the Holy Chapel and to worship the Crown of Thorns. Philip had thought of sending troops, if it please God, but never did so for the king's advisers remembered the earlier Crusades which had ended in disaster and that St Louis had, against everyone's advice, abandoned his kingdom to fight the infidels, and had died in Africa. The duty of a king was never to leave his kingdom unless it was in order.[148]

There were other monks sent by the Mongol khans to the Pope or to Christian kings and from these to the Mongol khans. The most famous of the Westerners were the Franciscans sent by the Popes: John of Montcorvin (Monte Corvino), in 1289, who was well received in China by the successor to Kublai, but faced hostility from the Nestorians. He became Archbishop of Peking. Andrew of Perugia, around 1310, worked at Quanzhou where he became bishop; Odoric of Pordenone in 1314, who has left a detailed account of his travels, crossed almost all of Asia, and lived for three years in Peking. John of Marignoli, in 1338, also travelled to Central Asia, India and China, and was briefly Archbishop of Peking, returning to Avignon in 1353; there were many others.[149] Roman Catholicism was more or less tolerant of the Nestorian groups which had lived for generations in China, but the Catholic presence did not last very long. In 1370, the archbishop named by the Pope for the archbishopric of Peking could not occupy his see, for after the fall of the Mongol Yuan dynasty, the new, purely Chinese Ming dynasty showed little goodwill at first towards foreign religions. Christians of all churches were compelled to leave or to mix in discreetly with Chinese tradition (Buddhism, on the other hand, was already assimilated into these traditions). The next representatives of Roman Catholicism in China were the Jesuits, the Italian Matteo Ricci who would arrive in 1582 and the German Adam Schall, in 1620.

> *The admiral of the fleet, Zheng He, a Muslim from Yunnan, recruited as a child to become a eunuch in the service of the state, led these diplomatic missions to the coast of Siam, Java, Ceylon, India, the Persian Gulf, East Africa and Arabia. They sailed as far as Mogadishu, Aden, Jeddah and the port of Mecca.*

The cyclical process was beginning once again. The Yuan dynasty had become degenerate, and fallen into disorder and ruin. Central power was weakened, and a vast movement of national liberation, which had begun in South China, overthrew the Mongol dynasty. After a period of infighting between nationalist or self-interested rebel chiefs, one of these took power in 1368, founding a new dynasty, the Ming. He quickly reconquered the rest of Chinese territory and devoted himself to restoring all the fundamentally Chinese values; although a Buddhist himself, and an ex-monk, he returned the Confucian cult to its supreme position, and protected scholars. This national restoration was completed by his successor Yongle (1403–1424), who devoted himself to making the Chinese Empire a great power once again, controlling its furthest territories and its neighbours and creating a powerful navy to press on with its imperial plans across the seas.

Between 1405 and 1433, seven naval expeditions were organized to "barbarian" lands. The admiral of the fleet, Zheng He, a Muslim from Yunnan, recruited as a child to become a eunuch in the service of the state, led these diplomatic missions to the coast of Siam, Java, Ceylon, India, the Persian Gulf, East Africa and Arabia. They sailed as far as Mogadishu, Aden, Jeddah and the port of Mecca.

The Chinese envoys contacted thirty-seven countries. They established diplomatic relations with the sovereigns, exchanged gifts and tribute, and sometimes even engaged in a military operation against an insolent king, or a pirate who would be taken back as a prisoner to the Chinese capital. Foreign princes would send a brother or an uncle with a letter confirming their status as vassal to the emperor.[150] These were similar practices as had existed during the Han and Tang dynasties in their relations with the kingdoms of the Western Territories. Commercial considerations were not overlooked. Unfortunately, this policy of maritime expansion and contacts with the outside world was abandoned after 1433. "The world policy of the Yongle emperor was not continued. China withdrew into itself," letting go its chance to make its mark on land and at sea, writes René Grousset, who observes the same withdrawal in the world of thought with the establishment of Confucianism as the official doctrine. The same immobility is observed in painting which became very academic and lacking in creativity. In the scientific field, "When the Ming came to the throne (1368), China and the West were more or less on the same level from the point of view of equipment and technology. By the fall of the dynasty, in 1644, it would become apparent that Europe already possessed modern science and the accessories which go with that, while China remained in the Middle Ages…"[151]

For some historians, what has retrospectively been called the Silk Road no longer existed after the Portuguese, having sailed round Africa and the Cape of Good Hope in 1498, established themselves in the ports of India and the East Indies. With the discovery of America, part of European imports and exports went to the New World. The arrival of the sea powers in Asia—first of all Portugal, then Holland and England—attracted to the sea routes and to the ports of India, Indonesia and China the flow of trade which for a long time had favoured the land routes. The transcontinental exchange currents along the Silk Road lost their vitality. For other historians, the "Silk Road", in the historical acceptance of the term, no longer existed by the end of the Mongol Empire. For yet others, the "Silk Road" ended with the Tang dynasty in the 10th century.

> *The term "Silk Road" has sometimes been given to any land or sea route between East and West followed at any given moment by merchants.*

These conceptions take into account the network of land routes, but separate them from the sea routes as if they were completely independent of one another. But the contrary would appear to be the case, for the commercial network was created by the interconnection of the two systems, at least from the beginning of the Christian era. On the whole, they supported each other and would not have been fully functional one without the other.

From a different perspective, the term "Silk Road" has sometimes been given to any land or sea route between East and West followed at any given moment by merchants. That is to say anything which took a traveller—by any mode—between the Greenwich meridian and that of Vladivostok, since the time of Alexander the Great, if not of Herodotus, or even as far back as the first Egyptian mummy with three threads of silk in its hair.

Let us translate the expression in terms of volume of trade. This volume was the result in part of political events, and in part of the technical evolution of methods of transport. Among the former were civil unrest, banditry and war, which threatened the safety of transport (this only reappeared with control by a powerful state); the closure of a country's borders (China and Japan are good examples of this); openness towards foreign lands, scientific curiosity, tolerance, material wealth; the monopoly of large commercial companies sustained by a powerful state, as was the case in the 17th, 18th and 19th centuries; embargoes, blockades, prohibitions on exports, exclusions, xenophobia; or more or less freedom of trade; and, above all, the presence or absence of supply and demand, according to the wealth of the potential customers. Among the methods of transport were progress in navigation, which would modify the balance of relative advantages and disadvantages between land transport and sea transport over distances such as those which separate Europe from eastern Asia.

The monopolies, de facto or by right, belonged to the large predators, be they states or pirates. From the 15th century on, these predators were those who had the most advanced navy, the largest, fastest and best-made ships, and those with the most sophisticated weapons, the cannon being a determining factor. Could China, under the Ming, have asserted itself in this role? It turned away from it. So the Portuguese arrived, dominating the 16th century thanks to their naval superiority, before being challenged and then eliminated in the 17th century by the Dutch and the English. Arriving directly from Europe by sailing round Africa, without having to unload and reload the merchandise, and suffering the inconveniences of exclusions or intermediaries in the Red Sea or the Gulf of Oman (eventually they controlled Hormuz), the Portuguese established their agencies in the large ports of India and Indonesia, and even of China. They brought their influence to bear on the local authorities, sometimes by force, and drove off rival ships, obtaining monopolies and concessions. Naturally, they became wealthy. In the 16th century, it was at Lisbon that the Europeans bought their spices.

> *It is obvious that in 1500, after the discovery of the New World and the circumnavigation of Africa by the Portuguese, the economic geography of the world had changed. The notion of "Silk Road" could no longer be applied.*

If one therefore considers the volume of commercial exchange, in so far as it can be evaluated, it appears that the period of the decline of the Mongol Empire, the devastation of Tamerlane's conquests and the disasters which hit Europe (the Hundred Years' War and the Black Death), constitute a blank page in the picture of trans-Eurasian trade. But this void may be due only to our own ignorance, because we have not read texts in languages which are not accessible to us; it is a blank in our European eyes. Nevertheless, it is obvious that in

1500, after the discovery of the New World and the circumnavigation of Africa by the Portuguese, the economic geography of the world had changed. The notion of "Silk Road" could no longer be applied.

The 15th and 16th centuries, with the Reformation and the Renaissance, with the great inventions (or rather their discovery in Europe: the compass, instruments of navigation, the rudder, printing), mark the end of the European Middle Ages and the beginning of what historians call modern times. Conventionally, we bring the Middle Ages to a close with the capture of Constantinople by the Turks in 1453; this break obviously can only be applied to Western Europe, because what we define as the Middle Ages lasted for several centuries more in the rest of the world.

In Europe, rival powers, precariously balanced, wrested control of the seas and of trade from one another. This was no longer a time when one wrote in Greek or Latin which could be read from the English coast to that of Syria (in the way that right across the Chinese Empire the same text written in Chinese characters can be read by people speaking many different dialects). Geographers and historians wrote in their mother tongue, and to follow the history of trade, it would be necessary to know six or seven languages and live in the libraries and archives of six or seven different countries. Some maps were still in Latin, but, to give just one example, the famous map of the world known as the *Catalan Atlas of Charles V* (a manuscript of 1375 kept in the library of the French king Charles V and now in the National Library in Paris), was written in Majorcan Catalan. How can one trace the trade network of eastern products in all their European ramifications? Here we shall only follow the evolution of the silk trade, of sericulture, and the silk industry in France, for which documentation is more easily accessible than in many countries.

ITALY

At the time of Marco Polo's return to Venice, sericulture, which was flourishing in Sicily, moved to Italy, first to Lucca, and from there to the whole peninsula, particularly to Venice, Florence, Milan and Bologna, around 1314. The workers from Lucca, driven from their home by a civil war, set up their workshops in these cities. From then on, the Italians held the monopoly on the silk trade with France, Germany and England. They succeeded both in producing silk themselves and in controlling the trade of silk from the Middle East. This soon became such an essential preoccupation for their governments that it induced the Venetians to take the matter up with the Pope: "In 1368, the trade of silks, gold cloth and other costly products from Alexandria with Europe through the intermediary of the Italians was still so considerable that the Italian communes, threatened with complete ruin because of an overseas war, concentrated their efforts on persuading the Pope to put an end to the war engaged against the king of Cyprus and the sultan of Egypt, a war during which much wealth had been lost."[152] Trade took precedence, and was more important than political or religious concerns. The Italians, for several centuries, would travel up and down Europe, selling on the markets of Montpellier or Lyons their *nachiz* cloth from Lucca or their Cypriot damasks. (Since the crusaders had finally lost Acre in 1291, Cyprus had become a Christian emporium in the eastern Mediterranean, and had enjoyed an industrial and commercial boom). From Cyprus too, came gold-braided embroidery which the Italians would soon imitate; from Tana on the Don, from Sudak in the Crimea, came silks bought from the Tartars, produced in China or in Central Asia, or Mongol Persia. These *tartaires*, as they were known, and these silk cloths with gold stripes, which Marco Polo may have made fashionable, would also be copied by Italian weavers.

The history of the introduction of sericulture into France must be seen against a background of military reprisals and protective customs duties. From the 14th century on, the government realized that too much money was leaving the kingdom to pay for luxury cloth sold by the Italians, particularly at the great fairs of Lyons and Champagne. The majority of the merchants at these fairs came from Genoa, Florence and Lucca. They had become wealthy through trading brocade and velvet, a fabric which would be extremely popular for three centuries (except for a few brief periods, Westerners would always be fond of stiff fabrics with heavy, majestic folds). Lyons was such an important fair at the time that the Italians thought of settling down there. They could now buy silk thread since the Popes, established at Avignon at the beginning of the 14th century, had introduced the cultivation of the mulberry tree and the breeding of silkworms. But the French silk industry was not developing and continued to rely on imports.

FRANCE

In 1466, King Louis XI (1461–1483) allocated a sum of two thousand *tournois* to pay for the salary of skilled silk workers, both men and women, whom he hoped to attract to the city of Lyons in order to give a boost to the French silk industry.[153] However, for various reasons, the project failed and it was not in Lyons that the industry first prospered, but at Tours where the king transferred it a few years later. Several workshops were also set up in Nîmes, Avignon and Paris.

François I, both to ruin defeated Italy and to promote French industry, prohibited the import into France of fabrics of gold and silver in 1517. Faced with the threat of poverty, the Italians living in Lyons attempted to manufacture in their adoptive city the cloths for which there was still a great demand among the French nobility and bourgeoisie.

In 1536, François I gave two Italian merchants working in Lyons, the Piemontese Etienne Turquet and the Genoese Bathélémy Nariz, patent letters allowing them to establish workshops in that town. As competent workers were lacking in France and existed only in Italy, they requested and obtained permission to bring silk workers and their families from Genoa. They were exempted from all taxes and duties on the condition that they settled in Lyons for their entire lives. In 1540, the Société Commerciale de la Fabrique Lyonnaise was founded, which would later become the famous Fabrique de Lyon. Lyons had a monopoly on the import and trade of all raw silk.

The weaving industry began to develop, first producing enough to satisfy demand within France, and soon entering into the competitive European market, challenging the Italian silk industry. But there were never enough workers, despite Italian immigration, and the highly specialized workforce required in the workshops making velvet and other delicate fabrics had to be trained on site. The division of labour between men, women and children, was characteristic of specialization in the West: women were in charge of the reeling, spinning and spooling; men would weave; and the children would carry out all the auxiliary tasks. The rules of the profession prevented women from becoming weavers, a more highly paid job, in the openly admitted aim of guaranteeing a constant and sufficient body of low-paid workers.

To feed this growing industry—7,000 looms around 1600 and 10,000 in the 1660s—more and more raw silk had to be produced: mulberry trees were planted and silkworms bred throughout the Languedoc, Beaujolais and even in the Lyons area. Despite this, the French silk industry never freed itself from the obligation of importing raw silk, from Italy (Piedmont and Sardinia), Spain, Turkey, and, from the 19th century on, mainly from the Far East.

The Lyons silk industry developed greatly in the 17th century; improvements made to the Italian loom in 1605 allowed the easier manufacture of certain fabrics. To protect themselves from fluctuations in fashion, the manufacturers had diversified production, adding to the luxury products which sold more readily and widely, and perfecting mixed cloths in which silk was added. But, ironically, while

> *[The] forced emigration of Protestants not only deprived France of a valuable workforce but also established rival enterprises among the enemy.*

Christian morality had come to terms with luxury and silk more than a millennium before, it was a purely religious event which was to deal a serious blow to the French silk industry: the Revocation of the Edict of Nantes by Louis XIV in 1685. This led to the emigration of more than 300,000 Huguenots from France, among them a number of silk manufacturers and bankers who took with them their know-how and their capital. They were welcomed in the neighbouring Protestant countries, in Switzerland (Basel and Zurich), Germany, Holland and England, where they set up silk factories. In England, the Huguenot refugees from Tours, the Lyons area, Nîmes and the Cévennes settled, among other places, in the London borough of Spitalfields. They brought their expertise, their manufacturing secrets and their capital, all of which was crucial to the development of the English textile industry. The same occurred in Holland. Both countries were rivals to France in politics and commerce, and this forced emigration of Protestants not only deprived France of a valuable workforce but also established rival enterprises among the enemy.[154]

The French silk industry flourished again in the 18th century, from 1717 until the Revolution in 1789. It had reached "a pre-eminent position in the world in terms of technology, commerce, and above all artistry", writes J. Vaschalde[155] (but is China included in the world?). The reign of Louis XV was, for the arts, a reign of grace and good taste; great artists set to decorating textiles; the court, nobility and rich bourgeoisie constituted an affluent clientele; and the renown of French taste and the quality of the Lyons products spread throughout the European courts. Catherine II of Russia would order her fabrics from a Lyons manufacturer.

THE CHINESE INFLUENCE

The fashion then was for large motifs which were veritable tableaux (the drawings of these motifs were kept strictly secret). Dresses were very loose, with panniers, which required huge lengths of cloth. Popular motifs were fruits and trees, seashells and bird feathers. Chinese motifs appeared for the first time, with pagodas, bamboo bridges and figures. This was not the best of Chinese art, but what arrived in Europe at the time was the export porcelain and lacquer from Qing dynasty workshops, the last dynasty of Manchu origin, which had taken over the Chinese Empire in 1664.

> *Tea began to spread across the world. It was now so much part of daily life in England that it would soon become a more determining factor in British commercial policy than silk itself.*

This wave of Chinese motifs reflects new contacts between Europe and the Far East. This was the period of the East India companies, this was the century of England, following that of the Dutch. Porcelain and tea were shipped down river on junks and transferred in Canton or in the ports of Fujian onto large clippers. These porcelains decorated the salons of London, Amsterdam and Paris, having crossed the Atlantic Ocean from the Cape of Good Hope to the coasts of Brittany, Normandy, the south of England or Holland. The sea journey was longer than ever, and a return trip took years. But sailing was safer, the ships were larger and could carry freight, water and food for long crossings, the sails had been perfected, the sailors had better equipment, the maps had improved and the seas were more familiar. Tea began to spread across the world. It was now so much part of daily life in England that it would soon become a more determining factor in British commercial policy than silk itself. France discovered it through Holland, and the nobility was beginning to develop a taste for it. China was the only tea producer in the world, and remained so until the 19th century.

At the same time that Chinese garden motifs were being delicately placed on the pannier dresses of the Marquise de Pompadour, another more traditional aspect of Chinese civilization was generating unexpected interest in the West. Once again, this was a religious matter: Confucian concepts had begun to enter Catholic France with what was known as the debate over rites. The two opposing sides in this quarrel were on the one hand, Confucian rites, and particularly the cult of the ancestors, and on the other, Louis XIV and the Pope; mediating between the two were the Jesuit missionaries in China.

There were a few Jesuits present in China, following on from Matteo Ricci and Adam Schall. They were almost always scholars—mathematicians, astronomers, cartographers, painters—whose knowledge was greatly appreciated by the Chinese emperors. They worked as scientists and missionaries, and were also the first Sinologists. During the 18th century, the Jesuit Fathers wrote reports and personal letters to their superiors and colleagues in Europe. Intended also as letters for the edification of the faithful, they were full of snippets of information on China which the Europeans regarded as "curious". These letters were compiled and published in book form as part of the Jesuit publication program. The greatest of these collections was the *Lettres édifiantes et curieuses* published in Paris between 1702 and 1776, with later additions and reprints.[156]

The conversion of the Chinese to Christianity always faced the same problem: the Chinese would not give up the Confucian rites of filial piety. The Jesuits, with a knowledge of Chinese civilization, did not consider this idolatry. They attempted to demonstrate to the European Catholics that the Confucian rites were not strictly speaking a cult, as they did not include the notion of a divinity; they were simply gestures without any religious significance, and were perfectly compatible with the obligations of a Christian. But the Pope saw things differently, and an impassioned debate followed. Many questions were raised about the nature of Confucianism; its similarities with Greco-Roman rites were emphasized, and China generated more interest than ever, though within this Catholic viewpoint. The Jesuits were opposed by the Franciscans and Dominicans, the foreign missions and King Louis XIV. Finally, the papacy condemned the Confucian rites in two bulls, in 1715 and 1742 (this condemnation was lifted in 1938 by Pius XII). The Jesuit order itself was suppressed in France in 1764 and in Rome in 1773, only to be re-established in 1814.

The Jesuits left China for a while, but the secular world in France was also developing a new philosophical interest in things Chinese. The physiocrats of François Quesnay's (1694–1774) ideas of governance, and Voltaire himself, admired its political and social system. It was Confucianism which was the object of their adoration, which they compared favourably to the political and social order of contemporary France that finally led to the Revolution. But their conception of China was abstract and theoretical, and they knew nothing of the real situation there.

Let us return to the silk industry in France, which was going through several crises. The fashion for *indiennes*, printed calicos from Persia or India, dealt a severe blow to the Lyons silk production. At the end of Louis XVI's reign, the serious economic situation, heavy customs duties and emerging competition from other European countries, led to a crisis even before the French Revolution. In 1789, 20,000 unemployed Lyons workers were living on public charity. The Revolution deprived the silk industry of its affluent customers from the court, the aristocracy and the church, and the suppression of the corporations in 1791 disrupted the Lyons industry further. In 1793, there were only 3,000 working looms in Lyons.

During the First Empire (1804–1814) the silk industry revived, thanks to a new clientele: silks, now slightly less luxurious, had become widespread among other social classes. There was less demand for sumptuous cloth and more for silks at an affordable price. In 1801, the introduction of the Jacquard loom reduced the necessary number of weavers by half, which presented serious social problems, inseparable from technological progress: this was the dawn of what historians call the Industrial Revolution. From then on, the French silk industry would have to navigate skilfully between fashions which demanded constant changes in textures, colour and motifs, and which would periodically give up silk for cotton, linen or wool, and the difficult balance of cost prices, linked to the price of raw silk. From the 19th century on, the problem of cost price encouraged the silk manufacturers to look for cheaper raw silk; logically, one would expect this to come from less far away. But another change was on the horizon with the advent of the steam engine: once English steamers had replaced sail ships, the result was an enormous drop in both incurred risk and in travel time. This, added to the relatively low price of raw materials in the Far East, once again encouraged the Western silk manufacturers to buy Chinese raw silks in Canton and Shanghai.

Chapter Eighteen

From the Last of the Sailing Ships to the Eurochrysalid and the Transgenic Worm

I n the 18th century, the southern coasts of China were visited more by the English than by the French. This was the period the English call the Old Trade (between 1700 and 1834). British merchants, acting on their own behalf, and then for the East India Company which held the trade monopoly, would regularly drop anchor off Canton, in front of the "Bogue", the labyrinthine estuary of the Pearl River, and buy mainly tea and then silk from Chinese agents. Off the Bogue, they would sometimes be joined by French ships, as well as Dutch, and from 1783, American clippers which travelled around Cape Horn. But the biggest customer in China was undeniably England, which paid for its tea and silk in silver coinage, and then more and more in opium from India or Persia. Silk, like tea, was a product of great value which weighed very little, and England would undoubtedly have imported more of it had the Chinese government not set a quota on the amounts which could leave the empire. Foreign captains, who could load as much tea as they wanted, were forbidden from taking more than 140 *piculs* (about eight and a half tons if one reckons the *picul* at around

> *Silk, like tea, was a product of great value which weighed very little, and England would undoubtedly have imported more of it had the Chinese government not set a quota on the amounts which could leave the empire.*

60 kilos) of silk per ship, unless they bought a special licence on top of the usual customs duties on departure; the cost price therefore remained quite high. Indeed, the organization of foreign trade from Canton was such that products there were on the whole relatively expensive.

The 18th century was, for the Far East, a period of obstinate and conscious closure to external contact, a period of systematic suspicion and great chauvinism, particularly on the part of China and Japan. The latter had only limited commercial exchange with Westerners, and then only with the Dutch, who were confined to the island of Deshima, from which they were forbidden to set foot on Japanese soil. Most products were not allowed to enter Japan, except for goods of absolute necessity such as metal or medicines. China had also closed its territory to all Europeans following the regrettable attitude of the Portuguese in the 15th and 16th centuries. China tolerated certain forms of exchange only and even then under arbitrarily fixed conditions. This at first applied to the southern ports, but was later limited to Canton alone, where all commerce with the Western Barbarians was exclusively in the hands of the Cantonese merchant guild known as Co-Hong (*Gonghang*), a sort of private agency recognized by Peking. Under the proviso of never breaking the rules set by the Co-Hong, Her Majesty's subjects sold their opium and their precious metal, and took on tea and silk. At the end of the 18th century, they also bought an excellent cotton cloth known as "nankeen", named after its town of origin.

The rules which could not be broken included the following: entering into the bay with warships; landing with knives and swords, firearms, or European women; travelling upriver along the Pearl River without authorization; disembarking large numbers of people; contacting anyone without the permission of the Co-Hong; and trading prohibited merchandise.

This corporate organization of the Co-Hong excluded official contact: no diplomatic representation backed up the private dealings, and merchants dealt with other merchants. Diplomatic representation was recognized by the Chinese emperor only in the case of vassal states. By 1838, this attitude had contributed greatly to the deterioration of relations between the Chinese and English. Until then, it has to be said, merchants on both sides were relatively satisfied with existing arrangements. Opium came along to spoil things, and controversies over etiquette then added fuel to the fire. The result was war.

Opium had been used in Chinese medicine since the Tang period at least, but did not take on its pernicious form as a drug until the 18th century. The first edict prohibiting it is dated 1729. The Chinese government, for moral and health reasons, but also to prevent opium from draining the wealth of the empire, intervened several times to limit or to prohibit the purchase of opium from the East India Company. But the sale of opium mainly grown in India was, for this company, an important source of revenue.

Once prohibited, the trade turned into a smuggling operation, and was no less prosperous. Cases of opium were sold with false content declarations and the provincial governors shut their eyes to these dealings, in return for substantial bribes. Forbidden or not, opium had an important clientele in China, including the imperial court's entourage.

Faced by the sheer magnitude of the smuggling and the attitude of the English merchants, the emperor sent Lin Zexu, a senior official, to Canton specifically, to deal with this problem. In 1839, he demanded the delivery of all opium cases stocked in the docks of the foreign warehouses and in the holds of ships. There were more than 20,000 of them, each weighing 120 kilos. All were completely destroyed. This was the beginning of the Opium Wars which marks the beginning of a sixty-year struggle between China and the Western powers. The former attempted to preserve its commercial status quo, its policy of territorial prohibition and its trade in dribs and drabs. The latter, meanwhile, attempted by every means to force the Chinese market open, to obtain advantageous customs tariffs and all sorts of commercial benefits. The government in London sent troops to seize Shanghai and Nanking. China capitulated and in 1842 signed with England the Treaty of Nanking, inaugurating the era of the gunship.

Under this treaty, England obtained everything it wanted, the opening of the Five Ports—Canton, Shanghai, Amoy, Fuzhou and Ningbo—to British commerce, the right to live and trade there, very moderate customs tariffs, most favoured nation status, the transfer of the island of Hong Kong and the right of extraterritoriality, that is the right not to be judged by Chinese justice in cases of crime. The Chinese government was no longer master in its own home.

The opening of the Five Ports to trade was soon extended to other Western powers. France had fewer commercial interests in China than Britain, but it did have another preoccupation of a different nature, the Catholic missions. It obtained, in the wake of the Treaty of Nanking, in 1844, through the Treaty of Whampoa, the right to preach the Catholic religion in the open ports, a right which was extended to the Protestants in 1846.

This was an unexpected outcome after a long period during which Christianity had had great trouble in maintaining itself in a country which defended its civilization, its social and political system, and its Confucian philosophy, against foreign influence, and which did not intend to have other ways of life dictated to it by Westerners convinced they held the Truth.

The Jesuits had been recalled from China, and since 1785, replaced by the Lazarists. But the French Revolution, the suppression of church congregations, and the wars of the French Empire, had reduced the presence of French missionaries in China. Missionary activity took off again, but was very much held in check by the various prohibitions of Chinese law. From 1841, however, the Jesuits returned.

After 1844, Catholic missions were to play an important role in Franco-Chinese relations and in French public opinion. In 1838, the Vatican had ended the *Padroado*, the system according to which a 16th-century Pope had divided the world between Spain and Portugal, giving the latter exclusive control of the missions in India and throughout the Far East. The Portuguese mission in China, dependent on that of Goa, had found its activities limited for a long time to Macao by the Chinese government. The Vatican and the Sacred Congregation of Propaganda took direct control of the Chinese missions.

Protestantism was introduced into Chinese territory at the beginning of the 19th century, mainly by British and American missionaries. In those areas where missionaries were not able to travel, it was spread through the large-scale distribution of copies of Chinese-language Bibles. The treaties of 1844 and 1846 had opened the door to Protestants as much as to Catholics.

These treaties, which had been imposed on China by force, were never really accepted or observed by the Chinese governments, or by the population. Various incidents, refusals, and the execution of a missionary, finally led to another military expedition, a Franco-British one this time. The 1860 campaign brought foreign armies into the heart of Peking itself, leading to the plunder and burning of the Summer Palace, and ended with the Treaty of Tianjin, according to which the British and the French, including their missionaries, obtained the authorization to live in China, with guarantees for the safety both of their goods and of themselves, as well as for Chinese Christian converts.

This uneasy relationship between the two parties would last, with numerous other military episodes and treaties, until the First World War. The "unequal treaties", as they have been called by Chinese historians, to a large extent fostered recent Chinese xenophobia. They left a black mark in the collective memory, and caused the demise of the dynasty which had allowed China to be humiliated in this way. For a long time, young Chinese patriots would demand the abolition of the "unequal treaties", abhorrent remains and symbols of the colonial period, and these sentiments return time and again in the writings of the Communist period. Perhaps this residual national bitterness has only finally been subsumed with the recent return to China of the territories of Hong Kong and Macao.

Europe still could not compete with China when it came to silkworm breeding, in terms of cocoon thread yield and volume of silk production, and regularly had to buy 50 per cent of its raw silk from the Chinese.

Another aspect of almost a century of Catholic missionary activity in China was the obvious and regrettable association in people's minds between the missions, merchant and cannons. This was to be expected given the circumstances in which the treaties were imposed on an unwilling country, the spirit in which these events occurred, the way in which the missions made use of their own governments' backing (and vice versa), and all of this backed by military force. For a long time the West would be rebuked for this, and it is probably the reason why all outbursts of patriotism in China tend to lead to Chinese Christians—relatively numerous since the missionary zeal of the 19th century—being treated with distrust, suspected almost of being traitors and conceivably prepared to become foreign vassals.

In the world of commerce, once the ports had been opened, the potential for buying and selling was extended. Foreign interests were represented by consuls and trade was normalized and profitable. From the very first treaties, the Western merchants and industrialists turned in large numbers to China as a supplier of raw silk.

Europe still could not compete with China when it came to silkworm breeding, in terms of cocoon thread yield and volume of silk production, and regularly had to buy 50 per cent of its raw silk from the Chinese. In addition, the opening of the Suez Canal, in 1869, greatly diminished the distance and cost of maritime transport, which had already improved with the introduction of steamships. This contributed notably to massive arrivals in Europe of silk from the Far East. Around 1900, China exported a total of some 4,800 tonnes of raw silk a year, whereas before the Opium Wars, the East India Company itself had never succeeded in buying more than 5,400 bales a year, approximately 220 tonnes if one reckons the weight of each bale at about 41 kilos. The largest buyer of raw silk seems to have been France: over half the raw silk exported from Shanghai, the largest point of export; 37,000 bales (approximately 1,517 tonnes) out of a total of 71,000 were shipped to Lyons.

At the end of the 19th century, the second largest buyer of silk, and the country with the biggest trade turnover with China, was Britain. In a single year they bought 13 million gold francs worth of tea and silk, and sold 150 million francs worth of various worked goods, particularly cheap cotton cloth made in Manchester with Indian cotton, at an unbeatably low price thanks to technical innovations in the British textile industry. While England sold to China more than it bought from it, France did the opposite: in 1897, it imported 124 million gold francs worth of silk, and sold just under 4 million francs worth of various goods to the Chinese. The other European countries, and in particular Germany and Italy, had much less trade with China, while the United States preferred to buy its supplies in Japan.

It should be noted that Western buyers were relatively disinterested in silk woven in China and preferred to buy silk in skeins, or undyed silk. Around 1900, the Chinese export of raw silk, in terms of value, was five times superior to that of woven silk. It is also interesting to note that Westerners imported from China a large quantity

Western buyers were relatively disinterested in silk woven in China and preferred to buy silk in skeins, or undyed silk.

of unreeled cocoons and of silk cut-offs, which the Chinese made into silk padding for clothes and covers, and which the Europeans turned into thread of a relatively good quality, known as "schappe".

There were, however, two fabrics which were particular to China, and which held the attention of both English and French buyers. The first was crepe, and in 1845, Father Huc wrote in his famous account, *Travels in Tartary, Thibet, and China*, that Europe could not yet match China in this domain. The second was raw silk pongee, very much in fashion during the First World War.

The preference for thread rather than for silks can be explained by market requirements. Lyons was suffering from social problems, especially from unemployment, and desperately needed to provide work for its silk workers. Reading the reports of experts, one becomes aware of the inferior quality of weaving and even of reeling in a large part of decadent China at the end of the 19th century. A particularly convincing eye-witness account is provided in the report of a mission sent to China by the Lyons Chamber of Commerce in 1895–1897.[157] It made a very detailed inquiry into the silk industry of Sichuan, one of the most important silk-producing provinces in China at the time (they estimated that there were some 7,000 working looms in the provincial capital, Chengdu). The experts described the production of cocoons there as a home industry: "There is not a single family, from the poorest up to the yamen of the great mandarins, where silkworms are not bred. However, the amounts produced are never very large, only one or two ounces at the most."

The hatching of the "grains", kept on bamboo paper suspended from the ceiling of the house, was assisted by a method also used in France at the same period: for about a week, the pieces of paper to which the eggs had affixed themselves would be worn by women in their bodices and by men in their hats. It was also in a family setting that subsequent operations were carried out, including setting the newly hatched caterpillars in their little baskets, feeding them on freshly cut mulberry leaves, inspecting them closely for thirty-five days during their period of transformation, and stifling the cocoons in steam above the kitchen pot. The French experts emphasized the spirit of routine of the Chinese who never tried to improve anything, declaring invariably: "This is how my ancestors did it and if I changed anything, it would bring bad luck." They were also very superstitious, avoiding at all costs allowing the silkworms to see lightning or hear thunder; while the presence of a dead person, or of someone who had seen a dead person or a snake, was thought to harm them. Yet they neglected certain conditions of hygiene and temperature control which the French breeders considered of great importance. Nevertheless, the price of the cocoons was inexpensive since the caterpillars were generally bred by women in their free time, or by the old and the young who were too weak to carry out agricultural work. Even in Europe, the problem of breeding silkworms on an industrial scale was only solved much later.

In Sichuan around 1900, when the peasants had gathered a few bucketfuls of cocoons, they would either sell them as they were or would reel them themselves. They could also turn to one of the itinerant workers who travelled from village to village, as weavers used to in Europe.

The time was gone when the Chinese spun the best silk in the world and jealously guarded their secrets.

The reeling equipment was obviously extremely primitive and the result, according to the Lyons experts, left much to be desired: there was a lot of waste, and the thread was so uneven that to export it was sometimes necessary to reel it again before spinning. Already at this stage of production, the French experts noticed that quality could be improved and suggested the setting up in Sichuan of a European-style filature. They even ordered the necessary equipment, but this never arrived and the model mill only ever existed on paper. The time was gone when the Chinese spun the best silk in the world and jealously guarded their secrets. Now, through too much reliance on routine, and because of the torpor in which China seems to have been plunged at the end of the Manchu dynasty, the Chinese artisans once reputed as the most skilled in the world produced only a mediocre silk. The Westerners had arrived there not to steal a secret but to take advantage of a beneficial environment, a suitable climate, a cheaper workforce and favourable customs duties, in order to transplant their own methods to China. In addition, this carelessness, this sluggishness, which provided such a contrast to the spirit of unceasing research and constant betterment which characterized the Westerners of the industrial era, would soon bring about the collapse of the Chinese market through Italian and Japanese competition. Around this time, a widespread disease among silkworms had a disastrous effect, lowering both the quality and quantity of silk obtained from the eggs.

> *China, continuing its age-old routine of egg selection by exposure to frost and snow, was not capable of detecting this disease, and soon found itself left behind.*

Europe first, and then Japan, the first of the Asian countries to adopt Western technology, managed to neutralize this disease, pebrine, relatively fast, in particular by examining the "grains" under a microscope to eliminate the bad lines at the egg stage, and to rebuild healthy breeds.* But China, continuing its age-old routine of egg selection by exposure to frost and snow, was not capable of detecting this disease, and soon found itself left behind. It could no longer produce more than a pound of reeled silk for every six or seven pounds of cocoons, whereas the microscope system used by the Italians allowed them to produce a pound of silk for every three or four

---

* In a novel by the Italian author Alessandro Baricco called Silk, published in 1996, a young Frenchman from a silk-rearing village in the south of France sets off for Japan in 1861. The disease affecting the silkworms had begun then to spread across Europe, but Japanese larvae were still untouched by it. However, the Japanese government forbade the export of silkworm eggs. The French merchant succeeded in taking some out secretly, making four trips in all between 1861 and 1864, which not only brought him wealth, but benefited all the silkworm breeders of his village. Later, Pasteur discovered how to make healthy breeds of larvae and Japan authorized the sale of eggs to foreigners. Thus, this fictional buying of clandestine eggs in Japan was probably inspired by a true event which occurred in 1861.

> *The rescue of European sericulture was in large part due to the work of the French scientist Louis Pasteur, who tackled the problem of pebrine, the silkworm disease, in 1865.*

pounds of cocoons. As a result, between 1902 and 1904, the West, which in the 19th century had bought half of its silk in China, was only buying 27 per cent there, whereas it was buying 20 per cent from Japan and 25 per cent from Italy.

The rescue of European sericulture was in large part due to the work of the French scientist Louis Pasteur, who tackled the problem of pebrine, the silkworm disease, in 1865. From then on France was to play an important role in silkworm breeding, not only through this scientific success, but also through the conscious dissemination abroad of the knowledge which had been acquired by its cocoon producers, particularly in Corsican sericulture. In 1880, the cultivation of the mulberry tree began in the agricultural penitentiaries in Corsica, and Corsican silkworm larvae became highly sought after. In 1886, the Corsican Joachim Aloisi left for Asia after a trip to the silk-producing region of the Gard in southern France. He passed through Tiflis, then Samarkand, Bukhara, Tashkent and Khodjent in Uzbekistan. He introduced the Corsican silkworm into Central Asia, as well as machinery for cocoon processing, and taught French sericulture methods. In 1890, he published a manual for silkworm breeding in Russian, Uzbek, Armenian and Georgian. He obtained from the shah of Persia and from the Russian government the monopoly on the sale of silkworm eggs, two-thirds of which came from Corsica and a third from mainland France, and finally became director-general of a technical college for silk making in Turkestan.[158]

We have mentioned Japan, which has so far appeared very little in this study. Japan had always voluntarily abstained from seeking contacts outside the Far East. However, it had belatedly opened to the outside world. From the middle of the 17th to the middle of the 19th century, it had kept all foreign nations at arm's length. It had quickly eliminated the Portuguese who had tried to establish trade and missions there, tolerating only a few Dutch agents on the island of

Deshima, off Nagasaki, and a few Chinese agents in Nagasaki itself. The volume of authorized trade was strictly controlled, and anything foreign was the object of great suspicion. The opening of Japan began only in 1853, under pressure from the United States. America, as a developing power, a self-liberated colony, did not share the colonial imperial attitude of the European kingdoms, and its past did not arouse in Asian states the same suspicion or hostility as that which marked relationships with the British, the Portuguese, the Dutch and then the French. The mission of the American Commodore Perry in 1853 opened three Japanese ports to trade, first with the United States, and in 1859, with four other countries, Great Britain, Holland, France and Russia. In addition, in 1868, the arrival of Emperor Meiji marked the beginning of radical political changes, particularly in relations with the outside world, as well as an unprecedented desire to acquire as fast as possible the scientific and technological knowledge

> *Japan was known for a particular wild silk, produced by the yama mayu, a worm from the oak tree which formed a magnificent green cocoon; the silk from this cocoon used to be exclusively reserved for the emperor and his family.*

which had given the Western countries their high level of military power.

By 1905, European imports of silk from China had decreased to less than 25 per cent. But China appeared to refuse to understand that Japan presented a dangerous threat to its silk trade. From 1860 on, Japanese silk could occasionally be bought in Chinese ports. Japan was known for a particular wild silk, produced by the *yama mayu*, a worm from the oak tree which formed a magnificent green cocoon; the silk from this cocoon used to be exclusively reserved for the emperor and his family. For a long time, its sale had been forbidden to foreigners on pain of death. Apart from this special category, Japanese raw silk, as fine as the Chinese, was, until 1900, sold mostly to the United States. The Japanese made great efforts to assimilate modern technology, and this, combined with their own skills as silk breeders, soon opened the world market to them. While China was struggling with the silkworm disease, Japan was winning the price battle.

The same negligence and shortcomings of the Chinese workmen were also apparent in their weaving, and in 1896 the French experts remarked upon the inferiority of the textiles, caused by the primitive character of the tools and machinery used. Weaving was carried out almost as a home industry, and Chinese customers, as much tied to routine habits as were the artisans, were not discriminating. "The very premises where these operations are carried out are completely inappropriate. More often than not, the machines are set up in basements, where the light of day is scarce. Even taking into account this incredible negligence, this voluntary ignorance of any improvement, of all development, of the meticulous care which is given in Europe to these branches of the silk industry, one must however admit that the Chinese possess innate qualities of dexterity, skill, and above all patient application which would allow them to make much of their workforce."

> *"The Chinese are ... faithful to tradition. It would never occur to them to suggest to the merchant or to the manufacturer a change in design, a modification in the making of a cloth. They will continue to buy the same type of cloth, the immutable, eternal cloth which their ancestors had already used before them and which their descendants would use for the same clothes, the same decoration."*

But despite these qualities and because of these defects, the Chinese silks show "the worst appearance: faulty manufacture, badly finished off pieces, with warps which run and wefts which score the cloth. The selvages form bumps or unravel. The cloth is heavy, thick, irregular, and yet does not resist to wear and tear."

"Despite all these defects, the Chinese are content with this, and faithful to tradition. It would never occur to them to suggest to the merchant or to the manufacturer a change in design, a modification in the making of a cloth. They will continue to buy the same type of cloth, the immutable, eternal cloth which their ancestors had already used before them and which their descendants would use for the same clothes, the same decoration." In other words, the Chinese textile industry was of no interest other than for "purely documentary and descriptive" reasons. And, for these experts: "our industrialists would be wrong to seek inspiration or lessons there". There was no doubt: the capital of fine silks was definitely not located in China, but in France and in other European centres, or even in Japan.

> *There was no doubt: the capital of fine silks was definitely not located in China, but in France and in other European centres, or ... Japan.*

It has to be admitted that China was going through a difficult period of political troubles and economic distress, and that in every field production was inevitably irregular and often dropping off. It had taken China so long to become industrialized that it could not hope to compete with Japan, then in full economic swing. It continued to live in some ways as it always had, and to reel cocoons because that was as natural as breathing.

THE IMPACT OF WAR

In Europe too, of course, the textile industry was suffering from the consequences of war, and, as is normal for any luxury product, silk weaving diminished during the First World War. Maritime transport was disrupted, and European trade in general slowed down. This was not a time to be thinking about silk, this was a time for shredded linen, blue work cloth, blankets and socks for the trenches. Meanwhile, northern China was sinking into civil war.

After the armistice came the carefree years; the mourning veils had not yet been put away when, in a world undergoing complete change, a wave of luxury swept the European capitals. There was enormous waste. Fashion, ever-changing, was demanding more and more diverse outfits: the days of the trousseau which would last a lifetime, and which would be handed down from mother to daughter, were over. In 1925, styles had to be changed with every season, there was no time to mend, to make things last, everything had to be new. Silk had a new place in fashion, not so much in quality but in quantity, or perhaps because it was less expensive, and because Japan, thanks to low salaries, was flooding Europe with cheap cloth. It did not matter that it was less hard-wearing since clothes were no longer kept until they were worn through, and perhaps the feel of silk between one's fingers corresponded to some sensual appetite of a society busily enjoying life to the full. After an era of bourgeois austerity, silk was once more endowed with that erotic value which is so apparent in the *Thousand and One Nights*, that feeling also of malaise and turmoil left by fragile and quickly burnt-out lives. At this period, silk discarded much of its majestic and sumptuous appearance. It was worn in secret, against the skin, to be felt, as feminine lingerie, as men's shirts, stockings, as bed sheets of Chinese crepe, as soft, light, gentle silks. At the same time, a vast industry of hard-wearing lingerie was being created, which did not need ironing. Machinery transformed silk into fine stockings, but to supply the modern European factories, it was necessary to turn to Chinese and Japanese raw silk. In 1921, China exported 16,000 tonnes of silk products, white and yellow raw silk, thread, schappe, cocoons, wild silk, discards, etc. But all of that represented only one-fifth of the total value of its exports.

Japan had won the sericulture battle. In 1930, Japanese cocoon production was eight times that of 1880, and two-thirds of the raw silk produced was exported. The silk trade had become as important to Japan as it once had been to China. In volume, this trade tripled between 1913 and 1929; around 1930, two out of every five Japanese peasant families bred silkworms at home, and the cocoons were sold to the mills in the nearby towns. In addition, the demand for labour was increasing, and the same families were sending their young daughters to work in the towns. The quality and cost price of Japanese silk ensured a foremost place in the world market, and neither the appearance of the first synthetic textiles nor the collapse of prices between 1925 and 1929 prevented silk from representing 36 per cent of Japanese exports.

In China, industrial methods were adopted very slowly at first, and mainly in Canton and Shanghai, the two most Europeanized ports, with the largest foreign population. In the early 1920s, the industrial silk factories, or filatures, and the cocoon-producing families were concentrated around these two great export centres.

The industrial operation, as in Japan, began with reeling.[159] Something of the old reputation of Chinese silks still existed, mainly in the case of untreated silks: the finest white silk in the world was said to came from Wuxi, in Jiangsu (west of Shanghai, near the north bank of Lake Taihu). The majority of white silk cocoons were produced in the Yangzi Valley and the province of Guangdong. Yellow silk cocoons came from Sichuan, Shandong and Yunnan. Wild silk was much appreciated at this time. In the 20th century, it came mainly from Manchuria and to some extent from Shandong. Its popularity increased after the invention of a new whitening process (wild silks naturally are either dull or on the contrary too bright in colour) which allowed it to be dyed afterwards in the most delicate shades. In addition, a new use was found for it in European industry: it had just been discovered that it was the best substance for covering aeroplane wings. Another very popular fabric was wild silk pongee from Shandong, very hard-wearing and in an attractive natural colour. European buyers even complained about being unable to buy sufficient amounts of it, and of not receiving their shipments within the agreed deadlines or in the agreed quantities. But it was too late, wild pongee from Shandong was already having to face strong competition from Japanese pongee.

In addition, around 1923, about 75 to 80 per cent of Chinese silkworms were again affected by disease. Faced with this threat, it was at last decided to begin scientific research into the problem. Shanghai spearheaded this movement,

In 1923, Yokohama was considered the largest silk warehouse in the world.

and the International Committee for the Improvement of Sericulture in China bought untainted silkworm larvae in France and Italy and tried to rebuild a healthy race. They managed to reduce to 8 or 12 per cent the proportion of affected larvae in laboratories, but costs were very high. Laboratories were created in several universities, and sericulture courses were organized. But it was again too late; China managed to improve the situation to some extent, but Japan had gained a head start. In 1923, Yokohama was considered the largest silk warehouse in the world.

The craze for silk between the two World Wars led to a corresponding demand for raw silk. The spread of machinery in the Far East allowed production to be increased. In China and in Japan, this also led to a transformation inherent to a modern economy. The traditional home industry adapted to village life and to the family unit gave way in the large towns to the daily hell of the large silk factories, with all the abuses created by poverty in an overpopulated nation that had been in a state of civil war for practically fifty years, in all or part of its territory.

In 1924, the fate of the children employed in the textile industry at last moved public opinion: the report of the Shanghai Child Labour Commission, sponsored by the Shanghai Municipal Council, revealed that in Shanghai filatures a third of the personnel, mostly female, was represented by children, many of whom were no more than six years old. Their task was to brush from the cocoons the exterior layer which could not be reeled, and then to pass the cocoons into the reeling machines, an operation carried out in hot steam above basins of water near boiling point. The children worked for twelve hours a day, from six in the morning to six in the evening, arriving in addition a quarter of an hour before the adults in order to get prepared. They were paid about half the salary of an adult. The basins of water created a particularly unhealthy, humid atmosphere, and combined with the summer heat, it was not uncommon for workers to faint. In these "steam filatures", tuberculosis was rampant among both children and adults. Yet twenty-five years previously, the French experts had noted that the weavers and spinners of Sichuan were the corporation with the highest salaries. In 1924, an attempt to head off Japanese competition had led to social abuses that held the seed of their own destruction. China was then still as the well-known writer Lu Xun described it in a preface to a collection of his short stories: "Imagine an iron house having not a single window and virtually indestructible, with all its inmates sound asleep and about to die of suffocation. Dying in their sleep, they won't feel the pain of death. Now if you raise a shout to wake up a few of the lighter sleepers, making these unfortunate few suffer the agony of irrevocable death, do you really think you are doing them a good turn?"[160] That suffocating chamber was the China of which even Chiang Kai-shek said, "It is a comatose country, we are a comatose nation."

The events which followed—worldwide stock market crashes, the Japanese aggression, a World War, a civil war—did nothing to help Chinese sericulture. During the Japanese invasion, more than 133,400 hectares of farms planted with mulberry trees were wiped out and more than half the silk factories destroyed in bombardments. In 1949, there were only two silk factories left in Shanghai, with a total of 348 spindles, in a status of semi-paralysis, whereas at the time of its greatest prosperity Shanghai had more than 106 factories with 25,000 spindles. Quality had dropped in proportion, and technology had not progressed in twenty years.

In Japan, France and Italy, the silk industry had been dormant for more than ten years. At the end of the Second World War, the appearance on the market of nylon and other synthetic fibres led to a loss of interest in natural silk. The lingerie industry, in particular stockings, completely abandoned the use of silk. The new textiles took over the market because of their sheer practicality (hard-wearing, fast-drying and requiring no ironing), despite being often unpleasant to wear (a disadvantage which was gradually eliminated to a large extent).

The history of the last fifty years of the silk trade reflects the extreme complexity of the modern economy, the competition to find markets, the fear of producing surpluses and of economic crashes.

In ancient times and in the Middle Ages, demand was always more or less equal to supply and products were bought up very rapidly. The 20th century has been the century of the salesman, of publicity and price collapses. Luxury industries react with a particular sensitivity to these constant fluctuations. Between the wars, once business had taken off again, came the threat of over-production and its trail of social problems.

An interesting study is that of the luxury industry, particularly that of silk, in Communist countries. When the Chinese Red Army crossed the Yangzi in 1950, the cloth merchants in the Far East melancholically sold their last bolts of brocade, telling their customers that these were the last ones, that there would be no more, and that from then on China would no longer produce fine silks. And indeed, the China of Mao Zedong was soon dressed in thick blue cottons. Understandably, the main concern of the Five-Year Plan was heavy industry, the guarantee of future prosperity, followed by the necessity to provide enough food to feed everyone.

On the world market, there was no longer any question of China competing with Lyons or Japan. Only raw silk sold well. Nevertheless, after a few years, the Chinese government decided to focus once again on the production of silk, stimulating silkworm breeding, the cultivation of the mulberry tree, the production of raw silk and weaving. In the 1980s, even luxury fabrics reappeared, the era of blue cotton was over and Chinese magazines began advertising silk and embroidered silk clothes. A big effort had been made on the technological front, and dyeing—long the weak spot in the Chinese silk industry—had been improved.

From 1957–58, China produced 11,000 tonnes of raw and luxury silk and 200 million metres of silk cloth, whereas in 1949, according to the Chinese press, production was only 3,000 tonnes of silk and 50 million metres of silk cloth. This was sold to seventy countries, both in the East and the West, although the government of the People's Republic of China was still not recognized by all Western states. The slogan at the time was "beat Japan and outdo France".

By 1984, China supplied more than half the world's production of raw silk, about 30,000 out of a total of 52,000 tonnes, well ahead of Japan, India, the USSR, South Korea and thirty other countries. This world production of 52,000 tonnes represented only 0.2 per cent of the total production of textile fibres. In 1994, China produced 32,000 tonnes of raw silk, of which 80 to 90 per cent was sold, again well ahead of India, Brazil and a few other countries. As for France, it supplied only 600 tonnes in 1994.

China swamped the world market by slashing prices, thanks to a highly underpaid workforce. However, this could not last. On the one hand, the domestic demand for silk was constantly on the increase because of the improvement in standards of living, "which could lead to an increase in prices or to shortages on the world market", according to an article published in 1994.[161] On the other hand, "history has shown the world that countries which become industrialized abandon sericulture, as was the case in Europe and more recently in Japan, and one can imagine the same thing occurring one day in China, hence the importance of setting up alternative channels".[162]

EUROCHRYSALID

A solution to the problem of reviving French and European raw silk production was sought in the 1990s in Lyons through scientific research. The project was known as Eurochrysalid and was aimed at developing new breeds of silkworm, resistant to disease, and producing better quality thread than the Chinese larvae. Research focused on the hybridization of about sixty varieties of silkworm. It was hoped that within a decade French dependence on Chinese silk would be reduced to 25 per cent.

Until then there had been no hope of creating a French sericulture which could compete with the very low Asian prices because of high labour costs: in order to feed the silkworms, it is necessary to hand pick the mulberry leaves, and to choose them according to the age of the caterpillars, an operation which is repeated over and over again. In the 1970s there had been several inconclusive attempts to re-establish silk factories in the Cévennes, an area which, before 1860, that is before the Franco-Chinese treaties and the opening of the Suez Canal, had been prosperous thanks to this industry. Some people even consider today that sericulture disappeared completely from France in 1968. However, one silkworm factory, the Magnanerie de Saillans, in the department of Drôme, was founded in 1991 with the stated aim of preserving the cultural heritage of sericulture and silk workshops and transmitting expertise in this field.

The key to the future seems to be diversification. On the one hand, manufacturers have to branch out into other textiles (one large silk firm has become the world's leading weaver of glass-fibre and only devotes a small part of its activities to silk). On the other hand, non-textile applications of cocoons have to be developed. The chrysalis can be used in medicine and cosmetics, and chrysalis oil is made under the name of "silk protein", a substance which is almost identical to human skin, and therefore valuable for skin grafting, surgical thread, etc. In addition, silk is an excellent insulator used around the doors of space shuttles; silk waste can be used to make beauty creams, and certain medicines such as synthetic insulin can be extracted from it.[163]

Quality and creative inventiveness have been the strong points of the French silk industry. Now, at the beginning of the 21st century, it is trying to create a

> The Silk Road no longer exists and has not existed for a long time; it no longer existed when a German geographer, Ferdinand von Richthofen, retrospectively gave that name, at the end of the 19th century, to the traditional trade routes, almost unchanged since ancient times.

cloth which hopefully will provide silk with the same resistance as synthetics while preserving its unique qualities. Recently a transgenic caterpillar has been produced from a spider gene placed in a silkworm gene, and the result is a more resistant silk.

All sorts of things have been exchanged with China since the end of the 19th century, cannon shots, missionaries, books, students, revolutions, technology, silk, porcelain, tea, tourists, engineers, translators, democracy, Marxism and other "isms". This was done by sea, then by air. Of course the Silk Road no longer exists and has not existed for a long time; it no longer existed when a German geographer, Ferdinand von Richthofen, retrospectively gave that name, at the end of the 19th century, to the traditional trade routes, almost unchanged since ancient times. He had himself used them in Central Asia, then a region which had become poor and had remained in the Middle Ages, stuck between the immobile and decadent China of the last emperors and the empire of the last tsars. It was as if time had become petrified there.

Caravans of camels trundled slowly from one oasis to another, carrying tea in bricks or in leaves, felt, cloths of silk or cotton, wool, cereals and many everyday objects. Entire herds of horses sold by the nomads from the steppes travelled towards the Great Wall, and certain princes still sent their caravans of tribute to the Chinese emperor. But ancient cities, libraries, huge sections of still unknown civilizations lay dormant under the sands, and nobody yet knew it.

It was then that the second Silk Road came into existence, that of the explorers, the archaeologists, the nomadic adventurers, many with their passion for art history or enamoured of the terrifying scenery, escaping for a while from their sophisticated civilization; later came the journalists or rather the travel writers, and then, much later, the tourists.

Chapter Nineteen
The Second Silk Road: Explorers, Archaeologists and Reporters

*T*he 20th century was a time of worldwide exploration, and particularly of exploration into the past through archaeology. In Asia, in the first decades of the century, archaeology was the private hunting ground of a few Western powers operating far from home. One could dub this early period the era of *"passions and thieves ad majorem scientiae gloriam"*.

When the outermost frontiers of the British Empire reached the Himalaya, the Karakoram and the Hindu Kush, on the periphery of Central Asia, political and military considerations, as well as the defence of the empire, kindled a keen interest in events in these little known regions, difficult of access, belonging to states which were not among Britain's firmest allies; zones in which it was believed that Russia, then pursuing its conquest of Turkestan, was trying to exert its influence. This was the time of the Great Game, played by three countries, England, Russia and China. It was also the period of Colonel T. G. Montgomerie's pundits, those Indian agents who, masquerading as Buddhist or Hindu pilgrims, would secretly draw up maps of regions where Europeans were not allowed, all of this within the larger context of the Survey of India's map-making project.[164] A number of British officers spent years watching the frontiers, riding around on horseback, collecting information on every imaginable topic; some of them were scholars, and we owe them much of our knowledge of these regions. Among the rumours that these informers brought back, of gossip overheard in bazaars, were stories of ancient cities buried in the desert sands of the Taklamakan. And what a desert! It was renowned as lethal—no one who entered it returned. The maps were marked "Unexplored". The entire region depended politically on the Chinese government. There were many dangers and no certainty of actually finding anything.

The first to cross this desert was not an Englishman but a Swede, Sven Hedin, one of the rare geographers and explorers to have also crossed northern Tibet from north to south through its most arid section, the western high plateau. His first expedition to Central Asia was in 1893–1897, when he crossed the Taklamakan, almost dying of thirst. In the middle of the desert, in the region of the Keriya River, which flows from south to north and disappears into the sands without ever reaching the Tarim depression, he did indeed find ruins: houses, walls, statues, remains of fruit trees: this was the site of Karadong. The first account of an exploration in the Taklamakan was a publication in Swedish in 1898. Later Sven Hedin made other similar discoveries, in particular the site of Loulan, near Lake Lop Nor.

In the heart of the Tarim depression, or in the series of deserts which Marco Polo generally termed the "Lop desert" and which the ancient Chinese called *liusha*, ("flowing sands", or the "river of sand"), which stretched from Kashgar to Lanzhou, or more frequently, on the edge of these deserts, ruins have been discovered, or rediscovered, unearthed and studied. These sites are frequently located near the present-day oasis-towns. They were often the capitals of small principalities, ancestors of the modern towns nearby, belonging to the period when Central Asia was Buddhist. But around 1900, none of that was yet known, though the English archaeologists were keeping an eye out.

The sites of Khotan, Dandan-Uilik, Dunhuang and Miran are all associated with the name of Marc Aurel Stein; this naturalized Englishman of Hungarian origin was as English as could be in his sense of humour, his affection for Queen Victoria and for his dog who accompanied him on his travels. He was a scholar, an Orientalist, an archaeologist-explorer and a historian. While two or three British officers were attempting at the same period to identify the route followed by Alexander the Great on his journey to India, Stein was following in the footsteps of the Chinese pilgrim Xuanzang, whom he called his "patron saint".

The accounts which these explorers wrote on returning from their missions are on a par with the most extraordinary adventure stories, as much for the physical exploits as for the scientific discoveries made. In those days, the equipment available was not as convenient and practical as is it today, and neither was transport. Stein took two mules with him to carry his glass photographic plates. No help was to be had anywhere in case of need. In 1906, as his expedition was entering the heart of the desert north of Abdal, slightly north-west of Miran, well away from any known track, the caravan lost its way, and could not find the source of water it was expecting. His guides and porters refused to continue, but they had come too far to turn back, and Stein knew that they could not cover the return distance without water. Their only hope of survival was to carry on. To compel his companions forward—the only reasonable option—he purely and simply threatened to kill them if they did not continue. They carried on and survived.

Apart from dying of thirst, one could also die of hunger. One day when there was only oatmeal to eat, his Chinese coolies refused the porridge because it was not one of the "five cereals" considered traditional human food. Stein announced to them that he, a scholar, had discovered an old Chinese text in which it stated that the rites authorized the consumption of oatmeal in cases of absolute necessity, and so the coolies were able to appease their hunger with the porridge. Stein, like Hedin before him, had great stamina; while his companions fell ill and returned home, he continued on. When the others slept, he would write his notes, stopping only once the ink froze. During one of his explorations, in Tibet, his foot froze and he had to ride for eight days, with the gangrene spreading, before arriving at a small field hospital in India where it was partially amputated. Luckily, archaeological expeditions were not always so hazardous. Fewer people died on them than climbing Everest.

Yutian, 630 to Khotan, 1906. More than twelve centuries separated Xuanzang on his pilgrimage to the holy Buddhist sites and Aurel Stein on his pilgrimage in the footsteps of Xuanzang. They followed the same road to the same oases; the route had hardly changed. The rare human beings whom Stein met on the way, the fishermen of the Lop Nor salt lake dressed in fur robes, a Mongol rider with a dagger inlaid with coral, caravaneers singing beside their camels loaded with felt, Xuanzang could have met their direct ancestors, identical in everything (although the Lop Nor had certainly become smaller). During a year of archaeological exploration, Stein would forget the centuries which had passed, and this same impression of suspended time was shared by all the travellers who crossed this region of the world before the 1960s.

Travel accounts convey the adventures well, but how can one express the beauty, the poetry and the emotion of an archaeological discovery? What Stein discovered during his years of exploration, nobody had ever even imagined. After the colours of the Tarim and its particular scents, out of the immensity of the landscape, there would emerge from the sand dead poplars, an indication of ruins, and then the remains of ramparts, forts, houses, a Buddhist monastery. At the back of the dead halls were murals, statues, divinities, figures which were slightly Indian, slightly Iranian, mostly Buddhist; paintings reminiscent of Greco-Roman art or with Turkish or Chinese physical features, becoming more Chinese as one progressed eastwards, still depicted in bright colours, preserved in the desert dryness; at times, there were seals resembling Greek coins, Chinese silks, documents written in Chinese or in other languages on wooden tablets, antique coins. An Orientalist familiar with Chinese history would find himself plunged into the world described by Xuanzang, or by Faxian two centuries before him—or perhaps to a yet earlier time.

Near the small sub-prefecture of Dunhuang, in Gansu, Stein visited a monastic complex of ancient constructions and caves which contained numerous murals and statues. Dunhuang, on the edge of the desert along the great road west, had been a large Buddhist centre from the 4th to the 11th century AD at least. When he arrived, Stein learned that in one of the caves a hoard of ancient manuscripts had recently been discovered, probably hidden and walled up during a war or an invasion. In 1906 or 1907, he obtained permission to visit the cave from the Daoist monk guarding it. And he discovered to his amazement an immense deposit of manuscripts, many of them on paper, as well as woodblock engravings.

The paintings in all the sites he had visited had been magnificent; but here surely history itself was revealed in these manuscripts. What was Stein's reaction? To cart them off, to take them back to England.

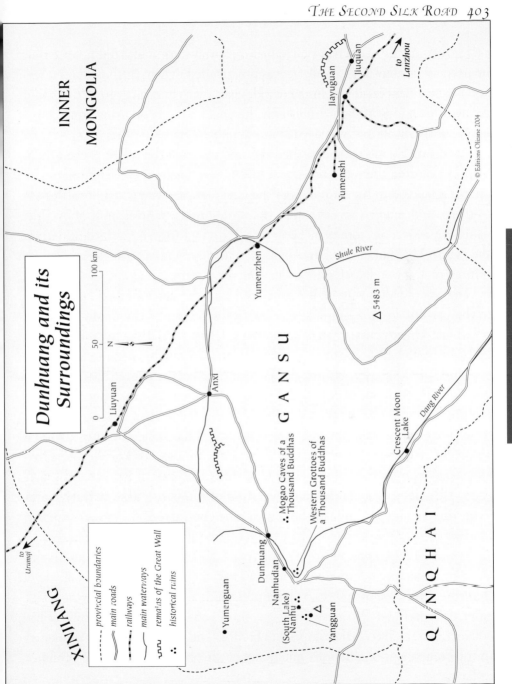

Dunhuang and its Surroundings

INNER MONGOLIA

Dunhuang and its Surroundings

100 km

50

N

0

Liuyuan

Anxi

XINJIANG

to Urumqi

G A N S U

Yumenzhen

Shule River

△ 5483 m

Jiayuguan   Jiuquan

to Lanzhou

Yumenshi

© Editions Olizane 2004

provincial boundaries
main roads
railways
main waterways
remains of the Great Wall
historical ruins

Mogao Caves of a Thousand Buddhas

Western Grottoes of a Thousand Buddhas

Crescent Moon Lake

Dang River

Dunhuang

Nanhudian

Yumenguan

Nanhu (South Lake)

Yangguan

△

QINGHAI

He was in Chinese territory. He had no authorization and did not see that he need ask for any. First of all, he was practically English. In those days it was good to be a British subject in the world. Caucasians in Asia or in Africa could get away with most things. Admittedly, he could not rely on using armed force here, but surely all that was needed was simply to bribe an official?

At Miran, Stein's team detached the frescoes from the walls, packed them up and exported them discreetly out of Chinese territory. At Dunhuang, he offered a present to the custodian of the caves, chose, wrapped and carried off even more discreetly over twenty cases of statues, fabrics and, above all, manuscripts. It took more than a year for all this loot to arrive at its destination, the British Museum in London. Among the manuscripts was the earliest known printed text, a woodblock print of the *Diamond Sutra*, dated 868.

The site of Dunhuang is also associated with the name of Paul Pelliot, one of the greatest French Sinologists, sent to the region by the Ecole Française d'Extrême-Orient. His extraordinary gift at languages and his incredible memory had been noticed when he was still very young. During his mission to Central Asia in 1906–1909, after visiting Kucha, he learned of the existence of a treasure of manuscripts at Dunhuang, and arrived there a few months after Stein. He too was authorized by the keeper to examine the documents. In this dark cave, which can still be seen today—empty—he found himself confronted by some 15,000 to 20,000 documents, many of them in Chinese. His knowledge of this language and of history allowed him to identify the texts as he sorted through them all, selecting from this massive store of religious, administrative and historical documents a pile of those which he considered absolutely essential. And what was his reaction? To cart them off, to take them back to France.

Pelliot did not know of Stein's purchases. He made a secret deal with the Daoist custodian, and for a paltry sum was allowed to wrap up and take with him case after case of statues, silk banners and, above all, manuscripts. The cases discreetly left Chinese territory, under the supervision of one of his collaborators, and were then shipped to France. The manuscripts were deposited in the French National Library and many of the objects in the Musée Guimet in Paris.

For nearly a century, scholars have studied the Stein and Pelliot collections. The latter has travelled only twice since then, the first time, in 1940, to be sheltered somewhere in France far from the threat of bombardments. The second time was in 1946 when it was brought back to Paris. The Stein Collection was unharmed during the Second World War.

The British and the French were not the only ones to seize, with more or less discretion, and with the support and financial backing of their governments, these precious and irreplaceable remains from ancient Central Asia.[165] There were German missions too, in the first two decades of the 20th century: Albert Grünwedel, Theodor Bartus and Albert von Le Coq explored the region of Turfan and Qotcho (Karakhoja, present day Gaochang), where they found Manichaean manuscripts and Nestorian remains. At Bezeklik were beautiful Buddhist murals and these they detached from the walls, as Stein had done elsewhere, wrapped them up, and carried them discreetly out of Chinese territory. They arrived in Berlin in good condition, nearly two years later, where they were admired in the museum until they were partially destroyed by the Anglo-American bombardments of 1944. The German mission also returned with many cases of manuscripts.

> *The manuscripts and printed sheets which were collected and illegally exported from China by Westerners during the period between 1900 and 1915, all of them invaluable documents on the history of China, of Central Asia, of Buddhism and other religions, are at present dispersed between eight different countries.*

Russian explorers crossed the region of Turfan, then moved to a completely new area, the site of Karakhoto, far to the north-east of Dunhuang, on the Etsin-gol River, in modern Gansu, near the Mongolian border. They brought back a more modest harvest, kept in the Hermitage Museum in Saint Petersburg. A Japanese mission, led by Count Otani, also visited several sites in the Tarim. The English watched his movements closely as they suspected his motives to be more than purely archaeological.* The Great Game was still continuing, but with four players now instead of three, as the Japanese had begun their policy of hegemony over the Far East.

The manuscripts and printed sheets which were collected and illegally exported from China by Westerners during the period between 1900 and 1915, all of them invaluable documents on the history of China, of Central Asia, of Buddhism and other religions, are at present dispersed between eight different countries. They are written in Chinese, Sogdian, Sanskrit, Tibetan and other languages, not all of them deciphered (there were even fake languages, invented by clever dealers in Central Asia, and intended for Europeans keenly interested in buying ancient manuscripts). This was not theft carried out by bandits, but operations organized by national institutions. One can understand the bitterness which the Chinese have harboured over this. Now that there are so many ways of reproducing texts, so that entire collections of ancient manuscripts and entire years of the great daily newspapers of the 19th century exist on microfilm and are kept in our national libraries, would it not be possible to carry out some sort of restitution in this form, at least for the unique or rare texts? Or, better still, by means of the even greater efficiency which computers can now offer? Reproductions have in fact begun to be exchanged between certain Chinese and foreign institutions.

With the First World War, all the British, French and Germans in Central Asia were called back to Europe. The turmoil which followed the Russian Revolution, the insecurity and political instability, isolated Central Asia. Around 1920, the Chinese Republican government put an end to archaeological research conducted by foreigners.

Just before the Second World War, archaeological digs began in the USSR in Khorezm, on the lower reaches of the Amu-Darya River. There too a large segment of ancient history was unveiled, ranging from the 7th century BC to the arrival of Islam; Zoroastrianism, Buddhism, Manichaeism, castles and ramparts, frescoes, statues, carved wood and coins were rescued from oblivion.

* The story of foreign archaeological expeditions in Chinese Central Asia between 1898 and 1920, put in its political context, has been told in Peter Hopkirk's excellent book, Foreign Devils on the Silk Road.

The name of Sergei Pavlovich Tolstov is closely tied to these finds. Then, after the war, archaeological research developed in Uzbekistan, revealing the city of Penjikent and part of Sogdian civilization.

Because of the Cold War between East and West, the Soviet republics of Central Asia and the west of China became completely inaccessible to Western Europeans and Americans for about thirty years. Nevertheless, thanks to exchanges between libraries which received works from the USSR, Western Europe was not completely cut off from what was being published in Moscow and Leningrad in the field of Soviet archaeology.

Among the Western institutions dedicated to the archaeology of Central Asia during the period from 1920 to 1940 was the French Archaeological Delegation in Afghanistan, which concentrated on ancient Bactria and the Kushan Empire, following up on the work carried out by A. Foucher around Taxila in the 1920s. From 1933 to 1946, it worked in the Begram area, 80 kilometres north of Kabul. The campaigns led by Joseph Hackin in 1937–1939 brought to light what has subsequently become known as the "Begram Treasure", a fabulous hoard of objects from the Roman Empire, India and China, including coloured glass, carved ivory and bone, plaster medallions, lacquered objects, coral branches, all proofs of the existence of international trade in the Kushan period. Some of these can be admired today in the Musée Guimet in Paris. The objects which were housed in the Kabul Museum have in large part been either destroyed or pillaged in recent years by the Afghans themselves during their civil war. It was also the French Archaeological Delegation in Afghanistan which brought to light in 1966–67 the treasure of Ai Khanum which we have referred to in chapter 10 of this book.

Another treasure discovered in Afghanistan in 1978 was that of Tillya-Tepe (the "hill of gold"), located near Sheberghan, near the left bank of the Amu-Darya River, just north-west of Balkh, near the Turkmen border. The team which discovered it was a joint Afghan and Soviet mission. V. I. Sarianidi, a Soviet archaeologist sent by the Archaeological Institute in Moscow, worked for nine years in the area alongside his Russian and Afghan colleagues. At Tillya-Tepe, a site where the oldest levels date back to the second millennium BC, eight tombs were unearthed. They probably belonged to Kushan men and women of high rank, who were buried with over 20,000 gold objects and precious stones, and innumerable small gold decorations which must originally have been sewn on to their clothing. Diadems, necklaces, bracelets, belt buckles, daggers, all in gold and turquoise, in which one can detect Greek, Iranian, Indian and Scythian influence, as well as Greek style cameos and intaglios, Parthian coins, Chinese bronze mirrors, all dating to the Kushan period. These were taken to the Kabul Museum in 1978. The archaeologists meant to return at the end of the winter of 1979, but war was already sweeping across the region and the unfinished work was stopped. They did not see their discoveries again until 1982, in the Kabul Museum, to photograph them.[166]

Where are all these treasures today? Twenty years of war, first against the USSR and then a civil war between the Taleban and their opponents, have been the cause not only of considerable human losses and of the ruin of the country, but have led to the disappearance through destruction or theft of a large part of the cultural heritage of Afghanistan. This includes both the architectural heritage and the objects uncovered in archaeological digs. The Kabul Museum was destroyed in bombardments and emptied of its contents; most of the stolen objects reappeared a few days later in the Peshawar bazaar and from there reached private collections, writes O. Bopearachchi in the March 2002 issue of the *International Institute for Asian Studies Newsletter*. Thieves have also helped themselves secretly to the excavation sites themselves: the thirty thousand antique coins (dating back to the 6th century BC) found at five different sites which had been kept in the Kabul Museum have completely disappeared, as well as the treasure of Mir Zakah, a site near Gardez in the north-east of the country, which included some five hundred and fifty thousand gold, silver, and bronze coins. The latter was almost certainly the source of the six bags weighing around 50 kilos each which O. Bopearachchi examined in the Peshawar bazaar in February 1994. The site of Ai Khanum has been completely pillaged, dug up and destroyed. Coins, carved ivories, medallions, bronzes and intaglios have been scattered around the world, among wealthy amateurs. We can hope that a few will reappear on the market, but it is also to be feared that many of the gold coins will have been melted down.

To all this one has to add the iconoclastic fanaticism of the Taleban regime, determined to annihilate all traces of Buddhism. On the 26th of February 2001, Mullah Mohammed Omar, the political and religious head of the Taleban in Afghanistan, ordered the destruction of all Buddhist statues and remains throughout the country, releasing a frenzy against these so-called harmful idols which violate the Koran, against all the

Mullah Mohammed Omar, the political and religious head of the Taleban in Afghanistan, ordered the destruction of all Buddhist statues and remains throughout the country, releasing a frenzy against these so-called harmful idols which violate the Koran, against all the "idolatry" which had preceded Islam.

"idolatry" which had preceded Islam. In March, the news channel of the Arab world, Al-Jazeera, in Qatar, announced that the two giant Buddhas of Bâmiyân, treasures of Greco-Buddhist art, had just been blown up with explosives and mortars. This act provoked a very strong world-wide reaction, perhaps a disproportionate one considering the suffering of the Afghan population itself, but one which has triggered on an international level the will power to do the utmost to save the Afghan artistic heritage in the future. "We have witnessed, for the first time in human history", wrote O. Bopearachchi, "the state taking the initiative to decree its subjects to destroy their own past. The state became the worst enemy of its own culture and heritage, leading the way to the destruction of the efforts of several generations of archaeologists, numismatists and art historians, and the collective memory of three thousand years of the history of the Afghan people."

The giant Buddhas (55 and 38 metres tall), carved into the cliff face of the Bâmiyân Valley, 230 kilometres north-west of Kabul, probably dated from the 4th or 5th centuries AD. They were the symbols of all the peaceful values of Buddhism, but had been the victims of iconoclasm previously, in some past century when they had lost their faces. In 1997, the Taleban had already threatened to harm them. Despite the early promises of the Taleban government not to destroy them, they did not survive for long "in a country in which they had become strangers who were not able to flee".

Since then, the attacks on 11th September 2001 against New York and Washington, and the American military response against the Taleban in Afghanistan have completely changed the situation. Kabul has been taken back from the Taleban, a new government put in place, and diplomatic representations and Western organizations have once again returned to the country; aside from the political and economic emergency, cultural concerns have surfaced again, with the question of the archaeological heritage first on the list. Foundations are ready to be set into action. And in June 2002 came mention of a long-awaited discovery: that of the site of the Greek city of Bactra (Balkh) in Bactria, dating back to the time of Alexander.

The ex-Soviet republics of Central Asia became independent states in 1991 and were completely reorganized. In 1995, a research centre founded by the French Ministry of Foreign Affairs, the French Institute of Central Asian Studies (IFEAC) was established in Uzbekistan. In 2000, a joint French and Uzbek archaeological mission working at Samarkand made an exceptional discovery at the nearby site of Koktepe, unearthing an intact tomb of a Sarmat princess dating from the beginning of the Christian era. Among the finds was an imported Chinese mirror, an example of the economic and cultural role played by the nomads in the heart of Central Asia.[167]

As for the sectors of the Silk Road in Chinese territory, in Xinjiang and Gansu, the government of the Chinese Republic had definitely re-established its control over them even before the Communist period. In 1914, the Dunhuang Research Institute was founded, dedicated to the study and preservation of the remains in the area, including the famous Mogao Caves, the caves of a Thousand Buddhas, and their 45,000 square metres of murals and hundreds of statues, mostly Buddhist, created between the 5th and the 10th century AD. After the long period of isolation which followed the establishment of the Communist regime in 1949, three decades during which there was no possibility of collaboration or exchange between scientists in China and those of the capitalist world, Deng Xiaoping once again opened the door to the West in 1978 with his reform policies. In 1979, "the first bus of British tourists stopped in front of the caves of the Thousand Buddhas".* A new phase was beginning; since then,

---

* Peter Hopkirk finished his book, Foreign Devils on the Silk Road, with the words: "The last shred of mystery and romance had finally gone from the Silk Road." Fortunately, we can now say, twenty years on, that he was wrong!

international colloquies on art history and archaeology have been organized regularly at Dunhuang as well as in other centres in Gansu and Xinjiang. Researchers from various countries meet there, including France, Great Britain, Germany and Japan, whose museums and institutes still house important collections of manuscripts, paintings, sculptures and other rare objects which were seized by the old expeditions in Chinese Central Asia. Photos and microfilms, as well as scientific publications, are exchanged across the world: the international scientific community has begun to link up.

In the Uighur Autonomous Region of Xinjiang, the Institute of Archaeology and Heritage of Xinjiang, in collaboration with a French team from the National Centre of Scientific Research led by H.P. Francfort, investigated, between 1991 and 1994, the site of Karadong, which had previously been visited by Hedin and Stein. This was a cultivated oasis, abandoned towards the end of the 3rd century AD, which included two Buddhist sanctuaries. In 1994, the archaeologists came across, in the nearby dried-up delta of the Keriya River, the site of Djumbulak Kum, a fortified city dating from the middle of the first millennium BC. The tombs there contained many objects, all the more interesting in that no trace of habitation from this period had previously been found in Xinjiang. These were agriculturalists and breeders, who practised irrigation, weaving and metallurgy.[168] The Taklamakan, the River of Sand, the Gobi have not yet yielded all their secrets; how many cities in the sand, mummified princes and walled-up libraries are still sleeping there, just as the clay soldiers of the First Emperor had slept for two millennia, despite being located only a short distance from the very large city of Xi'an (Chang'an).

The Chinese government is paying more and more attention to the preservation of its cultural heritage, particularly as the Qing dynasty failed to defend it from foreign predators.

The Chinese government is paying more and more attention to the preservation of its cultural heritage, particularly as the Qing dynasty failed to defend it from foreign predators at a time when China was in a position of weakness, and there is still much bitterness over this. If China now appeals to foreign specialists, it does so with the full intention of keeping absolute sovereignty over the objects found.

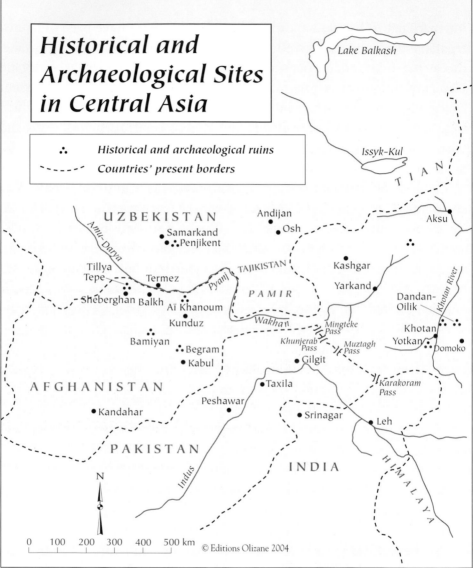

Historical and Archaeological Sites in Central Asia

∴   *Historical and archaeological ruins*
- - - - -   *Countries' present borders*

Lake Balkash

Issyk-Kul

TIAN

UZBEKISTAN

Andijan
Osh

Aksu

Amu-Darya

Samarkand
Penjikent

Kashgar

Khotan River

Tillya Tepe
Termez

Pyanj TAJIKISTAN

Yarkand

Sheberghan Balkh
Aï Khanoum

PAMIR

Dandan-Oilik

Kunduz

Wakhan

Mingteke Pass

Khotan

Bamiyan
Begram

Khunjerab Pass

Muztagh Pass

Yotkan
Domoko

Kabul

Gilgit

AFGHANISTAN

Taxila

Karakoram Pass

Kandahar

Peshawar

Srinagar

Leh

PAKISTAN

INDIA

HIMALAYA

N

Indus

0   100   200   300   400   500 km

© Editions Olizane 2004

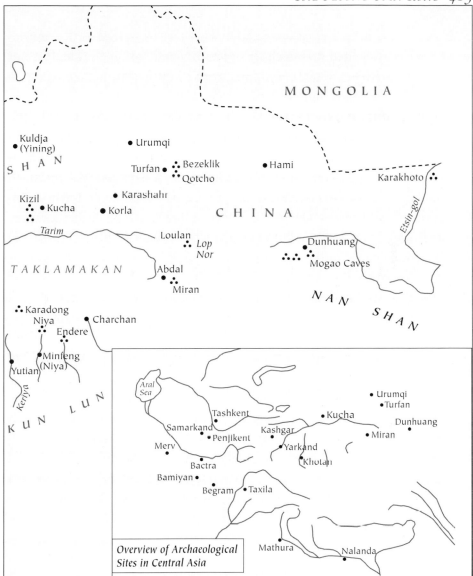

MONGOLIA

Kuldja
(Yining)
SHAN
• Urumqi
Turfan • Bezeklik
• Qotcho
• Hami
Karakhoto
Kizil
• Kucha
Karashahr
• Korla
CHINA
Tarim
Loulan
Lop
Nor
TAKLAMAKAN
Abdal
Miran
Dunhuang
Mogao Caves
NAN
SHAN
Etsin-gol
Karadong
Niya
Endere
Charchan
Minfeng
(Niya)
Yutian
Keriya
KUN LUN

Aral
Sea
• Urumqi
• Turfan
Tashkent
• Kucha
• Dunhuang
Samarkand
Kashgar
• Penjikent
Yarkand
• Miran
Merv
Khotan
Bactra
Bamiyan
Begram • Taxila
Mathura
Nalanda

Overview of Archaeological
Sites in Central Asia

Concern over the preservation of national heritage has spread to all countries and is closely associated with feelings of identity and national pride. It is not incompatible with economics, as a fine artistic heritage attracts tourism, an important source of revenue for a rich state, and an essential one for a poor one. Little by little, the notion of a World Heritage is taking shape, as distinct from each individual's attachment to his national heritage, and its protection is the concern of the community of nations. Since its founding, UNESCO has taken charge of or supervised a number of important preservation projects which have mobilized specialists and important financial resources, and major sites such as the Mogao Caves at Dunhuang, the giant Buddhas of Bâmiyân (destroyed in March 2001), or the site of Lumbini are gradually being added to the list of World Heritage Sites. In the case of China, UNESCO has played a significant role in presenting to the world and in preserving the historical remains located along the Silk Road with its program called "Silk Roads—Roads of Dialogue", which lasted from 1990 to 1997. During these years, colloquies, meetings, trips, exhibitions and cultural events succeeded one another along the ancient land and sea routes, bringing together nations and cultures in a spirit of peaceful exchange, mutual understanding, tolerance and humanitarianism.

Is archaeology the last great adventure on these land routes? Its roots certainly sprang out of 19th-century Romanticism, with its complex attraction to the past; these cultured men, brought up in the world of Greco-Latin civilization, discovered with fascination and stupefaction statues made in a Greek style, Hellenistic influences going back to the time of Alexander. This was also a time of curiosity about ancient Chinese history, which was beginning to be studied seriously in Europe. Romanticism brought with it a taste for wide-open spaces, unlimited landscapes, wild scenery and a lack of people (little sympathy was shown for the locals living in these spaces). This strange attraction which Westerners have for the desert may have deep roots in Biblical memories of the first centuries of Christianity, and is always surprising to the Chinese. Aestheticism in the face of nature and works of art was also part of the make-up of the explorer-adventurer in Central Asia at the beginning of the 20th century.

The Western or Muslim travellers of antiquity and the Middle Ages, right down to the 17th century, almost never mentioned the beauty of the landscape in their tales. Nature for them was either a source of food or of danger, not of aesthetic enjoyment; the beauty which held their attention was in the form of architecture, sumptuous costume and jewellery. They did not feel at ease when away from fellow men. The dominant feeling then was understandably one of danger. This taste for infinite space and wild landscapes is a recent one which appears prominently in Western tales of the 19th and 20th centuries, and which has played a role in the appeal—one might say the calling—of travel, felt not only by archaeologists but also by a new generation of wandering knights, the travel writers–reporters, living a free and independent life, relatively solitary, surviving thanks to the sales of their books, photos, articles or conferences. After the First World War, many of them were attracted to Soviet and Chinese Central Asia, and their books are still read and reprinted today.

Ella Maillart (1903–1997) was one of them, a young Swiss woman who decided at the end of the First World War to leave the West and its decadent civilization; fifty years on, this would be called rejection of the consumer society. She was at first attracted to sailing and to the Pacific Ocean, but through the whims of fate and her reading, she ended up travelling in the USSR before crisscrossing Asia for a large part of her long life. At twenty, she dreamt of "going to live among the nomads, in the steppes, to become a child of Nature in some distant corner of the world, to share the life of primitive beings, still pure of all contact with our foolish materialism". But after her first Russian trip, Central Asia appeared on the horizon, in 1932. "Turkestan and Central Asia exerted on me an invisible attraction, inspired by my reading." Readings in Russian, no doubt. Perhaps she had seen the works of Nikolai Prjevalsky, a zoologist-explorer who, in the last quarter of the 19th century, had crossed, among other areas, the still unknown regions of northern Tibet, modern Qinghai and Dzungaria where he one day caught sight of the rare wild horse, the ancestor-horse to which he gave his name and which has now been saved from extinction. Today Nikolai Prjevalsky is almost a national hero in Russia, as Ella Maillart is in Switzerland.

She made several trips to Russian and Chinese Turkestan, and published accounts of her travels. At the same time, Peter Fleming, a reporter with *The Times* in London, was also crossing Chinese and Soviet Asia. They travelled together for a few months in 1935, from Peking to Kashmir, one speaking good Chinese, and the other Russian, each respecting the other's need for solitude. Peter Fleming gives his account of the journey in *News from Tartary* which was published in 1936; the parallel account by Ella Maillart was published in 1937 as *Oasis interdites*—both became bestsellers.

At the time when these two travellers undertook their journeys, a few metalled roads existed, but these only linked up the main localities and it was often necessary to use trails or to travel on horseback. Paul Pelliot had been able to do most of his trip from Paris to Dunhuang by train, crossing Russian Europe and Asia on the Trans-Siberian railway and Ella Maillart had travelled on the Trans-Caspian; further south, however, there existed only roads or trails. To take the train from Gansu to Urumqi, one would have to wait for 1961; to Korla, 1984; and to Kashgar, 1999. Nevertheless, in the 1920s, the telegraph had already reached a few places.

But by the mid-1930s war was threatening everywhere. The Japanese had begun their conquest of Asia. Insecurity, the weakening of Chinese central power and xenophobia were little by little driving the foreigners out. Then, after the Japanese defeat, there was the growth of Communist power and civil war.

When Chinese Central Asia became accessible once more to foreigners, thirty years later, a new category of traveller, the tourist, arrived from all corners of the world by plane, train or bus. In Soviet Central Asia, Uzbekistan had opened up slightly earlier, in the 1970s. Very soon, the term "Silk Road", which no longer represented a reality, was used by travel agencies, and was synonymous with great cultural fulfilment and fabled landscapes.

Chapter Twenty
Roads and Bridges, Tourism and Pipelines

Tourism has been accused of all evils. It harms ethnic identity, generates mistaken and superficial viewpoints, humiliates the host country, destroys its environment, creates pernicious money-based relations between people; it is a danger to cultural heritage, spreading contagious bacilli and viruses, upsetting the balance of prices; all of this and more has been said about this new aspect of our lifestyle! Certainly, tourism has its down side, but in many countries it is the only way of travelling for most people, for those who have no diplomatic passport, no work contract; to go to a foreign land, one can easily obtain a tourist visa, valid for two or three weeks, or for two or three months, but to live there any longer is another matter. Therefore, one becomes a tourist, whether one wants to or not. For a while, one has to wear that label. Furthermore, at certain times or in certain regions of China or of some other country, individual tourism may not be permitted. The foreign visitor has no choice but to go through an agency and to travel as part of a group. An independent tourist, who does not speak Chinese, will have trouble obtaining a train ticket or a hotel room.

It was therefore on tourist visas and as part of organized trips that thousands of travellers wanting to visit Central Asia arrived in China from 1979 on. In general, people conjured up a picture of the Silk Road in their minds, reinforced by the message sent by advertisements, which corresponded to Chinese Central Asia or Soviet Central Asia, whereas in reality one should restore its full meaning, "from Italy to Xi'an". Afghanistan, which had been relatively accessible in the 1960s, was shut again at the end of the 1970s, and Iran, which played such an important role in the ancient history of the Silk Road, was also isolated. Therefore, the main areas which could be visited were, and still are, Gansu, Xinjiang and Uzbekistan.

Europeans along with Japanese and Americans were among the early visitors. They had various reasons for travelling and were amateurs of art or history, hikers, or younger generations of Sinologists, more and more numerous and better trained than earlier ones. There were also travel writers, pleased to discover a new world. This world was new to the Chinese themselves too, as for a long time they had not been free to travel where they wished and were inquisitive about their own cultural heritage; the Cultural Revolution was now behind them, and they were beginning to enjoy travelling, even in their own Far West, once so heavily laden with painful connotations of war, exile and banishment.

But long-distance travel is expensive. One of the most remarkable features of society in the Western world and Japan since 1960 has been the development of mass tourism, with travel to far-off places made possible by aeroplanes and charter flights. This tourism has benefited from the growth of the affluent classes and a period of thirty years of economic prosperity, fostering a clientele increasingly difficult to satisfy and whose intellectual curiosity is continually fed and stimulated by reading and television and tempted by the development of the travel book. There are also other reasons, such as more leisure time, a greater freedom of movement for the young, who are attracted by other civilizations and adventure and who possess more money than before, as well as the new phenomenon of a class of retirees enjoying long-distance travel. These are new habits which have now become well entrenched. They sustain numerous industries and create an infinite number of jobs, in the hotel business, bus and charter companies, tourist agencies, tour operators, guides, publishing and photography. All of this has occurred in China too, where after its opening, the term "Silk Road" began to appear everywhere. There and abroad, the term has been over-used, bandied about at every occasion, and not only in advertising. It can be found in many journalists' writings, and thus has become fashionable (one wonders what it will refer to in two hundred years' time).

The expression "Silk Road" is completely absent from ancient texts, Chinese as well as non-Chinese, as far as we know. The Chinese talked of the road west, the road of the Western Territories; others referred to the road to China, whatever the word used to designate China. Since 1978, Chinese writers have used it regularly. But there are cases where, surprisingly, it does not appear, as we shall see.

Around 1986, Chinese magazines latched onto the term "Silk Road" (*si lu, sichou zhi lu*) in the physical sense—a modern, tarmacked road which could be travelled in all seasons—for the road linking Kashgar to Islamabad in Pakistan. It was opened to foreigners in 1986, or at least accessible to them from May to November. Work on it had finished in 1978, and for the transport of goods the road was open and cleared of snow all year round. If the expression "Silk Road" began to appear then, it is probably because this coincided with the wave of development of international tourism in China, and because Pakistan too wanted to enter the galaxy of tourism; in any event, the term was highly evocative. Indian and Pakistani authors have also adopted the term and it is true that this road more or less follows one of the old trade routes.

But it is also more commonly known geographically as the Karakoram Highway, abbreviated as KKH, as it crosses the massif (and not the pass) of the Karakoram. Leaving Kashgar, where the two great roads of north and south Xinjiang come together, it passes through Tashkurgan—where certain people locate Ptolemy's Stone Tower—the Khunjerab Pass at 4,594 metres above sea level, the Hunza Valley, Gilgit and Kohestan, to end in Islamabad. It provides access to the sea for the landlocked province of Xinjiang by connecting it on the Pakistani side to the road and railway network to Karachi. On the Chinese side, the closest connection with a railroad at the time was at Urumqi or Korla, but Kashgar is linked by the southern Xinjiang road to Yarkand and Yecheng, and from then to the Xinjiang–Tibet road which skirts round the north of the Himalaya and ends up in Assam. Thus it was possible to travel by bus or lorry into the heart of Central Asia from the Gulf of Oman.

This road of 800 kilometres in length, technically very difficult to construct, was built by the Pakistanis from Islamabad to Gilgit, and from Gilgit to Kashgar by the Chinese, at great human and material cost. Hundreds of workers lost their lives. The road was constructed as the result of an agreement between the two countries, and as part of geopolitical rather than real commercial concerns.

The construction and maintenance of technically difficult and expensive modern roads, particularly ones at high altitude and in desert terrain, has been a specific feature of Chinese foreign policy since the creation of the People's

Republic. Very often, this form of construction has been carried out in the context of Chinese aid to technically less advanced nations. China built the Kathmandu–Lhasa road, the Kashgar–Gilgit road and others, under the watchful and worried eye of the great non-Communist powers. And of course, within their own territory, the first concern of the leaders of the People's Republic was to build modern roads, and if possible railway lines, in their remotest, economically less advanced and politically less secure zones: Tibet, Qinghai, Xinjiang. For the Chinese government, these roads were a method of controlling and integrating the population as much as an essential feature of economic development.

The KKH is a striking example of the improvements made in transport and of the contrast between "before" and "after": crossing the gorges of the Kei River, which used to take six days, is now done in 70 minutes; the trip from Rawalpindi to Gilgit, which represented 23 stages on horseback, is now reduced to 17 hours by bus; the distance from Gilgit to Hunza, once three days of riding, is now two hours by jeep. And the dangers incurred are much fewer.

Apart from its importance for Sino-Pakistani trade, this road has had a positive effect within each country and in each of the regions concerned. It has also helped to attract foreign tourists: Kashgar is now frequently visited and the landscape crossed is exceptional. In addition to the classic form of tourism, a particular type of tourism has also prospered: the pilgrimage to Mecca. This road is now regularly used by Muslim pilgrims of Chinese nationality, numerous in Xinjiang and Gansu, who travel by bus to Islamabad, from where an Islamic organization takes them to Mecca.

Mountain roads such as the KKH or the Kathmandu–Lhasa road are fragile and costly to maintain; they are slow and, in the frontier region of Pakistan, there are regularly rumours of bandits and landslides. For heavy goods, the only cost-effective means of transport over these long distances is by rail, but the nearest connection, in 1986, was at Korla, at the other end of Xinjiang. Since 1984, this had been the westernmost point which could be reached by rail in the People's Republic of China, in fact it is an embryonic branch line off the Lanzhou–Urumqi line, which has now been extended to Aksu and Kashgar. Similarly, in 2002, the government announced that work had started on the long-planned and long-postponed Qinghai line, which is set to join Xining to Lhasa, via Golmud.

Railways, trade and geopolitics have been intermingling since the 1950s over the question of the North Xinjiang line which today links Lanzhou to Turfan, Urumqi, Alatau-Drujba on the Sino-Kazakh border and Aktogay, in the ex-Soviet republic of Kazakhstan, where it joins what was once called the "Turksib", the Turkestan–Siberia railroad. In order to understand the implications of this we must return to the still recent period when Asia was divided between two powerful giants, both of them Communist, the USSR and the People's Republic of China.

After its founding, the PRC relied very heavily on aid from the USSR. One of the expressions of the good relations between the two powers was the project for the construction of a railway line between Xi'an and the USSR, directly linking Xinjiang to Kazakhstan, that is to say to the Soviet railway network. This was a project with huge potential for two countries which were both characterized by immense distances and inadequate communications infrastructures. The vast Western Territories of the Chinese Republic were totally deprived of railway lines, and until then any linking up with the Soviet network could only be done way off, in the north-east of China, which added several thousand kilometres to any trip.

In order to save those thousands of kilometres, the idea was to extend the Chinese railway line from Lanzhou through Hami, Turfan and Urumqi, as far as the Soviet border and the gateway to Dzungaria, that is the Alatau Pass. This is a depression about twenty kilometres wide which separates the autonomous Mongol district of Bortala, in Xinjiang, north-west of Urumqi, from the district of Taldy-Kurgan, on the Kazakh side, then a Soviet Socialist Republic. The line, which would cross the frontier at a point symbolically named Drujba, which in Russian means "friendship", would continue in Soviet territory with a section linking up with the Turkestan–Siberia line at Aktogay, midway between Alma-Ata and Semipalatinsk. This line, which itself joins the Trans-Siberian further north, was opened in 1931 and links Semipalatinsk to Alma-Ata, Loguvaya, Chimkent and Arys; at Arys, it connects with the Tashkent–Orenburg line.

The 1950s was a time of pioneers, as much on the Russian as on the Chinese side: egged on by vivid propaganda, youths from Byelorussia, Leningrad, Moscow, Kazakhstan, of thirty-six nationalities in all, arrived by the carriage-full in the "virgin lands" of Kazakhstan. Thousands of young enthusiastic volunteers (as they were described in the *Pravda* of 29th April 1961), "answering the call of their heart and the orders of the Komsomol", rushed forward to plant sugar beet and cereals, set up fisheries on the lakes, and work on this new building site of Socialism, the "Road of Friendship", the Turksib-Xinjiang junction.

In China, meanwhile, the development of the Far West was being carried out both economically and in terms of political integration; part of the population of Shanghai, for example, was forced to settle in Urumqi. The new Lanzhou–Xinjiang railway line, which had just been opened, was filled with "volunteers" who were going to develop the desert lands and particularly the oil fields. From both sides of the frontier, the official propaganda tried to fire up the enthusiasm of the young for this pioneering task, entrusted to a courageous elite, devoted to a great national and Communist cause; this "Road of Friendship" would be the crowning symbol of "friendship between two brother nations".

From Lanzhou to the border, the Xinjiang line would stretch across 2,350 kilometres. In April 1961, 2,000 kilometres of it were finished, and Urumqi had almost been reached. Villages were mushrooming up along the line, wrote the special correspondent of the *Pravda*. The city of Yumen, named for the nearby Jade Gate in the Great Wall, had become a centre of oil production, and Lanzhou a complex of refineries. The railway line was essential to the development of the oil industry in Gansu and Xinjiang, and to the development of these two regions in general.

The Russian railway line reached the frontier in April 1961 (hence the article in the *Pravda*), having overcome enormous difficulties: heat, salt-leached earth, lack of water, and fearsome winds, famous in the region, which sometimes compelled the line-laying workers to remain shut up in their wagons for days on end. At certain periods, they could only emerge eight or ten times a month. One engine driver, Alexey Petrovitch Ambrosenko, was decorated with the title of Hero of Socialist Work.

And there was the enormous station, "as white as a palace", of Drujba, the frontier post. All that was needed now was the Chinese, and they would soon arrive. The correspondent of the *Pravda*, M. Domogatzkikh, wrote with the customary lyricism of Soviet style, "Very soon, right here, where caravans once halted on the Silk Road, the railway lines of our two countries will meet in an iron handshake."

The Chinese arrived thirty-one years late. In 1961–62, relations between China and the Soviet Union cooled down considerably. The USSR ended its economic aid and recalled all its technicians from China. The cold persisted. A direct railway link was no longer desirable. The medals of the "Work Heroes" were a reward for vain sacrifice. The Sino-Soviet border became a border of conflict, an iron curtain within the Communist world.

The Russians more or less maintained their section of the useless line, occasionally sending a train along it. The Chinese did not extend their line northwards but built a section leaving Turfan to the south-west as far as Korla, which it reached in 1984 and stopped.

Then came the thaw, the great political opening of the People's Republic of China in 1978–1980 and new commercial relations with the USSR. The new agreements led to the resumption of work on the North Xinjiang line in 1985, with financial help from the Soviet government. The construction carriages set out again from Urumqi. On 1st December 1990, President Jiang Zemin cut the ribbon at the inauguration of the Urumqi–Alatau section. The first train travelled down it on 2nd September. On the 12th, the Soviet and Chinese railway networks were effectively connected, with one restriction, however: the railway gauges are not the same. Freight and passenger services on the line began some time later.

The conclusion of this project was marked by ceremonies and hailed in the Chinese press. The illustrated periodical *China* published an article in January 1991 entitled "The second railway 'bridge' between Asia and Europe", which stated: "A new transcontinental railway line from Lianyungang, a port in the province of Jiangsu, to Rotterdam in Holland, is being set up little by little and due to open in 1992. The construction of the western section of the Lanzhou–Xinjiang line, from Urumqi to Alatau, is finished. It is linked to the Soviet network."

The first railway "bridge" is of course the Trans-Siberian. Lianyungang is a port located just north of Shanghai, opposite Korea and Japan (the magazine *China* was to feature this port in November 1991). In 1991, Rotterdam was, in terms of commercial trade, the largest port in the world. In the spirit of these articles, this was therefore not merely a Sino-Soviet railway line but a transcontinental artery running from sea to sea, from the China Sea to the North Sea. This was a completely different vision from that of 1960. In the meantime, the world had opened up on the other side of the Urals and the aim was no longer to become integrated into the Soviet world, but into the global network. The way now seemed open to free commercial flows which would generate great prosperity.

The Lianyungang–Rotterdam line stretches across 10,000 kilometres, 4,100 of which are in the People's Republic of China. It is about 2,000 kilometres shorter than the Trans-Siberian, and 5,000 marine miles shorter than the maritime route via the Indian Ocean and the Suez Canal. The trip from Beijing to Moscow is reduced by a sixth, that is by 24 hours. The cost of transporting goods was to be reduced by 20 per cent, and the time of transport by 50 per cent compared to the maritime route. The Urumqi-Alatau junction opened a new frontier to Chinese trade, it revolutionized trans-Asian communication and was hailed as the most important transcontinental route since the Suez Canal had been built a hundred years ago.

The Chinese press also underlined the importance of this junction for the local economy: it opened up northern Xinjiang, while Kazakhstan would benefit from new export possibilities between Alma-Ata and Urumqi for its metals and chemical products, a trade which until then had been carried out by lorry.

The vocabulary which appears in the Chinese communiqués (never a matter of chance) in connection with this long-awaited junction is a good indicator of the various changes in the situation: in 1961, the line was called the "Road of Friendship" and the "Sino-Soviet railway line"; in 1985, it was the "railway of North Xinjiang"; in 1990 and 1991, the "Asia–Europe railway bridge". There are no more references to the Silk Road, although no occasion to make them is usually missed, and this line does actually follow one of the ancient routes. No

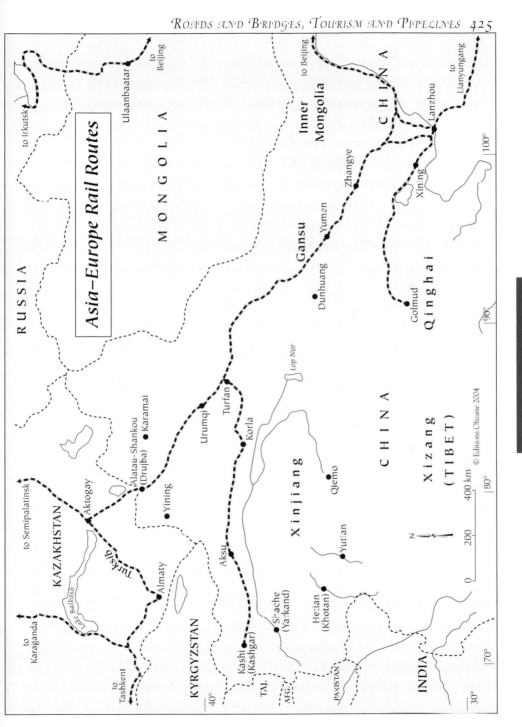

Asia–Europe Rail Routes

© Editions Olizane 2004

reference either to tourism; all that is mentioned is trade, reduction of transport costs and time, and integration into the global economy. The Chinese government is even said to have turned a deaf ear to a Russian project of a "Silk Road" tourist train which would have taken travellers from Xi'an to the historic cities of Central Asia and on to Europe.[169]

But then a new event occurred: the first train had only just travelled along it in 1990 when the political map of Asia was completely changed. Of the two great empires which had until then shared this part of the world, one had collapsed and broken into pieces, thereby multiplying its borders. During the last six months of 1991, all the Socialist Soviet Republics of Central Asia became independent one after the other, while the other republics of the Federation were separating through the same process. Finally, at Christmas 1991, the USSR was dissolved. In its stead appeared the Commonwealth of Independent States (CIS). There was now a multitude of independent republics, with as many borders, laws, visas, controls and customs. From now on, the Uighur Autonomous Region of Xinjiang gave on to eight foreign states instead of four, the USSR having been replaced by Tajikistan, Kyrgyzstan, Russia (CIS) and Kazakhstan. In addition, in 1990, the People's Republic of Mongolia had become more independent from its Russian "big brother". Strategy had to be rethought all over again.

After a period of hesitation, the position of the five ex-Soviet republics is beginning to take new shape. Kazakhstan, where 40 per cent of the population is of various Russian origins, 40 per cent is Kazakh and the remaining 20 per cent is a mixture, has remained tied to the government in Moscow by treaties and agreements (the presence on its territory of rocket launching sites and of Soviet nuclear bases weighs heavily in this), while maintaining its independence by diversifying its economic partners. It has great mineral resources (ferrous metals), as well as oil and natural gas. Its situation neighbouring China, with which it shares a long border, has suddenly increased the regional, bilateral importance of the new railway, particularly since Chinese policy has emphasized the development of cross-border trade. In 1990 and 1991, the Chinese government, pursuing its policy of reform and opening, boosted the liberalization of trade and particularly of cross-border trade, on all its frontiers (even opening the door with India a crack, after keeping it closed for thirty years), giving much more autonomy to the provinces and regions in their direct links with their neighbours. Foreign trade, powerfully stimulated, began taking off.

But this does not make the Xinjiang railroad, even linked to the Turksib, a "global artery", the "Asia–Europe railway bridge", an axis between the China Sea and Rotterdam, as was hoped in 1985 and 1990. Its future depends on relationships between the new states and their powerful neighbours.

The partnership between China and Kazakhstan (its capital is no longer Alma-Ata or Almaty, but was transferred in 1987 to Akmola, ex-Akmolinsk, ex-Tselinograd or "city of the virgin lands", in the north-east of the Republic, and finally named Astana), is flourishing and appears to be firm. China's demand for oil is constantly on the increase and becoming acute, and its own production is insufficient. In 1999, Kazakhstan sent 500,000 tonnes of oil to China by rail. Demand then doubled for the year 2000. The speed of rail transport, which was originally 40 km/h on this line, has been increased to 140 km/h. Nevertheless, to respond to the increase in demand, an agreement was signed in August 2000 between Astana and Beijing over the construction of an oil pipeline linking western Kazakhstan to Xinjiang. Kazakhstan is an obvious commercial partner for Xinjiang, almost half of whose exports consist of cotton.

There is one natural feature common to all the ex-Soviet republics of Central Asia which represents a serious handicap to them: they are all land-locked countries, as is Afghanistan. When it lost the Baltic states, the USSR lost its window on the sea, and the Ukraine, which gives onto the Black Sea, has distanced itself from Moscow. How efficient could an axis from the China Sea to Rotterdam be nowadays if barriers are set up halfway across it? In periods of disagreement, frontiers mean taxes, quotas, prohibitions, problems over prices, money-changing, banks. Once again, it will be necessary to draw up treaties regulating trade and transit, which always profit the more powerful. Once again, we will see blackmail to the point of suffocation by some, poverty for others. The history of certain other countries without access to the sea has shown this only too well. "Borders are a sequel from barbaric times", said Nursultan Nazarbaev, the President of Kazakhstan, in 1990.

The Chinese government of the 1990s opened its frontiers to trade and foreign investment, partly privatizing its economy, setting up a "socialist market economy". Deng Xiaoping had proclaimed a few years previously: "Get rich!" Increasing the standard of living had become his main weapon, his saving ideology, in controlling the remote foreign regions such as Tibet and Xinjiang. In these regions, where Chinese power is barely tolerated for more than one reason, economic development has been neglected and the standard of living is much lower than in eastern China.

Tibet has been resisting Chinese control continually for forty years; Xinjiang, where the majority of the population is Muslim, has known sporadic unrest, which is becoming more and more frequent, as evidenced by the growth in Uighur separatism. The Uighur account for 8 of the 18 million inhabitants (7 million are Han Chinese). Xinjiang is surrounded by Muslim states, some of which are home to Uighur communities. There is therefore much in terms of religion, culture, ethnic (Turkish) origin, language and past history, which is shared with the ex-Soviet Muslim republics, where the growth of Islam is sharply on the rise.

From the beginning of the 1990s, Turkey, Iran, Pakistan and Saudi Arabia have set up contacts with these ex-Soviet republics, opening embassies, proposing aid or commercial agreements, long-term credit which can be reimbursed in kind, sending Muslim preachers, Korans by the ton—even copies of the *Thoughts* of Imam Khomeini—and opening their universities to students. At the same time, they offered access to the sea by opening up their ports to the oil and natural gas of which three of the five republics have plentiful reserves. Some analysts sensed that this could lead to the birth of some form of great economic community of Muslim states stretching from the Great Wall to Turkey, a community which would follow a different path from Marxism, different from the materialist atheism of Western countries: the way of Islam. Many dreamt of a renaissance of the Silk Road which would once again turn Central Asia into a centre of culture and trade. They dreamt of a new caliphate, a caliphate in which a humanistic Islamic civilization would flourish once more, stimulating a great intellectual boom, as it had done in the past.

In what sands, in what Taklamakan, have these humanistic dreams vanished? And how does one say "Great Game" in Chinese, Kazak, Turkmen, Uighur, Persian, Turkish, Urdu, Pashtu, Arabic, Russian? The Great Game is currently being played by many players, through conferences of five or ten members, armed terrorist groups, civil war, in which the stakes are Islamic fundamentalism and oil and natural gas reserves.

Today, Afghanistan has exported war to neighbouring Tajikistan, where neo-Communists and Muslim fundamentalists struggle for power; to Uzbekistan and the "happy valley" of Ferghana which has become a fundamentalist fief; to Tajikistan where three Islamic movements operate clandestinely; to Kyrgyzstan and Uzbekistan, supported by Afghanistan or by the Wahabite sect from Saudi Arabia, financed by drug trafficking. The devastating combination of terrorism and repression is spreading everywhere. Central Asia has become a "breeding ground for terrorist groups and extremists and the last bastion of terrorism in Asia".[170] And all these republics are suffering from economic recession.

The new Russian government has been trying to re-impose its hegemony over the region. With Tajikistan's consent, it maintains armed forces in that country on the Afghan frontier, and has recently increased their numbers. The representatives of Russia, China, Tajikistan, Kyrgyzstan and Kazakhstan held a meeting in Dushanbe in July 2000, agreeing to fight together against drug and weapons trafficking and to prevent the incursion of Islamist extremists. This common policy of the "Shanghai group" (created in 1996 to solve frontier problems) is also aimed at creating an obstacle to the influence of the United States in the region. For the United States is also present in this Great Game, keeping watch over the risk of destabilization of the entire region, which would have short- and long-term repercussions on their own interests. In this region which stretches from the Caspian to Kazakhstan, lie reserves of oil and natural gas indispensable in the near future to the ever-increasing energy needs of the industrialized countries.

Since this chapter was originally written in March 2001, for the French version, the geopolitical importance of this region has been forcibly impressed on the world: the terrorist attacks on New York and Washington led to an

American military response in Afghanistan. Land and air operations were conducted with the aim of ousting the Taleban regime and capturing those who allegedly ordered the attacks, Osama Bin Laden and the heads of the Al-Qaeda network. All these events have been amply described and commented on in the media and need not be told again here. But their consequences do not concern only the United States and Afghanistan itself, today freed of its Taleban domination, but also Pakistan, all the states of Central Asia, China and Asian Russia—to mention only Asia.

The Americans have gained a foothold in Central Asia: with Russian consent, they have been able to use bases in Tajikistan, Kyrgyzstan and Uzbekistan to carry out military operations in Afghanistan. This scenario was indeed difficult to imagine just a few years beforehand. The perception of an "Islamic" danger (along with all the less transparent aspects which accompany it and everything which this danger can be used as a pretext for doing) has led to a reshaping, a new balance of alliances. The recent warming of relations between the United States of George W. Bush and the Russia of Vladimir Putin has finally settled the Cold War and led to a common struggle against radical Islamic terrorism, seen as a major worldwide danger.

Xinjiang is at risk of being involved through contagion in an explosive situation of religious anti-Chinese nationalism. These last few years, the rapid development of Muslim extremism, the proximity of Tajikistan and of the civil war in Afghanistan, the intensification of separatist aspirations and of anti-Chinese actions in Xinjiang, all of these have increased Beijing's fear of losing control of the area and of the destabilization of the whole of western China.

But Xinjiang, with its reserves in the Tarim Basin, in Dzungaria and in the area around Turfan, is so rich in oil and natural gas that it is bound to become the main supplier of Chinese needs in years to come; it also possesses other mineral resources. In addition to a hardening of the position of the police, the Chinese central government has adopted a different weapon: increasing the standard of living of the population, so that it will compare favourably with that of neighbouring countries, and will lessen the gap with that of the most developed regions of China itself.

This policy is also followed with regard to Tibet. Thus the 10th Five-Year Plan (2001–2005) includes the development as a priority of the west of China, "particularly those regions inhabited by national minorities", with large-scale investment by the state, and a particular effort made to improve means of transport. The aim is to attract to the south of Xinjiang Chinese—especially the young and technicians—from various regions of the country with a high demographic rate. This effort on transport in Xinjiang, particularly in the sector located to the south of the Tianshan chain (less developed than the northern part, Dzungaria), has materialized in the form of a new railway line: the South Xinjiang line, from Korla to Kashgar.

We have mentioned the branch line which left from Turfan station, on the North Xinjiang line, and which stopped in 1984 at Korla, 476 kilometres from Turfan. Work on it began again in 1996, as part of the 9th Five-Year Plan. The line travelled south of the great east–west road on which Luntai and Kuche (Kucha) are located, joining it at Aksu, then passing south of it before joining it again at Kashgar, 970 kilometres from Korla.[171] The line reached Kashgar at the beginning of December 1999. On 6th December of that year, Li Peng, the President of the Permanent Committee of the National Assembly, officially inaugurated the line. The event was celebrated in the national press, and the editions of the *Renmin Ribao* (*People's Daily*) of 6th and 7th December devoted half of their front page and of the columns inside to it. "For the various ethnic groups in Xinjiang, the South Xinjiang railway is the railway of hope, the railway of enrichment, the railway which unites, the railway of development [...] the ardent hope of the people of Xinjiang."

The railway which "unites", because it will tie this region more closely to Central China, to the *neidi*, the "inner lands", a term used to designate China proper when looking at it from its outer regions, to indicate clearly that these regions are just as Chinese as the rest, and not foreign lands. The road of "hope and enrichment" because until then this was a poor region, despite its production of cotton and its animal husbandry (the oil and natural gas of the Tarim depression are recent discoveries, and until now only the reserves north of the Tianshan, in Dzungaria, were exploited), so poor in fact that half the districts received assistance provided by the state or the provincial government (the population in southern Xinjiang, unlike that of the north, is almost entirely Uighur). "This is the dawn of our victory in eliminating poverty in south Xinjiang", because insufficient means of transport were stifling development, and because this railway would change everything. It will allow this Far West, which had been neglected for too long, to be opened up; transport costs of goods by rail (chemical fertilizers, pesticides, refined oil products, cotton, fruit) are three times lower than by road. The economic activity of the urban areas has been stimulated all along the railway line as it progressed westwards, attracting businesses and commerce. And, finally, foreign investors and capital have already arrived. In ten years, it is reckoned, southern Xinjiang will have completely changed. And they conclude, it will be, "Another transcontinental bridge between Asia and Europe!"

On 7th December 1999, Li Peng made a long declaration on the local Xinjiang radio about the necessity of maintaining stability among the ethnic groups in China, and invited people to do their utmost for the development of the Chinese West through the spread of science and culture.

The railway and this new policy have certainly helped stimulate the development of the region, and have led, according to recent observers, to a wave of Chinese immigration from various parts of the country. Also, in order to answer China's growing needs for oil and natural gas, a massive project for a gas pipeline stretching 4,167 kilometres, linking the gas production sites in the Tarim Basin with the city of Shanghai, was announced in August 2000. This project also included a gas pipeline linking Shanghai to the production sites of Changqing, near Jingbian in Shaanxi province. Together, these two pipelines are slated to provide gas to eastern China. The Jingbian–Shanghai section is now complete; the first gas was successfully piped into Shanghai in October 2003. The immense Tarim–Shanghai gas pipeline is due to be completed in early 2005.

Oil constitutes a strategic energy reserve; the 5,500 kilometres of international borders with eight different nations form a strategic zone of national importance; added to this is the risk of separatism and of Islamic fundamentalism. The necessity of controlling this immense territory (amounting to a sixth of the People's Republic), and of exploiting the very heart of the desert has required the construction of a new road, which crosses the Taklamakan from end to end, linking Minfeng, on the great south road, between Khotan and Qiemo, with Korla and further on with Turfan. Finished in 1995, it follows the new railway line for a short distance. Other roads are planned, as well as other railway lines, towards Kyrgyzstan and Uzbekistan, for example. Of course, more and more air routes have also been opened in the Chinese Far West.

But as more roads, railways and flights are created, so there are more travellers in search of archaic forms of travel: there will always be someone in the world travelling from Beijing to Kathmandu on a bicycle, or from Paris to Moscow on horseback, or swimming across the Atlantic, or crossing Australia on foot. Even the Taklamakan Desert was crossed on foot, from Khotan to Aksu, in October 1987, by a Fujicolour expedition. This is one of the more disconcerting aspects of technological progress. But would a trekker, prepared to walk for days behind his camel for the sheer joy of discovering by chance, in the middle of the desert, the half-buried remains of a fortified village still unknown to archaeologists, make such an effort to find himself gazing at a field of oil derricks in the heart of the Taklamakan, with roads and lorries all around? We can imagine the disappointment of the romantic trekker each time he or she reads of constructions and roads, but the trekker would be mistaken: for the desert is vast and, with imagination, one can still hear through the wind in the eternal desert the bells of the caravans, the mumbled prayers of the Buddhist monks and even the demons which Faxian, Xuanzang and Marco Polo told us of. And in the Taklamakan, there are still ancient cities buried in its sands.

Ancient manuscripts in a variety of languages found at Dunhuang, China

Notes

1   *In 699 or 700 according to different authors; 54 according to P. Gignoux in the* Encyclopaedia Universalis *of 1985; 53 on the map of* The Historic Mediterranean 800 BC to AD 1500 *of the* National Geographic Society, 1985.

2   PLUTARCH, Plutarch's Lives, *translated by Bernadotte Perrin, Loeb Classical Library, Heinemann, London, 1984, volume 3, "Pericles and Fabius Maximus, Nicias and Crassus", pp. 385–423. Plutarch was born around 50 AD and died circa 125;* FLORUS L., Annaei Flori Epitome rerum Romanorum (Epitome of Roman History), Book I, *translated by Edward S. Forster, Loeb Classical Library, Heinemann, London, 1966. Florus lived during the reigns of Trajan and Hadrian, at the end of the 1st and beginning of the 2nd centuries AD.*

3   LUBEC G. *et al., "Use of silk in ancient Egypt", in* Nature, *vol. 362, no. 6415, 4 March 1993, p. 25;* NOBLE WILFORD J., "New Finds suggest even earlier Trade of fabled Silk Road", The New York Times / Science Times, 16 March 1993.

4   New York Times / Science Times, *op. cit.*

5   RAPIN, C. *"L'incompréhensible Asie centrale de la carte de Ptolémée: propositions pour un décodage", pp. 201–225, in* Alexander's Legacy in the East. Studies in Honor of Paul Bernard, *ed. C. Altman Bromberg, O. Bopearachchi, F. Grenet, Bulletin of the Asia Institute, new series 12, 1998 (published 2001).*

6   *For the archaic period, we have followed* ZHANG Qiyun, Zhonghua wu qian nian shi (5000 Years of Chinese History), *published in Taipei, 1976, vol. 1.*

7   The Book of Odes, *translated by Bernhard Karlgren, Museum of Far Eastern Antiquities, Stockholm 1950, ode no. 57 p. 38*

8   BAN GU *(died 92 AD),* Qian Han shu, *chapters 6, 22, 25, 61, 96. English translation and commentary by DUBS Homer,* The History of the Former Han, *Baltimore, 1944;* SIMA QIAN *(145–86 BC),* Shiji, *chapter 123. Passages from this chapter have been translated in* LESLIE *and* GARDINER, The Roman Empire in Chinese Sources, *Bardi, Rome, 1996 pp. 33–35.*

9   Shiji *123 (Liezhuan 63), translated in* LESLIE *and* GARDINER, *op. cit. p. 34.*

10   History of the Former Han, *op. cit., chapter 96;* Shiji, *op. cit., chapter 24, 123.*

11   *On the spread of alfalfa and the vine, see:* BOULNOIS L., "Chevaux célestes et salive de dragon", *in* Diogène, *no. 167, 1994, pp. 18–42.*

12 On the "blood-sweating" horses, see DUBS H., The History of the Former Han, op. cit., pp. 132–135, 1944, appendix 5: "The Blood-Sweating Horses of Ferghana".

13 For both historical and legendary tales about Central Asian horses, and celestial and divine horses, see History of the Former Han, op. cit., chapter 6, 22, 25, 61; Shiji, op. cit., chapter 24; DUBS H., 1944, op. cit., pp. 19, 75, 110–111; CHEN LIANG, Silu shihua, Lanzhou, 1983, chapter 5, pp. 27–32; Jiuquan shihua, 1984, Gansusheng Jiuquan diqu "Jiuquan shihua", pp. 95–97. On Gesar's horse, see STEIN R.-A., Recherches sur l'épopéeet le barde au Tibet, PUF, Paris, pp. 119, 535 ff., 1959; DAVID-NEEL A., LAMA YONGDEN, The Superhuman Life of Gesar of Ling, translated by Sydney Violet,Shambala, 1981.

14 XUAN ZANG, Da Tang Xiyuji. Translated by BEAL SAMUEL, Si-yu-ki, Buddhist Records of the Western World, London, 1884, reprinted New Delhi, 1983, p. 20.

15 CHEN LIANG, 1983, op. cit., p. 28; History of the Former Han, op. cit., chapter 6; Jiuquan shihua, op. cit., 1984, pp. 95–97.

16 CHEN LIANG, ibid.; History of the Former Han, op. cit., chapter 22, 25, 61; Jiuquan shihua, ibid; DUBS H., op. cit., 1944, pp. 19, 75, 110, 111; Shiji, chapter 24.

17 CHEN LIANG, op. cit., 1983, pp. 30–31; History of the Former Han, chapter 6; DUBS H., op. cit., 1944, pp. 75, 110, 111.

18 STEIN R.-A., Recherches sur l'épopée et le barde au Tibet, 1959, p. 119.

19 The history of the war over the Dayuan horses is given in chapter 123 of the Shiji and in chapter 96 of the History of the Former Han; both these sources have been cited and commented on by later authors.

20 See DUBS H., op. cit., 1944, p. 108, as well as CH'U T'UNG-TSU, Han Social Structure, University of Washington Press 1972, pp. 328–332 for a discussion of the convict in Han times.

21 According to CHEN LIANG, op. cit., 1983, p. 41, it should be located along the middle reaches of the Kabul River.

22 JOSEPH NEEDHAM, Science and Civilisation in China, Vol. 5, Part 2, p. 219.

23 See p. 213 of RAO Zongyi's article in: WU Jialun, JIANG Yuxiang, Gudai xinan sizhou zhi lu yanji, Chengdu, 1990.

24 SANG Xiuyun, p. 194 in: WU Jialun, JIANG Yuxiang, op. cit., 1990.

25   *The Later Han dynasty lasted from 25 to 221 AD. Chapter 118 on the Western countries has been translated into French by the Sinologist Edouard CHAVANNES: "Les pays d'Occident d'après le Heou Han chou", T'oung Pao, 1907, sér. 2, vol. 8 (no. 1), pp. 149–234. See LESLIE and GARDINER, 1996 chapter 4 pp. 41–55 for transaltions of relevant passages from several chapters of the* Hou Han shu.

26   *In:* AL-MUQADDASI, The Best Divisions for Knowledge of the Regions, *translated by Basil A. Collins, Centre for Muslim Contribution to Civilization, Garnet Publishing, Reading 1994, p. 215.*

27   *IBN BATTÛTA, Travels of Ibn Battûta, AD 1325–1354, translated by Gibb H. A. R., 5 vols., Defrémery C. and Sanguinetti B. R., Hakluyt Society, London, 1958–2000, vol.1 pp. 25–26*

28   *SCHOFF Wilfred H., The Periplus of the Erythrean Sea. Travel and Trade in the Indian Ocean by a Merchant of the First Century, London, Bombay and Calcutta, Longmans, Green and Co., 1912, reprinted New Delhi 1972; CASSON Lionel, The Periplus Maris Erythraei. Text with introduction, translation and commentary, Princeton, 1989; ROBIN C., "L'Arabie du Sud et la date du Périple de la mer Erythrée (nouvelles données)", in* Journal Asiatique, *no. 1–2, 1991, vol. 279, pp. 1–30; FUSSMAN G., "Le Périple et l'histoire politique de l'Inde", in* Journal Asiatique, *no. 1–2, 1991, vol. 279, pp. 31–38; C. Robin adopts a late 1st century date, without however absolutely discounting the first half of the 3rd century; G. Fussman and L. Casson favour the first half of the 1st century, around the year 40 AD according to the former, and 20 to 50 AD according to the latter.*

29   *DIOSCORIDES, born at Anazarbos in Cilicia, 1st century AD. Bilingual Greek and Latin edition:* Pedacii Dioscoridis Anazarbaei opera quae extant omnia *(with a Latin commentary by Jean-Antoine Saracenus, Francfort, 1598); PAUL of AEGINA, translated from the Greek by Francis Adams, The Seven Books of Paulus Aeginata, London, Sydenham Society, 1844–1847.*

30   *ZHAO Rugua. Zhu fan zhi. English translation by Friedrich HIRTH and W. W. ROCKHILL: CHAU JU-KUA, His work on the Chinese and Arab trade in the 12th and 13th centuries, entitled Chu-fan-chi, St Petersburg, Imperial Academy of Sciences, 1911;* NEEDHAM, op. cit., *p. 137, vol. 5, part 2.*

31   *CHARAS Moyse, Pharmacopée royale galénique et chymique. Published by the author in Paris, at his home in Faux-Bourg-Saint-Germain, rue des Boucheries, at the Vipères d'Or, 1676; CAP, Biographie pharmaceutique. Moïse Charas, Paris, 1840.*

32   *COEDÈS, op. cit., 1910. LESLIE and GARDINER 1996 pp. 245–246.*

33   See FILLIOZAT J., *"Pline et le Malaya"*, in Journal Asiatique, no. 1/2, 1974, tome 262, pp. 119–130; ANDRÉ J., FILLIOZAT J., Pline l'Ancien, *op. cit.*, 1980, pp. 47, 117.

34   See BOPEARACHCHI O., *"La circulation des monnaies d'origine étrangère dans l'antique Sri Lanka"*, in Res Orientales, 1993, vol. 5, pp. 63–87.

35   FILLIOZAT J., Les relations extérieures de l'Inde. *"1. Les échanges de l'Inde et de l'empire romain aux premiers siècles de l'ère chrétienne."* Pondichéry, Institut français d'Indologie, 1956; DUPUIS J., Histoire de l'Inde, Paris, Payot, 1963, pp. 56–57.

36   MALLERET Louis, *"Rapport préliminaire sur les fouilles d'Oc-Eo"*, in Bulletin de l'Ecole Française d'Extrême-Orient, vol. 45, no.1, 1951; L'archéologie du delta du Mékong, Paris, EFEO, 1959–1963.

37   PTOLEMY, The Geography, *translated and edited by Edward Luther Stevenson, Dover, New York 1991;* PTOLEMY, Geography, Book 6, *original text with English and German translations by Susanne Ziegler, Wiesbaden 1998.*

38   *Among other recent works, see CRIBB J., "The early Kushan Kings: New Evidence for Chronology",* in ALRAM M., KLIMBURG-SALTER D. Ed., Coins, Art, and Chronology. Essays on the pre-Islamic History of the Indo-Iranian Borderlands, *Vienna, 1999, pp. 177–205; or the Masters thesis of BOUCHER Daniel J.,* Buddhist Translation Procedures in Third-century China: A Study of Dharmaraksa and his Translation Idiom, *Masters thesis, University of Pennsylvania, 1996.*

39   PTOLEMY, The Geography, *translated and edited by Edward Luther Stevenson, Dover, New York 1991, p. 33. The sections of Ptolemy's Geography on Asia can also be found in* PTOLEMY, The Geography, Book 6, *original text with English and German translations by Susanne Ziegler, Dr. Ludwig Reichert Verlag, Wiesbaden 1998.*

40   ANDRÉ et FILLIOZAT, *op. cit.*, 1980, p. 89.

41   See RAPIN, C., *op. cit.*

42   See BOULNOIS L., *"Démons et tambours au désert de Lop. Variations Orient-Occident"* in Médiévales, no. 22–23, pp. 91–115, 1992.

43   PTOLEMY, *op cit.*, 1991, pp. 37–38

44   See WU Jialun et JIANG Yuxiang, *op. cit.*, 1990, particularly the articles by JIANG Yuxiang, RAO Zongyi, SANG Xiuyun.

45   Les Trésors de l'Iran, Skira, Genève, 1970, pp. 129–130, 133–135, 282.

46   See BEAL S., Si-Yu-Ki. Buddhist records of the Western World, vol. I pp. 54–68 and 173–175.

47   BEAL, op. cit. p. 75.

48   Les Trésors de l'Iran, op. cit., pp. 129–130.

49   The Kautiliya Arthasastra, translated by Kangle R. P., University of Bombay, 1972, Part II. A rearranged translation of the text by L. N. Rangarajan was published in 1992 in the Penguin Classics series under the title The Arthashastra.

50   Quoted in KAUTILYA, The Arthasastra. Le traité politique de l'Inde ancienne, extracts selected by Marinette DAMBUYANT, Paris, 1971, p. 208.

51   See LIU Xinru, Ancient India and Ancient China. Trade and religious exchanges AD 1–600. Delhi, 1988, reprinted 1991.

52   See LIU Xinru, op. cit., pp. 92–101.

53   See LIU Xinru, op. cit., p. 54.

54   Shiji, chapter on "Sima Xiangru".

55   See the unpublished doctoral thesis of MANANDHAR S., Bijoux et Parures traditionnels des Néwar au Népal. Une approche anthropologique et historique, Université de Paris X, 1998, p. 339.

56   See REINACH S., "Le corail dans l'industrie celtique" in Revue celtique, no. 20, janvier–avril 1899, pp. 1–31.

57   See HUBERT H., Les Celtes et l'expansion celtique, reprinted Paris, 1974, p. 129.

58   See REINACH S., 1899, op. cit.; HUBERT H., 1974, op. cit.; CUNLIFFE B., The Celtic World, London, 1990; KONDAKOF N., TOLSTOI J., REINACH S., Antiquités de la Russie méridionale, Paris, 1891; Or des Scythes. Trésors des Musées soviétiques, Paris, 1975 (Exhibition at the Grand Palais, Paris, 1975); ELWERE C., L'Europe des Celtes, Paris, 1992; TOLSTOV S. P., Po drevnim del'tam Oksa i Jaksarta, Moscow, 1962.

59   NEEDHAM J., Science and Civilisation in China, vol. 5, part 2. Cambridge, 1974, p. 270.

60   On the evolution of terms referring to glass, see LIU Xinru, 1988, op. cit., pp. 59–61.

61   BEAL vol. 2 pp. 318–319

62   CHEN YU Ed., Dunhuang de chuan shuo, Shanghai, 1986, pp. 131–134.

63 On this series of panels, currently in the British Museum in London, see WHITFIELD R.,
FARRER A., Caves of the Thousand Buddhas. Chinese Art from the Silk Route, London,
1990, pp. 140, 141, 160, 162; BUSSAGLI M., La peinture de l'Asie centrale, Genève,
1963, pp. 56–57; L'Asie centrale, histoire et civilisation, Paris, 1977, fig. 122.

64 See Uzbekistan, Moscow, 1967.

65 LIU Xinru, 1988, op. cit., p. 70.

66 According to MICHEL F., Recherches sur la fabrication et le commerce des étoffes de soie,
d'or et d'argent, Paris 1852–1854.

67 PAUSANIAS, Description of Greece, translated by J. G. Frazer, 6 vols, Macmillan, London
1913, vol. 1 p. 324

68 Seres... qui aquarum aspergine inundatis frondibus vellera arborum adminiculo depectunt liquoris
et lanuginis teneram subtilitatem humore domant ad obsequium. See COEDÈS, 1910, op.
cit., pp. 84–85.

69 "[...] et abunde silvae sublucidae, a quibus arborum fetus aquarum asperginibus crebris velut
quaedam vellera molientes ex lanugine et liquore mixtam subtilitatem tenerrimam pectunt,
nentesque subtegmina conficiunt sericum ad usus antehac nobilium, nunc etiam infimorum
sine ulla discretione proficiens". See COEDÈS, 1910, op. cit.

70 See COEDÈS, op. cit.

71 See COEDÈS, op. cit., p. 77.

72 AMMIANUS MARCELLINUS Book 23; see COEDÈS, op. cit., p. 97; quoted in part in
LESLIE and GARDINER 1996 p. 246.

73 See RAPIN C., "Relations entre l'Asie centrale et l'Inde à l'époque hellénistique" in Cahiers
d'Asie Centrale, no. 1/2, 1996, "Inde-Asie centrale. Routes du commerce et des idées",
pp. 35–45.

74 See GRENET F., RAPIN C., "Alexander, Ai Khanum, Termez: remarks on the spring
campaign of 328", in Alexander's Legacy in the East, op. cit.

75 On the translation of Buddhist texts into Chinese during the first centuries of the Christian era,
see: WRIGHT A. F., Buddhism in Chinese History, Stanford University Press, 1959;
BOUCHER D. J., Buddhist Translation Procedures in Third-Century China: A Study of
Dharmaraksa and his Translation Idiom. Masters thesis, University of Pennsylvania, 1996.

76 BOUCHER D. J., Buddhist Translation Procedures in Third-Century China, op. cit., 1996.

77 Fo guo ji, *translated by LEGGE James*, A Record of Buddhistic Kingdoms, being an Account by the Chinese Monk Fa-Hein of Travels in India and Ceylon (AD 399–414) in Search of the Buddhist Books of Discipline, *Oxford, 1886, reprinted New York 1965, New Delhi 1998.*

78 *See CHEN Hanseng, "Gudai Zhongguo yu Nipoerdi wenhua jiaoliu gong yuandi wu zhi shiqi shiji", in Lishi yanjiu, no. 2, 1961, pp. 95–109; HUANG Shenchang, "Han yu gudai Zhongguo yu Nipoerdi wenhua jiaoliu", in Lishi yanjiu, no. 1, 1962, pp. 92–108.*

79 *LEGGE, A Record of Buddhistic Kingdoms, p. 103*

80 *LEGGE, op. cit. pp. 113–114*

81 *See CHEN LIANG, Silu shihua, 1983, op. cit. pp. 41–44.*

82 *See the following article by FILANOVIC M. I., USMANOVA Z. I., "Les frontières occidentales de la diffusion du bouddhisme en Asie centrale", in Cahiers d'Asie Centrale, no. 1/2, 1996, "Inde–Asie centrale. Routes du commerce et des idées", pp. 186–201.*

83 *Among others, see GIGNOUX P., "Controverse religieuse dans l'Iran sassanide", in Le Monde de la Bible, no. 119, mai-juin 1999, "La Bible et l'Asie à la rencontre du bouddhisme", pp. 22–24.*

84 *See TAJADOD N., Les porteurs de lumière, Paris, 1993, pp. 224–229.*

85 *See extracts in COEDÈS, op. cit.*

86 *N. TAJADOD, op. cit., pp. 244–248.*

87 *See ROBIN C., "Les religions de l'Arabie avant l'islam" in Le Monde de la Bible, no. 129, Sept–Oct 2000; and in the same volume: BRIQUEL CHATONNET F., "Un prosélytisme juif? Le cas de Najrân".*

88 *See the English translation by Roger C. Blockley,* The History of Menander the Guardsman, Liverpool, Francis Cairns, 1985.

89 *See TREMBLAY X., Chrétientés englouties. Le christianisme de Sérinde, 1999, pp. 71–74.*

90 *See COSMAS INDICOPLEUSTES, Cosmae Indicopleustae Christianorum opinio de mundo...; McCrindle, J.W. The Christian Topography of Cosmas, an Egyptian Monk, Burt Franklin: New York, 1887.*

91 *See HIERONYMUS, De virginitate opuscula sanctorum doctorum, Ambrosii, Hieronymi, et Augustini, 1562; pp. 61–62; and Saint JEROME, Select Letters, translated by F. A Wright, Loeb no. 262, Harvard University Press 1932.*

92 *See MAZAHERI A., La Route de la Soie, 1983, pp. 483–484.*

93   SCHAFER E. H., The Golden Peaches of Samarkand, A Study of T'ang Exotics, 1963, p. 158.

94   MAALOUF A., The Gardens of Light, *translated by Dorothy Blair, Interlink, 1999, from the original French*, Les jardins de lumière, *1991, p. 212.*

95   LIN Tienwai, A History of the Perfume Trade of the Sung Dynasty, 1960, pp. 40–41, 74–76.

96   *See* RAY H. P., La chrétienté dans l'Asie du Sud. Commerce et conversion, 1999, *pp. 63–65.*

97   RAY H. P., *ibid.*

98   *See* THOMAZ L. F., Hypothèses sur les premiers chrétiens dans l'Inde des Malabars, *1999, pp. 53–57.*

99   *See* SALLES J.-F., La tradition de saint Thomas apôtre en Inde, *1999, p. 59–61.*

100 SALLES J.–F., *op. cit.*

101 *The story is told in chapter 221 of the* Xin Tang shu.

102 *Chinese dictionaries list several types of golden peach, according to place of origin and textual source. These are the peaches to which E.H. SCHAFER refers in his* The Golden Peaches of Samarkand. A Study of T'ang Exotics, *published in 1963, a fundamental (and inexhaustible) work on the history of relations as well as cultural and material exchange between China and other countries during the Tang dynasty.*

103 *On this period of great Tibetan power, see* BECKWITH C. I., The Tibetan Empire in Central Asia, *Princeton, 1987.*

104 BECKWITH C. I., 1987, *op. cit., pp. 139–140.*

105 *See* LIU Guojun, ZHENG Rusi, L'histoire du livre en Chine, *Pékin, 1989.*

106 *See* LOMBARD M., L'islam dans sa première grandeur (VIIIe-XIe siècle), *Paris, 1971, pp. 209–211.*

107 MAALOUF A., The Crusades through Arab Eyes, *Schocken, 1989, from the original French,* Les croisades vues par les Arabes, *Paris, 1983, p. 70.*

108 LIU Guojun, ZHENG Rusi, 1989, pp. 67–68.

109 ZHANG Guangda, "Trois exemples d'influences mazdéennes dans la Chine des Tang", *in* Etudes chinoises, *no. 1–2, vol. 13, 1994.*

110 RAGUIN Yves, s.j., "La stèle de Xi'an", in Le Monde de la Bible, no. 119, 1999, pp. 82–83; FORTE Antonino, "The Edict of 638 allowing the Diffusion of Christianity in China", in Pelliot Paul, L'inscription nestorienne de Si-Ngan-Fou, Paris 1996 pp. 349–373, and FORTE A.,"On the so-called Abraham from Persia, a Case of Mistaken Identity", in op. cit., pp. 375–428.

111 From the French edition of MARDRUS J. C., Le Livre des Mille et Une Nuits, Ed. de la Revue Blanche, aris, 1899–1904.

112 LOMBARD M., L'islam dans sa première grandeur, 1971, op. cit., p. 214.

113 SCHAFER E. H., The Golden Peaches of Samarkand, op. cit., pp. 63–64.

114 SCHAFER E. H., 1963, op. cit., p. 263.

115 LOMBARD M., 1971, op. cit., p. 197.

116 See for example NEEDHAM J., Science and Civilisation in China, vol. 5, part 2, Cambridge, 1974, particularly pp. 134–154.

117 Voyage du marchand arabe Sulayman en Inde et en Chine rédigé en 851, translated from the Arabic by Gabriel FERRAND, Paris, 1922.

118 LOMBARD M., L'islam dans sa première grandeur..., op. cit., pp. 211–213.

119 LOMBARD M., ibid.

120 See NEEDHAM J., op. cit., section 2 of vol. 5: "Spagyrical Discovery and Invention: Magisteries of Gold and Immortality".

121 NEEDHAM, op. cit., pp. 122–123.

122 See note 344 by S. Yerasimos, p. 352 of vol. 2 of the 1980 edition of the French text by Louis Hambis, Marco Polo, Le Devisement du monde, Paris, 1998.

123 Quoted in FRANCK and BROWNSTONE, The Silk Road, a History, Fact on File Publications, New York and Oxford, 1986 p. 239

124 See LE GOFF Jacques, Saint Louis, chapter entitled "L'illusion mongole", Paris, 1996.

125 LE GOFF J., 1996, op. cit.

126 RUBRUCK, William of, The Mission of Friar Willaim of Rubruck, His Journey to the Court of the Great Khan Möngke 1253–1255, translated by Jackson Peter, with notes and introduction by Jackson Peter and Morgan Peter, Hukluyt Society, London, 1990.

127 LE GOFF J., Saint Louis, op. cit.

128 *See note 83 by Yerasimos in the 1980/1998 edition of the French Hambis version of the text*, Le Devisement du monde, *volume 1, chapter 25.*

129 *Subsequent quotes from Marco Polo's text come from the translation by William Marsden*, The Travels of Marco Polo the Venetian, *Doubleday & Co., New York, 1948.*

130 *The quotes from Ibn Battûta come from the English translation by H. A. R. Gibb*, The Travels of Ibn Battûta, AD 1325–1354, *Cambridge Hakluyt Society, vol. 2 pp. 485–486, 497, 503*

131 The Song of Roland, *tr. by John O'Hagan*, Epic and Saga. *New York, P. F. Collier & son [c 1910], Series: Harvard classics ; no. XLIX.*

132 *See among others* HEDDE Ph., *"Notice sur le manuscrit de Théodulfe"*, in Annales de la Société d'agriculture, sciences, arts et commerce du Puy, pour 1837–1838, *Le Puy, 1839, pp. 168–224.*

133 *See* PSEUDO-CALLISTHENES, Le roman d'Alexandre. La vie et les hauts faits d'Alexandre de Macédoine. *Traduit et commenté par Gilles* BOUNOURE *et Blandine* SERRET. *Paris, 1992; chapters 39 and 40 of Book 2.*

134 The Histories, *Book 3.102–5, translated by Aubrey de Sélincourt, revised by A. R. Burn, Penguin Classics, 1954, pp. 246–247.*

135 *See* BOULNOIS L., Poudre d'or et monnaies d'argent au Tibet..., *Paris, 1983, pp. 48–57.*

136 *See* MANDEVILLE John, The travels of Sir John Mandeville, *together with* The Journal of Friar Odoric, *Everyone's Library, 1928 ;* KOHANSKI *Tamarah*, The book of John Mandeville, *an edition of the Pynson text, with commentary on the defective version, Arizona Center for Medieval and Renaissance Studies, 2001.*

137 *Ibn Battûta, vol. 2 pp. 491–492.*

138 *See the note by P.–Y. Badel in his commentary of Marco Polo.* La description du monde, *1998, op. cit., p. 429.*

139 *See note in chapter 35 of the French Hambis edition.*

140 *On this siege, see* ROSSABI M., Khubilai Khan, his Life and Times, *University of California Press, Berkeley, 1988.*

141 ZHAO Rugua, Zhu fan zhi, *translated and annotated by* F. HIRTH *and* W. W. ROCKHILL, Chau Ju-kua: His Work on the Chinese and Arab Trade in the XIIth and XIIIth Centuries, entitled Chu-fan-chi, *St-Petersburg, 1911.*

142 *See* WOOD Frances, Did Marco Polo Go to China?, *Secker and Warburg, London, 1995, pp. 149–151.*

143 The City of Light *by Jacob d'Ancona, translated by David Selbourne, Abacus, 1998.*

144 *See the introductions and Dossier in the French edition*, La cité de lumière, *translated by P. E. Dauzat, Fayard, Paris, 2000.*

145 GROUSSET R., Histoire de la Chine, *Paris, 1942, p. 253.*

146 *See* LELIÈVRE D., Le dragon de lumière, *Paris, 1996.*

147 ROUX J.-P., Les explorateurs au Moyen Age, *Paris, 1985, pp. 131–134.*

148 *See among others* FAVIER J., Philippe le Bel, *Paris, 1978, p. 19.*

149 ROUX J.-P., *op. cit.;* GROUSSET R., Histoire de la Chine, *op. cit., pp. 304–308.*

150 LELIÈVRE D., *op. cit.*

151 GROUSSET R., Histoire de la Chine, *op. cit., p. 324.*

152 MICHEL F., Recherches sur la fabrication et le commerce des étoffes de soie, d'or et d'argent au Moyen Age, *Paris, 1852–1854.*

153 *For more details, see* KENDALL P.M., Louis XI, *Phoenix Press, 2001.*

154 GWYNN R.D., Huguenot Heritage. The History and Contribution of the Huguenots in Britain, *London, 1985.*

155 *In* Les industries de la soierie, *Paris, 1961, p. 16.*

156 Lettres édifiantes et curieuses de Chine par des missionnaires jésuites 1702–1776. *Chronology, introduction, and notes by I. and J.-L. Vissière, Paris, 1979.*

157 CHAMBRE DE COMMERCE DE LYON. *La mission française d'exploration commerciale en Chine (1895–1897), Lyon, 1898.*

158 *See: "Aspects de l'activité agricole et maritime de la Corse à la période de la navigation à voile", 8e partie, dans le* Bulletin de la Société des sciences historiques et naturelles de la Corse, *no. 589, 1968; and* GORSHENINA S., La route de Samarcande, L'Asie centrale dans l'objectif des voyageurs d'autrefois, *Geneva, 2000, pp. 162, 165.*

159 *The production of silk cocoons as a home industry in rural areas in China around 1930 is described by* MAO DUN *in a short story called "Spring Silkworms".*

160 LU XUN, Selected Works, *translated by Yang Xianyi and Gladys Yang, vol. 1, Foreign Languages Press, Beijing, 1980, preface to "Call to Arms" (Nahan), p. 37.*

161 *Article by Y. LE FORESTIER in* Le Figaro, *13–14th August 1994, in an interview of several personalities from the silk world.*

162 Ibid., interview of the head of a team of geneticists from the Institut National de la Recherche Agronomique, l'Unité Nationale Séricicole, based in Lyons.

163 According to an article in Le Monde, dated 11th December 1993.

164 On the Great Game see HOPKIRK Peter, The Great Game, Oxford University Press, Oxford, 1990; MEYER Karl and BRYSAC Shareen, Tournament of Shadows, The Great Game and the Race for Empire in Asia, Little, Brown & Co., London, 1999.

165 HOPKIRK Peter, Foreign Devils on the Silk Road, Oxford University Press, Oxford, 1980.

166 See SARIANIDI V. I., "The Golden Hoard of Bactria", in National Geographic Magazine, no. 3, vol. 177, March 1990, pp. 50–75.

167 Personal communication from Claude RAPIN.

168 See the exhibition catalogue: C. DEBAINE, FRANCFORT et A. IDRISS eds., Keriya, mémoires d'un fleuve. Archéologie et civilisation des oasis du Taklamakan, Paris, 2001.

169 See the article by RASHID Ahmed in the Far Eastern Economic Review, 12th July 1990.

170 RASHID Ahmed, "Asking for Holy War", in the Far Eastern Economic Review, no. 45, vol. 163, 9th November 2000, pp. 28, 30.

171 So far, we have only been able to consult a map of this new line published by N. Becquelin in an article entitled "Xinjiang in the Nineties", published in The China Journal of July 2000.

Right, above: Stucco images of the Buddha surrounded by bodhisattvas and disciples, Dunhuang, China

Right, below: Aurel Stein (centre) with his faithful terrier, Dash, pictured with field companions during March 1908 in the southern Taklamakan east of Hetian. On Stein's right is Chiang who helped negotiate the Dunhuang manuscript 'deal' with the Daoist priest Wang Yuanlu.

161. STUCCO IMAGE GROUP, REPRESENTING BUDDHA BETWEEN DISCIPLES, BODHISATTVAS, AND DVARAPALAS, IN CAVE-TEMPLE CH. III., 'THOUSAND BUDDHAS' SITE.

296. MY COMPANIONS AND MYSELF AT ULUGH-MAZAR, IN THE DESERT NORTH OF CHIRA.

From left to right, sitting : Chiang-ssŭ-yeh, myself with 'Dash,' Rai Bahadur Lal Singh. Standing : Ibrahim Beg, Jasvant Singh, Naik Ram Singh.

The Silk Road Today

Gateway to the Mogao Caves at Dunhuang (Wong)

Travelling the Silk Road

Bradley Mayhew graduated in Oriental Studies (Chinese) from Wadham College, Oxford University in 1992. He has travelled and trekked across Chinese and Russian Central Asia, Tibet, Iran, Mongolia and Ladakh. He has worked as a consultant for several travel companies and has led adventure tours along the Silk Road. He is also the author/co-author of the Odyssey guide to Uzbekistan, as well as over a dozen Lonely Planet guides, including those to Central Asia, Tibet, Mongolia, Shanghai and Southwest China, and has lectured on Central Asia to the Royal Geographical Society. He currently lives in Montana, USA.

*A*nyone who has read tales of Silk Road merchants, Buddhist pilgrims and Central Asian explorers, or marvelled at the exploits of Alexander the Great, Sven Hedin or Marco Polo, will at some point have wondered what it must be like to travel in their footsteps to those distant, exotic and almost mythical lands. Most of us who have fondled a creased map of inner Asia have traced our fingers in wonder over its monochrome yellow deserts and white glacial peaks. Murmuring the words 'Samarkand', 'Bactria' or 'Kashgaria', names so resonant with history that they simply define the exotic and remote, is enough to quicken the pulse of a certain type of traveller.

The good news for all of us seduced by the romance of the Silk Road is that these outlandish lands have never been more reachable. Today's travellers need not raise an expedition to reach the cave art of Dunhuang, nor dodge bands of roving slave traders to taste Turkestan's forbidden fruits. Tourists to Central Asia can sleep in a converted caravanserai or ride one of Ferghana's famous horses out to an eco-friendly yurt camp. Anyone with the requisite fistful of visas can take the golden road to Samarkand, travel by rail across the Eurasian landmass or journey by jeep over the high snowswept passes of the Tian Shan.

Central Asia is indeed an epic canvas crisscrossed by the ghosts of past travellers. From hardy pilgrims like Xuanzang and Faxian to marauding figures like Tamerlane and Genghis Khan, the modern tourist travels always in the footsteps of history. Stand at the base of Bukhara's Kalyan Minaret and feel a frisson of excitement when you remember that Genghis Khan once stood less

Left: A mulberry tree stands in the courtyard of the Kalyan Mosque with the Kalyan Minaret soaring to the right, Bukhara, Uzbekistan. (Grover)

than a stone's throw away. It's not difficult to catch echoes of a Sogdian trader in the faces of today's Tajik merchants, or glimpse the Turkic hordes in the eyes of a Kyrgyz or Kazak nomad.

The Silk Road is more than a string of tourist sites; it's a journey between cultures. As you progress along the Silk Road the land shifts and faces change; cheekbones rise and fall and noses become more prominent; eyes change hue and hats change shape. Chinese yields to Indo-European, and Turkic mixes with Persian, as Central Asia bleeds into the Middle East.

If you are ready to book your trip to the Silk Road but are not quite sure where that airport is exactly, the first conundrum to come to terms with is that there is no Silk Road; at least no single route, or road. Modern travellers have to cobble together a route based on issues such as transport, budget, security and visas, just as the original traders did. This chapter offers some pointers on how to do that and suggests sources of additional information.

If you do decide to make a Silk Road journey then expect some mediocre hotels, questionable food and volatile politics. But come prepared also to be

seduced by the graceful hand-over-the-heart greeting of a turbaned Uzbek elder and bewitched by the sophistication of an azure Timurid dome. Few journeys shimmer in the distance with such romance and expectation.

ITINERARIES

The Silk Road was a trans-continental network of routes that stretched for thousands of miles. Traders would never cover more than one or two legs at a stretch before handing over to other local middlemen and the modern traveller would be wise to take heed. Concentrate on a section and leave wanting to come back for more.

Air Hubs

To get to Xi'an you'll have to fly to Beijing, Shanghai or Hong Kong and catch a domestic flight. Urumqi has international flight connections to and from Islamabad, Tashkent, Almaty, Bishkek and Dushanbe, as well as domestic flights to destinations all over Xinjiang and throughout China. Tashkent is Central Asia's major air hub, closely followed by Almaty, though there are a few international flights to Bishkek and Ashgabat.

For schedules see the following airline websites:

www.air-astana.kz

www.airchina.com.cn/english

www.britishmediterranean.com

www.cxa.web.ur.ru (Xinjiang Airlines)

www.flyariana.com/ (Afghan Ariana)

www.klm.com

www.lufthansa.com

www.tajikistan-airlines.com

www.thy.com (Turkish Airlines)

www.turkmenistanairlines.com

www.uzbekistanairways.com or www.uzbekistan-airways.biz/

Left: Kyrgyz horsemen play tug-of-war with a goat carcass, Xinjiang, China. (Wong)

Following pages: The massive fortress of Jiayuguan marks the western extremity of the Great Wall of China, Gansu province, China. (Wong)

CHINA

The classic route along the Chinese Silk Road generally starts in Xi'an, China's first true imperial capital, and travels along the Hexi Corridor, edging between the Gobi and the Tibetan Plateau, up into Chinese Turkestan, currently known as Xinjiang.

Xi'an is famously home to the Terracotta Warriors of Qin Shihuangdi but has many more archaeological treasures to offer so allow a couple of days here.

Most itineraries then take an overnight train to **Lanzhou**, on the dusty banks of the Yellow River, and make a visit to the provincial museum and a night market. From June to October it should be possible to take the two-hour boat trip to the Buddhist caves of Bingling Si. If you have a couple of days up your sleeve, the huge Tibetan monastery of Labrang and the Hui Muslim town of Linxia combine to offer an excellent side trip south.

From Lanzhou an overnight train runs to Jiayuguan and the spectacularly located fortress that marked the symbolic end of the Chinese Empire at

Jiayuguan Pass. A half-day side trip to the westernmost end of the Great Wall offers a fine counterpoint if you visited the eastern wall near Beijing.

Another overnight train (or summertime flight) replaces the three-week plod faced by Silk Road camel caravans, passing through the ruined beacon towers of the Jade Gate (Yumen) to Liuyuan. From here it's two hours by bus to one of the artistic highlights of western China, the **Mogao Caves of Dunhuang**.

Next stop Xinjiang. Yet another overnight train or flight takes you 400 kilometres to Urumqi or Turfan. Urumqi is a modern Chinese city that rarely stirs the soul. **Turfan**, however, is a charming and relaxed Uighur town, lined with shady trellises covered in vines. Excellent and easily arranged side trips to the ruins of Karakhoja (Gaochang), Yarkhoto (Jiaohe), the Bezeklik Caves and Astana Tombs offer plenty of diversions, and you can reward your sightseeing efforts with a cold Xinjiang beer or a bottle of locally produced sweet and fruity red Loulan wine.

Above: Bazaar at Kucha, Xinjiang, China (Wong)
Left: Bezeklik Caves, Xinjiang, China (Wong)

From Turfan or Urumqi there are two main routes to Kashgar. The northern route is the more established, passing through Kucha and Korla. The southern route is a more arduous route along the southern underbelly of the Taklamakan Desert, passing the archaeological sites frequented by Aurel Stein and Albert von Le Coq. The railway link to Kashgar was opened in 1999 and now offers a comfortable overnight train ride from Urumqi.

Kucha has an interesting Friday bazaar and those with a deeper interest in Serindian art can hire transport (around US$50 for a half day) through CITS to several cave complexes such as Kizil, Kizil Kara, Kumtura and the ruined town of Subashi.

Kashgar is without doubt one of the most interesting towns in Central Asia. Its fantastic Sunday bazaar, the most interesting in Asia, may now be overrun with tourists but the town's backstreets shelter the cultural soul of the Uighur people, making this an endlessly fascinating city.

Off the Beaten Track

If you like getting off the beaten track consider these offbeat gems, though bear in mind that the hassles of independent travel increase in proportion to the distance you travel off the main tourist routes.

Khotan is a rewarding destination. Its Sunday market rivals Kashgar's, the old town is partly intact and the nearby ruined Silk Road towns of Melikawat and Yotkan are relatively easy to visit with a taxi driver and guide. In contrast you'll need travel agency help to arrange a trip to the ruins of Niya or Rawak as special permission (and high fees) are required. Overnight buses run from Urumqi along the desert highway and mercifully there are also daily flights. Buses run on to Kashgar but it's better to stop in the interesting Uighur bazaar towns of Karghilik and Yarkand en route.

The **Maijishan** grottoes, south of the train line at Tianshui, half way between Xi'an and Lanzhou, constitute China's fourth largest Buddhist cave complex, scenically carved on the side of a circular outcrop. Getting there can be a bit inconvenient.

Clockwise from top right: Silk cocoons being boiled to loosen the sericin; Uighur man weaving their traditional silk ikat; a wooden wheel for reeling silk hangs on the wall with woven silk ikat; Uighur woman throws and twists silk thread. (Wong)

CENTRAL ASIA

If you decide to travel overland between China and Central Asia you have several choices. From Kashgar there are three main onward routes; to Pakistan over the Khunjerab Pass and down the spectacular Karakoram Highway; or to Kyrgyzstan over the Torugart or Irkeshtam passes. The Torugart is one of the most exciting and scenic ways into Central Asia but finicky border requirements mean travellers need to arrange transport in advance on both sides of the border through a travel agency in order for border guards to allow you to cross.

In 2003 the Irkeshtam Pass between China and Kyrgyzstan opened, thus allowing a more direct (and authentic) Silk Road route between Kashgar, Osh and the Ferghana Valley of Uzbekistan. The route offers glimpses of such Pamir giants as Peak Lenin (7,134 metres) and best of all, there are none of the logistical complications attached to the Torugart Pass. This route allows the traveller to take the Pamir Highway from Dushanbe in Tajikistan to Sary Tash in the Kyrgyz Alai Valley, cross the Irkeshtam Pass to Kashgar and then take the Karakoram Highway to Tashkurgan and Pakistan, making this probably the world's greatest mountain drive. A minor detour from this road takes you along the Wakhan Valley and the Shugnan branch of the Silk Road. Marco Polo travelled along this valley before crossing the Sarikol Pamir into what is now modern-day Xinjiang.

A fourth road exists between the Karakoram Highway in China, north of Tashkurgan, and Murghab in the Gorno-Badakhshan region of Tajikistan, over the 4,362-metre Qolma Pass. The Chinese authorities have not yet opened this road to international traffic but when they do (and this should be soon) travellers will be able to travel directly along the Pamir Highway from Dushanbe to Murghab and then join the Karakoram Highway near Tashkurgan, making this another superbly scenic option.

Coming back to earth, the most reliable crossing into Central Asia is from Urumqi, either by train or bus through the Dzungarian Gap. Direct trains run between Urumqi and the cosmopolitan Kazak city of Almaty, or you can break

Right: Khiva's Tash Khauli Palace, completed in 1838, comprises three courtyards. Five decorative halls, or iwans, *are the highlight of the third and largest courtyard, which was the harem. (Grover)*

the trip at the Uighur town of Yining in the Yili Valley, stopping at gorgeous Sayram Lake en route.

For Silk Road khanates, beaconing minarets, cloistered bazaars and epic Islamic architecture, Uzbekistan forms very much the heartland of Central Asia. Tashkent is a largely Soviet creation, rebuilt after a massive 1966 earthquake. Tamerlane's capital at **Samarkand** contains the region's most audacious architecture and the name alone resonates with romantic allure. The town's huge Registan Square and ruined Bibi Khamun Mosque are joined by some of the region's most exquisite artistic touches at the tombs of the Shah-i-Zindah.

Descend the steps into the crypt of the Gur-i-Emir to touch Tamerlane's tomb.

The most atmospheric of the Silk Road cities is without doubt **Bukhara**, whose old town backstreets hide a wealth of hidden tombs, shrines and madrassahs. Must-sees include the Ark, formerly home to the Emir of Bukhara; the Kalyan Minaret, which stopped Genghis Khan in his tracks in 1220; and the gorgeous decoration of the Ismael Samani Mausoleum— it's worth planning a couple of extra days here. Stay in one of the many stylish bed and breakfasts in the old town and take tea with the *aksakals* ('white beards', or elders) of the poolside Lyab-i-Hauz teahouse.

The remotest of the khanates was **Khiva** and today it's a flight or long drive across the monotonous and stony Kara Kum Desert. The most intact of the Central Asian citadels, it's also the most sterile, having been preserved by the Soviets as an open air museum. A long day trip from Khiva could take you to Kunya-Urgench, once one of the Islamic world's major intellectual centres until razed by Mongols in the 13th century, but this raises some bureaucratic headaches as it requires a Turkmen visa.

Many people head home from Uzbekistan, taking advantage of Tashkent's international air connections, but it is possible to continue into the bizarre republic of Turkmenistan, dominated by the personality cult of President Saparmurat Niyazov, 'Father of the Turkmen'. With a visa it's not too difficult to stop in **Merv** (Mary) to visit the impressive Seljuk-era Sultan Sanjar Mausoleum. The Turkmen capital **Ashgabat** holds few draws except for its colourful Tolkuchka Bazaar and the chance to shop for a 'Bukhara' carpet. To get a Turkmen tourist visa you need a visa invitation and are currently required to hire a guide for the duration of your time in the country.

Off the Beaten Track

If you are headed to or from the Torugart Pass, a stop at the almost perfect **Tash Rabat Caravanserai** in Kyrgyzstan is an absolute must (you can stay in a basic yurt camp here for a couple of dollars). Son-Kul is a beautiful high-altitude lake, fringed with shepherd's yurts and herders, a short detour off the main highway from the pass to the capital Bishkek. Along this route you could also visit the Burana Tower and the petroglyphs of Cholpan-Ata. Explorers can get travel agency help in Karakol to seek out the remote Bedel Pass, a one-time Silk Road thoroughfare.

Tamerlane's home town of **Shakhrisabz** is a good day trip from Samarkand. This traditional Uzbek town has the ruins of some of Tamerlane's most monumental architecture. With travel agency help (and a Tajik visa) another day trip runs to the Sogdian city of Penjikent just over the border. Tajikistan is a little-known gem that offers some of the most spectacular mountain scenery in Asia.

Preceding pages: Tash Rabat Caravanserai between Naryn and the Torugart Pass, Kyrgyzstan (Grover)

Hire a car or taxi along the golden road between Samarkand and Bukhara and you can fit in stops at the impressive portal of the Rabat-i-Malik Caravanserai and the rarely visited tapering minaret of Vabkent.

Those with a special interest in archaeology have two options for some exploring. From Khiva it's possible to hire transport to the 2,000-year-old ruins of Toprak Kala or Ayaz Kala, where you can stay in desert yurts. Real die-hards could consider a trip to strategically sensitive Termez, on the Afghan border. The town has several archaeological sites that date from the earliest movements of Buddhism into the region.

If stability improves in Afghanistan it will be possible to continue south to Mazar-i-Sharif, and on to the near mythical Silk Road lands of Balkh and Bactria, but at the end of 2003, the nearest reliable land crossing to Afghanistan is through southern Tajikistan. Currently, the safest places to visit within Afghanistan are Kabul, the destroyed Buddhas of Bamiyan and the glorious former Timurid capital of Herat.

WESTWARDS FROM CENTRAL ASIA: MASHAD TO ISTANBUL

Despite the ethnic, historical and artistic links that bind Central Asia to Persia, crossing from Turkmenistan into Iran remains a little-travelled option. The easiest way (assuming you have an Iranian visa) is to fly from Ashgabat to the holy Shia city of Mashad, from where you can continue overland. By land there are two road border crossings (again if you have the

Little Buddha of Bamiyan, Afghanistan

requisite visas), at Serakhs and Bajgiran. You'll need to arrange transport or take one of the shared taxis to/from both borders.

One interesting diversion from Mashad is to the fine Rabat Sharif Caravanserai near Serakhs on the Turkmen border. Further west is the town of Nishapur and the tomb of Persian poet Omar Khayam. Also worth a stop en route to Tehran is the Gonbad-e-Kabus, a remarkable funeral tower that rises sheer from the Turkmen plain.

Iran's most glorious sites—Isfahan, Shiraz, Persepolis, Yazd and the ruined city of Bam—lie well south of the most direct overland route across Iran but shouldn't be missed, so this is the time for some detours. (Tragically, Bam was levelled by an earthquake in December 2003.) Despite media perceptions of the country the Iranian people are some of the most hospitable and welcoming in the world, though women should respect certain dress codes. With Iraq currently off-limits to travellers, the main overland route swings north-west to Tabriz (with its famous mosque) and crosses into Turkey's Kurdish south-west.

One other offbeat option is to travel westwards from Turkmenistan via the Caucasus, though this raises its own visa and security problems. Ferries sail across the Caspian Sea between Turkmenbashi and Baku in Azerbaijan, from where you can wind your way through the mountain valleys of Mskhetia to Tbilisi in Georgia and either on to the Russian Volga or to the beautiful north-eastern region of Turkey, with its ruined Armenian cathedrals and Black Sea port at Trabzon. The Selim Caravanserai in the Vayots Dzor region of southern Armenia is probably the best preserved Silk Road site in this region.

Georgian girls in traditional dress

Decorative courtyard of the 17th-century mosque of Masjed-e Emam, Isfahan, Iran (Grover)

SILK ROAD BY RAIL

The 'Iron Silk Road' offers trips of an epic proportion only rivalled by its more famous cousin, the Trans-Siberian railway. Rail is definitely the most convenient way to travel through China up the Hexi Corridor from Lanzhou to Turfan or Urumqi. A recent spur now continues 24 hours on to Kashgar. From Urumqi there are also two trains a week to Almaty (40 hours), via part of the Turksib railway. From Almaty, lines continue down to Tashkent and on to Khiva or Ashgabat. Epic transcontinental routes converge from the major Central Asian capitals to Moscow, taking in the transition from Asia to Europe at a clanking 60 kilometres per hour.

Boosters have been trying for years now to pull together a rail connection from Tashkent/Ashgabat to Iran but at the time of writing, endless wrangling over transit regulations meant that the single international test run has never been repeated.

In general, Central Asian trains are not as safe or comfortable as those in China. Currently the only train frequented much by tourists is the overnight run from Tashkent to Bukhara. Occasional tourist charter trains traverse the region in style.

Jiaohe, west of Turfan, Xinjiang, China (Wong)

Organized Tours and Travel Websites

The following companies offer Silk Road tours of some description or another and can arrange private itineraries:

Exodus, 9 Weir Rd, London SW12 OLT, UK, tel (020) 8675 5550, email info@exodus.co.uk, www.exodus.co.uk; 21 days Tashkent to Beijing over the Torugart Pass, tours in Iran and Tibet/Chinese Silk Road combinations.

Explore, 1 Frederick St, Aldershot, Hants GU11 1LQ, UK, tel (01252) 319448, email info@explore.co.uk, www.explore.co.uk; 25-day Beijing–Bukhara trip and interesting Central Asia and Xinjiang loops.

Geographic Expeditions, 2627 Lombard St, San Francisco, CA 94123, USA, tel (800) 7778183, email info@geoex.com, www.geoex.com

MIR Corporation, 85 South Washington St, Suite 210, Seattle WA 98104, USA, tel (206) 6247289, (800) 424 7289, email info@mircorp.com, www.mircorp.com

Regent Holidays, 15 John St, Bristol BS1 2HR, UK, tel (0117) 921 1711, email regent@regent-holidays.co.uk, www.regent-holidays.co.uk

Silk Road Tours, Vancouver, Canada, tel (1-888) 881-7455, (604) 925 3831, email travel@silkroadtours.com, www.silkroadtours.com; Iran travel specialists with Silk Road tours.

Silk Road Tours, 371 Kensington High Street, London W14 8QZ, UK, tel (020) 7603 1246, email sales@silkroadtours.co.uk, www.silkroadtours.co.uk

Silk Road Travel Management Ltd, Suite 1602, Chinachem Century Tower, 178 Gloucester Road, Wanchai, Hong Kong, tel (+852) 2736 8828, fax (+852) 2736 8000, email webmaster@the-silk-road.com, www.the-silk-road.com

Silk Steps, Tyndale House, 7 High St, Chipping Sodbury, Bristol, BS37 6BA, UK, tel (01454) 888850, fax (01454) 888851, email info@silksteps.co.uk, www.silksteps.co.uk/

Steppes East, 51 Castle Street, Cirencester, Gloucestershire GL7 1QD, UK, tel (01285) 651010, fax (01285) 885888, email sales@steppeseast.co.uk, www.steppeseast.co.uk

Archway at the remains of Hadrian's Temple on the Curetes Way, Ephesus, Turkey (Woolfitt)

Sundowners Travel, Suite 15, Lonsdale Court, 600 Lonsdale Street, Melbourne 3000, Australia, tel (03) 9672 5300, fax (03) 9672 5311, www.sundownerstravel.com

The Trans-Siberian Express Company, 2 Tabley Court, Moss Lane, Over Tabley, Knutsford, Cheshire WA16 0PL, UK, tel (01565) 754 540, fax (01565) 634 172, email mail@gwtravel.co.uk, www.gwtravel.co.uk

Wild Frontiers Adventure Travel Ltd, 40a, Peterborough Road, London SW6 3BN, UK, tel (020) 7736 3968, fax (020) 7751 0710, email office@wildfrontiers. co.uk, www.wildfrontiers.co.uk

Travel Agencies for Central Asia

The following agencies can organize part or all of your trip through the Central Asian region. They and their websites are a good source of information, travel information and visa invitations, and can help with accommodation and transport bookings.

ARMENIA

Armintour, 1 P. Byuzand Street, Yerevan, 375010, Armenia, tel (3741) 582282, email armint@arminco.com

AZERBAIJAN

Improtex Travel, 16 Samed Vurgun Street, Baku, 370000, Azerbaijan, tel (99412) 931728, email improlcc@intrans.az

GEORGIA

Caucasus Travel, 5/7 Shavteli Street, Tbilisi, 380005, Georgia, tel (995 32) 987400, email georgia@caucasustravel.com, www.caucasustravel.com (site under construction at time of going to press)

IRAN

Iran Pars Tour Operator, IPTO Building, 1/F No. 12, 13th Street, Miremad, Motahari Avenue, Tehran, Iran, tel (9821) 8737135, 8737087, email iranparstour@apadana.com

Pasargad Tours, 146 Africa Avenue, Tehran, 19156, Iran, tel (9821) 2058833, email info@pasargad-tour.com, www.pasargad-tour.com

KAZAKHSTAN

Stantours, Kunyaeva 163/76, Almaty, Kazakhstan, tel (3272) 631344, email info@stantours.com, www.stantours.com

Turan-Asia, 66/8 Ablay Khan Avenue, Almaty, 480004, Kazakhstan, tel (3272) 730371, 730596, email turanasiakaz@asdc.kz, www.turanasia.kz

KYRGYZSTAN

Asia Silk Tours, Kievskaya 23–19, Bishkek, Kyrgyzstan, tel (996-312) 624361, email contact@centralasiatravel.com, www.centralasiatravel.com

Celestial Mountains, Kievskaya 131–2 , Bishkek, Kyrgyzstan, tel (996 312) 21-25-62, email celest@infotel.kg, www.celestial.com.kg

ITMC Tien-Shan, 1–a Molodaia Gvardia St, Bishkek, Kyrgyzstan, tel (996 312) 651404, 651221, email itmc@elcat.kg, www.itmc.centralasia.kg/

Kyrgyz Concept, 100 Razzakov St, Bishkek, Kyrgyzstan, tel (996 312) 661331, 210556, email akc@elcat.kg, www.concept.kg/about/

TURKMENISTAN

Ayan Travel, 108-2/4 Magtumkuli Ave, Ashgabat, Turkmenistan, tel (993-12) 352914, 350797, email info@ayan-travel.com, www.ayan-travel.com

DN Tour, 48/1 Magtumguly Ave, Ashgabat, Turkmenistan, tel (99312) 470121, 479217, email dntour@online.tm, www.dntour.com

Latif, 36A Khoudaiberdiev St, Ashgabat, Turkmenistan, tel (99312) 415077, 415087, email info@turkmenistan-travel.com, www.turkmenistan-travel.com/

TAJIKISTAN

Great Game Travel, 19 Echo Hill, Royston, Herts SG8 9BB, UK, tel/fax (1763) 220049, email michael@thegreatgame.co.uk, www.greatgametravel.co.uk, www.traveltajikistan.com

Sayoh-Tajikistan State National Travel Company, 14 Pushkin Street, Dushanbe 734095, Tajikistan, tel/fax: (992-372) 231401, email sayoh@traveltajikistan.com, www.traveltajikistan.com/sayoh

UZBEKISTAN

Asia Travel, 91 Chilanzor St, Tashkent, Uzbekistan, tel (998-71) 1735107, email attour@online.ru, www.asia-travel.uz

Semi-nomadic herders journey each summer to this lofty lake, the Son-Kul, in Kyrgyzstan. (Grover)

Dolores Tour, Ivleva kochasi 14, Tashkent, Uzbekistan, tel (998-71) 1208877, email info@dolorestour.com, www.sambuh.com, www.advantour.com/

Great Silk Road Tour Operators Group, 1, Kuk-Saray Sq., Samarkand, 703057, Uzbekistan, tel (998-662) 331735, 332770, fax (998-662) 311735, email silk@intal.uz, www.silktour.uz

Sairam Tourism, 13-a Movarounahr St, Tashkent, Uzbekistan, tel (998-71) 1337411, 1333559, email silkroad@sairamtour.com.uz

Salom Travel, Bukhara, Uzbekistan, www.salomtravel.com/

Sogda Tour, 1 Kuk-Saray Sq, Samarkand, Uzbekistan, tel (998-662) 331735, email silk@naytov.com, www.silktour.uz

XINJIANG
Caravan Cafe, 120 Seman Road, Kashgar, Xinjiang, PRC 844000, tel (86 998) 298 1864, 298 2196, email info1@caravancafe.com, www.caravancafe.com, www.asianexplorations.com

WHEN TO GO

Central Asia's continental climate translates into extremes of temperatures. Summer brings sizzling heat to much of the region, particularly the deserts of Xinjiang, Turkmenistan, Uzbekistan and Iran, while much of Central Asia freezes solid in sub-Siberian winters. April/May and September/October are the premium times to make a trip if high-altitude trekking is not in your itinerary. The catch is that the Khunjerab Pass (between China and Pakistan) is only open between May and October and the Torugart and Irkeshtam crossings are only reliable during similar dates, even though they are technically open year-round.

A Christian gets directions from a Muslim on the road between Marmaris and Dalayan in Turkey. (Woolfitt)

Accommodation: Modern-Day Caravanserais

Standards of accommodation along the Silk Road have improved greatly in recent years. Most Chinese towns have comfortable three star accommodation which though not luxurious offers clean rooms, hot water and decent dining. For a taste of upmarket but traditional-style accommodation, the Silk Road Hotel Management Co. Ltd., owned by Silk Road aficionado Peter Wong, offers a unique experience of 'culture hotels' in Dunhuang, Xining and Turfan (www. the-silk-road.com/hotel).

The major Central Asian cities have international standard hotels such as the Hyatt in Bishkek, Intercontinental, Sheraton and Le Meridien in Tashkent and others. The smaller Uzbek towns of Samarkand and Bukhara offer an excellent collection of bed & breakfasts, with prices around US$20 per night. Beyond this there is a scattering of private hotels. Bottom of the heap are the old Soviet hotels which offer little more than broken fittings, bad plumbing and suspicious service.

There are a few gems, such as the Hotel Khiva, whose rooms occupy the former student cells of the Amin Khan Madrassah in Khiva's old town and the Chini Bagh in Kashgar, in the grounds of the former British consulate and steeped in the history of the Great Game.

Food

Even in Gansu and Xinjiang you'll find Chinese food omnipresent, often in the shape of Hui (Chinese Muslim) noodles. Lanzhou-style noodles are famous throughout the country; watch the noodles being stretched and pulled by hand as they have been since before pasta was even a glimmer in an Italian mind.

The quintessential Central Asian meal runs along the lines of a round of grilled mutton *shashlyk* (kebabs) on a plate of hot sesame seed nan bread, followed by sweet Turfan grapes or a Hami melon, washed down with a cold Xinjiang beer or a pot of

kok chai (green tea). The introduction of Middle Eastern spices like cumin are just one thing you can thank the Silk Road for. Xinjiang-style *suoman* is available everywhere and mixes Mediterranean tomatoes and peppers with Chinese noodle squares, stir-fried in a wok; an early form of fusion cuisine. Hot *gizhde* nan are bagel-like rolls, delicious when hot straight out of the oven.

The welcome effect of Chinese culinary influence ends abruptly at the old Soviet borders, where a more malign Russian influence takes hold. In ex-Soviet Central Asia the kebabs seem ropier, the dumplings greasier and the Soviet canteen smell more pervasive, just one reason for the growing popularity of Turkish restaurants in all the Central Asian republics. One traveller described ex-Soviet Central Asian cuisine, not entirely unfairly, as a choice between mutton fat with rice (*plov*), mutton fat on a stick (*shashlyk*) or mutton fat in a soup (*shorpa*).

Iran brings a more sophisticated cuisine, benefiting from the introduction of rose water, pistachio and saffron. Kebabs are joined by yoghurt, stews (*khoresht*) and fragrant pilaus.

Above: Uighur men dry raisins in a mud hut in Turfan (Wong)
Left: Buying nan bread at a typical food market in Xinjiang (Wong)

VISAS

As far as red tape is concerned, the high point for Silk Road travellers came just after the Mongol invasions in the 13th century. The subsequent *pax mongolica* meant that a traveller could travel the breadth of Asia with only one 'visa', a golden plaque issued by the Mongol khans.

Today even the splintering of the Soviet Empire has done little to facilitate entry requirements in the region, which run the gamut from a convenient formality (Kyrgyzstan, China and Uzbekistan) to requiring advance planning (Kazakhstan and Tajikistan) to downright obstuctionist (Iran and Turkmenistan). Currently citizens of most Western countries do not need an invitation to get visas for Kyrgyzstan, China, Turkey and, most recently, Uzbekistan. Invitations are required for Iran, Kazakhstan, Turkmenistan and Tajikistan. Travel agents can help for a fee, particularly if you book some travel arrangements with them. A multi-country Silk Road trip will require months of visa hunting so leave plenty of time.

EMBASSY WEBSITES

The following websites offer visa guidelines:
Afghanistan
www.embassyofafghanistan.org/

China:
www.china-embassy.org
www.chinese-embassy.org.uk

Kazakhstan
www.kazakhembus.com/

Kyrgyzstan:
www.kyrgyz-embassy.org.uk
www.kyrgyzstan.org

Tajikistan:
www.tjus.org
www.botschft-tadschikistan.de/

Turkmenistan:

www.turkmenistanembassy.org/
www.britishembassytm.org.uk/

Uzbekistan:

www.uzbekconsulny.org
www.uzbekistan.org
www.uzbekistanembassy.uk.net/
www.uzbekistan.de/

TRAVEL ADVISORIES

The Silk Road traverses some volatile parts of the world, as indeed it always has done. Silk route travellers have for centuries adapted their travel routes to avoid bandits and detour around hostile empires, and today's travellers will have to do likewise. Plague and war are almost as current in the 21st century as they were in the 5th.

To get an idea of the security in the areas you intend to travel through, it's necessary to piece together information from various sources. Do a search on news stories for those regions to get a feel for the political climate. Check the **British Foreign and Commonwealth Office** (www.fco.gov.uk/travel), **US State Department** (www.travel.state.gov/travel_warnings.html) or **Australian Department of Foreign Affairs and Trade** (www.dfat.gov.au/travel/) for up-to-the-minute advice, travel warnings and consular information sheets. They offer a detailed breakdown of regions, not just states, though they tend to err on the side of caution. At time of going to press, all three advise against travel to Afghanistan and Iraq, and all three recommend caution when travelling to Tajikistan, particularly the border areas.

GENERAL INFORMATION WEBSITES

The Central Asian travel agency websites (see earlier) generally offer the best travel overviews. The following websites are also useful:

www.kabulcaravan.com (Excellent travel site on Afghanistan)

www.kabulguide.com (Focused practical information on visiting Kabul)

www.silk-road.com (Online Silk Road learning by the Silk Road Foundation, with lectures and historical articles, and links with a scholarly bent; the practical information is dated)

www.silkroadproject.org (Yo Yo Ma's Silk Road Project, with lots to explore in this labyrinthine site)

www.times.kg (The Times of Central Asia—a first-rate news site on Central Asia, though you need to subscribe to get the full stories. Based in Bishkek, Kyrgyzstan)

www.eurasianet.org (News stories, cultural items and some travel links)

www.asia.si.edu/exhibitions/online/silkroad/default.htm

www.asia.si.edu/exhibitions/online/cave/default.htm

www.asia.si.edu/exhibitions/online/luxuryarts/default.htm (Arts of the Freer and Sackler Silk Road galleries from the National Museum of Asian Art)

www.depts.washington.edu/uwch/silkroad/exhibit/index.shtml (Online Exhibitions of Art of the Silk Road at the Seattle Museum)

www.depts.washington.edu/uwch/silkroad/index.shtml (Online information on the Silk Road in Central Asia)

www.silkroaddance.com/ (Silk Road Dance Troupe)

http://idp.bl.uk/ (International Dunhuang Project. Excellent, though somewhat complicated, site with interesting background text and searchable database of Dunhuang images spread around the world)

http://203.10.106.20/hsc/textiles/default.htm (Textile Arts of Central Asia at the Powerhouse Museum in Australia)

www.unesco.org/culture/silkroads/ (UNESCO)

www.askasia.org/silk_roads/SilkIndx.htm (Teacher's kits for Silk Road study)

www.silkroadtog.com (Silk Road Tour Operators Group; with a newsletter and links to member travel agencies)

Oxiana is an email list devoted to travel in Central Asia. Once you've joined (send a blank message to oxiana-subscribe@yahoogroups.com) you can read articles pertaining to the region and post travel-related queries.

TRAVEL-RELATED BOOKS
Guidebooks

Odyssey's *Silk Road* guide is a detailed guide to the Chinese section of the Silk Road. Odyssey also publishes individual guides to *Mongolia*, *Uzbekistan*, *Kyrgyzstan*, *Iran*, *Georgia* and *Turkey*, and an upcoming Silk Road map. For additional practical travel information, Lonely Planet produces a *Central Asia* guide (3rd edition 2004) , as well as a useful *Central Asia Phrasebook*. Trailblazer do a nuts and bolts *Silk Road by Rail* and a new general guidebook to *The Silk Roads*, aimed very much at backpackers.

Armchair Reading

The following is a short list of recommended travel literature that is essential reading material for any Silk Road adventure:

Bissell, Tom, *Chasing the Sea*, Pantheon, 2003

Byron, Robert, *The Road to Oxiana*, Oxford University Press, 1982

Danziger, Nick, *Danziger's Travels: Beyond Forbidden Frontiers*, Harpercollins, 2002

Elliott, Jason, *An Unexpected Light: Travels in Afghanistan*, Picador, 2001

Fleming, Peter, *News from Tartary: A Journey from Peking to Kashmir*, Northwestern University Press, 1999

Glazebrook, Phillip, *Journey to Khiva: A Writer's Search for Central Asia*, Kodansha International, 1996

Hedin, Sven, *My Life As an Explorer: The Great Adventurer's Classic Memoir*, Kodansha International, 1996

Hopkirk, Kathleen, *A Traveller's Companion to Central Asia*, John Murray

Kaplan, Robert D, *Eastward to Tartary*, Vintage Departures, 2001

Knobloch, Edgar, *Monuments of Central Asia: A Guide to the Archaeology, Art and Architecture of Turkestan*, I.B. Tauris, 2001

Kremmer, Christopher, *The Carpet Wars: From Kabul to Baghdad: A Ten-Year Journey Along Ancient Trade Routes*, Ecco, 2002

Maclean Fitzroy, *Eastern Approaches*, Puffin, 2000

Thubron, Colin, *The Lost Heart of Asia*, Perennial, 2000

Walker, Annabel, *Aurel Stein: Pioneer of the Silk Road*, Hong Kong University Press, 1999

Whitfield, Susan, *Life Along the Silk Road*, University of California Press, 2001

Wood, Frances, *The Silk Road: Two Thousand Years in the Heart of Asia*, University of California Press, October 2003

Wriggins, Sally Hovey, *Xuanzang: A Buddhist Pilgrim on the Silk Road*, Westview Press, 1998

Large Format Art & Photo Books

Harvey, Janet & Rivers, Victoria Z, *Traditional Textiles of Central Asia*, Thames & Hudson, 1997

Juliano, Annette L, Lerner, Judith A & Alram, Michael, *Monks and Merchants: Silk Road Treasures from Northwest China*, (large format to accompany exhibition of the same name), Harry N Abrams, 2001

Ma Yo Yo et al, *Along the Silk Road* (Asian Art & Culture (no. 6), University of Washington Press, March 2002

Sumner, Christina & Feltham Heleanor, *Beyond the Silk Road: Arts of Central Asia*, Publishers' Group West, 2000; in conjunction with Australia's Powerhouse Museum's collection of Central Asian arts and crafts

Tucker, Jonathan B, *The Silk Road: Art and History*, Philip Wilson Publishers, 2003

Weng, Wei-Chuan, et al, *Bazaars of Chinese Turkestan: Life and Trade Along the Old Silk Road*, Oxford University Press, 1997

Yamashita, Michael, *Marco Polo: A Photographer's Journey*, White Star Publishers, 2002

Both Nelles and Viaggi dell' Elefante produce good maps of Central Asia.

A treasure trove of books, from left to right, top: Jonathan Tucker's The Silk Road: Art and History, celebrating the cultural heritage of countries on the Silk Road; Along the Silk Road, celebrating the music, art and history of the Silk Road past and present; and Michael Yamashita's highly acclaimed photographic journal of his travels in the footsteps of Marco Polo.

Below: Odyssey guides to some of the world's most exotic and fascinating destinations, whether you make the journey in person, or whether you take flight purely in your mind and soul.

National Geographic magazine (www.nationalgeographic.com) has some excellent articles on the Silk Road. Subject matter includes the travels of Marco Polo (three parts, May–July 2001), Silk and the Silk Road (January 1984), Xinjiang (March 1996), the Buddhist cave art of Kyzyl (April 1996) and the Mongol conquests (December 1996), as well as some great early articles such as the Mogao Caves of Dunhuang (1951) and Nomads of Central Asia (1936).

MUSIC

Music is one of those intangible arts that travelled, fused and morphed in cultural combinations along the Silk Road. There are few things more evocative of a desert highway or a Central Asian bazaar than music.

Yo Yo Ma's Silk Road Project brings together a collection of musicians and composers from along the Silk Road to explore and incorporate each others' musical traditions. So far the ensemble has produced two CDs. *Silk Road Journeys: When Strangers Meet* is closer to classical than world music. *The Silk Road—A Musical Caravan* (Smithsonian Folkways) is a two-CD collection offering traditional music that gives a good overview of the lands of the Silk Road.

Two recommended recordings of modern Central Asian music are Uzbek singer and dutar player Sevara Nazarkhan's *Yol Boisin* and the lilting Turkmenistan band Ashgabat's *City of Love*, both on the excellent Real World Records label. Yulduz Usmanova is another Uzbek musical star to look out for.

For a more traditional recording try *Music from the Oasis Towns of Central Asia* (Global Style), a collection of Uighur musical pieces from Xinjiang, or *Persian Classical Music* (Nonesuch), also by various artists, from Iran.

A Kyrgyz family relaxes in their akhoi, *or collapsible felt tent, in the Chinese Pamir, just north of Kucha.* (Wong)

Above. Amphorae, originally for storing olive oil, honey, wine or seed at Fethiye, Turkey. Such amphorae were stored with their bases sitting in a slight indentation in the earth floor of a barn or storeroom. (Woolfitt)

Following page: The 10th-century Armenian Church of the Holy Cross, built by King Gagik I, on the island of Akdamar in Lake Van, Turkey. The rich stone relief carvings on the exterior of the church show a variety of biblical scenes in vivid detail. (Woolfitt)

Silk Road Treasures Nearer to Home

This guide to the museums has been prepared by Angela Sheng, an independent scholar who specializes in intercultural exchanges along the Silk Road. She studied in Toronto, at the Sorbonne in Paris, and received her Ph.D. in Oriental Studies from the University of Pennsylvania. She was Assistant Curator of Asian Textiles at the Royal Ontario Museum for ten years before her husband's career took them to Japan. While there she taught Chinese history and art history at Keio University and Temple University. Since joining the 1996–98 Yale-Beijing University sponsored Silk Road Project, she has been lecturing, researching and publishing on the transfer of art and technology between China and Central Asia.

Numerous museums in the United States house rare examples of art from the Silk Road in their permanent collections. Some also continue to expand their holdings. These include the Metropolitan Museum of Art in New York, the University of Pennsylvania Museum of Archaeology and Anthropology in Philadelphia and the Museum of Fine Arts in Boston on the northeast coast; the Freer Gallery of Art, Smithsonian Institution, Washington, D.C.; the Cleveland Museum of Art, the Art Institute of Chicago and the Oriental Institute (also in Chicago) in the mid-west; and on the west coast, the Asian Art Museum in San Francisco and the Los Angeles County Museum.

The Metropolitan Museum of Art
1000 Fifth Avenue at 82nd Street
New York, New York 10028-0198
Phone: 212-535-7710
http://www.metmuseum.org

University of Pennsylvania Museum of Archaeology and Anthropology
3260 South Street, Philadelphia, PA 19104
Phone: 215-898-4000
http://www.museum.upenn.edu/

Museum of Fine Arts, Boston
Avenue of the Arts, 465 Huntington Avenue
Boston, Massachusetts 02115-5523
Phone: 617-267-9300
http://www.mfa.org/sitemap.htm

Freer Gallery of Art, Smithsonian Institution
Jefferson Drive and 12th Street
SW Washington D.C. 20013-7012
Phone: 202-633-4880
http://www.asia.si.edu/

*Brass ewer inlaid with gold
and silver, 13th century, in the
Victoria and Albert Museum*

Preceding page: Detail, Majnun Approaches the Camp of Layli's Caravan, *from a manuscript of the* Haft Awrang *of Jami, Iran, 1556–65, now housed in the Freer Gallery of Art.*

The Cleveland Museum of Art
11150 East Boulevard, Cleveland, Ohio 44106
Phone: 1-888-262-0033
http://www.clemusart.com/

The Art Institute of Chicago
111 South Michigan Avenue, Chicago, Illinois 60603
Phone: (312) 443-3600
http://www.artic.edu/aic/visitor_info/index.html

The Oriental Institute
1155 East 58th Street, Chicago, IL 60637
Phone: 773-702-9514
http://www-oi.uchicago.edu/OI/default.html

Asian Art Museum of San Francisco
200 Larkin Street, San Francisco
CA 94102
Phone: 415.581.3500
http://www.asianart.org/

Los Angeles County Museum of Art
5905 Wilshire Boulevard
Los Angeles, CA 90036
Phone: 323-857-6000
http://www.lacma.org

Outside the United States, some of the world's top museums that are accessible for Silk Road art and archaeology are listed in alphabetical order of their cities: Berlin, Istanbul, London, Lyons, New Delhi, Paris, Riggisberg, Stockholm, St Petersburg, Tokyo, Urumqi and Xi'an.

Pottery warrior figure on horseback, Western Han dynasty (206 BC to 8 AD); unearthed in 1965 at Yangjiawan, Shaanxi province, China.

The Museum of Indian Art (Museum für Indische Kunst)
Takstrasse 40, 14195 Berlin-Dahlem, Germany
Phone: (49) 30-830-1361
Fax: (49) 30-830-1502
http://www.smb.spk-berlin.de/mik/e/s.html

This museum houses the famous Turfan Collection: wall paintings, sculptures, textiles and manuscripts dating from the 2nd to the 12th century that four German expeditions brought back from Turfan, Hami, Kucha and Karashahr on the northern Silk Road in the early 20th century. These expeditions were spearheaded by a scholar of Indo-Tibetan Buddhism, Albert Grünwedel (1856–1935). He was the first person to recognize that the cave paintings found in Kumtura and Kizil near Kucha were early Central Asian Buddhist. Many examples are on display.

The collection also highlights a group of rare Uighur Buddhist wall paintings dated to the 9th century. Albert von Le Coq (1860–1930), a Huguenot entrepreneur turned linguist and museum volunteer, had cut them out of the Bezeklik Thousand Buddha Caves northeast of Turfan. After they arrived in Berlin for safekeeping, however, some were lost to Allied bombing in the Second World War. Only their reproductions are preserved in von Le Coq's *Chotscho* (1913). The remaining pieces correspond to the conspicuous blanks in Bezeklik.

Bodhisattva painting on silk, Khocho, 9th to 10th century AD

Von Le Coq also discovered many rare manuscripts made of palm leaves, paper and birch bark inscribed in many languages. Among them, the illuminated Manichaean texts dated to the 8th and 9th centuries offer vivid evidence of religious pluralism along the Silk Road.

The Topkapi Palace Museum (Topkapi Sarayi)
Sultanahmet, Eminonu, Istanbul, Turkey
Phone : (90) 212-512-0480
Fax : (90) 212-528-5991
http://www.ee.bilkent.edu.tr/~history/topkapi.html

The exquisite Chinese export porcelains here attract collectors and Silk Road aficionados alike. A selection of 10,700 pieces are exhibited in the kitchens opposite the Harem in the second courtyard and in the kitchen designed by the famous Turkish architect, Sinan, in the fifth courtyard. These rare pieces of tableware entered the palace as gifts, spoils of war or through trade. Although some merchants had transported these fragile objects overland, most preferred to ship them via the maritime Silk Road routes. Detailed palace accounts show that they were carefully preserved in the treasury. With the possible exception

Tugra (monogram) of Suleiman the Magnificent, Topkapi Palace, Istanbul (Woolfitt)

of the Chinese Imperial Collection in the National Palace Museum in Taipei, the 2,000 pieces of early celadon shine with an unsurpassed beauty. The Ottomans called them "merteban". Chinese artisans made them in the Longquan (dragon spring) district south of Shanghai during the 13th to the 15th centuries. The underglazed blue pieces came from kilns located further inland in Jingdezhen from the 14th to the 19th centuries. Ceramicists in both places made ewers in the style of 6th-century Sassanian wine jugs. While some bowls were already decorated with Arabic exaltations to please their destined owners, other pieces such as vases received additional gold embellishment at the palace.

The British Museum
Great Russell Street, London WC1B 3DG, UK
Phone: (44) 020-7323-8299; http://www.thebritishmuseum.ac.uk/

Paintings, prints, textiles and other artefacts from Central Asia held in the Department of Oriental Antiquities at the British Museum came from Marc Aurel Stein's (1862–1942) three expeditions there in 1900–01, 1906–09 and 1913–16. He published detailed descriptions of these objects in his monumental works: *Ancient Khotan* in 1907, *Serindia* in 1921 and *Innermost Asia* in 1928. Because Stein had received funding from both the Indian government and the British Museum, the artefacts that he had removed from China were divided between the National Museum in New Delhi and the British Museum in London.

Besides his indomitable spirit, Stein is perhaps best known for his having chanced upon thousands of scrolls and textiles previously sealed inside a small cave, popularly known as the "Library Cave" (Cave 17) in the Buddhist complex outside the town of Dunhuang. Many of these superb Buddhist paintings on silk and woodblock-printed images on paper, dated to the 9th and 10th centuries, are now available for viewing at the British Museum, some in the Stein Room. The manuscripts found by Stein are housed at the British Library (consult the website of the International Dunhuang Project, http://idp.bl.uk/).

Right: Buddhist banners painted on silk gauze, over 1 metre in length, depicting the life of the Buddha. Acquired by Stein and lodged in the British Museum.

Preceding pages: View of a gallery in the Topkapi Palace Museum showing one of the finest carved marble sarcophagi ever discovered, known as Alexander's Tomb but now thought to be that of an unnamed high-ranking commander. (Woolfitt)

While in London, also visit the Victoria and Albert Museum, which houses an extensive collection of Asian, South Asian and Islamic art.

Victoria and Albert Museum
Cromwell Road, South Kensington, London SW7 2R2, UK
Tel: (44) 020-7942-2197
http://www.vam.ac.uk/sitemap

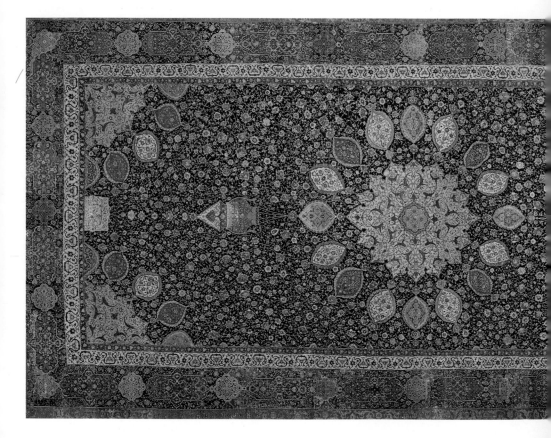

Above: The famous Ardabil carpet, one of a pair originally laid in the ancestral shrine of the Safavid dynasty that ruled Iran during the 16th and 17th centuries, now lodged in the Victoria and Albert Museum.

Following page: Persian velvet weave in silk and silver threads on a gold ground, 16th–17th century, depicting young men smelling flowers among cypress trees, flowering plants and fishponds, formerly in the Treasury of Jaipur, now lodged in the Victoria and Albert Museum.

Textile Museum of Lyons (Musée des Tissus de Lyon)

34 rue de la Charité, Lyons, F-69002, France
Phone: (33) 4-7838-4200; Fax: (33) 4-7240-2512
http://www.musee-des-tissus.com/

Created in 1864 by the Chamber of Commerce and Industry of Lyons, this museum initially continued the tradition of the Museum of Art and Industry, highlighting

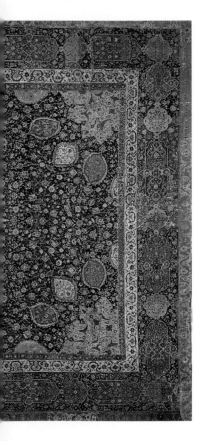

the local silk industry. The building itself is the 18th century Palais de Villeroy, the residence of the Governor of Lyons. The collection soon grew to include rare examples of European and non-European textiles, the latter mostly from ancient Egypt (Coptic), Persia, China and Japan. This extensive collection illustrates well the kind of silks traded along the ancient Silk Road.

Textile historians, notably Monsieur Gabriel Vial, have been able to study many artefacts in depth, for example, a fragment dated to the 7th century, with the rider on a winged horse within a pearl roundel (otherwise known as the "Pegasus"), which corresponds to similar motifs on Astana finds of the same period sometimes on display in Urumqi.

This important collection has enabled a systematic textile analysis of all weaves and methods of textile ornamentation. Indeed, it led to the founding of the Centre International d'Etudes des Textiles Anciens (CIETA), which publishes scholarly research in its *Bulletin*. The centre has also published standardized dictionaries of textile terms in many Western languages. Many textile curators take intensive courses here.

The National Museum of India
Janpath, New Delhi 110 011, India
Phone: (91) 11-301-8415
http://www.nationalmuseumindia.org/index.html

Less well-known but no less important than the Stein Collection in the British Museum are some 11,000 treasures that Stein deposited in New Delhi after his three expeditions to Chinese Central Asia in the early 20th century. They include mural paintings, paintings on textiles and paper, terracotta figurines, wood carvings, coins, glass beads, textile fragments and documents in Kharosthi (an ancient Central Asian script that perished in the 5th century). This collection offers an invaluable comparison with the Stein Collection in London and the Pelliot Collection in Paris.

One can also study the origins and early development of Buddhist art abundantly represented at this museum. In the Maurya-Shunga Gallery stand sculptures of the 2nd to 1st century BCE. Some had been used to embellish stupas at such places as Bodhgaya where according to legend the historical Buddha had attained enlightenment three centuries earlier. In the Kushana and Gupta galleries one can view exquisite examples of Buddhist deities represented in the distinct styles of Mathura (pink terracotta), Gandhara (grey schist) and Gupta schools. Foreign, mostly Hellenistic, elements are successfully integrated with indigenous designs.

National Museum of Asian Art-Guimet
(Musée National des Arts Asiatiques-Guimet)
6, place d'Iéna
75116 Paris, France
Phone: (33) 1-5652-5300
http://www.museeguimet.fr

Comprehensive in both historical and geographic scope, this museum collection features superb Silk Road art. The extensive collection resulted from three early French archaeological missions to Central Asia, led by Dutreuil de Rhins in 1890–1895, Paul Pelliot in 1906–09 and Joseph Hackin in 1931–32. The Pelliot

Collection of paintings, manuscripts and textile fragments from Dunhuang, mostly dated to the 9th and 10th centuries, offers comparison with the Stein materials in London and New Delhi. Whereas the Stein Collections have inspired sporadic research, the Pelliot Collection moved the French to pioneer the field of Dunhuang studies outside China during the period when China was largely closed to the West. After the Cultural Revolution ended in 1976, the Chinese actively pursued Dunhuang studies as well.

When Hackin went to excavate sites in Afghanistan in the 1920s and 1930s, he returned with incredible treasures from Begram, an area reached by Alexander the Great in the 4th century BCE. They include Mathura-styled ivory carvings, Greco-Roman glassware and Han Chinese lacquerware. The French archaeologists' early start continues to give them an edge in the field. The organization of this museum's holdings reflects the systematic effort with which the French have tried to link arts of various cultures adjacent to the Silk Road, from Tibet and Nepal to Korea and Japan.

Abegg Foundation (Abegg-Stiftung)
CH-3132 Riggisberg, Switzerland
Phone: (41) 31-808-1201 (closed during winter)
http://www.abegg-stiftung.ch

Set in the rolling hills near Bern, this private art historical institute is dedicated to the research of historical textiles and boasts a resplendent Silk Road collection that amply rewards a visit. Werner and Margaret Abegg, who founded the institute in 1961, began collecting ancient textiles long before it grew fashionable. To better study their early specimens, including some rare Egyptian and Persian fragments, they built up an impressive library and a state-of-the art textile conservation laboratory where many of the world's leading textile conservators have since been trained. To complement these textiles, they also purchased contemporaneous artefacts, such as early Iranian rhytons in bronze and lapis lazuli, dating from the 5th to the 7th centuries.

Expanding their interest in the evolution of textile motifs and technology, their nephew, Dominik Keller, has guided the recent acquisition of some major textile finds from Chinese Central Asia. Dating from to the 2nd century BCE to the mid-4th century CE, these wool fragments from Shanpula (near Khotan on the southern Silk Road in the Uighur Autonomous Region of Xinjiang) provide important evidence of Saka-Khotanese culture. They predate Sassanian and Sogdian silks of the 7th to the 9th centuries and later Chinese export silks, also at Abegg. All the textiles are exhibited within their historical context along with a substantial collection of paintings, sculpture and applied arts. Scholarly publications accompany major exhibits.

The National Museum of Ethnography (Etnografiska museet)
Djurgårdsbrunnsvägen 34, Stockholm, Sweden
Phone: (46) 8519-550-00
http://www.etnografiska.se

Nowhere else could one find more complete documentation of a Silk Road explorer than this museum where the Royal Swedish Academy set up a foundation to manage the estate of Sven Hedin (1865–1952). Hedin began his studies at the University of Berlin under the distinguished geographer, Ferdinand von Richthofen, who had first coined the term "Silk Road" to describe the network of overland routes connecting ancient Rome and China. This may account for Hedin's travels to Persia and Russian Central Asia well before receiving his doctorate in 1892.

Between 1893 and 1935, he made four expeditions to Central Asia, charting maps of many areas in Pamir, Taklamakan, Tibet and the Himalaya. The mystery of the dried-up Lop Nor lake led him to discover the ancient ruins of Loulan. Between 1927 and 1935, he went to the Gobi Desert and Turkestan with other German, Danish, Swedish and Chinese scientists. Besides his own prolific publications, he also collaborated with others to complete thirty-five volumes of scientific studies between 1937 and 1949. All of his maps, photographs and notes are kept here, whereas most objects that he brought back for ethnographic study have been repatriated to China and are stored at the National History Museum in Beijing. Some were also donated back to the Sven Hedin Foundation from the United States.

The State Hermitage Museum
34 Dvortsovaya Naberzhnaya (Palace Embankment)
St Petersburg 190000, Russia
Phone : (812) 311-3420
http://www.hermitagemuseum.org/

Russian imperial rule in the 18th and 19th centuries, and then in the 20th century the Soviet control of the Eurasian steppes and Central Asia, resulted in a wealth of treasures housed at this museum. Early tribute to the throne and later archaeological excavations led to many studies of nomadic art and cultures, notably: Scythian art in the Crimea, Kuban Basin, and in the valleys of

The Hermitage on the Neva River; on the right the golden dome of St Isaac's Cathedral stands behind the spire of the Admiralty.

the Dnieper and Don rivers, dating from as early as the 8th and 7th centuries BCE; and Scythian-Sakae art in the Altai mountains, dating from the 6th to the 4th centuries BCE (see "Prehistoric Art" on the website). The ancient nomadic art works, such as gold objects carved with animal motifs (see "The Golden Rooms" on the website), greatly help us better understand later artefacts.

In addition, the Central Asian collection (see "Oriental Art" on the website) includes wall paintings, sculptures, ivories, wood carvings, bronzes, coins, ceramics, jewellery and textiles that date from the 4th millennium BCE to modern times. Especially valuable are the Sogdian wall paintings of the 7th and 8th centuries from such places as Penjikent (near modern Samarkand). They show considerable Indian and Chinese elements both in form and style. Their collection of Sassanian art is also exceptionally rich, providing useful comparisons.

The Tokyo National Museum
13–9 Ueno Park, Taito-ku, Tokyo, 110-8712, Japan
Phone: (81) 03-3822-1111; http://www.tnm.jp

Recipients of Silk Road influences via China since the mid-1st millennium, the Japanese have gone out of their way to preserve many artefacts dating from the 7th and 8th centuries that show a strong Central Asian influence. Most were deposited at the Imperial Repository, Shosoin, and a Buddhist temple, Horyuji, both in Nara near Kyoto. Whereas the Shosoin treasures remain largely inaccessible, one can now easily admire the Horyuji collection at the museum's Horyuji Gallery, newly renovated in 1999. This collection includes numerous extant gilt-bronze Buddhist statutes and Buddhist sutras, as well as bronze ewers and textile fragments used for Buddhist rituals.

The museum also houses important archaeological finds from Chinese Central Asia that the Otani missions brought back in the early 20th century. Sponsored by Count Kozui Otani, the spiritual leader of the Buddhist Pure Land Sect, Zuicho Tachibana, a naval officer, and Eizaburo Nomura, a military officer, went together and separately to Turfan, Korla, Karashahr, Loulan, Charkhlik, Niya, Keriya, Khotan, Kucha and Kashgar. Their finds range from Buddhist texts and ritual objects to mural paintings, clay sculptures and textiles, offering a valuable comparison with the Stein Collections in London and New Delhi, as well as the Pelliot Collection in Paris. The museum also holds a strong collection of Indian, Chinese and Korean art for in-house comparisons.

While in Tokyo, the Ancient Orient Museum, which collects, researches and publishes archaeological finds from the Middle East, also merits a visit. The Ancient Orient Museum is located in the Sunshine Building, 7th Floor, 1–4 Higashi-Ikebukuro 3-chome, Toshima-ku, Tokyo 170-8630, Japan. Phone: (81) 3989-3491, Fax: (81) 3590-3266.

Xinjiang Regional Museum
No. 132 Xibei Road, Urumqi, Xinjiang Uighur Autonomous Region, PRC 830000
Phone: (86) 991-453-3561
http://www.travelchinaguide.com/attraction/xinjiang/urumqi/museum.htm

Recently renovated to national level, this regional museum holds some of the best artefacts that Chinese archaeologists have unearthed since 1959. One of the most famous is the four thousand year-old mummy called the "Loulan Beauty". Her Caucasian bone structure has raised controversial questions about the indigenous population in antiquity; her beautiful wool clothing attests to an already well-developed level of weaving tradition. Other outstanding artefacts include more mummies; objects made in jade (mostly nephrite from Khotan); wooden slips inscribed with Kharosthi (ancient Central Asian script that survived until the 5th century); lively ceramic figures dancing, playing music, doing daily chores or riding; silk flowers, a paper coffin, and many clothing and textile fragments in complex weaves developed during the 6th and 7th centuries when many Sogdian immigrants worked in Turfan.

Nearby, the little known Institute of Archaeology also displays newly excavated artefacts. Funded by the Japanese, the two floors provide up-to-date finds in every medium imaginable. Of particular interest is the collection of small, carved gold objects used to embellish costumes and horses that are related to Scythian and Sakae art. The Xinjiang Institute of Archaeology is at 4B South Beijing Road, Urumqi, Xinjiang, PRC 830000. Phone (86) 991-383-7146.

Shaanxi History Museum

No. 91 East Xiao Zai Road
Xi'an, Shaanxi, PRC 710061
http://www.sxhm.com/english/1-1.htm

The Shaanxi History Museum opened in 1991, eighteen years after Premier Zhou Enlai first suggested that such an establishment was needed to exhibit the province's archaeological treasures. Occupying a large site in Xi'an's southern suburbs close to the Big Goose Pagoda, the museum, housed

Bronze vessel with loop handle from the Shang dynasty (13th to 11th centuries BC); unearthed in 1971 i[n] Jinyang, Shaanxi province, China.

in a complex of striking Tang-dynasty style pavilions, is an absolute must for every visitor to the city.

The exhibits here represent the very best of the museum's collection, the greater portion of which remain stored in its underground warehouse. The permanent exhibition on the ground and first floors is supplemented by touring exhibitions—usually two—in the basement. Included elsewhere in the palatial-style buildings are lecture theatres, conference rooms, a library, research laboratories and an extensive restoration centre.

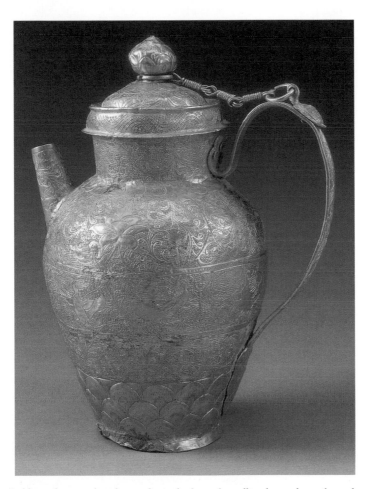

Gold pot decorated with mandarin ducks and scrolling lotus plants from the Tang dynasty (618–907 AD); unearthed in 1969, Shaanxi province, China.

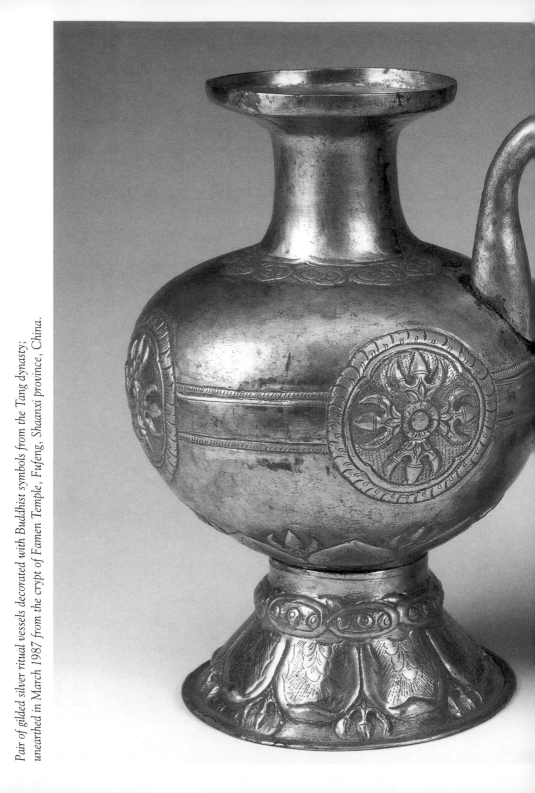

Pair of gilded silver ritual vessels decorated with Buddhist symbols from the Tang dynasty; unearthed in March 1987 from the crypt of Famen Temple, Fufeng, Shaanxi province, China.

A Tang-dynasty band of musicians on a camel in tri-colour pottery,
now in the Shaanxi History Museum, Xi'an, China.

Comparative Place Names

This comparative place name list has been compiled from various sources including gleanings from Herbert Herrmann's An Historical Atlas of China *(first printed in 1935 and republished in 1966), which I found to be an amazing work that proved more reliable than many later attempts. Places and regions mentioned in the book whose names remain unchanged to the present day have been excluded from this list. Otherwise the ancient name is listed first with the corresponding current name or possible location following. I hope this attempt will aid readers in tracing the complexities of references within the text.*

Judy Bonavia-Boillat

A

Adulis = near port of Massawa, Ethiopia

Aduly (see Adulis)

Aeolian (Islands) = Lipari Islands, north of Sicily, Italy

Afrasiab/Afrasyab = near Samarkand, Uzbekistan

Ai Khanum = in ancient Bactria, located on the Afghanistan/Tajikistan border where the Pyandzh and Kokcha rivers meet, north of Kunduz. This site could be Ptolemy's Euratidia.

Ain-Djaldt (battle site) = in Galilee, Israel

Akka = Acre, Israel

Akmola/Akmolinsk/Astana = Tselinograd, Kazakhstan

Alatau (see Drujba)

Alexandria-Margiana = probably to the south-east of the southern shores of the Caspian Sea, within borders of Turkmenistan (or the old site of Merv).

Alexandria of Aria/Aria = Herat, Afghanistan

Alexandria Oxiana (Oxus) = possibly once situated near Termez, on the Afghan–Tajikistan border.

Antioch = Antakya, Turkey

Antioch of Margiana (see Alexandria-Margiana)

Anxi = Persia (may be Parthian dynasty of the Arsacids)

Anxi = an ancient Chinese protectorate in present-day Xinjiang, China.

Apologus = situated at the mouth of the Euphrates River, in present-day Iraq.

Aquileaus/Aquileia – situated near present-day Trieste, Italy.

Argaris = once situated on the eastern coast of India.

Aria/Alexandria of Aria = Herat, Afghanistan

Arikamedu (see Virampatnam)

Arretium = Arezzo, Italy

Artaxa (Artachat) = situated just south of Erevan, Armenia

Artachat (see Artaxa)

Astana (see Akmola)
Atlakh = near Dzhambul,
    Kazakhstan
Ayas (see Layas)
Axum = near Asmara, Ethiopia

B

Bactra = Balkh, Afghanistan
Bactria = occupied a region roughly
    to the south-south-west of the
    Amu-Darya River, part of present-day
    Afghanistan and Turkmenistan.

*The 15th-century shrine of Khwaja Abu Nasr Parsa,
Balkh, Afghanistan*

Badascian = Badakhshan, Afghanistan
Bakare/Bacare = an ancient port on the south-west coast of India.
Baldach/Baudac = Baghdad, Iraq
Balkh = a city in ancient Tokharestan, in present-day northern Afghanistan.
Barbaricum/Barbaricon = an ancient port, thought to have been just south of Karachi, Pakistan.
Barygaza = said to correspond with present-day Bharuch, just north of Surat, on the north-west
    coast of India.
Baoshan = Yongchang, Yunnan province, China
Beiting/Beshbalyk = near Jimushaer (Jimsar), Xinjiang, China
Bender-el-Kebir (see Berenicê)
Berenicê = an ancient and modern port on the Egyptian coast of the Red Sea.
Beshbalyk (see Beiting)
Bettala = Puttalam, Sri Lanka
Bolor (kingdom) = situated in the Pamir, near present-day Tajikistan.
Bosi = Persia
Bythinia/Bithynia = a state located east of the Bosphorus, along the southern Black Sea coast,
    Turkey.
Byzantium (see Constantinople)

C

Cacanfu = Hejian, Hebei province, China
Calliana = possibly also called Gozurat, an ancient port in present-day Gujerat state, India.
Callinica = possibly Rakka or Ar Rqqah, on the left bank of the Euphrates River, Syria.
Cambaluc (see Khanbaligh)
Cane (see Kane)

Cappadocia = a state located on the present-day border of Turkey and Armenia.

Carrhae (Battle of) = near the Turkish town of Haran, near the Syrian border.

Caugigu = probably northern Vietnam.

Champa = Vietnam

Cherman (see Kierman)

Chrysê (Island) = Sumatra, Indonesia

Ciarcian (province) = Qiemo (Charchan), Xinjiang, China

Cilicia = a region in present-day Turkey.

Cînapati (Zhinapudi) = a town or state founded by the Kushans in the Punjab, India.

Cipangu = Japan

Chang'an = Xi'an, Shaanxi province, China

Comedoi (mountains) = region of the Hindu Kush, Afghanistan

Condifu (see Tundifu)

Constantinople = Istanbul, Turkey

Coptus = once situated on the River Nile, near Luxor, Egypt.

Ceos (Island) = once the Hydrussa of the Greeks, now the Island of Kea, Aegean Sea, Greece.

Cranganore (see Kodungalur)

Ctesiphon = once situated on the eastern bank of the lower Tigris River, Iraq. Also once known as Seleucia.

Cuigiu = possibly Yibin, Sichuan province, China

Curmos = Hormuz, Iran

D

Da Qin = see also Lijian and Folin: ancient Chinese names for the Roman Empire.

Dadu = Beijing (Peking), China

Dandan-Ulik/Dandan Oiluq (archaeological site) = east of present-day Hetian, Xinjiang, China

Daxia (kingdom) = old Bactria of Hellenized Persian Empire

Dayuan (kingdom) = in Ferghana Valley, south-east Uzbekistan. (Also known as the kingdom of Kokand during the Muslim period.)

Deshima (Island) = was a specially constructed island in Nagasaki harbour, Japan, where Dutch traders did business with Japan between 1639 and 1854.

Dian = Kunming, Yunnan province, China

Djambul = Dzhambul, Kazakhstan

Djumbulak Kum (archaeological site) = on Keriya River, Xinjiang, China

Drepanum (Cape) = Trapani, Sicily, Italy

Drujba (Alatau) = Druzhba on Kazakhstan/Chinese border, at the Dzungarian Gate

Dsimsa = Jimusaer, Xinjiang, China

Dufar = situated in present-day Oman.

E

Ecbatana = Hamadan, Iran

Edessus = Urfa, Turkey

Emamshahr = possibly present-day Damghan, Iran (Parthian Hecatompylos)

Ephesus = an ancient Ionian Greek city, once located on the Aegean Sea coast of present-day Turkey.

Euripe (Straits) = Evvoikos Canal, Greece

Ershi/Eulshe = capital of ancient Dayuan. Ruins near village of Markhamat, north-east of Ferghana, Uzbekistan.

Erythraean Sea = name used in first Christian era to designate the Red Sea and part of the Indian Ocean, from Cape Guardafui as far as the western coast of India.

Etsin-gol (River) = Hei He (River), Gansu province, China

Euboea (Island) = a large Greek island in the Aegean Sea which subsided, leaving a few islets, including Kea (Pliny's Ceos).

F

Fansur (kingdom) = Island of Sumatra, Indonesia

Ferghana (see Dayuan)

Folin = see also Lijian and Da Qin: ancient Chinese names for the Roman Empire.

Fortunate (Islands)(also known as Islands of the Blessed) = thought by some to refer to Madeira or the Canary Islands.

Fustat = Cairo, Egypt

G

Gaindu (province) = Xichang region, southern Sichuan province, China

Gates of Dzungaria (see Drujba)

Gaul (Gulf) = Gulf of Lions, France

Ghinghin Talas = a region located around present-day Urumqi, Xinjiang, China.

Giogiu/Ginguy = Zhuoxian, Hebei province, China

Graviscae = once existed on the western coast of Italy.

Gruganj/Gurganj = Kunya-Urgench, Turkmenistan

Above: Cave complex at the ruined town of Subashi, Xinjiang, China (Wong)

Right: A terracotta charioteer with outstretched arms that once held the reins of his steeds; excavated from Pit One of the Qin Terracotta Army Museum, Xi'an, China.

H

Harran = once near Urfa, Turkey

Hecatompylos (see Emamshahr)

Hemodi (mountains) = an ancient term for part of the Himalaya mountain range.

Hierapolis = situated north-east of Aleppo, Syria

Himyar (kingdom) = included Yemen and beyond. (The capital of the Himyar kingdom was called Zafar).

Hippone = near Bone, Algeria

Hippuros = an ancient port in present-day Sri Lanka.

Hisn el-Ghurab (see Kane)

Hydrussa (Island) = Island of Kea, Greece

Hyrcania = a region bordering the Caspian Sea north of present-day Tehran, Iran.

I

Iasd (see Yasdi)

Illyria = covered much of Austria, Hungary and the eastern coast of the Adriatic Sea (under the Roman Empire).

Issedon Scythia = Kashi (Kashgar), Xinjiang, China

Itil (in kingdom of Khazaria) = once situated where the Volga River enters the Caspian Sea, near present day Astrakhan?

J

Jaxartes (River) = Syr-Darya

Jenan = possibly Vietnam

Jibin (kingdom) = thought to be either present-day Kashmir or the region of Kabul.

Jiecha = perhaps Skardu, in Baltistan, in Pakistan-administered Kashmir.

Jimsar/Jinmancheng (see Beshbalyk)

Jourganie = Georgia

Juliopolis = thought to have been situated very close to Alexandria, Egypt.

K

Kai-Pi-Shi (see Kapisa)

Kalahbar = an ancient port in Java, Indonesia

Kamara = an ancient port on the south-west coast of India.

Kamarupa = Gauhati, Assam, India

Kane = an ancient incense port, once situated between Aden and Mukalla, on the Gulf of Aden, Yemen.

Kangju (kingdom) = in the region of ancient Sogdiana between Amu-Darya and Syr-Darya rivers with its capital at Samarkand (also called Marakanda and Afrasiab), Uzbekistan.

Sand dunes outside Dunhuang, China (Wong)

Kapilavastu (kingdom) = situated between present-day Gorakphur, northern India and the Kathmandu Valley, Nepal.

Kapisa (kingdom) = north of Kabul, Afghanistan

Karakhodja (see Qotcho)

Karakhoto = once situated near the present-day Dong He and Xi He (rivers) in northern Gansu province, China.

Karakorum = west of Ulaanbaatar, Mongolia

Karashahr = Yanqi, Xinjiang, China

Kashi (see Shule)

Kedjaran/Kedjaweran = an ancient town situated on the Iranian coast of the Persian Gulf.

Keriya = Yutian, Xinjiang, China

Kerya (see Keriya)

Kham = on the border of eastern Tibet and Sichuan province, China.

Khanbaligh/Khanbaliq (see Dadu)

Khanfu = Guangzhou (Canton), Guangdong province, China

Kharashahr = Yanqi, Xinjiang, China

Khazaria (see Itil)

Khorassan (state) = in present-day region of Khorasan, Iran.

Khorezm (kingdom) = situated in the region of present-day Khorezmskaya, on the Amu-Darya River, Uzbekistan.

Khotan = ancient Yutian, modern Hetian, Xinjiang, China

Kierman/Cherman = Kerman, Iran

Kin-sai/Quinsay = Hangzhou, Zhejiang province, China
Kodungalur (see Muziris)
Koft (see Coptus)
Kokand (see Dayuan)
Kom = Qom, Iran
Kufa/Koufa = old capital of a caliphate which was replaced in 762 by Baghdad, modern Iraq.
Kuft (see Coptus)
Kulam of Malaya = an ancient port in southern India, probably present-day Quilon
Kundrang = Cochinchina

L

Lajazzo (see Layas)
Langabalus (Islands) = perhaps the Nicobar Islands in Bay of Bengal, India.
Layas = Payas, just north of Iskenderun, Turkey
Leuke Come = an ancient port on the Red Sea.
Liangzhou = Wuwei, Gansu province, China
Lijian = see also Da Qin and Folin: ancient Chinese names for the Roman Empire.
Lijian = probably Inching, near Wuwei, Gansu province, China.
Loulan (kingdom) = situated around Lop Nor, Xinjiang, China.
Lu (kingdom) = situated in Shandong province, China.
Lumbini (see also Kapilavastu) = the ancient site of Buddha's renunciation, in present-day
   Kathmandu Valley, Nepal.

M

Magadha = ancient kingdom situated in present-day Bihar state,
   India (see also Palimbothra/Palibothrs/Pataliputra).
Male = probably the port of the ancient south-western coastal
   region known as Male, present-day Kerala state, India.
Manbij (see Hierapolis)
Mangi = South China
Maniolae (Islands)(the so-called
   "Stone of Heracles" a group of
   ten islands) = probably the
   Nicobar Islands, Bay of
   Bengal, India.
Maracanda = Samarkand, Uzbekistan
Marghinan = Marghilan, near
   Ferghana, Uzbekistan

Terracotta army horse of the Qin emperor, Xi'an (Wong)

Margiana/Margyane (see Mary)

Mary = Melkyda (see Nelcynda)

Merv = possibly present-day Giaur-Kala south of the Tedjen River or Murgab River, or in the district of Mary, Turkmenistan.

Minnagara = an ancient port on the mouth of the Indus River, near present-day Karachi, Pakistan.

Miran (archaeological site) = west of Ruoqiang (Charkhlik), Xinjiang, China

Mosul (kingdom) = in region of Mosul, modern Iraq

Mosyllon/Mosyllum = probably the port of Ras Hafun, Somalia.

Mutifili/Mutfili = kingdom of Telingana, once located on the Coromandel Coast between Madras and Machilipatnam, India.

Muza = possibly Moka (Mukalla), Yemen

Muziris/Muzeris (Kodungalur) = thought to be later known as Cranganore on old British maps, on south-western coast of India, just north of Cochin.

Mylapore = a site near Madras, India where Saint Thomas is purported to be buried.

Myos Hormus = once situated on the Red Sea coast north-east of present-day Thebes, Egypt.

N

Nelcynda/Neakyndon/Nincildea/Melkyda = an ancient port just east of present-day Kottayam, India.

Nicea = Iznik, Turkey

Nisibis/Nisibin = Nusaybin, Turkey

O

Occlis/Okclis/Ocilia = once situated on the western coast of the Straight of Bab al Mandab, probably in present-day Djibouti.

Oc-Eo (archaeological site) = near Gulf of Thailand, Vietnam

Omiritis = the earlier Himyar kingdom, present-day Yemen

Ommana/Omana = an ancient port on the Gulf of Oman, Oman.

Onion (mountains) = Pamir mountain range

Opone = an ancient port close to the present-day port of Ras Hafun, Somalia.

Oxus (River) = Amu-Darya River

Oxus (see Alexandria Oxiana)

P

Paikend = once located near Bukhara, in present-day Uzbekistan.

Palaesimundu (Island) (see Taprobane)

Palimbothra/Palibothrs/Pataliputra = Patna, India (Pataliputra was capital of the kingdom of Magadha)

Pem/Pera = later called Keriya, now Yutian, Xinjiang, China
Pergamom = Bergama, Turkey
Perimula = ancient name of a promontory on south-east coast of India.
Phoenicia = present-day Lebanon
Piao (kingdom) = an ancient Burmese kingdom on the border with Yunnan province, China.
Poduke = ruins not far from Pondicherry, Coromandel Coast, India
Pontus/Pontus Euxinus = Black Sea
Promontory of Spices = Cape of Guardafui, Somalia
Purushapur = Peshawar, Pakistan
Purple Isles = may be the Canary Islands, Atlantic Ocean
Ptolemais/Ptolemais Theron = once in the vicinity of Port Sudan, Sudan.
Pyandjikent/Pendjikent (Sogdiana) = Pendzhikent, Uzbekistan
Pyanj (River) = Pyandzh River on Afghan–Tajikistan border

Q
Qana (see Kane)
Qi (kingdom) = an ancient kingdom in Shandong province, China
Qiong (kingdom) = an ancient kingdom in Sichuan province, China
Qiuci (kingdom) = near Kuche (Kucha, Kuqa), Xinjiang, China
Qomul = Hami, Xinjiang, China
Qotcho = Gaochang, near Turfan, Xinjiang, China
Quift (see Coptus)
Quinsay (see Kin-sai)
Qushi (kingdom) = included present-day Turfan, Xinjiang, China

R
Rayy/Ray/Rey = Tehran, Iran
Rekem = the site of Petra in Jordan.

S
Saminid (kingdom) = a kingdom which once included present-day Uzbekistan.
Sarandan/Zarandan (region) (see Baoshan)
Sarai = probably close to present-day Volgagrad, on Volga River, Russia.
Scier Shihr = Yemen.
Serica/Seres = China
Sera Metropolis = capital of China

Central Asia's quintessential architectural ensemble,
Registan Square in Samarkand, Uzbekistan (Grover)

Serendib (see Taprobane)

Shangdu (Xanadu) = Duolun (To-lun), Inner Mongolia, China (summer capital of the Mongol khans)

Shanshan (kingdom) = perhaps once located south-west and west of Lop Nor, Xinjiang, China.

Shengdu = ancient Chinese name for northern India.

Shizi (see Taprobane)

Shu (kingdom) = Sichuan province, China

Shule = Kashi (Kashgar), Xinjiang, China

Sicile = Island of Sicily, Italy

Sidon = Saida, Lebanon

Sielediba (see Taprobane)

Silingiu = Xining, Qinghai province, China

Sin/Sin al-Sin/Sin-i Kalan = Guangzhou (Canton), Guangdong province, China

Sindu = considered the ancient gateway to India, seemingly located in the Indus River estuary.

Sindufu = Chengdu, Sichuan province, China

Siraf = a port destroyed around 970 AD, near modern Taheri, Persian Gulf, Iran.

Sogdiana (see Kangju)

Sopatma = an ancient port on the Coromandel Coast, India, near Pondicherry.

Spasinou Charax = once situated on the Tigris River estuary, near Abadan, Iran.

Styria = Austria

Suoche/Suoqu/Shache (see Yarkand)

Sudak = also once called Soldaia, on the Crimean coast of the Black Sea.

Syagros (Cape of) = Cape of Ras Fartak, Yemen

T

Talas (River)(Battle) = in region of Dzhambul, Kazakhstan

Tana (kingdom) = near Mumbai (Bombay), India

Tana = once situated near Rostov-on-Don, Russia.

Tangut (kingdom) = covered modern Gansu and Ningxia provinces, China

Taprobane = Ceylon/Sri Lanka/Serendib (Taprobane was the ancient Greek name for the island.)

Taraz = near present-day Dzhambul, Kazakhstan

Tauris = Tabriz, Iran

Tchertchen = Qiemo (Ciarcian), Xinjiang, China

Tebet = Tibet, China

Tedjen (River) = Tedzhen River, Turkmenistan

Telingana (kingdom) = either on the Cormandel Coast between present-day Madras and Machilipatnam, or in the region of the Irrawaddy estuary, present-day Burma.

Tenduc = in region of present-day Hoechst, Inner Mongolia, China

Tianzhu = India

Tiaozhi = possibly once located just north of Bushehr, on the Persian Gulf, Iran.

Tillya-Tepe (archaeological site) = near Sheberghab (Shibarghan), Afghanistan

Tokharestan/Tokharistan (also known as Bactria) (see Bactria)

Toli (kingdom) = probably in the region of present-day eastern Tajikistan and its border with Xinjiang, China.

Trebizond (Trepezus) = near Trabzon, Turkey

Tsin = China

Tundifu = Dongping, Hebei province, China

Turkomania = part of present-day eastern Turkey

Tyre = Tyr, Lebanon

A tea plantation in Trabzon, Black Sea coast, Turkey (Woolfit)

U

Urgench (old town) = Kunya-Urgench, Turkmenistan

V

Varahch = near Bukhara, Uzbekistan

Virampatnam = Arikamedu (archaeological site), just south of Pondicherry, Coromandel coast, India

W

Weili (kingdom) = present-day Weili Xian (county), just south of Korma, Xinjiang, China

Western Territories (see Xiyu)

X

Xiyu = the name given to those territories which lay west of China around the 2nd century BC

Y

Yancai = an ancient Allan country situated north of the Caucasus.

Yarkand = Shache/Suoche, Xinjiang, China

Yasdi = Yazd, Iran

Yiwu = Hami, Xinjiang, China

Yotkan = near Khotan, old capital of Yutian, modern Hetian, Xinjiang, China

Yutian (see Khotan)

Yuehzhi (Da Yuezhi) (kingdom) = once occupied the territory of ancient Daxia, Bactria, part of present-day Afghanistan and Turkmenistan.

Z

Zafar (see Himyar)

Zaitun = Quanzhou, Fujian province, China

Zanj = Zanzibar, Tanzania

Zhezhe = probably in the valley of the Talas River, present-day northern Kyrgyzstan

Zhinapudi (see Cînapati)

Following pages: Mountain goats overlook part of the Great Wall that was built by the state of Zhao around 300 BC, Inner Mongolia.

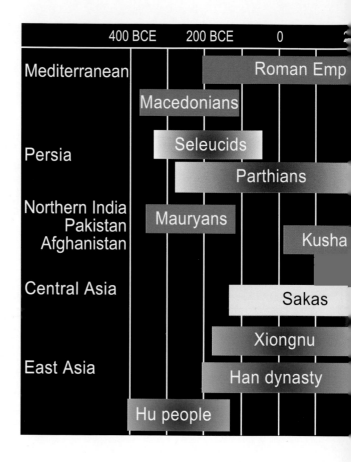

Silk Road Timeline

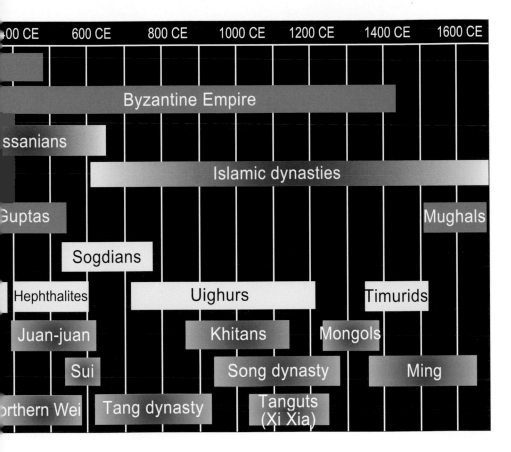

Silk Road Cultures

Full credit and gratitude goes to the team of John Szostak, Lance Jenott and Daniel Waugh who contributed this timeline image, reprinted with their kind permission. This timeline is one part of the exhibit "Silk Road Seattle", a collaborative public education project exploring cultural interaction across Eurasia from the 1st century BCE to the 16th century CE. "Silk Road Seattle" is sponsored by the Walter Chapin Simpson Center for the Humanities at the University of Washington. For more information please visit:

<http://depts.washington.edu/uwch/silkroad/exhibit/index2.html>.

Bibliography

The number of publications on various aspects of the history of the Silk Road is such that it would take a lifetime to read them all, and this number is constantly on the increase. There are over a thousand studies and articles on the subject just in English and French, without mentioning doctoral theses, to which one could add thousands more in Chinese, Japanese, German, Russian, Italian and other languages. The list below includes all the works referred to in this study, as well as some recent publications of particular interest. Further bibliographies are to be found in the works below.

PUBLICATIONS IN ENGLISH

AL-MUQADDASI, *The Best Divisions for Knowledge of the Regions*, translated by Basil A. Collins, Centre for Muslim Contribution to Civilization, Garnet Publishing, Reading, 1994.

ALLAN N.J.R., "Highways to the sky: the impact of tourism on South Asian culture" in *Tourism, Recreation, Research*, vol. 13, no. 1, pp. 11–16, 1988.

ALLAN N.J.R., "Kashgar to Islamabad: the impact of the Karakorum highway on mountain society and habitat" in *Scottish Geographical Magazine*, vol. 105, no. 3, pp. 130–141, 1989.

ALRAM Michael, KLIMBURG-SALTER Deborah E. (ed.), *Coins, Art, and Chronology. Essays on the Pre-Islamic History of the Indo-Iranian Borderlands*, Verlag der Österreichischen Akademie der Wissenschaften, Wien, 1999 (Österr. Akad. der Wissens., Philosophisch-historische Klasse Denkschriften, Band 280).

ALLCHIN F.R. and HAMMOND Norman eds., *The Archaeology of Afghanistan from Earliest Times to the Timurid Period*, Academic Press, London, 1978.

BBC FOREIGN BROADCAST INFORMATION SERVICE, *Summary of World Broadcasts. Part III, Far East. Daily reports; Weekly economic reports.* (These daily and weekly printed reports supply an English translation of selections from the written press and radio broadcasts from the People's Republic of China).

Left: Kyrgyz yurts dot the landscape near the Pamir, where China borders Tajikistan, Afghanistan, Pakistan and India. (Wong)

BARICCO Alessandro, *Silk*, translated from the Italian by Guido Waldman, Vintage Books, 1998 (original published by Seta, Milan, 1996).

BEAL Samuel, Si-yu-ki, *Buddhist Records of the Western World*, translated from the Chinese of Hiuen Tsiang (AD 629), Kegan Paul, Trench, Trubner, London, 1884. Reprinted Chinese Materials Center, San Francisco, 1976, and New Delhi, 1983.

BECKWITH Christopher I., *The Tibetan Empire in Central Asia: A History of the Struggle for Great Power among Tibetans, Turks, Arabs, and Chinese during the Early Middle Ages*, Princeton University Press, Princeton, 1987.

BECQUELIN Nicolas, "Xinjiang in the Nineties" in *The China Journal* (Canberra), pp. 65–90, July 2000.

BOUCHER Daniel J., *Buddhist Translation Procedures in Third-Century China: A Study of Dharmaraksa and his Translation Idiom*. Master thesis, University of Pennsylvania, 1996.

BROMBERG C. Altman, BOPEARACHCHI O., GRENET F., (ed.) *Alexander's Legacy in the East. Studies in Honor of Paul Bernard*, Bulletin of the Asia Institute, 12, 2001, no. 49.

CABLE M. and FRENCH F., *Through the Jade Gate and Central Asia*, Constable, London, 1927.

CASSON Lionel, *The Periplus Maris Erythraei*. Text with introduction, translation and commentary, Princeton University Press, Princeton, 1989.

CHAU JU-KUA: His works on the Chinese and Arab trade in the 12th and 13th centuries entitled *Chu fan-chï*, translated from the Chinese and annotated by Friedrich HIRTH and W.W. ROCKHILL, Imperial Academy of Sciences, St Petersburg, 1911.

COSMAS INDICOPLEUSTES, "Cosmae Indicopleustae Christianorum opinio de mundo, sive Topographia christiana", in *Collectio nova patrum et scriptorum graecorum...*, vol. 2, Claude Rigaud, Paris, pp. 113–346, 1707; English translation by McCrindle, J.W. *The Christian Topography of Cosmas, an Egyptian Monk*, Burt Franklin: New York, 1887.

CH'U T'UNG-TSU, *Han Social Structure*, University of Washington Press, Washington, 1972.

CRIBB Joe, "The early Kushan Kings: New evidence for chronology", in ALRAM M., KLIMBURG-SALTER D. (ed.), *Coins, art and chronology...* (see ALLAN), pp. 177–205.

CUNLIFFE Barry, *The Celtic World*, BCA, London, 1990.

DAVID-NEEL Alexandra, LAMA YONGDEN, *The Superhuman Life of Gesar of Ling*, translated from the French by Sydney Violet, Shambala, 1981.

DUBS Homer H., translator of BAN GU (PAN KU), *The History of the Former Han Dynasty*, Kegan Paul, Trubner, London, 1938; Waverly Press, Baltimore, 1944.

DUBS, Homer H., *A Roman City in Ancient China*, The China Society, London, 1957.

FLEMING Peter, *News from Tartary. A journey from Peking to Kashmir*, Jonathan Cape, London, 1936; Macdonald Futura, London, 1980.

FLORUS L., *Annaei Flori Epitome rerum Romanorum (Epitome of Roman History)*, Book I, translated by Edward S. Forster, Loeb Classical Library Heinemann, London, 1966.

FORBES R.J., *Studies in Ancient Technology*, vol. VIII, E.J. Brill, Leyde, 1971.

FORTE Antonino, *"On the so-called Abraham from Persia, a Case of Mistaken Identity"*, pp. 375–428.

FORTE Antonino, "The Edict of 638 allowing the Diffusion of Christianity in China", in PELLIOT Paul, pp. 349–373, *L'inscription nestorienne de Si-Ngan-Fou*, Paris 1996.

FRANCK Irene M. and BROWNSTONE David M., *The Silk Road, A History, Fact on File Publications*, New York and Oxford, 1986.

GAULIER S., JERA-BEZARD R., MAILLARD M., *Buddhism in Afghanistan and Central Asia*, Brill, Leyde, 1987.

GROUSSET René, *The Empire of the Steppes*, Rutgers University Press, 1988.

GROUSSET René, *The Rise and Splendour of the Chinese Empire*, Barnes & Noble Books, 2000.

GROUSSET René, *In the Footsteps of Buddha*, Routledge, 1971.

HEDIN Sven, *Across the Gobi Desert*, Greenwood, 1968.

HEERS Jacques, *Marco Polo*, Fayard, Paris, 1983.

HERODOTUS, *The Histories*, translated by Aubrey de Sélincourt, revised by A. R. Burn, Penguin Classics, 1954.

History of Civilisations of Central Asia, UNESCO Publishing, Paris (series of 6 volumes, vol. I, The Dawn of Civilisation: Earliest times to 700 BC; vol. II, The Development of Sedentary and Nomadic Civilisations: 700 BC to AD 250; vol. III, The Crossroads of Civilisation, AD 250 to 750; vol. IV, Part 1; Part 2, The Age of Achievement AD 750 to the End of the Fifteenth Century,), 2000–2002 (vols. V and VI forthcoming).

HOLT F. L., *Alexander the Great and Bactria, The Formation of a Greek Frontier in Central Asia*, E.J. Brill, Leyde, 1988 (Supplement to *Mnemosyne, Bibliotheca classica batava*).

HOPKIRK Peter, *Foreign Devils on the Silk Road*, Oxford University Press, Oxford, 1980.

HOPKIRK Peter, *The Great Game*, Oxford University Press, Oxford, 1990.

HOUSTON M., *Ancient Greek, Roman and Byzantine Costume and Decoration*, Black, London, 1947.

Hudud-Al-'Alam. The Regions of the World, A Persian Geography, 372 A.H.–982 AD, translated from the Persian and explained by V. MINORSKY. 2nd ed. with a preface by V.V. Barthold; translated from the Russian... ed. by C.E. BOSWORTH, Luzac, London, 1970.

IBN BATTÛTA, *Travels of Ibn Battûta*, AD 1325–1354, translated by Gibb H.A.R., 5 vols., Defrémery C. and Sanguinetti B. R., Hakluyt Society, London, 1958–2000.

ISPAHANI M.Z., *Roads and Rivals. The Politics of Access in the Borderlands of Asia*, Tauris, London, 1989.

JACOB D'ANCONA, *The City of Light*, Little, Brown and Co., London, 1997; translated and annotated by David SELBOURNE.

(JEROME) (SAINT JEROME), *Select Letters*, translated by F.A. Wright, Heinemann, 1933.

KENDALL Paul Murray, *Louis XI*, George Allen and Unwin, London, 1971, reprinted Phoenix Press, 2001.

KIRCHER Athanasius, *China illustrata*, Johannes Jansson van Waesberg,

193. GIGANTIC ROLL OF PAPER, WITH SANSKRIT AND 'UNKNOWN LANGUAGE' TEXTS IN BRAHMI SCRIPT, FROM WALLED-UP TEMPLE LIBRARY, 'THOUSAND BUDDHAS,' TUN-HUANG.
Scale, one-fifth.
A shows the roll, which is over seventy feet long, partially opened.
B shows the silk painting on top of outer side.

Amsterdam, 1667 (reprinted Ratna Pustak Bhandar, Kathmandu, 1979).

KOESTLER Arthur, *The Thriteenth Tribe*, Popular Library, 1978.

KOHANSKI Tamarah, *The Book of John Mandeville*, an edition of the Pynson Text, with commentary on the defective version, Arizona Center for Medieval and Renaissance Studies, 2001.

KREUTZMANN Hermann, "The Karakoram Highway: The impact of road construction on mountain societies", in *Modern Asian Studies*, vol. 25, no. 4, pp. 711–736, 1991.

LAUFER Berthold, *Sino-Iranica: Chinese Contributions to the History of Civilisation in Ancient Iran*, with Special References to the History of Cultivated Plants and Products, Field Museum of Natural History, Chicago, 1919; reprinted Ch'eng Wen, Taipei, 1973.

LAUFER Berthold, "Asbestos and Salamander. An essay on Chinese and

Hellenistic folklore" in LAUFER B., *Sino-Tibetan Studies*, vol. I, pp. 219–293, New Delhi, 1987.

LE GOFF Jacques, *Saint Louis*, Gallimard, Paris, 1996.

LEGGE James, *The Chinese Classics*, London, 1861–1872, vol. IV, *The She King*; reprinted Hong Kong University Press, 1960.

LEGGE James, *A Record of Buddhistic Kingdoms, being an Account by the Chinese Monk Fa-Hein of Travels in India and Ceylon (AD 399–414) in Search of the Buddhist Books of Discipline*, Oxford, 1886, reprinted New York 1965, New Delhi 1998.

LESLIE D.D. and GARDINER K.H.J., *The Roman Empire in Chinese Sources*, Bardi, Rome, 1996.

LIU Xinru, *Ancient India and Ancient China. Trade and Religious Exchanges AD 1–600*, Oxford University Press, Delhi, 1988 (reprinted 1991).

LUBEC G., HOLAUBEK J., FELD C., LUBEC B., STROUHAL E., "Use of silk in ancient Egypt", in *Nature* (London), vol. 362, no. 6415, p. 25, 4 March 1993.

LU XUN, *Selected Works*, translated by Yang Xianyi and Gladys Yang, Foreign Languages Press, Beijing, 1980.

MAALOUF A., *The Crusades through Arab Eyes*, Schocken 1989, from the original French, *Les croisades vues par les Arabes*, J.–C. Lattès, Paris, 1983.

MAALOUF A., *The Gardens of Light*, translated by Dorothy Blair, Interlink, 1999, from the original French, *Les jardins de lumière*, J.–C. Lattès, Paris, 1991.

MAILLART Ella, *Forbidden Journey*, Century Paperback, 1987.

MAILLART Ella, *The Cruel Way*, Beacon Press, 1987.

MAILLART Ella, *Turkestan Solo: A Journey Through Central Asia*, Long Riders' Guild Press, 2001.

MANDEVILLE John, *The Travels of Sir John Mandeville*, together with *The Journal of Friar Odoric*, Everyone's Library, 1928.

MAO DUN, *Spring Silkworms and Other Stories*, translated by Sydney Shapiro, Cheng & Tsui, 1999.

MARDRUS J. C. and MATHERS E. P. eds., *The Book of the Thousand Nights and One Night*, 2 vols., Routledge, 1994.

MARSDEN William, *The Travels of Marco Polo the Venetian*, re-edited by Thomas Wright, Doubleday & Co., New York, 1948.

MENANDER PROTECTOR, *The History of Menander the Guardsman*, translated by Roger C. Blockley, Francis Cairns, Liverpool, 1985.

MEYER Karl and BRYSAC Shareen, *Tournament of Shadows, The Great Game and the Race for Empire in Asia*, Little, Brown & Co., London, 1999.

MORRIS Colin, *The Papal Monarchy, The Western Church from 1050 to 1250*, Clarendon Press, Oxford, 1991.

MORSE Hosea Ballou, *The Chronicles of the East India Company Trading to China 1635–1834*, Oxford University Press, 1925; reprinted Cheng Wen, Taipei, 1975.

MOULE A.C., PELLIOT P., *The Description of the World*, Routledge, London, 1938.

NEEDHAM Joseph, *Science and Civilisation in China*, Cambridge University Press, Cambridge, 1954–1990 and ff. (see in particular vol. V: "Chemistry and Chemical Technology. Part 2, Spagyrical Discovery and Invention", 1974).

NOBLE WILFORD John, "New finds suggest even earlier trade on fabled Silk Road" in *The New York Times/Science Times*, 16 March 1993.

PAUL OF EGINA, *The Seven Books of Paulus Aeginata*, transl. from the Greek by Francis ADAMS, Sydenham Society, London, 1844–1847.

PAUSANIAS, *Description of Greece*, translated by J. G. Frazer, 6 vols, Macmillan, London 1913.

PLINY THE ELDER, *Natural History*, bilingual Latin-English text, translated by H. RACKHAM, Loeb Classical Library, London, 1952.

PLUTARCH, *Plutarch's Lives*, translated by Bernadotte Perrin, Loeb Classical Library, Heinemann, London, 1984.

PROCOPIUS OF CESAREA, *Secret History*, transl. Williamson G. A., Penguin Classics, 1969.

PTOLEMY Claudius, *The Geography*, translated and edited by Edward Luther Stevenson, New York Public Library 1912, reprinted Dover, New York 1991.

PTOLEMY Claudius, *Ptolemy, Geography, Book 6*, original text with English and German translations by Susanne Ziegler, Dr. Ludwig Reichert Verlag, Wiesbaden 1998.

QUINN-JUDGE S., "Parting of the ways", in *Far Eastern Economic Review*, vol. 154, no. 4, pp. 16–18, 3 October 1991 (with several other articles on "Soviet Empire: Key to Central Asia").

RASHID Ahmed, "The New Silk Road", in *Far Eastern Economic Review*, vol. 149, no. 28, 12 July 1990.

RASHID Ahmed, "Asking for Holy War", in *Far Eastern Economic Review*, vol. 163, no. 45, pp. 28–30, 9 November 2000.

ROSSABI Morris, *Khubilai Khan, His Life and Times*, University of California Press, Berkeley, 1988.

ROSTOVTSEFF M.I., *The Social and Economic History of the Roman Empire*, Oxford University Press, 1957.

RUBRUCK, William of, *The Mission of Friar Willaim of Rubruck, His Journey to the Court of the Great Khan Möngke 1253–1255*, translated by Jackson Peter, with notes and introduction by Jackson Peter and Morgan Peter, Hakluyt Society, London, 1990.

SARIANIDI V.I., "The Golden Horde of Bactria", photographs by L. Bogdanov and V. Terebenin, in *National Geographic Magazine*, vol. 177, no. 3, pp. 50–75, March 1990.

SCHAFER E.H., *The Golden Peaches of Samarkand. A Study of T'ang Exotics*, University of California Press, Berkeley and Los Angeles, 1963.

SCHOFF Wilfred H., *The Periplus of the Erythraean Sea. Travel and trade in the Indian Ocean by a merchant of the First Century*, transl. from the Greek and annotated by Longmans, Green and Co., London, Bombay and Calcutta, 1912.

STARCKY J., *Palmyre*, Adrien Maisonneuve, Paris, 1952.

STEIN Marc Aurel, *Ruins of Desert Cathay: Personal Narrative of Explorations in Central Asia and Westernmost China*, Macmillan, London, 1912, reprinted Dover Reprints, 1989.

STEIN Marc Aurel, *Sand-buried Ruins of Khotan*, Fisher and Unwin, 1903, reprinted Asian Educational Services, 2000.

WATT George, *A Dictionary of the Economic Products of India*, (1st ed: 1889), reprinted Cosmo Publ., Delhi, 1972.

WESSELS C.S.J., *Early Jesuit Travellers in Central Asia 1603–1721*, Martinus Nijhoff, La Haye, 1924 (reprinted Asian educational services, New Delhi, 1992).

WHITFIELD Roderich, FARRER Anne, *Caves of the Thousand Buddhas, Chinese Art from the Silk Route*. With contributions by S.J. Vainker and Jessica Rawson, British Museum, London, 1990.

WOOD Frances, *Did Marco Polo Go to China?*, Secker and Warburg, London, 1995.

WOOD Frances, *The Silk Road: Two Thousand Years in the Heart of Asia*, University of California Press, 2003.

WRIGHT A.F., *Buddhism in Chinese History*, Stanford University Press, 1959.

YAMADA Kentaro, *A Study of the Introduction of An-Hsihsiang in China and that of Gum Benzoin in Europe*, Kinki University, 1954.

YAMADA Kentaro, *A Short History of Ambergris by the Arabs and Chinese in the Indian Ocean*, Kinki University, 1955.

YULE H., *Cathay and the Way Thither*, Hakluyt Society, London, 1866; reprinted 1915.

PUBLICATIONS IN FRENCH

ANDRÉ J., FILLIOZAT J., *Pline l'Ancien, Histoire Naturelle. VI. 2e Partie* (L'Asie centrale et orientale, l'Inde). Texte établi, traduit et commenté, Les Belles Lettres, Paris, 1980.

ANDRÉ J., FILLIOZAT J., *L'Inde vue de Rome*. Textes latins de l'antiquité relatifs à l'Inde, Les Belles Lettres, Paris, 1986.

ANQUETIL J., *Routes de la soie*, Lattès, Paris, 1992.

Asie centrale. Aux confins des empires, réveil et tumulte, Ed. Autrement, Paris, 1992 (Série Monde H.S. no. 64) (edited by C. POUJOL with the collaboration of P. GENTELLE; various authors). L'Asie centrale. Histoire et civilisation, *Imprimerie nationale*, Paris, 1977. "L'Asie centrale: vers un nouveau 'grand jeu'? Dossier" in *La Revue internationale* et stratégique, pp. 67–207, no. 34, été 1999 (various authors).

BADEL Pierre-Yves, *Marco Polo, La description du monde*, Edition, traduction et présentation par Pierre-Yves BADEL, Librairie générale française, 1998 (Livre de poche—Lettres gothiques)

BARTHOLD W., *Histoire des Turcs d'Asie centrale*, Adrien Maisonneuve, Paris, 1945.

BIBLIOTHÈQUE NATIONALE, *A la découverte de la Terre*. Dix siècles de cartographie. Trésors du Département des cartes et plans, Bibliothèque Nationale, Paris, 1979.

BOPEARACHCHI Osmund, "La circulation des monnaies d'origine étrangère dans l'antique Sri Lanka" in *Res orientales*, vol. 5, 1993.

BOULNOIS Lucette (=Luce), *Poudre d'or et monnaies d'argent au Tibet* (principalement au XVIIIe siècle), Ed. du Centre national de la recherche scientifique, Paris, 1983.

BOULNOIS Lucette, "Démons et tambours au désert de Lop. Variations Orient-Occident" in *Médiévales*, no. 22–23, pp. 91–115, 1992.

BOULNOIS Lucette, "Nouvelle route de la soie" in *Asie centrale. Aux confins des empires, réveil et tumulte*, pp. 98–109, Ed. Autrement, Paris, 1992.

BOULNOIS Lucette, "Chevaux célestes et salive de dragon. Transferts de culture matérielle sur les (routes de la soie) avant le XIIe siècle" in *Diogène*, no. 167, pp. 18–42, juillet–septembre 1994.

BRIQUEL CHATONNET Françoise, "Un prosélytisme juif? Le cas de Najrân" in *Le Monde de la Bible*, no. 129, pp. 34–35, sept–octobre 2000.

CAGNAT René, JAN Michel, *Le milieu des empires. Entre URSS, Chine et Islam; le destin de l'Asie centrale*, R. Laffont, Paris, 1990 (nouvelle éd.).

CAP, *Biographie pharmaceutique*. Moïse Charas, Paris, 1840.

CHAMBRE DE COMMERCE DE LYON, *La mission française d'exploration commerciale en Chine (1895–1897)*, Lyon, 1898.

CHAVANNES Edouard, "Les pays d'Occident d'après le Heou Han chou" in *T'oung Pao*, Sér. 2, vol. 8 (no. 1), pp. 149–234, March 1907 (with a facsimile of the Chinese text).

CHAVANNES Edouard, "Un traité manichéen retrouvé en Chine", in *Journal asiatique*, 1912 et janvier–février 1913.

CHRISTENSEN A., *L'Iran sous les Sassanides*, E. Munksgaard, Copenhague, 1936.

COEDÈS George, *Textes d'auteurs grecs et latins relatifs à l'Extrême-Orient depuis le IVe siècle av. J.-C. jusqu'au XIVe siècle*, translated by G. Coedès, E. Leroux, Paris, 1910.

CORDIER Henri, *Les voyages en Asie au XIVe siècle du bienheureux frère Odoric de Pordenone*, introduction and notes by Henri CORDIER, E. Leroux, Paris, 1891.

CORDIER Henri, "L'Extrême-Orient dans l'atlas catalan de Charles V, roi de France" in *Bulletin de géographie historique et descriptive*, pp. 19–63, 1895.

DEBAINE-FRANCFORT Corinne, IDRISS Abduressul, *Keriya, mémoires d'un fleuve. Archéologie et civilisation des oasis du Taklamakan*, ed. Findakly, Paris, 2001.

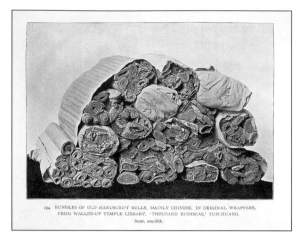

194. BUNDLES OF OLD MANUSCRIPT ROLLS, MAINLY CHINESE, IN ORIGINAL WRAPPERS, FROM WALLED-UP TEMPLE LIBRARY, ·THOUSAND BUDDHAS,· TUN-HUANG.
Scale, 000-6th.

DERMIGNY L., *La Chine et l'Occident. Le commerce à Canton au XVIIIe siècle*, 1719–1833, SEVPN, Paris, 1964.

DJALILI Mohammad-Reza et KELLNER Thierry, *Géopolitique de la nouvelle Asie centrale*, Presses Universitaires de France, Paris, 2001.

DRÈGE Jean-Pierre, "Les débuts du papier en Chine", in *Comptes rendus des séances de l'année 1987 de l'Académie des Inscriptions et Belles-Lettres*, juillet–octobre, pp. 642–650.

DRÈGE Jean-Pierre, *Marco Polo et la Route de la Soie*, Gallimard, Paris, 1989.

DRÈGE Jean-Pierre, BÜHRER E.M., *La Route de la Soie: paysages et légendes*, Biblioarts, Paris, 1986.

DRÈGE Jean-Pierre, "Les routes orientales du papier", in *Les routes de la soie, Patrimoine commun, identités plurielles*, Ed. UNESCO, Paris, pp. 53–63, 1994.

ELWERE Christiane, *L'Europe des Celtes*, Gallimard, Paris, 1992.

Ethnies (Des) aux nations en Asie centrale, Revue du Monde musulman et de la Méditerranée, no. 59–60, 1991 (1/2) (articles par 11 auteurs).

FAVIER Jean, *Philippe le Bel*, Fayard, Paris, 1978.

FERRAND Gabriel, *Relations de voyages et textes géographiques arabes, persans et turcs relatifs à l'Extrême-Orient du VIIIe au XIIIe siècle*, Leroux, Paris, 1913–1914.

FERRAND Gabriel, *Voyage du marchand arabe Sulayman en Inde et en Chine, rédigé en 851, suivi de remarques par Abû Zayd Hasan (vers 916)*, translated from the Arabic with an introduction, glossary and index, Bossard, Paris, 1922.

FILANOVIC M. I., USMANOVA Z.I., "Les frontières occidentales de la diffusion du bouddhisme en Asie centrale" in *Cahiers d'Asie centrale* no. 1/2, *Inde–Asie centrale. Routes du commerce et des idées*, pp. 186–201, 1996.

FILLIOZAT Jean, *Les relations extérieures de l'Inde. Les échanges de l'Inde et de l'empire romain aux premiers siècles de l'ère chrétienne*, Institut français d'Indologie, Pondichery, 1956.

FILLIOZAT Jean, "Pline et le Malaya", in *Journal asiatique*, tome 262, no. 1/2, pp. 119–130, 1974.

FRANCFORT Henri-Paul, "Les pétroglyphes d'Asie centrale et la route de la soie", in *Les routes de la soie, Patrimoine commun, identités plurielles*, Ed. UNESCO, Paris, pp. 34–52, 1994.

FUSSMAN Gérard, "Le Périple et l'Histoire politique de l'Inde", *Journal asiatique*, tome 279, no. 1/2, pp. 31–38, 1991.

GAGÉ J., *La montée des Sassanides et l'heure de Palmyre...*, Albin Michel, Paris, 1964.

GHIRSHMAN Roman, *L'Iran des origines à l'Islam*, Payot, Paris, 1951; 2e éd.: Albin Michel, 1976.

GIES Jacques, "Un témoignage du bouddhisme impérial Tang à Dunhuang", in *Les routes de la soie, Patrimoine commun, identités plurielles*, Ed. UNESCO, Paris, pp. 65–79, 1994.

GIGNOUX Philippe, "Controverse religieuse dans l'Iran sassanide" in *Le Monde de la Bible* no. 119, *La Bible et l'Asie à la rencontre du bouddhisme*, pp. 22–24, mai–juin 1999.

GODART J., *L'ouvrier en soie, monographie du tisseur lyonnais, étude historique, économique et sociale*, Thèse, Université de Lyon, Faculté de droit, Lyon, 1899.

GORSHENINA Svetlana, *La Route de Samarcande. L'Asie centrale dans l'objectif des voyageurs d'autrefois*, translated from the Russian by Habiba Fathi, Claude Rapin, Frantz Grenet, Olizane, Geneva, 2000.

HALLBFERG Ivar, "L'Extrême-Orient dans la littérature et la cartographie de l'Occident des XIIIe, XIVe et XVe siècles, étude sur l'histoire de la géographie", in *Göteborgs Kungl. Vetenskaps-och… Vitterhets Samhälles Handlingar*, tome IV, no. 7/8, VIII–573, p. 1906.

HAMBIS Louis, *La Haute-Asie*, Presses Universitaires de France, 2e édition, Paris, 1968.

HAMBIS Louis, *Marco Polo, La description du monde*, C. Klincksieck, Paris, 1955; reprinted as *Marco Polo, Le devisement du monde, Le livre des merveilles*, Texte intégral établi par A.–C. MOULE et P. PELLIOT, version française de L. HAMBIS, introduction and notes by S. YERASIMOS, ed. François Maspéro, Paris, 1980; reprinted *La Découverte*, Paris, 1998.

HEDDE P., "Notice sur le manuscrit de Théodulfe", in *Annales de la Société d'agriculture, sciences, arts et commerce du Puy pour 1837–38*, pp. 168–224, 1839.

HUBERT Henri, *Les Celtes et l'expansion celtique*, 1932; rééd. Albin-Michel, Paris, 1974.

Inde–Asie centrale. Routes du commerce et des idées, Cahiers de l'Asie centrale, no. 1/2, 1996 (articles by 21 authors).

JAN Michel, *Le voyage en Asie centrale et au Tibet*. Anthologie des voyageurs occidentaux du Moyen Age à la première moitié du XXe siècle. Introduction, chronologie, bibliographie, index des noms de personnes et de lieux établis par Robert Laffont, Paris, 1992.

KONDRAKOF N., TOLSTOI J., REINACH S., *Antiquités de la Russie méridionale*, E. Leroux, Paris, 1891.

LELIÈVRE Dominique, *Le dragon de lumière. Les grandes expéditions des Ming au début du XVe siècle*, France-Empire, Paris, 1996.

LEROUDIER E., *Histoire de la fabrique lyonnaise des étoffes de soie*, M. Camus, Lyon, 1934 (Extrait des Annales franco-chinoises, no. 28–30).

Lettres édifiantes et curieuses de Chine par des missionnaires jésuites 1702–1776, Chronologie, introduction, notices et notes par Isabelle et Jean-Louis VISSIÈRE, Garnier-Flammarion, Paris, 1979.

LÉVI Sylvain, "Les missions de Wang Hiuen-ts'e dans l'Inde", in *Journal asiatique*, mars–avril et mai–juin 1900.

LIU Guojun, ZHENG Rusi, *L'histoire du livre en Chine*, ed. en langues étrangères, Beijing, 1989.

LOMBARD Maurice, *L'Islam dans sa première grandeur (VIIIe–XIe siècle)*, Flammarion, Paris, 1971.

MAILLARD Monique, *Grottes et monuments d'Asie centrale. Essai sur l'architecture des monuments civils et religieux dans l'Asie centrale sédentaire depuis l'ère chrétienne jusqu'à la conquête musulmane*, Librairie d'Amérique et d'Orient Jean Maisonneuve, Paris, 1983.

MAILLART Ella, *Oasis interdites*, Grasset, Paris, 1937 (reprinted editions 24 Heures, Lausanne, 1982).

MALLERET Louis, "Rapport préliminaire sur les fouilles d'Oc-Eo", in *Bulletin de l'Ecole Française d'Extrême-Orient*, vol. 45, no. 1, 1951.

MALLERET Louis, *L'archéologie du delta du Mékong*, Ecole française d'Extrême-Orient, Paris, 1959–1963.

MANANDHAR Sushila, *Bijoux et parures traditionnels des Néwar au Népal. Une approche anthropologique et historique*. Thèse de doctorat, Université de Paris X, 1998 (unpublished).

MASPÉRO Henri, "Le royaume de Ta-ts'in", in *Mélanges posthumes sur les religions et l'histoire de la Chine. III. Etudes historiques*, Civilisations du Sud, Paris, 1950.

MAZAHERI Aly, *Les Trésors de l'Iran*, Skira, Genève, 1970.

MAZAHERI Aly, *La route de la soie*, SPAG Papyrus, Paris, 1983.

MEUWESE Catherine, *L'Inde du Bouddha vue par les pèlerins chinois sous la dynastie Tang (VIIe siècle)*, Calmann-Lévy, Paris, 1968.

MICHEL Francisque (or: FRANCISQUE-MICHEL), *Recherches sur la fabrication et le commerce des étoffes de soie, d'or et d'argent et autres tissus précieux en Occident, principalement en France, pendant le Moyen Age*, Imprimerie Crapelet,

Paris, 1852–1854. Also *Des Scythes, Trésors des musées soviétiques*, edition des Musées nationaux, Paris, 1975.

PELLIOT Paul, *Trésors de Chine et de Haute Asie*. Centième anniversaire de Bibliothèque Nationale, Paris, 1979.

PELLIOT Paul, *Recherches sur les chrétiens d'Asie centrale et d'Extrême-Orient, II, 1. La stèle de Si-Ngan-Fou*, ed. de la Fondation Singer-Polignac, Paris, 1984.

PELLIOT Paul, *L'inscription nestorienne de Si-Ngan-Fou*, Paris 1996.

PHILIPE Anne, *Caravanes d'Asie (du Sin-Kiang au Cachemire)*, Julliard, Paris, 1955.

PRJEVALSKI N., *Mongolie et pays des Tangoutes*, Hachette, Paris, 1880.

PSEUDO-CALLISTHÈNE, *Le Roman d'Alexandre. La vie et les hauts faits d'Alexandre de Macédoine*, trad. et commenté par Gilles BOUNOURE et Blandine SERRET, Les Belles Lettres, Paris, 1992.

RAGUIN Yves, "La stèle de Xi'an", in *Le Monde de la Bible*, no. 119, pp. 82–83, mai–juin 1999.

RAPIN Claude, "Relations entre l'Asie centrale et l'Inde à l'époque hellénistique", in *Cahiers d'Asie centrale* no. 1/2, *Inde–Asie centrale. Routes du commerce et des idées*, pp. 35–45, 1996.

RAY Himanshu Prabha, "La chrétienté dans l'Asie du Sud. Commerce et conversion", in *Le Monde de la Bible*, no. 129, pp. 63–65, sept–oct 2000.

RAYNAL abbé G.T., *Histoire philosophique et politique des établissements et du commerce des Européens dans les deux Indes*. (1re éd.: Amsterdam, 1770; autres éd.: Amsterdam, 1773; Amable Costes, Paris, 1820).

REINACH Salomon, "Le corail dans l'industrie celtique", in *Revue celtique*, tome 20, pp. 1–31, janvier–avril 1899.

REINAUD J.–T., *Relations politiques et commerciales de l'Empire romain avec l'Asie orientale (l'Hyrcanie, l'Inde, la Bactriane et la Chine) pendant les cinq premiers siècles de l'ère chrétienne*, Imprimerie impériale, Paris, 1863.

"Remise des pièces de fouilles d'Oc-Eo au Musée national du Viêt-Nam, Saigon, le 25 mai 1959", in *Bulletin de la Société des études indochinoises*, vol. 34, no. 1, 1959.

RENOU Louis, *La Géographie de Ptolémée*. L'Inde (VII, 1–4), texte établi par L. Renou, thèse présentée à la Faculté des lettres de l'Université de Paris, Edouard Champion, Paris, 1925.

RENOUVIN Pierre, *La question d'Extrême-Orient 1840–1940*, Hachette, Paris, 1946.

RIBOUD K., VIAL G., *Mission Paul Pelliot. XIII. Tissus de Touen-Houang conservés au Musée Guimet et à la Bibliothèque Nationale*, Paris, 1970.

RIBOUD Krishna, "Découvertes récentes de soieries en Chine: dynasties des Royaumes combattants et des Han", in *Les routes de la soie, Patrimoine commun, identités plurielles*, ed. UNESCO, Paris, pp. 21–33, 1994.

ROBERT Jean-Noël, *De Rome à la Chine: sur les routes de la soie au temps des Césars*, Belles Lettres, Paris, 1993.

ROBIN Christian, "La civilisation de l'Arabie méridionale avant l'Islam", in CHELHOD J. et al., *L'Arabie du Sud, Histoire et civilisation*, tome I, pp. 195–223, Maisonneuve et Larose, Paris, 1984.

ROBIN Christian, "L'Arabie du Sud et la date du Périple de la mer Erythrée (Nouvelles données)", in *Journal asiatique*, tome 279, no. 1/2, pp. 1–30, 1991.

ROBIN Christian, "Les religions de l'Arabie avant l'Islam", in *Le Monde de la Bible*, no. 129, pp. 29–33, sept–octobre 2000.

ROUX Jean-Paul, (en collaboration avec Sylvie-Anne Roux), *Les explorateurs au Moyen Age*, Fayard, Paris, 1985.

SALLES Jean-François, "La tradition de saint Thomas apôtre en Inde", in *Le Monde de la Bible*, no. 119, pp. 59–61, mai–juin 1999.

SCHWARTZ J., "L'Empire romain et le commerce oriental", in *Annales*, janv–février 1960.

STAVISKIJ B. Ja., *La Bactriane sous les Kushans: problèmes d'histoire et de culture*, trad. du russe, Librairie d'Amérique et d'Orient Jean Maisonneuve, Paris, 1986.

STEIN R.–A., *Recherches sur l'épopée et le barde au Tibet*, Presses Universitaires de France, Paris, 1959.

TAJADOD Nahal, *Les porteurs de lumière. I, Péripéties de l'Eglise chrétienne de Perse IIIe–VIIe siècle*, Plon, Paris, 1993.

THÉVENOT Melchissedec, *Relation de divers voyages curieux, qui n'ont point été publiés...*, Paris, 1663.

THIRIET Freddy, *Histoire de Venise*, Presses Universitaires de France, Paris, 1961.

THOMAZ Luis Filipe, "Hypothèses sur les premiers chrétiens dans l'Inde des Malabars", in *Le Monde de la Bible*, no. 119, pp. 53–57, mai–juin 1999.

TREMBLAY Xavier, " Chrétientés englouties. Le christianisme de Sérinde", in *Le Monde de la Bible*, no. 119, pp. 71–74, mai–juin 1999.

TSING TUNG-CHUN ou TSENG T'ONG-TCH'OUEN, *De la production et du commerce de la soie en Chine*, Thèse de doctorat, Université de Lyon, Faculté de droit, Geuthner, Paris, 1928.

VASCHALDE Jean, *Les industries de la soierie*, Presses Universitaires de France, Paris, 1961.

VILLEHARDOUIN Geoffroy de, *La conquête de Constantinople*, Chronologie et préface par Jean DUFOURNET, Garnier-Flammarion, Paris, 1969.

WEI Tsing-sing (Louis), *La politique missionnaire de la France en Chine 1842–1856*, Nouvelles éditions latines, Paris, 1960.

WHEELER M., *Les influences romaines au-delà des frontières impériales*, Plon, Paris, 1960.

ZHANG Guangda, "Trois exemples d'influences mazdéennes dans la Chine des Tang", in *Etudes chinoises*, vol. 13, no. 1/2, pp. 203–219, printemps–automne 1994.

ZHANG Hai ou, "Le second pont ferroviaire entre l'Asie et l'Europe", in *La Chine*, no. 1, pp. 20–21, 1991.

Publications in Chinese

BAN GU, *Qian Han shu* (*History of the Former Han*). See in particular *juan* (chapters) 6, 22, 25, 61 and 96. For an English translation', see DUBS H.H. above.

BANG Xiexuan, *Dunhuang de gu shi* (*Ancient Tales from Dunhuang*), Zhongguo qingnian chubanshe, Beijing, 1985.

CHEN LIANG, *Silu shihua* (*On the History of the Silk Road*), Gansu Renmin chubanshe, Lanzhou, 1983.

CHEN YU, *Dunhuang de chuan shuo* (*Oral Tales from Dunhuang*), Wenyi chubanshe, Shanghai, 1986.

DONGFANG Shuo, *Hainei shizhou ji* (*Tales of the Ten Islands in the Sea*), (included in *Gu shi wen fang xiao shuo*, 1925).

FAN YE, *Hou Han shu* (*History of the Later Han*). See in particular chapter 118.

FAXIAN, *Fo guo ji*. For an English translation, see LEGGE J.

HUANG Shengchang, "Han yu gu dai Zhongguo yu Nipoer de wenhua jiaoliu" (Cultural Exchanges in Ancient Times between China and Nepal), in *Lishi yanjiu* (*Historical Studies*), no. 1, pp. 92–108, 1962.

JIANG Yuxiang, "Gudai Zhongguo xinan 'Sichou zhi lu' jian lun" (Brief Considerations on the 'Silk Road' in *South-West China in Antiquity*), in WU Jialong, JIANG Yuxiang, *Gudai xinan sizhou zhi lu yanjiu*, pp. 30–41.

Jiuquan shi hua (*On the History of Jiuquan*), by an editorial team from Jiuquan, Gansu (preface dated 1984, endnote 1987).

Li Yanzhou, *Bei shi* (*History of the Northern Dynasties*). See in particular chapter 97.

LIN TIENWEI, *Song dai xiangyao maoyi shi kao* (*A History of the Perfume Trade of the Sung Dynasty*), Zhongguo xueshi chubanshe, Hong Kong, 1960.

LIU Manchun, "Han Tang jian sichou zhilu shande sichou maoyi (The Silk Trade along the Silk Road in the Han and Tang Periods)", in *Si lu fang gu*

(*Searching for Antique Remains along the Silk Road*), edited by the Silk Road Research Team, Gansu renmin chubanshe, Lanzhou, pp. 84–96, 1982.

RAO Zongyi, "Shu bu yu Cinapatta, Lun caoqi Zhong, Yin, Mian zhi jiaotong (The Cloths of Shu and Cinapatta: on Relations between China, India, and Burma in Antiquity)", in WU Jialun, JIANG Yuxiang, *Gudai xinan sizhou zhi lu yanjiu*, pp. 201–233.

SANG Xiuyun, "Shu bu Qiong zhu zhuan zhi Daxia lujing de lice (A Superficial View of the Itinerary along which the Cloths of Shu and the Bamboos of Qiong reached Daxia)", in WU Jialun, JIANG Yuxiang, *Gudai xinan sizhou zhi lu yanjiu*, pp. 175–199.

Shijing (Book of Odes). For an English translation, see LEGGE James, *The Chinese classics*, vol. IV, *The She King*.

WU Jialun, JIANG Yuxiang, *Gudai xinan sichou zhi lu yanjiu (Research into the South-Western Silk Road in Antiquity)*, Sichuan Daxue chubanshe, Chengdu, 1990.

XUANZANG, *Da Tang Xiyu ji*. For an English translation, see BEAL S. *Si-yu-ki, Buddhist Records of the Western World*.

ZHANG Qijun, *Zhong Hua wu qian nan shi (5000 Years of Chinese History)*, Huagang chuban youxian gongsi, Taibei, 1976.

ZHAO Rugua, *Zhu fan zhi (Topography of all the Barbarian States)*. For an English translation, see Friedrich HIRTH and W.W. ROCKHILL (under CHAU JU-KUA).

PUBLICATIONS IN RUSSIAN

BIČURIN Nikita Jakovlevič, *Sobranie svedenij o narodakh obitavšikh v Srednej Azii v drevnie vremena (Collected Information on the Peoples of Central Asia in Ancient Times)*, Izdatel'stvo Akademii nauk SSSR, Moscow-Leningrad, 1950–1953 (1st ed 1851).

GAFUROV B.G., *Istorija Tadžikskogo naroda… s drevnejšikh vremen do velikoj oktabr'skoj socialističeskoj revoljucii 1917 g. (History of the Tajik People from Ancient*

Times until the Great Socialist October Revolution of 1917), 2nd ed, Gospolitizdat, 1952.

Kazakhstan, Izdatel'stvo, Mysl', Moscow, 1970.

Kirghizija, Izdatel'stvo, Mysl', Moscow, 1970.

MURZAEV E.M., *Gody iskanij v Azii (Years of Research in Asia)*, Izdatel'stvo, Mysl', Moscow, 1973.

NIZAMUTDINOV I., *Iz istorii sredneaziatsko-indijskikh otnošenij (IX–XVIII vekov) (History of Relations between Central Asia and India, (9th–18th centuries)*, Izdat, Uzbekistan, Tashkent, 1969.

PEVCOV M.V., *Putešestvie v Kašgariju I Kun-lun' (Voyage to Kashgaria and the Kunlun)*, Gosudarstvennoe izdatel'stvo geografičeskoj literatury, Moscow, 1949.

PIGULEVSKAJA N.V., *Vizantija i Iran na rubeže V–VI vekov (Byzantium and Iran between the 5th and 6th centuries)*, Izdat. Akademii nauk SSSR, Moscow, 1946.

PIGULEVSKAJA N.V., *Vizantija na put'jakh v Indiju, iz istorii torgovli Vizantii s vostokom v IV–VI vv (Byzantium on the Road to India according to the History of Byzantine Trade with the West in the 4th to 6th centuries)*, Izdat. Akademii nauk SSSR, Moscow, 1951.

PRŽEVAL'SKIJ N.M., *Tret'e putešestvie v Central'noj Azii, iz Zajcana čerez Khami v Tibet i na verkhov'ja Želtoj Reki (Third Trip to Central Asia, from Lake Zaisan to Tibet and the Upper Reaches of the Yellow River, passing through Hami)*, St Petersburg, 1883.

Skul'ptura i živopis' drevnego Pjandžikenta (Sculpture and Painting from Antique Penjikent), by the Institute of the History of Material Culture of the Academy of Sciences of the USSR, and the Institute of History, Archaeology and Ethnography of the Academy of Sciences of the Tajik SSR, Izdat. Akademii nauk SSSR, Moscow, 1959.

TOLSTOV S.P., *Po sledam drevnekhorezmijskoj civilizacii (On the Traces of the Ancient Civilization of Khorezm)*, Izdat. Akademii nauk SSSR, Moscow-Leningrad, 1948.

TOLSTOV S.P., *Po drevnim del'tam Okca i Jaksarta (In the Antique Deltas of the Oxus and Jaxartes)*, Izdat. Vostocnoj literatury, Moscow, 1962.

Turkmenistan, Izdatel'stvo, Mysl', Moscow, 1969.

Uzbekistan, Izdatel'stvo, Mysl', Moscow, 1967.

PUBLICATIONS IN OTHER LANGUAGES

DIOSCORIDES, *Pedacii Dioscoridis Anazarbaei opera quae extant omnia (ex nova interpretatione Jani-Antonii Saraceni Lugdunaei, Medici)*, Sumtibus haeredum Andreae Wecheli, Claudii Marnii, et Ioan. Aubrii, Francofurti, 1598 (bilingual Greek and Latin text).

(JEROME) (SAINT JEROME) HIERONYMUS, *De virginitate opuscula sanctorum doctorum, Ambrosii, Hieronymi, et Augustini,* apud Paulum Manutium..., Romae, 1562.

Oriente poliano, studi e conferenze tenute all'Istituto italiano per il Medio ed Estreme Oriente in occasione del VII centenario della nascita di Marco Polo, 1254–1954, Is.M.E.O., Rome, 1957 (various authors, articles in French, English, Italian and German).

Index of Geographical Names

Please note: Museums and related institutions are listed under the cities in which they are located.

Index

Make the most of your journey with ODYSSEY books, guides and maps

Distributed in the United Kingdom and Europe by:
Cordee Books & Maps
3a De Montfort Street, Leicester, UK, LE1 7HD
Tel: 0116-254-3579   Fax: 0116-247-1176
www.cordee.co.uk

Distributed in the United States of America by:
W.W. Norton & Company,Inc.
500 Fifth Avenue, New York, NY 10110
Tel: 800-233-4830   Fax: 800-458-6515
www.wwnorton.com

For all distributors, please visit: www.odysseypublications.com

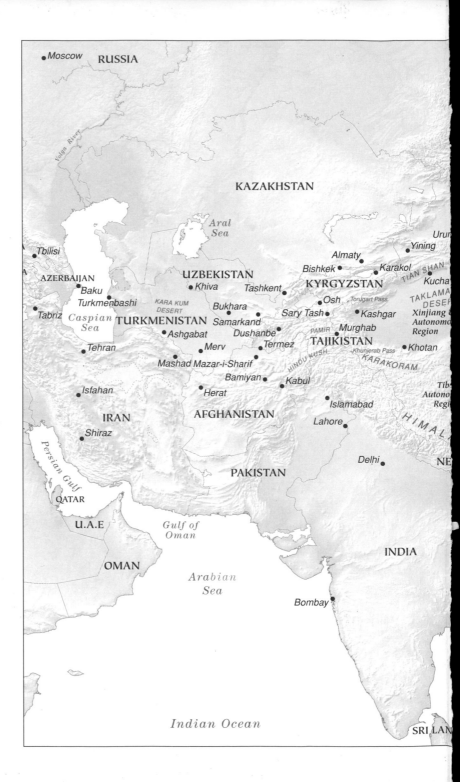